FOR REFERENCE USE (7 Vols 3780 1975

(Please do not remove from Libra

UNITY LIBRARY & ARCHIVES
A history of the expansion of C
REF BR 145 .L3 v.1

0 0051 0012473 6

D1287405

A History of
The Expansion of Christianity

Volume I
THE FIRST FIVE CENTURIES

FOR REFERENCE USE ONLY
(Please do not remove from Library)

A History of

THE EXPANSION OF CHRISTIANITY

(Volume I)

THE FIRST
FIVE CENTURIES

by

KENNETH SCOTT LATOURETTE

*D. Willis James Professor of Missions
and Oriental History in Yale University*

ΛΑΜΠΑΔΙΑ ΕΧΟΝΤΕΣ ΔΙΑΔΩΣΟΥΣΙΝ ΑΛΛΗΛΟΙΣ

HARPER & BROTHERS PUBLISHERS

New York and London

UNITY SCHOOL LIBRARY
Unity Village
Lee's Summit, Missouri 64063

THE FIRST FIVE CENTURIES

Copyright, 1937, by Harper & Brothers

Printed in the United States of America

All rights in this book are reserved.
No part of the book may be reproduced in any
manner whatsoever without written permission.
For information address
Harper & Brothers

EIGHTH EDITION

L-V

BR
145
L359h
v.1

ref.
BR
145
.L3
v. 1

In memory of

HARLAN PAGE BEACH

1854-1933

Contents

Chapter VI

Chapter VII

Chapter VIII

Introduction

IN ONE of the parables of the New Testament the "Kingdom of God" is compared to a mustard seed, "which, when it is sown in the earth, is less than all the seeds of the earth: but when it is sown, it groweth up, and becometh greater than all herbs." It is also said that "the Kingdom of God . . . is like leaven, which a woman took and hid in three measures of meal, till the whole was leavened." Whether the originator of these parables meant to identify the Kingdom of God with the Christianity which arose out of his life and teachings may be debatable. Certainly, however, they may with startling aptness be applied to it. Christianity claims as its founder and preëminent figure one whose public career was at most three years and perhaps only one year in length. He did not commit his teachings to writing, but contented himself with uttering them orally, subject to misunderstanding, garbling, and oblivion through faulty human memories. He deliberately sought the support not of the mighty, but of the humble. Whatever his dreams about the ultimate future may have been, he contented himself in his own lifetime with only the very minimum of organization among his followers. Christianity began as a small Jewish sect, looked at askance by the leaders of the nation, numerically one of the least considerable of the many faiths and religious societies of the recently founded Roman Empire. Yet geographically it has spread more widely than any other religion in all the millenniums of mankind's long history. The largest group which has claimed to embody it, the Roman Catholic Church, is to be found in more countries and peoples than any other organization, political, economic, or ecclesiastical, ever known to man. Several other Christian Churches have adherents in a large proportion of the nations of the globe. In its influence, too, Christianity has been notable. Exact measurements are difficult and frequently impossible. Who can determine, for instance, precisely how far the family of twentieth-century Europe or America has been moulded by it, to what extent nineteenth- and twentieth-century democracy is its product, or even to what degree the abolition of human slavery in the nineteenth century among Western peoples can be ascribed to it? Yet that into all three of these Christianity has entered no one with a knowledge of the facts can well deny. The Christian leaven has to a greater or less extent modified every environment into which it has penetrated.

Strangely enough, never has anyone undertaken in an inclusive and thorough fashion to tell the story of the expansion of Christianity—of the permeation of the meal by the leaven. Histories of many phases of Christianity we have had in almost unbelievable number and in prodigious quantity. Histories of the Christian Church abound, of the intellectual garb in which believers have clothed their faith, of individual Christian organizations, of the Church in particular lands, of eminent leaders, and of movements which owe their impulse to Christianity. We have had narrated, too, many portions of the story of the spread of Christianity. A huge library would be required to contain all the books which have been written on one phase or another of it—on the history of Christian missions in particular ages, countries, or peoples, on particular organizations which have made it their object to further that spread, and of individuals who have given their lives to propagating the faith. We have histories of Roman Catholic missions and of Protestant missions. Yet never has anyone undertaken to cover the entire sweep of the geographic spread of the Christian faith. Not even *The Acts of the Apostles*, that earliest surviving history of the propagation of Christianity, attempted an inclusive narrative. It tells us nothing, for example, of the origin of the important Christian group or groups at Rome and stresses the work of one missionary, Paul.

Such an inclusive task, if it were to be performed completely, would be impossible for any one man. The mass of existing materials is so vast, and the knowledge of all the languages involved so encyclopædic, that one lifetime is entirely too short to compass it. To accomplish it fully through a group of scholars would be an undertaking which for sheer magnitude would dwarf most existing literary compilations.

Comprehensively conceived, the story must include the spread of Christianity into all the peoples and regions where it has had adherents. It must cover not only the winning of converts among nations and tribes previously non-Christian, but the transplanting of the faith by migrations of individuals and groups calling themselves Christian and the building of an ecclesiastical structure by them and for them in the lands to which they have gone—notably in the Americas, Australia, New Zealand, and in North and South Africa. It must comprise not only the deliberate efforts to propagate the faith, but also the unpremeditated processes, frequently incidental to other movements by which Christian influences have made themselves felt.

The account, too, should raise and seek to answer a number of questions which either must form an integral part of it or are very closely related to it. The most important of these are seven in number.

Of course it must be asked: *What was the Christianity which spread?* Obviously this query belongs close to the outset, for early in the narrative one must seek to know what the faith was at the inception of its remarkable geographic extension. Just what was this mustard seed at the time it germinated? The question is not one, however, which can be answered and then dismissed. Like other religions, in the course of its history Christianity has taken many forms. Each time that it enters new territory, we must seek to determine the form and the content of that which was now in process of propagation. Thus the Protestantism transferred to the English colonies in North America in the seventeenth and eighteenth centuries was not the same as the Roman Catholicism which, at that very time, the French were planting in other portions of that continent, and neither was identical with primitive Christianity. Protestantism is obviously multiform: usually more than one type has entered a particular area. Nor, whatever may be said of its doctrines, is Roman Catholicism always the same. Its expressions in organization and rites vary. In practice what it means to one age or individual or group that professes it may markedly differ from that which it signifies to another. Thus the Catholicism of the Irish missionaries to the Anglo-Saxons was so far from being identical with that of the contemporary Italian missionaries to England, that a serious disagreement developed, and that which the Spanish *conquistadores* brought to the New World in the sixteenth and seventeenth centuries was, as it actually operated, in some ways at variance with that which Roman Catholics from the United States have taken to the Far East in the twentieth century. So, too, the Christianity of the learned which finds expression in books is usually quite different from that of the less educated but nominally Christian masses.

A second question must be raised again and again: *Why did Christianity spread?* What enabled the mustard seed to grow into a plant which is "greater than all herbs"? Was it the soil, the quality of the seed itself, the method of planting and cultivation, or was it a combination? To put the question in another way and to subdivide it, what was it among the peoples and in the countries from which Christianity moved which helped to account for the impulse to spread it, and what was it in the regions to which it was taken which was partly responsible for the results? What was there in the conditions of the times which made it possible for it to gain adherents? What elements in Christianity itself gave it vitality? What motives led its converts to accept it? To what extent were the methods employed responsible for the successes achieved? How far is the spread attributable to purely religious factors and how far must it be assigned to other circumstances? Again, no one answer can be given which holds true for all times, places, and individuals. The conditions which prepared the ground for the rapid increase of Christianity in the Græco-Roman world were many of them quite distinct from those which paved the way for its triumph among the peoples of Northern Europe. In any age the motives which lead one individual to accept the faith may be entirely different from those which induce his neighbour to take the same step. Since Christianity itself is not always the same, the qualities within it which account for its ability to win men and women are not uniform. The methods of its agents have shown great variety. The diversity, however, does not necessarily rule out the persistence of characteristics which Christianity may have possessed from the outset and in most or all of its forms. A striking feature of its history has been its possession of certain traits and ideals which in all ages have impressed upon even its most diverse forms a striking family likeness.

The obverse of this second main question is another: *Why has Christianity suffered reverses and at times met only partial successes?* Why did it fall before Islam in so much of the Mediterranean basin and Western and Central Asia, and, more recently, in Russia, before Communism? Why did Nestorianism win so few adherents in China, and, indeed, in most of its territory in Asia, and then all but disappear? Why, in the twentieth century, after being continuously present in India and China for a longer time than was required to win the majority of the population of the Roman Empire does Christianity still enroll numerically only a very small proportion of the peoples of either land?

In the fourth place it must be asked: *By what processes did Christianity spread?* Obviously this question is intimately related to the second and in many instances the two must be dealt with together. The answer involves a narrative of missionary operations, the biographies of the leading missionaries, the accounts of the origin, development, and operations of the various orders, congregations, societies, committees, and boards which have actively undertaken the task of propagation, the methods employed, the opposition encountered, and the results which have ensued. The larger proportion of the space of most of the existing histories of missions is devoted, quite naturally, to this question.

With these four questions any narrative of the expansion of Christianity must inevitably be concerned. The other three are quite as imperative, although some of their ramifications at times lead the investigator into fields seemingly remote from the main current of his story and introduce him to intricate and baffling problems, more than one of which does not admit of satisfactory or final solution.

The fifth, then, of the main questions has to do with results: *What effect has Christianity had upon its environment?* Some phases of the answer are usually fairly obvious and require no great acumen to determine and record.

The approximate number of professed adherents to the Church, the institutions and movements which are evidently and directly traceable to the missionaries or the communities of Christians which they have called into being are often, although by no means always, readily ascertained. The accurate answers to many other and often more significant queries are not so easily arrived at. How far was the disappearance of slavery and of the gladiatorial contests of the Roman Empire due to Christianity? To what extent are the Crusades to be ascribed to the Christian impulse? To what degree, if at all, can the geographic discoveries by European peoples from the fifteenth to the twentieth century be said to have been due to Christianity? For instance, did Prince Henry the Navigator send his expeditions along the coast of Africa, and did Columbus venture westward at least in part because they were professed Christians? Is there any causal connexion between Corpernicus's faith as a churchman and his formulation of the astronomical system which bears his name; or between Isaac Newton's Christian belief and the discovery of his laws of motion; or between the initial observations which underlie the Mendelian laws of heredity and the fact that they were made in the garden of a monastery? In other words, to what extent, if at all, can the development of the scientific approach in Western peoples be ascribed to Christianity? Or again, is modern capitalism, as some have claimed, at least in part the fruit of Calvinism? Can the developments in international law and organization in the past four centuries be attributed in any degree to the Christian impulse? Is it anything but a coincidence that the earliest formulations of international law in our modern age were by a churchman in Spain and by Hugo Grotius, a devout Christian, and that he to whom, more than any other, the League of Nations owes its inception, Woodrow Wilson, came from the family of a clergyman and was himself an earnest Christian? How far has Christianity left its stamp on Western codes of law, on European art, music, and literature? Can such movements as the French Revolution and Russian Communism, both vigorously opposed to organized Christianity, historically be traced even in part to Christian sources? How far can what is often known as "American idealism" be attributed to Christianity? To what extent, if at all, is the decline of population in some of the Pacific islands in the nineteenth and twentieth centuries because of the Christian missionary? To what degree have Christian missions been responsible for the impact of European peoples upon Africa and Asia in the past hundred or more years? In what fashion have they modified it? All these and many other problems are of extreme importance to him who would appraise the effect of the Christian leaven. Yet none of them are easily answered and to some of them no well-balanced and accurate reply is possible.

The sixth main question, *the effect of the environment on Christianity*, of the meal on the leaven, is of similar importance and often equally difficult to answer with accuracy. It is clear that Christianity bears the indelible impression of the Jewish faith in which it was cradled and with which it has so continuously been in contact and often in conflict, but the exact extent of that debt is not always readily determined. Roman Catholic Christianity in its very name, in the seat of its central government, and in its official language gives evidence of its obligation to the Roman Empire. Again, however, it is not a light task to measure the effect upon it of that state which was the first and in many respects the most notable of its great conquests. Shall we appraise the famous saying, "The Roman Catholic Church is the ghost of the Roman Empire," as merely a clever phrase, or does it contain an accurate statement of fact? What effect did that Mediterranean world into which Christianity was born have upon the faith in the years in which its ritual, doctrines, and organization were taking form? To what extent, if at all, were the mystery religions which were such prominent rivals copied, either consciously or unconsciously, by the victor? How far do Roman Catholicism and the Eastern Orthodox churches reflect Greek thought? What is their debt to Neoplatonism? To what extent was the Roman Catholic Church feudalized in the European Middle Ages? What did the Byzantine Empire do to the Greek Orthodox Church? How far was the Russian Church Russian? To what extent does the Gregorian Church mirror Armenian national thought and institutions, and the Coptic Church bear the marks of pre-Christian Egypt? Is Protestantism, as someone has declared, the reaction of the Teutonic mind to Christianity, the product of the assimilation and moulding of the faith by nearly related peoples in Germany, the Netherlands, Scandinavia, England, Switzerland, portions of France, and the Scotch lowlands? To what extent is the nascent Christianity in negro Africa, in India, in China, in Japan, and in the Pacific islands beginning to display the influence of the traditional cultures of these lands and peoples? In what respects does the Christianity of the negroes of the United States incorporate the characteristics of its adherents? How far is the Protestant Christianity of the United States the product of its prolonged contact with the advancing frontier? Has the Roman Catholicism of that land been affected by the dominant Protestantism? To what degree, if at all, are the various Christian Churches, especially the Protestant denominations, class institutions incorporating the customs, beliefs, and prejudices of particular social and economic groups? Toward the answer of most of these inquiries interesting facts may be assembled and stimulating suggestions made, but to most of them in the present state of our knowledge definitive answers are impossible.

The seventh and final outstanding question is: *What bearing do the processes by which Christianity spread have upon the effect of Christianity on its environment, and of the environment upon Christianity?* How far may mediæval and modern Europe be ascribed to the methods employed in the conversion of its peoples? Obviously, at the best it only imperfectly embodies the ethical and spiritual ideals expressed in such early Christian documents as the Gospels and the Epistles. To what extent may this often superficial and far from thoroughgoing transformation be traced to the processes by which nominal conversion was accomplished? How far, if at all, is the Roman Catholicism of twentieth-century Latin America the product of methods by which Christianity was brought into that huge and important region in the fifteenth, sixteenth, seventeenth, and eighteenth centuries? Are the characteristics peculiar to Christianity in the United States due to the different ways in which it was introduced and propagated in that country? To what degree must one attribute the relatively small size of the Christian communities in India, China, and Japan, and the influence, disproportionately large when compared with the numerical strength of Christianity in these lands, and especially of Protestant Christianity, to the missionary methods of the nineteenth and twentieth centuries? Again the answers are often difficult or impossible of determination, all the more so because the fifth and sixth groups of questions, with which the seventh is closely related and upon which it is frequently dependent, are so baffling. As a rule this seventh question will be dealt with incidentally under the others and not in a separate section. However, it is not for that reason considered unimportant.

Manifestly, in undertaking to narrate the history of the expansion of Christianity, especially in any such sense as is implied in these seven groups of questions, the author is embarking upon an almost preposterous enterprise and runs the grave risk of being both superficial and inaccurate. If, however, at the very outset the inevitable limitations of such a work are frankly recognized, a certain value may attach to a survey which results from allowing as many of the facts as possible to pass through one mind. For more than a quarter of a century the author has had the privilege of living with much of the pertinent literature. During most of that time he has had constant access to one of the world's richest collections of printed material related to the subject, in the libraries of Yale University and especially the Day Missions Library. He has made use of several of the leading collections germane to his history in Asia, the United States, and Europe. He has had the continuous privilege of covering the entire field in his teaching, with the advantage which that brings of preparing the material for orderly presentation and of the criticisms and suggestions of students. He has known a large number of the leaders of the missionary enterprise of his adult years, both Protestant and Roman Catholic, and has discussed with them, often repeatedly and at great length, the issues involved. For a brief period in his early manhood he was himself a missionary. He has participated in the councils of some of the bodies which have shared in the formulation of the policies of Protestant missions. He has had the benefit of association with scholars whose major interests lie in or close to the subjects discussed. Many of the most helpful of these associations have, naturally, been with his colleagues on the faculty of Yale University, but numbers of them have been with members of other academic communities in Asia, Europe, and America. By no means all of these specialists have been committed to the Christian faith and some have brought the contribution, often very important, of those who are frankly in disagreement with it. To those who have been of most assistance the author's gratitude is expressed in more detail elsewhere. To all of them together the following pages are indebted for much of whatever value they may possess. Without them the work would have been impossible.

The limitations of the ensuing volumes must be clear to any who give them a careful perusal. While the author has sufficient familiarity for reading purposes with the majority of the languages in which the major part of the material is found, including nearly all those of Western Europe, with many of the tongues employed by Christianity in the course of its spread he has not even a nodding acquaintance. He knows only one of the languages native to Asia, and none of negro Africa or of the Pacific islanders. Literature in these mediums of thought is, therefore, closed to him except as it has been translated into one of the languages of Western Europe or has been utilized by those writing in a Western European tongue. Of the Slavic languages he has used only Russian. Moreover, even in the languages which he can use, the limitations imposed by the brevity of human life have precluded reading more than a small fraction of the available material. While many primary sources have been covered, the author has had to rely partly upon so-called secondary works, those books and articles which result from the investigations of others.

Among the chief limitations must be the writer's own presuppositions. The author is not conscious of any thesis which he desires to establish. He has set himself to the objective investigation of the facts and has been eager to see them as they actually are and to hear and to record what they have to say. However, no historian can write without bias, and he who professes to do so is either deceiving or self-deceived. The very selection of facts out of the endless and infinitely multiple stream of daily happenings in itself involves judgment as to what is significant. An author is not always cognizant of his own predilections and prejudices, and if he is, in his effort to guard against them he may not give them their due weight.

So far as the present writer is aware, the features of his background and convictions which may colour his narrative are to be found in the facts that he is American, a Protestant, has long been and still is an active participant in the Christian missionary enterprise, and that he is at the same time a historian trained in the modern methods of that craft. His American environment may have led him to give disproportionate weight to Christianity in the Western Hemisphere and to the part of Americans, and especially of American Protestants, in the Christian missions of the nineteenth and twentieth centuries. His American Protestantism may have led him to look for and stress the facts which are of interest to one with that rearing, particularly those which have to do with moral transformation and with social, economic, and political changes. Almost certainly his Protestantism, which is of the non-liturgical type and in the stream of what is usually called Evangelicalism, derived from the revivals of the eighteenth and nineteenth centuries, has prevented him from understanding fully the great branches of the Christian Church which are more nearly in the historic Catholic tradition, whether Roman Catholic, Anglo-Catholic, Russian, or Greek Orthodox.

Yet the author has been trained in the school of modern history which looks askance at the supernatural and sees in the flow of events simply mechanical and human factors—geographical, climatic, economic, political, social, æsthetic, and intellectual. Most members of this school decline to affirm any cosmic significance in human history. If in the story of the human race they discern any determining cause or causes (and many of them are unable to do so) they find them in some factor or combination of factors which by themselves cannot be labelled as "supernatural." Usually they seek causes, but believe them to be only in preceding events, in human nature, and in the physical environment. It is from this standpoint that these volumes are written.

In many ways this training and the Christian view of history are incompatible. The Christian sees in history the hand of God and centres his faith about events which he holds to be the acts of God in time. For him the human drama has a meaning. The author has been unable to avoid calling attention from time to time to facts which he regards as insufficiently accounted for on the assumptions of the school of history in which he has been reared. These facts, he believes, afford one basis—although not the only one—for adherence to the Christian explanation. The two viewpoints may sometimes seem to clash. Often the Christian interpretation of history will appear to be ignored.

Occasionally the Christian will obtrude himself in what may appear a rude or jarring manner. A synthesis is possible if the Christian interpretation be accepted, but not, the author is convinced, if it be rejected. That synthesis, however, is not attempted in this story. It is left to other volumes or to other pens.

The main chronological divisions of the narrative seem to be marked out by the course of events, and by these the succeeding volumes will be organized. They are three in number. At the outset are the first five centuries of the Christian era, in which Christianity was winning the Roman Empire. By about the year 500 by far the majority of the population of the Empire had become professedly Christian. Christianity, too, had here and there begun to spread outside the boundaries of Roman rule, chiefly in Asia and in Ireland.

Second is a period stretching roughly from the year 500 to the year 1500. In it Christianity won the adherence of the peoples of Northern Europe. These included the tribes whose invasions are usually said to mark the downfall of the Roman Empire, and those other peoples, still farther north, who either did not penetrate to the basin of the Mediterranean until long after the date traditionally given for the collapse of Rome or whose movements never stretched that far south. The process of conversion was one which required fully a thousand years. Even by 1500 in large regions it was almost entirely nominal and in some portions of Europe confessedly pagan peoples survived. In these centuries, too, came the extension of Christianity to the south and east far beyond the limits of the old Roman domains. On the south was the barrier of the Sahara which effectively insulated the black peoples of Africa from the spread of practically every cultural influence. Christianity, however, was carried up the most nearly traversable route, the Nile, and became strong in Nubia. Chiefly, but by no means entirely in the form of what is generally called Nestorianism, Christianity also penetrated much of Asia, into Persia, into the central part of the continent, and into India and China. In the thousand years between 500 and 1500, moreover, in the rise and spread of Islam, Christianity experienced what until the triumph of Russian Communism in 1917 was its most serious territorial reverse. Islam, while deeply indebted to its older rival, won from it much of Western and Central Asia, most of Northern Africa, and the larger part of the Iberian Peninsula. Eventually it gained a substantial foothold in South-eastern Europe. Christianity did not supinely retreat before it, but survived in large areas under Moslem control. Against Islam, too, Christianity registered a persistent counter-advance, spectacularly in the Crusades which won for Latin Christianity precarious footing on the east coast of the Mediterranean, less spectacularly and not much more successfully in the closely associated work of religious orders and individual missionaries, notably the Franciscans and Dominicans and Raymond Lull, and with eminent success in the Iberian Peninsula. For a brief time, too, in the thirteenth and fourteenth centuries, in a series of efforts which were heroic and romantic. but without large or lasting results, the Orders of Preachers and Brothers Minor, then in the flush of their youth, carried Latin Christianity into Central Asia, India, and China.

The third period is the one which spans the years from about 1500 to the present time and seems not yet to have closed. In it, transported by the peoples of Europe, Christianity has attained by far its widest geographical extent. The period is, in turn, divided into two others, one reaching from about 1500 to about 1800 and the other from about 1800 to the present. The first of these was introduced by the age of geographical discoveries which carried Europeans into the Americas and Asia. In it Roman Catholicism was the form of Christianity most active in propagating the faith. This it did largely under the ægis of the Spanish and Portuguese governments and to a less extent under the French. In no small degree it owed its vitality to the new burst of religious life which came with the Roman Catholic reformation of the sixteenth century. It won large sections of the New World and small groups in negro Africa. It made its presence felt in Asia by attracting to itself the majority of the Filipinos, by a brief and stormy career in Japan, by establishing Christian communities, most of them relatively small, in China, India, Ceylon, Burma, Indo-China, and the East Indies, and by endeavouring, with mixed success and failure, to bring into communion with Rome the adherents of some of the non-Roman churches of the Near East. The Russian Orthodox Church, propelled by the wave of Russian exploration and conquest, obtained scattered posts as far east as China and even Kamchatka and Alaska. It also registered gains in South Russia. In this enormous extension of the faith the newly born Protestantism shared to only a slight extent. However, in the English colonies in the Americas and the West Indies, in the Dutch possessions in the Americas, the East Indies, Ceylon, and South Africa, and in a Danish-German-English mission in India, it achieved beginnings which were later to prove of outstanding significance. As the eighteenth century wore on, the tempo of missionary enthusiasm and activity slowed down. The decay of Spain and Portugal, the dissolution of the Society of Jesus, the Enlightenment, and then the French Revolution dealt what seemed for a time to be fatal blows.

In the closing years of the eighteenth century, however, and swelling to full flood in the nineteenth and the opening years of the twentieth century, came a new access of life which was to make of these decades the most remarkable era in the history of the expansion of Christianity. European peoples, equipped increasingly with the mechanical appliances which the great age of scientific discoveries gave them, penetrated every corner of the globe, carrying with them their civilization. At the same time Westerners experienced a fresh religious awakening, most spectacularly in Protestant circles, but also in several of the Roman Catholic lands. The phenomenal increase of the white population, largely by migration, in the United States, Canada, Australia, New Zealand, South Africa, Siberia, and the southern part of South America was matched by efforts, to a high degree successful, to hold these emigrants to the faith of their fathers and to build among them strong ecclesiastical organizations. Wherever Europeans penetrated, Christianity also went, the missionary frequently being the advance guard of the invasion. In the Americas, Christianity was offered enthusiastically to most of the hitherto untouched tribes of pagan Indians. It gained the negro populations which had resulted in the New World from African slavery. It was brought to the large majority of the islands of the Pacific, in many instances gathering most of the population into its fold. It placed its representatives among a large proportion of the tribes of Africa. It won substantial minorities in Japan, Korea, China, Indo-China, Burma, India, Ceylon, and Madagascar. In the Near East the Christian Churches of the West, both Protestant and Roman Catholic, gained adherents from the Eastern Churches. Everywhere Christian missionaries had a share in introducing Western forms of education. In hundreds of instances they reduced languages to writing and began in them the creation of a literature. In many places they were pioneers of Western medicine and of the European and American humanitarian movements of the nineteenth century. Christianity, in other words, spread with expanding European peoples and cultures and affected more or less profoundly their impact upon the non-European world. Never has any other faith or any other set of ideas and ideals possessed so elaborate and far-flung an organization for propaganda. Measured by the number of professional missionaries, in the nineteenth- and twentieth-century spread of Christianity Protestantism and Roman Catholicism have been represented in about equal strength. In results, however, they have registered marked differences. The Russian Orthodox Church is the only other branch of Christianity which has been at all aggressive in that period (although some others have been carried by migration to America), and its activities have been limited chiefly to Russian territory, to Japan, and to emigrants in the United States and Canada.

This, then, is the chronological framework around which our narrative is to be organized. About a sixth of our space will be given to the first period, another sixth to the second, about a sixth to the first part of the third, and the remainder, about a half, to the years since 1800. Thus about two-thirds of the pages are devoted to less than the last quarter of the time that Christianity has been among men. To some, accustomed to the traditional divisions of the history of the Church, this proportion may seem distorted. It has, however, been deliberately adopted and from conviction. Since 1500, and especially since 1800, Christianity has been introduced to more different peoples and has made larger territorial agains than in all the rest of its history. In these nearly four and a half centuries, too, it has suffered a major geographical reverse. Complex as was its environment and diverse as were the peoples among whom it spread in the first fifteen centuries of its history, since 1500 it has been carried into many more different environments and among a far greater number of peoples and tribes. Church history which follows traditional patterns is rightly concerned largely with the earlier centuries, when Christianity developed the creeds and the main features of the organization to which the majority of Christians have since adhered. In any well-rounded story of the spread of Christianity, however, as contrasted with its internal history, the proportions must be quite different and, so the author believes, approximately the ones which will be followed in the ensuing chapters.

In connexion with each of these periods and often in their subdivisions material will be sought which bears on each of the seven major questions which have been propounded. In many instances no definitive answer will be attempted. Facts which seem significant will be noted and assembled. It is to the first four that the major amount of space will be devoted: What was the Christianity that spread? Why did it spread? Why did it sometimes lose ground? By what processes did it spread? It is upon the fourth that the chief emphasis will fall. Yet the remaining three questions cannot be ignored. To many, indeed, it will seem of primary importance to attempt to determine the effect which Christianity had on its environment, the effect of the environment upon Christianity, and the manner in which these two sets of results were modified by the processes through which Christianity spread. Even if most of the answers given must be tentative, no account of the history of the expansion of Christianity which professes comprehensiveness can neglect them. Around them cluster some of the most vital and perplexing problems with which men have wrestled.

It must again be emphasized that in many respects this book is breaking new ground. It will probably display both the virtues and the defects of a pioneer effort. For large sections of its story no monographs have prepared the way by preliminary spade work. We have, for example, no satisfactory survey of the expansion of Christianity in the United States, or in Australia or Canada. Nor does any single work deal satisfactorily with Roman Catholic missions in India in the nineteenth and twentieth centuries. No one book specializes in any competent fashion on Roman Catholic missions in Japan for that period. Particularly in the effects of Christianity on its environment and of the environment on Christianity dependable studies are few. This work, then, is a new venture. The author can only hope that it will prove stimulating and not too misleading, and that in it will be seen, from these fresh angles, the history and the nature of the world's most widely spread religion.

The value of such a work must lie largely in the attempt to tell the entire story of the expansion of Christianity. Many correlations and interpretations are made possible by such a comprehensive narrative which the detailed studies of separate areas and periods must miss. It should, moreover, be possible to propound many questions the very asking of which will have worth. Even when the answers are unobtainable, the queries themselves possess importance. In many of the generalizations and correlations here offered and in numbers of the problems propounded the author can lay no claim to originality. However, a large proportion of the interpretations and generalizations ventured and of the questions asked are, so far as the author is aware, entirely new. In these the work must be expected to make one of its main contributions. Such generalizations and interpretations must, of course, be based upon the assemblage of a vast number of facts. Without these latter they would be worthless. The data so gathered, with the appropriate references to sources, will, it is hoped, be of use for purposes of reference to both amateurs and specialists. Bringing together, as they seek to do, the outstanding features of the entire course of the spread of Christianity, these volumes make possible the propounding of questions and the suggestion of answers and generalizations for which a work of lesser scope would be an inadequate background or provide a distorted perspective. Some of these are assembled in the concluding chapter. The majority, however, are in appropriate places through the body of the work.

Into one field, it must be noted again, these volumes do not enter. They do not seek to discuss the cosmic significance of the events they record. This is not because the author is unaware of the importance of this question or blind to the bearing of his story upon it. From the very beginning of Christian history men have been endeavouring to relate the facts of the career of Jesus and of the lives of his followers to the nature of the universe and to the place of mankind in it. More than that, many have formed profound convictions on these issues. Millions have believed that Jesus is convincing evidence that at the heart of the universe, as its creator, sustainer, and governor, is one who has made men in his likeness, who strives, in love and through his own vicarious suffering, to purge men from their imperfections and sins and to bring them into an eternal and growing fellowship with himself. They have held that in Jesus men may see the face of God himself. They believe that in the spread of Christianity is the continued effort of the God who once in time showed himself perfectly in Jesus. To them the entire course of the history of this planet is a drama which has as its central theme the creation by God of beings whom he wishes to grow in likeness to himself, and of his effort through the life, death, and resurrection of Jesus and through the continued operation of his Spirit to bring that purpose to perfection. Over the validity and the details of this interpretation men have been debating since the beginning of the Christian era. It is not because he deems these questions trivial that the author does not enter upon their discussion. He is convinced that they are of supreme importance. Nor has the author omitted their discussion because he has formed no opinions on them. He has profound convictions, and ones which are in accord with many which the majority of thoughtful Christians have held through the more than nineteen centuries of Christian history. Here and there the ensuing volumes contain hints as to what these are. However, in the answers to these questions the author could scarcely hope to make any fresh contribution. They have been discussed by many far more competent than he and in a voluminous literature. The author has deliberately confined himself almost entirely to the narrative of the facts of the expansion of Christianity, and to pointing out their part in the shaping of cultures. It is this phase of the history of the Christian movement which has been the most nearly neglected by other writers and where the need exists for fresh insight and interpretation. As has been said, moreover, the author is here resolutely avoiding any attempt to prove the Christian thesis. He has endeavoured to conform to that kind of objectivity extolled by the school of history in which he has been trained.

The story here told is by no means finished. In spite of the reverses suffered through Russian Communism and of much loss of ground among large groups in other supposedly Christian lands, Christianity is still advancing on many of its geographic frontiers. Forecasting the future is always uncertain and no attempt will be made to embark on so hazardous an adventure. Since about the year 1500 the fate of Christianity has been largely identified with that of the peoples of Northern and Western Europe. It is they who in the discoveries, conquests, and migrations of the past four and a half centuries have carried Christianity to every corner of the globe. If, as is often suggested, the day of their supremacy is dying, and if, as many believe, they are becoming less zealous and convinced champions of their traditional faith, then it may be that future generations will be able to discern somewhere in the twentieth century the end of the era which began in 1500. Such evidence as exists to support these assertions we must eventually record and attempt to evaluate.

The author cannot close this introduction without expressing his profound appreciation of the kindness of the many scholars and librarians who have assisted him in his task. Even to mention their names would extend these pages to undue length. Some, however, have been of such outstanding assistance that the author craves the privilege of recording specifically both his debt and his gratitude. For this first volume the author is under deep obligation to Mrs. Charles T. Lincoln, whose careful typing of an often almost illegible manuscript and whose suggestions as to literary style have been invaluable, to the librarians of Yale University and particularly to Professor R. P. Morris for their unfailing courtesy, and to Professors R. H. Bainton, E. R. Goodenough, C. H. Kraeling, and C. E. Raven, all of whom read large portions of the typescript and whose comments aided immensely in the final revision.

A History of
The Expansion of Christianity

Volume I
THE FIRST FIVE CENTURIES

Chapter I

THE BACKGROUND OUT OF WHICH CHRISTIANITY CAME AND THE ENVIRONMENT INTO WHICH IT WAS BORN

TO GAIN perspective and to see the place of Christianity in the history of mankind we must begin at a very remote period. So far as man knows, he is the only creature on this planet who possesses a religion. He may not have been able to enter sufficiently into the consciousness of others to discover what may be an attitude akin to what he calls religious. He has, to be sure, repeatedly called upon animate creatures and inanimate objects to join with him in worship.[1] That, however, is not the result of precise information. While the insight of the poet may approach nearer to the truth than the cold-blooded observations of the scientist, proof is wanting that in these instances it has done so.

Moreover, even man may have been late in arriving at a religious consciousness. The early stages of his story are still obscure. We do not yet know the point in our ancestry where what may safely be called human appears. Nor does agreement exist as to the length of time which has elapsed since that occurred. One estimate conjectures that a creature which may be termed human emerged about the middle of what the geologists denominate the Oligocene age and that this was perhaps 1,200,000 years ago. From this ancestry, so the same conjecture goes on to say, came, at the beginning of the Pliocene, possibly half a million years ago, a being which in size of brain approached the present human standard.[2] Not until long after this do we possess evidence that man had practices which can be termed religious. Palæolithic man seems in places to be religious. Mousterian (Neanderthal) man, from his care in the burial of his dead, appears to have believed in an after life, and Mousterian culture, so one time scale has it, lasted in Western Europe from perhaps 40,000 to 20,000 B.C. The Aurignacian, which followed it, and later races developed the burial rite still further and are said to have employed magic and phallic symbols.[3]

[1] See, for example, such a passage as Psalm 148.
[2] Keith, *The Antiquity of Man*, Vol. II, pp. 711-713, 733, 734; MacCurdy, *The Coming of Man*, pp. 18-46.
[3] MacCurdy, *Human Origins*, Vol. II, pp. 169-174; Keith, *The Antiquity of Man*, Vol. I, p. xvi; Keith, *New Discoveries Relating to the Antiquity of Man*, p. 200.

1

An elaborate religious development seems to have waited for the appearance of a more complex culture and to have gone hand in hand with it.

What we think of as civilization was very late in coming to birth. Not until well after the last ice age in Europe was nearing its end, possibly ten to twelve thousand years ago, did human communities emerge which we would esteem civilized.[4] Their beginning may have been due to the declining rainfall, or perhaps the shifting of the zone of rainfall, which accompanied the shrinking of the ice caps. The change of climate turned into a desert the erstwhile well-watered region of the Sahara in which primitive man had hunted and fished, and made more precarious his livelihood in Central Asia.[5] This alteration in his environment appears to have forced man to take refuge in the valleys of Mesopotamia, the Nile, and the Indus and there to win his food through tilling the soil. Agriculture led to more settled communities and to a more highly organized society. The use of metals began to enter about 4000 B.C. and worked a further revolution.[6] Copper led the way, followed by bronze, and, about 1300-1200 B.C., iron.[7] The development of writing brought additional changes. By about 3000 B.C. three centres of what we may call human civilization had arisen —along the Nile, in Mesopotamia, and in the Valley of the Indus[8] and along the rocky hills and now arid valleys which border the Indus Valley on the West.[9] Apparently, too, the settlements along the Indus and the Euphrates were connected by communities of a similar culture across what are now Baluchistan and Persia.[10] Another centre was in the Yellow River Valley in the present China. What may be termed civilization probably, although by no means certainly, emerged here several centuries later than in the other three fertile valleys.[11]

Religion seems to have been an integral part of each of these four cultures and probably shared their development. In each region it early displayed characteristic and distinctive features which persisted, although with modifications, for millenniums.[12] Religion, therefore, at least in any elaborate form, like civilization, has been a comparatively late phenomenon in the life of mankind. Compared with the brief span of a single human existence, it is old. It came, too, long before written records began to be made, and so before what we have

[4] Keith, *The Antiquity of Man*, Vol. I, pp. 39, 40.
[5] *Ibid.*, Childe, *New Light on the Most Ancient East, passim.*
[6] Breasted, *The Dawn of Conscience*, pp. 9-11.
[7] MacCurdy, *The Coming of Man*, pp. 72-77.
[8] Childe, *New Light on the Most Ancient East, passim.*
[9] Arthur Keith in *Asia*, Nov., 1934, pp. 649-652.
[10] *Ibid.*
[11] Latourette, *The Chinese: Their History and Culture*, Vol. I, pp. 32-42.
[12] On Mesopotamian and Egyptian religion see Breasted, *The Dawn of Conscience,* especially pp. 13, 18-22, 312-330, 336-343.

traditionally spoken of as history. Seen, however, against the background of the total period of man's life on the earth, so far as our records now enable us to say, it is a recent feature in man's growth.

Most of the chief religious systems of mankind are, moreover, of even later origin. The larger proportion of them emerged out of earlier ones and trace their beginnings to men of marked individuality and force of character. The majority of them arose after 1000 B.C. Before that time distinctive religions had begun to develop in Egypt, Mesopotamia, India, and China. In Egypt, indeed, the native religion reached its maturity in the twelfth and thirteenth centuries B.C. Morality had been linked to religion, and, under one of the rulers, apparently a most original and remarkable individual, a form of monotheism had developed.[13] Before 1000 B.C., too, must be placed Moses. After 1000 B.C., however, come the Hebrew prophets, the rise of Confucianism, Taoism, Buddhism, and Zoroastrianism, and the entire course of Greek philosophy. Indeed, Confucius, the creators of Taoism, the Buddha, Zoroaster, some of the greatest of the Hebrew prophets, all the Greek philosophers, Jesus, Mani, and Mohammed lived, dreamed their dreams, and did their work after 650 B.C.

It is interesting and highly important that Christianity was among the last of the religions which have succeeded in spreading widely. Of the faiths which won adherents from among many races only Manichæism and Islam were younger. Confucianism, Taoism, Buddhism, Zoroastrianism, and the outstanding Greek philosophers were all older. One of the most remarkable and yet least noted facts of human history is that the origins of all but two of the organized religions which today hold the allegiance of large sections of mankind and the foundations of most of the philosophic systems which have most profoundly influenced men are in the thirteen centuries between 650 B.C. and A.D. 650. These two, Judaism and Hinduism, are of earlier birth but underwent extremely important modifications during these years. Here and there, since A.D. 650, new faiths have arisen, such as that of the Sikhs in India. None, however, has succeeded in winning the allegiance of more than a very few millions. Within the older faiths fresh movements have broken forth—among them most of the monastic orders within the Roman Catholic Church, some of the variations of Hinduism and Buddhism, and the many forms of Protestantism. It is, indeed, one of the indications of vitality that from a religion creative personalities continue to emerge. These become responsible for modifications in their inherited faith, attract to themselves followers, and are the founders of fresh groups. If in any faith they cease to appear, that faith is either somnolent or moribund. The multiplicity of fresh movements within existing religions

[13] Breasted, op. cit., pp. 18-22, 312-330.

since A.D. 650 is ample witness to the continued vigour of these systems. It seems, however, significant that whereas the thirteen centuries before A.D. 650 saw the beginnings of most of the highly organized religions which have won the allegiance of mankind, in the nearly thirteen centuries since that date no new faith has arisen which has so gripped the imagination of millions in many lands and climes as have Confucianism, Buddhism, Christianity, and Islam.

The problem is complicated by the fact that in the past two centuries new movements have sprung up, not religious in the usually accepted sense of that term, which have evoked much the same kind of enthusiastic devotion from individuals and vast populations as have these historic faiths. Nationalism, democracy, communism, socialism in several of its various forms, and fascism have absorbed men's loyalties. In their more extreme expressions, nationalism, socialism, communism, and fascism have insisted on the prior and undivided allegiance of their adherents even at the expense of loyalty to the traditional religions. If they have tolerated the older faiths at all, it has been with reluctance. Usually they have at least insisted upon controlling religious teaching and organization. When we come to that stage of our story we shall find them at times seeking to uproot all religion as an enemy and at others striving so to control it as practically to eliminate it. They have sought to provide their adherents with a philosophy of life which makes the historic religions superfluous or which regards them as irreconcilably antagonistic. In other words, they have convictions as to what is most desirable and as to the way in which human life is to be most satisfactorily lived; they are based upon assumptions as to the nature of the universe and of man which in their inclusiveness resemble what we have usually termed religion.

Parallel with these new movements has recently been a loss of confidence in the traditional faiths. This had its origin in the Occident and has spread to the remainder of the world. In the Occident it has coincided with the development of the scientific approach and the appearance of modern mechanical appliances and is to be found both among the educated and the uneducated. In non-Occidental peoples it has appeared chiefly among those groups which have been most permeated by Western ideas. Men have become sceptical about the interpretation of life and of the universe given by the historic religions and believe that what is really desirable can be better obtained through scientific and mechanical devices and through human intelligence, unassisted by super-human beings.

What, then, is the significance of these facts? Some would declare that they indicate that what has traditionally been known as religion is a stage through which mankind has passed and from which it is now emerging. They would say that the birth of so many of the existing religious systems in the thirteen centuries between 650 B.C. and A.D. 650 is evidence of a certain world-wide climate of opinion which is now vanishing. They would point to the fact that all of these were regarded by many of their contemporaries as heresies, and represent the original and daring reflection of great individuals upon the crude stuff of religion which had come down from antiquity. The historic religions were, so this theory would assert, the partial emancipation of civilized man from the superstitions and immature beliefs of his palæolithic and neolithic ancestors. This interpretation would appear to be supported by the fact that more of these religions were born in the first half of the thirteen hundred years than in the latter half, and that in the areas in which they arose they synchronized roughly with man's emergence from a fairly primitive into a more complex stage of civilization. Those who hold to this position would go on to say that the present departure from these faiths is part and parcel of the process by which man is now advancing into a new stage of civilization, and that whether we like it or not the old must be discarded as part of the furniture of an outgrown past. They would declare that Christianity is a transient episode in human history and that the title of these volumes had better be *The Rise and Decline of Christianity*.

Others would declare that in this history of religion we see the double process of man's groping after God and of God's education of man. They would say that God was always seeking to reveal himself to man and that, as he found men fitted to be the channels of that revelation, he disclosed himself and his truth through them. Moslems would say that while God had spoken through many prophets, Mohammed was his perfect mouthpiece. Christians hold that Jesus is that perfect revelation. They would say that the fact that so few creators of new religions have appeared since Jesus is because mankind has in him so complete a revelation of God that no other has been necessary. Such later leaders outside the Christian stream as Mani and Mohammed, some of them would explain as due either to a lack of understanding of Jesus or to human imperfection. They declare that Jesus in his life and teachings set up a standard of religious living, of ethics, and of social relations which is still far ahead of the practice of mankind. They maintain that if his insights were embodied fully in individual lives and in human institutions we would have a perfect human society. They hold that Jesus discloses the ideal toward which God calls men, toward which he is working, and toward which men should strive. They see in the expansion of Christianity progress, however slow, toward that goal. Some view the losses which Christianity has suffered from time to time as due either to human perversity—the inevitable accompaniment of man's moral freedom—or to reactions against types of Christianity which so obscured or inadequately reflected the spirit of its professed master that an outraged human conscience was justified in seeking to discard them. They point out, and here the facts seem to be clearly with them, that never has Christianity displayed such vigour as in the nineteenth and twentieth centuries.

The announced purpose of these volumes does not permit a discussion of the question of which of these interpretations is correct, or of whether some other must be sought. He would be strangely obtuse, however, who did not recognize the existence of the issues and who did not see their importance for any comprehensive search for an understanding of the history of mankind.

Whatever the reasons, the systems of organized religion arrived comparatively late in man's career, and many of them came after the beginnings of organized states and cultures. Of these religions Christianity is among the youngest. When it appeared, therefore, Christianity found itself in a world which was already possessed of religions, some of them centuries old.

Contrasted with the total course of human history, therefore, Christianity has been but a brief time on this planet. Even in comparison with most of the religious systems existing today it is youthful. It has had, accordingly, only a relatively short period in which to spread and to make its dreams effective. Its ethical ideals are so revolutionary and, if carried out in full, would involve so drastic a reorganization of the lives of individuals and of society that it is not surprising that in the less than twenty centuries in which it has been in existence it has not won the world to complete conformity to its pattern. It is important to recall that even in this brief span, as the succeeding chapters will show, it has spread more widely than any other organized religious faith which mankind has known, and that never has it been propagated over so extensive an area or won adherents among so many different peoples as in the past century and a half. Even when full account has been taken of recent geographical losses and of the widespread questioning of its claims in lands which have been traditionally known as Christendom, the fact remains that in the past three or four generations Christianity has been more prominent in the total picture of the race's cultural life than ever before.

In understanding Christianity and in seeking to determine the reasons for the great influence which it has come to have it is necessary to recall the environment into which it was born. Many of the characteristics of what we call Christianity can be appreciated only as we see the setting out of which it arose and in which it first found itself. Here are to be found some of the causes of the prominence which it has achieved.

First of all it must be remembered that Christianity had its origin in the

Mediterranean world. At the time of Christ the basin of the Mediterranean and the lands immediately adjacent to it formed the centre of the most powerful and complex culture which man had yet developed. To it contributed the civilizations of Egypt and Mesopotamia, the two areas (with the possible exception of the Indus Valley and Iran) where mankind had earliest attained an ordered, settled society, with cities, commerce, the arts, literature, and religions which were beyond the primitive stages. In it were or had been the Minoans, the Phœnicians, the Jews, the Greeks, the Romans, and other peoples who had attained to advanced culture and had made distinct contributions. Into it poured influences from Persia, and, to a less extent, from India. Any faith, therefore, which could capture the allegiance of the Mediterranean world would have a much better chance of shaping the rest of the human race than would one in any other of the centres, such as India and China, where civilization had developed. In its subsequent spread Christianity has been intimately associated with the extension of the influence of the culture of the Mediterranean basin. It has been neither the sole heir nor the sole vehicle for that culture. Islam, for example, has shared that distinction. As we shall see later, moreover, the spread of the culture which had its beginning and early growth in the Mediterranean world must probably be ascribed very largely to the intimate relation which it came to have with Christianity. However, it is clear that to that close association Christianity has been indebted for much of its geographic expansion. More often than not, the two have entered a new area hand in hand, each reinforcing the other. When once Christianity had captured the ancient world, its prospects for world-wide extension were enormously enhanced.

Christianity has seldom since succeeded in becoming the predominant faith of any people which at the time of their conversion possessed an advanced civilization. Its victories in Northern Europe were among folk of relatively simple culture. In the New World, in Mexico and Peru, it met distinct cultures which were some distance removed from their primitive stages. Here it won, but that was because the cultures which might otherwise have offered opposition were wiped out by invaders who employed it as one of their agencies of conquest. A religion and its associated culture seem to be so closely intertwined that the one can be accepted only by destroying or profoundly altering the other. Christianity's triumph in the Græco-Roman world was accompanied, as we shall see, by revolutionary alterations in that world and also by changes in Christianity. Never has Christianity been adopted where the pre-Christian culture remained intact. In some regions of high civilizations, as in Persia, India, China, and Japan, it has won the allegiance of minorities. It has often obtained the adherence of entire peoples of primitive or nearly primitive cultures, but only as these peoples, in accepting it, abandoned their own culture and adopted, at least in part, that with which Christianity was associated.

Even in the Græco-Roman world cultural disintegration had set in before Christianity attracted more than a minority. It was largely because the established civilization was dissolving, weakened by many other factors than the attack of Christianity, that the faith was able to win. In the process of becoming predominant it absorbed so many elements of the surrounding culture that ever afterward it has been largely identified with it.

In all this, it must be added, the experience of Christianity is by no means exceptional. No other faith has ever obtained the undivided allegiance of a people of high culture unless associated with military conquest. It was only after the Arabs had established themselves by force of arms that Islam achieved wide acceptance in the southern and eastern portions of the Mediterranean basin and in Persia. It was because of conquests by Moslem peoples that Islam acquired so strong a foothold in India and even there its gains were chiefly from among the depressed classes and other sections of the population which were near the primitive stages of culture. In China, where at first sight Buddhism seems purely by peaceful propaganda to have won a vast and highly cultured folk, only a small minority, mainly the monks and nuns, ever gave it their unreserved allegiance. The vast majority adopted a few Buddhist beliefs and practices, but without changing the essential structure of their cultural life. Confucianism, a native faith, associated with the origin of Chinese civilization, remained dominant.

At the time when Christianity began and in the first three centuries of its existence more than at any preceding era conditions in the Mediterranean world prepared the way for the spread of a new religious faith throughout the entire extent of that area. Nor, indeed, after the three centuries in which Christianity succeeded in establishing itself as the strongest religion in that region, did conditions ever again exist there which quite so favoured the entrance and general acceptance of a new faith.

At the outset must be noted the political unity. At the time of the birth of Jesus, Augustus, building on the structure begun by Julius Cæsar and on foundations laid by a long succession of Roman conquests, was creating the Roman Empire. His rule brought peace to a world which had long been distraught by wars between the contending states, by civil strife between factions and ambitious leaders, and by the piracy which had flourished in the time of disorder. The Roman boundaries embraced a larger proportion of the Mediterranean basin than had ever before been united under one rule. For two centuries, under the empire so established, this vast region was to enjoy internal peace to a degree which it had never before known and which, for so prolonged a period, it has never seen repeated.[14]

Peace was accompanied by the growth of roads and commerce. The Roman roads are famous. They made possible more extensive and more rapid travel than in many sections had ever before been possible. The suppression of piracy increased the sea-borne commerce.[15] Political unity and the removal of burdensome restrictions favoured trade.[16] Roads and commerce facilitated the movements of groups, individuals, and ideas.[17] It was not an accident that Christianity expanded first along the trade routes and had most of its earliest strongholds in cities from which commerce radiated.[18]

Moreover, the propagation of ideas was furthered by the wide use of the Greek language. From at least the time of Alexander the Great and the subsequent extension of Greek culture, the Greek tongue gained currency along the avenues of commerce and in a large proportion of the chief cities. In Roman times in the eastern and to a somewhat less extent in the western portions of the Empire Greek was spoken and read extensively in many of the chief centres of population.[19] Even the Roman, conqueror though he was, had long borrowed from Greece. Many Romans were familiar with the Greek language.[20] This Greek, moreover, although it had arisen out of several dialects, had a common form in all the far-flung Greek-using communities in the world of commerce.[21] Any religion, therefore, which could gain a foothold in the Greek-using sections of the population and could create a literature in Greek would have an opportunity to reach most of the provinces of the Empire.

In the West Latin had a growing use and this, in the later stages of its spread around the Mediterranean, proved favourable to Christianity.

Then, too, the Roman rule was indifferent to the existence of most religions and ideas. To be sure, as we shall see later, complete tolerance did not exist. From time to time the state exerted itself to restrict or to stamp out some cult

[14] Rostovtzeff, *A History of the Ancient World,* Vol. II, pp. 294, 295.
[15] On the growth of trade by land and sea, see Rostovtzeff, *Social and Economic History of the Roman Empire,* pp. 65-68, 145-148.
[16] McGiffert, *A History of Christianity in the Apostolic Age,* p. 154.
[17] Friedländer, *Roman Life and Manners under the Early Empire,* Vol. I, pp. 300-322.
[18] See, for example, Map 1 at the end of volume two of Harnack, *The Mission and Expansion of Christianity,* where the cities are shown in which Christians are known to have been by A.D. 180.
[19] Rostovtzeff, *A History of the Ancient World,* Vol. II, pp. 173, 224; Lebreton in Descamps, *Histoire Générale Comparée des Missions,* pp. 17, 18.
[20] Dill, *Roman Society from Nero to Marcus Aurelius,* pp. 89-91.
[21] Angus, *The Mystery Religions and Christianity,* pp. 15-22.

or organization which it deemed detrimental to the public good. As a rule, however, it offered no check to the spread of religions.

Thanks partly to these facilities, the Roman Empire saw an extensive inter-change of ideas. Local customs and institutions were slow to die and in many places persisted, but throughout its course the area and peoples comprised in the Empire tended toward cultural unity. Cultural unity naturally made for religious unity and the dominance of a single faith. A religion which had at once vitality and adaptability had, therefore, an opportunity for universal acceptance.

None of these factors, however, whether peace, political unity, commerce, linguistic unity, a fair degree of tolerance, or a growing uniformity of culture, is sufficient to account for the rapidity of the expansion of Christianity. In other areas of the earth's surface similar conditions have not always been accompanied by the extensive acceptance of a new religion. For instance, in the China of the T'ang, although for nearly three centuries all these factors were present, and although Christianity, Manichæism, and Islam gained entrance, none of the three won any large following. Additional reasons must be sought which facilitated the triumph of a new faith. These are to be found in large part in the social and religious situation.

An outstanding characteristic of the world which Christianity entered was a growing cosmopolitanism. For at least three centuries before the birth of Christ this movement had been in progress. The Persian conquests had paved the way for it, but its inception is usually dated from Alexander the Great. Although the empire which he built broke apart almost immediately after his death, the spread of Hellenistic culture continued under the Greek rulers who made them-selves heirs of the various portions of his realm. The Roman Empire occupied a much larger proportion of the Mediterranean basin than had Alexander. The unity of its government, the commerce and travel which it fostered, and its comparative tolerance furthered the disintegration of old cultural units. Greece and Rome were both city states. Alexander and his successors and the Romans, therefore, encouraged the founding and growth of cities. In a certain sense the Empire into which Christianity entered was a congeries of semi-autonomous cities held together by the rule of Rome. No longer, however, were they fully independent politically. Bound together by a growing commerce and under one central administration, in art, institutions, and ideas they tended to conform to one pattern. Local peculiarities were weakened. In this unified world, moreover, thousands of individuals were torn loose from their hereditary *milieu*. As merchants, as slaves, or as soldiers, they found themselves in alien environments. Uprooted from their accustomed soil, the migrants tended to borrow from one another and to abandon or alter their inherited cultures. The Roman Empire was a vast melting-pot in which each ingredient tended to modify and to be modified by every other.[22] The city meant less to the citizen than it had in early Greek or Roman times. The individual often felt lost and sought solace in a religion adapted to his needs and in voluntary, unofficial organizations.[23]

For a considerable period before the advent of Christianity, the traditional state and family cults of Greece and Rome had been losing their hold. Increasingly they were unable to satisfy some of the needs for which a large and probably growing proportion of the population looked to religion. The decay of the older faiths was due to a variety of factors. In part these were found in a changing standard of ethics which regarded the stories told of the Olympian gods by the traditional mythology as morally revolting.[24] The attempt to make the myths more palatable by allegorizing them only partly succeeded. Especially did the intellectuals find difficulty in accepting the inherited beliefs. In Greece this had been true as early as the fifth century B.C. For some, loyalty to the city had formerly taken the place of devotion to the gods,[25] and the weakening of the city state now cast many an individual adrift in his affections. The desire for a cosmic reference in religion superseded the local cults with their limited geographic significance and rendered them ineffective. In Rome, contact with ideas from Greece and the East brought an undercurrent of scepticism toward the official deities.[26] The ceremonies were maintained as a matter of public policy, but no test was applied to insure the endorsement of the existence of the gods by those officiating.[27]

Not only did the centuries immediately before that in which Jesus was born witness a loss of faith in the cults of the state. The age into which he came saw in Rome, the very centre of the Mediterranean world, a most serious moral condition. No very close connexion need be supposed to have existed between the decay in the official religion and the state of morals. The state faith and ethics were not intimately associated.[28] However, both customary religion and ethics were undermined by the irruption of fresh ideas from the East and by the decimation of the old Roman stock through the prolonged wars which Augustus ended. Moreover, the destructive civil strife which preceded the

[22] Case, *The Social Origins of Christianity*, pp. 119-121; McGiffert, *A History of Christianity in the Apostolic Age*, p. 154.
[23] Willoughby, *Pagan Regeneration*, pp. 263-267.
[24] Murray, *Five Stages of Greek Religion*, pp. 59-101.
[25] Murray, *op. cit.*, pp. 59-101; Breasted, *Ancient Times*, pp. 372, 373.
[26] Hardy, *Christianity and the Roman Government*, p. 9.
[27] Merrill, *Essays on Early Christian History*, pp. 33-37.
[28] *Ibid.*

pacification of the world by Augustus was not friendly to most of the virtues. Then, too, wealth was pouring into Rome. Conquests with their spoils and their tribute followed by peace and its commerce brought vast riches to many in the capital of the world. With wealth came luxury, much of it crude. The sturdy virtues of Rome's simpler days were honoured more by breach than by observance. Those who pictured the times had many tales to tell of wanton and lavish display, of senseless cruelty to slaves, of infanticide and abortion, and of the disregard of marriage ties.[29] Doubtless some of this was not seen in its true perspective. Among the writers of the period were those who bewailed the degeneracy. Their existence gives evidence that conscience was not entirely quiescent.[30] We have, too, in the letters of Pliny the Younger glimpses into circles which were not seriously infected by the prevailing vices.[31] We hear of benevolent institutions founded by private generosity.[32] Yet when the pictures of satirists and moralists are discounted and compared with the reports of those who had no interest in the reform of manners, and after account is taken of the worthy lives of which we know, the attested facts are far from pleasant. No doubt, for instance, can well exist of the bald obscenity of the stage or of the brutal slaughter in the arena.[33] It is not strange that in many a disgust developed and a desire for some means of emancipation from the grossness of the age.

Before Christianity was long on its way, and when it had not yet begun to have an influence except on a very few, what seems to have been an improvement in morality had begun.[34] Certainly the preaching of morality by word and pen was widespread.[35] Clearly, too, a marked religious awakening was in progress. Christianity had the first stages of its phenomenal growth in an age and an Empire in which were marked ethical movements and great religious hunger and activity.[36] It made its way in a world in which many preachers of ethics were being heard and where many thousands were seeking through religion protection for society, guidance in their private affairs, solace for their ills, immediate contact and union with the divine, an escape from the trammels

[29] Epictetus, *Discourses and Manual*, edited by Matheson, Vol. I, pp. 11, 74; Dill, *Roman Society from Nero to Marcus Aurelius*, pp. 12, 58-99; Willoughby, *Pagan Regeneration*, pp. 278-298.

[30] Dill, *op. cit.*, pp. 22-30, 141-195.

[31] Dill, *op. cit.*, pp. 141-195.

[32] Dill, *op. cit.*, pp. 193-195.

[33] Dill, *op. cit.*, p. 86.

[34] McGiffert, *A History of Christianity in the Apostolic Age*, p. 156; Dill, *Roman Society from Nero to Marcus Aurelius*, pp. 1, 2, 6, 7.

[35] Dill, *loc. cit.*; Nock, *Conversion*, pp. 99-121.

[36] Willoughby, *Pagan Regeneration*, pp. 1-4; Rostovtzeff, *A History of the Ancient World*, Vol. II, pp. 335, 336.

and the corruption of the flesh, and an assured road to personal immortality. In this ethical, philosophical, and religious ferment is one of the chief reasons for Christianity's remarkable spread.[37]

In its attempts to meet these needs Christianity had many competitors. It did not enter a religious vacuum. In a later chapter we will seek to determine the reasons for its success against its rivals. We will also endeavour to appraise the impress left on Christianity by the systems and ideas which vied with it for supremacy. Here we must sketch briefly what these competitors were and through them attempt to gain something of an insight into the moral, intellectual, and spiritual atmosphere in which Christianity first drew its breath and in which it won its first victories.

First of all, before these various rivals of Christianity are enumerated, it must be noted that they reacted on one another. The times were ones of syncretism and eclecticism. In an Empire in which the boundaries separating peoples, cultures, and states had been weakened or eradicated, this was almost inevitable. Philosophies, religions, deities, magical practices, beliefs and ideas which heretofore had been largely local in their following, were now thrown together in a vast melting-pot. The individual might still be trained in the hereditary religion of his group. If, however, he lived in a city or on a trade route he early became aware of other faiths. Eclecticism abounded. Both the thoughtful and the superficial, impressed by the multiplicity of competing cults and philosophies, despaired of finding complete truth in any one of them. Rather, they constructed philosophies for themselves by combining elements from a number of existing systems. For many, perhaps for the majority, eclecticism implied a conscious or unconscious scepticism. It was because men had no faith in any one system that they sought salvation in several. Philosophies and cults borrowed from one another. Names and attributes were transferred from god to god. Ceremonies were copied. Sometimes this was probably a conscious attempt on the part of a leader in one cult or philosophy to appropriate what seemed to him admirable in another. Sometimes it may have been from a desire to offer all that made other cults or philosophies attractive. It was more often due to a cultural atmosphere in which ideas from a great variety of systems were current and were almost unconsciously adopted.[38]

Instances of this syncretism will appear again and again in our story. One of its most prominent exemplars was Plutarch. The greatest Hellenist of the

---

[37] Angus, *The Mystery Religions and Christianity*, pp. 4, 5; Case, *The Social Origins of Christianity*, pp. 115, 116.

[38] Many books dealing with the period touch on this tendency to eclecticism and syncretism. Among them see Farnell, *Outline History of Greek Philosophy*, p. 144; Glover, *Conflict of Religions in the Early Roman Empire*, p. 89.

latter part of the first century and the first quarter of the second century after Christ, he possessed a wide knowledge of the literature of his day. His was not an original mind of the first quality. Like many of the more thoughtful of the day, he was deeply interested in both morals and religion. He was influenced by Platonism, Stoicism, and Epicureanism, and yet was fully committed to none of them.[39]

While a given thinker might bear the label of a particular philosophic school, it was sometimes difficult to tell from his writings to which of several he really adhered. Room, too, could be made for ancient popular myths by the device of allegorizing. In these stories of the gods, originally so naïve, a hidden meaning was detected and they could, accordingly, be fitted into almost any system of thought or religion.

Probably few, if any, systems succumbed without a struggle to the tendency to sacrifice their individuality.[40] In Judaism and Christianity especially vigorous attempts were made to preserve intact the historic heritage. In none, however, was the effort completely successful.

To turn, then, to the chief of the many systems which the Roman Empire knew and with which Christianity had to deal.

At the outset may perhaps be placed the religion maintained by the state. In Rome the last century of the Republic had seen a weakening of the official cult. However, a deep-seated conviction still existed that the welfare of society depended quite as much upon the favour of the gods as upon human effort. Many looked to some kind of saviour god for deliverance from the turmoil which immediately preceded the establishment of the Empire. Augustus devoted much attention to the revival of the old forms.[41] Early in the Empire, too, came the development of the worship of the Emperor. The longing for a saviour who would bring peace to the earth had seemed to have fulfilment in Augustus. In his lifetime, therefore, the belief arose that he was an incarnation of divinity. His image was erected and religious honours paid to his *genius*.[42] This was not an especially revolutionary innovation. The East had long been accustomed to the idea of a connexion between the ruler and divinity. The Greeks had hero cults. The two streams coalesced in Alexander, who

[39] Plutarch's *Morals, Ethical Essays*, translated by A. R. Shilleto, London, 1898; Plutarch's *Morals, Theosophical Essays*, translated by C. W. King, London, 1898; Dill, *op. cit.*, pp. 384-440.

[40] La Piana, *Foreign Groups in Rome during the First Centuries of the Empire*, p. 325, thinks that the idea that each people was bound to have its own religion died very slowly.

[41] Fowler, *The Religious Experience of the Roman People*, p. 456.

[42] Rostovtzeff, *op. cit.*, Vol. II, pp. 203, 204; Taylor, *The Divinity of the Roman Emperor*, *passim;* Scott, *The Identification of Augustus with Romulus-Quirinus*.

became a deified hero ruler.[43] It was not strange that Julius and Augustus Cæsar should occupy the same rôle. The precedent so established was followed by the development of a cult of the Emperor, which included some of the imperial relatives.[44] The official cult also continued the worship of the ancient gods Jupiter, Juno, and Minerva.[45] As an integral part of it was the reverence for *Roma*.[46]

For this religion temples were erected, not only in Rome itself, but in the many cities of the Empire. The shrines were among the public buildings, and their construction, adornment, and maintenance were matters of civic pride.[47] In the provinces the upkeep of the temples and the celebration of the ceremonies of the cult of Rome were especially the charge of the aristocracy and of the official classes who prided themselves on their Roman citizenship and upon whom fell the burden of civic duties.[48] The ruling classes looked upon them as an integral part of the established order, and regarded any attack upon them or any refusal to endorse them as a threat to the very existence of the state and of society. It was this conviction, as we shall see later, which gave rise to the most severe persecutions which Christianity encountered.

The age in which Christianity appeared saw not only the revival of the official cult, but a widespread dissemination of Greek philosophy. The era of creative and original thinking had largely passed. For more than two centuries no important system of thought had appeared. After the third century B.C. the only new school of any consequence was what we term Neoplatonism.[49] Its very name, however, indicates that it was not a fresh creation, but an outgrowth of a predecessor. The centuries in which Christianity was first spreading were not ones in which the Mediterranean world was endeavouring with intellectual daring to explore the mysteries of the universe. Many of the more thoughtful were, rather, seeking to bring about an orderly society in a vast area which, after long centuries of war, had become, for the first time, a political unit. Their interests were practical. They concerned themselves not with searching for fresh answers to the questions which had fascinated the great Greek minds, but centred their attention chiefly upon administration, upon morals and the cultivation of character, and upon putting into effect principles which

[43] Case, *The Evolution of Early Christianity*, pp. 197-218.
[44] Willoughby, *Pagan Regeneration*, pp. 15-18.
[45] Rostovtzeff, *A History of the Ancient World*, Vol. II, p. 334.
[46] Rostovtzeff, *op. cit.*, Vol. II, pp. 204, 205.
[47] Case, *The Social Origins of Christianity*, pp. 99, 100.
[48] La Piana, *Foreign Groups in Rome during the First Centuries of the Empire*, pp. 283-288; Leclercq, *L'Afrique Chrétienne*, Vol. II, p. 93.
[49] See any history of philosophy. Such a sketch as Murray, *The Five Stages of Greek Religion*, especially pp. 105-152, will suffice.

they accepted as already established.[50] Intellectual speculation there was, to be sure, but it tended to be ancillary to these eminently utilitarian purposes.

This attitude may have been partly the effect of the Roman mind, concerned as it was with the problems of organizing and governing society rather than with inquiry into the ultimate nature of the cosmos. To be sure, the emphasis of philosophy on ethics was not new. Several centuries before, Socrates and the Sophists had been interested in them, as had been other great minds between them and the Empire. However, the Empire saw little or none of original thinking such as had accompanied the development of the historic systems. Its early centuries, rather, were marked not by efforts to blaze fresh trails and found new schools but by attempts to propagate existing philosophical systems, to make their findings the possession of the masses, and to emphasize their ethical teachings.

The first two centuries or so after Christ, then, witnessed the popularizing of philosophy, its widespread dissemination, and the endeavour to bring about through it an elevation of morals.[51] Teachers of philosophy were numerous. Lecture halls where they held forth were familiar features of the cities.[52] In the climax of the movement for moral reform through philosophy, in the age of Marcus Aurelius, men philosophically trained were found in the highest official positions and in charge of great prefectures.[53]

Many had ceased to have confidence in the capacity of the human mind, unaided, to arrive at reliable answers to the questions which perplexed them. They looked, rather, to some divine revelation, made preferably in remote antiquity and possessing the hoary sanctions of age. The individual, longing for personal immortality, searched for it through religious channels. This led, as we shall see, to a remarkable growth of certain kinds of religion. It also tended to transform philosophy and to make it contributory and subordinate to religion. As a result, the philosophical development of the Roman Empire culminated, on the one hand, in Neoplatonism, which was quite as much a religion as a philosophy, and on the other in Christian theology.[54]

The chief schools of Greek philosophy represented in the Roman Empire were the Epicureans, the Peripatetics (followers of Aristotle), the Pythagoreans, the Stoics, the Platonists, and the Neoplatonists.

Epicureanism, although it persisted as a separate school into the fourth century,

[50] Uhlhorn, *The Conflict of Christianity with Heathenism*, p. 93; Nock, *Conversion*, pp. 99-121; Dill, *Roman Society from Nero to Marcus Aurelius*, pp. 289-333.
[51] Goodenough, *The Theology of Justin Martyr*, pp. 31, 32.
[52] Dill, *op. cit.*, pp. 289-333.
[53] Dill, *op. cit.*, pp. 6, 7.
[54] Nock, *Conversion*, pp. 99-121; Goodenough, *op. cit.*, pp. 232, 233; Halliday, *The Pagan Background of Early Christianity*, pp. 168-209.

never succeeded in appealing to large numbers. Its following was chiefly among the educated and the upper classes. Its founder emphasized affection, taught that man can be happy in spite of suffering, and himself met defeat and hardship with high courage. He never counselled the pursuit of pleasure, but lived simply and sought the deliverance of mankind. Yet his philosophy was not primarily one of conquest, but of escape.[55] While its originator by no means denied the existence of the gods, Epicureanism was sceptical of popular superstitions. Some of its adherents held religion to be an incubus on the human soul and were frankly atheistic.[56] It may have contributed slightly to the spread of Christianity by throwing doubt upon the validity of some of the religious beliefs which the latter also attacked.[57]

The Peripatetics, although they continued the tradition of Aristotle which was to be of outstanding importance in the Europe of the Middle Ages, were not as prominent as were some of the other schools in the centuries in which Christianity was first making its way.[58]

The Pythagorean strain was present, mainly among the Neopythagoreans. The Neopythagoreans, of whom we begin to obtain fairly clear information about the first century B.C., cultivated an earnest personal religion based on revelation and tending to asceticism. They influenced some of the Neoplatonists and at Rome had close association with Stoicism.[59] As a body the Pythagoreans seem to have disappeared in the second century after Christ, perhaps by being merged in the revived Platonism.[60]

In the two centuries in which Christianity was first winning a foothold in the Empire, Stoicism was probably the chief agency of moral reform. It was, to be sure, much modified from the original Greek school which is known by that name. Thanks to the eclecticism of the times and to the personal views and interpretations of some of its leading exponents, it eventually bore the impress of some of the other philosophies. Although monistic, increasingly it used the terminology of dualism derived from Platonism. In the Christian era its most prominent representatives were successively Seneca, Epictetus, and the Emperor Marcus Aurelius Antoninus. In all three of these the moral element was much more prominent than the speculative. They were not profound or original

[55] Murray, *Five Stages of Greek Religion*, pp. 105-152; see also on Epicureanism, Zeller, *Stoics, Epicureans, and Sceptics*, pp. 382-485.
[56] R. D. Hicks in Hastings, *Encyclopædia of Religion and Ethics*, Vol. V, pp. 325-330; Case, *The Social Origins of Christianity*, p. 88; Whittaker, *The Neo-Platonists*, p. 19.
[57] Case, *The Evolution of Early Christianity*, pp. 255-278.
[58] *Ibid.*
[59] J. Burnet in Hastings, *Encyclopædia of Religion and Ethics*, Vol. XVI, pp. 520-530; Whittaker, *op. cit.*, pp. 21, 22; Nock, *op. cit.*, p. 167.
[60] Nock, *op. cit.*, p. 167.

metaphysicians or daring intellectual investigators. They were concerned chiefly with living in the world in which they found themselves and in assisting others to do so. Seneca was the wealthy aristocrat and statesman, the tutor of Nero. Epictetus, on the other hand, was a Greek, originally a slave and later a freedman, delicate in health and lame.

Marcus Aurelius led the busy life of the ruler of a vast empire in which he was seeking to maintain order and which he was guarding against the incursions of barbarians. In him Stoicism had its last noteworthy exponent. With him, too, came to an end the succession of high-minded, conscientious rulers who played so important a part in the prosperity of the second century after Christ. They were products of that reform in morals which characterized their age. After them followed a century of domestic strife, barbarian invasions, and foreign wars. After them, too, came that decline in the culture of the Empire which they had delayed, but which all their nobility of character and all the morality of their age had been powerless to avert.[61] In Marcus Aurelius, indeed, one can see the shadow of impending doom. Possessed of a strong sense of public duty, upright, stern in his self-admonitions, living as under the eye of a God who desires righteousness, there seems to have been about him no enthusiasm. Although he believed in God and in God's care for men, he was weighted down by sadness, the burden of empire, and the certain expectation of death. In his meditations, as he recorded them, is disclosed one who seems constantly to be adjusting himself to the thought of death and fortifying himself to endure the ills of life. There is no sense of joyous expectation, either for himself, his friends and neighbours, or for the world as a whole. In him can be caught a glimpse of an age which was fearful of approaching demise and was steeling itself to meet it.[62]

Yet the Stoics left their mark permanently not only upon the civilization of the Empire, but upon that of Europe. Theirs was a philosophy which held that all men are equal by divine right, declared that in the sight of God a slave is of as much value as a monarch, taught the universal brotherhood of man, extolled justice, mercy, and friendship, and maintained that all, as the sons of God, are entitled to share the goods of life. Their humanitarianism left an indelible impress upon Roman law and, through it, upon succeeding centuries of those extensive portions of Europe which incorporated

their beliefs

---

[61] On Stoicism in the Roman Empire see Arnold, *Roman Stoicism;* Dill, *Roman Society from Nero to Marcus Aurelius,* pp. 289-333; Epictetus, *Discourses and Manual* (edited by Matheson); Goodenough, *The Theology of Justin Martyr,* pp. 18-20; Zeller, *Stoics, Epicureans, and Sceptics,* pp. 37, 38; Halliday, *The Pagan Background of Early Christianity,* pp. 132-141.

[62] *The Thoughts of Marcus Aurelius,* translated by Jackson; Alston, *Stoic and Christian in the Second Century.*

that law into their legal systems. Their ideals helped to soften the lot of the slave and to mitigate the harshness of some other existing social institutions.

Christianity eventually triumphed in a society whose morals and whose outlook on life had been profoundly influenced by Stoicism. Many of the latter's standards were not unlike its own. It is often difficult to determine what changes in the later Roman Empire and which of the ethical ideals of European civilization are historically due to Christianity and which to Stoicism. Certainly, as we shall see, while Stoicism as a living school of thought perished, it left its imprint upon the victor.[63]

The Stoics, important though they were, appealed chiefly to aristocratic circles. The education of the masses in morals was largely the work of the Cynics. This school traced its origin to the influence of Socrates and so could boast a fairly long history. In the early centuries of the Christian era its chief representatives were popular preachers. Frequently, perhaps as a rule, they were men of little education. Living simply, they went from place to place, haranguing an audience wherever they could gather one, in the streets, on the porches of temples, or in public squares. Unkempt, rude in speech, they were often regarded with contempt and dislike. Recruited in part from the rebels against society, their own morals were sometimes not above reproach. Many of them, however, were sincere and deeply in earnest, and some were men of education. They denounced pretence and ostentatious display of wealth. To them the usual objects for which men strove were anathema. They poured scorn, too, on much of the popular religion, upon reverence for idols, and upon divination. One of them of the first and second centuries after Christ, in the course of a long life, adjusted quarrels between individuals and cities and is said to have been held in universal deference.[64]

The latest and last of the great philosophical schools of the world which Christianity captured was what we know as Neoplatonism. As its name indicates, many of its basic ideas were Platonic in their origin and descent. As a formal school Platonism had not attained the prominence in the early Roman Empire which Stoicism enjoyed. In its contribution to this new development, however, it displayed a new and vigorous life. In the last centuries of paganism, just before the religious and philosophic systems which are grouped under that head were erased by triumphant Christianity, Neoplatonism was the most prominent of the schools. Under it the ancient re-

[63] The references for Stoic influence on Christianity are many and will be found more fully in a later chapter. Among them see Hatch, *The Influence of Greek Ideas and Usages upon the Christian Church*, p. 168; Dill, *op. cit.*, pp. 234-283.

[64] Dill, *Roman Society from Nero to Marcus Aurelius*, pp. 334-383; R. M. Wenley, in Hastings, *Encyclopædia of Religion and Ethics*, Vol. IV, pp. 378, 383.

ligion made its last stand. In it the attempt was made to synthesize pagan thought and religion. It believed profoundly in one transcendent God and its adherents sought, by the road of the mystic, to attain to union with him. It also made room for the gods of the traditional polytheism and for much of the demonology of popular belief. Unlike the elder philosophies, whose leading exponents had passed off the scene before Christianity had risen to prominence, its creators and interpreters were aware of the new faith, and among them were those who levelled against it the most skilful and formidable intellectual attacks which the Church had yet met.

their belief

Many of the leaders of Neoplatonism were high-minded, widely read, austerely ascetic, deeply religious mystics, whose sincerity, intellectual power, and beauty of character could not but have a profound effect upon those who knew them. Such a one was Plotinus, the first great figure in the school. Born early in the third century after Christ, probably in Egypt, he studied for many years in Alexandria, that intellectual capital of the Græco-Roman world. The one who had the greatest influence on him, Ammonius Saccas, is by some accounted the originator of the school. Ammonius, it is interesting to note, is said to have been reared a Christian, but to have abandoned that faith for philosophy. It is certain that for a time he was the teacher of Origen, who had so much to do with the shaping of Christian thought. Although trained at Alexandria, Plotinus spent most of his mature years in Rome. His pupil, Porphyry, composed what the Church regarded as the most dangerous written argument against Christianity. Iamblichus followed Porphyry in the succession, and the school, which had representatives in many centres of the Empire, included holders of the chair of Plato in Athens and Hypatia of Alexandria, famous for her beauty, modesty, eloquence, and learning. Neoplatonism was to leave an indelible mark upon Christian theology and mysticism and in the life of its successful rival remains today a force with which to reckon.[65]

Philosophy, then, in the forms with which Christianity came in contact with it, was not merely a group of intellectual systems. It was also leading in the moral education of the educated and of the masses. It was increasingly religious. It was both a cause and a product of the movements for moral reform and of the religious hunger which characterized the age in which Christianity first made its way. Hundreds of teachers were spreading it. In lecture halls, where the well-to-do came to listen, in streets, in squares, in the porticoes of public buildings where the itinerant Cynic held forth, the

[65] On Neoplatonism see especially W. R. Inge, *The Philosophy of Plotinus,* and Thomas Whittaker, *The Neo-Platonists.*

public was made familiar with its tenets. Fragments of the philosophical vocabulary ran current in the speech of the time. Although schools borrowed
quite shamelessly from one another and in the process technical terms tended
to be used in more than one sense, and although as they passed from lip to
lip these terms lost their clearly defined outlines, something of their original
significance must have clung to them and so passed into the thinking of the
majority.

The state cults and philosophy, however, by no means constituted all of
the religious picture. Christianity had to reckon with many other elements
in it. Not only the uneducated masses, but also the majority of the cultured
believed in gods, spirits, dreams, miracles, astrology, portents, divination, and
oracles. All the philosophical systems had to take account of them. Although
some ridiculed, others made room for them, sought to justify them intellectually, and endeavoured to fit them into their explanation of the universe.
Divinities were almost infinite in number. Many were petty. Some were
benevolent and some malevolent. Some were well defined in their characteristics and others ill defined. One of the most widely spread of the cults was
that of Æsculapius. His shrines were centres of healing. The practice of
incubation—of sleeping in his temples—was one of the favorite means of
meeting him and experiencing his therapeutic powers. There were sacred
wells and trees. Societies of a religious character abounded. Guilds bringing
together members of particular occupations usually had religious features. In
a world where deities were omnipresent, miracles which evidenced their power
were expected. The gods were believed to disclose themselves in dreams.
Even a Marcus Aurelius thanked them for revealing to him in his sleep a
remedy for illness. If gods were multitudinous, spirits of various kinds were
even more so. What was termed demon possession was common, and disease
was often ascribed to it.[66]

Confidence in astrology was widespread. Astrology as the Græco-Roman
world knew it was largely of Babylonian provenance. In Babylonia had developed an interest in astronomy, and a body of astronomical and mathematical
knowledge had been accumulated. The specialists had been priests and, not
unnaturally, they sought to integrate with religion what they had observed
about the stars and about numbers. They came to think of the universe as
closely articulated and orderly. Human affairs, being part of the universe,
were intimately related to the sidereal system. It was, accordingly, possible

[66] Glover, The Conflict of Religions in the Early Roman Empire, pp. 12, 13; Dill, op. cit.,
pp. 443-483; Friedländer, Roman Life and Manners under the Early Empire, Vol. III,
pp. 84-218; Case, Experience with the Supernatural in Early Christian Times, pp. 3-15.

to gain light on men's future through a knowledge of the heavens. With this, too, were associated theories of numbers. Greek contacts with Babylonia, especially after the conquests of Alexander, brought these tenets and practices into the Hellenistic world. They spread throughout that heir of Hellenism, the Roman Empire. Augustus resorted to astrology. Tiberius was thoroughly committed to it, and its experts were confidants and advisers of the mighty. Professional astrologers were, to be sure, frowned upon by the law, but in practice they were tolerated except when they were believed to menace the welfare of the state. For many astrology was associated with an ironclad fatalism. A man's career was determined by decrees which he could not alter. All that he could hope to do was to discover what his future was to be.

Astrology had intimate relations with Neopythagoreanism and Stoicism. For example, Posidonius of Apamea, of the second and first centuries b.c., made much of it. A Stoic, but, in accordance with the syncretizing spirit of the day, influenced by other systems, including those of Plato and Aristotle, he interwove astrology with his philosophy. He regarded with reverence and awe the heavens as revealed by astrology, and through their contemplation was led into mystic ecstasy. Posidonius contributed to shaping both Stoicism and Neopythagoreanism.

These two philosophies were not alone in showing the effect of astrology. It was part of the intellectual and religious atmosphere of the age, and although they might not formally tolerate it and might even denounce it, few, if any, cults and schools entirely escaped its influence.[67]

Portents, oracles, divination, and other signs by which men might read the future were rejected by Epicureans, Cynics, and Aristoteleans, but Platonists, Pythagoreans, and Stoics held to them. The Stoics especially, who maintained the solicitude of God for men, regarded divination as a proof of Providence and the gods. If this were true of so many of the educated, the prevalence of these convictions among the uncritical masses must have been even more marked.[68]

Of all the cults of the religiously eager age in which Christianity first gained a foothold, none were more popular or widespread than those which are known as the mystery religions. Full information concerning them is as yet unobtainable. The members were under a vow of secrecy, and the literature, most of it only for the elect, has largely disappeared. Our knowledge is, ac-

[67] Cumont, *Astrology and Religion among the Greeks and Romans*, pp. 8, 30, 36-72, 75-99, 140; Cumont, *Oriental Religions*, pp. 179ff.; Friedländer, *op. cit.*, Vol. I, pp. 185-188; Kennedy, *St. Paul and the Mystery Religions*, pp. 6-8, 24, 26.
[68] Friedländer, *op. cit.*, Vol. III, pp. 122-134.

cordingly, fragmentary. The mysteries had their rise in a number of different regions, as widely separated as Anatolia, Persia, and Egypt. In many ways they differed, but in purpose and in the main outlines of their beliefs they displayed a remarkable similarity. This likeness was furthered by a tendency to borrow from one another as they mingled in the syncretistic Græco-Roman world. In general their purpose was to free their members from the bondage of the flesh and to assure them a blissful immortality. This they achieved through union with saviour-gods who had died and risen again. The union was obtained through an initiation ceremony and through rites, such as a common meal, in which the members participated. The mystery cults were rich in symbolism. They professed to achieve redemption for their members from the mortality, the impurity, and the evil in which men were enmeshed. They were highly emotional and some were orgiastic. They promised to satisfy the current craving for knowledge of the divine through exclusive information and processes of which they claimed possession. They offered a symbolic sacramental drama which through its emotional effects would lead the neophyte into a new exaltation of life.[69]

Geographically they were widely extended. However, they were not universal,[70] and seem to have spread partly in connexion with the settlements of members of the racial and national groups in whose lands they had originated. They followed, too, the main arteries of travel and were often disseminated by troops. All seem to have been present in Rome, but that was primarily because of the cosmopolitan character of the population of the metropolis. Sooner or later representatives of every race of the Empire found their way to the capital, bringing with them their peculiar cults.[71] The mystery faiths did not always have an easy course. Sometimes they faced official persecution.[72] They attained, however, to great popularity.

The reasons for the success of the mystery religions are to be found partly in the social conditions and the intellectual and spiritual temper of the times, and partly in the nature of the cults. The age was one, as we have seen, when large numbers of men were uprooted. The compact city states had been partly merged into one vast empire. Men's geographical and political horizons had broadened, and the old social and political groupings had been weakened or dissolved. The individual, thus cast adrift, was seeking security.

[69] Angus, *The Mystery Religions and Christianity*, pp. 38-75; Willoughby, *Pagan Regeneration*, pp. 274-278.
[70] Nock, *Conversion*, pp. 131-133, 192.
[71] La Piana, *Foreign Groups in Rome during the First Centuries of the Empire*, pp. 188-197.
[72] La Piana, *op. cit.*, p. 288.

A great longing existed for assurance of personal immortality. The old city cults, carried over into the state cult, offered no satisfaction. The state religion and many of the ancient beliefs could not promise blissful immortality, but spoke, if at all, only of an utterly unattractive future beyond the grave. A widespread feeling existed in the Hellenistic and, for that matter, in much of the ancient world, that man, by his very nature, is doomed to misery and that except through some miracle by which he comes to share in the nature of the gods he cannot attain to happiness hereafter. The gulf between man and God is abysmal and can be crossed only in a unique fashion. Philosophy, while appealing to many, and in some of its forms holding out a hope of immortality, was usually intellectually cold and emotionally unattractive. Many, too, had lost faith in the ability of the human intellect, unaided, to answer the riddle of the universe and were seeking a self-revelation of the divine. The mystery cults were for the individual. They offered fellowship in this life and held out the promise of a happy immortality. To those looking for an authentic word from the divine, the mysteries gave what professed to be a revelation supported by the sanction of remote antiquity. To those left unsatisfied by the intellectual approach of philosophy, they offered warm emotion.[73]

The mystery cults, as has been suggested, were of ancient origin and from either Greece or the Orient. Many a region from the Adriatic to Persia and from Greece and Asia Minor to Egypt developed one or more of them. From Attica came the Eleusinian mysteries, from Thrace the Dionysian and Orphic movements, from Anatolia the Great Mother of the Gods, from Syria the Syrian goddess and the cult of Aphrodite and Adonis, from the Nile Valley Isis and Osiris, and from the plateau of Iran Mithraism.[74]

The Eleusinian mysteries, developed at Eleusis, near Athens, were associated with Demeter and with the story of the carrying off of her daughter to the underworld by Pluto, her grief and anger in which she blasted the world so that it brought forth no crops, the restoration of her daughter, the permission for the land once more to be fruitful, and the necessity laid upon the daughter of spending part of each year in the lower regions. Obviously here was a myth inspired by the alternation of fruitful spring and summer

[73] Murray, Five Stages of Greek Religion, pp. 155-206; Angus, The Mystery Religions and Christianity, pp. 5, 144-234; Willoughby, Pagan Regeneration, pp. vii, 278-298; Dill, Roman Society from Nero to Marcus Aurelius, pp. 484-528; Angus, Religious Quests of the Graeco-Roman World, pp. 24-46; Baillie, And the Life Everlasting, pp. 121-131; Kennedy, St. Paul and the Mystery Religions, p. 72; Cumont, Oriental Religions, pp. 196-211. See also on the mystery religions, Reitzenstein, Die hellenistischen Mysterienreligionen, passim.

[74] Willoughby. Pagan Regeneration, pp. 23-34.

with sear autumn and winter. The rites connected with the cult were wide-spread and set forth the myth in the form of a drama. Initiation involved no alteration in the manner of life of the participant and no ethical revolution, but was a privilege which assured immortality to those so fortunate as to participate in it. Rites similar to those of Eleusis were celebrated in many other places, either stimulated by Eleusis or having a common parentage with it.[75]

Apparently of Thraco-Phrygian origin, Dionysus and his cult were carried to Greece long before Alexander. The god of wine and of animal and vegetable life, he was given many names, among them that of Bacchus. The ceremonies connected with him were orgiastic. His devotees drank of the fruit of the vine and tore apart the flesh of a slain bull (closely associated with the god) and devoured it, still dripping blood. Thus they partook of the life of the god. A sacred dance induced possession by the god's spirit. The dancers were mostly women, called mænads. The possession of the nature of the god and the transformation of the person by it were only temporary and ceased with the passing of the ecstasy. It was, however, supposed to be a foretaste of a happy future life which the devotees were to share with Dionysus. The cult spread to Italy in the second century B.C. and in the first century of the Christian era was widely extended in the Græco-Roman world. Under the Empire Bacchic associations made up of the initiates of the cult were accused of being centres of moral corruption and of murder, forgery, and political conspiracy. The initiates were youthful, and though at first only women had been admitted, men later were also encouraged to join. So objectionable to the state did these associations become that towards the close of the second century a determined effort was made to stamp them out.[76]

Closely related to Dionysus were Orphism and the Orphic sects. These were associated with the name of Orpheus, but their origins are obscure. Whether Orpheus was an historical personage has been disputed. He was pictured as a musician who by his playing charmed men and beasts. He was also a theologian and a herald of religious change who had suffered martyrdom—the form of his death varying in different accounts. If historical, he seems to have been a philosopher and religious reformer. Certainly the cults which bore his name were less orgiastic, more ethical, and represented more

[75] Rohde, *Psyche*, pp. 217-229; Farnell, *Cults of the Greek States* (most of the third volume is devoted to Demeter and her cult); Willoughby, *op. cit.*, pp. 36-67.
[76] Farnell, *Cults of the Greek State*, Vol. V, pp. 85-344; Farnell, *Outline History of Greek Religion*, p. 56; Rohde, *Psyche*, pp. 253-334; Willoughby, *Pagan Regeneration*, pp. 68-89; Hardy, *Christianity and the Roman Government*, p. 8; Spencer, *Beyond Damascus*, pp. 239, 438; Harrison, *Prolegomena to the Study of Greek Religion*, pp. 364-454.

mature thinking than those of Dionysus. They were, however, built around the myth of Dionysus and so were a development from it. The myth recounted how Zagreus, the son of Zeus, was born of Persephone in the form of a bull. Destined to be the ruler of the world, he was dismembered and eaten by the jealous Titans. Athena, however, saved his heart and Zeus swallowed it. When, therefore, Semele bore a son, Dionysus, to Zeus, he was Zagreus reborn. Orphism intellectualized this story. It had a set of writings giving detailed instructions in ritual and theology. Dualistic, it taught that fundamental differences existed between soul and body and afforded a means of purifying the former from the taint of the latter. It believed in the transmigration of souls, but taught a way of escape from the endless cycle by initiation, cleanliness, and asceticism. After the meal of raw flesh which formed part of the initiation its adherents remained vegetarians. When once freed from its impurities and the contamination of the body, the soul, liberated from the chain of rebirths, lives for ever in bliss like God. The votaries of Orphism formed private associations. Orphism had a centre in Athens, but it was probably also to be found in Italy as early as the sixth and the fifth centuries B.C. Certainly it was there in the first century of the Christian era. The distinction between soul and body which was one of its cardinal assumptions, with the accompanying conviction that body and matter are evil from which the divine element in man, his soul, must be cleansed, constituted one of the most widespread features of Hellenistic thought. It was part of the intellectual and spiritual atmosphere of the Græco-Roman world. As such it modified other mystery cults and later helped to shape Christian belief and practice.[77]

Magna Mater, or the Great Mother of the gods, was the centre of a widespread cult. The cult was found in Asia Minor, whence it seems to have come to Rome. It was also in Crete and its extension to Greece appears to have been closely connected with contacts with that island. It took different forms and *Magna Mater* was known under various names. Like the Eleusinian mysteries and the Dionysiac and Orphic cults, it had its basis in a nature myth which dramatized the death of vegetation in the winter and the revival of the spring. The main outline of the customary myth recounted the love of Cybele, the *Magna Mater,* for the virgin-born shepherd Attis. Attis died, slain either by his own hand or by that of another (if by his own, by emasculation). The goddess mourned for him and effected his resurrection, and he became immortal

[77] Harrison, *Prolegomena to the Study of Greek Religion,* pp. 455-659; Rohde, *Psyche,* pp. 335-361; Willoughby, *Pagan Regeneration,* pp. 90-113; Guthrie, *Orpheus and Greek Religion. passim.*

and deified. Although not originally a part of it, the *taurobolium*, borrowed through the syncretism of the times, became associated with the cult. In the *taurobolium* a bull was killed and the devotees bathed in the blood as a means of dying to the old life and being born again. Regeneration might also be effected by a different kind of union with the deity, a mystic marriage. Participants in the mystery mourned for Attis. At the climax, excited by barbaric music, wild dancing, and the sight of blood, they might follow the example of Attis and emasculate themselves as an act of devotion to the Great Mother. Following this came the day in which the resurrection of Attis was celebrated, when the initiates, in an ecstasy of joy, felt themselves united to Attis through the ceremonies and their self-mutilation. Having experienced a new birth and shared in the resurrection of Attis, they now participated in his immortality. There was also a lay membership for men and women which did not involve mutilation, but had an initiation in which communion was established with the deity.

A very similar cult with a Babylonian prototype was found in Syria and Cyprus and had as its god who died and rose again a young deity called by the Greeks Adonis. Still another cult with the goddess Atargatis and her consort Hadad possessed a Syrian habitat and was celebrated with rites closely resembling those of the Great Mother.

All these were religions of redemption in which, in connexion with a saviour god, initiates were reborn into a new and immortal life. By the time that Christianity was beginning its course they were spreading from their native homes to various parts of the Græco-Roman world and were met by it in more than one region.[78]

Still another and similar cult, that of Isis, had Egyptian sources. Its roots were in the myth of Isis and Osiris which, like the others, seems to have taken its rise in the recurring dying and revival of plant life. Osiris was represented as an early king who had led in introducing civilization. He had been killed by his brother, and his wife, Isis, had travelled about mourning and looking for him. Having found his body, she revived it, whereupon Osiris was transferred to the lower world and reigned as ruler of the dead. Out of this myth and its accompanying rites and beliefs arose, under Hellenistic influence, a cult in which Osiris was replaced by Serapis and in which the emphasis shifted to Isis. The syncretic religion thus developed became a compound of Egyptian elements and of others from the mysteries of Greece and Asia Minor. The

[78] Willoughby, *Pagan Regeneration*, pp. 114-142; Farnell, *Cults of the Greek States*, Vol. III, pp. 289-305; Ramsay, *The Cities and Bishoprics of Phrygia*, Vol. I, pp. 87-92; Dill, *Roman Society from Nero to Marcus Aurelius*, pp. 2, 546-559; Frazer, *Adonis Attis Osiris*, pp. 3-49, 182-193, 217-261.

cult had as a centre the Serapeum at Alexandria and spread widely not only in Egypt, but through the eastern and western borders of the Mediterranean. Membership in the community was by an initiation which probably included a ritual death and resurrection, dramatized, by which the neophyte became identified with the god and was given assurance of immortality.[79]

The latest of the mystery religions to achieve wide popularity in the Roman Empire was Mithraism. Associated with the Persian faith, it spread into Armenia and Asia Minor. In the process it acquired elements from Babylonia and Asia Minor. In the latter region, for example, it came in contact with the *Magna Mater*. It was carried westward to Rome, where it arrived late enough to avoid the persecutions which had attended the advent there of some of its predecessors. In Rome it acquired adherents from the aristocracy and remained strong in those exclusive circles until late in the fourth and early in the fifth century. However, it owed its dissemination chiefly to slaves and military colonists and especially to soldiers. Probably it never attracted many adherents in the Hellenistic world, the sections of the Empire's population in which Christianity made its first large gains. It attained its greatest strength in the Danubian provinces and in Germany. In the Roman Empire the devotees formed religious guilds or societies to which admission was by initiation. The central figure was Mithra, a god of Oriental origin. He was usually represented bestriding a bull and slaying it. Since from the dying bull issued the seed of life for the world, this act became the symbol of regeneration. The cult practised baptism and had a sacramental meal. In contrast to most of the mysteries, it made stern ethical demands on its votaries. It prized abstinence and asceticism. The places of worship were in the form of crypts or underground caverns, small in size and capable of accommodating only a limited number of worshippers. Membership was restricted to men, although in some places a cult open to women seems to have had a close connexion with the faith. Unlike Christianity, Mithraism made a place for the traditional divinities of the Græco-Roman world. At Rome it was especially popular under the Emperor Commodus, at the end of the second century. It was associated with the worship of the sun, a type of monotheism which was in vogue in the later days of Roman paganism. By the end of the third century it had begun to decline, but it remained strong until toward the close of the fourth.

Of all the mystery cults, Mithraism proved the most serious competitor of Christianity. The two showed many resemblances. Both had baptism, a sacramental meal, a belief in immortality, a resurrection, a last judgment, a heaven

[79] Dill, *op. cit.*, pp. 560-584; Willoughby, *op. cit.*, pp. 169-195; Breasted, *The Dawn of Conscience*, p. 95; Frazer, *op. cit.*, pp. 267-400.

of bliss, and a hell of misery. Both made strong ethical demands on their adherents. Both organized into conventicles. Both observed Sunday and celebrated December 25th as a great feast. In the earlier centuries of its existence Christianity seems to have concerned itself very little with Mithraism, possibly because the latter was strongest in official circles and the army, where the former had few adherents. Later the rivals clashed, especially in the Rhone Valley, North Africa, and Rome, and some of the Church Fathers saw in Mithraism a malign imitation of Christianity. How far Mithraism influenced the victor is not clear. Only in Christian art can transference be clearly proved.[80]

These, then, are the chief of what are usually called the mystery religions. Some had developed in the Hellenistic atmosphere and all were influenced by it. While having much in common, they were by no means identical in their teaching or in constituency. They seem to have owed their popularity chiefly to their promise to insure their adherents a blissful immortality. They were very widespread and, as in the case of philosophy, their main teachings and some of their technical terminology probably became current in everyday speech and thought.

The mysteries are often declared to have influenced Christianity. Some have affirmed, indeed, that in the Greek-speaking part of the Empire, filled as it was with the ideas associated with them, Christianity became just another mystery religion. The discussion of that question will be entered upon in a later chapter. Here, however, it may be said that the voluminous extant Christian documents of the first four centuries have comparatively little about them, and that, as a rule, the Christian apologists devoted very little space to refuting them.[81] As rivals of the new faith they seem not to have bulked nearly so largely in the thought of educated Christians as did pagan philosophy and the gods of the state cult. This comparative neglect of the mysteries in Christian writings may have been because cultured Christians did not regard them as serious competitors. Certainly in a number of ways the mystery cults differed markedly from Christianity and lacked some of the features which gave to the latter its victory. Several of them seem to have been weak in their ethical content and so did not have the stamina which a sturdy moral system usually possesses. As a rule they were unable to present a theology and a philosophy which brought conviction to those in search of an intellectually tenable interpretation of the universe.

[80] On Mithraism see Cumont, *The Mysteries of Mithra;* Geden, *Select Passages Illustrating Mithraism;* Dill, *op. cit.,* pp. 585-626; Willoughby, *Pagan Regeneration,* pp. 143-168; Harnack, *The Mission and Expansion of Christianity,* Vol. II, pp. 317-323.

[81] The author has remarked this in his own reading of early Christian writings. It is also noted in Glover, *The Influence of Christ in the Ancient World,* p. 8.

Some of them appealed chiefly or entirely to one sex and not to both, as did Christianity.[82]

To much the same general stream of religion as the mystery cults belongs Hermeticism. We know it through a literature which claims as its author Hermes Trismegistus, who was probably purely mythical. Numbers of fragments have survived, but the chief works which we possess are included in what is called the *Corpus Hermeticum*. The movement of which these documents were an expression was of Egyptian origin and development and seems to have begun at least as early as the second century B.C. Most of the literature, however, was written in the first three centuries of the Christian era. Although of Egyptian birth, it was largely Hellenistic in its thought and Greek and Latin in its language. In part of it the Hebrew cosmology was an important factor. Its influence spread widely in the western part of the Empire. Platonism is the chief ingredient, but, true to the syncretizing tendency of the day, other elements entered, among them Stoicism, Hellenistic Judaism, Neopythagoreanism, and just possibly Christianity. Like the mystery cults, the Hermetic literature presented a religion of redemption. This redemption it declared to be from the trammels of the flesh and matter; it was thoroughly dualistic. Redemption resulted in immortality. Hermeticism had a strong ethical quality: it favoured asceticism and opposed sensuality, injustice, avarice, envy, deceit, anger, and malice. It inculcated meditation, and spoke of a theophany and of ecstasy. Its doctrines it believed to be divinely revealed. It taught a mixture of polytheism, pantheism, and monotheism and took account of astrology. Usually it held that God was not the direct creator of the world, but that he acted through intermediaries. In this latter respect it closely resembled the Gnosticism which played so strong a part in the Christian movement and of which we shall have much to say later.[83]

Gnosticism, to which Hermeticism was related, we know almost entirely in the forms in which it sought to incorporate Christianity. It was, however, pre-Christian in origin. It was dualistic, bridging the gulf between the eternal good on the one hand and evil matter on the other by means of emanations or spirits. It sought salvation, the purging of the human soul from the stain of matter,

[82] Nock, *Conversion*, pp. 56, 57; La Piana, *Foreign Groups in Rome during the First Centuries of the Empire*, p. 333; B. S. Easton in *An Outline of Christianity*, Vol. I, pp. 211-216; Angus, *The Mystery Religions and Christianity*, pp. 235-314; Lake, *Landmarks in the History of Early Christianity*, pp. 73-80.

[83] Angus, *Religious Quests of the Græco-Roman World*, pp. 321-375; Willoughby, *Pagan Regeneration*, pp. 196-224; St. George Stock in Hastings, *Encyclopædia of Religion and Ethics*, Vol. VI, pp. 626-629; Dodd, *The Bible and the Greeks*, pp. 99-248; Scott, *Hermetica*, giving the texts and their translations; Kroll, *Die Lehren des Hermes Trismegistos*.

but this was to be only for the few who had been fortunate enough to acquire the secret knowledge which made its attainment possible.[84]

One important stream of religious development remains to be noted. Whatever the explanation of the emergence of Christianity at a particular point in human history, it has always been clear that it was an outgrowth of Judaism.

Judaism has been so often described that it would be superfluous to go into it in any detail. However, a brief summary of its development, and especially of its outstanding characteristics in the century in which Christianity was born, is essential to any comprehensive understanding of the nature and the spread of this its daughter faith.

Many of the features of Judaism must be ascribed in large part to the geographic and cultural setting in which it arose. Its traditional national home was on and near an important highway between some of the most powerful cultural centres of the ancient world. Along this road moved the commerce and the armies of Egypt, Babylonia, Assyria, and Persia, to be followed later by Alexander and the Greeks and, still later, by the Romans.[85] Near by were the Phœnicians and the Philistines, the latter representing the Minoan culture. The Jews were, therefore, subject to the influence of all the cultures which helped to shape the ancient Mediterranean world. On them the Hittites left their stamp, as did other peoples with whom they mingled in Palestine. East of them, too, was the desert, with its nomads and oases. Yet, living on hills and highlands above the trade routes, the Israelitish peoples, and especially those on the Judean uplands around Jerusalem, were sufficiently independent of the international thoroughfare to assimilate and make their own the many influences which passed by them, to place their stamp upon what they received, and to utilize it as a stimulus to a culture of their own. In the Jewish faith are to be observed, however, contributions from numbers of the different religions and cultures which had touched them. In it elements from Egypt, Babylonia, Syria, and Persia are to be found. Later Greek ideas had their effect. The desert background can also be discerned. As they spread throughout the ancient world, some by forcible deportation and some by voluntary migration, the Jews became even more subject to alien influences.

The tribes which we know under the collective name of Israel were originally a semi-nomadic, pastoral people. Just when they began their conquest of Palestine is not certainly known, although one estimate places the time in the fourteenth century B.C.[86] Certainly it continued for several centuries and was

[84] E. F. Scott in Hastings, *Encyclopædia of Religion and Ethics*, Vol. II, pp. 230-242.

[85] For a map of these trade routes, see Smith, *Atlas of the Historical Geography of the Holy Land*, p. 9.

[86] Oesterley and Robinson, *A History of Israel*, Vol. I, pp. 72-80.

not easily accomplished. Before them the land had been occupied by several different racial groups. Some of these prior inhabitants had a much more complex culture, with agriculture, fortified towns, and better arms than the invaders could boast. During the course of their conquest, moreover, the Israelites faced conquerors from the sea, the Philistines, who represented the ancient Ægean culture which had been so strong in Crete, Greece, and Asia Minor and were much better armed than the rude tribesmen. During the long period of the conquest Egypt seems to have exerted a more or less vague suzerainty over Palestine, although its cultural effect upon Israel apparently was not nearly so great as that of Mesopotamia. At first masters only of the hills, eventually the Israelitish peoples spread to the fertile plains, learned agriculture, and took on something of the less primitive civilization of their neighbours. Some of them became town and city dwellers. In the process they intermarried extensively with the many different races who shared the land with them and absorbed some of their manners and beliefs. In time they formed a united monarchy which for a brief period achieved some degree of prominence. Soon, however, it divided and shrank. Eventually, in the eighth and the sixth centuries B.C., even these two frail states were erased by the major powers of the time, Assyria and Babylon.

Under the Persian Empire, which followed not many years after the extinction of the last of the two petty states, the Jews regained a degree of self-government. For a relatively short time in the second and first centuries B.C., under the Greek rulers who succeeded the Persians, the Jews attained to a certain amount of autonomy and set up a small state governed by their priests. This in turn became subject to the growing Roman Empire. Desperate revolts in the early centuries of the Christian era led only to the final destruction of the traditional architectural symbol of religious unity.[87]

Politically neither the Jews nor their ancestors were of major importance. The states which they organized were relatively small and insignificant. But for their religion and the coherence which it gave them, the Jews would probably long since have been forgotten—except, perhaps, by a few historians and archæologists. Indeed, aside from their religion and its closely related ethical principles and social forms, the Jews and their progenitors seem to have developed no distinctive culture of any consequence. It was not because of association with a politically powerful people or because of its connexion with a many-sided

---

[87] A prodigious literature exists on the history of the Jews and their ancestors. The chief sources for pre-Christian times are the Old Testament and the discoveries made by nineteenth- and twentieth-century archæology. A good survey of the known facts is in Oesterley and Robinson, *A History of Israel*. An older, semi-popular account is Kent, *A History of the Hebrew People*.

and strong civilization that Judaism made upon the rest of the human race the marked impression which it did. To be sure, Judaism as such has never won any very extensive bodies of adherents outside the racial group which has regarded it as its inherited faith. Moreover, beginning with the empires of Alexander's successors, the wide geographic extension of the Jews has been largely through commerce. However, the Jews have owed their coherence to their religion, and their faith has profoundly influenced Islam and Christianity, the two religions of mankind which have expanded the most widely. Even though, chiefly because of its identification with a particular race, Judaism has failed to win many non-Jews, it has been the source of impulses which have affected a larger proportion of the human race than have those from any other religion.

Here is not the place to go at all fully into the reasons for this phenomenon. They must be sought primarily in geography and in the nature of Judaism itself. Fortunately for its future, Judaism had its origin and early development on and near some of the most important trade routes of the ancient world. Fortunately, too, its home was in the Mediterranean area, in which the civilization developed which was to have the widest extension of any that mankind has yet produced. This geographic advantage, however, was shared by several other faiths.

It was the nature of Judaism which proved the greatest asset. This it was which bound the Jews together and nourished the distinctiveness which amid all their dispersions and wanderings has kept them apart from other peoples.

Even before Christianity arose from it, the Jewish religion had had a long history and had displayed a marked development. Its beginnings and much of the course of its early history are shrouded in the obscurity of time. It seems clear that at the outset the Israelites thought of Yahweh, their god, as a tribal divinity. He had chosen them and they had accepted him on the basis of a contract or covenant in which each assumed certain obligations. Among his other acts for this his people, Yahweh aided them in war against their enemies. In time, although just how early we do not know, the peoples of Israel came to think of Yahweh as the creator and Lord of all the earth and its denizens. They never ceased, however, to believe themselves to be, in a peculiar sense, his especial favourites. This conviction passed over into Christianity and has displayed itself again and again, notably in certain national churches and in particular sects. Long before the time of Christ, however, some of "the peculiar people" had come to believe that their God, as Lord of all, cared for all men and that those who had been blessed with a knowledge of him and his will were under obligation to share that knowledge with all the earth.

The Israelites, and their successors, the Jews, also held that they owed certain obligations to Yahweh. Some of these were ritual observances, such as male circumcision, the keeping of the Sabbath, and formal worship. Worship, many of their leaders were convinced, was due to Yahweh alone: Yahweh was a "jealous" God who would not tolerate honours to other divinities. This exclusive worship of Yahweh did not win easily, but only by a prolonged struggle, and the intolerance of Jewish—and Christian—monotheism is an eloquent testimony to the intensity of the battle.

To Yahweh the loyal Israelite owed more than fidelity to prescribed rites. There were ethical duties, particularly in relations of men to one another. Yahweh was interested in his people as a whole. He also had his eye on the individual, was concerned when the weak or the humble were maltreated by their more powerful neighbours and superiors, and demanded justice and mercy. This moral content, this union of religion with the duties which man owed to his fellow, was one of the outstanding features of the faith.

For the majority of Jews no distinction in importance existed between ritual and the ethical relations of men. Both were obligations due to God. Both were prescribed in written laws.

As a marked feature of the religion of Israel, and closely associated with this emphasis upon the righteousness which Yahweh required of his people, were the prophets. These, too, appeared very early and their calling had a long development. They were believed to be, when filled by his Spirit, the mouthpieces of Yahweh. At the outset they may not have been very different from those found in many other faiths who, possessed by a divine afflatus, speak for the god. In Israel, however, they underwent a striking evolution. From among their number, or sometimes quite outside the ranks of the professional prophets, arose those who, unafraid and with great vigour, denounced the sins of rulers and people. Usually unpopular with the majority and some of them persecuted and even killed, they were the leaders and inspirers of the minority. Through them is chiefly traced the moral passion which has been one of the outstanding features of Judaism. Not all—perhaps none—of their ideas were original with them. The high courage and boldness with which they enunciated them, however, were outstanding. Remarkable, too, was the fact that they were not confined to one or two centuries. Their long procession continued for at least a thousand years. The tradition became firmly embedded of the individual, impelled by what he is convinced is the spirit of the One God, proclaiming to the hostile multitude the ethical duties which he believes God demands of men, and denouncing men's iniquities.

It is the vision of the individual, as the mouthpiece of God, standing alone or with the few, persecuted, but with the support of God, which is firmly embedded in Judaism and which passed on into Christianity. With it went, too, the glorification of martyrdom. Prophets, because they are individualists, are annoying to group authority and to administrators, whether in state or religious organization. In post-Christian Judaism they are seen only irregularly and infrequently. In Christianity more frequently than not ecclesiastical officials have frowned upon them and for centuries large Christian groups have not known them. Yet in Christianity prophetism in one form or another has continued to reappear. Especially in early Christianity and in Protestantism the recurrence of the divine voice to the individual has been striking and characteristic.

It was not alone as arraigners of men before the bar of divine judgment that prophets acted. Many also carried a message of repentance and therefore of hope. To them, God had the same mercy that he demands of men. By some of them, as by many of their fellow countrymen, Yahweh was thought of as an Oriental monarch surrounded by his ministers, absolute and to be approached only with awe. However, he not only commanded men's obedience but he was also forgiving. By some few, God was thought of as a husband suffering over the sins of a faithless wife and yearning for her repentance and healing, or as a father longing for the return and moral remaking of his wayward children.

All of these features of the Jewish religion had appeared before the "Exile"— the marked point in the history of the people brought by the extinguishment of political independence by Assyria and Babylonia and the carrying into captivity of the more influential elements of the population.[88] In their main outlines they were present, although in modified form, in the days when Christianity had its beginnings.

The extinction of the little kingdoms of Israel and Judah and the attendant and subsequent migrations, voluntary and involuntary, chiefly to Egypt and Mesopotamia, led to important additions and alterations in the inherited faith. The autonomous state had disappeared. The bond which now held the Jews together was almost purely religious and not, as before, both political and religious.[89] Many Jews were absorbed into the peoples among whom they lived.[90] The political tie having been destroyed, the individual tended to be more prominent. Religion became more an individual matter and not so

---

[88] On pre-Exilic history, besides the appropriate sections of the Old Testament, see Oesterley and Robinson, *A History of Israel,* Vol. I; H. P. Smith, *The Religion of Israel,* pp. 1-195; Kent, *A History of the Hebrew People;* Dawson, *Progress and Religion,* pp. 148-155; Moore. *Judaism,* Vol. I, pp. 421, 500; Vol. II, pp. 16-38; Oesterley and Box, *The Religion and Worship of the Synagogue,* pp. 229-254.

[89] Lietzmann, *Geschichte der alten Kirche,* Vol. I, pp. 10 *et seq.*

[90] Moore, *op. cit.,* Vol. I, p. 113.

exclusively a concern of the group.[91] Each might now think of God as interested in him personally. Individual repentance of individual sins became more common.[92] A belief in personal immortality, previously vague or non-existent, developed, although slowly and late.[93] The horizons of many were broadened and, as in the Book of Jonah, some Jews came to think of their people as having an obligation to call all men to repentance.

When, under the Persians, a small Jewish state was again set up, it was ruled by priests and was largely religious in purpose.[94] The centre was Jerusalem with its temple. On the basis of the ethical monotheism of the prophets, priests and scholars further developed ritual and law.[95] God was regarded with such awe that his personal name, Yahweh, was less and less used, and he was called instead by a term which we translate as Lord.[96] Perhaps under Persian influence the belief in angels, spirit messengers of God, was elaborated, with special names, such as Gabriel, for the more important of them. Perhaps also aided by Persian example, belief in spirits of evil grew.[97]

Sometime during or after the Exile, just when is not known, the synagogue emerged. It seems to have taken on definite forms in the fourth and third centuries B.C. Perhaps it first arose among the Jews in foreign lands. By the time of Christ it was to be found not only among the Jews of the Dispersion, but in Palestine and even in Jerusalem. It was for worship and instruction. The worship was without the sacrifices of the temple and the ritual consisted of prayers and reading from the Scriptures, both the Law and the Prophets. Often, if a competent person were present, the service included a homily. Frequently a school was attached to the synagogue for more detailed instruction. The synagogues became the characteristic centres of Judaism and so played an extremely important part in the perpetuation of the faith.[98] They were to have an important rôle in the early spread of Christianity and probably helped to determine Christian organization and ritual.[99]

As the centuries passed, other developments in the inherited faith were seen.

[91] Charles, *Religious Development between the Old and the New Testaments*, pp. 65-72.
[92] Moore, *op. cit.*, Vol. I, p. 113.
[93] R. H. Charles, *A Critical History of the Doctrine of a Future Life in Israel, in Judaism, and in Christianity*; B. S. Easton in *An Outline of Christianity*, Vol. I, pp. 153-155.
[94] Schürer, *Geschichte des jüdischen Volkes im Zeitalter Jesu Christi*, Vol. I, pp. 181-184.
[95] Streeter, *The Four Gospels*, p. 367.
[96] Moore, *op. cit.*, Vol. I, pp. 424, 425.
[97] Moore, *op. cit.*, Vol. I, pp. 401-404, 438, 439; Oesterley, *The Jewish Background of the Christian Liturgy*, p. 143.
[98] Moore, *op. cit.*, Vol. I, pp. 281-307; Oesterley, *The Jewish Background of the Christian Liturgy*, pp. 36-82; Oesterley and Box, *The Religion and Worship of the Synagogue*, pp. 309-318.
[99] Moore, *op. cit.*, Vol. I, pp. 308-322.

A canon of writings regarded as authoritative was built up, the basis of what later was taken over by Christians as their Old Testament. This was supplemented by oral tradition and by voluminous interpretation and exegesis. The additions were in progress before the advent of Christianity and out of them arose the Talmudic literature, which, however, did not take on its permanent form until some centuries after the time of Christ. As Hebrew, the language of the canon, ceased to be understood by the masses, Targums, or translations and paraphrases of the originals, were made in Aramaic, the vernacular.[100] The *midrash* arose, an exposition of a morally edifying character. It was to influence Christian literature, notably some passages in the Gospels which were cast in its style.[101]

A type of literature which was to have an especially marked effect upon Christianity was the apocalypse. Apocalypses, or revelations, believed to be divinely inspired and often coming in a vision or a dream usually interpreted to the seer by an angel, purported to foretell the future. Some took the name of an ancient worthy and professed to have been disclosed to him. Just how wide a circulation they had is not known. They were frowned upon by many of the rabbis, but, to judge from the number which have come down to us, must have been immensely popular in certain circles. Most of the surviving examples were written between 200 B.C. and 100 A.D., but some of their ideas are to be found as early as 400 B.C. Many are Jewish and others Christian. The apocalyptic writers had a philosophy of history which looked towards a culmination of the human drama in an act of God. Repeatedly this took the form of a resurrection of the dead, in some apocalypses general and in others limited. Often there was a grand assize in which the wicked were condemned and the righteous vindicated and rewarded. An ideal society in which righteousness, peace, and plenty were to prevail was to be set up, according to some in Palestine and according to others in a new universe, spiritual in character, which was to follow the destruction of the present world. The details and even the main features varied from apocalypse to apocalypse or within the same book, but in general the apocalyptists agreed that God's righteousness was to be vindicated and the age-long problem of evil to find its answer by judgment upon wickedness and the establishment of a morally perfect order in which good was at last triumphant.[102]

[100] Oesterley and Box, *op. cit.*, pp. 44-73.
[101] *Ibid.*, pp. 74-97.
[102] Moore, *Judaism*, Vol. II, pp. 279-286, 377-395; Oesterley and Box, *op. cit.*, pp. 211-228; Charles, *Religious Development between the Old and the New Testaments*, pp. 8-21, 40-45, 185-252; Charles, *The Testaments of the Twelve Prophets, passim;* Scott, *The Kingdom of God in the New Testament*, pp. 19-21; Levison, *The Jewish Background of Christianity*, pp. 46-56.

Apocalypticism made a deep impress upon Christianity. Some, indeed, maintain that Christianity was born of this strain of Judaism.[103] Others, however, while not denying the presence of apocalypses in Christian thought and literature, contend that since the literature was mostly in Hebrew, not Aramaic, it could not have been widely current nor especially familiar to the populace from which Jesus drew his early followers.[104]

No other of the apocalypses seems to have had so great an effect upon Christianity as the Book of Enoch. Certainly several New Testament writers show a familiarity with it and quote from it, and some of the post-Apostolic Church Fathers refer to it.[105] The book, written probably before 64 B.C., has several distinct parts. In it an eternal kingdom is pictured as established after the resurrection and the final judgment and in a new heavens and a new earth.[106]

Closely associated with the apocalypses was the conception of a Messiah. Here again great diversity was seen. The Messiah is found outside apocalyptic thought. In some forms of the apocalyptic hope he does not appear at all. In others he is pictured as a king of the Davidic line who is to lead the peoples of Israel to final victory over their enemies. In still another he is a pre-existent heavenly being, at the right hand of God until the time comes for him to act. Then he is to descend from heaven, banish or exterminate the unrighteous, and set up an eternal and perfect kingdom in which the righteous dead, through the resurrection, are to share in the blessedness of the righteous living.[107] In the Book of Enoch, moreover, occurs the title, "The Son of Man,"[108] whose historical connexion with that phrase in the New Testament has been much debated. Just how wide a currency the Messianic hope had among the Jews in the time of Jesus we do not know. As in the case of the apocalypses, we have no way of determining how far it remained characteristic chiefly of certain schools of thought or, perhaps, of sects, and how far it entered generally into popular religion.[109] The conception of the Messiah has been prominent in

---

[103] Charles, *Religious Development between the Old and the New Testaments*, pp. 32-34.
[104] Scott, *The Kingdom of God in the New Testament*, pp. 30-34.
[105] Charles, *The Book of Enoch*, pp. lxxxi-xcv.
[106] Charles, *The Book of Enoch, passim;* Charles, *Religious Development between the Old and the New Testaments*, pp. 59, 60.
[107] Scott, *The Kingdom of God in the New Testament*, pp. 23-26; McGiffert, *A History of Christianity in the Apostolic Age*, pp. 8, 9; B. S. Easton in *An Outline of Christianity*, Vol. I, pp. 153-155; Charles, *The Testaments of the Twelve Patriarchs*, pp. xv-xvii; Charles, *Religious Development between the Old and the New Testaments*, pp. 74-85; Mathews, *The Messianic Hope in the New Testament*, pp. 3-54; Moore, *Judaism*, Vol. II, pp. 323-376; Oesterley and Box, *The Religion and Worship of the Synagogue*, pp. 196-210.
[108] Charles, *The Book of Enoch*, pp. cix, 56.
[109] Schweitzer, *The Quest of the Historical Jesus*, p. 8.

Christianity and, under its Greek form, the Christ, has passed over into its very name.

When Christianity began, Judaism was by no means uniform. Often it is said to have displayed two main divisions, Palestinian and Hellenistic. By the first is meant that which prevailed in Palestine and which, supposedly, had been less subject to alien influences than the second. Hellenistic Judaism was that which predominated among the Jews outside the homeland, where the inherited faith had been modified by the pervading Greek culture which had acquired such currency and prestige under Alexander and his successors. However, geographically these two divisions are only rough approximations of the facts. Greek influences were felt in Palestine: even in Jerusalem were synagogues of Hellenistic Jews and some of the religious festivals prominent in Palestine may have been largely indebted to Greek example. Outside Palestine it is possible that types existed which differed from those in Judea and on which Greek culture had had little effect. Moreover, neither Palestinian nor Hellenistic Judaism was a unity. Each displayed varied forms.

Some of the divisions of Palestinian Judaism loom large in the early stages of Christian history. Those most prominent in our records are the Pharisees and the Sadducees. Chronologically prior to them were the *Chasidim*, characterized by strict adherence to the Law.[110] The *Chasidim* were deeply religious, and from the stream represented by them seem to have come the Pharisees, the apocalyptists, and the Essenes. The Pharisees continued the precedent of the *Chasidim* and held firmly to the historic Law, resisting the Hellenizing tendencies which were permeating much of the nation. To the Law, presumably in part from zeal for it, they added various interpretations and traditional observances. Personal immortality, with rewards for the good and punishments for the evil, had a place in their belief. Of all the schools, theirs enjoyed the greatest popularity with the masses. To them more than to any other party of their time was due the transmission of the tradition which ultimately resulted in the orthodox Judaism of later centuries. To them, too, Christianity originally apparently had more likeness than to any other and with them had its most violent differences.[111] The Sadducees were comparatively few and were confined to aristocratic circles in whose hands rested the control of the temple at Jerusalem. Worldly minded, they seem to

---

[110] Oesterley and Robinson, *A History of Israel*, Vol. II, pp. 314-321; Schürer, *Geschichte des jüdischen Volkes im Zeitalter Jesu Christi*, Vol. I, pp. 186-190.

[111] Josephus, *Bell. Jud.*, Vol. II, 162, 166; Josephus, *Antiq.*, Book XIII, Chap. X, section 6, Book XVIII, Chap. I, sections 3-6; Oesterley and Robinson, *op. cit.*, Vol. II, pp. 317, 318; Moore, *Judaism*, Vol. I, pp. 59-68; McGiffert, *A History of Christianity in the Apostolic Age*, p. 4; Schürer, *op. cit.*, Vol. II, p. 389.

have temporized with the surrounding Hellenism. Yet in some respects, they tended to conservatism and rejected such innovations as the belief in personal immortality and the traditions added to the Law which constituted part of Pharisaism.[112] The Essenes do not appear, at least not by name, in the pages of the New Testament, but by some they have been said to have had a large part in shaping early Christianity. They held high ethical standards to which they enforced strict adherence. They admitted members only after a probation, observed a certain community of goods, and a large proportion of them were celibates.[113] In spite of conjectures and assertions, however, any historical connexion between them and Christianity has yet to be demonstrated.

These three schools probably by no means exhaust all the varieties of Palestinian Judaism at the time of Christ.[114] When the new faith first appeared Palestine displayed much pulsing religious life and had in it a variety of currents. The struggle against the Hellenizing efforts of the Seleucids had intensified adherence to the national faith. Synagogues gave the masses instruction in the historic religion. In the century or two before the Romans arrived the Jewish people and Jewish beliefs and customs had been spreading into Galilee and east of the Jordan.[115] Under the Roman rule the land seems to have prospered. The Romans displayed their customary religious tolerance of local cults and interfered with religious zealots only when the latter's activities seemed to threaten public order. Not until shortly after the time of Christ did they run the risk of offending popular sensibilities by attempting to introduce the imperial cult to Judea.[116] Underneath, however, was a seething tide of unrest—of what in the nineteenth and twentieth centuries would be called nationalism. Only a generation or so after the time of Jesus it was to break out in the desperate revolt, as much religious as nationalistic, which led to the destruction of Jerusalem and its temple.

It was in the midst of this scene that Jesus grew to manhood, lived, and taught, and that the first Christian communities came into existence. It was not strange that a new Jewish sect should be born. What was unique, however, and quite without parallel in either earlier or later Jewish history was that this sect should break away from Judaism and become a religion far more inclusive and far more widely extended than the parent stock.

As we have suggested, Judaism was not confined to Palestine. For centuries

[112] Josephus, *Bell. Jud.*, II, 164, 165; Josephus, *Antiq.*, Book XVIII, Chap. I, sections 3-6; Oesterley and Robinson, *op. cit.*, Vol. II, p. 322; Schürer, *op. cit.*, Vol. II, p. 406.
[113] Josephus, *Bell. Jud.*, II, 119-161; Josephus, *Antiq.*, Book XVIII, Chap. I, sections 3-6; Oesterley and Robinson, *op. cit.*, Vol. II, pp. 323-328.
[114] Bacon, *The Gospel of the Hellenists*, p. 94.
[115] Schürer, *Geschichte des jüdischen Volkes im Zeitalter Jesu Christi*, Vol. II, p. 1.
[116] Schürer, *op. cit.*, Vol. I, pp. 482, 483.

Jews had been found outside their traditional home. Many had been carried captive to Mesopotamia. Others had migrated voluntarily, some of them to Egypt. The successors of Alexander, the Seleucids in North Syria and the Ptolemies in Syria and Egypt, had founded cities. They had offered special privileges to settlers. Partly as a result of these favours and partly for other reasons, some of the new cities in time possessed important Jewish elements.[117] Alexandria had a particularly large Jewish population.[118] Younger and smaller was the Jewish community in Antioch, but, for its bearing on the history of Christianity, very important.[119] Jews became numerous at Rome, partly through captives, but apparently chiefly through migration. We hear of them in many parts of the Roman Empire and even outside it, as, for instance, in South Arabia.[120]

Wherever they went, at least some and probably the majority of the Jews carried their faith with them. Synagogues were established for worship and instruction. Yet the Jews could scarcely fail to be affected by their environment. No closely knit organization existed to enforce orthodoxy, and, until after the time of Christ, no one school was generally accepted as standard. To be sure, the Law and the Prophets seem generally to have been revered, but they were subject to interpretation. The temple at Jerusalem formed a tangible centre of the faith, but the Sadducees in charge probably had no inclination, even had they possessed the power, to impose uniformity on the far-flung colonies of the Dispersion. Moreover, the atmosphere of the times, as we have so often suggested, encouraged the interchange of ideas and customs. It would have been surprising indeed, therefore, if the faith of the Jewish populations outside Palestine had not in part taken on the complexion of their surroundings and if Jewish sects and schools of various kinds had not sprung up.[121]

Of these alien influences that of Hellenism was the most potent. In the cities which arose in the wake of the conquests of Alexander, Hellenistic manners, customs, language, and thought were prominent. Many of the Jews who settled in them, therefore, acquired Greek as a second tongue or even lost all knowledge of the speech of their fathers. Translations of their scriptures into

[117] Schürer, op. cit., Vol. III, pp. 2-9; Levison, The Jewish Background of Christianity, p. 11.
[118] Schürer, op. cit., Vol. III, pp. 19-28.
[119] Kraeling, The Jewish Community at Antioch, passim.
[120] Schürer, op. cit., Vol. III, pp. 2-9.
[121] Moore, Judaism, Vol. I, pp. 102, 103; Oesterley and Box, The Religion and Worship of the Synagogue, Vol. I, pp. 3-8. On interesting ways in which the worship of Yahweh mingled with other cults in Syria and Asia Minor see Cumont, The Oriental Religions in Roman Paganism, pp. 62, 252.

Greek were made, that known as the septuagint being the best known but by no means the only example.[122] With the use of the Greek language must also have come much of Hellenistic ideology and modifications of the inherited faith.

Of the Hellenistic Jewish thinkers the most famous was Philo. An older contemporary of Jesus and Paul, he came from one of the leading Jewish families of Alexandria. In that cosmopolitan Jewish-Hellenistic atmosphere with its pervading syncretism he set himself to the reconciliation of Judaism with Greek thought. This for Philo seems to have been more than an intellectual undertaking. He was himself a mystic, to whom the object of the soul's striving was an immediate vision of God. On him Platonism, Stoicism, and Pythagoreanism as well as his inherited Judaism left their stamp. Of the Greek philosophies, Platonism and Stoicism made the deepest impressions. Among other purposes of his writings was the attempt, through the Logos, to bridge the gulf between the God who is pure being and the world of becoming.[123]

In modern accounts of Hellenistic Judaism we hear much of Philo, but he was only one representative of the tendencies which were in that offshoot of the ancestral faith. The Judaism which resulted from contact with Hellenism probably took many forms, but in the lapse of the centuries the features of most of them have been blurred and even the very existence of some has been forgotten.

The Judaism of the time of Christ, and especially Hellenistic Judaism, had much of the missionary about it. In the religious ferment of the Græco-Roman world many Gentiles were attracted to Judaism. Some became full-fledged converts. Others did not identify themselves with the Jewish community or accept all the ritual requirements of the Law but observed with varying degrees the worship of the Jewish God.[124]

In many ways Hellenistic Judaism both proved a distinct advantage to Christianity and exercised marked influence upon it. The early Christians used its translations of the Scriptures. Apparently it was Hellenistic Jews who first bore the Christian message to the Gentiles and who led the way in ridding Christianity of the features which tended to keep it a Jewish sect. So far as our records tell us, it was a Hellenistic Jew, Paul, who was the chief figure

[122] Oesterley and Robinson, *A History of Israel,* Vol. II, pp. 175-182, 306; Moore, *Judaism,* Vol. I, pp. 88, 101; Oesterley and Box, *op. cit.,* pp. 28-43.

[123] Moore, *Judaism,* Vol. I, pp. 211-214, 357; Kennedy, *Philo's Contribution to Religion,* pp. 6, 11-95, 134, 135, 153-210; Willoughby, *Pagan Regeneration,* pp. 225-262; Goodenough, *By Light, Light, passim.*

[124] Matt. xxiii:15; Schürer, *op. cit.,* Vol. III, pp. 37, 122; Goodenough, *The Theology of Justin Martyr,* pp. 33-56; McGiffert, *A History of Christian Thought,* Vol. I, pp. 16, 17; Moore, *Judaism,* Vol. I, pp. 323-353; Lake, *The Earlier Epistles of St. Paul,* p. 62.

in universalizing the Christian faith and in making the membership of the Christian communities predominantly Gentile. To the synagogues of the Dispersion the early Christian missionaries often went to make the initial presentation of their message. From among the Jewish members and Gentile adherents of these synagogues came many of the first Christian converts. To Hellenistic Judaism, moreover, Gentile Christianity appears to have owed some of its concepts.

Great though the assistance of the Judaism of the Dispersion undoubtedly was in the initial stages of the spread of Christianity, and marked though its impress may have been upon the new faith, it is noteworthy that no form of Hellenistic Judaism made anything like the extensive appeal to the Gentile world that Christianity eventually did. This may have been because Christianity became the heir of Hellenistic Judaism and absorbed or supplanted the latter while it was still spreading. Yet it was Christianity and not what is usually termed Hellenistic Judaism which eventually won the Græco-Roman world.

This chapter has dealt with a long period of time and has attempted to describe complex movements. Inevitably, therefore, it has had to avoid details and to paint its pictures with broad strokes. Perhaps enough has been said, however, to place the inception of Christianity in its proper perspective and to make clear the setting of its early spread.

Christianity arrived late in human history and was preceded by a prolonged development, both in religion and in other phases of civilization. Compared with the total span of mankind's career, its course thus far has been very brief. At the very outset it was favoured by the region and the time into which it was born. It came into being in the Mediterranean world, the largest of the various centres of civilization. Back of it lay the centuries of religious growth out of which Judaism had sprung. Judaism itself had selected, and used as a stimulus to something new and original, much from the previous religious experience of mankind, and to this Christianity fell heir. Christianity, too, arose almost contemporaneously with the Roman Empire and had the advantage of the peace and the political, cultural, commercial, and linguistic unity which that regime created or furthered. Then, too, the first period of Christianity's expansion coincided with the weakening of many of the accustomed social, political, and religious patterns of the Mediterranean basin. Cast adrift from their old moorings, men were searching for security. A religious ferment was stirring men's spirits. As the centuries passed and the decay of ancient civilization and of the Roman Empire itself continued, individuals more and more sought salvation through religious channels and old resistances to the advance of a new religion were progressively weakened. Never before in the history of the race had conditions been so ready for the adoption of a new faith by a majority of the peoples of so large an area.

All of these propitious circumstances, however, did not necessarily mean the triumph of Christianity. It was only one of many systems competing for the allegiance of the Græco-Roman world and some of its rivals apparently had fewer handicaps. We must postpone until a later chapter a consideration of the reasons for the ultimate victory of this particular faith.

Chapter II

CHRISTIANITY AT ITS INCEPTION

WHAT was Christianity at the outset? We have sketched some of the main outlines of the Græco-Roman world into which it was born and in which, in the course of its first five centuries, it triumphed. We have seen that this world was in process of change, that old institutions were crumbling, and that many individuals were seeking fellowship, an answer to the questions which disturbed them, and a solution for their own ills and those of society. This fellowship many, especially in the great cities, were finding in voluntary associations. For the answers to their questions they were turning to philosophy and religion. Philosophy was given more and more an ethical and a religious tinge, and religion was asked to assure, on the one hand, the safety of organized society and on the other the immortal security of the individual. As in the state political unity had been achieved, so in religion and philosophy some sort of universal system was being sought. Towards this universalism many of the best minds and noblest spirits were reaching through the processes of syncretism. Into this scene came Christianity, at the beginning one of the most inconspicuous of the many cults of the complex and cosmopolitan urban centres. Within three centuries it had not only become more powerful than all its many rivals, but it had successfully withstood the attempts of the state to extirpate it. Within five centuries it was the official faith of the Empire and numbered among its adherents the vast majority of the population. What was this faith which had this remarkable spread?

First of all it must be said that no single picture would be valid for all the five centuries or for all individuals or all portions of the Empire. The stream which flowed from primitive Christianity early divided into many different channels. As it increased in volume the courses through which it ran became more numerous and its waters took on varied colours from the soils they traversed. To focus our attention on these many branchings and tints is not the purpose of this book. Notice them we must, but we shall content ourselves chiefly by asking what the stream was at its source and in its higher courses and then, in a later chapter, by describing its main branches.

As we have suggested, Christianity had its rise in Judaism and for a brief time seemed to be merely another sect or school of that faith. Nor has it ever separated itself completely from this Jewish background, even though from time to time numbers of Christians, notably Marcion and some of the Gnostics, would have had it do so.

Always Christianity has looked back to Jesus as its founder and has esteemed him its dominant figure.

By some scholars the prominence assigned to Jesus is alleged to be historically untenable. They say that he had little to do with either the origin or the growth of Christianity. They declare him to be a shadowy figure about whom our reliable information is scanty. Our records of him, so they assert, are at best very brief. Being based on oral tradition, they were subject to interpolations and were distorted by the purposes, the presuppositions, and the lack of comprehension of the transmitters. We can never, therefore, so it is argued, be absolutely sure that in any of the reported sayings of Jesus we have his exact words, nor can we be certain of even the general tenor of his teachings. He did not write a book nor concern himself with organization. He was an artisan from a small village and never travelled beyond the very limited boundaries of Palestine. Out of touch with the great minds of antiquity, his outlook, so it is declared, was at best that of a deeply religious Palestinian Jew. He was earnest, no doubt, but not a creative spirit of the first water to whom we can look as the source of so far-flung and potent a religion as Christianity.[1]

It must be said that this view, while sometimes attractively and persuasively stated, either quite ignores or unduly minimizes certain important facts. The oral tradition on which our Gospels are based was very early committed to writing, part of it probably about a generation after the events and sayings they record.[2] These Gospels are not biographies in the modern sense of that term. They are but little interested in chronology and are silent on the major part, measured in years, of the life of Jesus. Fragments of discourses, pithy sayings, parables, and incidents, some of them put together without regard for the correct sequence, make up large portions of the first three, and the fourth is chiefly an interpretation. Yet when all this is said, the fact remains that we have a sufficient amount of material to give a clear picture of the

[1] Some of these positions are recorded in Schweitzer, The Quest of the Historical Jesus, passim. The problem is also dealt with in Case, The Historicity of Jesus.

[2] See discussions of the nature of these documents in Bacon, The Story of Jesus, passim, and Case, Jesus. A New Biography, passim. Torrey, The Four Gospels: A New Translation, passim, but especially pp. xi, 256, declares that all four are Greek translations of Aramaic originals which must go back at least before 70 A.D. and perhaps to about 60 A.D. or before. This view, however, is not widely accepted.

main characteristics of the one of whom they tell. Even if we did not have these four Gospels, we could gain from the letters of Paul, written within a generation after Jesus, a fairly full picture of the main purport of the teachings of Jesus, the nature of his death, and the accepted belief about his resurrection.[3] Indeed, one fairly radical scholar has declared that for few figures of antiquity do we possess as much indubitably historical information as we do for Jesus and that there are few from whom we have so many authentic discourses.[4] We are probably much nearer to his exact words, for instance, than to those of Socrates.[5] Moreover, while Jesus did not travel widely, neither did Socrates or Plato. Palestine was not a remote corner of the world, for through it ran some of the chief trade routes of the Roman Empire, and Nazareth, where Jesus was reared, was near one of them. Then, too, Jesus was obviously familiar with the religious heritage of his people. In the Jewish Scriptures he came into intimate contact with some of the greatest religious geniuses and some of the most eminent formulations of ethical principles that the human race has known. In Judaism, as we have seen, were caught up contributions from most of the chief cultures of the ancient East, but assimilated into a unique and distinctive religion.

It must also be said that whether historically correct or not, the pictures of Jesus given in the four books with which the New Testament opens have through the centuries been regarded by the vast majority of Christians as authentic and authoritative. The figure, the sayings, and the deeds as there recorded have, accordingly, entered into the very warp and woof of Christianity. No reasonable doubt can exist that with Jesus the movement which we call Christianity appears, and that for the vast majority of Christian leaders the words, deeds, death, and resurrection attributed to him have ever been, at least in theory, the norm to which beliefs and actions have been referred and by which they have been judged. Of the Gospel records the masses of Christians may repeatedly have been ignorant and from them the leaders of the Church have in practice often departed, but the ideal has always been there. From Jesus came the impulse which gave Christianity its origin, and what men believed he said and did have been the accepted standards of that faith.

Of the childhood and early manhood of Jesus we know very little. It is clear that he was reared in Galilee in the village of Nazareth, in the hills above the plain of Esdraelon with its stirring memories and not far from one

[3] Porter, *The Mind of Christ in Paul*, deals with this question, maintaining the essential identity of the picture of Jesus given in the first three Gospels with that to be inferred from Paul's letters.

[4] Schweitzer, *op. cit.*, p. 6.

[5] *Ibid.*

of the main thoroughfares of antiquity. He was known as "the carpenter," and his mother and at least four brothers and two sisters survived into the days of his public career.[6] Joseph does not appear after the stories of the childhood and it is fair guess that he had died before Jesus fared forth to preach, and that possibly the support of the fatherless family had devolved upon the latter as the oldest son. It is often assumed that Jesus knew grinding poverty, but this is not demonstrated. It is even suggested, although without clear proof, that he may have come from a home which in the village was regarded as one of comfort or even modest affluence.[7] That he knew the life of common folk intimately is clear from his recorded words. It is also certain, as we have suggested, that he had acquired or been given a training in the literature of his people and had meditated long and deeply for himself on religious and ethical issues. He seems especially to have been nurtured on or impressed by Deuteronomy, the Psalms, and Isaiah. He was a lover of the out-of-doors and was keenly sensitive to nature in its varying moods. He was quick to take in impressions. Apparently his glance was penetrating.[8] His parables and pithy remarks make it clear that he thought, not in abstract terms, but in pictures. He possessed a keen appreciation of the ludicrous and some of his sayings sparkle with humour.[9] In all these respects Jesus stands out strongly on the pages of the first three Gospels, in some of them quite distinct from the writers and other figures of the New Testament. Until after he had begun his public career he seems not to have impressed his fellow villagers as especially unusual: when he returned to visit them they appeared astonished at the alteration which had taken place in him since the quiet years of his life among them.[10] This change and his public career were inaugurated through contact with John the Baptist.

Of John the Baptist we have only brief glimpses.[11] An ascetic who seems to have kept away from towns and to have made no effort to spread his message by preaching tours, he nevertheless attracted large crowds. He proclaimed an impending judgment and called on men to forsake their sins before it should come. Those who heeded and repented he baptized. He seems to have preached no new ethical precepts, but to have assumed that those taught in

[6] Mark vi:3.

[7] E. F. Scott in *An Outline of Christianity*, Vol. I, p. 38.

[8] See an interpretation in which some of these facts are brought out in Glover, *The Jesus of History*, especially pp. 25-62.

[9] As in Matt. vi:2; Luke vii:31, 32.

[10] Luke iv:22; Mark vi:2.

[11] Our knowledge of him is limited to a few passages in the New Testament, especially the Gospels, and to Josephus, *Ant.*, xviii, 5, 2.

the synagogues were valid.[12] It is said that when asked he gave specific counsel, but in the conduct he advocated was nothing new.[13] He appears to have owed his vogue to his announcement in striking fashion of the nearness of the crisis which the apocalyptists pictured and to his appeal to consciences trained to accept as standard the ethical demands of the Jewish Law. Fearless, rugged, and with a sturdy sense of social justice, he impressed his contemporaries as in the succession of the ancient prophets. It would be interesting to know whether there was any relation between John's plea for moral reform and that which was being made in so much of the Roman Empire by the philosophers. No proof of such a connexion is known and probably none existed, but the approximate coincidence is important. Christianity, continuing as it did much of the ethical emphasis of John, was congenial to the temper of some of the more earnest souls of the age.[14] John gathered about him disciples whom he trained in ascetic practices and methods of prayer.[15] A violent end was put to his ministry by his arrest and execution by a local princeling, Herod the Tetrarch. Herod was moved, so one account has it, by John's denunciation of his marital relations[16] and, according to another, by his fear that John's following might precipitate a political insurrection.[17]

John seems to have given rise to a movement or movements which continued after his death,[18] but we know very little about them. How far they prepared the way for the spread of Christianity and how far they opposed it remains in doubt. It is interesting that the Mandeans, who continued into modern times in the present Iraq as a distinct religious group, seem at the outset to have had some contact with the movement inaugurated by him.[19]

Our accounts agree that the inception of the public career of Jesus was associated with the preaching of John. Jesus himself was baptized by John and that act was accompanied by what was for him a momentous and epoch-making religious experience. Apparently because he was forced to think it through and to discover and adjust himself to its implications, he went away from the haunts of men for a period of engrossing meditation marked by

[12] Moore, *Judaism*, Vol. I, pp. 518, 519.
[13] Luke iii:10-14; Lietzmann, *Geschichte der alten Kirche*, Vol. I, pp. 29-32.
[14] Whether John's message was primarily eschatological is a matter of debate. Burkitt, *Christian Beginnings*, pp. 13-18.
[15] Mark ii:18; Luke xi:1.
[16] Mark vi:17.
[17] Josephus, *Ant.*, xviii, 5, 2.
[18] Acts xix:1-5; K. Kundsin, *Topologische Überlieferungsstoffe im Johannes-Evangelium*, p. 26. However, Burkitt, *Christian Beginnings*, p. 17, believes that John's followers did not form a separate sect.
[19] Kraeling, *The Origin and Antiquity of the Mandeans*, in *Journal of the American Oriental Society*, Vol. XLIX, pp. 195-218.

inner conflict. From the baptism and the wilderness he emerged with a clear sense of mission and with a message and bearing of authority. The oldest of our Gospels connects the beginning of his preaching with the arrest and imprisonment of John[20] and it has been suggested that in this sudden termination of John's activities Jesus heard a divine call to take up the work so tragically broken off.[21] Another tradition declares that he was preaching while John was still at liberty, but tactfully sought to avoid any appearence of competition.[22] Certainly Jesus held his predecessor in high esteem.[23] Unquestionably, too, their messages showed similarity. Both, for instance, advocated repentance.[24]

However, and also indubitably, in many ways Jesus was strikingly different from John. While simple in his tastes, quite independent of any attachment to property, and inured to hardship, Jesus was distinctly not a professional ascetic: he "came both eating and drinking."[25] Nor does he seem to have taught any set system of devotions as John appears to have done.[26] What we call "the Lord's Prayer" was probably meant more as a suggested outline than a fixed formula, and was given, so one account has it, at the instance of his disciples.[27] Although he spoke of judgment, it was not accorded the sombre prominence that it held in John's teaching. John remained aloof from the main centres of human habitation, but Jesus deliberately frequented them. We hear of no miracles wrought by John, while they are prominent in the accounts of Jesus. The contrast is significant, for it fits in with what we are told of Jesus's eagerness to discover and heal the morally and physically ill and deformed. Jesus called men to repent, as John had done, but he also sought them out where they lived. He had stern words for the proud, the self-righteous, the hypocritical, the uncharitable, the unmerciful, the evil-minded, and the cowardly, but he had infinite tenderness for those who were conscious of their need, longed for their renewal, and inspired them with courage and hope.[28] In the unlikenesses to John are to be found some of the chief characteristics of Jesus and so, through his example, of the faith which claimed him as its author.

To these features must be added others. Jesus had for God the reverence and awe that we associate with the Hebrew tradition. We sometimes forget the frequency with which he spoke of the condemnation passed by God on

[20] Mark i:14.
[21] Bacon, *The Story of Jesus,* p. 132.
[22] John iii:21-23; iv:1-3.
[23] Matt. xi:7-11.
[24] Mark i:4, 15.
[25] Luke vii:33, 34.
[26] Luke xi:1.
[27] Luke xi:1-4. But see also Matt. vi:9-13.
[28] Luke vii:36-50; xviii:9-14.

wickedness and the wicked:[29] his was no easy-going Deity with whom men might trifle. However, he had much to say of the goodness and kindness of God and his favourite term for him was Father. As Father men might trust him and his care and Jesus called on them to imitate him in his impartial kindness toward the evil and the good.[30] He did not seek to answer all of men's questions about God. There still remained, for example, the mystery of the sufferings and the seemingly unanswered prayers of the righteous.[31] Yet he did teach men that they should trust God, even when they could not fully understand his ways. He taught that God forgives and he also insisted that a prerequisite to that forgiveness is a man's forgiveness of his fellows.[32] He had a strong sense of social justice, but he wished that men would go beyond justice in active care for one another.[33] For place and power as man had traditionally valued them he had no use: his standards of greatness were the reverse of those commonly held in most if not all of the cultures which had so far developed. To him the really great were not those who could command the submission of their fellows, but those who, however humble, unselfishly and lovingly served.[34] He appears to have accepted unquestioningly the Jewish Law,[35] but he insisted that its ritual was meant to benefit men and he set an example of interpreting it in practice in such fashion as would not be incompatible with obvious human needs.[36]

Jesus spoke a great deal of the Kingdom of God, or the Kingdom of Heaven. This term he apparently inherited from the apocalyptists, although it is not prominent in such of their writings as have come down to us.[37] At any rate the phrase appears to have been so familiar to the audiences which Jesus addressed that it did not seem strange to them and he could assume their knowledge of it.[38] To him the Kingdom of God was both a present fact[39] and a future consummation.[40] Men were to accept it one by one and were to become citizens of it by their own volition.[41] It was not a state with physical boundaries,

[29] Matt. viii:12; xviii:21-35.
[30] Matt. vi:25-34; v:43-48.
[31] Luke xviii:1-8.
[32] Matt. vi:14, 15.
[33] Matt. v:38-42.
[34] Mark x:35-44; Matt. x:11.
[35] Bacon, *Studies in Matthew*, p. 357, notes that Paul cited no instance from the life of Jesus in his support of his own rejection of the Law.
[36] Mark ii:23—iii:5.
[37] Scott, *The Kingdom of God in the New Testament*, p. 36.
[38] Scott, *op. cit.*, pp. 11-15.
[39] Luke xxii:20, 21. See also McGiffert, *A History of Christianity in the Apostolic Age*, pp. 20-24.
[40] Mark i:15.
[41] Luke xviii:15-17, 29.

but embraced men who continued to mingle in ordinary society. Yet Jesus also looked forward to the time when, by the act of God, the present age would be swept away and the Kingdom of God would come. When he expected this to take place has been a matter of debate. Some believe that he anticipated its very early arrival, at the latest in the lifetime of some of his disciples.[42] Others contend that the apocalyptic elements in his sayings were heightened by his followers in the years just after his death.[43] Some of the words attributed to him may be interpreted as implying that he surmised that the final act in the drama of the present age might be greatly delayed.[44] Whether present or future, long deferred or imminent, to his mind the Kingdom of God clearly had implications for social relations. The members of the Kingdom were to act towards their fellows in accordance with certain principles. Chief among these was love. The citizens of the heavenly order were to practise active goodwill to those about them, with forgiveness, kindness, and humility.

It is also clear that Jesus thought of himself as Messiah,[45] although scholars are not agreed as to when the consciousness of this special mission came to him, or whether he ever made a proclamation of his claim to the general public. He assumed for himself what seems to have been an unusual designation, the Son of Man, for which the chief precedent appears to have been in the books of Daniel and Enoch. Many conceptions of the Messiah were, as we have seen, in popular circulation, but he adopted none of them in its entirety, giving, rather, his own content to the term. Out of his inner experience had come a conviction, differing at least in part from what he had inherited, of what his function as Messiah was to be. Even to his most intimate friends it seemed strange and forbidding.[46] He also appears to have believed that men's ultimate welfare was bound up with their relation to him and claimed the personal loyalty of his disciples.[47]

[42] They base their assertions on such passages as Mark i:15; Luke ix:27; Mark xiii:30; Luke xxii:18.

[43] Scott, op. cit., pp. 58-60.

[44] As in the parable of the virgins, where five are called wise apparently because they were prepared for a longer delay in the coming of the bridegroom than was expected. Matt. xxv:1-13.

[45] McGiffert, op. cit., pp. 20-24; Scott, op. cit., pp. 121-125; Mathews, The Messianic Hope of the New Testament, p. 69; Burkitt, Christian Beginnings, pp. 25, 26. Schweitzer, The Quest of the Historical Jesus, p. 8, declares, however, that the whole account of his last days at Jerusalem would be unintelligible if we had to suppose that the masses entertained a shadow of a suspicion that Jesus held himself to be the Messiah.

[46] Matt. xvi:13-23. Charles, Religious Development between the Old and the New Testaments, pp. 91-94, believes that Jesus consciously combined and applied to himself the conception of the Son of Man found in Enoch with that of the suffering servant found in Isaiah.

[47] Matt. viii:35-38; Matt. xix:28, 29.

It is significant that Jesus did not attempt, as Messiah, to bring in the Kingdom of God by political means. In a community seething with nationalistic aspirations and where many were restive under the relatively mild rule of the Romans, Jesus made no effort to organize revolt, as some of his fellow countrymen expected the Messiah to do. Apparently at the very outset of his public career he had faced that issue in his own mind and had deliberately come to the conclusion that God expected his kingdom to be of a non-political kind and that the Messiah, as his agent, must pursue paths quite different from those which some of the apocalyptists had marked out for him.[48] Far from organizing a revolt against Rome, Jesus enjoined, in somewhat cryptic fashion, continued acceptance of its rule,[49] and on at least one occasion took a decidedly friendly attitude toward one of its representatives.[50]

Along with this conviction of the non-political nature of his mission goes another notable feature of the activities and teachings of Jesus. Apparently he was but little concerned with organization. In the few brief months in which he had to work, and especially as powerful opposition developed and his cause was threatened with disaster, he might have been expected to have set about devising and bringing into existence some kind of body under competent leadership either to overcome the opposition or to carry on after his death. This, apparently, he either did not do at all or did not stress. He had about him a chosen group of intimates,[51] and on one occasion[52] he is reported to have assembled and sent out a number of preachers, but the former seems not to have been planned as the beginning of anything more elaborate, and the latter appears to have been thought of as a purely temporary measure for a specific purpose. On two occasions he is said to have used the word "church,"[53] but it is a fair question whether this may not have been put on his lips by a later generation. Certainly the fact that the word is found in only one of our Gospels, and then merely in two sayings, is clear evidence that in the minds of those who compiled our records he was not thought to have emphasized it.

Why Jesus made so little of organization must be a matter of conjecture. It may be that he expected the early end of the present age and the speedy inauguration of the final stage of the Kingdom of Heaven by the direct act of God. If so, organization would have been unnecessary and would even have

---

[48] Luke iv:5-8. See also such popular estimates by non-experts as Simkovitch, *Toward an Understanding of Jesus,* and Curtis, *Civitas Dei,* in which Jesus is held deliberately to have rejected the measures usually advocated by the Jewish nationalists.
[49] Mark xii:13-17.
[50] Matt. viii:5-13.
[51] Mark iii:14.
[52] Luke x:1-17.
[53] Matt. xvi:18, xviii:17.

implied a lack of faith. It is conceivable that he gave instructions to his disciples about an organization which have not found their way into our records. That, however, seems against almost the entire tenor of the sayings which have come down to us. It is more probable that with his profound faith in God he believed that in his own good time and way the Father would bring in the Kingdom, and that the Kingdom did not come in such tangible form that men could say "lo, here, or lo, there,"[54] but that, at least until the great final deed of God, it would spread in unorganized and, perhaps, quite unspectacular fashion. It looks as though Jesus had a profound distrust of elaborate organized effort or at least an indifference to it as a means of bringing in a better day.

It is one of the strange and momentous facts of history that out of a movement begun by one who paid so little attention to organization and administration has come the Roman Catholic Church, geographically more widely spread than any other body that mankind has ever seen, and that not only the Roman Catholic Church, but many other elaborate ecclesiastical structures have emerged from it. Into some of the reasons for this phenomenon we must go in later chapters.

We must also note that Jesus made no frontal attack upon any of the social evils of his day in an attempt to eliminate them. He preached love and himself healed individuals who had been maimed morally or physically by the society in which he lived. He denounced injustice, callousness to need and suffering, the lack of a forgiving spirit, impurity even of thought, pride, ostentation, and any shadow of dishonesty or pretence. However, he did not directly oppose slavery or war as such, nor institute any campaign to abolish prostitution, nor found institutions for the relief of the poor. Yet from no other single individual have impulses gone out which have contributed to so many of the efforts which men have made to rid society of what they have deemed social ills.

The question is often raised as to what was new in the teachings of Jesus. For practically all, if not all, of the specific precepts and beliefs attributed to him it is possible to find precedent in the pre-Christian literature of his people.[55] What Jesus did was to penetrate into the heart of the moral and religious concepts which he had inherited from the past and to pick out what seemed to him essential. He performed this not in any systematic fashion. He wrote no

---

[54] Luke xvii:20, 21.
[55] As by the Jewish Rabbi, G. Friedländer, *The Jewish Sources of the Sermon on the Mount, passim.* See also an eminent Jewish scholar, C. G. Montefiore, *Rabbinic Literature and Gospel Teachings.* On the novelty of the Message of Jesus, see Scott, *The Gospel and Its Tributaries,* pp. 1-22.

book in which he attempted to give permanence to his ideas. We have no record of his ever formulating an ordered, comprehensive body of teaching which he asked his disciples to commit to memory. He even had no brief creed which he inculcated as a summary of his beliefs. His discourses were meant mostly for specific occasions. What men recalled and transmitted were chiefly parables, illustrations, and pithy sayings. They were impressed by what he said and did. What seems to have made its deepest mark on his intimates was the man himself, and for him they came, even in his lifetime, to have the most exalted regard.[56] The novelty of Jesus must be sought not so much in fresh principles, but in his phraseology, in what he emphasized, and especially in what he was as revealed in his words and deeds. Indeed, it has been one of the causes of the persistence of the influence of Jesus that he did not express himself in metaphysical or scientific formulas, which must either have been too far ahead of his contemporaries to be understood by them or else too entangled with contemporary systems to be freed from them as the latter were outgrown, but in stories and sayings which are timeless. Even the apocalyptic symbolism which he used had the advantage which poetry gives over prose.[57]

Jesus most certainly seems to have thought of himself as inaugurating a movement which, while having its roots in the past, was yet different. He who had been made a scribe in the Kingdom of God, so he said, brought forth out of his treasures things both new and old.[58] He also hinted at the destruction which the new wine would work in the old containers.[59] Moreover, the Pharisees thought of him as sufficiently revolutionary to constitute a menace to what they believed to be the heritage of Israel. It is significant that the records of the life of Jesus as they have come down to us give more space to his conflict with the Pharisees than with any other of the Jewish schools or groups of the time, and this in spite of the fact that it was not they but the Sadducean priests in charge of the temple who were immediately responsible for his death. The controversy with the Pharisees may have been heightened in the telling, but that it was prominent appears incontestable. The Pharisees represented the stream out of which Jewish orthodoxy was shortly to develop. With them Jesus appears to have had closer affinity than with any other Jewish group. Certainly some of the early Christians came from among them.[60] Yet

[56] Mark viii:27-30.
[57] Scott, *The Kingdom of God in the New Testament*, p. 118; Schweitzer, *The Quest of the Historical Jesus*, p. 400.
[58] Matt. xiii:52.
[59] Matt. ix:16, 17.
[60] Acts xv:5.

the main body of Pharisees seem to have regarded Jesus as threatening at least some of what they esteemed as most precious and authentic in the Jewish faith and Jesus held them to be distorters of true religion. The difference was chiefly a matter of proportion, but this proved of fundamental importance. To the Pharisees all the Jewish Law, its ritual and taboos and the duties of man to man, were important, and they had elaborated these by tradition and exegesis. To Jesus the inherited rites were valid,[61] but they must always be secondary to human life and welfare and, accordingly, to the duties which men owe to one another.[62] He united the ancient commands to love God and one's neighbour, declaring that they resembled each other.[63] Love of God he placed first, but it and love for one's neighbour obviously could not be incompatible. Jesus seems to have implied, moreover, that men must be the judge as to when the rites and taboos should be ignored. It is also interesting to note that in the accounts of those whom he declared to have been "saved" or "found," such as a woman of the street,[64] a Zaccheus,[65] and the prodigal son,[66] Jesus ignored their relation to the ceremonial Law. It is only the fact of a deep-seated change of life, of moral transformation, which he mentioned. The tenor of the individual life was to him of more importance than outward conformity, whether to a code of morals or a system of ceremonies. He looked to the thoughts and motives of men's acts and insisted that these be such as could bear scrutiny by a righteous God.[67]

All of this prepared the way for the universalizing of Christianity. Jesus himself restricted his labours almost entirely to the Jewish people.[68] His attitude towards rites, however, and his insistence upon the primacy of motive over the outward act, led naturally to a break with ceremonies set down in an inherited written Law. Once that break was made, it would be difficult to confine his message to any one race or nation. His conception of God and the kind of love for men which he showed could not be confined to any one group or region. Jesus himself specifically foreshadowed this on a number of occasions. His discourse at Nazareth in which he called attention to the care of Old Testament prophets for non-Israelites,[69] his interest in the centurion[70] and the

---

[61] Matt. v:18, 19; Mark i:40, 45.
[62] Luke xi:42; Mark iii:1-6.
[63] Mark xii:28-34.
[64] Luke vii:36-50.
[65] Luke xix:1-10.
[66] Luke xv:11-32.
[67] Matt. v:8, 27-32; Luke xi:37-41.
[68] Matt. xv:24.
[69] Luke iv:25-27.
[70] Luke vii:2-11.

Syro-Phœnician woman,[71] and the parable in which he immortalized a Samaritan[72] as an instance of one who, rather than professional religious leaders of the Jews, had kept the commandment of love for his neighbour, indicate a vision larger than the horizons of one nation. It was not an accident that the impulse given by Jesus led to the creation of the only direct outgrowth of Judaism which has ever broken the bounds of the parent faith and race and become universal in its appeal and scope. It must never be forgotten that of all the many schools which Judaism developed in the course of its long history, Christianity is the only one which has become preponderatingly non-Jewish in membership and has had an extensive geographic spread. This must be traced back to Jesus. The preaching of the Christian Gospel to the Gentiles and the freedom from the inherited Jewish ceremonies begin so early that they cannot be ascribed to any one disciple of Jesus, not even Paul, but must be attributed to the life and message of Jesus himself.

It must, moreover, be recalled that Jesus gave a distinctive designation to his message—Gospel, or "Good News." This in itself is an indication that he thought of his mission as registering a fresh start, and is also a clew to what he believed its nature to be. To be sure, he is reported to have had stern words to say of the tragic fate of the unrighteous and unrepentant,[73] but he also encouraged men and women to repent, through him went a power which made them over in a new abounding life physical and spiritual, and one of his phrases remembered by his disciples was, "be of good cheer."[74] He compared himself and his disciples to a wedding party.[75] He knew privation, temptation, and suffering,[76] but one of the dominant impressions he seems to have made was of confidence, faith in a dependable God, and joy.[77]

Closely related to what Jesus called the "Good News" were his miracles, especially those of healing. While scholars have debated the authenticity of some or all of them, no doubt can exist that they hold a prominent place in our records and so in the picture of Jesus which his intimates transmitted to the early disciples. Several of the diseases healed seem so like nervous disorders which we now know to be subject to sudden cure that many even of the sceptical are willing to admit the possibility of a large proportion of the miracles. It is clear from our records that Jesus did not perform them to

[71] Matt. xv:21-28.
[72] Luke x:25-37.
[73] As in Matt. xviii:32, 35, xxv:41-46.
[74] Matt. ix:2, xiv:27.
[75] Mark ii:19.
[76] Luke xxii:28; ix:58. Also the story of Gethsemane and the Crucifixion.
[77] As in Mark iv:35-41.

prove the validity of his message, but rather out of a desire to help the unfortunate and the suffering. At times he even sought to keep them from the knowledge of the public,[78] perhaps because he felt that they tended to obscure his message or throw it out of proportion.[79] Apparently, however, he regarded them as evidence of the power of God[80] and as characteristic of his mission.[81] He also insisted that healing was wrought through faith, which men themselves might have, rather than through any power which resided in him alone.[82] That in itself would be a message of joy and would tend toward the continued reappearance of miracles in the movement which he inaugurated.

All four Gospels make much of the death of Jesus and the events immediately preceding it. This emphasis upon his martyrdom is shared by most of the other books which compose the New Testament. The cross, moreover, has become the symbol of the Christian faith, and the vast majority of Christians have continued to dwell upon it and the incidents surrounding it. Our records, however, do not disclose fully the motives of Jesus or exactly what he believed to be the significance of his death. Obviously he deliberately came to Jerusalem knowing that death awaited him. It also seems clear that the deed which precipitated action against him was his cleansing the temple of those who made gain out of the worshippers and the worship. For a brief time he kept out of the temple those whom he had expelled. Apparently he wished, in this fashion, to make clear, at the very centre of the faith of his people, at least one of the reforms in religious practice which he believed necessary. It was a daring gesture to the nation. Yet he must have known that, barring the direct intervention of God, if he remained in Jerusalem this act would mean his death. The Sadducean clique which controlled the temple would regard him a menace to their power and would seek to do away with him. Although they were so numerous that his enemies feared to take him by day, he did not organize his followers to hold by force what he had won. Nor did he, the demonstration made, retire quietly, as, apparently, he could easily have done. To be sure, he would probably have had to go beyond the confines of Palestine, at least for a time, for neither Galilee nor Judea was now safe. That he would not, or at least did not do. He held a final supper with his intimates, went to a garden to pray, was there arrested through the perfidy of one of the Twelve, and was brought by the high-priestly group to the Roman governor, Pilate, for formal trial. Pilate, always faced with the possibility of riots

[78] Mark i:43.
[79] Mark i:38, 45.
[80] Luke x:11.
[81] Luke vii:18-23.
[82] Mark v:34; Luke vii:50, xviii:42.

in a region seething with nationalistic aspirations, and especially at the Passover festival, when the city was thronged with pilgrims and feeling ran high,
apparently was persuaded that the best way to keep the peace was to dispose
of the accused promptly and vigorously, although our accounts represent him
as acting only under pressure and as convinced of the harmlessness and innocence of the prisoner. Jesus was crucified before his followers had time to
gather, even had they been disposed to do so. So far as the casual spectator
late on the afternoon of the execution could have seen, the work of Jesus had
ended in failure. His had been a mad plan, pursued in a manner which foredoomed it, and the end had been inevitable and not so much tragic as pitiful.
Entrenched ecclesiastical privilege, badly alarmed for the moment, had sought
aid of the civil authorities. The latter had done what seemed to them prudent
and the dreamer had been effectively removed.

One of the most remarkable facts of human history, however, is the repercussions which this event has had. Any attempt to discover why this has been so
would quickly take us out of the realms to which the modern historian is supposed to restrict himself and translate us into the regions of metaphysics and
theology. Over the significance of the cross men have been meditating—and
debating—for centuries. He would be strangely obtuse who did not recognize
the magnitude of the issues involved. They lead us at once into fundamental
questions about the very nature of the universe itself. Is the universe on the
side of the worldly priests, intent on preserving their position and perquisites,
and of a Pilate, or is it on the side of Jesus? Or is it unknowing or indifferent?
Into the answer we must not seek to go. Nor must we attempt to determine
why this particular tragedy should have risen to such prominence as the classic
incentive for such questions. Thousands of other idealists who have sought the
welfare of their fellows have been done to death by entrenched privilege and
prudent administrators. Why has the death of Jesus exerted such exceptional
influence? Again the historian must recognize the fact that the answer may
elude him if he seeks for it only in the areas to which he and his fellows are
accustomed to confine themselves.

One answer even the modern historian may verify by the tests which his craft
is accustomed to use. It was the conviction of the resurrection of Jesus which
lifted his followers out of the despair into which his death had cast them and
which led to the perpetuation of the movement begun by him. But for their
profound belief that the crucified had risen from the dead and that they had
seen him and talked with him, the death of Jesus and even Jesus himself would
probably have been all but forgotten.

What were the experiences which gave rise to this conviction? Any attempt to answer that question at all fully must be aside from our present purpose. The accounts with which the New Testament supplies us cannot easily be woven into a consistent whole. For instance, the Fourth Gospel gives as apparently the first recorded appearance of the risen Jesus that to Mary Magdalene,[83] the First Gospel makes it to two women,[84] while Paul, whose record is the earliest which we have in its present form, declares expressly that the first appearance was to Peter.[85] The Third Gospel places all the appearances in and near Jerusalem, the First and Fourth locate some of them in or near Jerusalem and some in Galilee, and the original Mark, whose ending we do not have, seems to indicate that they were in Galilee.[86] A good many modern scholars are inclined, therefore, to place them in Galilee[87] and at least one of them holds that they all followed upon the contagion of Peter's vision.[88] Whatever the precise order or localities or the nature of the experiences which gave rise to it, no doubt can exist of the inspiring and ineradicable conviction of the early Christians. They were persuaded that Jesus had risen from the dead, that many of their number had seen him, and that after a given time the appearances had ceased. Even Paul, while believing that his contact with Jesus on the Damascus road was as valid as the others, regarded it as exceptional.[89] Yet, while they held that a particular type of appearance of Jesus had ended, the Christians were sure that Jesus lived on and that valid messages continued to come from him to them.[90] Without these convictions the history of Christianity would be very different from what it has been—if, indeed, there would have been any history at all.

The life, character, teachings, deeds, death, and resurrection of Jesus were the starting point of Christianity, the impulse from which came the movement in its many ramifications whose spread is the subject of these volumes. They have been, however, not the kind of impulse which is given and then forgotten. They have continued to be the professed standard of reference of the many branches of Christianity. In its nineteen hundred years, Christianity has taken on many forms in many different environments. Through them all, however, has run the influence of the written records of the life of Jesus. Varied interpretations have been given these records. They have been read with emphases

[83] John xx:11-18.
[84] Matt. xxviii:1-10.
[85] I Cor. xv, 4.
[86] Mark xvi:7.
[87] Weiss, *Urchristentum*, p. 11.
[88] Bacon, *The Story of Jesus*, pp. 290-295.
[89] I Cor. xv:8.
[90] As in Acts xvi:7 and Rev. i:1, 9-20. For a brief argument for the authenticity of the resurrection appearances, see B. S. Easton in *An Outline of Christianity*, Vol. I, pp. 116-123.

which have differed from age to age, from person to person, and from ecclesiastical body to ecclesiastical body. Yet they have been a persistent element in Christianity and have had no small part in determining the characteristics of its many types.

The Christianity which spread in the Græco-Roman world arose, then, out of impulses given by the career of Jesus. However, that religion was never merely the words and deeds of Jesus, but these in the forms in which they were remembered and transmitted, the experiences of individual Christians, and the interpretations given the memories and the experiences. It follows, therefore, that from the outset Christianity has been varied. It has not been a single system of beliefs and practices which has expanded. Even a casual perusal of the New Testament discloses differences, as, for instance, between the Gospel of John and that of Mark, between the Gospels of Matthew and Luke, and between the Epistle of James and that to the Hebrews. The multiplicity of forms was encouraged by two early factors. The first has already been noted—the absence of any systematized body of doctrine or any elaborate organization formulated by Jesus and transmitted by him as authoritative. The second seems to have been closely related to the first, the experiences which the Christians ascribed to what they usually termed the Holy Spirit or the Spirit. Jesus himself had set the example of speaking and acting as he believed God directed him.[91] Early tradition declares that after the resurrection and ascension of Jesus the disciples assembled in Jerusalem had a remarkable empowering by the Holy Spirit. Certainly the primitive Christian communities displayed a fresh outburst of enthusiasm and of prophetism. Prophecy was, indeed, one of the most distinctive features of early Christianity.[92] Men and women believed that the Spirit spoke directly to them and that the messages had divine authority. However, those who live in the conviction that they have direct access to God often tend to be individualistic. A movement in which they are prominent shows great diversity. To this early Christianity was no exception.

What all the varieties of this early Christianity were we do not know. We hear much of certain strains, but of others we have only tantalizing hints[93] and from them can conjecture that still others existed of which no traces survive. For a few, however, our records are sufficiently full to enable us to determine their main outlines. They are the ones which entered into the main stream of what came to be the faith of the majority. To these, then, we must now turn.

In general, Christianity during the first two generations of its existence is

[91] As in Luke iv:16-21; Mark xiv:36-39.
[92] As in Acts xi:27, xv:32, xxi:9, 10; Romans xii:6, 7; I Cor. xiv:32, 36, 37; I Thes. v:20. See also Lindsay, *The Church and the Ministry in the Early Centuries*, p. 90.
[93] As in Acts xviii:24-26; I Cor. i:12; I John iv:1, 2; Rev. ii:6, 15.

usually said to have displayed chiefly two forms, Jewish and Hellenistic. As we shall see a little later, by A.D. 100 it may have begun its spread into other cultural environments, as, for instance, non-Jewish Aramaic-using communities. Moreover, each of the two streams displayed more than one current. Especially did that which flowed into the Hellenistic world show variations. For our purposes, however, we need fix our attention only on the broad outlines of the two.

So far as we know, the earliest Christian community or communities constituted a Jewish sect. Our record of them as they first existed is tantalizingly brief, mainly the first few chapters of the book of Acts. Nor are we sure how far we can depend upon it. For instance, almost certainly we do not have in the speeches there reported verbally accurate written transcripts and we can only conjecture how near they are to the originals.[94] From statements in Paul's letters[95] and from deductions which we may make from the emphases in the first three Gospels, whose underlying documents must have arisen in this Jewish-Christian community, we can supplement and correct the picture.[96] It seems clear that these early Jewish Christians had their centre at Jerusalem and that they conformed to the generally accepted rites and practices of their fellow Jews.[97] Their chief distinguishing characteristic was their conviction that Jesus was the Messiah. They may have prayed to him.[98] It seems probable that they also called him Lord, although precisely what they meant by the title is a matter of debate. The designation of Jesus in that fashion by men who had eaten and drunk with him, convinced Jewish monotheists though they were, is remarkable evidence of the impression he had made on them. These Jewish Christians emphasized the death and resurrection of Jesus and looked for his reappearance, as Messiah, to inaugurate a new age.[99] They were marked, too, by the experience of the Holy Spirit, which, among other things, led to emotional

[94] Ropes, *The Apostolic Age*, p. 75. Even Torrey, who contends that the first fifteen chapters of Acts are a translation of an early Aramaic original, says that the main source of the original document is oral tradition (*The Composition and Date of Acts*, p. 58).

[95] As in Galatians i:16-ii:21.

[96] Ropes, *op. cit.*, p. 74. Burkitt, *Christian Beginnings*, p. 62, speaks of how little we know of the details of the religion of the Jewish Christians.

[97] Acts i-xv, especially ii:46, xi:2, xv:1-21.

[98] Weiss, *Urchristentum*, p. 26, points out that the early Aramaic formula, *Maranatha*—"Our Lord come"—probably originated in the early Jewish-Christian community and was both a prayer and a designation of Jesus as Lord.

[99] Acts ii:36, iii:20, 21. See also Mathews, *The Messianic Hope in the New Testament*, pp. 141-148; McGiffert, *The God of the Early Christians*, p. 22; Weiss, *Urchristentum*, p. 22; Case, *The Evolution of Early Christianity*, p. 336. Scott, *The Kingdom of God in the New Testament*, pp. 134-139, says that the effect of the departure of Jesus was to heighten the hope of the Kingdom of God on its apocalyptic side. The apocalypticism of the early Church was more fully elaborated than that of Jesus and the Messiah was always made central in it.

excitement, to "speaking with tongues," and to a large number of prophets.[100] For a time, possibly brief, they practised community of goods.[101] We may gather from the first three Gospels, for which at least some of the material must have been collected by them, that they treasured the deeds and sayings of Jesus. They seem also to have been characterized by joy. The Christian message was to them, as it had been to Jesus, "Good News."

Hellenistic Christianity seems to have begun at Jerusalem,[102] but it early developed an important centre at Antioch.[103] It differed from Jewish Christianity mainly by not being a Jewish sect. In it Christianity quickly cast aside enough of its Jewish swaddling-clothes to become a universal religion, not confined to Judaism. Its leader of whom we know most, Paul, had much to do with shaping it, but it antedated him[104] and he may not have had as important a part in creating it as we usually suppose. It broke with Jewish ritual obligations,[105] and received members into fellowship without their first becoming Jews—a step made natural, as we have suggested, by the example of Jesus. It took on many forms, even at an early date, and was much more varied than Jewish Christianity seems to have been. To some of the more prominent of these forms we must revert in later chapters. Its adherents, both Jews and Gentiles, coming, as they did, out of a Hellenistic environment and continuing to live in it, brought with them many concepts and practices from that syncretizing background, so manifold in its manifestations. Upon it Hellenistic Judaism exercised a profound influence.

The main streams of Jewish and Hellenistic Christianity had much in common. Both believed in Jesus as risen Lord,[106] regarded him as authoritative, and looked for his early return. Both had the experience of the Holy Spirit. Both valued as standard ethical principles inherited from Judaism and Jesus. Both observed certain rites, especially baptism,[107] and the Lord's Supper.[108]

Very early, indeed, the conviction arose of a Christian community. Christianity has been the most quarrelsome of religions. No other faith has shown

[100] Acts ii:1-13, viii:17, x:44.

[101] Acts iv:32.

[102] Acts vi:6, 11-13. Bacon, Stephen's Speech, p. 219, says that the report of Stephen's speech seems to proceed from a type of universalism more radical in some respects than Paulinism itself.

[103] Acts xi:19-30, xii:1, 2.

[104] See the references in footnotes 102 and 103.

[105] See on this point, among others, Paul's letter to the Galatians.

[106] Ephesians iv:4-6; Bacon, The Founding of the Church, p. 47.

[107] Ephesians iv:4-6. We are not sure of the origin of Christian baptism. Christ in his lifetime seems to have baptized no one and it would be interesting to know how the practice came into the Church. Schweitzer, The Quest of the Historical Jesus, p. 18. See also Reitzenstein, Die Vorgeschichte der christlichen Taufe, passim.

[108] Acts ii:46; I Cor. xi:17-29.

so many acrimonious divisions. This has been in part a sign of vitality. It seems also to have been a logical outgrowth of the individualism bred by the belief in the Holy Spirit. Yet from the outset Christians have seemed to hold that they should form one community and that in their divisions they were doing violence to the spirit and message of their Lord.[109] The bitterness of the struggles between groups calling themselves Christian has been enhanced by the contradiction between the individualism born of the experience of the Holy Spirit and the dream of an inclusive community. The way of reciprocal love, advocated as the sign of unity,[110] has in practice been so frequently ignored that the resulting strife has been prominent. The ideal of unity in love has never been entirely forgotten, however, and has reappeared from time to time as a not ineffective factor.

It must also be noted that none of these early Christian communities, whether Jewish or Hellenistic, made any serious effort to transform the life of the entire Græco-Roman world. From their ethical standards and the prominence of the Kingdom of God found in the teachings of Jesus they might at first sight have been expected to seek to revolutionize society. They were, indeed, accused of that purpose.[111] In time they produced profound changes. These did not arise, however, from a deliberately conceived program for a thoroughgoing replacement of the existing order. Christians expected that transformation to be wrought, but not by their own efforts. It was to be in sudden, apocalyptic fashion by their returning Lord. In this they had the example of Jesus in his earthly life, for, as we have seen, he made no effort at planned social revolution, but specialized on winning individuals. Christians, at the outset a minority group, cultivated those virtues which could be practised in their own circles and did not seek to shape the Empire as a whole.

This, then, was Christianity as it was at the beginning of its expansion. It regarded as its founder and authoritative Master one who had come out of Judaism and who had emphasized in that faith what seemed to him central and valid. Yet Christianity was a new creation. It bore the stamp of a great religious and ethical genius. The death of Jesus and the conviction that he had risen from the grave became integral parts of the faith of his followers and have, ever since, given Christianity some of its outstanding features. The immediate disciples of Jesus were Jews and the first Christian communities constituted a Jewish sect. Within much less than a generation, however, Christianity had broken its Jewish chrysalis and had emerged into the Hellenistic

[109] I Cor. i:10-13; Ephesians iv:3-5; John xvii:11.
[110] John xiii:34, 35; xv:12, 17.
[111] Acts xvii:6.

world as one of the faiths which, in a time of religious ferment, were competing for the allegiance of the newly formed Roman Empire. Equipped with its Jewish heritage, with the insights and the compelling person and the death and resurrection of its founder, and with the fresh and unusually vital experiences and enthusiastic convictions of its earliest leaders, Christianity, at first one of the smallest and youngest of the competitors, was, within three and a half centuries, to be clearly the victor, and within five centuries to be the almost undisputed religious master of the Mediterranean world.

Chapter III

THE SPREAD OF CHRISTIANITY BEFORE CONSTANTINE: THE GEOGRAPHICAL EXTENSION

THE first great geographic triumph of Christianity was the winning of the cultural area into which it was born, the Mediterranean world. For such an achievement it is almost always impossible to give exact terminal dates. To do so even approximately involves ascertaining when the process of conversion was completed and that in turn presupposes a definition of conversion. If by conversion is meant the formal acceptance of a faith, even though that act may not be accompanied by any very profound insight into the nature of the religion and no marked change of conduct, then the Roman Empire may be said to have been won by about A.D. 500. If a more precise date is desired, perhaps A.D. 529 will serve. It was in that year that the Emperor Justinian I closed the ancient schools of philosophy at Athens, an act symbolic of the end of the toleration of what had once been important rivals of Christianity. It is interesting, too, that about A.D. 529 Benedict of Nursia, accompanied by a small band of disciples, moved from Subiaco to Monte Cassino, later the chief centre of the rule that prevailed in those monastic communities upon which fell so much of the burden of winning Western and North-western Europe in the succeeding major period of the expansion of Christianity. In 496, moreover, occurred the baptism of Clovis, a landmark in the conversion of the peoples of North-western Europe. About A.D. 500, then, one stage in the spread of Christianity was ending and another beginning.

However, the importance of the year 500 as marking the end of an era can easily be exaggerated. Long before then the vast majority of the population of the Roman Empire had nominally associated themselves with the Christian Church and for some time thereafter the Empire contained those who were still frankly pagan. Some time before A.D. 500, moreover, Christianity had taken on most of the forms which determined its outstanding features in the centuries ahead. Some of its leading creeds had been formulated, the territorial monarchical episcopate had been developed, and most of the greatest of the thinkers had lived and written who, as the Fathers, were revered by later generations of Christians as having given the authoritative interpretations to the faith.

The winning of the Roman Empire, then, required approximately five centuries. It had, however, two main stages, divided by the reign of Constantine the Great, A.D. 306-337. In the first of these Christianity was making its way as a religion without formal official toleration and latterly in the face of strenuous efforts of the Emperors to extirpate it. Under Constantine began the official steps by which Christianity became the state religion. Beginning with the reign of Constantine, and except for the brief reaction under Julian, Christianity was sponsored by the government and eventually became the sole official cult.

This change in the status of Christianity had important consequences for both the nature of the Christianity which spread and the processes and success of the Christian propaganda. For example, the state now threw its weight on the side of unity in the Church, it sought to control the Church as an agent for its ends, and it accorded the Church prestige and privileges which helped to alter the quality of both the membership and the leaders. Then, too, before Constantine the Church, although, after the state, the most powerful organization in the Empire, still embraced only a minority of the population. Beginning with Constantine, accessions so flooded the Church that before A.D. 500 the vast majority of the citizens of the Empire had become Christians. The change in status also profoundly affected the extension of Christianity outside the bounds of the Empire. The reign of Constantine, therefore, begins a new chapter. Since, however, it is chiefly significant as a step toward the completion of the conversion of the Empire, a process already well begun, it is not a major dividing point.

As the narrative progresses we shall see that neither of these two stages was a unit. Each embraced what may be called subordinate steps, and for neither is the story free from complexities. Some of the variations and diversities will appear as we proceed, but numbers can either only be surmised from the imperfect records which remain or in an account as comprehensive as ours must be passed over with a cursory notice.

It is interesting that during the centuries in which Christianity was becoming dominant in the Mediterranean world Buddhism, still prosperous in India, was spreading in Central Asia, China, and Korea, and was about to enter Japan. Never, to be sure, did it occupy in the cultural circle of China quite the place of exclusive prominence which Christianity came to hold in the Roman Empire and Western Europe. Perhaps, however, there is more than a coincidence in the fact that these two faiths, both combining otherworldliness with highly ethical emphases, were making rapid headway at about the same time. No conclusive evidence exists of the influence of the one upon the other, but it may be that conditions then existed throughout most of civilized mankind which made such faiths welcome. Certainly, after about A.D. 200, both in the basin of the Mediterranean and in China the rapid spread of Christianity and Buddhism seems to have been due in part to the weakening or disintegration of existing institutions which might otherwise have offered effective resistance to the advance of new religions. In both the expansion of Christianity in the Roman Empire and of Buddhism in China, moreover, the major factor was not force of arms or association with commerce or with a superior culture, but religious vitality. Both are examples of religions winning primarily, although not exclusively, because of their spiritual appeal.

In the Roman Empire, however, the victory of Christianity was much more nearly complete than was that of Buddhism in China. Although it modified the religious beliefs and ethical practice of China, Buddhism became the exclusive faith of only a small minority of the population—the monks, nuns, and a few lay folk. The land remained predominantly Confucian. In the Mediterranean world Christianity supplanted all its rivals except Judaism, the faith of a small minority. To be sure, the victor was modified by the systems which it displaced, but none of these survived as organized cults.

The first stage of the spread of Christianity through the Roman world, or until Constantine, seems in turn to subdivide itself into at least three others. The initial one includes approximately the first generation after Jesus, or what is sometimes called the Apostolic Age. In it the new faith was being extended largely among Jews and those Gentiles who had some touch with Judaism. The agents were often from the immediate entourage of Jesus or those who had caught the contagion through direct contact with them. By the second period, from the latter part of the first century after Christ to the close of the second century, the hope of converting the Jews had proved illusory and Christianity was spreading almost entirely among non-Jews and chiefly in the cities. Christians were still so much in the minority that only occasionally do they seem to have attracted much public notice. In the third period, beginning with the close of the second century, or, to be more exact, with the death of the Emperor Marcus Aurelius and the accession of Commodus (A.D. 180), the Empire was racked by internal disorder, pestilence, and foreign wars. In the fears and pessimism which these engendered and in the weakening of existing institutions, many turned to Christianity and its growth was very rapid. By Constantine the Church had become the chief internal rival of the state, and next to the state the most powerful institution in the Empire.

For the spread of Christianity in the Apostolic Age the surviving traces are tantalizingly brief. To be sure, we have the New Testament, made up of documents of the first and the early part of the second century after Christ. Compared with the extant sources of information for several other contemporary religions of the Empire they are fairly extensive.[1] This is as we would expect, for the records of a victor are more likely to be preserved than are those of its defeated rivals. Of the origin of many important Christian communities, however, we know little or nothing. For instance, we have no information of the precise time or manner in which the highly influential Church in Alexandria arose. Of the even more prominent Church in Rome we know something, but just how it came to be or who founded it we cannot say.

This is not surprising. At the outset Christianity was one of the smallest of the many cults with which the Græco-Roman world teemed. It would have been extraordinary if the little groups of believers had attracted much attention from those who wrote most of the literature of the time, and it would have been still more remarkable had there survived many of such scanty notices as were probably made.

Because of the fragmentary nature of our records, we may be in danger of giving such as we possess undue prominence and so of distorting the story. It is entirely possible, for example, that Paul did not have as prominent a part in the propagation of Hellenistic Christianity as the space devoted in the New Testament to his letters would lead us to expect.

Short though the records are, they not only afford us remarkable insight into the character of the earliest forms of Christianity and of the processes by which they spread, but, because of the veneration with which they have been regarded by successive generations of Christians, they have enjoyed a rôle of incalculable importance in shaping Christianity through the ensuing centuries and have helped to give it continuity and to hold before it its primitive ideals.

As we have seen, the Christian community seems to have had its first centre in Jerusalem.[2] Even though at least some of the appearances of the risen Jesus were in Galilee, the headquarters of the movement were quickly established in the holy city of the nation. It would be interesting to know whether groups of disciples survived in Galilee, where Jesus spent so much of his public career. We hear at an early date of Christians there.[3] It is conceivable that the Christian community at Damascus arose from contacts with Galilee, for it was nearer the latter than to Jerusalem.[4] It is very possible that the appearance of the risen

---

[1] Harnack, *The Mission and Expansion of Christianity*, Vol. I, p. x.
[2] Acts i-vi.
[3] Acts ix:31.
[4] Acts ix:1-19; B. S. Easton in *An Outline of Christianity*, Vol. I, pp. 174-178.

Jesus to the "above five hundred brethren" of which Paul speaks[5] was in Galilee and that the majority of these remained there.[6] It seems not unreasonable, moreover, to surmise that much of the tradition of the deeds and words of Jesus which has gone into our Gospels owes its preservation to Galilean Christians. Our evidence, however, is tantalizingly inadequate.[7]

If the reports given us in Acts are authentic, the leaders of the Jerusalem group were active as preachers of their faith.[8] In spite of occasional persecution, the community grew rapidly.[9] It early attracted adherents not only from Palestinian Jews but from those of Hellenistic background.[10] We even hear of one Gentile, a proselyte to Judaism, who held office in the community.[11] As we noticed in the last chapter, most of the first Christians seem to have had no intention of separating from Judaism. Like the members of most young sects, they were ardent and at times very annoying to those who constituted the established order.[12] At least one of the leaders of the Pharisees, however, is reported to have looked upon them with somewhat guarded tolerance.[13] Indeed, with their emphasis on the resurrection of Jesus, some of the Pharisees may have regarded them with no unfriendly eye.[14] We hear, too, of converts from the Pharisees.[15]

However, very soon at least one member of the young community, Stephen, developed tendencies which pointed to a speedy and decisive break with Judaism. He seems to have put forward views of the traditional rites of the nation and of the Mosaic law which no Jew, certainly no Jew of Pharisaic or Sadducean background, could tolerate and which aroused the ire of the more conservative even of the Hellenistic Jews.[16] Certainly, in view of the attitude which many

[5] I Cor. xv:6.

[6] Weiss, *Urchristentum*, p. 98.

[7] Burkitt, *Christian Beginnings*, p. 89, says that there is no evidence in early times of any Galilean Christianity. On the other hand, Streeter, *The Four Gospels*, p. 233, says that we know from the rabbis that for centuries Capernaum was a great centre for *Minim*, or Christians, and that probably, therefore, some of the Twelve made the city their headquarters.

[8] Acts ii:1-42; iii:1-26; v:12-25; vi:8-10.

[9] Acts ii:41; v:14.

[10] Acts vi:1-6. It is conceivable that the Andronicus and Junias, Jews bearing Greek or Græco-Latin names, mentioned by Paul in Romans xvi:7 as having been Christians before his conversion, were also members of the Jerusalem community. Dodd, *The Epistle of Paul to the Romans*, pp. 237, 238.

[11] Acts vi:5.

[12] Acts iv:1-21; v:17-32.

[13] Acts v:33-39.

[14] As in Acts xxiii:6-9.

[15] Acts xv:5.

[16] Acts vi:8-14. However, it must be said that McGiffert, *A History of Christianity in the Apostolic Age*, pp. 86-89, holds, from the content of his speech, that Stephen did not question the continued validity of the Jewish Law or suggest in any way the call of the

of the Gentile Christians were soon to take, the reported charge against Stephen appears highly significant—that he had been heard to say "that this Jesus of Nazareth shall destroy this place and shall change the customs which Moses delivered unto us."[17] It is also of more than passing importance that this first Christian martyr of whom we have record appears to have paid with his life for the contention that Christianity was not just another school of Judaism, but was something new and would supersede the parent faith. Christianity had started on its course as a supra-national religion.

It was probably no accident that the first Christian missionaries outside Judea of whom we know were those "scattered abroad" by the persecution which followed the death of Stephen. The preaching of one of these to the Samaritans appears to have been most significant.[18] It seems a not unreasonable conjecture that many of them shared Stephen's views. Certainly the one whose name looms most prominently, Philip, is first heard of in close association with Stephen.[19] The guess may also be hazarded, but with much more tenuous foundation, that those who were followers of "the Way" in Damascus whom Paul was sent to harass[20] were singled out because they were known to sympathize with Stephen. As possible evidence is the report that it was at Damascus that Paul, in spite of his initial strong impulse to bear witness of his new-found faith to the Jews, came to the conviction that his mission was to the Gentiles and that the first of the Damascus Christians who is said to have seen him is reported to have beheld in him a future missionary to the Gentiles.[21] It is clear that not all the Christians were compelled to flee from Jerusalem as a result of the persecution,[22] and it is probable that their opponents distinguished between those who shared the views of Stephen and those who were content to remain within Judaism.

From the character of the evidence, much of this must be in the nature of an hypothesis which cannot be proved or disproved. Our records declare, however, that Philip won to the faith a highly placed eunuch of Ethiopia[23] whose race

---

Gentiles. He believes that he did not anticipate Paul's treatment of the Jewish Law or a free Gentile Christianity.

[17] Acts vi:14. See also Acts vii:48-50 and B. W. Bacon, Stephen's Speech: Its Argument and Doctrinal Relationship, in Biblical and Semitic Studies (Yale Bicentennial Publications, 1901), pp. 213-276.

[18] Acts viii:1-25.

[19] Acts viii:1-8, 26-40.

[20] Acts ix:1, 2.

[21] Acts ix:15.

[22] Acts viii:14.

[23] Acts viii:26-40. McGiffert, op. cit., p. 100, declares that the author of Acts did not regard this as a conversion of a Gentile, but of a Jew or a Jewish proselyte.

we do not know, and that some of those dispersed by the persecution which followed Stephen's martyrdom preached to "the Greeks" at Antioch.[24]

Probably it was not due to the genius of any one disciple, whether a Stephen or a Paul, that the infant religion so early outgrew its Jewish swaddling-clothes. Even our surviving records, fragmentary though they are, suggest that the venture into the Gentile world was made on at least two occasions which were largely and perhaps entirely independent of each other.[25] It is clear, too, that all four of our Gospels agree in ascribing the original impulse to Jesus,[26] even though the historicity of the words they attribute to him has been denied. It has been suggested[27] that such sayings as "Go not into the way of the Gentiles"[28] and "Ye shall not have gone over the cities of Israel till the Son of Man be come"[29] reflect the earliest attitude of the Apostles in Jerusalem. On the other hand, it must also be noted that at least some forms of the prevalent apocalyptic hope contemplated the extension of the Messianic Kingdom throughout the earth and the conversion of the Gentiles.[30] This might well have prepared the way for the preaching to the Gentiles of Jesus as the Messiah and the winning of them to a righteousness which did not involve conformity to the Jewish ritual law or incorporation into the Jewish nation. Hellenistic Judaism, too, from which Stephen, Paul, and other early missionaries to the Gentiles came, had long been winning converts from among the Gentiles. Whatever the predisposing forces in Palestinian and Hellenistic Judaism, the main incentive to the Gentile mission seems to have come from Jesus.

At Antioch arose the first important community of which we know where the prevailing form of Christianity had broken the restrictions which bound it to a racial religion.[31] Antioch, too, became the centre for the propagation of this type of the faith throughout at least part of the adjoining region. Founded by successors of Alexander, it was predominantly Hellenistic in culture. Situ-

---

[24] Acts xi : 19, 20.

[25] As in Antioch in Acts xi:20 and by Peter to Cornelius in Acts x:1-xi:18. It might be argued that both of these incidents could be traced to the impulse given by Stephen. Those who preached to "the Greeks" in Antioch being of those who had been expelled from Jerusalem in the persecution which arose because of Stephen might easily have derived their views from him. Peter, too, must have known Stephen's views. The story of his vision at Joppa might be held to indicate that Peter had been inwardly fighting the suggestion and had his doubts solved by the appearance of the messengers from Cornelius.

[26] Matt. xviii:18-20; Mark xvi:15, 16; Luke xxiv:47; Acts 1:8; John xii:20-32.

[27] Nock, Conversion, p. 187.

[28] Matt. x:5, 6.

[29] Matt. x:23.

[30] As in Isaiah xlix:6, lxvi:19-27; Enoch xc:20. See also the universalism in the book of Jonah.

[31] Acts xv:1—which makes it clear that the church in Antioch did not practise the test rite of circumcision. See also Gal. ii:11-13.

ated on the Orontes River twenty miles or so from the sea, on a fertile plain which separated the Lebanon from the spurs of the Taurus, through it passed some of the main trade routes of the East, and it became an important commercial city.[32] In its large body of Hellenistic Jews Christianity quickly gained a foothold and spread among the cosmopolitan population of the metropolis. It was natural that the new faith should move out along the channels of commerce which radiated from the city.

Within less than a generation, then, after the death of Jesus, Christianity had begun to be a part of the urban life of the Hellenistic world. This was to be expected. Born among the Jews, it was almost inevitable that, possessed of the enthusiastic vitality which it displayed from its very inception and with its original headquarters at Jerusalem, the religious capital, to which came Jews from the wide-flung Dispersion, it should quickly be carried to Jewish groups in the cities of the Empire. Bearing within itself, too, inherent qualities of universalism, it caught fire among some of those Jews who, affected by the syncretizing atmosphere of the Hellenistic world, were consciously or unconsciously ready for a faith which, while retaining the ethical and spiritual values of Judaism, was broader than any one nation and had as well the extraordinary attraction of Jesus.

The early entrance into the stream of Hellenistic urban life greatly facilitated the spread of Christianity. Greek-speaking communities existed in most of the main cities of the Empire and Hellenistic ideas and culture were dominant in extensive circles. The fact that Christianity gained this connexion made easy its access to the chief centres of Mediterranean civilization. The Græco-Roman world was a congeries of cities. A faith with its stronghold in them would tend to penetrate to the connecting towns and countryside.

It must also be noticed that the Hellenistic urban environment helped to determine the future form of the new faith, although the precise ways in which it did so must be left to a future chapter.

By no means all the Jews in the Hellenistic cities welcomed the new sect. It was to the synagogues that the early missionaries usually first made their way and gave their message, presenting Jesus, crucified and risen, as the Messiah, and interpreting the Jewish Scriptures as finding their fulfilment in him.[33] In nearly every place some accepted the new gospel. This was true both of the Jews and of the numbers of non-Jews who had become either full Jewish proselytes or were interested in Judaism. Seldom if ever, however, did the entire

[32] On Antioch see Bouchier, *A Short History of Antioch.*
[33] Acts xvii:1-3.

Jewish community concur. Usually a sharp conflict arose which ended in the separation of the Christians[34] into their own conventicles.[35]

Disappointing though this was to the Christian missionary,[36] it was not strange. In the cities of the Roman Empire the Jews formed distinct and sometimes unpopular communities.[37] Their religion gave them coherence and nourished a pride which in part compensated for the contempt of their neighbours. Now came a faith which claimed universalism and sought to wipe out the distinction between Jew and Gentile[38] even at the sacrifice of some of the customs which the Jew held most dear. It is not surprising that the majority, alarmed and enraged by this threat to what they cherished, should angrily reject the innovation and expel its messengers. Among immigrant minorities almost everywhere and in every age are the conservatives who fight against assimilation.

In this case the conservatives won. Before the end of the first hundred years of its existence, the new faith had become predominantly non-Jewish in its membership and the main currents of Jewish life and thought went on almost without reference to it. Clashes between the two religions there were, but most Christian apologists turned their attention to other rivals and most of the Jewish teachers who were shaping Jewish orthodoxy gave little heed to Christianity—except, perhaps, to react against Messianism.

In the spread of this universalized Christianity from Antioch the one who stands out most prominently in the surviving records is Paul. To him *The Acts of the Apostles* pays more attention than to any other of the early missionaries, and his letters loom large in the New Testament. He was connected either with the founding or the early life of several of the most prominent of the early Christian communities, including especially Antioch, Ephesus, and Rome. His letters are unusually self-revealing and we know him better than we do any other early Christian and, indeed, almost as well as we do any figure of antiquity.

Born in Tarsus, one of the cities where Hellenistic culture was strong, the son of a Roman citizen,[39] as a boy he was surrounded by that teeming urban

[34] On the various designations by which Christians were known—such as Nazarenes, Galileans, or "Poor"—and the names which they called themselves—"Believers," "Saints," "Brethren," "The Church of God"—see Harnack, *The Mission and Expansion of Christianity*, Vol. I, pp. 399-418. See also, on the designation of Christians, McGiffert, *A History of Christianity in the Apostolic Age*, pp. 109, 110; and Haines, *Heathen Contact with Christianity during the First Century and a Half*, p. 4.

[35] Acts xvii:1-5; xviii:5, 6; xix:9.

[36] Romans ix:1-5.

[37] As in Acts xvii:12-17.

[38] Eph. ii:11-14; Col. iii:10, 11.

[39] Acts xxii:25-28.

life in the midst of which he did so much to plant Christianity. Unusually sensitive, he must have carried with him through life impressions early received from it, many of them probably only half-conscious. He was, however, reared a Jew and a Pharisee,[40] perhaps all the more strictly so because his parents wished to keep him unspoiled by the syncretizing life about them. Sometime in his boyhood or early manhood he was sent to Jerusalem, to be instructed further in the faith as held by the Pharisees.[41]

What Paul looked like, either in his youth or when older, we cannot say.[42] That he was not particularly impressive except to those who knew him well seems probable.[43] Although he had been born in a Greek city and was known as "the Apostle to the Gentiles," and although his letters did much to shape the non-Jewish Christian Church, he seems not to have been especially at home in Greek thought or literature or particularly facile in his use of the language.[44] His methods of thinking and reasoning betray his Jewish background,[45] and he employed Aramaic, apparently easily.[46] Yet Greek was the medium of his extant epistles, he knew the Jewish Scriptures chiefly through the standard translation into Greek, the Septuagint,[47] and echoes of Greek thought and literature in his writings[48] show that he must have absorbed something of the atmosphere of the Hellenistic Orient. In contrast with Jesus, he was essentially a man of the city and we find him making few if any references to rural life. Unlike Jesus, moreover, he appears to have had no sense of humour. Jesus thought and spoke in vivid pictures, Paul more usually in abstract terms.

---

[40] Phil. iii:5; Acts xxiii:6. Deissmann, *Paul,* pp. 48-51, contends that Paul was from the unliterary artisan lower classes and remained one of them. Glover, *Paul of Tarsus,* p. 15, believes this probably to be mistaken. Foakes-Jackson, *The Rise of Gentile Christianity,* p. 87, thinks it likely that Paul belonged to the educated, wealthy, privileged classes. Montefiore, *Judaism and St. Paul,* pp. 1-129, argues that Paul's religious background cannot have been that of the Rabbinic Judaism which we know, of c. A.D. 500, but that either (and this he holds unlikely) the Rabbinic Judaism of Paul's youth was very different from that of A.D. 500, or else Paul's religious background was in many ways different from it. In any event, he believes, it was not against anything like the Rabbinic Judaism which we know that Paul preached.

[41] Acts xxii:3.

[42] See a discussion of the description given in the apocryphal *Acts of Paul and Thekla* and other suggestions in Glover, *op. cit.,* pp. 172-191.

[43] II Cor. x:10.

[44] Glover, *Paul of Tarsus,* pp. 172-191.

[45] As in Gal. iii:15-18, Eph. iv:8, 9. See Burkitt, *Christian Beginnings,* p. 106.

[46] Acts xxi:40-xxii:2. The "Hebrew" which he used was, of course, Aramaic, the speech related to Hebrew which was current in the Palestine of his time. Weiss, *Urchristentum,* pp. 131-135.

[47] Deissmann, *Paul,* p. 100.

[48] As in I Cor. viii:6, which seems to be Stoic in origin. Porter, *The Mind of Christ in Paul,* pp. 172-176; Raven, *Jesus and the Gospel of Love,* pp. 259-262; Dodd, *The Epistle of Paul to the Romans,* pp. xxxi-xxxii. See also Glover, *op. cit.,* pp. 18-23.

Sensitive, quick-tempered,[49] a mystic,[50] deeply affectionate[51] and dependent on friendship,[52] usually courteous,[53] subject to depths of despair[54] and to heights of exaltation,[55] capable of great joy[56] and yet haunted at times by fears and doubts,[57] he was constant in a purpose once formed,[58] displayed great resourcefulness, presence of mind, sound judgment, physical endurance, and powers of recuperation,[59] and was a leader.[60] Few men of the ancient Mediterranean world have so profoundly affected the course of history.

What integrated Paul's life, however, and lifted this almost neurotic temperament out of obscurity into enduring influence was a profound and revolutionary religious experience. Paul believed, and reiterated again and again, that contact with the living Jesus had transformed him[61] and that continued fellowship with Jesus was the source of his strength.[62] Apparently his first contacts with Christianity gave him a cordial dislike of the new faith.[63] Frank though he is in his letters, we can only conjecture the precise steps which led to the change. While holding himself to be blameless when judged by the exacting standard of the Jewish Law,[64] apparently he had felt himself living morally a divided and defeated life.[65] Although a persecutor of the Christians,[66] he seems to have come to suffer from inner misgivings as to the correctness of his course,[67] perhaps because he saw in some of his victims an inward radiance and peace for

[49] Gal. v, xii; Acts xiii:8-11.

[50] Deissmann, Paul, p. 79. Deissmann says (p. 246) that the words "in Christ," which incorporate so much of Paul's mysticism, occur 164 times in Paul's writings. See also Schweitzer, The Mysticism of Paul the Apostle.

[51] As his list of greetings shows, for example, in Rom. xvi:1-16. See also Gal. iv:19; Phil. i:3-8.

[52] I Thes. ii:17-20; v:25.

[53] As in his letter to Philemon. See also Foakes-Jackson, op. cit., pp. 94-95.

[54] II Cor. i:8-10. See also Spencer, Beyond Damascus, p. 247; Deissmann, Paul, p. 65. These moods may have been accentuated by bodily weakness or a nervous instability. Lietzmann, Geschichte der alten Kirche, Vol. I, p. 112.

[55] II Cor. xii:2, 3.

[56] II Cor. vii:7-9; I. Thess. ii:19; Phil. iv:10.

[57] II Cor. iv:8, vii:5.

[58] As in his pressing on to Jerusalem in the face of known danger and then on to Rome. Acts xx-xxviii.

[59] As in Acts xiv:19, 20, xvi:19-40. See also the list of his hardships in II Cor. xi:23-28. Also Foakes-Jackson, The Rise of Gentile Christianity, pp. 94, 95.

[60] As is shown often, including Acts xxviii:21-36.

[61] Acts xxii:3-16, xxvi:11-20; Gal. i:15, 16.

[62] Phil. iv:13; Gal. ii:20.

[63] Acts viii:1, ix:1; I Cor. xv:9.

[64] Phil. iii:6.

[65] Rom. vii:14-25. This seems clearly to be autobiographical. See also Spencer, Beyond Damascus, p. 21.

[66] Acts viii:1, ix:1; I Cor. xv:9.

[67] Acts xxvi:14.

which he longed but to which he was alien.[68] The inner struggle culminated in a decisive crisis just before he reached Damascus, where he had been sent on an errand of persecution. It may, indeed, have been precipitated by the fact that he was about to enter the city where he would have to take action against those who, perhaps unconsciously or only half consciously, he now felt in his heart of hearts to be right.

Whatever the inner processes of his mind, on the Damascus road Paul met with the experience which he never forgot and made a commitment of his life from which, so far as we know, he never for an instant wavered.[69] He believed that he had seen the risen Jesus.[70] For him all things were new.[71] He had become a "fresh creation."[72] The life so suddenly begun brought to him radiant joy, a growing inward peace[73] in spite of his tempestuous nature and the stress of his missionary career, and increasing patience.[74] It meant, too, an ardent love for God, for Jesus, and for those about him.[75] Confessedly the new life did not at once enable him to achieve moral perfection.[76] At times he was betrayed by his hasty temper and his intense nature into bitter denunciation of his opponents[77] which ill comported with his ideal of love.[78] Yet the controversial spirit partly arose from his deep love of those whom he believed his opponents had wronged. Certainly his conversion began an inner revolution and no superlatives were too great for him to use in praise of the love of God which had brought it about or for his newly found Master and Saviour. A hint of what the change meant to him can be seen in the exalted terms which he applies to Jesus.[79] For some of these no precedent can be found in the Messianic terminology of the apocalypses.[80] They bear vivid witness to what had happened within him.

With such an experience Paul could scarcely have avoided being a missionary.

---

[68] Acts vi:15, vii:54-viii:1.

[69] Three accounts of the conversion are given in Acts (ix:1-9, xxii:3-11, xxvi:9-18) and in Paul's own letters are references to it, as in I Cor. xv:8; Gal. i:1, 15-17. The experience has, naturally, interested many writers. Among them see Bacon, *The Story of St. Paul*, pp. 50-53; Ropes, *The Apostolic Age*, pp. 107-112; Glover, *Paul of Tarsus*, pp. 57-62; Deissmann, *Paul*, p. 23.

[70] I Cor. ix:1, xv:8.

[71] II Cor. v:17.

[72] II Cor. v:17.

[73] Phil. iv:7, 11.

[74] Gal. v:22, 23. Compare also his impatience in Galatians with Phil. i:15-18, written, supposedly, from Rome some years later.

[75] As in I Cor. xiii; Eph. iii:14-19.

[76] Phil. iii:12.

[77] As in Galatians.

[78] I Cor. xiii:7.

[79] As in Phil. ii:6-11; Col. i:15.

[80] Porter, *The Mind of Christ in Paul.* p. 25.

The burning love for God and man which that begot longed to see those whom he touched have the same joyous sense of being "in Christ."[81] He laboured for his fellow Jews[82] and deeply regretted the failure of the majority to become Christians.[83] It was, however, among the Gentiles and in the cities of Greece and the Hellenistic East that most of his efforts were expended.

Of some of these missionary journeys and labours we have written records. Of much, perhaps more, we have only hints. From a summary which he once gave of his hardships[84] we catch glimpses of events on which our other records are silent. We cannot construct a conclusive chronology of his life,[85] and while it is generally believed that he died in Rome, even that cannot be proved beyond the possibility of doubt.[86] Most of his missionary activity of which we know was in what we now call Asia Minor and in Greece and Macedonia. He spent much time in the commercial city of Corinth, a Roman colony noted for its luxury and licentiousness,[87] and in the important Greek city of Ephesus. He seems to have been especially successful in Macedonia: of none of his churches does he speak with greater satisfaction than of those in Philippi and Thessalonica.[88] The precise location of the communities he founded in Galatia is still a matter of debate.[89] It is also clear that we do not have a complete list of the cities and towns in which he worked.[90]

Paul's was the urge of a pioneer and he had a consuming desire not only to preach the Gospel, but to do so where no one else had been before him.[91] Although he was to have a profound effect upon Christian theology and literature, he was always primarily a missionary and only incidentally a theologian and author.

[81] Eph. iv:13-15.
[82] As in Acts xvii:1-3, xviii:1-4, xix:8.
[83] Rom. ix:1-3, x:1.
[84] II Cor. xi:24-28.
[85] There are some clues to chronology: as the coincidence of Paul's residence in Corinth with the proconsulate of Gallio (Acts xviii:12) and durations of periods of his life, as in Gal. i:18, ii:1; Acts xix:8, 10, xx:31, xxiv:27, xxviii:30. We know from these and other references that between his conversion and the time we finally lose sight of him in Rome the time elapsed must have been at least twenty-five years. It was undoubtedly longer, but just how much longer we do not know. McGiffert, *A History of Christianity in the Apostolic Age*, p. 422, thinks Paul's missionary campaign lasted ten or twelve years.
[86] See the First Epistle of Clement, v:3-7 (*Ante-Nicene Fathers*, Vol. I, p. 6); Lietzmann, *Petrus und Paulus in Rom, passim*, believes that in all probability Paul was martyred in Rome under Nero. See also Dodd, *The Epistle of Paul to the Romans*, pp. xxvi-xxviii.
[87] McGiffert, *op. cit.*, p. 262.
[88] McGiffert, *op. cit.*, p. 255.
[89] The North and South Galatian theories. See McGiffert, *op. cit.*, pp. 178ff.; Ramsay, *The Church in the Roman Empire*, p. 9.
[90] McGiffert, *op. cit.*, pp. 280-289, 422.
[91] Rom. xv:20.

The details of his labours need not be recounted here, for they have repeatedly been narrated. We must think of him as at first sent out by the Church of Antioch, but later as largely and perhaps entirely independent of it. From city to city he travelled, probably mostly on foot if by land. He took pride in supporting himself by his trade and not being dependent on his converts.[92] Usually he first presented his message in the synagogue, arguing from the Jewish Scriptures that Jesus was the Messiah, that these foretold the death and resurrection of Jesus, and that Jesus was soon to return.[93] As a rule he was given a hearing, occasionally over a considerable length of time.[94] Sooner or later, however, his preaching caused a division, the majority rejecting his novel interpretations.[95] One reason for the violence of the Hellenistic Jews against Paul may have been the fact that he drew away so many of the Gentiles whom, by earnest missionary effort, they had attracted to the synagogue.[96] While the Christian groups which Paul gathered were drawn in part from Jews, the larger proportion seem to have been non-Jewish.[97]

These communities Paul bore on his heart. He longed for their growth in Christian virtues, remembered their members by name, revisited them, and kept in touch with them by letter. How far he was an organizer is not clear. Believing that his converts were guided by the Spirit, organization, rites, and ceremonies seemed to him relatively unimportant.[98]

Paul's was a comprehensive vision. He shared the conception of a Church which embraced all Christians, sought to promote the unity of that Church and to heal its divisions, and to bind in sympathy the communities which he had founded with the mother one at Jerusalem risked the certain danger of what proved to be his most famous imprisonment.[99] In his journeys in Asia Minor, Macedonia, and Greece his efforts centred on those cities along the main trade routes where there were Jewish colonies and from which the faith

[92] Acts xviii:3, xx:33, 34; I Cor. ix:1-19.
[93] As in I Thess. i:9, 10; Acts xiii:16-41, xvii:3. Most of Romans ii may be the substance of an address which he often gave to Jews and so may represent his teaching to them. Dodd, *The Epistle of Paul to the Romans*, p. 35.
[94] As in Acts xix:8.
[95] That it was probably only the minority which he won is shown by the fact that we have no record of Paul ever continuing indefinitely in a synagogue or of the transition of a synagogue into a church. The majority of Jews and proselytes, therefore, remained unconvinced.
[96] Lake, *Earlier Epistles of St. Paul*, p. 37.
[97] As is seen in I Thess. i:9, 10 and I Cor. xii:2, which indicate that the majority of the Christians in Thessalonica and Corinth were Gentiles and had come directly out of paganism into Christianity. However, the passages do not preclude the possibility that the transition may have been made by the way of Judaism. See Case, *The Evolution of Early Christianity*, pp. 176, 177.
[98] McGiffert, *op. cit.*, p. 272.
[99] This conception of unity is seen in I Cor. i:10-17, xii:12-14; Eph. iv:1-16; Col. i:18.

could spread to outlying districts.[100] His deliberately planned trip to Rome and his dream of following it by one to Spain[101] show something of the wide sweep of his geographic horizons. Whether he ever reached Spain we do not know. So far as our assured information goes, the curtain falls on him while he was in Rome.[102]

As the Christian missionary of the Apostolic Age of whose labours and inner mind we know the most, Paul has been at once the prototype, the model, and the inspiration of thousands of successors. Through the esteem in which his writings have been held he has profoundly influenced the ideals of those of his profession who came after him.

Paul was by no means the only missionary of the first generation after Jesus. Of some we have the names and know a little of their activity. Of still others we have hints and we can venture conjectures about the existence of many concerning whom our existing documents tell us nothing. The surviving records are manifestly incomplete and probably, for a well-rounded picture of the expansion of the faith in the first generation after Jesus, are ill-proportioned. From what we possess emerge some of the outlines, many of them vaguely discerned, of a rapid spread of the new message among the cities of the eastern part of the Empire, possibly outside its borders, and in the west at least as far as Italy.

The important commercial and political metropolis of Antioch was the centre from which radiated more missionary journeys than those of Paul. We know that Barnabas, of whom we hear first as a member of the Jerusalem community,[103] after his separation from Paul went with Mark to his native island of Cyprus.[104] It would be very strange if Paul and Barnabas were the only leaders of missionary tours from Antioch and if the only directions in which Antiochene missionaries travelled in these thirty or forty years were west and north-west. It seems reasonable to suppose that they also went at least eastward, possibly to Mesopotamia. While, for example, we have no clear proof of the presence of Christianity in Edessa at so early a date, it would be rather remarkable if the new faith had not made its way along the caravan route to that important city, where a Jewish population provided it a natural foothold.

[100] Deissmann, *Paul*, p. 246.

[101] Rom. xv:24.

[102] Acts xxviii:30, 31. The earliest clear statements of Paul's martyrdom in Rome under Nero are in Origen of Alexandria (Eusebius, *Ecclesiastical History*, III, 1) and in Tertullian, *Scorpiace*, 15. Yet a reference which may imply both the Spanish journey and the Roman martyrdom is much earlier than either, in I Clement, v. On the Spanish journey and the death in Rome see Lietzmann, *Petrus und Paulus in Rom*, especially pp. 242-245. On the Spanish journey see McGiffert, *op. cit.*, pp. 416-421.

[103] Acts iv:36, 37.

[104] Acts xv:39.

From Paul we learn that among the Christians of Corinth were those who said, "I am of Cephas, and I of Christ."[105] Whether this means that Peter had been there and that some had come to Corinth who had been acquainted with Jesus in Palestine is not certain. We hear more than once of Apollos, an Alexandrian Jew, as a missionary.[106] Whether he had been introduced to Christianity at Alexandria we do not know, and, if he had, we know still less of how the faith came to be planted in that city. It is clear that at first Apollos was preaching a different form of Christianity from that proclaimed by Paul,[107] so presumably he learned it from another source than Antioch. Apparently, too, Paul knew that Peter and the brothers of Jesus were travelling about, living at the expense of the Christians,[108] and it would be remarkable if while doing so they were not seeking to spread the faith.

We have hints in Paul's letters of those who were propagating types of Christianity with which he vigorously disagreed, on the one hand some who wished all followers of Jesus to conform fully to the Jewish Law[109] and on the other some who went far in assimilating Christianity to pagan beliefs and who possibly represented the Gnostic strain which later became a major problem for the Christian communities.[110] It is quite possible that the first group worked only among Christians and that the latter arose out of the Pauline converts, but it is also possible that both were active in trying to spread their forms of the faith among non-Christians as well as Christians.[111] Indeed, from one of Paul's statements it seems fairly clear that some who disagreed with him were proclaiming a Christian message to non-Christians.[112]

From such books in the New Testament as James, Hebrews, the Gospel of John and the Johannine Epistles, Jude, the Petrine Epistles, and Revelation, we know of types of Christianity which, while not radically different from that of Paul, were not identical with it. Some of these variations may have arisen in churches founded by Paul, but others may be evidence of the propagation of strains of Christianity which, while not disagreeing violently with that which stemmed from Paul, yet had little direct connexion with him. When Paul declares that "from Jerusalem and round about even unto Illyricum I have fully preached the gospel of Christ" and with the next breath goes on to add "making it my aim so to preach the gospel, not where Christ was already

[105] I Cor. i:12.
[106] Acts xviii:24-28; I Cor. i:12.
[107] Acts xviii:24-26.
[108] I Cor. ix:5.
[109] As in Acts xv:1 and Galatians.
[110] Col. ii:18, 19.
[111] Weiss, *Urchristentum*, p. 150.
[112] Phil. i:15.

named, that I might not build upon another man's foundations,"[113] it seems
a reasonable conjecture that he knew of other missionaries at work in the wide
area of Palestine, southern and western Asia Minor, and the southern portions
of the Balkan Peninsula, and that he went only to those centres where they
had not been. It is possible, indeed, that the reason why Paul did not go into
Bithynia, passed by Mysia, and from Troas went to Macedonia[114] was because
Christian missionaries had preceded him in these regions.[115] Certainly the document which is called the First Epistle of Peter speaks of Christians in Bithynia,
Pontus, and Cappadocia,[116] and yet we do not know how they came there. They
seem to be thought of as Jews of the Dispersion and presumably were in
the cities.

We know of Silas and Timothy as companions of Paul,[117] but they may also
have laboured in some other places than those where they accompanied him.
We hear, too, of Christians at Tyre[118] and probably at Sidon,[119] but how they
became such we are not informed. We also read of Christians at Puteoli,[120]
a port near the present Naples, but of the beginnings of the community there
and of the more important church in Rome we have no information except
that they were prior to the arrival of Paul. Since Puteoli was on a trade route
from the East and since to Rome as the capital of the Empire came many
migrants from the Orient, the communities in both probably arose from
Christians who were there for business purposes and who, if missionaries, were
so only incidentally. We hear, too, of Christians on the island of Crete,[121]
although we do not know their origin. Since the memory of the existence of
some of the groups of which we have learned was preserved only incidentally,
because, for example, Paul passed through the cities where they were found,
it is highly probable that numbers of other communities existed to which we
have no reference in our scanty records.[122]

The later tradition which narrates the activities of various members of the

---

[113] Rom. xv:19, 20.

[114] Acts xvi:7, 8.

[115] Bacon, *The Gospel of the Hellenists*, pp. 60, 61.

[116] I Peter i:1.

[117] Acts xv:40, xvi:1, xvii:4-15; Phil. i:1; I Thess. i:1. It has been questioned whether
the Silvanus of I Thess. i:1 is the same as the Silas of the Acts. McGiffert, *op. cit.*, p. 230,
believes them the same but notes that this has been doubted.

[118] Acts xxi:3, 4.

[119] Acts xxvii:3. "Friends" of Paul are mentioned here and presumably they were
Christians.

[120] Acts xxviii:13, 14.

[121] Titus i:5; Harnack, *The Mission and Expansion of Christianity*, Vol. II, pp. 93, 229.

[122] For a list of the places in which Christianity is known to have been planted in
the Apostolic Age, see Harnack, *op. cit.*, Vol. II, pp. 91-94.

original group of the Twelve Apostles in widely different parts of the world[123] has not been proved to have any basis of fact. Of the Twelve the only ones of whom we have indubitably authentic reference as being outside Palestine is Peter.[124]

This, then, in all too brief form, is the story, often told, of the spread of Christianity during the first generation after the death of Jesus. Before the time when the last of those who could remember their Master had died, the faith had had important experiences which were largely to determine its future. It had begun with Judaism and some at least of its followers had hoped to win the adherents of the parent religion. Even a Paul, who so epitomized the Gentile mission and who aroused so much antagonism among the majority of his fellow Jews, did not despair of the eventual conversion of his race.[125] Some basis existed for regarding this dream as not entirely preposterous. The early Jewish Christians insisted that their faith was the fulfilment and not the enemy of that of their fathers.[126] In Judaism was a strong tradition of Messianism, and Jesus, the Christians insisted, was the Messiah whose life, death, and resurrection were clearly foretold by the Scriptures which all accepted as authoritative.[127] Many Jews, too, were longing for the turning of the Gentiles to God as they knew him and were seeing, in apparent confirmation, thousands of non-Jews who were either becoming full proselytes or were conforming to a greater or less extent to the demands of the Law. To the optimistic, Judaism might well have seemed on the road to becoming universal in its appeal. The syncretism and religious hunger of the times favoured this process: never had the influence of Judaism been wider. At least some of the Jews who had become Christians might anticipate that through the Gospel the goal was at last to be reached and that the barrier between Jew and Gentile was to be broken down by both becoming "one new man" "in Christ Jesus."[128] In the brief course of this one generation this hope was proved vain. The majority of Jews refused the proffered Messiah.

This refusal had consequences of major importance for both Christianity and Judaism. Christianity realized in practice the universalism which had been the dream of some of the Jews for the past hundreds of years and is the only offshoot of Judaism which has ever done so. In the process it moved out into the

---

[123] Eusebius, *Ecclesiastical History,* Book III, Chap. I; Schmidlin, *Katholische Missionsgeschichte,* pp. 40-44.

[124] Gal. ii:11.

[125] As in Rom. xi:15, 24.

[126] As in Luke xxiv:25-27; Acts ii:22-36, xxvi:6-7.

[127] As in Acts ii:22-36, xvii:31, xviii:27, 28.

[128] Eph. ii:11-15.

Hellenistic world, so marked by syncretism and by a mixture of philosophies and mystery cults. Carrying with it only a relatively few Jews, inevitably it was profoundly affected by the Hellenistic atmosphere. The Christianity which spread in the following years was, therefore, somewhat different from that of the primitive Jewish communities. Yet the main stream of Christianity still flowed in the channels charted by Judaism and by Jesus and his immediate followers. The majority of Gentile Christians regarded the Jewish Scriptures as authoritative, thought of themselves as the true spiritual heirs of Israel, claimed for themselves the promises which the Hebrews held that Yahweh had made to them,[129] and treasured and read repeatedly one or more of the Gospels and the letters of Paul and of others of the first-century Christians. Christianity attracted from Judaism many and perhaps most of the latter's Gentile adherents.[130] It could offer to the Gentile all that Judaism could promise and more, yet without some of the conditions which rendered the latter repellent. Judaism, reacting, and shaken to the core by the political rebellions of the first and second centuries, the crushing defeats at the hands of Vespasian, Titus, and Hadrian, and the unsuccessful revolts of A.D. 116 and 117 in Cyrenaica, Egypt, and Cyprus,[131] retired within itself, continued the development of its Rabbinic forms, largely ceased its efforts to win the Gentiles, and remained even more exclusively racial.[132]

For the second subdivision of the pre-Constantinian period of the spread of Christianity, the century or so that elapsed between the Apostolic Age and the death of Marcus Aurelius, our records of the spread of the faith are even less satisfactory than are those for the generation immediately after Jesus. We have fragments of information concerning the Christian communities, but we know very little of the process by which new ones were founded or by which converts were won to the existing groups. We do know that Christianity continued to expand. Having been fairly launched into the stream of Hellenistic life, it made its way along the main trade routes to the cities and regions touched by Hellenism and before long overpassed the boundaries of Hellenism as it previously had those of Judaism. Yet it continued its triumphal march in the Hellenistic portions of the Mediterranean world. In the flux of the times, when old institutions and ideals were disintegrating, it had the advantage of association with the Hellenism which was dominant in so much of the ancient

---

[129] Rom. ix:6-8; Gal. iii:7, 9, vi:16; Phil. iii:3. The Christians held that, the Jews having been rejected by God, they themselves had become the chosen people. Harnack, *op. cit.*, Vol. I, p. 69.

[130] Müller, *Kirchengeschichte*, Vol. I, p. 50; Moore, *Judaism*, Vol. I, p. 107.

[131] Moore, *Judaism*, Vol. I, pp. 90-93, 107.

[132] Moore, *Judaism*, Vol. I, p. 107. On the failure of the mass of Jews to be won to Christianity, see also Case, *The Social Origins of Christianity*, pp. 27, 28, 38, 39, 65-68.

world. As has frequently happened in the history of mankind, a religion was winning adherents in a period of cultural instability and in connexion with a set of ideas and an attitude of mind which had social or political prestige. Until after A.D. 180, however, Christian communities remained relatively small and obscure. To the eye of the casual observer they were only one of the many cults which came out of the ancient East and found lodgment among the cosmopolitan populations of the great cities. We have, accordingly, but scanty references to Christianity in such pagan books and letters as have reached us from that period. For the late years of the first century and the early decades of the second century the surviving Christian literature is only slightly less tantalizing in its brevity.[133]

Our records, unsatisfactory though they are, suffice to show that by A.D. 180 Christians were in all the provinces of the Empire and in Mesopotamia. Already, moreover, the main outlines of that organization were appearing which attempted to give concrete reality to the vision of an inclusive community which seems to have been present in Christianity from the beginning.[134]

In the little over the century and a quarter between the death of Marcus Aurelius and the espousal of the faith by Constantine, Christianity, as we have suggested, enjoyed a remarkable growth. The Empire was torn by civil strife. The prosperity under the strong Emperors of the second century was followed by suffering and insecurity.[135] Many, afraid, sought refuge in religion. The weakening or disintegration of time-honoured patterns of society and inherited beliefs made relatively easy the spread of new faiths. The mystery cults, especially Mithraism,[136] flourished, and Neoplatonism was taking form and becoming popular. Christianity, profiting by these conditions, rapidly increased the numbers of its adherents.[137] Some of the rulers of the period, indeed, were not unfriendly to it.[138] However, with its Empire-wide organization, its exclusive demands on its adherents, and its abhorrence of the state religion, the Church, while still embracing only a small minority of the population, seemed to some of the Emperors a public menace. Bent on restoring order in the realm and saving society, they sought to exterminate it. There followed, then, a series of persecutions more severe than any the Church had yet known. The Church

[133] Streeter, *The Four Gospels*, p. 2.
[134] Harnack, *The Mission and Expansion of Christianity*, Vol. II, pp. 94-96.
[135] Rostovtzeff, *A History of the Ancient World*, Vol. II, p. 305ff. See also the first volume of Gibbon, *The Decline and Fall of the Roman Empire*.
[136] The Emperor Aurelian, for instance, officially instituted the cult of *Sol Invictus* and proclaimed a Latinized Mithraism as the state cult—Ferrero, *The Ruin of Ancient Civilization and the Triumph of Christianity*, p. 65.
[137] Ferrero, *op. cit.*, pp. 70-72.
[138] Healy, *The Valerian Persecution*, p. 52.

withstood the shock, and Constantine, probably from a mixture of motives, made his peace with it.

For the years between Marcus Aurelius and Constantine, as in the previous hundred years, our records of the spread of Christianity are very meagre. Indeed, for the entire pre-Constantinian period it is impossible to reconstruct even the main outlines of the manner in which the faith attained its remarkable position. In numbers of regions we possess no information concerning those who introduced it. To be sure, legends exist, but they are usually late and undependable. We know almost as little of the methods by which Christianity expanded as we do of the names of those who propagated it. The dependable Christian documents which survive, although impressive in their total bulk, give slight space to the manner in which the religion was disseminated. The chief interest of the writers was elsewhere. No period in our whole story is more important. The position which Christianity won in these centuries insured its future and largely determined the forms which it has since assumed. Yet our knowledge of the processes by which this position was achieved is obviously fragmentary and woefully inadequate. Any detailed treatment and even any summary, therefore, must be very disappointing.

The story of the spread of Christianity from the end of the Apostolic Age until Constantine can best be pursued topically and the two chronological divisions into which the period falls can be treated together. First we will describe the progress of the faith region by region. Then, in the following chapter, we will inquire into the means and methods of its spread. Next we will say something about the reasons advanced by Christians in advocacy of their faith. That is to be followed by an account of the objections urged by the opponents of Christianity and by a summary of the attitude of the state and of the great persecutions. Finally we will seek for the reasons for the triumph of Christianity over its many rivals.

Palestine, the scene of the life of Jesus and the first home of the faith, was very slow in becoming Christian. At first sight it is surprising that Christianity had for centuries only a slight foothold in the land of its birth. This seeming anomaly is, however, easily explained. Jesus in his own lifetime was not accepted by the majority of his fellow countrymen. After his death only a small minority of the Jews entered the new sect. The Jewish population, therefore, which must have made up a large proportion of the inhabitants of the land, was relatively untouched. Since, probably, the majority of such Christians as existed in Palestine belonged to the branch of the Church which held to Jewish customs, it would have been strange if many of the Gentile population had been attracted. As late as Constantine Palestine remained predominantly non-Christian. Such few Christians as there were seem to have been mostly Greek-speaking or at least bilingual. Many of them appear not to have been natives, but immigrants from other regions and, presumably, had been Christians before entering Palestine.[139]

In Phœnicia the new faith seems to have been stronger than in Palestine. Here were Christians at a very early date.[140] In Tyre especially was a strong Church. However, it appears probable that here, as in most of the Empire, Christianity was predominantly Greek-using and that, therefore, it was confined largely to the cities, particularly on the coast, and to the Greek-speaking portions of the urban population.[141]

We have seen that Antioch was, so far as we know, the first great stronghold of Hellenistic Christianity. For centuries it continued to be a prominent Christian centre. From it, as was natural from so important a commercial metropolis, Christianity expanded in various directions. Yet whether by the time of Constantine even here Christians formed a majority of the population is very doubtful.[142] In Antioch the Church was predominantly Greek. How soon Christianity had an extensive following among those whose tongue was Syriac we do not know. Probably from an early time it was bilingual. However, for many years the chief nucleus of Syriac-speaking Christianity was east of Antioch, in Edessa. Presumably, therefore, the Syriac-using Christians of Syria owed their faith to it more than to Antioch. It seems reasonable to suppose that the Greek-speaking sections of the towns of Syria derived from Antioch much of such Christianity as they had. Obviously Christianity was fairly widespread before Constantine. The names of the sees of the twenty bishops from Syria who attended the Council of Nicæa in A.D. 325 indicate the presence of the faith in towns and cities in several different parts of the region.[143] While we do not know to just what extent Christianity had supplanted the native religions, clearly it was already well and widely rooted.

Even in Apostolic times the island of Cyprus could boast some Christians.[144] By the time of Constantine Christianity seems to have been fairly strong, possibly with several bishops.[145]

It was in Asia Minor that, by the beginning of the fourth century, Christianity had been adopted more widely than in any other large section of the

---

[139] Harnack, *The Mission and Expansion of Christianity*, Vol. II, pp. 97-120.
[140] Acts xi:19, xxi:2-4, 7, xxvii:3.
[141] Harnack, *op. cit.*, Vol. II, pp. 120-125.
[142] Bouchier, *A Short History of Antioch*, p. 153, seems to believe that by Constantine Christians were in a majority in the city, but this is probably a mistake.
[143] Harnack, *op. cit.*, Vol. II, pp. 125-140.
[144] Acts xi:20, xiii:4-12, xv:39.
[145] Harnack, *op. cit.*, Vol. II, pp. 140-142.

Empire. The strength of Christianity in this region, one of the richest in the Empire,[146] could not but be significant. Here, in Ephesus, was one of the most influential early strongholds of the faith. Here, too, were the Churches mentioned in the Apocalypse.

For the relatively rapid progress in Asia Minor a number of reasons have been ascribed. Paul spent much of his missionary career there. Here were strong Greek cities, centres of that Hellenistic culture in which Christianity so soon became acclimatized. In the early centuries of the Christian era, the native races, very diverse, were adopting Græco-Roman cultures and the native cultures with their religious cults were disintegrating. In such an atmosphere, Christianity, coming with the conquering culture, met less formidable opposition than in some other regions. It seems, indeed, to have registered its most rapid growth not in the Greek cities, although there it was fairly strong, but in the sections where the disorganization of existing customs was proceeding under the impact of the invading culture. Where Hellenistic education was unknown the new faith seems to have made little or no progress. As Hellenistic education spread, those who adopted it tended to regard the older religions as mere superstitions and were open to the message of a new religion. Then, too, the many Jews of the region appear to have attracted a number of Gentiles who were thus made ready for Christianity. Upon some of the Jews themselves their hereditary faith sat rather lightly and they were, accordingly, relatively open-minded to the message of the Christian missionary.[147]

As has been suggested, Christianity penetrated various parts of Asia Minor with differing degrees of rapidity. On the west coast, in the province of Asia and in the adjoining provinces of Phrygia and Bithynia, it was early quite strong. For instance, one of the few as well as one of the fullest references to Christianity in non-Christian writers of the first century and a quarter of the faith's existence is in the much-quoted letter of the younger Pliny to the Emperor Trajan.[148] This missive, an official one of report and inquiry, written from

[146] Mommsen, *The Provinces of the Roman Empire*, Vol. I, p. 387.

[147] Harnack, *op. cit.*, Vol. II, pp. 182-184; Ramsay, *The Cities and Bishoprics of Phrygia*, Vol. I, pp. 96, 137, Vol. II, p. 674; Ramsay, *The Church in the Roman Empire*, pp. 41, 146, 147.

[148] Pliny, *Epistolæ*, x:97. The Latin text is in *G. Plinii Cæcilii Secundi Epistolæ*, ed. M. Döring, Vol. II, pp. 378-389. English translations are in Merrill, *Essays in Early Christian History*, pp. 179, 180 and in Ayer, *A Source Book of Ancient Church History*, pp. 20-22. Lucian, writing after the middle of the second century, makes his hero, Alexander of Abonotichus, describe his native country, Pontus, as "filled with Epicureans and Christians" (*Luciani Samosatensis Opera*, ed. J. T. Lehmann, Vol. V, p. 85, in *Alexander seu Pseudomantis, c. 25*). See also Orr, *Neglected Factors in the Study of the Early Progress of Christianity*, p. 51.

Bithynia, and in the second decade of the second century,[149] speaks of Christianity as having spread widely in the towns and even in the countryside. From the beginning of the third century Christians seem to have been dominant in the cities of Phrygia.[150] Yet on the great plains of Axylon and North Galatia the faith made slow progress and until the third or fourth century paganism was the religion of the majority.[151]

Except for the work of Paul, of which we hear only imperfectly, we have almost no information of the processes by which Christianity won its way in Asia Minor or of the missionaries who propagated it. Yet from records about the Quartodecinian controversy and Montanist developments we know of the increasing importance of the new faith. Fortunately, too, we have a fairly full account, part of it from his own pen, of one who in the third century had much to do with the adoption of Christianity by the majority of the population of a section of Pontus. Long before his time the faith had gained footholds in that region,[152] but he seems to have been responsible for the completion of the process of conversion. Gregory Thaumaturgos, or Worker of Wonders, was a native of Pontus, the scion of a prominent and wealthy pagan family. At the age of fourteen he lost his father, and his mother had him trained in rhetoric and public speaking—as was usual among youths of his social position. From this he went on to the study of law as a further preparation for the duties to which his birth predestined him. Travelling for this purpose, at Cæsarea in Palestine he came in touch with Origen, the famous Christian teacher of Alexandrian rearing. Origen helped to instil in him a respect for Greek philosophy. By that road and through the winsomeness of his own character, the famous teacher led the young aristocrat into the Christian faith. For Origen Gregory continued to have the greatest respect and affection. After five years with him he returned home.

About A.D. 240, somewhat against his will, Gregory was made bishop of his native city. Once in the position, he gave himself to it with energy and devotion. Aided by his brother, Athenodorus, bishop in another city of Pontus, he set about finishing the work of conversion. When he died, about A.D. 270, after approximately thirty years in office, it is said that in contrast with the seventeen Christians whom he found on his accession to the episcopal see, only seventeen of the populace remained pagan. Such numbers are probably more rhetorical than accurate, but it seems clear that under him something approaching a mass

[149] Harnack, op. cit., Vol. II, pp. 186-188.
[150] Ramsay, The Cities and Bishoprics of Phrygia, Vol. II, pp. 502-504, 511; Ramsay, The Church in the Roman Empire, pp. 146, 147.
[151] Ramsay, The Church in the Roman Empire, pp. 146, 147.
[152] I Peter, i:1; Harnack, op. cit., Vol. II, p. 203.

conversion took place. Coming as he did from the governing classes whose leadership the citizenry was accustomed to follow, and, apparently, possessing force of character and determination, it is not surprising that he met with success. Again and again, in the case not only of Christianity but also of other faiths, conversion of the masses has followed the espousal of a religion by some dominant figure in the ruling classes.

Gregory's methods were well adapted to his purpose. To pagan miracles he opposed Christian ones and exposed the fraudulent practices of the priests. He encouraged the Christians to celebrate festivals in honour of the martyrs, substituting these for the feasts of the old gods.[153] By such means the transition from the old to the new was eased and popularized, even though in the process Christianity acquired some of the beliefs and trappings of the cults which it supplanted. Gregory seems frankly to have recognized the fact that for the masses any demand for a complete break with the past would either prevent conversion or could not be realized. However, although he sought to render the passing from the old to the new as painless as possible, he did seek to make the adoption of the new something more than nominal and to hold up to his flock certain standards of action. We find him, for instance, disciplining Christians who under pressure of an invasion of the Goths compromised their faith and were guilty of deeds unworthy of the Christian name.[154]

The presence of Christianity in Crete and in some of the islands of the Ægean in or before the days of Constantine is well established.[155] Of its strength and of its introduction and progress we know almost nothing.

Nor can we draw any accurate picture of the extent of Christianity in Greece and the Balkan Peninsula before the time of Constantine. Of groups of Christians in some of the chief cities in the days of Paul we have, of course, information. We catch glimpses which assure us of the continued existence of Christian communities in such centres as Corinth, Athens, and Thessalonica. We know that the faith spread into the Peloponnesus, Thessaly, Byzantium, Pannonia, Dalmatia, and Moesia. Christians appear to have been present in some of the legions in the Danubian provinces. It seems probable, however, that at the accession of Constantine Christians were still very much in a minority.[156]

[153] *Ante-Nicene Fathers*, Vol. VI, pp. 5, 6, 21-39, which gives a summary of the life of Gregory and a translation of Gregory's oration and panegyric addressed to Origen. See also the panegyric life by Gregory of Nyssa in Migne, *Patrologiæ Græcæ*, Vol. XLVI, pp. 893-958.

[154] Gregory Thaumaturgos, *Canonical Epistle* (translation in *Ante-Nicene Fathers*, Vol. VI, pp. 18-20); Duchesne, *Early History of the Christian Church*, Vol. I, p. 319.

[155] Harnack, *op. cit.*, Vol. II, pp. 229, 230; Eusebius, *Ecclesiastical History*, Book III, Chap. IV.

[156] Harnack, *op. cit.*, Vol. II, pp. 230-239; Duchesne, *op. cit.*, Vol. I, p. 188; Zeiller,

For Egypt much more than for Greece our knowledge of the early stages of the Christian movement is unsatisfactory. We have a report, given cautiously as hearsay, that Mark was the first to be sent to Egypt to proclaim the Gospel.[157] The early missionary, Apollos, was called an Alexandrian Jew,[158] but we do not know that he acquired his Christian faith at Alexandria. If he did, as we have suggested, the form of Christianity to which he had there been introduced must have differed from that which Paul preached.[159] By the end of the second century the Church was already strong. There had been "a gospel according to the Egyptians" and several strains of Christianity were represented, including some which the main stream regarded as heretical. In Alexandria itself a famous catechetical school developed which was to have among its teachers such distinguished scholars as Clement and Origen. In Alexandria the Christianity was predominantly Greek. Before the time of Constantine, however, it had spread elsewhere in Egypt and among the indigenous populations. Translations of parts of the Scriptures had possibly been made into more than one dialect of the non-Greek vernacular, the faith was found in Upper as well as in Lower Egypt, and the foundations of a native Egyptian (or Coptic) Church had been laid.[160]

On the north shore of Africa west of Egypt, and especially in and around Carthage in the present Tunis and Algeria, Christianity was very strong by the time of Constantine. Indeed, here and in Asia Minor appear to have been the two greatest numerical strongholds of the faith at the end of the third century. The population was a mixture of older stocks which we call collectively the Berbers, with such later arrivals as Phœnicians and Italians. As a rule the Berbers formed the masses of the rural population, the Phœnician or Punic elements the urban proletariat and middle classes, and the Italians the owners of estates and the upper classes in the cities. These social classifications are not exact and some fusion of the various elements took place.[161] Under Roman

---

Les Origines Chrétiennes dans la Province Romaine de Dalmatie, pp. 1-95; Zeiller, *Les Origines Chrétiennes dans les Provinces Danubiennes de l'Empire Romain*, pp. 27-120.

[157] Eusebius, *Ecclesiastical History*, Book II, Chap. XVI.

[158] Acts xviii:24-26.

[159] *Ibid.*

[160] Harnack, *op. cit.*, Vol. II, pp. 158-179; Duchesne, *op. cit.*, Vol. I, p. 240; Müller, *Kirchengeschichte*, Vol. I, pp. 50, 102. On some early fragments of Christian literature, probably dating from the second and third centuries, and discovered within the present generation, see Kenyon, *Recent Developments in the Textual Criticism of the Greek Bible*, pp. 32, 33, 51-63; Grenfell, Drexel, and Hunt, editors, *New Sayings of Jesus and Fragment of a Lost Gospel from Oxyrhynchus;* White, *The Sayings of Jesus from Oxyrhynchus.*

[161] Leclercq, *L'Afrique Chrétienne*, Vol. I, pp. 12-15; Mommsen, *The Provinces of the Roman Empire*, Vol. II, pp. 330-334; Harnack, *op. cit.*, Vol. II, p. 297.

rule, notably in the imperial age, the region became very prosperous. After the ruin of the Phœnician regime in the Punic wars, the Romans, especially beginning with Augustus and continuing into the second century after Christ, encouraged the colonization of the country by Italians. Cities multiplied, and particularly in the third century Romanization proceeded apace. The Roman culture centred in the cities. The agricultural labour, upon which the prosperity of this urban life depended, was performed chiefly by the non-Latin-speaking native populations.[162] As in so much of the Empire, the peak of prosperity was attained in the second century. In the third century decay set in and by the end of the century municipal self-government was disappearing.[163] Still, up to the fourth century cities and presumably the countryside seem to have continued to grow in population.[164]

From what direction Christianity first came to North Africa we do not know. It may have been from the East, with which the region had traditional commercial contacts. A large number of Jews seem to have made their way thither and possibly the faith won its first foothold among them.[165] Apparently the original language of the Christian community was Greek.[166] Long before the age of Constantine, however, Latin had taken its place, and North Africa became the first main home of Latin Christian literature. Here laboured such early eminent Latin writers on Christianity as Tertullian and Cyprian. Here important Christian books, including probably at least parts of the Bible, were put into Latin, and Christianity first moved prominently into the Latin world.[167] In North Africa, too, was the home of Augustine, who had so much to do with shaping the thought of the Christianity of the West. The progress of Christianity seems to have been especially rapid in the third century (a phenomenon common to many other portions of the Empire), with what was probably something like a mass movement into the Church.[168] Just why this took place is not clear. Possibly it was because the rapid Romanization of the region with the weakening of old institutions made the populace more receptive to new ideas. It may have been that, as so largely throughout the Empire, the disorder

---

[162] Rostovtzeff, *A Social and Economic History of the Roman Empire*, pp. 280-293.

[163] Leclercq, *op. cit.*, Vol. I, pp. 301, 302.

[164] Rostovtzeff, *op. cit.*, p. 329.

[165] Leclercq, *op. cit.*, Vol. I, pp. 31-42, 66-70. Excavations show that for some time Jews and Christians used common cemeteries and so must have lived on fairly amicable terms. Donaldson, *Church Life and Thought in North Africa, A.D. 200*, p. 11.

[166] Harnack, *op. cit.*, Vol. II, p. 277. Tertullian wrote his first four treatises in Greek. Leclercq, *op. cit.*, Vol. I, pp. 91-101.

[167] Harnack, *op. cit.*, Vol. II, p. 279; Donaldson, *op. cit.*, pp. 179-182; Mommsen, *op. cit.*, Vol. II, pp. 373-376; Buonaiuti, *Il Cristianesimo nell'Africa Romana*, pp. 1-233.

[168] Leclercq, *op. cit.*, Vol. I, p. 43. It is interesting that both Tertullian and Cyprian were born pagans.

of the third century drove those whom the times had made fearful or insecure to the Church for consolation, fellowship, and material assistance.[169] The Church was strongest in the cities and in the Latin-speaking portions of the population, but it also made some progress among the non-Latin-speaking groups. The Punic stock became at least in part Christian, but very little Christian literature appears to have been produced in its tongue, only a small minority of the bishops of whom we know bore Punic names, and the conversion of that portion of the populace may have been partial or superficial. The conversion of the Berber elements seems to have been even less complete. Presumably it was among those of Italian provenance whose daily speech was Latin that the faith became most firmly rooted. This element, although dominant in wealth and in political power, was probably much in the minority. It was from this stratum that the mass of Latin Christian literature proceeded which had so profound an influence upon Christianity in the Occident. Indeed, it has been declared that the Punic and Berber populations became Christian only to the degree that they became Latinized and that the Latin language was the sole vehicle of Christian preaching. Possibly, as the great landed proprietors, Romano-Africans, became Christian, some of them furthered the conversion of the people on their estates.[170] In later centuries, however, when disasters overwhelmed the Romano-Africans, Christianity suffered greater loss than in Egypt, where it had become entirely at home among the older Egyptian, or Coptic, peasant stock which made up the bulk of the population. This probably helps to account for the survival of Christianity in Egypt when Moslem invaders became the rulers and for its disappearance in other parts of North Africa when a similar fate overtook that region.

Although it was in North Africa that the faith first moved out most markedly from the borders of Hellenism and became at home in the Latin world, it was natural that Latin Christianity should make its headquarters not there but in Rome. As we have seen, the origins of the Christian community at Rome are wrapped in obscurity. That Christians were there before the arrival of Paul (not later than A.D. 62 and not earlier than A.D. 58)[171] is, of course, indubitable.

---

[169] Leclercq, *op. cit.*, Vol. I, pp. 301, 302.

[170] Mesnage, *Le Christianisme en Afrique* (Vol. I), *Origenes, Développements, Extension*, p. 273; Mesnage, *Évangélisation de l'Afrique. Part que Certaines Familles Romano-Africaines y ont Prise, passim;* Duchesne, *Early History of the Christian Church*, Vol. I, p. 285; Leclercq, *op. cit.*, Vol. I, pp. 46, 91-101; Harnack, *op. cit.*, Vol. I, pp. 279, 297. However, in the time of Augustine, in his diocese, that of Hippo, the clergy in certain localities needed to know Punic. Leclercq, *op. cit.*, Vol. I, pp. 91-101. We also have the suggestion that the Donatists, of whom we are to say more in a later chapter, were recruited from non-Roman Christian elements. Beaver in *Church History*, Vol. IV, pp. 123-133.

[171] J. H. Ropes in *An Outline of Christianity*, Vol. I, pp. 316, 317.

It was, indeed, almost inevitable that the faith should early make its way to the Eternal City. From the many parts of the Empire came immigrants and sojourners to the capital. The numerous Oriental cults had their followings in the foreign-language groups, and some of them won adherents from the native Latin-speaking population. Among these cults was Christianity. Of them all, it was the only one which really succeeded in acclimatizing itself and becoming Roman.[172]

How long before Paul Christians appeared at Rome we do not know. There is the story, not generally accepted as authentic, that Pilate reported to Tiberius the teachings, miracles, and crucifixion of Jesus and that the latter in turn conveyed the information to the Senate.[173] We have in Suetonius a brief statement that the Emperor Claudius (A.D. 41-54) drove the Jews out of Rome because of the uproar among them raised by a certain Chrestus.[174] Whether by this Chrestus is meant Jesus Christ is not certain.[175] There is nothing improbable in the identification, for often elsewhere the coming of the Christian message aroused bitter dissension in the synagogues.[176] It is possible that the Prisca and Aquila whom Paul met at Corinth and who were among those who had removed from the capital because of the action of Claudius[177] had been Christians before leaving Rome.[178] There is even a conjecture that the Church of St. Prisca on the Aventine is on the site of their house and that the Coemeterium Priscillæ in the catacombs takes its name from her.[179] If, as is sometimes questioned,[180] the long list of friends attached to Paul's letter to the Romans[181] originally belonged in it and not to another epistle, the Roman Church in his day was a fairly numerous body and included several whom he had known as Christians elsewhere.

The tradition that Peter came to Rome and was martyred under Nero[182]

[172] La Piana, *Foreign Groups in Rome during the First Centuries of the Empire*, pp. 183, 184.

[173] Eusebius, *Ecclesiastical History*, Book II, Chap. 2; Tertullian, *Apology*, Chap. 5 (translation in *Ante-Nicene Fathers*, Vol. III, p. 22).

[174] C. Suetonii Tranquilli, *Vita Divi Claudii*, c. 25. The Latin is "Judaeos impulsore Chresto assidue tumultuantes Roma expulit."

[175] Weiss, *Urchristentum*, pp. 274, 275; Duchesne, *op. cit.*, Vol. I, p. 40; Dodd, *The Epistle of Paul to the Romans*, pp. xxvi-xxviii.

[176] As in Acts xiv:1, 2, xvii:1-9.

[177] Acts xviii:1-3.

[178] Dodd, *op. cit.*, pp. xxvi-xxviii.

[179] Lake, *The Earlier Epistles of St. Paul*, pp. 332, 333. Lake dissents from this conjecture of de Rossi (*Bull. di Archeologia Cristiana*, 1888, pp. 129ff. Cited from Lake).

[180] Dodd, *op. cit.*, pp. xvii-xxiv.

[181] Romans xvi:3-15.

[182] First Epistle of Clement (translation in *Ante-Nicene Fathers*, Vol. I, p. 6); Eusebius, *Ecclesiastical History*, Book II, Chap. 14).

has been challenged,[183] but even non-Roman Catholic scholars incline to the conviction that it is dependable.[184] It is highly unlikely, however, that he was the founder of the Roman Christian community.[185]

From the temper of Paul's letter to the Church in Rome it seems that the latter was more nearly in accord with Jewish Christianity than was Paul, but did not occupy an extreme position.[186] It is certain that for many years the language of the Church was Greek. Toward the end of the second century Victor, a native of Africa, but of Latin stock and speech, became bishop. He and perhaps other Christians from Africa strengthened the Latin element. Yet not until the first half of the third century did the Roman clergy become predominantly Latin.[187] The many Christians coming to Rome from different sections of the Empire brought with them divergent types of Christianity. Probably nowhere else did the faith display so many different forms. It appears to have been the growing predominance of the Latin element with its Roman sense of order which led to the submergence of these differences and to that achievement of unity which became one of the sources of strength of the Roman Church.[188]

One estimate of the size of the Church shortly after A.D. 250, based upon contemporary statistics of the number of clergy and widows supported by it,[189] places it as at least 30,000,[190] but this is admittedly conservative, and other conjectures are higher.[191]

We need not here enter upon a description of the leading place which the Church of Rome came to occupy among the Christian communities of the Empire. It is clear, however, that it early had such a position.[192] Already, for example, in the second century it was sending financial aid to many Christians

[183] Merrill, *Essays on Early Christian History*, pp. 24-27, 281-333.
[184] Shotwell and Loomis, *The See of Peter*, pp. 56-58; Dodd, *op. cit.*, pp. xxvi-xxviii. For a Roman Catholic writer see Duchesne, *op. cit.*, Vol. I, pp. 45, 46. See, too, Lietzmann, *Petrus und Paulus in Rom*, *passim*.
[185] Dodd, *op. cit.*, pp. xxvi-xxviii.
[186] B. S. Easton in *An Outline of Christianity*, Vol. I, p. 302.
[187] La Piana, *The Roman Church at the End of the Second Century*, in *Harvard Theological Review*, Vol. XVIII (1925), pp. 201-277; Harnack, *The Mission and Expansion of Christianity*, Vol. II, pp. 241, 242; Dodd, *op. cit.*, p. 8.
[188] La Piana, *Foreign Groups in Rome during the First Centuries of the Empire*, p. 394.
[189] In an epistle of Bishop Cornelius of Rome given in Eusebius, *Ecclesiastical History*, Book VI, Chap. 43.
[190] Shotwell and Loomis, *The See of Peter*, p. 215, and Harnack, *op. cit.*, Vol. II, p. 248. Both give this figure.
[191] See other estimates in Harnack, *op. cit.*, Vol. II, p. 248, footnote 1; Gibbon, *The Decline and Fall of the Roman Empire*, Bury edition, Vol. II, p. 542; Orr, *Neglected Factors in the Study of the Early Progress of Christianity*, pp. 78-81.
[192] Eusebius, *Ecclesiastical History*, Book IV, Chap. 23; Harnack, *op. cit.*, Vol. II, pp. 250, 251.

suffering in the mines and to many Churches, including such distant ones as those in Syria, Cappadocia, and Arabia.[193]

Of the founding and development of Christianity in Central and Southern Italy in the pre-Constantinian period we possess very little information. We know no more of the communities in Sicily and Northern Italy. By the middle of the third century Italy seems to have had about one hundred bishoprics. Since the second half of that century saw, in general, a still more rapid growth of the Church than the preceding decades had witnessed, the number of bishops must have been very much larger by the beginning of the fourth century. This probably means that by then nearly every town of importance contained some Christians. In Sicily there were Christians, possibly in the second century, and certainly in the third. In Northern Italy the new faith was much more retarded. It seems to have entered chiefly not from the South, but from Dalmatia and the East, up the valley of the Po.[194]

We know even less of the beginnings and growth of pre-Constantinian Christianity in Spain than we do in North Africa and Italy. In Spain the process of Romanization had set in strongly much earlier than in Africa and, as was to be expected, was particularly advanced in the South and the East.[195] Yet by the time of Constantine Christianity had not attained to anything like the vigour which it showed among the Latin-speaking population of North Africa nor, so far as we know, had it produced any outstanding leaders or literature. This was not because the official Roman religion had achieved any very great popularity, for, with the exception of the cult of the Emperor, it seems to have been fairly weak. Nor was it because of the resistance offered by the cults of the native deities, for these had been largely assimilated to the Greek and Roman pantheon, and the mystery religions, especially that of Isis, had made headway.[196]

We know nothing of the introduction of Christianity to Spain, although legend or tradition pictures the Apostle James as labouring there, declares that Paul made the projected voyage of which he speaks in his letter to the Romans,[197] and reports that Peter sent seven bishops to the country.[198] Possibly Christianity first entered through Jewish communities in the coast cities.[199] It seems clear that early in the third century it was fairly firmly established in

[193] Eusebius, op. cit., Book IV, Chap. 23; Harnack, op. cit., Vol. II, p. 250.
[194] Harnack, op. cit., Vol. II, pp. 251-260.
[195] Mommsen, The Provinces of the Roman Empire, Vol. I, pp. 74-78.
[196] Bouchier, Spain under the Roman Empire, pp. 109-125.
[197] Romans xv:24.
[198] Leclercq, L'Espagne Chrétienne, pp. 27-42.
[199] Bouchier, op. cit., pp. 173-178.

the South.[200] When we do begin to catch clear glimpses of the Church in Spain, it was already old and sufficiently well developed to have bishops.

The picture of the quality of the Spanish Christians is not particularly heartening, for it portrays a bishop who apostatized during the Decian persecution (A.D. 250) and after the danger had passed resumed his office.[201] From Cyprian, in the third century, we hear of Spanish bishops who left their dioceses to undertake long voyages and engage in commerce.[202] The canons of a council held at Elvira (almost certainly the present Granada), probably about A.D. 300, disclose a Christian community which compromised with idolatry, homicide, and adultery, and yet with sufficient conscience to legislate against these departures from accepted standards.[203]

Although Spanish Christianity does not at first appear in an especially favourable light, and although in its early days it did not take anything approaching the prominent place which the North African Church possessed, it seems to have become more firmly rooted than the latter. Certainly it survived the onslaught of Islam as African Christianity did not and eventually expelled the invader. Into this difference in fate various factors probably entered. It may have been that in Africa the strength of the Church was also its weakness. The prominence of the African Church in the creation of a Christian literature in Latin may well have been closely associated with what seems to have been the leadership of the Latin-speaking stock of Italian descent and with a failure to win the affection of the masses among whom Punic and Berber blood predominated. Then, too, the African Church was torn by the prolonged and stormy Donatist schism, of which we are to speak in a later chapter. This division may have been on racial and class lines, in part a revolt of the non-Roman masses against the possessor classes. On the other hand, the very compromises with pagan standards by Christians in Spain may be evidence that there the faith had become inclusive in its appeal and more integrated with the life of the country.

For the regions of Gallica, Belgica, Germania, and Rhætia, which roughly coincide with what are now France, Belgium, the Rhine Valley, Southern Germany, and a part of Switzerland, we also are without precise knowledge of the introduction and initial growth of Christianity. Because of the close

[200] Tertullian, *Against the Jews*, vii (translation in *Ante-Nicene Fathers*, Vol. III, p. 158); Cyprian, *Epistle*, lxvii (translation in *Ante-Nicene Fathers*, Vol. V, pp. 369-372).
[201] Cyprian, *Epistle*, lxvii; Leclercq, *op. cit.*, pp. 49-52.
[202] Cyprian, *Epistle*, lxvii.
[203] Dale, *The Synod of Elvira and Christian Life in the Fourth Century*, passim; Hefele, *A History of the Christian Councils*, Vol. I, pp. 131-172; Leclercq, *op. cit.*, pp. 58-77; Harnack, *op. cit.*, Vol. II, pp. 300-306. The text of the canons of the Council is given in Dale.

commercial connexions of the lower part of the Rhone Valley with the Greek and the Syrian Orient, we may surmise that Christianity came fairly early and directly from the East.[204] This conjecture is supported by the fact that when we first learn of the faith in Gaul, in the second half of the second century, it is from Lyons and Vienne and the language of the community was predominantly Greek.[205] Syrian merchants were widely spread in Gaul and the Rhine Valley and if there were Christians among them they probably used Greek.[206] The Greek communities in Southern Gaul were originally colonies from Ionia, and it is quite possible that the Christianity of the Rhone Valley was derived from Ephesus. Irenæus, the first prominent churchman of Gaul of whom we know, as a boy, before coming to Lyons, sat at the feet of Polycarp in Smyrna, and it is unlikely that he was the only instance of a Christian immigrant from that region.[207] It is possible that in the New Testament we have reference to a companion of Paul going to Gaul.[208] However, our first indubitable information about Christianity there is of a persecution in Lyons and Vienne in A.D 177.[209] How long before the persecution Christianity had made its appearance we do not know. Irenæus, who belongs to the second half of the second century and lived and laboured in Lyons, calls himself a resident among the Ketae, and speaks of being "accustomed for the most part to use that barbarous dialect."[210] From this we may gather that he preached in Celtic and that the Church contained Christians of the native stock. However, from the fact that Irenæus wrote in Greek and that the recorded names of the martyrs were Greek and Latin,[211] the Celtic element, if present, must either have been small or partially assimilated to Græco-Roman culture.

The progress of Christianity in Gaul and the neighbouring provinces on the north must have been conditioned by the spread of Roman civilization. In Gaul the process of Romanization had begun under the Republic, before the time of Christ.[212] It proceeded less rapidly than in Spain, and the native gods gave way less quickly before the Roman deities. In the eastern part of Gaul

---

[204] Harnack, op. cit., Vol. II, p. 261; Duchesne, Fastes Episcopaux de l'Ancienne Gaule, Vol. I, p. 76.

[205] Harnack, op. cit., Vol. II, p. 261.

[206] Mommsen, op. cit., Vol. II, p. 152.

[207] Irenæus, Adv. Hær., Book III, Chap. 3; Eusebius, Eccles. Hist., Book V, Chap. 20; Streeter, The Four Gospels, pp. 71, 72.

[208] II Tim. iv:10. (While the word is usually translated Galatia, it may have been Gaul. Eusebius, Eccles. Hist., Book III, Chap. 4.)

[209] Eusebius, Eccles. Hist., Book V, Chaps. 1-4.

[210] Irenæus, Adv. Hær., Book I, Introd. (translation in Ante-Nicene Fathers, Vol. I, p. 316).

[211] Harnack, The Mission and Expansion of Christianity, Vol. II, pp. 261, 262.

[212] Mommsen, The Provinces of the Roman Empire, Vol. I, pp. 85-86.

the indigenous cultures disappeared more quickly than in the valleys of the Loire and the Seine. Moreover, the native cults may have provided the final rallying-points and bulwarks of Gallic nationality. However, the older tongues seem to have persisted longer than did the local gods, and the latter appear to have offered little serious resistance to Christianity.[213] In places, indeed, the Celtic language was spoken centuries after the collapse of Roman rule. It was the Church and not the Empire which completed the Romanization of the country.[214] More than one people and culture existed in Gaul before the Roman conquest. Not only were there the Celts, but in the South were Iberians and along the Rhine Germans.[215] In the latter half of the third century Gaul was afflicted by invasions of Germanic tribes and by strife among rivals for the imperial purple. Although the persecution of Diocletian did not severely affect the region, Christianity spread slowly during these years, and when Constantine came into power Gaul was probably still predominantly pagan.[216]

In Gaul, as elsewhere, Christianity apparently first found lodgment in the cities, probably, as we have suggested, through Jewish, Greek, and Syrian merchants. Most of these cities were in the South, in the valley of the Rhone, and in the North. The most prominent were the present Narbonne, Lyons, and, later, Trier.[217] Of the dioceses the approximate dates of whose foundation have been determined, only one, that of Lyons, falls within the second century, another, Arles, in the first half of the third century, four (Toulouse, Vienne, Trier, and Rheims) in the middle of the third century, and Rouen, Bordeaux, Cologne, Metz, Bourges, and Paris about the end of the third or the beginning of the fourth century.[218] Although the Churches in Trier, Cologne, Mainz, and Metz claim foundation through pupils of the Apostles, and although from a statement in Irenæus[219] it has been conjectured that at least Cologne and Mainz had bishops as early as A.D. 185,[220] they may not go back much if any farther than the middle of the third century.[221] At the outset they were, of course, small, and probably their tongue was Latin. Presumably they possessed few if any German and Celtic members and did not have adherents from among the rural

[213] Mommsen, *op. cit.,* Vol. I, pp. 111-115.

[214] Hauck, *Kirchengeschichte Deutschlands,* Vol. I, pp. 5-41.

[215] Mommsen, *op. cit.,* Vol. II, pp. 89-110.

[216] J. E. L. Oulton in Phillips, *A History of the Church of Ireland,* Vol. I, pp. 7-10.

[217] Mommsen, *op. cit.,* Vol. II, pp. 89-110.

[218] Duchesne, *Fastes Episcopaux de l'Ancienne Gaule,* Vol. I, pp. 31, 32.

[219] Irenæus, *Adv. Hær.,* Book I, Chap. 10 (translation in *Ante-Nicene Fathers,* Vol. I, p. 331).

[220] Harnack, *op. cit.,* Vol. II, p. 269.

[221] Hauck, *op. cit.,* Vol. I, pp. 5-41; Duchesne, *Fastes Episcopaux de l'Ancienne Gaule,* Vol. III, p. 9.

population.[222] In Aquitaine dates are lacking, but we know that three bishops from that region were present at a council in A.D. 314 and we may guess that other cities there also had Churches by that year.[223]

How early Christianity was introduced into Britain we do not know.[224] Tertullian, in the first decade of the third century, speaks of Christians there, but expert opinion differs as to the validity of this evidence.[225] It is, however, quite possible that Christians were there by the end of the second century. Perhaps the reports of the martyrdom of Albans at Verulam (St. Albans), and of two others elsewhere during the Diocletian persecution, arise from historic incidents.[226] We are certain that three bishops from Britain attended the Council of Arles in A.D. 314,[227] and it may be that the island held other bishoprics at this time.[228]

From this survey it is clear that within the first three centuries of its existence and while it was still frowned upon by the state, Christianity had spread to most and possibly to all the main divisions of the Roman domains. It had overpassed the boundaries of Judaism, and, far from being content to domicile itself only in Hellenism, it had won important footholds among the non-Greek peoples of Egypt and the Latin-speaking peoples of the West. Probably here and there it had also moved beyond the lines set by the use of Latin and had gained some adherents among the native and not yet fully Romanized populations in such regions as North Africa and Gaul. Although bearing the marks of its different environments, Christianity was already more inclusive than any one cultural tradition.

While found chiefly within the Roman Empire, by the end of its third century Christianity had begun to spill over the borders of even that most populous of the states of the day. This is not surprising. The political boundaries of the Empire were not water-tight. Beyond them, especially in the East, stretched trade routes by land and sea. The merchant from the Roman Orient was a not unfamiliar sight in the ports of India, and even from distant China came silks for the markets of the Mediterranean world.[229] With the merchant

---

[222] Hauck, *op. cit.*, Vol. I, pp. 5-41.

[223] Duchesne, *op. cit.*, Vol. II, p. 9.

[224] See a summary of the legendary accounts in Williams, *Christianity in Early Britain*, pp. 54-66.

[225] Tertullian, *Adv. Iudaeos*, c. 7. Williams, *op. cit.*, pp. 72-77, upholds the reliability of this reference. Harnack, *op. cit.*, Vol. II, p. 272, dismisses it as of no consequence.

[226] Bede, *Eccles. Hist.*, Book I, Chap. 7. See a full discussion, with reference to the sources, in Williams, *op. cit.*, pp. 101-11.

[227] See their names in Gee and Hardy, *Documents Illustrative of English Church History*, Vol. I, p. 1.

[228] Harnack, *op. cit.*, Vol. II, pp. 272-274.

[229] For this Eastern trade of the Roman Empire see a brief summary in Rostovtzeff, *Social and Economic History of the Roman Empire*, pp. 91-93, 147. A longer summary

went something of his culture—although the latter did not necessarily penetrate so far as did his goods. It would have been strange, therefore, if Christianity, rooted as it was in the main commercial cities of the Empire and to a certain extent among the migrant merchant and artisan classes, had halted at the Roman *limes*.

Sometime in the early centuries of Christianity the tradition arose that the Twelve Apostles had parcelled among themselves the known world. One form of this tradition declared that Thomas received the Parthians as his assignment; Matthew, Ethiopia; and Bartholomew, part of India.[230] Another version gave Scythia to Andrew.[231] We shall see in a moment the accounts which sent Thomas to India. We need not give credence to these reports to prove the early existence of Christian communities outside the Empire.

It was natural that the faith should soon win adherents in Edessa. Here was a city on the great trade routes which ran between the mountains of Armenia on the North and the Syrian desert on the South. Until the end of the second century it was outside the Roman Empire and within the sphere of influence of Parthia, one of Rome's most formidable rivals. On the border, it could expect attack from both sides, but for a time in the first centuries of our story it maintained an independent existence.[232] An interesting legend declares that King Abgar of Edessa wrote to Jesus himself asking him to come and cure him of a disease and had a reply, and that after the resurrection one of the Seventy arrived who healed the king and won the entire city to the faith.[233] Not far from Antioch, that early centre of missionary activity, it may be that Edessa received emissaries from the same Church which sent out Paul and Barnabas. A tradition, indeed, traces the succession of the Bishops of Edessa to Serapion, Bishop of Antioch A.D. 190-203.[234] Edessa was, moreover, an important centre of Greek culture.[235] What more natural than that a faith with an active missionary community in Hellenistic Antioch should there early win adherents? In Mesopotamia, too, were many Jews[236] and among them, as elsewhere, Chris-

---

is in Charlesworth, *Trade-Routes and Commerce of the Roman Empire*. See also Hudson, *Europe and China*, pp. 68-109.

[230] Socrates, *Eccles. Hist.*, Book I, Chap. 19.

[231] Eusebius, *Eccles. Hist.*, Book III, Chap. 1.

[232] Burkitt, *Early Eastern Christianity*, pp. 6-8; Bacon, *Studies in Matthew*, p. 14.

[233] Eusebius, *Eccles. Hist.*, Book I, Chap. 13; Book II, Chap. 1. Eusebius declares that the evidence for this was letters in the archives of the city. See also on this legend translations of documents in *Ante-Nicene Fathers*, Vol. VIII, pp. 648-665, 702-707, and of the *Acts of the Holy Apostle Thaddeus* (who is alleged to have done the preaching) in *Ante-Nicene Fathers*, Vol. VIII, pp. 558, 559.

[234] Burkitt, *Early Christianity Outside the Roman Empire*, p. 12.

[235] Bacon, *Studies in Matthew*, p. 14.

[236] *Ibid.*

tianity might well make a beginning. It might have come, for instance, from Damascus.

Whatever its debt to Hellenistic Antioch, the Christianity of Edessa was not predominantly Greek, but Syrian. The language of the city was chiefly Syriac, a tongue closely akin to the Aramaic of the Palestine of the time.[237] Here, spanning the end of the second and the beginning of the third century, lived Bardaisan, a convert who wrote vigorously and originally on his new faith and some of whose writings circulated in Syriac.[238]

The precise historical order of the introduction and growth of Christianity in Edessa we do not know, but one suggestion has it that the first adherents were among the Jews, probably before the middle of the second century, and that at first the Church contained a strong Jewish element; that by about the end of the second century Christianity became the state religion; and that when, about the beginning of the third century, the city passed under Roman dominion, a mission came whose authority and orders were from the Bishop of Antioch.[239] At the dawn of the third century few if any cities contained a larger percentage of Christians. By the beginning of the fourth century Edessa may have been predominantly Christian.[240]

Here was a centre of a Syriac type of Christianity, different in some ways from that prevailing in the Hellenistic world, and which spread into Mesopotamia and the edges of Persia. It was a beginning of that wide extension of the faith in the Tigris-Euphrates Valley, Persia, Central Asia, and China whose course we are later to trace.

We know too little of the founding and early growth of Christianity in Edessa and Mesopotamia to correlate them minutely and conclusively with the political vicissitudes of this region. Situated as it was on the border between the Roman Empire on the one hand and the Parthian and the latter's successor, the Sassanian Empire, on the other, Edessa was inevitably affected by the relations between its huge neighbours. Not until early in the third century was the independence of Edessa and the state of which it was the capital erased by Rome, and possibly its previous autonomy with freedom from the restraints placed by the Roman authorities on Christianity had favoured the acceptance of the faith. It may be, too, that here we have the earliest instance of what

---

[237] Burkitt, *Early Eastern Christianity*, pp. 6, 7.

[238] Eusebius, *Eccles. Hist.*, Book IV, Chap. 1; Burkitt, *op. cit.*, pp. 156-188; Harnack, *The Mission and Expansion of Christianity*, Vol. II, p. 144.

[239] Burkitt, *op. cit.*, pp. 22, 34-36; Adeney, *The Greek and Eastern Churches*, pp. 459-476.

[240] Harnack, *op. cit.*, Vol. II, p. 145; F. C. Burkitt, *Euphemia and the Goth*, pp. 15, 19. Yet long after the third century the city contained many pagans. Possibly as late as the sixth century the majority of the population was non-Christian. Schultze. *Geschichte des untergangs des griechisch-römischen Heidentums*, Vol. II, p. 270.

was often to be seen later in the spread of Christianity, the rulers becoming Christian and the majority of their subjects following their example.[241] In the absence of more detailed information, however, this must be conjecture.

Edessa seems to have been a point from which Christianity was carried farther into Mesopotamia and to the edges of Persia. It is possible that even in the first generation after Jesus the faith reached that region, for the account of the Pentecost experience given in Acts mentions among those who heard the Christian message "Parthians and Medes and Elamites and the dwellers in Mesopotamia."[242] It may be that Christianity first gained a footing among the Jews.[243] Certainly we hear of early leading Christians bearing Old Testament names.[244]

It seems probable that the Arsacids, who ruled the Parthian Empire in the early centuries of the Christian era, were fairly tolerant. At least some martyrdoms appear to have been due to local hostility rather than to a deliberate policy of the state.[245] The old faiths of Babylonia and Assyria seem to have disintegrated and so to have offered little opposition to the advent of a new religion.[246] The opposition of which we hear was chiefly from Zoroastrianism.[247] Even when in the first half of the third century a native Persian dynasty, the Sassanids, replaced the Arsacids and made Zoroastrianism the state cult, Christianity seems not for some time to have been singled out for persecution.[248]

Long before the opening of the fourth century Christianity had been disseminated widely in Mesopotamia, Babylonia, and east of the Tigris. By A.D. 225, or about the end of the Arsacid rule, more than twenty bishoprics are known to have existed in the Tigris-Euphrates Valley and on the borders of Persia. They stretched from near the Caspian to the Bahrein Islands in the Persian Gulf. The region of Adiabene, near the upper reaches of the Tigris, with its capital, Arbela, an old sacred city of the Assyrians, was early reached. We read of a missionary making converts there about A.D. 100. Yet the Christian groups seem usually to have been small and occasionally subject to active resistance

---

[241] Eusebius, *Eccles. Hist.*, Book I, Chap. 13, Book II, Chap. 1, par. 7.

[242] Acts ii:9.

[243] Adiabene, on the upper part of the Tigris, became Jewish in faith in the first century. Josephus, *Ant.*, Book XX, Chaps. 2-4. The conjecture that Christianity first spread among the Jews is to be found in Labourt, *Le Christianisme dans l'Empire Perse sous la Dynastie Sassanide*, pp. 16, 17; Sachau, *Die Chronik von Arbela*, p. 30; and Sachau, *Zur Ausbreitung des Christentums in Asien* (in *Abhandlungen der preussichen Akademie der Wissenschaften*, 1919), p. 5.

[244] Sachau, *Die Chronik von Arbela*, p. 30.

[245] Wigram, *An Introduction to the History of the Assyrian Church*, pp. 31-39.

[246] *Ibid.*

[247] Sachau, *Die Chronik von Arbela*, p. 30.

[248] Wigram, *op. cit.*, pp. 31-39.

from leaders of rival religions. We hear, for example, of repeated persecutions during the lives of the early Bishops of Arbela. However, the faith continued to gain strength. One of the persecuted bishops, in a time of enforced exile, is said to have won the population of the village in which he took refuge.[249] At Dura-Europos, on the Tigris, on the great road from Ctesiphon to Antioch and Palmyra, archæology has revealed a building which was used as a church at least as early as A.D. 232. It seems to have been first a part of a private house, of the sort of which we often hear in the New Testament. Presumably its membership was small. From the fact that the inscriptions on its walls are in Greek, it seems logical to assume that this and not Syriac was the language of the congregation.[250] Merchants and other travellers from a Hellenistic world which contained a growing proportion of Christians must have brought their faith with them. It is possible that some fled from the persecutions in the Roman Empire. Then, too, the captives made by the Persians in their raids toward the west, notably under the early Sassanids, may have included some Christians.[251] The preaching of the faith among the indigenous population was facilitated by the use of Syriac, the vernacular which prevailed from Syria to Babylonia.[252] How far eastward Christianity penetrated we do not know. In the second century it may have reached Bactria.[253]

Here, then, in a region outside the Roman Empire and only partially under Hellenistic influence, was a wide early extension of the Christian faith. Usually the Christian communities were small. Even in the capital, Seleucia-Ctesiphon, the Christians were few and probably did not have a bishop until about A.D. 280.[254] Yet this minority was reaching out, often with missionary zeal, and was augmenting its numbers.

One of the most interesting and important problems of our story, to which we must recur more than once, is the failure of these communities to win the same success that their co-religionists achieved in the Roman Empire. Why did they always remain a minority and eventually all but disappear? The answer is partly to be found in the religious policy of the Sassanids. As a native

---

[249] Sachau, *Die Chronik von Arbela, passim*, gives an introduction to and a translation of a document which is very important for the early history and which is also referred to by Mingana in *The Early Spread of Christianity in Central Asia and the Far East*, pp. 3-8.

[250] C. Hopkins in Rostovtzeff (editor), *The Excavations at Dura-Europos Conducted by Yale University and the French Academy of Inscriptions and Letters. Preliminary Report of Fifth Season of Work, Oct. 1931-March 1932*, pp. 238-253.

[251] Wigram, *An Introduction to the History of the Assyrian Church*, pp. 40-55.

[252] Sachau, *Zur Ausbreitung des Christentums in Asien*, p. 6.

[253] Mingana, *op. cit.*, pp. 3-8, with a reference to Bardaisan.

[254] Wigram, *op. cit.*, pp. 40-55.

Persian dynasty they endorsed Zoroastrianism.[255] This, led by a powerful hierarchy and supported by the monarchy, was able to offer more energetic and united resistance than could any of the religions of the Græco-Roman world. Moreover, the very success in the Roman Empire proved one of Christianity's greatest obstacles in the Persian realms. After its adoption by Constantine, it was regarded by the Persian rulers as the faith of their deadliest rivals. To be a Christian was to be under the protection of Rome. Weighed down by that incubus, Christianity was suspect and in the vicissitudes of Persian-Roman relations subject to repeated and often severe persecutions.

Not far from the regions with which we have just been concerned was Armenia. The name has been made to include an area of varying boundaries, but which centred in the south slopes of the Caucasus and the tableland north of the valley of the Tigris and Euphrates. In the period which we are considering, it was divided into Little Armenia, west of the upper reaches of the Euphrates, and Great Armenia, east of that river. A border state between the Roman and the Parthian and Persian Empires, and subject to invasion from both directions, it usually maintained its independence, even if somewhat precariously.

Christianity appears to have penetrated Armenia by the beginning of the third century, partly from Cæsarea in Cappadocia and partly from Antioch and Edessa. Great Armenia probably has the distinction of being the second state (Edessa being the first) and the first country of any size in which Christianity became the official religion.

The conversion of the land is said to have been the work of Gregory the Illuminator. Christianity seems to have entered long before his day.[256] In accounts which have come down to us it is difficult, if not impossible, to entangle the accretions of legend from the unvarnished facts. Precise dates, too, largely elude us. Gregory appears to have sprung from the aristocracy and to have acquired his Christian faith while in exile in Cæsarea. Returning to Armenia, after an initial persecution he won to the faith the king, Tradt, Tirdat, or Tiridates (c. A.D. 261-317).[257] The conjecture is hazarded that Tradt was moved by a desire to offset the influence of Persia and its Zoroastrianism, which under the Sassanids menaced the autonomy of the land. He had, indeed, freed his kingdom from the Persian yoke.[258] Whatever the motive, after his

[255] Ibid.

[256] Tertullian, c. A.D. 200, in Adv. Iud., Chap. 7, speaks of Christians in Armenia, although he does not specify whether it was Little Armenia or Great Armenia. See also Eusebius, Eccles. Hist., Book VI, Chap. 6; Conybeare, The Key of Truth, pp. viii, ix.

[257] On the dates of Tradt, see Gibbon, Decline and Fall of the Roman Empire (Bury ed.), Vol. II, pp. 563-565.

[258] On Tradt see Gibbon, op. cit., Vol. II, pp. 366-375.

first vigorous resistance, the king accepted the faith and with the consent o his nobles supported Gregory. The native religion seems to have been fairl strong, with a powerful priesthood and temples possessing large endowment The shrines were often transformed to the uses of Christian worship and th endowments transferred to the Church. Many of the pagan priests, or at leas of their sons, appear to have passed over into the clergy of the new faith, som of them becoming bishops. Schools were established to train the scions of th priesthood for their new clerical duties. Although Gregory called in Greek an Syrian missionaries to assist him, much of the conversion, *en masse* as it wa must have been very superficial. Gregory obtained episcopal ordination from Cæsarea and headed the national Church. In this office he was followed by hi lineal descendants. One of these latter, with the aid of a learned monk, devise a revision of an alphabet for the Armenian language, and with it as a mediur had a quantity of religious books translated from Greek and Syriac.

A people for whom religion was a matter of state had, under their natura leaders, transferred their allegiance from one cult to another. Naturally it too several generations for the new arrival to convey anything of its inward meanin to any but a favoured few. It may be questioned, indeed, whether more than small minority ever ceased to view it as the religion of the group. The majorit identified the Armenian Church and its Christianity with Armenian na tionalism.[259]

To the north of Armenia, in the Caucasus and on the northern shores of th Black Sea, some planting of Christianity was to be expected through contact with the Roman Empire. In the mountainous region of Georgia, north of th Armenian plateau and south of the main ridges of the Caucasus, traditio declares that the first Christian missionary was Andrew, one of the Twelv Apostles. A tradition also comes down of a few converts and martyrs in th generation after the Apostles.[260] The first report of missionary effort whic seems to have about it any trace of authenticity is from about the time of Co stantine. The story told is of a Christian captive, a woman, who by her prayer wrought works of healing which included in their beneficence the queen. I

[259] On the conversion of Armenia see Sozomen, *Eccles. Hist.*, Book II, Chap. 8; Harnacl *The Mission and Expansion of Christianity*, Vol. II, pp. 196-203; Adeney, *The Gree and Eastern Churches*, pp. 539-552; Duchesne, *Early History of the Christian Churc* Vol. III, pp. 362-378; Schmidlin, *Katholische Missionsgeschichte*, p. 98; Aufhause *Armeniens Missionierung bis zur Gründung der Nationalkirche*, in *Zeitschrift für Mi sionswissenschaft*, Vol. VIII (1918), pp. 80-87. A standard history often quoted is one the fourth century, Agathangelus, which is to be found in French translation in Langloi *Collection des Historiens Anciens et Modernes de l'Armenie*, Vol. I, pp. 97-195. See al Gelzer, *Die Anfänge der armenischen Kirche* (*Berichten der königl. sächs. Gesellscha der Wissenschaften, Sitzung vom 4 Mai, 1895*, pp. 109-174).

[260] Tamarati. *L'Église Géorgienne*, pp. 120-133, 149-151.

gratitude, so it is said, the king and queen built a church and asked Constantine for priests.[261] The Goths, to the north and west of the Black Sea, seem first also to have received Christianity from captives. In a raid into Asia Minor in A.D. 258 they carried away a number of Cappadocian Christians who persisted in their faith and sought to propagate it among their masters.[262]

Across the Jordan and southward into Arabia Christianity had penetrated before the close of the third century. We hear of a bishop whose Christology created a sensation, and of a synod held at his see, Bostra.[263] We have a report, too, of other doctrines put forth by Arabian Christians which differed from those held by the majority of the Church.[264] This may be evidence that the faith had spread among the non-Greek native population, who held views more in accord with their own background than with that of the Hellenistic world.[265] About A.D. 180, moreover, Pantænus, who went from Alexandria to "India" (by which is possibly meant Southern Arabia) found there those who had "a Hebrew version of Matthew's gospel."[266]

It is not improbable that before the end of the third century Christianity had arrived in India itself. The commerce between that country and the Roman East was largely through Alexandria and brought merchants from the Empire to India.[267] Since a strong Church existed in Alexandria, some contact of Indians with Christianity is entirely possible. If the region which Pantænus reached was really India and not Southern Arabia, then by the close of the second century Christians were there who attributed the first mission in their country to the Apostle Bartholomew.[268] Even if these Christians were in Southern Arabia, the fact of their existence would heighten the possibility of the spread of the faith across the Indian Ocean. We have also the well-known and detailed story of the introduction of the faith to India by the Apostle Thomas. The narrative is so interwoven with the miraculous that scholars are at least inclined to question it and many of them are disposed to dismiss it as having no basis in fact. How it arose at all becomes a subject of interesting speculation.[269] A vast quantity of

[261] Rufinus, *Historia Ecclesiastica*, Book I, Chap. 10; Duchesne, *op. cit.*, Vol. III, pp. 360, 361.

[262] Harnack, *op. cit.*, Vol. II, p. 239.

[263] Eusebius, *Eccles. Hist.*, Book VI, Chaps. 20, 33.

[264] Eusebius, *op. cit.*, Book VI, Chap. 37.

[265] Harnack, *op. cit.*, Vol. II, p. 154.

[266] Eusebius, *Eccles. Hist.*, Book V, Chap. 10.

[267] Rostovtzeff, *A Social and Economic History of the Roman Empire*, pp. 91, 147; Mommsen, *Provinces of the Roman Empire*, Vol. II, p. 327; Gibbon, *The Decline and Fall of the Roman Empire*, Vol. I, pp. 54, 55.

[268] Eusebius, *Eccles. Hist.*, Book V, Chap. 10.

[269] The account is contained in the *Acta Thomae* (English translation in *Ante-Nicene Fathers*, Vol. VIII, pp. 535-549). Burkitt, *Early Christianity Outside the Roman Empire*, pp. 63-86, suggests that the story was composed in Syriac and is an expression of a type

ink has been spilled in the attempt to prove that Thomas actually made converts in India, either in the North or the South or in both places.[270] To many, however, the arguments set forth are not convincing. The most that we can subscribe to with assurance is the entirely unsatisfying and banal statement that, as in so much of the ancient world, the origins of the Christian communities are shrouded in obscurity. We can neither demonstrate nor disprove the existence of Christians in India in the first three centuries.

A statistically minded age is inevitably interested in attempts to discover the numbers of professed Christians at various periods in the life of the faith. Or if, as is usually the case, precise figures cannot be obtained, we are eager to learn what proportion of the population bears the Christian label. Obviously, exact totals during the centuries we have been describing are out of the question. Percentages also elude us. Many estimates have been made, but none of them ought to claim even approximate accuracy. The evidence on which they are based is at best fragmentary. Occasional statements in contemporary authors, some of them pagan but more of them Christian, rare references to the number of clergy in a particular city or lists of bishops attending a synod, and here and there an inscription or some other bit of evidence from archæology constitute the basis for the conjectures. Under such circumstances the wide divergence in the guesses of various scholars need not surprise us. They vary from the familiar one of Gibbon, which placed the number of Christians at the time of Constantine at not "more than a twentieth part of the subjects of the Empire"[271] to one which estimates it at about the same date as one-half the population.[272] Most estimates give proportions ranging from one-twentieth to one-eighth of the population.[273]

---

of Christianity which was interested in preaching virginity and poverty and in the conversion of individual souls rather than in establishing a church.

[270] Zaleski, *The Saints of India*, pp. 37-99, contends that Bartholomew actually preached in India (pp. 177-190), that Pantænus reached India proper, and (pp. 105-173) that Thomas laboured in India. Dahlmann, *Die Thomas-Legende und die ältesten historischen Beziehungen des Christentums zum Fernen Osten*, also argues that Thomas was in India. So also does D'Cruz, *St. Thomas the Apostle in India*. Farquhar, *The Apostle Thomas in North India* and Farquhar, *The Apostle Thomas in South India* declare it quite probable that the Apostle Thomas was in both North and South India. Medlycott, *India and the Apostle Thomas* also argues, with much erudition, for the presence of Thomas in India. Rae, *The Syrian Church in India* thinks this unlikely, but contends that the author of the *Acta Thomae*, writing in the second century, believed that Christians were in India at that time. He also inclines to the opinion that Pantænus laboured in India. Part of the argument for the validity of the story of Thomas is evidence which leads some to support the historicity of the King Gudnaphar who looms so prominently in it. Adeney, *The Greek and Eastern Churches*, pp. 296, 297, holds that Christianity had reached North-west India as early as the third century.

[271] Gibbon, *op. cit.*, Vol. II, p. 65.

[272] Stäudlin, quoted in Harnack, *op. cit.*, Vol. II, p. 325.

[273] Harnack, *op. cit.*, Vol. II, p. 325, Schultze, *Geschichte des Untergangs des griechisch-*

Uncertainty also bedevils attempts at determining the proportional representation of the various classes in the Christian Church. We have, to be sure, contemporary statements in the form of generalizations. Among these are the famous one of Paul that "not many wise after the flesh, not many mighty, not many noble are called,"[274] and the charge of Celsus which Origen seeks to answer but does not deny, that Christianity obtained a hold chiefly on the ignorant.[275] Yet neither enables us to know whether the Church was a cross section of the population, in which, of course, the humbler classes would be in the large majority, or whether it drew disproportionately from certain groups. In later writers we find such contradictory opinions as the one summarized by Gibbon—which he admits is biased—that the Christians were "almost entirely composed of the dregs of the populace, of peasants and mechanics, of boys and women, of beggars and slaves"[276] and that of Ramsay, who declares that Christianity spread first among the educated more rapidly than among the uneducated.[277] We have a considerable amount of evidence bearing on the classes from which individual Christians came and on the penetration of the faith into particular groups. We possess very little information, however, which enables us safely to conjecture even the approximate ratio of the various social, economic, racial, and occupational strata in the membership of the Christian community. It is clear that even in the Apostolic Age a number of men and women of wealth, education, and social consequence entered the Church. The early Christian community in Jerusalem had not only the poor who needed assistance, but those of substance who sold their houses and lands to contribute to the common purse.[278] Paul speaks of Christians who gave out of their deep

---

römischen Heidentums, Vol. I, p. 23, footnote 3, and Schmidlin, *Katholische Missionsgeschichte*, p. 77, give a number of these. Harnack considers one-half quite excessive. Schmidlin thinks the proportion of Christians in the population about one-eighth. Orr, *Neglected Factors in the Study of the Early Progress of Christianity*, pp. 13-91, argues that the proportion was much larger than one-tenth. Schultze, *op. cit.*, Vol. I, p. 22, believes that at the accession of Constantine there were in the Empire about ten million Christians in a population of one hundred million.

[274] I Cor. i:26.

[275] Origen, *Contra Cels.*, Book I, Chap. 27.

[276] Gibbon, *op. cit.*, Vol. II, pp. 65, 66. We have a statement by Case, *The Social Triumph of the Ancient Church*, pp. 61-64, which declares that Christianity spread widely among the working classes and small tradesmen of the Empire, and that while a few persons of education and dignity were to be found in the churches, the majority of the Christians were slaves, common labourers, and people without recognized social standing. However, Case does not attempt to determine whether persons of prominence were proportionately less numerous than in society as a whole.

[277] Ramsay, *The Church in the Roman Empire*, p. 57.

[278] Acts iv:32-37.

poverty.[279] We also hear of converts of considerable local prominence.[280] Some of the epistles in the New Testament distinctly speak of wealthy Christians.[281] It is within the realm of possibility that as far back as the first century the faith had been accepted by some members of the most prominent families of Rome itself[282] and that a near relative of Domitian was a Christian and might, but for his untimely execution, have succeeded the latter to the imperial dignity.[283] It is certain that before Constantine Christians were occupying high official posts, including the governorships of provinces.[284] That scholars were entering the Church as converts or being reared in it is clear from the presence of such men as Clement and Origen of Alexandria and Tertullian of Carthage. Yet we have no way of determining whether people of consequence constituted a larger or a smaller percentage of the membership of the Church than of the population as a whole. We gain the impression that the numbers of prominent folk increased rapidly during the third century,[285] but we do not know whether they rose more quickly than that of the total membership.

It is clear that the faith spread first in the cities and that during the first three centuries it was predominantly urban rather than rural. We have very little information, however, as to whether the composition of the Church differed from city to city. We know, of course, that Christianity was first confined to the Jews and that when it moved into the Gentile world its accessions were chiefly among those of Greek speech and Hellenic culture. In the West it eventually entered the circles whose tongue was primarily Latin. In the Tigris-Euphrates Valley its home was chiefly among those of Syriac speech. Naturally, therefore, it tended in the Middle East to be identified with Greek civilization, in the West with Roman manners, and in the East, outside the Empire, with

[279] II Cor. viii:1-3.

[280] For a list of instances of this kind see Orr, *op. cit.*, pp. 104-110. Among them are the Centurion Cornelius (Acts xi:1-48), Manaen, foster-brother of Herod the Tetrarch (Acts xiii:1), the Proconsul Sergius Paulus of Cyprus (Acts xiii:6-12), Crispus, the chief ruler of the synagogue (Acts xviii:8), and Erastus, a city treasurer (Rom. xvi:23).

[281] James ii:1-13; I Tim. vi:17.

[282] For instances of this see Orr, *op. cit.*, pp. 113-136; Harnack, *op. cit.*, Vol. II, pp. 35, 36; Uhlhorn, *The Conflict of Christianity with Paganism*, p. 222; Schmidlin, *Katholische Missionsgeschichte*, pp. 74, 75; Workman, *Persecution in the Early Church*, p. 60.

[283] This was T. Flavius Clemens. He may have been at least an inquirer, and his wife, Domitilla, an adherent of the Church. See a discussion of this in Streeter, *The Four Gospels*, pp. 535, 536. The pertinent passages are in Suetonius, *Dom.* 15, and Cassius Dio, lxvii, 14.

[284] Eusebius, *Eccles. Hist.*, Book VIII, Chap. 1.

[285] Origen, *Contra Cels.*, Book III, Chap. 9, says, "At the present day, when, owing to the multitude of Christian believers, not only rich men, but persons of rank and delicate and high-born ladies, receive the teachers of Christianity, some perhaps will dare to say that it is for the sake of a little glory that certain individuals assume the office of Christian instructor."

those who used Syriac. It expanded with these cultures and aided in their dissemination.

Within these linguistic and cultural groups we are not sure what classes were most responsive. It appears clear that relatively few Christians were found in the army, partly because the attitude of the Church in the early centuries was unfriendly to military service as an occupation for Christians.[286] It also seems fairly certain that the Church contained more women than men, at least from the higher classes.[287] Beyond these broad generalizations and unanswered questions, however, our evidence does not as yet permit us to go.

Any summary of the spread of a faith which confines itself, as has this chapter, to a survey of the areas and classes into which the extension was effected is inevitably incomplete and therefore unsatisfying. It says little of the vivid and varied life in the midst of which the growth took place, and seems scarcely related to that world which was portrayed in the second chapter. It has only barely touched on the processes, the agents, and the methods by which the religion was propagated. It has said still less of the motives which led converts to embrace the faith. It has given nothing at all of the arguments used by Christians in their approach to non-Christians, of the reasons why Christianity made a more rapid growth than its rivals, of its effect upon those who accepted it and upon the culture of the ancient world, or of the changes which the faith itself underwent.

Yet a certain advantage may accrue from this segregating of one phase of the story. To one with imagination the amazing rapidity of the spread of Christianity must be apparent. The followers of Jesus began as a sect within Judaism. They succeeded in winning only a small minority of their fellow Jews. However, far from dying out or persisting only as a small cult, Christianity moved on into the stream of Hellenistic urban culture. In spite of the competition of the many cults and philosophies with which that world teemed, it quickly attracted a following, and, by the end of the third century of its life, in many of the cities of the East, especially in Antioch, Alexandria, and those in Asia Minor, it embraced an important minority of the population and in a few places probably a majority. Nor did it remain exclusively Greek. Long before the close of its third century it had made itself at home in the Latin-speaking portions of the West, notably in the capital of the Empire and in North Africa. In the West, as in North Africa and Gaul, it had begun to gain adherents

[286] C. J. Cadoux, *The Early Christian Attitude to War;* Harnack, *op. cit.,* Vol. II, pp. 52-64; Ramsay, *The Cities and Bishoprics of Phrygia,* Vol. II, pp. 717, 718.
[287] Harnack, *op. cit.,* Vol. II, pp. 64-84. On women in the early Church see Goltz, *Der Dienst der Frau in der christlichen Kirche,* Part I, pp. 5-57, Part II, pp. 1-21; Stöcker, *Die Frau in der alten Kirche;* Gottlieb, *Die Frau im frühen Christentum.*

among those whose primary tongue was not Latin. In the East it was becoming naturalized in Armenia and among peoples who spoke Syriac. It had acquired a foothold among still other folk, including those of the older Egyptian stocks, some of the peoples of Arabia, probably the Goths, and possibly the Georgians and the Indians. In speech and environment it was still predominantly Greek and in its heritage more Jewish than anything else. The vast majority of its followers were in the Roman Empire and practically all the remainder were in the political, cultural, or commercial spheres of influence of that Empire. Already, however, Christianity was cosmopolitan in its membership. Its rate of increase apparently was accelerated as the decades passed. Certainly it seems to have had a phenomenal growth in the third century. Within the Empire it had developed what was, after the state, the strongest and most widely spread organization. As we shall see in a later chapter, it had even proved itself stronger than the state. The latter had sought to exterminate it, but in vain. Whether the persecution could have been continued until the faith was stamped out we do not know. As it was, the state in effect capitulated and sought to make an ally of the foe which it had not succeeded in eliminating.

Never in the history of the race has this record ever quite been equalled. Never in so short a time has any other religious faith, or, for that matter, any other set of ideas, religious, political, or economic, without the aid of physical force or of social or cultural prestige, achieved so commanding a position in such an important culture. Others have gained far more adherents in the same length of time. Islam probably did so in its first three centuries, but that was chiefly because of the power and prestige which came from the success of its armies. Buddhism may possibly have attracted as many converts in its initial three centuries, but if so it was largely through the support given it by a great monarch, Asoka. It may be that in a similar span of years Manichæism spread over a wider area. Like Christianity, too, its growth was often in the face of persecution and without the support of the rulers. However, never did it loom so prominently in any populous or important state as did Christianity in the Roman Empire. In the nineteenth and twentieth centuries such sets of ideas as democracy, socialism, and the scientific method have drawn much more numerous followings over far wider areas. This, however, has been due partly to more rapid means of communication, partly to the prestige which has been theirs through affiliation with triumphant Western civilization, or because, as in the case of democracy, they have been associated with some prominent nation, such as France, Great Britain, or the United States, or through the fact that they have been fortunate in seizing the control of the political machinery of a particular nation. The phenomenal spread of Communism, far more rapid and

pectacular than was that of Christianity at the outset, has been due largely to
the capture of the government of the huge Russian Empire by what was origi-
ally a comparatively small group. In the number and extent of new areas
ntered Christianity itself has more than once surpassed the record of its own
rst three hundred years. This it did in the sixteenth and seventeenth and in
ne nineteenth and twentieth centuries. However, it then had the advantage of
ne armed support of powerful nations or of the prestige which accrued from
pparent identification with a conquering culture. In the ways we have indi-
ated, Christianity's record in the first three centuries is unique.

It is, moreover, to its progress in these three centuries that Christianity largely
wed its future success. In them it attained the position which shortly made it
upreme in the Roman Empire. It was partly because it became so integrated
vith the civilization of the Mediterranean world that it attracted the allegiance
f the barbarians of Northern Europe. They took over Christianity as a con-
tituent part of the more advanced culture of the South which they overran but
f which they stood in awe. It was through these same peoples of the northern
hores of the Mediterranean and of Northern Europe that Christianity achieved
ne geographical advances of the sixteenth, seventeenth, eighteenth, and nine-
eenth centuries which have made it the most widely professed faith of man-
ind.

This, of course, is not all the story. But for certain inward qualities Chris-
ianity could not have attained so outstanding a place in its first three hundred
ears or have held it and extended it in later centuries. It was, however, highly
ortunate for its future that it was born in the Roman Empire and into a
ivilization in process of flux, and that this cultural area should have been the
argest and most prominent which the human race had yet developed. But for
hat fact and for its initial successes Christianity might not have gained the
rominence which it now holds.

Chapter IV

THE SPREAD OF CHRISTIANITY BEFORE CONSTANTINI
AGENTS, METHODS, ARGUMENTS, OPPOSITION, THE COI
VERSION OF CONSTANTINE, AND REASONS FOR ULTIMAT
SUCCESS

FROM an account of areas and groups among which Christianity we
adherents in its first three centuries we turn to such closely related subjec
as the agents of the spread, the methods employed, the arguments advanced l
Christians to win adherents or to answer their opponents, the objections p
forward by the enemies of Christianity, the nature of the opposition, includir
the persecutions inflicted on Christians, and the reasons for the ultimate t
umph of the faith. For some of these topics our information is as fragmenta
as it is for the inception of most of the Christian communities. On sever
others the conclusions must be largely conjectural. All, however, are of gre
importance, and we must seek to summarize such facts as we possess and
draw from them such deductions as appear warranted.

For the agents of the spread our documents are very unsatisfactory. Abo
some generalizations we can be clear. It is obvious that we cannot expect to fir
duplicated in the first three hundred years the elaborate missionary machine
of the nineteenth and twentieth centuries. The latter, as we shall see in lat
sections of our story, arose out of conditions unparalleled in earlier ages. Whe
we attempt to move back from the last hundred and fifty years we find ou
selves in very different surroundings. Societies financed by the gifts of millio
of Christians and supporting missionaries are a recent phenomenon. We mu
therefore, be prepared for the spread of the faith by means unfamiliar to us.
is also certain that Christianity won converts through more than one type
person. We must not expect to discover that the gains were exclusively or ev
mainly through one class or profession.

It is probable, however, that for about the first two centuries types of Chri
tians existed one of whose chief functions it was to propagate the faith. It
clear that the authors of the Gospel of Matthew and the Acts of the Apostl
believed that the Eleven were especially commissioned to proclaim the Christia
message. Such, at least, seems to be the clear inference from the settings give

114

for the Great Commission.[1] We have seen that most of the Eleven quickly drop out of sight and appear again only in late and probably unauthentic reports. Of Peter alone do we hear by name as a peripatetic missionary. In the New Testament we read repeatedly of those who for longer or shorter periods made it their primary occupation to travel from place to place proclaiming the Gospel. They might settle for months or years in one city, winning converts and instructing the neophytes. Sooner or later, however, the urge would come to move on. Of these we know more of Paul than of any one else, but we catch glimpses of others—among them Philip, Barnabas, John Mark, Silas, and Apollos. The profession seems to have been thought of as one to which men were summoned by the Spirit and not by man,[2] although a group, under the direction of the Spirit, might commission them[3] or recognize their calling.[4] In the *Didache*, which belongs probably to the first half of the second century, we have a glimpse of those who put in their time travelling from church to church, but it is not clear that reaching non-Christians was one of their functions.[5] They may resemble those spoken of in the *Third Epistle of John*, but only from inference can it be said that these latter had a mission to pagans.[6] In the first half of the third century Origen speaks of those "who make it their business to itinerate not only through cities, but even villages and country houses that they might make converts to God."[7] While more obviously missionaries to non-Christians, these may have been in the spiritual heritage of those mentioned in the *Didache* and the *Third Epistle of John*.[8]

We have noted the prevalence of prophecy in the Early Church. Men and women spoke under the influence of the Holy Spirit and in a striking way carried on the Old Testament tradition. Prophets, indeed, are mentioned along with apostles as especially honourable.[9] They persisted for a few generations, notably in the Montanist movement of which we are to hear later, but in time disappeared. It is not clear that presenting the faith to non-Christians was even an incidental part of their functions. In Paul's time, however, non-Christians

---

[1] In Matt. xxviii:16-20, the Great Commission is expressly to the Eleven. While in Acts i:1-8 the charge is given to the "Apostles," that word is not expressly limited to the Eleven, although, from the use made of the term in the next few chapters, this seems to have been the meaning in the author's mind.

[2] At least Paul so regarded it, in I Cor. xii:1, 4-11, 28.

[3] Acts xiii:1-3.

[4] Gal. ii:6-9.

[5] *Didache* xi:3.

[6] III John, 5-8. Bacon, *The Gospel of the Hellenists*, p. 55, seems to think of these as missionaries, but only from the fact that they are spoken of as "taking nothing of the Gentiles" may we gather that their mission was at least partly to non-Christians.

[7] Origen, *Contra Cels.*, III, 9.

[8] *Ibid*. See also Harnack, *The Mission and Expansion of Christianity*, Vol. I, pp. 347, 348.

[9] I Cor. xii:28; Eph. ii:20, iii:5.

as well as Christians seem to have listened to them.[10] By their travels the apostles and prophets appear to have helped to bind together the various local Christian communities and to have been an important factor in achieving the unity and homogeneity which eventually characterized much of the Church.[11]

Teachers, classed with apostles and prophets in the Early Church,[12] remained prominent much longer than did the other two.[13] The earlier ones were probably more akin to what we know as catechists. Later they seem to have been more like philosophers. We know that they were the means of reaching at least some pagans. It was, it will be recalled, through one of the greatest of the teachers, Origen, that Gregory Thaumaturgos was won to the faith.[14] We read of another teacher, Pantænus, as being sent as a missionary "to the nations of the East."[15] As instructors of catechumens they must have had a large part in the extension of Christianity. Teachers of philosophy, many of them with lecture halls, were so familiar a feature of the Græco-Roman world that it must have been very easy for Christians to use this form of approach to non-Christians. We hear of Paul making an extended use of one of these halls,[16] and it is not strange that the most famous of Christian catechetical schools should have arisen in Alexandria, long prominent as a centre of Greek learning. Here seems to have been one of the factors responsible for the presentation of the Gospel as a philosophy and hence for the alteration of the form of the Christian message.

When the office of bishop arose, one of its functions seems to have been winning pagans to the faith,[17] although this was doubtless performed more energetically by some than by others.

The chief agents in the expansion of Christianity appear not to have been those who made it a profession or a major part of their occupation, but men and women who earned their livelihood in some purely secular manner and spoke of their faith to those whom they met in this natural fashion. Thus when Celsus denounces a religion which spreads through workers in wool and

---

[10] I Cor. xiv:24, 25. See also Acts xiii:1, where prophets and teachers are classed together.

[11] Harnack, op. cit., Vol. I, p. 342.

[12] I Cor. xii:28.

[13] Harnack, op. cit., Vol. I, p. 358; Lindsay, The Church and the Ministry in the Early Centuries, pp. 103-106.

[14] Gregory's Oration and Panegyric of Origen (translated in Ante-Nicene Fathers, Vol. VI, pp. 21-39).

[15] Eusebius, Eccles. Hist., Book V, Chap. 10.

[16] Acts xix:9, 10.

[17] So Ignatius in a letter to Polycarp encourages him "to exhort all men that they may be saved" (Ignatius to Polycarp, Chap. 1). So, too, Gregory Thaumaturgos as bishop was active in winning the pagans of his diocese.

leather and fullers and uneducated persons who get hold of children privately and of ignorant women and teach them, Origen does not deny that this occurs.[18] In the commerce and the travel which were so marked a feature of the Roman Empire, the faith must have made many new contacts through Christian merchants and tradesmen. It is significant that Christianity appeared very early in Puteoli, on the Bay of Naples,[19] on the route to Rome, and that while we do not know of the beginnings of the Church in Gaul, when we first meet it there, it is in a section which had commercial connexions with the Hellenistic East. Involuntary travellers such as slaves and Christians deported for their faith were also agents.[20] Martyrs by their example impressed many.[21]

It would probably be a misconception to think of every Christian of the first three hundred years after Christ as aggressively seeking converts. Such pictures as we have of these early communities in the New Testament and in the voluminous writings of these centuries warrant no such conclusion. In none of them does any hint occur that the rank and file of Christians regarded it as even a minor part of their duty to communicate their faith to others. It seems probable, however, that many must incidentally have talked of their religion to those whom they met in the round of their daily occupations.

Of the methods of spread we know something, although not so much as we could wish. In the first century we hear much of the public address, often given in the synagogue.[22] We read, too, of private conversations and of meetings with small groups.[23] In entering a town for the first time the missionaries usually sought out those best prepared to receive their message—Jews, and Gentiles who had been influenced by Judaism.[24] In the earlier decades at least some of the meetings of Christians were open to unbelievers. Later, because of fear of persecution, pagans were not admitted to services of worship. Still later, when days of peace came, non-Christians were permitted to attend portions of the services.[25] As time passed, provision was made for testing the sincerity and character of those applying for membership, and graded instruction was given in a catechumenate.[26] In the *Acts* we hear of baptism administered as soon as an applicant expressed his faith and his desire.[27] In the *Didache*, we read of a

[18] Origen, *Contra Cels.*, III, 55.
[19] Acts xxviii:13, 14.
[20] Jacquin in Descamps, *Histoire Générale Comparée des Missions*, p. 112.
[21] One example of this is in Eusebius, *Eccles. Hist.*, Book VI, Chap. 15.
[22] As in Acts xiii:14, xiv:1, xvii:1, 2, xviii:4.
[23] As in Acts viii:29-39, x:23, 24.
[24] As in Acts xiv:1, xvii:1-4.
[25] Uhlhorn, *The Conflict of Christianity with Heathenism*, pp. 368-388.
[26] Origen, *Contra Cels.*, III, 51, describes the process. See also Uhlhorn, *op. cit.*, pp. 368-388; Easton in *An Outline of Christianity*, Vol. II, p. 63.
[27] As in Acts ii:41, viii:36-38, xvi:33.

two days' fast as a preliminary.[28] By the third century we learn of a period o
three months preceding baptism spent in self-examination and frequent fasts.[2]

Just how or why baptism came to be the method of admission to the Chris
tian community we do not know. We have no record of Jesus himself admin
istering the rite. Our earliest accounts of the Christian groups which succeede
the death and resurrection of Jesus seem to show baptism accepted as the invari
able method of introduction to membership and to Christian discipleship.[3]
Some, however, believe that these accounts reflect the practice of the generatio
which gave them their present form and not that of the years immediatel
after Jesus.

Into the frequently discussed form of organization of the earliest Christia
communities we need not go. It is clear, however, that at least some of th
missionaries had a hand in it.[31] Paul's epistles are evidence that he kept i
touch by letter with the communities he had founded. While we do not hav
any other letters which we can indubitably show were from missionaries t
the churches they had brought into existence, there is no reason to deem Paul'
practice exceptional. Certainly we have many epistles to churches, even if no
by the founders.[32]

For the most part conversion at the outset seems to have been by individual
rather than by groups. We read, however, of households coming into the faith
together.[33] Such families might become nuclei to which those from the outside
attached themselves.[34] Not infrequently Christian communities continued to
worship in private houses.[35] Later we hear of what seem to be mass conver
sions, notably under Gregory Thaumaturgos and in Armenia.

All of this is what might be expected. The movement into any new cult
religious, political, or social, usually begins with a few hardy individuals who
have the courage and initiative to depart from the conventional mores. In the
Græco-Roman world of the first centuries of the Christian era this was less
difficult because, in the prevalent disruption of old manners and social forms

[28] *Didache*, vii.
[29] *Recognitions of Clement*, Book III, Chap. 67. The date of the *Recognitions* is dis
puted. See *Ante-Nicene Fathers*, Vol. VIII, p. 74; Lea, *A History of Auricular Confession
and Indulgences*, Vol. I, p. 8.
[30] Matt. xxviii:19; Mark xvi:16; John iii:5; Eph. iv:5.
[31] As in Acts xiv:23.
[32] Harnack, *op. cit.*, Vol. I, pp. 369-380.
[33] As in Acts xvi:15, xviii:8; I Cor. i:16, xvi:15.
[34] Dodd, *The Epistle of Paul to the Romans*, pp. 236, 237.
[35] As in Acts xii:12; Rom. xvi:5; Col. iv:15; Lindsay, *op. cit.*, p. 41. Recall, too, that
the Christian baptistry discovered in Dura-Europos was originally part of a private
house.—C. Hopkins in Rostovtzeff (editor), *The Excavations at Dura-Europos . .
Report of Fifth Season of Work, Oct. 1931-March 1932*, pp. 238-253.

often the hereditary groupings sat lightly upon the individual. However, the family or household often retained its traditional strength and it was reasonable to expect it to come into the faith as a unit. In the instances of mass conversion which we have noted, either a strong individual such as a Gregory Thaumaturgos, from the aristocracy and in an outstanding office, exerted all the influence of his position to bring about the change, or the political rulers made the adoption of the faith by the populace a matter of state policy. Moreover, as the Church increased in numbers, power, and prestige, as it did in the latter half of the third century, many thronged into it. The lengthening of the pre-baptismal term of probation and instruction was probably a recognition of this fact and of the difficulty of insuring the same strength of religious conviction that existed in the days when it required marked initiative to join a humble and unpopular minority. It is notable, however, that, except in Armenia and possibly Edessa, we do not know of the political heads of a community taking the lead in the work of conversion. This method, so frequent in later centuries, was rare before Constantine.

The motives which led men and women to accept Christianity must have varied greatly. Unfortunately, for relatively few conversions do we have a sufficient report to permit a determination of the reasons, and in such records as we possess autobiographical references by the educated probably form a disproportionate part. Any attempts at generalization, therefore, must be based largely on inference and may be very faulty. In the New Testament, the strongest impressions seem to have been made by miracles, by the appeal to Old Testament prophecy,[36] and, perhaps, by the belief in the early second coming of the Christ and the impending judgment. Again and again it was a miracle which brought interest and conviction. The visions which preceded the conversion of Cornelius,[37] the blinding of Elymas the sorcerer which convinced the Proconsul Sergius Paulus that Paul and Barnabas could invoke a mightier spirit than could he,[38] the earthquake followed by the magnanimous conduct of the prisoners which led to the baptism of the Philippian jailer and his household,[39] are only some of the many which come immediately to mind. It was prophecy which won the Ethiopian eunuch,[40] and the argument from prophecy seems again and again to have been used and to have persuaded many.[41] We know, too, that in preaching to non-Christians the second coming

[36] Nock, *Conversion*, p. 254.
[37] Acts x:1-48.
[38] Acts xiii:6-12.
[39] Acts xvi:25-34.
[40] Acts viii:26-36.
[41] As in Acts xiii:15-43, xvii:1-4.

and the judgment were employed[42] and presumably would not have been had they not proved effective. From *The Acts of Thomas* we may infer that one attraction was the hope of a heavenly reward for acts of charity. From *The Shepherd of Hermas*, long so popular in the Church and presumably primarily for Christians, we may possibly gather that part of the appeal was ethical, with future rewards and punishments. Arguments against idolatry,[43] the summons to repentance from sin, and the promise of forgiveness to the penitent were stressed[44] and, supposedly, did not always fall on deaf ears. Justin Martyr, an intellectual in quest of wisdom who had tried several of the philosophies of his time, was impressed by the heroism of the martyrs and by the Old Testament and became satisfied that in the Christian revelation he had found fulness of truth.[45] Clement of Alexandria, also an educated man, seems to have arrived at inward peace only after a search which took him to many Christian teachers,[46] but what finally brought him what he longed for we do not know. Theophilus of Antioch traces his conversion to a perusal of the Scriptures and to the fulfilment of their prophecies.[47] Tatian was convinced by reading the Scriptures, by the purity of the morality they inculcated, and the means which they provided for deliverance from sin.[48] Origen declares that many came into the faith suddenly, after an initial aversion to it, through a waking vision or a dream[49]—the sort of cataclysmic conversion which we find through the centuries both inside and outside of Christianity.[50] How far the economic motive entered we do not know. The generous aid given by the Church to its poor may have attracted some, but this charge seems not to have been made against the Church by its detractors, or at least not prominently enough to demand much if any attention from the apologists.

An extensive apologetic literature has come down to us from the first three centuries. Probably this does not afford a complete or even a well-proportioned picture of the reasons which led people to accept the faith. A disparity may well exist between the arguments which were put forward and those which brought

[42] As in Acts xvii:30, 31, xxiv:25; I Thess. i:9, 10.

[43] Acts xvii:22, 31; I Thess. i:9, 10. Possibly Romans i:18-32 represents the substance of addresses which Paul made to pagans.

[44] Luke xxiv:47; Acts ii:38.

[45] *Dialogue of Justin with Trypho, a Jew*, Chaps. 2-8. Goodenough, *The Theology of Justin Martyr*, pp. 57-65, thinks that Justin Martyr's account of this wandering from philosophy to philosophy was somewhat conventionalized by him.

[46] Eusebius, *Eccles. Hist.*, Book V, Chap. 11.

[47] *Theophilus to Autolycus*, Book I, Chap. 14.

[48] On Tatian see Puech, *Les Apologistes Grecs du IIe Siècle du Notre Ère*, pp. 148-171. *Address of Tatian to the Greeks*, Chaps. 29, 35, 42.

[49] Origen, *Contra Cels.*, Book I, Chap. 26.

[50] For some of these see the well-known work of William James, *Varieties of Religious Experience*. (New York, 1902.)

conviction. Almost certainly, moreover, the impulse which led many of the neophytes to embrace Christianity was not intellectual, but emotional. Then, too, many, perhaps most, of the arguments were designed not to win converts, but to remove prejudice and to meet attacks and accusations. However, the reasoning of the apologists must represent what was said orally to pagans as opportunity offered, or at least to the educated among the pagans, and probably is also what Christians said to one another in justification for their position. Moreover, the apologies are a window by which we can see into the nature of the Christianity which was being propagated and into the causes of the opposition.

It is from the second century that the earliest surviving works of the apologists come. Among the writers are Quadratus, Aristides, Justin Martyr, Melito, Tatian, and Athenagoras. Minucius Felix is of the second or third century. Late in the second and early in the third century came Clement of Alexandria, and in the third century Origen, Cyprian, and Tertullian.

In these second- and third-century apologists much less attention is paid to the Jews and to those influenced by them than in the Christian literature of the first century. We do have some space devoted to them—as in the *Dialogue of Justin Martyr with Trypho a Jew*,[51] in Cyprian's *Three Books of Testimonies against the Jews*, and in the writings of Novatian. We have a possible hint at Jewish-Christian controversy in the work of Celsus against which Origen entered the lists.

The recession of the Jewish-Christian controversy is not strange. By the time the apologists began writing, the effort to win over the majority of the Jews to Christianity had failed. Most of the Christians were from non-Jewish stock and it was to pagans that the Christian missionary effort was mainly directed. From pagans and not from Jews was now coming the chief opposition to Christianity. It may well be that after the first century the hatred of Jews for Christians abated. Occasionally there was acute hostility. Sometimes, however, relations were friendly.[52]

One of the arguments on which the apologists most frequently rang the changes was the irrationality of the prevailing polytheism and the immoralities in the familiar stories about the gods. In view of what is so often said of the influence of the mystery religions upon Christianity, it is a remarkable and significant fact that the apologists devote much less attention to them than to the state cult. They were, to be sure, mentioned, and their practices and beliefs

[51] This Trypho may have been a straw man set up as a literary device.—Goodenough, *The Theology of Justin Martyr*, pp. 90-98.

[52] Parkes, *The Conflict between the Church and the Synagogue*, pp. 125-150, argues for this point of view against the position of Harnack and Allard.

derided, but they did not loom as large in the eyes of the apologists as did some other opponents.[53]

Belief in the gods of the Græco-Roman pantheon may have been shaken, but the public cults of these deities were still dominant. The myths of which the gods were the centre were common property and were intertwined with literature, art, festivals, and the stage. Of these the apologists had much to say. One of them, for example, pours scorn on the morals depicted in the Homeric poems and on the theogony of Hesiod's *Works and Days*. He declares that by Greek mythology the gods are convicted of intemperance and the heroes of effeminacy.[54] Tertullian points to the follies and inconsistencies in the current worship, pillories the immoralities of the gods, and holds up to ridicule the Homeric poems which make the gods fight among themselves like pairs of gladiators.[55] The *Octavius* of Minucius Felix pokes fun at some of the stories of the gods and suggests that Plato was right in seeking to exclude Homer from the Republic.[56] Arnobius has no use for gods which are begotten and beget and which are confined to human forms. He insists that gods cannot have the vile natures attributed to them by pagan mythology.[57] He demands of the pagans the ground for their belief that their images accurately represent the gods and why, if the gods live, their statues must be locked up and placed under guard as though the deities were unable to protect themselves.[58] Clement of Alexandria declares that most of what is told of the gods is invented and pokes fun at the deification of fear, love, and joy. He pours contempt on the licentiousness of the gods and on the Egyptian practice of paying divine honours to animals.[59] He says that the gods are "inhuman demons, hostile to the human race . . . not only delighting in the insanity of men, but gloating over human slaughter," taking pleasure as they do in the spectacles in the arena.[60]

The traditional belief in the gods must, then, have been much stronger than some reports of its decay would induce us to believe. The widespread

---

[53] Among the Christian attacks on them is that in Clement of Alexandria, *Exhortation to the Heathen,* in which he pours scorn on the immoralities and cruelties contained in their myths and on what he regards as the absurdity of their ceremonies.

[54] *Discourse to the Greeks.* On this apocryphal work see Puech, *Les Apologistes Grecs du IIe Siècle de Notre Ère,* pp. 228-232.

[55] Tertullian, *Apology,* Chaps. 10-16.

[56] Minucius Felix, *Octavius,* Chaps. 21-23.

[57] Arnobius, *Adv. Gen.,* Book III.

[58] Arnobius, *Adv. Gen.,* Books IV, V, VI. A convenient translation of some of the arguments of Arnobius is in Wright, *Fathers of the Church,* pp. 142-156.

[59] Clement of Alexandria, *Exhortation to the Heathen,* Chap. 2.

[60] Clement, *op. cit.,* Chap. 3. Also on the vanity of idols see Cyprian, *Treatise VI* (translation in *Ante-Nicene Fathers,* Vol. V, pp. 465-469).

religious scepticism which undoubtedly existed might lead us to be surprised at the attention which the apologists paid to the current polytheism. They might even seem to be seeking to dodge the really serious objections to their faith by beating a dead dog. However, it is clear from the events that the inherited faith proved much more tenacious of life than might have been expected from a religion cumbered by so many puerilities. Even in its last stages, in the fourth century, it won converts back from Christianity. In spite of the weaknesses which spelled its doom it made a powerful appeal to the imagination and affection of many from among the most highly educated.[61]

As against the traditional polytheism, the apologists present monotheism and argue for it. *The Sole Government of God* declares that such Greek poets as Æschylus and Sophocles said that God is one.[62] In contrast with the images which are the work of men's hands Clement sets God, the maker of the heavens, the sun, the angels, and men.[63] Tertullian points out that the object of Christian worship is the One God who created the world, who, though he is spiritually visible, cannot be seen by human eye, who, though incomprehensible, is manifested in grace, and who, although our human faculties can conceive of him, is beyond our utmost thought.[64] Clement speaks of the mercy of God as shown in the incarnation, by which man, entangled in the fall of Adam and bound fast by corruption, had his hands unloosed and was set free.[65]

In attacking the prevailing polytheism the Christian apologists were dealing blows at one of the most vulnerable features of the life about them. Much of the intelligence and conscience of the age was offended by the weaknesses at which Christians were pointing the finger of scorn and was groping toward an ethical monotheism. While, however, these intellectuals and moralists were seeking by the familiar road of allegory to find a way to a reconciliation of their minds and consciences with the traditional faith and to retain the old forms while transcending them, the Christian apologists were endeavouring to make a clean sweep of the system and to replace it by the worship of a righteous God who could command man's respect, awe, and love. Theirs was the way not of compromise, but of revolution.

The apologists did not content themselves with belabouring a weakened and rather hollow polytheism. They also attacked the philosophies which controlled

---

[61] Nock, *Conversion*, pp. 156-158.
[62] *The Sole Government of God* (translation in *Ante-Nicene Fathers*, Vol. I, pp. 290-293).
[63] Clement of Alexandria, *op. cit.*, Chap. 4.
[64] Tertullian, *Apology*, Chap. 17.
[65] Clement of Alexandria, *op. cit.*, Chap. 11.

most of the best minds of the pagans. Thus the *Hortatory Address to the Greeks* declared that the Greek philosophers were guilty of sectarian wranglings and so were not safe guides. Even Plato and Aristotle, so it averred, disagreed and hence must have been ignorant. It pointed out what it believed to be inconsistencies and self-contradictions in Plato's doctrines. It said, moreover, that Moses was the source of some of Plato's ideas, including his doctrine of form.[66] Tertullian, while accepting some of the views of Plato and Aristotle, singled out for criticism what he held to be errors, especially in Plato. He also differed from the Pythagoreans on their doctrine of the transmigration of souls.[67] Tatian poured scorn on the follies of Diogenes, made fun of Zeno, and said that Plato was a gourmand, that Aristotle flattered Alexander, and that Heraclitus was self-taught and arrogant and died of smearing himself with cow-dung to cure dropsy.[68] Theophilus pointed out the discords in the views of the pagan philosophers and declared that Zeno, Cleanthes, and Diogenes advocated cannibalism and that Plato in *The Republic* held that wives were to be common.[69] All four of these apologists, it is important to recall, were converts to Christianity, and at least the first three had studied philosophy in their pre-Christian days. They may, therefore, be representative of many who had found the Greek thinkers unsatisfying and had become ardent advocates of Christianity. It may be that they did not really comprehend the systems which they criticized and were not throughly competent philosophers.[70] For them, however, philosophy as they understood it had proved sterile.

Origen encouraged the study of philosophy and, if we may judge from his method of dealing with the young Gregory who later became known as Thaumaturgos, insisted upon a broad reading in it, but made it lead to the Christian faith.[71]

The apologists dwelt on the immoralities of the pagans and on the change which had been wrought in Christians by their new life. Thus Justin Martyr pilloried the exposure of children by pagans and the rearing of boys and girls rescued from that fate for lives of prostitution. In contrast, he pictured Christians who formerly delighted in fornication but had become chaste, who once placed foremost the acquisition of wealth but now had brought their posses-

---

[66] *Hortatory Address to the Greeks,* Chaps. 3-7, 20, 29.
[67] Tertullian, *A Treatise on the Soul,* Chaps. 5, 6, 8, 10, 17, 24, 28-33.
[68] Tatian, *Address to the Greeks,* Chaps. 2, 3.
[69] *Theophilus to Autolycus,* Book II, Chap. 5, Book III, Chap. 5.
[70] Goodenough, *The Theology of Justin Martyr,* pp. 292, 293, declares that Justin Martyr's use of terminology shows that he had only a superficial and popular understanding of philosophical concepts.
[71] Gregory Thaumaturgos, *Oration and Panegyric Addressed to Origen.*

sions into a common stock to help those in need, who had once hated one another and destroyed one another because of differing customs and now, in the Church, lived peaceably with men of other tribes. Christians, so he said, prayed for their enemies and sought to persuade those who hated them unjustly to conform to the precepts of Christ that they might become partakers of the joyful hope of a reward from God.[72] Tatian accused the Romans of honouring sodomy[73] and declared that the Christians admitted both sexes, all ages, the wise and the unlearned, to instruction and kept every kind of licentiousness at a distance.[74] Tertullian challenged the critics to find one Christian who had been accused of sacrilege or seduction or who was an assassin, a cut-purse, or a stealer of the clothes of bathers. He declared that Christians were guiltless of lust and of some of the misdeeds of which pagan philosophers had been accused, or that if Christians fell into such sins they were cut off from the fellowship of the Church.[75] Athenagoras in denying the charges of immorality among Christians which were widely spread in the ancient world declared that those who had made them were themselves sodomites and adulterers, but that Christians believed in treating their neighbours as themselves and, since they were convinced that in a future life they must give an account to God of their deeds here, adopted a temperate and benevolent manner of life, when struck did not strike in return, and when robbed did not go to law.[76] Aristides said of Christians that they were not guilty of adultery or fornication, that they did not bear false witness or covet the property of others, that they honoured their parents and loved their neighbours, that they strove to do good to their enemies and to win as friends those who injured them, that if they saw a stranger they took him under their roof and rejoiced over him, and that he who had gave without reproach to him who had not.[77]

The apologists made much of Jesus. They stressed especially the passages in Moses and the Hebrew prophets which they believed foretold his coming, his birth of a virgin, his rejection by the Jews, his crucifixion, his resurrection, and his elevation to heaven.[78]

They argued at length on the validity of the belief in the resurrection and at

[72] Justin Martyr, First Apology, Chaps. 14, 27, 29.
[73] Tatian, Address to the Greeks, Chap. 28.
[74] Tatian, op. cit., Chap. 32.
[75] Tertullian, Apology, Chaps. 44, 46.
[76] Athenagoras, A Plea for the Christians, Chaps. 11, 12, 31-36.
[77] A translation of the passage is in McGiffert, A History of Christian Thought, Vol. I, pp. 123, 124.
[78] As in Justin Martyr, First Apology, Chaps. 21, 32-53; Justin Martyr, Second Apology, Chap. 10; Arnobius, Against the Heathen, II, 1-4.

least one of them adduced as an argument the historicity of the resurrection of Jesus.[79]

The apologists were by no means identical in their approach. It is possible to point out differences between them. On the whole, those in the East, living as they did in the midst of Greek thought, were inclined to deal more with philosophy, and those in the West, having to meet the practical Roman, were more at pains to answer the charge that Christians were enemies of civilization and destructive to the state. Those of the West were particularly insistent that Christians were loyal, that they prayed for the Emperor, and that it was not they who were a menace to civilization and the cause of the disasters which were overtaking the Empire, but that the pagans by their failure to honour God were the real danger and Christians the saviours of society.[80]

In spite of the variations in arguments the apologists display a remarkable family likeness. A perusal of them gives the impression of much parallelism. A possible explanation is that in them we have in written form the arguments widely used by Christians to answer their critics and to win adherents. In general they declared that intellectually and morally the current polytheism was contrary to man's best knowledge, that the ethical fruits of paganism were reprehensible, that the philosophies in which men sought salvation often contradicted one another, and that each had its weaknesses. In all this the apologists were but voicing doubts which were troubling many thoughtful souls. As a substitute for the systems whose defects were so palpable they did not offer, as did so many religious teachers, a syncretism which sought to blend into a whole the many heritages from the past, allegorizing such offensive features as they could not ignore. That effort made a strong appeal to many who had an emotional attachment to what had gone before, but it could never rid itself of the weaknesses which the Christians attacked. In an era in which many of the choicest spirits were groping their way toward monotheism the apologists offered a righteous God who commanded men's awe and moral respect. To an age which distrusted its own reason and looked to antiquity for authority they presented a faith bulwarked by a sacred literature older than the most ancient of the Greek thinkers. While they held that this faith was richer than the Greek philosophies, they represented it as agreeing with many of the best of

[79] As in *Fragments of a Lost Work of Justin on the Resurrection* (translation in *Ante-Nicene Fathers*, Vol. I, pp. 294-299) ; *The Treatise of Athenagoras the Athenian Philosopher and Christian on the Resurrection of the Dead* (translation in *Ante-Nicene Fathers*, Vol. II, pp. 149-162) ; *Theophilus to Autolycus*, Chap. 13 (translation in *Ante-Nicene Fathers*, Vol. II, pp. 92, 93).

[80] Tertullian, *Apology*, Chaps. 6, 30, 33. See a summary in Lindsay, *The Church and the Ministry in the Early Centuries*, p. 230.

the latter's insights To those seeking immortality through union with saviour gods they spoke of a saviour who was foretold by the Hebrew Scriptures, was the incarnation of the eternal God, died for man's redemption, and rose again. They told, too, of a future life with a judgment, with punishments, and with eternal bliss for the saved. They also argued that here and now Christians lived a life vastly superior in moral quality to that of the world about them.

Some apologists represented Christianity as not having come to destroy but to fulfil, and maintained that its essential principles were what humanity at its best had always held or sought.[81] Others were less conciliatory and none sought to disguise the fact that in many ways Christianity differed from all other faiths and systems with which pagans were familiar. It was, for example, peculiar to the Christian creed that Jesus had suffered voluntarily and for all men and that this sacrifice was itself the basis of salvation.[82] The apologists who were in the main stream of Christianity did not seek victory by compromising what they believed to be the distinctive tenets of their faith. That Christianity was affected by its rivals is indubitable. To the nature and extent of that influence we are later to return. We shall also see that many in the ancient world sought so to integrate Christianity with other systems that it would have lost many of its distinctive features. This trend those apologists who represented what came to be thought of as orthodox Christianity not only repudiated but fought. They might wish to show that Christianity was the true philosophy and the fulfilment of other systems, but they were not seeking a religious synthesis which would incorporate what they deemed the best from the various rivals and to which primitive Christianity would be only one of the contributors. To their mind Christianity was the only religion which was fully true. To them mankind was "naturally Christian" and other faiths had in them elements of truth, but in Christianity all the values seen in them were to be found and in the one complete and well-rounded form.

It is obvious that these arguments appealed to many. Either because of them or for other reasons, increasing thousands flocked into the Christian fold.[83]

Yet it is one of the commonplaces of history that the new faith met with more severe opposition than did any other in the Roman Empire. Its critics were many. The objections urged against it ranged from absurd reports

---

[81] Nock, *Conversion*, p. 250.

[82] Nock, *op. cit.*, pp. 232-242.

[83] Yet Uhlhorn, *The Conflict of Christianity with Heathenism*, pp. 265-270, declares that no evidence exists that the writings of these apologists influenced the pagans and that even Celsus gives no indication of having read them. That they are preserved, however, shows that they must have been highly valued by the Christians and presumably, since they were read at least by Christians, the latter would use their arguments in conversations with pagans.

charging its adherents with the grossest immoralities, to assertions that it was destructive to the state and to existing society and to arguments of a high intellectual order which sought skilfully for any weak spot in its defences.

We have by no means a complete record of the attacks which troubled the course of the spread of Christianity, but it seems clear that the first three centuries witnessed a fairly continuous dislike which from time to time broke out into local persecutions. Although the Christian communities existed only on sufferance and repeatedly officials took action against them, not until the third century did the state make a really serious effort to crush the growing Church. Then in successive attempts, the most determined of which was just before Constantine, the government set itself to the extermination of what had become a formidable menace. Constantine reversed the policy and with such effect that not even Julian, in his brief and futile effort to restore paganism, ventured again to follow the road of wholesale violence.

At first sight this persistent and envenomed opposition to Christianity appears surprising. The Roman Empire was usually tolerant and even hospitable to the many religions found within its broad domains. To be sure, the Roman state more than once sought to check the influx of foreign faiths to the Eternal City. On more than one occasion, too, the Jews met with sharp restrictions. The sanguinary wars against them, however, were provoked by Jewish insurrections and were not deliberate pogroms carried out against peaceable and unresisting subjects. In the bizarre medley of faiths and philosophies which so characterized the first three centuries of the Empire, competition was not unknown, but there was much of the attitude of live and let live. Christians, although never resorting to arms, even in self-defence, were the only element harassed by prolonged persecution.

On second thought, however, this active dislike is understandable. Most Christians were in closely knit groups some of whose rites were not open to outsiders and it was not strange that rumours of obscene practices should gain credence. Christians thought of themselves as a distinct people especially chosen by God,[84] and this won them no goodwill. Unlike most of the faiths of the time, they were hostile to other religions. Christians denounced the gods of paganism as immoral and as demons and poured scorn on idols. In contrast with the fairly broad tolerance which characterized other cults, they declared that they had final truth and would eliminate rival faiths. Such an attitude not unnaturally provoked anger. Because of its intransigency Christianity threatened the structure of society. The institutions and practices which it would uproot

[84] See a discussion of this with quotations from the sources in Harnack, *The Mission and Expansion of Christianity*, Vol. I, pp. 240-278.

seemed inextricably intertwined with civilization. The worship of the gods from which it weaned men was deemed essential to the welfare of mankind. Christians were, therefore, regarded as enemies of the human race.[85] The Jews constituted a similarly unassimilable element of the population, but after the first century they seem not to have been very active in seeking proselytes. Accordingly, they did not appear to menace the existing order. Christians, on the other hand, were aggressively missionary and so aroused resentment and alarm. Far from the persecutions being strange, it would have been remarkable if Christianity had not met with violent dislike and repressive measures. The only way to avoid such treatment was compromise either on the side of society or of the Church. Both could not remain true to their respective natures and be reciprocally tolerant. When they finally made peace it was because both had yielded—the state and society consciously so and most of the Church only half consciously.

As this last paragraph suggests, the reasons urged against Christianity by its critics and opponents were varied. We know of them chiefly not in the precise words in which they were phrased, but in the form in which they were quoted by the Christian apologists who sought to answer them.

At the outset Christians were regarded as Jews and shared in the dislike which was felt for that people.[86] While it was not long before the difference between the two became apparent, Christians suffered from this early prejudice.

An accusation which seems to have been very common is that Christians were guilty of flagrant breaches of good morals, especially in their secret services. The *Octavius* of Minucius Felix pays a good deal of attention to this charge. It represents the pagan as declaring that the secrecy with which Christians surround their cult is evidence that they must have something which will not bear the light of publicity. Into this fitted the esoteric marks by which Christians knew one another, and their reluctance to speak openly or to congregate freely. The fact that they called one another brother and sister and loved one another on the scantiest acquaintance was held to prove that their religion encouraged vice. It was also alleged that at their services Christians placed before the novice an infant covered with new meal which was then slain by the initiate and the blood and limbs consumed by those present. Then, too, it was said that at meetings in which the two sexes were present the Christians used a dog to

[85] See accusations to this effect summarized in Arnobius, *Against the Heathen*, Book I, Chaps. 1, 3. An enumeration of the causes of the hatred for the Christians is in Workman, *Persecution in the Early Church*, pp. 138-196. See also Tacitus, *Annals*, XV, 44.

[86] Merrill, *Essays on Early Christian History*, pp. 46-48. On the unpopularity of the Jews and the measures against them see Hardy, *Christianity and the Roman Government*, pp. 15-22; Askowith, *The Toleration of Jews under Julius Caesar and Augustus, passim;* Juster, *Les Juifs dans l'Empire Romain, passim.*

extinguish the light and in the ensuing darkness engaged in promiscuous relations.[87] It is, of course, easy to see how some of these rumours arose from the quite innocent practices of the Christians and the reticence which they had adopted as a protection against persecution.

Tertullian found it necessary to notice the accusation that Christians were utterly steeped in luxury, avarice, and depravity.[88]

It was easy to answer the canard that the Christian God had the head of an ass.[89] So, too, with the frequent assertion that Christians were atheists, arising out of their refusal to join in ceremonies to the gods which all but they and the Jews worshipped.[90] The apologist could here dwell on the grandeur of the one God whom Christians worshipped and the puerilities and immoralities of the current paganism.[91]

More difficult to meet was the objection that Christians were destructive to civilization. The maintenance of the worship of the gods was believed to be essential to the welfare of society.[92] Pagans did not demand that Christians believe in the gods, but held that if they failed to sacrifice to them the neglect would bring ill luck upon all, non-Christians as well as Christians. It was not strange that a connexion was seen between the public calamities which multiplied in the third century and the increasing strength of a religion whose adherents declined to participate in the state cult.[93] We shall see later that in the last days of paganism, when the Empire, especially in the West, was tottering to its fall, Christian apologists were compelled to face again and again the charge that the coincidence between the decline of loyalty to the old religion and the illnesses of the body politic was more than a matter of chance.[94] Even apart from their hostility to the sacrifices to the old gods, Christians seemed enemies of society. As heirs of the apocalyptists they talked of an impending and sudden destruction of the world. They tended to break up families, for their faith led to dissension even in those intimate circles. They avoided military

---

[87] The *Octavius* of Minucius Felix, Chaps. 9, 10. This charge in whole or in part had to be answered by Tertullian, *Apology*, Chap. 7. Irenæus had to meet the accusation that the Christians ate the actual flesh and blood of Christ (see fragments from his lost writings translated in *Ante-Nicene Fathers*, Vol. I, p. 570).

[88] Tertullian, *Ad Nationes*, Book I, Chap. 5.

[89] Tertullian, *Apology*, Chap. 16.

[90] Athenagoras, *A Plea for the Christians*, Chap. 3; Justin Martyr, *Second Apology*, Chap. 3.

[91] Athenagoras, *op. cit.*, Chap. 4.

[92] Hardy, *Christianity and the Roman Government*, p. 3.

[93] Tertullian, *Ad Nationes*, Book I, Chap. 9. This is one of the chief charges which Arnobius sought to meet in his *Against the Heathen* (see translation in *Ante-Nicene Fathers*, Vol. VI, pp. 405-543).

[94] This in the main was the accusation to which Augustine addressed himself in *The City of God*. His was the chief but not the only reply to this charge.

service and the holding of public office (for in both they would need to compromise with idolatry) and so were accused of neglecting their duty to the state. Their refusal to join in religious festivals and to attend the public spectacles seemed anti-social.[95]

Of such charges the apologists were forced to take account. They met them with various arguments. Tertullian, for instance, maintained that Christians were better subjects of the Emperor than were pagans, for they had never raised an insurrection or a riot and had never even plotted against him, but offered prayers to God that he might have a long life, brave armies, and a peaceful reign.[96] Melito, Bishop of Sardis, writing before the era of disasters, argued that the emergence of Christianity in the reign of Augustus had been a happy omen, and that the fact that since then prosperity had prevailed was proof that Christianity had made for the good of the Empire.[97] When, toward the close of the second century, this prosperity began to wane and calamities overtook the realm, such an answer no longer brought conviction. Tertullian boldly reversed the accusation and declared that pagans rather than Christians were responsible for the troubled state of human affairs, for they despised God and worshipped images. As evidence for this he pointed out that droughts, floods, and other misfortunes had been the lot of mankind long before the advent of Christianity, and that in spite of all the religious rites which the pagans had employed to avert them. Christians, he declared, had reduced the frequency of such ills.[98]

Still another set of charges held Christianity up to ridicule for its recent origin and contrasted it with the antiquity of its rivals.[99] Minucius Felix represented a pagan as saying that nothing can be certainly known, and that in face of this lack of assurance the best guide is the tradition of the fathers. The claim of the Christians to possess clear truth therefore appeared preposterous.[100] In an age when the intellectuals were despairing of the ability of the unaided human mind to arrive at truth, the confidence of the Christians, so largely an unlettered group and of recent origin, must have seemed absurd.

Celsus, in his *True Discourse* (written toward the latter part of the second

[95] Tertullian, *Apology*, Chap. 42; the *Octavius* of Minucius Felix, Chap. 12; Aristides, *The Four*, translated in Haines, *Heathen Contact with Christianity during the First Century and a Half*, pp. 27, 28, 70-73. It is not quite certain in this last that the Christians were the ones attacked. See also Hardy, *Christianity and the Roman Government*, pp. 35-37.

[96] Tertullian, *Apology*, Chaps. 30-33.

[97] Quoted in Eusebius, *Eccles. Hist.*, Book IV, Chap. 26.

[98] Tertullian, *Apology*, Chaps. 40, 41.

[99] Arnobius, *Against the Heathen*, Book II.

[100] The *Octavius* of Minucius Felix, Chap. 5.

century), which Origen was at such pains to answer, had much of the scorn of a cultivated heir of Græco-Roman culture for what he deemed an anti-social cult many of whose tenets either were not new or were intellectually ridiculous. Christians, in defiance of the law, he declared, formed secret associations.[101] Judaism, upon which the faith was based, was of barbarous origin.[102] The ethical precepts which it taught made no distinctive or original contribution, but were simply those found in existing philosophies.[103] Even the Christian attack on idolatry was not new, but had been anticipated by Heraclitus.[104] Christians, so he said, ignored reason and inculcated the precept, "Do not examine, but believe."[105] He found fault with the allegorical interpretation of the Scriptures which Christians, in common with many others of those centuries, were fond of employing.[106] In opposition to the Old Testament account of the creation he held that the world was uncreated.[107] He declared that Christianity was a religion of the vulgar and that its founder, the illegitimate son of a poor woman, had wandered to Egypt, where he had learned from the Egyptians the methods of working miracles, and that his disciples were despicable tax-gatherers and sailors with whom he fled from place to place, obtaining a precarious livelihood in a shameful and importunate manner.[108] He commented disparagingly on the failure of Jesus to use the divine power ascribed to him to discomfit the enemies who compassed his death or to take vengeance on those who insulted him. He pointed out that the disciples had fled and had left Jesus to die alone, and said that the supposed resurrection appearances were only in secret and to his followers and not to his judge and to others who were not predisposed to believe in them.[109] Christians, so Celsus declared, ran true to the precedent set by their founder, and in contrast with the mystery religions who invited only those with clean hands and prudent tongues proclaimed: "Everyone . . . who is a sinner, who is devoid of understanding, who is a child, and . . . whoever is unfortunate, him will the Kingdom of God receive."[110] He said that "to change a nature entirely is exceedingly

---

[101] Origen, *Against Celsus*, Book I, Chap. 1. See an attempt to restore the text of Celsus in Glöckner, *Celsi αληϑής λόγos*. See also Labriolle *La Reaction Païenne*, pp. 111-169.

[102] Origen, *op. cit.*, Book I, Chap. 2.

[103] Origen, *op. cit.*, Book I, Chap. 4.

[104] Origen, *op. cit.*, Book I, Chap. 5.

[105] Origen, *op. cit.*, Book I, Chap. 9.

[106] Origen, *op. cit.*, Book I, Chap. 17; **Book IV, Chaps. 48, 49.**

[107] Origen, *op. cit.*, Book I, Chap. 19.

[108] Origen, *op. cit.*, Book I, Chaps. 27, 28, 32, 62.

[109] Origen, *op. cit.*, Book II, Chaps. 9, 17, 33, 45, 63.

[110] Origen, *op. cit.*, Book III, Chap. 59 (translation in *Ante-Nicene Fathers*, Vol. IV, p. 487).

difficult"[111] and so all but denied the possibility of a moral conversion and implied that a community recruited from the unintelligent and the dregs of society could not command respect. He ridiculed both Jews and Christians for asserting that God made all things for the sake of man.[112] In a famous passage he compared the presumption of Jews and Christians in believing that God had revealed the future to them and that men, made by him, are like him, to that of bats or ants or worms who would fall to quarrelling among themselves as to who is the greatest sinner and who would believe that God, leaving the world and heaven, had become a citizen among them alone, that they were like God, and that all things existed for their sake.[113] He spoke disdainfully of Christians who, although giving no credence to pagan oracles, had confidence in the divine inspiration of the prophecies of the Old Testament.[114] His, too, was the not unfamiliar objection that every man should live according to the customs of his own country and should not, as did the Christians, abandon them for Jesus.[115]

Porphyry, who as a friend and pupil of Plotinus, its first great figure, represented that Neoplatonism which so appealed to the educated of the last years of paganism, wrote towards the close of the third century *Fifteen Books against the Christians*. The work itself was probably too large for general circulation, but it apparently provided an arsenal for many briefer attacks on Christianity. Certainly a number of Christians felt it necessary to attempt to refute it.[116] The full text has not come down to us, but from the replies which have reached us we know something of its arguments. Prophyry had an acquaintance with both the Old and the New Testament. In these he pointed out what he believed to be contradictions. He asked embarrassing questions. How can one reconcile the discrepancies in the genealogies of Jesus given in Matthew and in Luke? What is the explanation of the differences between the various Gospel narratives of the death and resurrection of Jesus? Is Peter Satan or a rock? Which saying is to be believed, "Lo, I am with you alway" or "Me ye have not always"? Why, in the healing of the Gadarene demoniac, was one man freed at the expense of frightening others? Why did Jesus grant the request of the demons? He said that although Jesus foretold for John and his brother the martyr's fate, John died a natural death. To his mind the disagreement between Peter and Paul was proof that their message was not from heaven.

[111] Origen, *op. cit.*, Book III, Chap. 59.
[112] Origen, *op. cit.*, Book IV, Chaps. 23, 28, 29, 58.
[113] Origen, *op. cit.*, Book IV, Chap. 23.
[114] Origen, *op. cit.*, Book VII, Chap. 3.
[115] Origen, *op. cit.*, Book V, Chap. 35.
[116] Foakes-Jackson, *Eusebius Pamphili*, p. 20.

Although Paul said "Bless and curse not," he reviled his opponents. Porphyry criticized Origen for his use of the method of allegory in interpreting the Scriptures. He differed from the Biblical account of the Creation. He declared that the Book of Daniel had been written in the time of Antiochus Epiphanes and that most of its prophecies, therefore, merely recorded what had already occurred. He said that on occasion the writers of the Gospels displayed their ignorance by ascribing to one prophet what had been written by another. He took exception to the claim that Christianity offered the only way of salvation and asked why, if that were the case, Jesus had not appeared earlier and what was to be the fate of those in distant lands who had not heard the Gospel. He could not accept the Christian identification of Jesus with the Logos and rejected the Christian teachings of the creation and ultimate destruction of the world and the resurrection of the body. Living as he did in the dualistic Neoplatonic tradition, with its belief that matter is evil, he held that a soul could be saved only by being freed from the body. He rose up in defence of the use of images. These, he maintained, were not thought of as the dwelling-place of a god, but were simply erected to bring the god to remembrance and to honour him. He argued for polytheism, declaring that God, as a monarch, must have many gods under him. He despised Christians for what he believed to be their lack of culture and held that many of them, regarding forgiveness as easy to win, repeatedly sinned.[117]

Not all these criticisms of Christianity led to violent persecution. They are, however, evidence of the resistance which the new faith met, a resistance which was not confined to any one class. Here was an aggressive new religion which declined to live in complacent tolerance of other beliefs and customs, but which in part withdrew its members from existing society and threatened much of what was held dear by those who prized the Greek and Roman traditions.

The menace of Christianity to the contemporary order, it must be noted, did not take the form of plots to overturn the government or of plans to reshape society by force. The Christians did not contemplate a violent revolution. Even when, in the fourth century, they became dominant and were given the support

[117] There is a large literature on Porphyry. A brief selected bibliography is to be found in Hulen, *Porphyry's Work Against the Christians: An Interpretation.* Hulen's monograph also contains a useful summary. Briefer accounts are by McGiffert in *The Nicene and Post-Nicene Fathers*, Second series, Vol. I, pp. 264, 265, and in Labriolle, *La Réaction Païenne*, pp. 223-296. Very important are Harnack, *Porphyrius "Gegen die Christen,"* *15 Bücher: Zeugnisse, Fragmente, und Referate (Abhandlungen der königlichen preussischen Akademie der Wissenschaften, phil.-hist. Klasse*, Berlin, 1916, No. I, pp. 1-115) and Harnack, *Neue Fragmente des Werks des Porphyrius gegen die Christen (Sitzungsberichte der preussischen Akademie der Wissenschaften*, 1921. Erster Halbband, pp. 266-284).

of the state, the eradication of paganism was attended by comparatively little loss of life and by no quick overturning of society. They indulged in no organized and explosive rebellions as did the Jews of the first and second centuries. The contrast with the French and the Russian revolutions is striking, and even with the initial conquests of Islam. To be sure, the Christians threatened certain features of the culture about them—polytheism, idolatry, the theatre and the public spectacles, and the practices which contravened their ethical standards. Until the fourth century, however, this attack seems always to have been verbal and not physical, and often as much by quiet withdrawal as by open denunciation. When they came into power in the fourth century Christians destroyed or disfigured pagan images and temples, and occasionally, in the ensuing riots, lives were lost, but they engaged in no deliberate decimation of their opponents or even in a policy of wholesale imprisonment or exile. No rebellions were aroused by the repeated and violent persecutions of the third century. The apologists insisted that Christians were loyal to the state.[118] They indulged in no violent denunciation of their enemies. As a rule their arguments were put forward temperately. Their attitude toward pagans, indeed, was more moderate and restrained than it sometimes was toward those fellow believers whom they deemed heretical. If the Christians indulged in bitter railing against their critics and persecutors, very few traces of it have reached us. Some of it is found in the New Testament[119] but comparatively little of it appears in the apologists. In general the latter were surprisingly temperate, especially in view of some of the charges hurled against Christians and of the persecutions which were so frequently their lot.

From the very beginning, as we have suggested, the course of Christianity was marked by persecutions and martyrdoms. No other of the faiths of mankind, religious or political, has quite so extensive a record of violent and bitter opposition to its growth. Jesus himself met it during most of his brief public career, and his cross is the prevailing symbol of the Christian religion. The Book of Acts has much to say of the persecutions which the early Christians endured. Its leading hero, Paul, derived his first recorded impression of the faith from a martyrdom, that of Stephen, and he himself suffered scourgings, stonings, and imprisonment. Early tradition declares that he came to his end by execution in Rome.[120] Peter, of whom we know more than we do of any other of the original Twelve, endured much at the hands of the established

[118] Allard, *Histoire des Persécutions pendant les Deux Premiers Siècles,* p. xviii, notes that the writings of the early Christian scholars contain no trace of hostility to Roman rule.
[119] As in Rev. xvii:3-6, xviii:1-3, xix:1, 2.
[120] Eusebius, *Eccles. Hist.,* Book II, Chap. 1; Tertullian, *Scorpiace,* 15; Lietzmann, *Petrus und Paulus in Rom, passim.*

order in Jerusalem in the early days of the Church, and what is also probably authentic tradition declares that he likewise met a martyr's death in Rome.[121] Again and again in the New Testament we have echoes of the persecutions which punctuated the history of the first century[122] and the canon closes with an Apocalypse which is redolent with the blood of the martyrs.[123] Some of the oldest of the letters which did not find a place in the canon are ascribed to a leading Christian while on his way to Rome for his martyr's crown.[124] Persecutions were by no means uncommon in the second century. In the third century they increased in violence and the most severe of all was immediately before the state finally capitulated and sought the support of a faith which it had not been able to crush. Then, when the Roman Empire became professedly Christian, persecutions continued in the Persian Empire and on new geographic frontiers of the faith.

This long experience with violent opposition left a permanent mark on Christianity. It led to the exaltation of passive martyrdom and of martyrs which, although not without parallels, is unequalled in the history of any other religion. Since fresh advances of Christianity into non-Christian territories have continued to be accompanied by the death of unresisting Christians, the emphasis has never been allowed to die.

Traditionally ten major persecutions in the Roman Empire are usually enumerated—under Nero, Domitian, Trajan, Hadrian, Marcus Aurelius, Septimus Severus, Maximinus the Thracian, Decius, Valerian, and Diocletian.[125] This classification is, however, partly misleading, for it does not distinguish between the differing natures of the various attacks. In general, the persecutions fall into two main chronological divisions, one embracing approximately the first two and a half centuries and the other beginning roughly with the middle of the third century and ending with the triumph of Constantine. In the first division, they were largely sporadic and local[126] and, so far as the state was concerned, probably chiefly because of a general policy which frowned on the growth of unauthorized organizations as possible centres of sedition. The number of martyrs may have been relatively small.[127] In the second, the Church

---

[121] First Epistle of Clement; Eusebius, *Eccles. Hist.*, Book II, Chap. 14; Lietzmann, *op. cit.*

[122] As in Matt. v:11, 12, xxiv:9; Mark x:39, xiii:9; Heb. xii:3; 1 Peter iv:12.

[123] As in Rev. vii:14, xiii:7, xvii:6.

[124] Ignatius. See translations of his epistles in *Ante-Nicene Fathers*, Vol. I, pp. 49-104, and on his martyrdom, *op. cit.*, Vol. I, pp. 127-131.

[125] Uhlhorn, *The Conflict of Christianity with Heathenism*, pp. 235-237.

[126] Workman, *Persecution in the Early Church*, pp. 62-66.

[127] Origen, *Against Celsus*, Book III, Chap. 8, says that up to his time the Christian martyrs could easily be numbered. He may, of course, have been in error. See also Hardy, *Christianity and the Roman Government*, p. 126; Goodenough, *The Church in the Roman*

was growing rapidly and awakened the active fears of several rulers who saw in it one of the major causes of the disasters which dogged the course of the Empire in the third century and who sought to extirpate it by vigorous measures throughout the length and breadth of the realm.

The first persecutions of which we know were, as was natural, by the Jews. Aside from the antagonism to Jesus shown by the Pharisees, these initial efforts at restraint were by members of that same ruling ecclesiastical group, the Sadducees, who had engineered the crucifixion. Their action was apparently taken because the Christians seemed to them to threaten the public order and the peace of the Sadducean priesthood.[128] The death of Stephen and the attacks which followed his death were probably the work of Hellenistic Jews and not of natives of Jerusalem or of the authorities, and were because of the anger aroused by the views of Stephen.[129] The later persecution by Herod is said to have been undertaken to please his Jewish subjects.[130] So far as we know, most of the violence which Paul encountered arose out of the irritation of Jews[131]— although we hear of disturbances raised because the Christian movement was threatening the livelihood of some who depended for their support upon religious practices which Christianity condemned.[132] In Paul's experience the Roman officials never took action against him on their own initiative, but only when forced to do so because he was accused of disturbing the peace.[133] Usually they were friendly[134] or at least neutral[135] and he inculcated obedience to them.[136] Never do the records of his life give any indication that they regarded Christianity as in itself contrary to the law or as something which, because of its nature or of either general or specific edicts or rescripts, must be suppressed.

This indifference of the Roman authorities was not of long endurance. Before the first generation of Christians had passed off the scene the Church had suffered the sharp persecution by Nero. The fullest early account of this is by Tacitus,[137] who was a child at the time and was not necessarily an eye

---

Empire, p. 37; Foakes-Jackson, in *An Outline of Christianity*, Vol. II, pp. 16-19; Merrill, *Essays on Early Christian History*, p. 50.

[128] Acts iv:1-23. See also McGiffert, *A History of Christianity in the Apostolic Age*, p. 83.

[129] Acts vi:8-viii:1. See also Foakes-Jackson, *The Rise of Gentile Christianity*, p. 65.

[130] Acts xii:1-19.

[131] As in Acts xiii:50; xiv:5, 19; xvii:5; xviii:12, 13; xxi:27-30.

[132] Acts xvi:16-23; xix:23-41.

[133] Acts xvi:19-24; xxi:27-33.

[134] As in Acts xiii:6-12; xxvii:43.

[135] Acts xviii:12-16.

[136] Rom. xiii:1-7. See also Dodd, *The Epistle of Paul to the Romans*, pp. 203-205, who points out that this was in opposition to the growing tendency in Judaism which culminated in the final outbreak.

[137] Tacitus, *Annals*, xv:44. This persecution has often been written about by later authors.

witness. He declares that Nero instituted measures against the Christians to avert from himself the popular suspicion of having set the fires which in A.D. 64 destroyed a large part of the city of Rome. He describes vividly the tortures to which the Christians were subjected—how, covered with the skins of beasts, they were torn by dogs, or were nailed to crosses and set on fire to serve at night as living torches. He declares that the Christians were killed not so much for incendiarism as for hatred of the human race, a phrase which seems to indicate that they were already unpopular and that the harsh treatment meted out to them was not unacceptable to the multitude.[138] The numbers killed, he says, were very large, and he reports that the pity of the citizenry was aroused by the feeling that their torments were inflicted not to serve the public interest, but to satisfy the cruelty of one man. The accuracy of Tacitus in connecting the fire with the persecution has been questioned, and it is at least possible that the two took place at quite different times and were entirely unrelated. Probably the anti-Christian action was brief. The loss of life, too, may have been much less than Tacitus would have us believe.[139] Ancient tradition has it that Peter and Paul both won their martyr's crown under Nero, although not necessarily at this time.[140] Peter is supposed to be buried in a tomb over which now rise the high altar and the dome of St. Peter's and in what were presumably once the gardens and the circus where the Christians were done to death.[141] Whether the Neronian persecution was confined to the city of Rome we do not know. If the Christians were widely disliked, the imperial action in the capital probably led to outbreaks against them elsewhere.[142] A brief statement in Suetonius gives some ground for suspecting that Nero's was more than a temporary or a local measure.[143]

Among these are Eusebius, *Eccles. Hist.*, Book II, Chap. 25; Allard, *Histoire des Persécutions pendant les Deux Premiers Siècles*, pp. 37-85; Hardy, *Christianity and the Roman Government*, p. 55; Merrill, *Essays on Early Christian History*, pp. 82-130. It may be that the brief statement in Suetonius, *Ner.* 16, who says that Nero persecuted the Christians, "a new and evil superstition," refers to this particular episode.—Hardy, *op. cit.*, p. 55. Juvenal, *Sat.*, i:155 *seq.*, may also be a reference to it.—Uhlhorn, *The Conflict of Christianity with Heathenism*, p. 247.

[138] J. H. Ropes in *An Outline of Christianity*, Vol. I, pp. 318-320.

[139] See an excellent discussion of the Neronian persecution and the reliability of Tacitus in Canfield, *The Early Persecutions of the Christians*, pp. 43-70.

[140] Eusebius, *Eccles. Hist.*, Book II, Chap. 25. See the footnote on this by McGiffert in *The Nicene and Post-Nicene Fathers*, Second Series, Vol. I, p. 129. See also the apocryphal "Acts of the Holy Apostles Peter and Paul" and "The Teaching of Simon Cephas in the City of Rome" in *Ante-Nicene Fathers*, Vol. VIII, pp. 477-485, 673-675; Shotwell and Loomis, *The See of Peter*, p. 75; Allard, *op. cit.*, pp. 77-81. Canfield, *op. cit.*, pp. 67, 68, gives the reference to the sources. See also Lietzmann, *Petrus und Paulus in Rom*.

[141] Allard, *op. cit.*, p. 49. Lietzmann, *op. cit.*, questions the authenticity of the tradition.

[142] Bacon, *Studies in Matthew*, p. 77; Allard, *op. cit.*, pp. 60-77; Uhlhorn, *op. cit.*, p. 251.

[143] Suetonius, *Ner.* 16.

After the age of the apostles we hear little of the Jews as persecutors of the Christians. To be sure, they have been charged with inciting Nero to his slaughter.[144] They are said to have assisted actively in the martyrdom of Polycarp (A.D. 156) and this is spoken of as their usual practice.[145] Barcochba, who in the second century led a Jewish rebellion against Rome, is reported to have harried the Christians.[146] So far as our very fragmentary sources inform us, however, the Jews were responsible for relatively little of the annoyance from which the Christians suffered. This was to be expected. When, as soon happened, the new faith began to draw converts primarily from the Gentiles rather than the Jews, Jewish irritation against it would tend to subside and to be replaced by that of non-Jewish communities.

The extent to which the Roman state took action against the Christians in the first two centuries of the Christian era is a matter of debate. Nor does any agreement exist as to the legal basis on which the measures were carried out. Various possibilities have been suggested.[147] Christians may have been haled into courts as violators of standing legislation against treason, sacrilege, membership in a foreign cult, and the practice of forbidden magic, or for belonging to an unauthorized association. The law made provision for the official registration of certain types of associations, but many existed which were not so recognized. Often they were tolerated, but from time to time suspicion might be aroused against them as possible centres of sedition and repressive measures instituted.[148] Christian groups came under the classification of unregistered associations, although later some Christians seem to have been granted a measure of sanction by forming burial clubs, a type of organization permitted by law.[149] It may have been, too, that special anti-Christian legislation was promulgated,

[144] Workman, Persecution in the Early Church, p. 57; Allard, op. cit., p. 43.

[145] Foakes-Jackson, The Rise of Gentile Christianity, pp. 192-199. See a translation of the Encyclical Epistle of the Church at Smyrna Concerning the Martyrdom of the Holy Polycarp in Ante-Nicene Fathers, Vol. I, pp. 39-44. The mention of the Jews is in Chaps. 13, 17, 18.

[146] Foakes-Jackson, op. cit., p. 191; Eusebius, Eccles. Hist., Book IV, Chaps. 6, 8.

[147] Linsenmayer, Die Bekämpfung des Christentums durch den römischen Staat, pp. 27-43; Case, The Social Triumph of the Ancient Church, p. 170; Duchesne, Early History of the Christian Church, Vol. I, p. 80; Hardy, Christianity and the Roman Government, p. 95; Canfield, op. cit., pp. 25-42.

[148] Merrill, Essays on Early Christian History, p. 48. Merrill says that the collegia illicita were usually not persecuted, but had no legal recognition, and that no valid indication exists of an interdiction in the first two centuries directed only against associations of Christians. See also Workman, op. cit., pp. 67, 70; Ramsay, The Church in the Roman Empire, p. 354; Hardy, op. cit., pp. 128-149.

[149] Uhlhorn, op. cit., p. 238; Healy, The Valerian Persecution, pp. 55-61 (who says that this use by Christians of the form of burial clubs is questioned); Workman, op. cit., p. 70; Duchesne, op. cit., Vol. I, pp. 278, 279.

perhaps beginning with Nero, specifically designating Christianity as illegal.[150] It is possible, moreover, that magistrates acted against the Christians on their own responsibility with the tacit or implicit approval of the Emperors.[151] Certainly in face of the widespread popular prejudice against Christianity reflected in the writings of the apologists, such official measures are not unlikely. It is often said that the motive for the official persecution of Christianity was political, but this is also questioned.[152]

For several generations after Nero much obscurity attends our knowledge of the persecutions. Even though no special or fresh anti-Christian legislation was enacted by him, his measures might well have been remembered, have served to confirm the opposition to Christians, and have given rise to or at least have strengthened the conviction that it was illegal to be a Christian.[153] Some evidence exists for believing that Titus took action against the Christians in connexion with his suppression of the Jewish revolt.[154] His predecessor, Vespasian, may also have been anti-Christian.[155] The successor of Titus, Domitian, has even more emphatically been accused of being among the persecutors. From the second century comes a statement in a Christian author which associates his name with that of Nero as one who "wished to slander" the Christian doctrine,[156] and this presumably means that he was thought of as having been a persecutor. Then, too, Domitian put to death his cousin, Flavius Clemens, and had the latter's wife, Domitilla, banished, presumably on the ground of "sacrilege."[157] Some ground exists for supposing that this sacrilege was associated with Christianity.[158] It has repeatedly been affirmed that the action against

[150] Workman, op. cit., pp. 52-55; Linsenmayer, op. cit., p. 65.

[151] Ramsay, op. cit., p. 209.

[152] For instance, Linsenmayer, op. cit., p. 17, says that basically the repression of Christianity arose more from political than from religious motives, but Allard, Histoire des Persécutions pendant les Deux Premiers Siècles, pp. xxxii, xxxiii, declares that the reason for the persecutions was not the incompatibility of the doctrines, manners, and type of life of the Christians with the institutions of the Roman world, but such low motives as the vanity, jealousy, and cupidity of Nero, the popular calumnies, the irritation of intellectuals, and loyalty to current "superstitions."

[153] Linsenmayer, op. cit., p. 65.

[154] Haines, Heathen Contact with Christianity during the First Century and a Half, pp. 50, 51. He quotes from Sulpicius Severus, Hist. Sac., II ad med., and says that the statement was probably from a lost book of Tacitus.

[155] Ramsay, op. cit., pp. 253-264; Linsenmayer, op. cit., pp. 66-70, says no martyrdoms can certainly be referred to the reign of Vespasian.

[156] Eusebius, Eccles. Hist., Book IV, Chap. 26, quoting Melito, Bishop of Sardis; Tertullian, Apology, Chap. 5.

[157] Dio Cassius, Domit., XIV.

[158] Eusebius, Eccles. Hist., Book III, Chap. 18, says that Flavia Domitilla and many others were exiled to the island of Pontia in the fifteenth year of Domitian (A.D. 95) because they were Christians. Another reference to the sources is Suetonius, Domit., Chap. 15. See also Ramsay, The Church in the Roman Empire, pp. 253-264; Hardy, op.

the Christians extended to the provinces:[159] the Apocalypse, which seems to speak of recent martyrdoms, is by some assigned to the reign of Domitian and is held to refer to the persecutions by him in Asia Minor.[160] Much of this, however, like so much else in this stage in the history of Christianity, rests upon conjecture, and there are not wanting those who declare that none of the evidence warrants the belief that the Emperor's violence reached beyond the aristocratic circles of Rome.[161] One opinion is that such sufferings as were endured by Christians under Domitian arose from the failure to distinguish between Jews and Christians in measures instituted against the former.[162]

A reference to Domitian's successor, Nerva (A.D. 96-98), may indicate that the latter relaxed the measures against the Christians.[163]

Evidence which has attracted much attention comes from the reign of Trajan (A.D. 98-117). This is correspondence between Pliny the Younger, while imperial legate in Bithynia, in Asia Minor, and the Emperor. In a letter to Trajan Pliny said that he found that not only in the cities but in the villages and in the countryside Christianity had made great progress. Those who pled guilty of being Christians he executed and those who recanted he freed. Those who were Roman citizens and persisted in their Christian faith he noted for dispatch to Rome. He spoke, too, of acting on a list of Christians sent him anonymously. He said that never having participated in the trial of Christians, he was ignorant of the customary procedure and penalties. He therefore desired imperial instructions. Trajan replied with a rescript which commended Pliny's procedure, stated that no universally applicable rule could be laid down, that Christians must not be sought out, that anonymous accusations should not be given recognition, that those denounced and proved to be Christians should be punished, but that those who denied adherence to that faith or recanted and proved their sincerity by worshipping the Roman gods should be pardoned.[164]

To some authors this correspondence has seemed proof of a more or less

---

cit., pp. 60-77; Allard, op. cit., pp. 122-132; Linsenmayer, op. cit., pp. 72-84; Canfield, *The Early Persecutions of the Christians*, pp. 79-82.

[159] Allard, op. cit., pp. 122-132; Linsenmayer, op. cit., pp. 82-84.

[160] *Eusebii Pamphili Chronici Canones* (ed. Fotheringham), p. 274; Allard, op. cit., p. 125; Linsenmayer, op. cit., p. 83; Streeter, *The Four Gospels*, p. 475; Sulpicius Severus, *Sacred Hist.*, Chap. 31.

[161] Merrill, *Essays on Early Christian History*, pp. 148-173; Canfield, op. cit., pp. 72-79.

[162] Uhlhorn, *The Conflict of Christianity with Heathenism*, p. 252.

[163] Dio Cassius, *Nerva*, 1.

[104] Pliny, *Epis. X* (*Epistularum ad Traianum Liber*), pp. 97, 98. A reference to this correspondence is in Tertullian, *Apology*, Chap. 2. Especially full is Hardy, *C. Plinii Caecilii Secundi Epistulæ ad Traianum Imperatorem*, particularly pp. 25, 210-217.

general persecution under Trajan.[165] Others, however, and this appears the more reasonable opinion, lean toward the conviction that it indicates no special or unusual proscription. Out of the great mass of letters these have chanced to survive and are probably exceptional only in that they have come down to us. For a year or so before this correspondence special action had been taken to suppress *collegia*, as possible centres of sedition. Christian conventicles came under this category. Pliny seems to indicate that measures against Christians were not unusual but that thus far he had not chanced to take part in them. It may well be that the procedure against them was already stereotyped and that, in the main, Pliny knew what it was and followed it. On the other hand it has been suggested that had trials of Christians been frequent or important Pliny would have been less in doubt and would not have deemed it necessary to direct an inquiry to the Emperor.[166] It appears clear that Christians, as Christians, were under legal disapprobation and that if they persisted in their faith they were to be executed.[167] Perhaps we have here one of many spasmodic efforts, brought about by some special occasion or some access of fear or strictness on the part of an Emperor, to repress unregistered organizations which might be sources of uprisings. Persecution under Trajan was not confined to Asia Minor, for we have references to martyrdoms elsewhere.[168]

Similar measures may have been taken again and again under several reigns and have fallen into oblivion because no record chanced to be preserved.[169] That may be the explanation of a statement in Tertullian[170] which some have thought arose only out of this particular incident. It may refer as well to other action at quite a different time.

Persecution occurred under the succeeding Emperor, Hadrian (A.D. 117-138). At least we hear of the martyrdom of a bishop of Rome in the latter part of this or the first of the following reign.[171] We have, too, a rescript of Hadrian to Minucius Fundanus, the Proconsul of Asia, which indicates that Christians were being proceeded against and that accusations were being made to the

---

[165] Linsenmayer, *op. cit.*, p. 85.

[166] Hardy, *C. Plinii Cæcilii Secundi Epistulæ ad Traianum Imperatorem*, p. 211. Ramsay, *The Church in the Roman Empire*, pp. 196-225, discusses the Pliny correspondence and would not agree with Hardy.

[167] Hardy, *op. cit.*, p. 212.

[168] Eusebius, *Eccles. Hist.*, Book III, Chap. 32; *Eusebii Pamphili Chronici Canonici* (ed. Fotheringham), p. 276; Canfield, *op. cit.*, pp. 99-102; *Ante-Nicene Fathers*, Vol. VIII, pp. 685-689. Under him, too, was possibly the famous martyrdom of Ignatius.—Allard, *op. cit.*, pp. 193-211.

[169] Something akin to this view is to be found in Ramsay, *op. cit.*, pp. 198-225; Hardy, *Christianity and the Roman Government*, pp. 88, 89, 95, 101, 106.

[170] Tertullian, *Apology*, Chap. 2.

[171] Irenæus, *Adv. Haer*, Book III, Chap. 3. On other martyrdoms under Hadrian see Allard, *op. cit.*, pp. 220-243.

authorities, denouncing some as Christians. Hadrian did nothing to halt the steps, but insisted that those innocent of the charge of being Christians should be protected and ordered the punishment of those bringing charges which they could not substantiate.[172] The authenticity of this rescript has been challenged, but experts tend to maintain its genuineness.[173]

The First Epistle of Peter (if that was really written, as the salutation indicates, to Christians in Asia Minor), the Apocalypse, Pliny's letter, and Hadrian's rescript, when taken together, may indicate that in Asia Minor, where Christianity was making particularly marked progress, persecution was frequent. Perhaps its intensity was due, at least in part, to the opposition aroused by the rapidity of the growth of the new faith.

Under both of the following Emperors, Antoninus Pius (A.D. 138-161) and Marcus Aurelius (A.D. 161-180), Asia Minor continued to be the scene of activities against the Christians. From a letter written by one or the other of them to the Commune of Asia and published in Ephesus we infer that the populace held the Christians responsible for a series of earthquakes then taking place and had been harrying them. The letter ordered the acquittal of any charged with being Christians and the punishment of their accusers.[174] It is said to have been during the reign of Antoninus Pius that the famous martyrdom occurred, in Smyrna, of the aged Polycarp. Polycarp was possibly the last survivor of those who had been instructed by the apostles and had talked with others who had known Jesus.[175] Under Antoninus Pius, moreover, Christians suffered in Rome.[176]

We know of more persecutions under Marcus Aurelius than under Antoninus Pius. Marcus Aurelius did not like the Christians,[177] but that was not unusual

---

[172] What purports to be the text, or at least a Greek translation of the text, is in Eusebius, *Eccles. Hist.*, Book IV, Chap. 9. The text in the Latin version of Eusebius by Rufinus may be taken from the original Latin rescript (Haines, *Heathen Contact with Christianity during the First Century and a Half*, p. 52).

[173] The rescript is also in Justin Martyr, *First Apology*, Chap. 68; Haines, *op. cit.*, p. 16; Uhlhorn, *op. cit.*, p. 262; Merrill, *Essays on Early Christian History*, pp. 202-216.

[174] Eusebius, *Eccles. Hist.*, Book IV, Chap. 13. The authenticity of this document has been questioned but has generally been accepted. Eusebius ascribes it to Marcus Aurelius, but the usual opinion is that it belongs under Antonnius Pius. See a footnote by McGiffert in *The Nicene and Post-Nicene Fathers*, Vol. I, p. 186; Haines, *op. cit.*, pp. 21, 22.

[175] Eusebius, *Eccles. Hist.*, Book IV, Chap. 15; *Encyclical Epistle of the Church at Smyrna concerning the Martyrdom of the Holy Polycarp* (translation in *Ante-Nicene Fathers*, Vol. I, pp. 39-44). See also Owen, *Acts of the Early Martyrs*, pp. 31-41. On the date, see McGiffert in *The Nicene and Post-Nicene Fathers*, Second Series, Vol. I, p. 188, and Allard, *op. cit.*, p. 315. Eusebius is possibly in error in ascribing the event to the reign of Antoninus Pius.

[176] Hardy, *Christianity and the Roman Government*, pp. 110-118.

[177] Marcus Aurelius, *Meditations* XI, 3, and possibly I, 6, III, 16; Labriolle, *La Réaction Païenne*, pp. 71-79.

for those in high places.[178] It has been both affirmed and denied that he took more vigorous measures against them than had his predecessors.[179] We hear of what are said to have been new decrees through which the Christians of Asia were suffering.[180] Incidentally we here catch a glimpse of one of the motives of those who accused them—the despoiling of Christians of their property. It was under Marcus Aurelius that Christians in Gaul, in Lyons, and Vienne, were harassed.[181] Probably, too, in this reign a Bishop of Athens suffered death[182] and Justin Martyr won in Rome the fate from which he derived his honoured title.[183] Marcus Aurelius was attached to the old order and was struggling to maintain the Empire against domestic foes and foreign invasion. Already those strains were beginning to be apparent which made the following century so sorrowful for the Mediterranean world.[184] It may well have been that he saw in the Christians one of the threats to the culture which he loved and, as a high-minded conservative to whom had been entrusted the preservation of the existing order and the prosperity of the realm, took action against them.

Under the rule of Commodus (A.D. 180-192), the unworthy and dissipated son of Marcus Aurelius, measures against the Christians continued, and in more than one quarter of the Empire.[185] However, the pressure was less than under Marcus Aurelius,[186] and later in the reign, thanks to the influence over Commodus of his favourite, Marcia, who was friendly toward the Christians, a number of those were freed who for their faith had been condemned to the mines in Sardinia.[187]

[178] See, for instance, a supposed letter of Hadrian to Servianus (which Harnack rejects), with text and translation in Haines, *op. cit.*, pp. 54, 55. Then there are the many expressions which we have noted as given in the Apologists.
[179] Allard, *Histoire des Persécutions pendant les Deux Premiers Siècles*, p. 349; Hardy, *op. cit.*, pp. 110-118; Ramsay, *The Church in the Roman Empire*, p. 336, gives a number of evidences of persecution under Marcus Aurelius.
[180] Eusebius, *Eccles. Hist.*, Book IV, Chap. 26. Eusebius quotes from Melito, Bishop of Sardis.
[181] Eusebius, *Eccles. Hist.*, Book V, Chaps. 1-4. On the date, see note by McGiffert in *The Nicene and Ante-Nicene Fathers*, Second Series, Vol. I, p. 390. Owen, *op. cit.*, pp. 53-70.
[182] Eusebius, *Eccles. Hist.*, Book IV, Chap. 23.
[183] *Ibid.*, Book IV, Chap. 16. A translation of an account of the martyrdom is in *Ante-Nicene Fathers*, Vol. I, pp. 305, 306. On the date of his death see McGiffert in *The Nicene and Post-Nicene Fathers*, Vol. I, p. 193, footnote 4. Goodenough, *The Theology of Justin Martyr*, pp. 74-77, places it between A.D. 163 and 167. See also Owen, *op. cit.*, pp. 47-52.
[184] Rostovtzeff, *A History of the Ancient World*, Vol. II, pp. 232-239.
[185] Tertullian, *Ad Scapulam*, Chaps. 3, 5; Eusebius, *Eccles. Hist.*, Book V, Chap. 21; Allard, *op. cit.*, pp. 460-479; Neumann, *Der römische Staat und die allgemeine Kirche bis auf Diocletian*, Vol. I, pp. 79-84, 283-291.
[186] Eusebius, *Eccles. Hist.*, Book V, Chap. 21.
[187] Allard, *op. cit.*, pp. 481, 482; Neumann, *op. cit.*, pp. 84-90.

Septimius Severus (A.D. 193-211) was responsible for fresh activity against the unpopular religion. In the early part of his reign he seemed disposed to be lenient. Many Christians were in his household, he himself is said to have been healed miraculously through a Christian slave, and his son, Caracalla, was reared by a Christian nurse.[188] In A.D. 202, however, his policy changed—for what reason can only be conjectured—and he issued an edict forbidding conversions to Judaism or Christianity.[189] The persecution which followed could scarcely be confined to neophytes, but included those who had longer been Christians. It was especially severe in Egypt and in North Africa. In Alexandria the father of the famous Origen was executed, his property confiscated, and his family left destitute.[190] Origen himself, then a youth of seventeen, wished martyrdom and was only prevented when his mother, by hiding his clothes, compelled him to remain at home.[191] In North Africa some of the faithful sought safety in flight or purchased exemption.[192] In Carthage occurred several martyrdoms of catechumens, that of Perpetua being especially notable.[193] In a Church where the expectation of the early return of Christ could easily be awakened, the severity of the persecution apparently led many to give credence to a writer who declared that the coming of Antichrist was imminent.[194] The Christians in Rome were, seemingly, not much troubled by the edict,[195] but it may be that the paucity of documents is responsible for this impression.[196] We hear of sufferings in Asia Minor, perhaps accentuated by the public attention attracted by the ecstatic Montanist movement.[197]

Under Caracalla (A.D. 211-217) persecution seems to have subsided, probably more because of the indifference and preoccupation of the Emperor than of any interest in the Christians. It has been suggested that his extension of Roman citizenship to the inhabitants of the Empire, a step taken for financial reasons, may have served as a restraint, for the Roman citizen had the right of appeal to the Emperor and this might delay procedure against Christians who invoked it.[198]

During the reign of Caracalla, indeed, began a period when for nearly a

---

[188] Tertullian, *Ad Scapulam*, Chap. 4.
[189] Allard, *Histoire des Persécutions pendant la Première Moitié du Troisième Siècle.* pp. 55-66.
[190] Eusebius, *Eccles. Hist.*, Book VI, Chaps. 1, 2; Allard, *op. cit.*, pp. 67-78.
[191] Eusebius, *Eccles. Hist.*, Book VI, Chap. 2.
[192] Tertullian, *De Fuga in persecutione.*
[193] Allard, *op. cit.*, pp. 119-126; Neumann, *op. cit.*, pp. 171-176.
[194] Eusebius, *Eccles. Hist.*, Book VI, Chap. 7.
[195] Allard, *op. cit.*, pp. 79-82.
[196] *Ibid.*
[197] Allard, *op. cit.*, pp. 135-142.
[198] Allard, *op. cit.*, pp. 161-163.

generation (except for the short reign of Maximinus Thrax, A.D. 235-238) Christians were comparatively undisturbed by the state. Some of the rulers and their relatives were from the East and represented a partial triumph of the Orient over the Occident. Most of them had little interest in maintaining the ancient Roman traditions. Syncretism, with a tendency toward monotheism, was the order of the day. Several of those in high places were distinctly friendly to Christianity. During his brief reign Macrinus (A.D. 217) was too preoccupied to pay much attention to the Christians.[199] Elagabalus (A.D. 218-222) interested himself in syncretism and in spreading the cult of the Sun—which was esteemed an emblem of the supreme God. He was not especially antagonistic and his disregard for the old gods of the state worked somewhat in favour of Christianity.[200] Alexander Severus (Emperor A.D. 222-235) is said to have been eclectic religiously and to have had in his domestic chapel statues of Orpheus, Abraham, Alexander the Great, a number of the Emperors, and Jesus.[201] His mother, Julia Mammæa, a powerful figure in the government, was looked upon by Christians as devout. She even sent for Origen, probably the foremost scholar and teacher of the Church of his day, and had him instruct her.[202] However, some martyrdoms occurred in this reign.[203]

Alexander Severus came to a violent end and was succeeded by one who had had something to do with his murder, Maximinus, a Thracian peasant who through physical prowess had climbed the first rung of the ladder which eventually led him to this perilous height. His persecution is said to have been because of his dislike for the entourage of his assassinated predecessor.[204] Since this contained many Christians, it is not strange that he took action against their fellow believers. Moreover, coming from Thrace, he represented a reaction against Oriental domination and all for which it stood and was vigorously pagan. It is interesting and perhaps significant that another persecutor of the next century, Galerius, came from the same general region, and that Decius, also a persecutor, was a native of Pannonia, north-east of Thrace. Maximinus directed his measures primarily against the heads of the Churches, and a number of martyrdoms are recorded during his short tenure of office.[205]

[199] Neumann, op. cit., Vol. I, p. 205.

[200] Linsenmayer, Die Bekämpfung des Christentums durch den römischen Staat bis zum Tode des Kaisers Julian (363), p. 117; Allard, Histoire des Persécutions pendant la Première Moitié du Troisième Siècle, pp. 173, 174.

[201] Allard, op. cit., p. 178.

[202] Eusebius, Eccles. Hist., Book VI, Chap. 21.

[203] Neumann, op. cit., pp. 309-318.

[204] Eusebius, Eccles. Hist., Book VI, Chap. 28. Bihlmeyer, Die "syrischen" Kaiser zu Rom (211-35) und das Christentum, is an interesting monograph on this period.

[205] Allard, op. cit., pp. 193-214; Neumann, op. cit., Vol. I, pp. 318-327.

Philip the Arabian (Emperor A.D. 244-249), who followed a few years after Maximinus and was again the Orient come into power, is by some regarded as the first Christian Emperor. He is said to have shared in the paschal vigil and, as a condition for entrance to that service, to have submitted to confession and assignment to the section reserved for penitents.[206] Under him, naturally, persecution of Christians would be discouraged. If any occurred it would be due to local conditions and would not receive imperial support.[207]

This generation or more of comparative rest witnessed a rapid growth of the Church. The time was one of marked distress for the Graeco-Roman world. Several of the Emperors were creatures of the army, and the army itself was mutinous and frequently indisposed to fulfil its duty of guarding the frontiers. Civil strife, invasions, and corrupt government threatened the ruin of the Empire and even of civilization.[208] The old structure of life was weakened. Under such circumstances the organized opposition to the spread of the unpopular Christian community diminished. It seems safe to conjecture, although it cannot be proved, that the disorders led many to turn to Christianity for security, if not for this life, at least for the life to come.[209]

In the year 250 came a sudden reaction and the most severe general persecution which the Church had yet experienced. With it began a new stage in the relations of the government toward the Church. Heretofore, although official measures had been taken against the faith, these had been more to restrict than to extirpate it. Martyrdoms, while usually spectacular and having a profound effect on the outlook of the Christian community, probably were relatively few. Now began a series of efforts to exterminate the faith, each entailing a great deal of suffering. Between these were breathing spaces, but only breathing spaces.

In October, 249, Decius became master of the Empire, and late in December of that year or very early in 250 edicts were issued which precipitated action against the Christians. The texts of the edicts have not survived and we are not sure of all their contents.[210] Nor can we be certain of the motives which

[206] Eusebius, *Eccles. Hist.*, Book VI, Chap. 34. It has, however, been seriously questioned whether Philip was a Christian.—Gregg, *The Decian Persecution*, pp. 43-45.

[207] A few martyrdoms under Philip are recorded (Neumann, *op. cit.*, pp. 330, 331). There was, too, a notable local persecution in Alexandria, said to have been due to mass violence stirred up by a pagan "prophet" (Eusebius, *Eccles. Hist.*, Book VI, Chap. 41. Eusebius quotes from a letter of Dionysius, Bishop of Alexandria).

[208] Rostovtzeff, *A History of the Ancient World*, Vol. II, pp. 306-310.

[209] Case, *The Social Origins of Christianity*, pp. 221-229, suggests that the Church, in the sense of solidarity which it had developed, gave its members a confidence and determination which enabled them to face the unhappy conditions of Roman society with more equanimity than did their neighbours.

[210] McGiffert in *The Nicene and Post-Nicene Fathers*, Second Series, Vol. I, p. 280, note 1; Gregg, *op. cit.*, pp. 70. 82-86.

impelled Decius. A Christian account declares that he was actuated by hatred of Philip.[211] This may have been an element in his decision, for he came to power after a victory over Philip's forces. Modern writers, however, are more inclined to see in his policy an attempt to extricate the Empire from the disasters which had overtaken it. Decius was acclaimed by non-Christian writers as a personification of the old Roman virtues.[212] Apparently he was making a determined effort to restore peace and prosperity and to do this by a renewal of old Roman manners. It is quite easy to understand how to him the Orientalism of Philip the Arabian and some of his predecessors would be abhorrent and why he reversed their policy of leniency to that Oriental cult, Christianity. In accordance with the Roman tradition he may have believed that the calamities of the times were due to a neglect of the sacrifices to the state gods. If so, a necessary road to recovery would be a reawakening of loyalty to these deities. He would therefore, require all citizens to sacrifice. To the carrying out of this policy the Jews and the Christians were the chief obstacles. The Jews had a traditional immunity and official effort was directed chiefly against the Christians. Christians were especially to be feared, because they had been displaying a rapid growth.[213]

Whatever the purpose of the imperial decrees, the disturbance to the Church was very great. Executions seem not to have been numerous, but many distinguished Christians were cast into prison and some died there. It was thus that the aged Bishop of Jerusalem succumbed. A similar fate overtook the Bishop of Antioch. Origen was jailed,[214] Fabianus, Bishop of Rome, was martyred.[215] Many Christians fled and suffered hardships in their places of refuge.[216] Some were sent to the mines.[217] Many others yielded to fear or to the pressure of friends, and apostatized.[218] Sacrifice to the gods was what was demanded and those who complied were given certificates showing their orthodoxy.

[211] Eusebius, Eccles. Hist., Book VI, Chap. 39.
[212] On pagan estimates of the character of Decius, see Allard, Histoire des Persécutions pendant la Première Moitié du Troisième Siècle, pp. 257, 258. See also Gregg, op. cit., pp. 16-21.
[213] On conjectures as to the motives which led Decius to act as he did, see G. T. Oborn, Why did Decius and Valerian Proscribe Christianity?, in Church History, June, 1933, Vol. II, pp. 67-77; Allard, op. cit., pp. 257-260; Linsenmayer, Die Bekämpfung des Christentums durch den römischen Staat biz zum Tode des Kaisers Julian (363), pp. 129, 130. Confirmation of the theory that the object of the persecution was to revive the state cult is seen in the evidence of a renewed interest in the Vestal Virgins as given in A. D. Nock, A Diis Electa: A Chapter in the Religious History of the Third Century, in Harvard Theological Review, Oct., 1930, Vol. XXIII, pp. 251-269.
[214] Eusebius, Eccles. Hist., Book VI, Chap. 39.
[215] Ibid.
[216] Eusebius, Eccles. Hist., Book VI, Chaps. 41, 42; Cyprian, Epistles, 4-13.
[217] Cyprian, Epistle 76.
[218] Eusebius, Eccles. Hist., Book VI, Chap. 41.

Some who had not so sacrificed purchased certificates testifying that they had done so.[219] It seems, indeed, that these certificates, or *libelli*, were required of all inhabitants of the Empire, citizens and non-citizens, Christians and non-Christians.[220] Decius was apparently making a determined effort to restore the worship of the state cult and wished to make all conform. Geographically the persecution was widely extended. We hear of it in Rome, in Gaul, in Spain, in North Africa, in Egypt, in Palestine, in Greece, and in Asia Minor.[221] It has been suggested that the St. George whose cult became widespread and who eventually was adopted as the patron saint of England was martyred in Asia Minor at this time.[222] In Pontus Gregory Thaumaturgos retired to a place of safety.[223] Cyprian, the Bishop of Carthage, also sought refuge outside his cathedral city, presumably not because of cowardice, for he met martyrdom bravely eight years later, but for what he deemed the best interests of his flock.[224]

The storm was of relatively brief duration. In 251 Decius fell in battle against the Goths. Before his death he had become engrossed in the defence of the Empire against the Gothic menace and the persecution had been allowed to lag.[225] Under a brief reign, that of Gallus (A.D. 251-253), the anti-Christian measures were revived in at least Italy, North Africa, and Egypt, perhaps induced by a pestilence which once more drove the terrified public to the altars of the gods and led to a wave of resentment against the Christians, who by their neglect of these rites might be supposed to have precipitated the disaster.[226]

After the still shorter reign of Æmilianus, Valerian came to the throne and held it for about seven years (A.D. 253-260). He was followed by his son Gallienus (A.D. 260-268) who had previously shared the rule with him. The times were again ones of great disorder—of invasions of Germanic peoples from the northern frontiers, of war with the Persians, of the continuation of the pestilence

---

[219] Leclercq, *Les Certificats de Sacrifice Païen sous Dèce, en 250* (*Extrait du Bulletin d'Ancienne Littérature et Archéologie Chrétienne*, Jan., 1914) ; J. R. Knipfing, *The Libelli of the Decian Persecution*, in *Harvard Theological Review*, Oct., 1923, Vol. XVI, pp. 345-390; Gregg, *The Decian Persecution*, pp. 153-159. Tertullian, *De Fuga in Persecutione*, declares that some churches bought themselves off *en masse*.

[220] J. R. Knipfing, *op. cit.*

[221] Allard, *Histoire des Persécutions pendant la Première Moitié du Troisième Siècle*, pp. 275-436; Gregg, *op. cit.*, pp. 91-266.

[222] Budge, *George of England*, pp. ix-xi.

[223] Gregg, *op. cit.*, p. 230. He draws from Gregory of Nyssa's Life of Gregory Thaumaturgos (Migne, *Patrologia Graecæ*, Vol. XLVI, pp. 893-958).

[224] Cyprian, *Epistles* 2 and 14.

[225] Gregg, *op. cit.*, p. 268.

[226] Gregg, *op. cit.*, pp. 274-278, drawing largely on Cyprian's *Epistles*; Allard, *Les Dernières Persécutions du Troisième Siècle*, pp. 1-31; Eusebius, *Eccles. Hist.*, Book VII, Chap. 1; Oborn, *Why did Decius and Valerian Proscribe Christianity?* in *Church History*, June, 1933, pp. 67-77.

which had disturbed the realm under Gallus, and of rival aspirants for the throne. Valerian himself at the age of seventy was captured by the Persians.

In the first part of Valerian's reign the Church enjoyed peace. It had been purified by the trials under Decius and its morale had improved.[227] To be sure, numbers of Christians had lapsed under pressure and the question of whether they should be reinstated was rending the Church in what came to be known as the Novatian schism. Since many held that those who had suffered for the faith could pardon those who had lapsed, the former were being besieged by the latter, and abuses were not unknown.[228] Yet by and large the Church seems to have been stronger than before the Decian measures. Valerian himself appeared friendly and his household contained many Christians.[229]

However, this peace proved only a lull before a fresh and even more violent outbreak. For some reason, Valerian changed his attitude and instituted a fresh persecution. The Bishop of Alexandria ascribed the new policy to the influence of Macrianus, a general and counsellor in whom the Emperor placed great confidence.[230] Macrianus appears to have been skilled in some of the pagan arts of foretelling the future and to have cast on the Christians, as men who had antagonized the gods, the blame for some of his failures.[231] It may well again, as in the case of Decius and Gallus, have been a persecution brought on in part by the belief that the catastrophes of the times were due to the neglect of the gods. Then, too, Valerian seems to have resembled Decius in embodying the old Roman virtues[232] and by the predisposition of that rearing he may have been prepared to heed the charge that Christians by their "atheism" were undermining the welfare of the state.

The storm broke in 257, its immediate cause being an imperial edict of that year. The text has not reached us, but its main outlines seem to have been an order that the heads of the Christian hierarchy were to do homage to the gods of Rome. If they persistently refused, they were to be exiled. Christians were warned that the death penalty awaited those who met in the assemblies of the Church or who even entered Christian cemeteries.[233] This attack, it will be

---

[227] Lindsay, *The Church and the Ministry in the Early Centuries*, p. 323.

[228] As in Cyprian, *Epistles* 4-13.

[229] Eusebius, *Eccles. Hist.*, Book VII, Chap. 10, quoting from a letter of Dionysius, Bishop of Alexandria.

[230] Eusebius, *Eccles. Hist.*, Book VII, Chap. 10, quoting from a letter of Dionysius, Bishop of Alexandria. See also the footnote by McGiffert in *The Nicene and Post-Nicene Fathers*, Vol. I, p. 298.

[231] See footnote by McGiffert in *The Nicene and Post-Nicene Fathers*, Vol. I, p. 298.

[232] Healy, *The Valerian Persecution*, pp. 75-104; Gibbon, *The Decline and Fall of the Roman Empire*, Vol. I, p. 253.

[233] Healy, *op. cit.*, pp. 130-154; Allard, *Les Dernières Persécutions du Troisième Siècle*, pp. 50-54; Eusebius, *Eccles. Hist.*, Vol. VII, Chap. 11.

noted, differed from that of Decius. The Decian edict had ordered all members of the Empire, Christian and non-Christian, to sacrifice to the gods. The edict of Valerian was directed avowedly and directly against the Christians and apparently sought to reach them by stamping out their organization. The ordinary member need not sacrifice, but the heads of the Church must do so. Moreover, specific action was taken against the associations of Christians. They had always been among the *collegia illicta,* which apparently meant merely that with others of their class they were not officially licensed and might be proceeded against at any time. Some of the Christians seem to have attempted to bring themselves within the protection of the law by forming funerary associations, a type of organization which could gain official recognition. Now by the edict Christian assemblies were singled out for proscription and the loophole of meeting as burial clubs was stopped up.[234] In 258 the first edict was followed by a second, still more drastic. Again we do not have the exact wording. From what is told us by Cyprian, it appears clear that the clerical leaders of the Church—bishops, priests, and deacons—were to be put to death; Christians of high rank in the state were to be deprived of their property, and if they persisted in their faith were to be killed; Christian matrons were to suffer confiscation of their goods and banishment; and Christian Cæsariani, or members of the imperial household, were to forfeit their possessions, be put in bonds, entered on the slave lists, and be sent to work on the imperial estates.[235] The edict was shrewdly designed. The Christians were too numerous all to be executed or banished. The Decian edict which had proceeded against them all had left the Church even stronger than before. If, however, the Christians could be deprived of their leaders they would, presumably, prove tractable.

The persecution which followed the promulgation of these edicts apparently extended to at least a majority of the provinces. We hear of it in Rome, in Gaul, in Spain, in North Africa, in Egypt, in Palestine and Syria, and in Asia Minor.[236] In Rome Xystus, or Sixtus, the bishop, was apprehended in the cemetery or catacombs of Prætextatus while seated in his chair and teaching, and was slain there with four of his deacons.[237] Two more of the seven deacons were killed on the same day, and, later, the last surviving deacon of the Roman Church, Lawrence, perished, although the traditional form of his execution, on a grid-

---

[234] Allard, *op. cit.,* pp. 51-53.
[235] Healy, *op. cit.,* pp. 155-248; Allard, *op. cit.,* pp. 76-85.
[236] Healy, *op. cit.,* pp. 155-248; Allard, *op. cit.,* pp. 55-144; Linsenmayer, *Die Bekämpfung des Christentums durch den römischen Staat,* pp. 148-158.
[237] Cyprian, *Epistle* 81.

iron, may not be historical.[238] In Africa Bishop Cyprian was killed[239] and a Bishop of Hippo was among the victims.[240] In Spain the dead included the Bishop of Tarragona, who is said to have been much loved by pagans as well as Christians, and two of his deacons, who were taken to the amphitheatre and burned at the stake.[241] In Asia Minor the martyrdoms may have been augmented because of the Montanists, for this sect made it a duty to let their faith be known.[242] It is suggested, however, that in one part of Asia Minor, Phrygia, martyrdoms were rare during the third century, and that this may have been because of the reluctance of officials to proceed against the Christians and of the studious use by the Church of outward forms which would give the least cause for legal action against it.[243] In the main, the persecution under Valerian seems to have been more severe than that under Decius. Certainly it lasted longer. However, the capture of the Emperor by the Persians in 260 brought it to an end.[244]

The son and successor of Valerian, Gallienus, reversed the policy of his father. He is said to have published formal edicts of toleration.[245] The texts have not survived, and some doubt exists as to whether the report is true.[246] He seems certainly, however, to have issued rescripts to various bishops.[247] Their meaning is not entirely clear, but they appear either to have recalled the Christians from their hiding-places or to have returned to them their places of worship.[248] Another rescript allowed some others of the bishops to regain possession of their cemeteries.[249] Why Gallienus should have taken these steps we do not know. Clever, versatile, a voluptuary, apparently with no especial concern for the fate of the Empire, he was presumably not one to act either from deep interest in Christianity or from concern for the welfare of the state. It has been suggested that his attitude was due to his attachment to Plotinus, the leading figure among the Neoplatonists, and perhaps from his hope that the

[238] Healy, *The Valerian Persecution*, pp. 179-181; Mason, *Historic Martyrs of the Primitive Church*, pp. 193, 194. Mason quotes from Ambrose, *De offic. minist.*, i, 41, ii, 28.
[239] See a translation of the *Acts of Cyprian* in Owen, *Acts of the Early Martyrs*, pp. 92-99.
[240] Leclercq, *L'Afrique Chrétienne*, Vol. I, p. 214.
[241] See *Acts of SS. Fructuosus and His Deacons* translated in Owen, *op. cit.*, pp. 100-104; Leclercq, *L'Espagne Chrétienne*, pp. 53-57.
[242] Ramsay, *The Cities and Bishoprics of Phrygia*, Vol. II, pp. 490, 491.
[243] Ramsay, *op. cit.*, Vol. II, p. 501.
[244] Eusebius, *Eccles. Hist.*, Book VII, Chap. 13.
[245] *Ibid.*
[246] Case, *The Social Triumph of the Ancient Church*, p. 187.
[247] Eusebius, *Eccles. Hist.*, Book VII, Chap. 13.
[248] Note by McGiffert in *The Nicene and Post-Nicene Fathers*, Vol. I, p. 302.
[249] Eusebius, *Eccles. Hist.*, Book VII, Chap. 13.

Christians might amalgamate with these latter.[250] Whatever his motives, he was the first Emperor who we know granted formally to Christians permissions which resembled toleration. Even had he wished to do so, however, he was in no position to enforce general toleration, for his rule was challenged by many aspirants for the purple.[251] Macrianus, for instance, the alleged instigator of the Valerian persecution, possibly continued the anti-Christian policies in the portion of the realm over which for a brief time he had power.[252]

For the next generation or so the most vigorous and successful of the Emperors —Claudius II (268-270), Aurelian (270-275), Probus (276-282), and Diocletian (284-305)—were from the peasant stock of Illyria. They arose out of the army and Illyria was a fertile recruiting-ground for the legions of this period. They fought valiantly and in the main successfully against the barbarian invaders and sought to restore internal unity and order. Diocletian became the reorganizer of the Empire. He did much to extricate it from the ills which in the third century threatened its existence and to him more than to any other one man the Mediterranean world owed the reprieve which for more than a century postponed collapse.

In the main, the forty-three years which elapsed between Valerian and the year 303 were ones of comparative peace for the Church. The state had failed in its effort to break up the Church and from the ordeal the Christian movement emerged more vigorous than ever.[253] In the ensuing years it seems to have increased in numbers and to have consolidated its strength. Here and there even the majority of the members of municipal councils became Christians.[254] The Church's opponents had by no means admitted its triumph. Occasional martyrdoms punctuated the years. Thus in Rome and in several other places in Italy during the reign of Claudius, probably during his absence from the city, the Christians were held responsible by pagans for the misfortunes of the times. It may have been, too, that a conscious reaction took place against the toleration of Gallienus. Certainly some Christians perished.[255] From his early background, Aurelian favoured Mithraism and sought to unite the Empire in the worship of the Sun. In 274 he is said to have issued an anti-Christian edict.

---

[250] Healy, op. cit., pp. 266-272.

[251] Linsenmayer, op. cit., p. 160.

[252] Allard, Les Dernières Persécutions du Troisième Siècle, pp. 177-182. It was probably under Macrianus that Marinus suffered the martyrdom in Cæsarea in Palestine of which Eusebius tells (Eccles. Hist., Book VII, Chap. 15).

[253] Goodenough, The Church in the Roman Empire, p. 38.

[254] Eusebius, Eccles. Hist., Book VIII, Chap. 1; Grégoire, La "Conversion" de Constantin, in Revue de l'Université de Bruxelles, 1930-1931, pp. 231-272.

[255] Allard, op. cit., pp. 202-205.

Some deaths of Christians are attributed to him, notably in Gaul,[256] and we also hear of martyrdoms in Italy and in the Orient.[257] From the reign of Probus we have the report of martyrdoms in Phrygia, due to the open contempt of a Christian for a pagan festival.[258] We are told, too, of attempts to purge the army of Christians.[259] In general, however, the Church had a generation or so of comparative peace.

Again a lull was followed by a fresh tempest, still more violent than any which had preceded it. Christians, although growing in numbers and in some places in the majority, still constituted only a minority of the total population. The very fact that the Church was, next to the state, the strongest organization in the Empire must in many quarters have aroused suspicion and resentment. Yet Christians were prominent in the imperial household, and the wife of Diocletian and his daughter, who was also the wife of Galerius, one of the two Cæsars, were, if not Christians themselves, at least well disposed.[260] It was, therefore, a sudden reversal of policy when, in his late fifties, in A.D. 303, Diocletian issued edicts ordering the destruction of the churches, the burning of the Scriptures, the degradation of Christians who held places of honour, and deprivation of freedom of household servants who persisted in a profession of the obnoxious faith.[261] After an interval, of what length we do not know, appeared a second edict ordering the imprisonment of the rulers of the churches. Later decrees, sometimes called the third edict, offered release to those who sacrificed, but prescribed torture for those who refused.[262] A fourth edict against the Christians seems to have been issued by Maximian, Diocletian's colleague, in 304.[263]

Why Diocletian took action against the Christians has long been a matter of conjecture. The general supposition is that he was urged to it by Galerius and agreed to it somewhat reluctantly.[264] The motive of Galerius is by no

---

[256] Allard, *op. cit.*, pp. 233-242; Holmes, *The Origin and Development of the Christian Church in Gaul*, pp. 79-81.

[257] Allard, *op. cit.*, pp. 243-261.

[258] Allard, *op. cit.*, pp. 279-293.

[259] Eusebius, *Eccles. Hist.*, Book VIII, Chap. 4.

[260] Eusebius, *Eccles. Hist.*, Book VIII, Chap. 1.

[261] Eusebius, *Eccles. Hist.*, Book VIII, Chap. 2. There is some doubt as to the meaning of the last provision in the edict. See note by McGiffert in *The Nicene and Post-Nicene Fathers*, Second Series, Vol. I, p. 324; Allard, *La Persécution de Dioclétien et le Triomphe de l'Église*, pp. 148-170.

[262] Eusebius, *Eccles. Hist.*, Book VIII, Chaps. 1, 6; Mason, *The Persecution of Diocletian*, pp. 103-138; Allard, *op. cit.*, Vol. I, pp. 215-227.

[263] Mason, *op. cit.*, pp. 212-222.

[264] See the discussion of this, with references to the sources, in Mason, *op. cit.*, pp. 94-100; Allard, *op. cit.*, Vol. I, pp. 148-152. One source is Lactantius, *De Mortibus Persecutorum*, Chaps. 10-14.

means clear. He was born in the Balkans, not far from the present Sofia, of a fanatically pagan mother and was himself ardently loyal to the old faith.[265] One interesting suggestion is that he was moved by political considerations. He wished, so it is said, to insure himself the succession to the supreme power. He needed the support of the army, and that body was predominantly pagan. While his seat was in the East, where Christianity was strong, he wished also to win the West, where paganism still predominated. Hence his anti-Christian attitude.[266] This may help to explain the anomaly of a severe persecution in Asia Minor, where the Christians constituted a large minority and perhaps a majority of the population, and a somewhat lighter persecution in parts of the West, where Christians were still, except possibly in North Africa, in the minority. It may be, too, that Galerius had the contempt of a rough military man of frontier rearing for those of what seemed to him the effete cities of the East who professed a faith which appeared to him peculiarly odious. It is also surmised that a plot of the Christians to balk him in his desire for the succession may have been the exciting cause.[267]

Whatever the factors which led to the persecution, it was more serious and prolonged than any which the Church had yet faced. Even though the edicts contemplated the death penalty only as a last resort, torture was freely applied to induce the prisoners to sacrifice and fatalities from it were not uncommon. Then, too, direct executions were by no means unknown. In Nicomedia, where Diocletian had his home, the leading church building was destroyed even before the promulgation of the first edict.[268] There, too, we hear of a Christian tearing down the edict and paying for his temerity with his life.[269] Any detailed account of the persecution would carry us beyond the purpose of this book. It lasted for more than a decade, but it differed in intensity from region to region and ended much earlier in some areas than in others. The story, too, is inextricably mixed with the confused struggle for power which followed the abdication of Diocletian in 305 and ended only with the elimination of the last of the rivals of Constantine in 323. None of the contestants could avoid the religious issue and each had his own policy. Sometimes, too, the same man varied his attitude. The growth of Christianity is seen in the mounting prominence of the faith in the politics of the time. More than ever it proved a factor with which the rulers were forced to reckon.

[265] Mason, *op. cit.*, pp. 53-58.

[266] Grégoire, La *"Conversion"* de Constantin (in *Revue de l'Université de Bruxelles,* 1930-1931, pp. 231-272).

[267] McGiffert, in *The Nicene and Post-Nicene Fathers*, Second Series, Vol. I, pp. 397-400.

[268] Allard, *op. cit.*, Vol. I, pp. 154-157. He draws from Lactantius, *De Mortibus Persecutorum*, Chap. 12. Mason, *op. cit.*, pp. 101, 102, draws from the same source.

[269] Eusebius, *Eccles. Hist.*, Book VIII, Chap. 5.

The course of the persecution was both confused and dramatic.[270] We hear of a fire in the imperial palace at Nicomedia which was ascribed to the Christians and of wholesale martyrdoms which followed.[271] Eusebius declares that he himself saw wild beasts leave unharmed Christians among whom they had been loosed, but turn upon those who were goading them on.[272] We hear of a town of Christians in Asia Minor which was surrounded by soldiers and then burned with its inhabitants.[273] The names have come down to us of a number of bishops who sealed with their lives their loyalty to the faith.[274] While the leaders of the Church usually strove to restrain those who craved martyrdom,[275] we hear of numbers who rushed in to seek that honour.[276] Upon many pagans the heroism of the victims must have made an impression and it is not surprising to read of the conversion of at least two thoughtful men, both experts in philosophy and formerly critics of the Christians, because of what they had witnessed.[277]

The persecution probably extended from Britain to Arabia. The execution of Alban,[278] if historical, is evidence of violence in Britain. We hear of the destruction of Christian books in Spain, of the confiscation of the property of the Roman Church, the scattering of its archives, and the deaths of many of its members.[279] In North Africa we know of violation of Christian burial-places, of martyrdoms, and of the demolition of ecclesiastical property and archives.[280] We hear of martyrdoms in the Balkans.[281] The sufferings were especially prolonged in the East, for here the anti-Christian policy of the state continued much longer than in the West. Christians in Egypt, Palestine, and Syria bore again and again the brunt of the displeasure of their rulers.[282] It was too much

---

[270] Accounts by authors who lived through the persecution and witnessed in part what they recorded are Eusebius, *Ecclesiastical History;* Eusebius, *Martyrs of Palestine* (the shorter form of which is often attached to the *Eccles. Hist.*); Lactantius, *De Mortibus Persecutorum* (text in *Corpus Scriptorum Ecclesiasticorum Latinorum*, Vol. XXVII, pp. 171-238). Among more recent accounts are A. J. Mason, *The Persecution of Diocletian;* P. Allard, *La Persécution de Dioclétien et le Triomphe de l'Église;* O. Hunziker, *Zur Regierung und Christianverfolgung des Kaisers Diocletianus und seiner Nachfolger 303-313*, in *Untersuchungen zur römischen Kaisergeschichte*, Vol. II, 1868, pp. 113-286.

[271] Mason, *op. cit.*, pp. 118-121, the material for which comes from Lactantius, *De Mortibus Persecutorum*, Chap. 14.

[272] Eusebius, *Eccles. Hist.*, Book VIII, Chap. 7.

[273] Eusebius, *Eccles. Hist.*, Book VIII, Chap. 11.

[274] Eusebius, *Eccles. Hist.*, Book VIII, Chap. 13.

[275] McGiffert, in *The Nicene and Post-Nicene Fathers*, Second Series, Vol. I, p. 8.

[276] As in Eusebius, *Eccles. Hist.*, Book VIII, Chap. 9.

[277] Arnobius and Lactantius. See Allard, *op. cit.*, Vol. I, pp. 213-221.

[278] Bede, *Ecclesiastical History*, Book I, Chap. 5.

[279] Allard, *op. cit.*, Vol. I, pp. 183-186, 358-399, 437-446.

[280] Allard, *op. cit.*, Vol. I, pp. 190-213, 426-436.

[281] Allard, *op. cit.*, Vol. I, pp. 226-320.

[282] Allard, *op. cit.*, Vol. II, *passim;* Eusebius, *Martyrs of Palestine, passim.* Also on the martyrs, see Workman, *The Martyrs of the Early Church*, pp. 123-152.

to hope that all Christians would stand the test without flinching. We read of apostasies. Some only after enduring torture sacrificed to the gods. Some yielded while in prison. Some sent pagans or slaves to sacrifice for them. Others faltered at first, but later repented and gave themselves up to the authorities.[283]

Constantius Chlorus, who governed Gaul, Spain, and Britain, had no stomach for the persecution, and conducted it only perfunctorily. When, in 305, on the abdication of the two Augusti, Diocletian and Maximian, he was raised from the rank of Cæsar to that of Augustus, he seems to have allowed it to lapse.[284] After his death (306) that policy, so far as we know, was followed by his son Constantine, who succeeded to the control of his territories. Certainly Constantine is said to have dealt leniently with the Christians.[285] It may have been fortunate for the Church that its ordeal was briefest in the West, where in numerical strength it was weaker than in most parts of the Empire. Maxentius, the son of Maximian, who for a few years ruled in Rome until his defeat by Constantine (312) and who for his profligacy and cruelty was execrated by both pagans and Christians, for a time favoured the Church[286]—perhaps an attempt to conciliate the Christians who were so strong in the East without antagonizing too greatly the pagans who were still dominant in the Eternal City.[287] In the East Galerius retained his hostility to the Christians until near his death. Then, a sick man, in 311 he issued an edict of toleration.[288] Measures against the Christians were continued by Maximinus Daza, who ruled in Egypt and Syria and, later, in Asia Minor.[289] Maximinus died in 313 and shortly before his death reversed his policy and granted toleration.[290] The last of the persecutions of this stormy epoch was by Licinius, who on the division of the Empire between himself and Constantine ruled in the East from 313 to his defeat by the latter in 323. It began about 319, probably because Licinius suspected the Christians of complicity with his colleague and rival. Although Licinius expelled some of the Christians from his household and a few bishops were put to death in his dominions, his persecution was never especially severe.[291]

[283] The Canonical Epistle (of Peter, Bishop of Alexandria, who was beheaded under Maximin), translated in Ante-Nicene Fathers, Vol. VI, pp. 269-279.

[284] Eusebius, Life of Constantine, Book I, Chap. 16; Mason, op. cit., p. 246.

[285] Lactantius, De Mortibus Persecutorum, Chap. 24; Allard, op. cit., Vol. II, p. 67.

[286] Eusebius, Eccles. Hist., Book VIII, Chap. 14; Grégoire, La "Conversion" de Constantin.

[287] McGiffert, in The Nicene and Post-Nicene Fathers, Second Series, Vol. I, p. 336, footnote 1.

[288] Eusebius, Eccles. Hist., Book VIII, Chaps. 16, 17, Book IX, Chap. 1.

[289] Eusebius, Eccles. Hist., Book IX, Chaps. 2-8.

[290] Eusebius, Eccles. Hist., Book IX, Chap. 10.

[291] Eusebius, Life of Constantine, Book I, Chaps. 50-56; Uhlhorn, The Conflict of Christianity with Heathenism, pp. 438-440; Sozomen, Eccles. Hist., Book I, Chap. 2; Adeney, The Greek and Eastern Churches, p. 38; Allard, op. cit., Vol. II, pp. 293-320.

The decisive turning-point in the relations of the Church and the Empire, as we have suggested, was the reign of Constantine. In this a determining factor was the attitude of the Emperor himself. As we have said, Constantine, following the policy of his father, had never been antagonistic to Christians. When he faced his struggle with Maxentius, he realized that the latter relied on pagan magic and so felt the need of similar power to offset it. Constantine told the historian Eusebius that, after noon, as he was praying, he had a vision of a cross of light in the heavens bearing the inscription "Conquer by this," and that this was confirmed by a dream in which God appeared to him with the same sign and commanded him to make a likeness of it and use it as a safeguard in all encounters with his enemies.[292] How accurately this experience is reported we do not know. If it is a dependable account of what happened, it is clear that Constantine, in the spirit of many in his age, was seeking to counter the supernatural support of Maxentius with a more potent weapon of the same kind. Eusebius declares that he himself saw the standard which was made in response to this vision—a spear overlaid with gold, on which a cross was formed by a transverse bar, with a wreath of gold and precious stones enclosing the monogram of Chi and Rho, for the name of Christ. The staff also bore an embroidered cloth and a portrait of the Emperor and his children.[293]

The victory over Maxentius confirmed Constantine in his faith in the efficacy of this aid and sealed his friendship with the Christians. This was followed, probably in 313,[294] by the famous so-called Edict of Milan, which is said to have granted toleration to Christians, to have allowed conversions to Christianity, and to have provided for the restoration to the Christian communities of the church property alienated during the persecutions.[295] What actually was done at Milan is in dispute. Some have denied that an edict was issued. The consensus

---

[292] Eusebius, *Life of Constantine*, Book II, Chaps. 27-29. Lactantius, *De Mortibus Persecutorum*, Chap. 44, the earliest account of the event, speaks only of a dream. Adeney, *op. cit.*, pp. 32-34.

[293] Eusebius, *Life of Constantine*, Book I, Chap. 31. For a brief discussion of the Labarum and a fairly long bibliography on it, see Baynes, *Constantine the Great and the Christian Church*, pp. 9, 10, 60-65. There is some doubt as to the time when the Labarum was introduced and it has been questioned whether originally it was meant to have a Christian significance. What seems to be the earliest version of the adoption of the Labarum is in Lactantius, *De Mortibus Persecutorum*, Chap. 44, who places it before the decisive battle with Maxentius at the Milvian bridge, near Rome. With this agrees Alföldi, *The Helmet of Constantine with the Christian Monogram* (*Journal of Roman Studies*, Vol. XXII, 1932, pp. 10-23).

[294] For a discussion of the date, see Mason, *op. cit.*, pp. 327, 328, where 313 is upheld. McGiffert, in *The Nicene and Post-Nicene Fathers*, Second Series, Vol. I, p. 379, footnote 2, says it was late in 312.

[295] The alleged terms of the "edict" are in Eusebius, *Eccles. Hist.*, Book X, Chap. 5.

of opinion holds that at least some important measures were there determined on behalf of the Christians.[296]

What motive actuated Constantine has also been a matter of debate. It is sometimes assumed that political considerations were uppermost.[297] It is suggested that Constantine wished to conciliate the East, where Christians were extremely influential, without alienating the pagan majority in the West. Certainly, as we shall see, he did not go over completely to the Church, but remained in part pagan. In 314, when the cross for the first time appeared on his coins, it was accompanied by the figures of *Sol Invictus* and *Mars Conservator*. To the end he retained the title and office of *pontifex maximus* and so remained the head of the pagan state cult.[298] It is even conjectured that Licinius, and not Constantine, was chiefly responsible for whatever was determined on at Milan.[299] Moreover, Constantine's steps in behalf of the Church were not all taken at one time. After the elimination of Licinius left him the sole master of the Empire, he came out for Christianity more decidedly than before. It may be that until then he feared to do so too pointedly lest the pagans should side with his rival. When all the qualifications have been made, however, the acts immediately preceding and culminating in whatever was done at Milan in 313 still remain the most significant of the many milestones in the road by which the Church and the state moved toward co-operation. Christianity was as yet the faith of a

[296] For a brief summary of the controversy, with a fairly full bibliography, see Baynes, *Constantine the Great and the Christian Church*, pp. 11, 69-74. Baynes says that there never was an Edict of Milan, but that at Milan Constantine and Licinius agreed on a policy of complete religious freedom and that the text was settled of a rescript which was to be put in force by Licinius on his return to the East. The action had already been anticipated, so Baynes says, by letters of Constantine to his officials, beginning as early as 312, and Constantine shared with Galerius responsibility for the latter's edict of 311. Coleman, *Constantine the Great and Christianity*, p. 29, believes that at Milan was issued either an edict or a rescript. One of the most provocative and most frequently mentioned contributions to the discussion is O. Seeck, *Das sogenannte Edikt von Mailand* (*Zeitschrift für Kirchengeschichte*, July, 1891, Vol. XII, pp. 381-386). The contention of this brief but important paper is that there was no Edict of Milan, that what was done was not issued by Constantine but by Licinius, and that it was meant not for the entire Empire but only for the Orient. See also Henri Grégoire, *La "Conversion" de Constantin* (*Revue de l'Université de Bruxelles*, Vol. XXXVI, 1930-1931, pp. 231-272).

[297] Schmidlin, *Katholische Missionsgeschichte*, p. 91, hints at an admixture of political motives. Baynes, *op. cit., passim*, after going into the question and the divergent interpretations, concludes (pp. 29, 30) that Constantine definitely identified himself with Christianity and was convinced that he had "a personal mission entrusted to him by the Christian God." For a summary of various views of the motives of Constantine, see Coleman, *op. cit.*, pp. 20-23. Coleman himself (*op. cit.*, p. 78) believes that it is clearly proved that political considerations did not enter into Constantine's adoption of the Labarum.

[298] Alföldi, *The Helmet of Constantine with the Christian Monogram* (*Journal of Roman Studies*, Vol. XXII, 1932, pp. 10-23); Adeney, *op. cit.*, p. 39.

[299] Grégoire, *La "Conversion" de Constantin*.

minority, and it still was to face an important reverse under the Emperor Julian, but as we look back now, from the vantage of sixteen centuries, it is clear that the favour of Constantine proved decisive and that his acts shortly before and at his meeting with Licinius at Milan were determinative.

It is interesting that few if any of the non-Christians of the time, at least of those whose writings have come down to us, were aware that Constantine's action marked the beginning of the end of Christianity's rivals. Not until a generation or so later, after the failure of Julian to restore the old gods, did pagans seem clearly to see that Christianity was the victor.[300]

Would Christianity have triumphed without Constantine? If Constantine had not actively favoured it, would some other Emperor soon have done so? Like many other tantalizing questions of history, no answer can be satisfactorily validated. However, certain facts seem pertinent. After the abdication of Diocletian and Maximian, all the major aspirants for the supreme honours in the state, even those who had persecuted it, came to terms with Christianity. Before his death Galerius, who appears to have instigated the original action by Diocletian, issued an edict of toleration. In this he was followed by Maximin, who had seemingly been quite as implacable. Maxentius, although far from Christian in his moral life or his religious practices, was conciliatory. Licinius for years was favourable. Apparently every ruler of consequence had recognized that persecution had failed and that any one who hoped to control the Empire or even an important part of it must make his peace with the Church. It seems probable, therefore, that if Constantine had not come to power or had been less friendly some other ruler would presently have arisen who would have set about making Christianity the religion of the state.

At first sight it may have seemed that the preceding pages have devoted an entirely disproportionate attention to the criticism and persecutions of Christianity. The story has been often told. Why should it be narrated again, even in such summary fashion? On second thought, however, it must be clear that in any well-rounded account of the expansion of Christianity these have a highly significant place.

First of all, they give some indication of the opposition against which the faith made its way. Other religions in the Roman Empire met persecution, both from the populace and from the government. As has been suggested, however, no other faced such stubborn and long-continued resistance and then achieved so signal a victory.

More significant is the light which the story sheds on the revolution which Christianity proposed making in the structure of the Græco-Roman world. It

[300] Coleman, *op. cit.*, p. 66.

can scarcely be repeated too often that Christianity met with such cordial and varied dislike because it set itself against so many of the patterns of the society into which it was born. The opposition, as we have seen, brought not one but a number of accusations. Those trained in ancient philosophy disdained the new religion partly because, from the standards of the schools, some of its beliefs seemed preposterous. The populace disliked the Christians because they refused to participate in so many of the accepted practices, religious and social, which the masses accepted or supported as a normal and desirable part of life. The denunciation of the current polytheism and idolatry threatened beliefs and customs which were intertwined with the very structure of civilization. It seemed impossible to disentangle business, amusements, the family, and the state from the ceremonies and convictions which the Christians denounced. As we have noted, repeatedly it was urged that the disasters threatening the existence of civilization were due to the neglect by the Christians of the state cult. The Christians, moreover, were not primarily a racial group, as were the Jews. The latter, after the crushing of the great rebellions of the first and second centuries, accepted their position as a subject minority and made no very great effort either to achieve political independence or to win converts. The state could tolerate them without fear for its existence. The Christians, on the other hand, congregated in unregistered associations which attracted a rapidly growing body of adherents from all races and classes. More than any other of the many cults which were spreading in the ancient world, their requirements for admission menaced the established order.

Also of importance was the effect of the persecutions upon the Church. They did not prove severe enough to crush it. Whether a more prolonged or more determined effort might have done so we do not know. From the later disappearance of Christianity in some lands where it became strong, it is conceivable that more drastic measures might here have been followed by a similar outcome. As it was, the persecutions both weakened and strengthened the Church. Many Christians denied their faith and later, in the controversies which arose over the issue of the restoration of repentant apostates, the Church was rent by severe schisms. Yet in the main the Church emerged more vigorous for the ordeal. The fear of opprobrium and suffering probably served as a deterrent to many who might lightly have joined themselves to it. Those who in seeking baptism faced the possibility of martyrdom were not likely to be easily weaned from their faith. In the intervals of prosperity, and in spite of the requirement of a prolonged catechumenate, many thronged into the Church. At the first threat of persecution numbers denied their faith. However, the apostasy would almost certainly have been much greater had not the major persecutions of the third and fourth centuries been preceded by many smaller ones. Through meeting milder attacks the Church had built up an internal resistance which enabled it to withstand more severe ones. Both consciously and unconsciously it prepared its members for the martyr's fate. The rewards accruing from such a confession were urged, and punishments for apostasy, both temporal and eternal, magnified.[301] The founder of the faith had been executed. Deeply ingrained was the conviction that Christians were happy if they would share that experience, not merely in some symbolic manner or through self-mutilation, as did the initiates into the mystery cults, but by voluntary submission to suffering imposed by others.[302] The driving force so given had much to do with the temper of the Church through all succeeding ages and with the ability to persist and spread in face of bitter and often sanguinary opposition.

Why is it that Christianity won? Why, among all the many cults and philosophies which competed in the Græco-Roman world and in spite of more severe opposition than was encountered by any other, did this faith outstrip them all? What reasons account for the fact that, in the course of three centuries, a religion which began as an obscure Jewish sect with no influential backing in high places, developed an organization second only in extent to that of the Empire, forced the state to come to terms with it, and within another two centuries became the one official religion, held the nominal allegiance of the vast majority of the population of the Mediterranean basin, and then outlived the Empire which had sought to uproot it? The question has often been asked and many answers have been given.[303] Closely allied with it are three other problems. Why, of the several Jewish sects, was Christianity the only one which proved successful in achieving a permanent place outside the parent stock? Why did that parent stock, of all the religious groups in the Roman Empire, prove the most resistant to the new faith and why was it never absorbed by it? Why did Christianity make headway first in the cities and in the elements touched by Hellenistic Judaism and Hellenism?

To these questions no single reply will suffice. A number of factors contributed to the result. One, as we shall suggest, was determinative. Without it

[301] See a treatment of this in D. W. Riddle, *The Martyrs: A Study in Social Control.*
[302] As in John xv:20; II Tim. ii:10, 11.
[303] Some of the many are to be found in Gibbon, *A History of the Decline and Fall of the Roman Empire,* Chap. 15; Lecky, *History of European Morals,* Vol. I, pp. 387-390; Case, *Social Origins of Christianity,* pp. 73-78; Nock, *Conversion,* pp. 104, 210, 211; Goodenough, *The Church in the Roman World,* pp. 4-7; Toynbee, *A Study of History,* Vol. I, pp. 56, 57; La Piana, *Foreign Groups in Rome during the First Centuries of the Empire,* pp. 399-403; Angus, *The Mystery Religions and Christianity,* pp. 271-314; Holl, *Urchristentum und Religionsgeschichte,* pp. 14-21; Harnack, *The Mission and Expansion of Christianity,* Vol. I, pp. 86-289.

the others would have been insufficient. Yet it may be that without the others that main factor would have proved unequal to bringing about the eventual triumph of Christianity. The answer is not simple, but complex.

One factor has been suggested—the endorsement of Constantine. Had that Emperor been less able or had his reign been brief, his support might not have led to such consequences. It was no minor cause of the part that Christianity was later to play in the world that the Church obtained the active endorsement of the head of the most powerful state of the time and that the particular monarch who initiated the policy stood out as among the ablest of the imperial succession and enjoyed a sufficiently long tenure of office to place the Church firmly in its new position. Had he been a weaker man or had he died soon after he granted toleration, the inevitable reaction might have embarrassed the Church much more than it did. As we have suggested, however, the Church was growing so rapidly before Constantine and the persecutions had so clearly failed of their purpose that he seems merely to have hastened an already probable consummation. To account for this victory of Christianity one must go back of Constantine and seek for the causes of growth before his day and of the attraction of the faith for him.

Another factor, and one which we have mentioned more than once, appears to have been the disintegration of society. From at least the time of Alexander the Mediterranean world had been in a state of flux. The passing of the old was hastened by the wars which culminated in the founding of the Roman Empire and was further accelerated by the Empire itself. The construction of a universal state could not but dissolve the barriers which divided people from people. In the consequent intermingling of individuals and ideas old cultures, with their religions, were weakened. In the great cities especially were thousands of deracinated individuals, some of them slaves, some freedmen, and some merchants, who had been separated by force or voluntarily from their hereditary milieu. Often insecure, subject to oppression from the powerful, presumably many of them welcomed the fellowship afforded by the strong Christian organization and the security which the faith promised for the life to come. It is notable that Christianity had its first strongholds in the large cities, where these conditions were particularly prominent. The disintegration of existing cultures had become especially marked in the hundred and thirty years between Marcus Aurelius and Constantine. The disasters of these decades had weakened the established order, had made it less able to resist the inroads of a new faith, and had started many men on a quest for the sort of security which an authoritative religion seemed to offer. Had Christianity been born in a vigorous young culture whose adherents were confident of its virtues, it might have met a different fate. Then, too, at first the government was relatively indifferent and did not exert itself to support the state religion against this rival. Later, when it became alarmed and took drastic measures, it proved too weak to crush the Church. In Persia, as we shall see in later chapters, Christianity confronted a state religion actively sustained by the crown and never became the faith of more than a minority. Yet it must be remembered that Christianity was only one of many competing cults in the decaying Roman Empire. Some of these, notably Neoplatonism, had the endorsement of a much larger proportion of the upper classes than did the eventual victor. Why was it that of all these rivals Christianity gained the day?

A third cause of Christianity's victory was the organization which it developed. No one of its rivals possessed so powerful and coherent a structure as did the Church. No other gave to adherents quite the same feeling of coming into a closely knit community. To be sure, that organization was far from perfect. Never, unless possibly in the first generation after Jesus, and probably not even then, had all who called themselves Christians been embraced within a single visible fellowship. Long before Constantine, sectarian differences developed and leaders of rival Christian bodies engaged in reciprocal recrimination. Yet for a combination of inclusiveness, strength against attack, and flexibility, the Christian Churches were without parallel among the religious bodies in the Græco-Roman world. In this respect the nearest approach to them was Judaism. It was probably in part to this fact that the parent faith owed its survival. However, it did not equal its victorious scion. The Church proved able to instil in its members a loyalty and a feeling of solidarity which proved inestimable assets in the struggle for existence. Yet what was the source of this organization and of its strength?

A fourth reason for Christianity's success is to be found in its inclusiveness. More than any of its competitors it attracted all races and classes. Even in the days of its most active proselyting activities Judaism never quite escaped from its racial bonds, and after the second century infrequently overpassed them. It usually remained an encysted minority. Christianity, however, gloried in its appeal to Jew and Gentile, Greek and barbarian. The philosophies never really won the allegiance of the masses. In spite of attempts at popularization they appealed primarily to the educated. It was one of the charges against Christianity, however, that it drew the lowly and unlettered multitude.[304] The

---

[304] This was one of the charges of Celsus.—Origen, *Against Celsus*, Book III, Chap. 59. It is this hold of the Church on the affections of "the internal proletariat" to which Toynbee ascribes the victory of Christianity over the Empire.—*A Study of History*, Vol. I, pp. 56, 57. It must be noted, however, that it would be an oversimplification and a reading back into ancient times of modern concepts to see in the victory of Christianity a pro-

essence of its teachings was so simple that all could understand, and in its story of the life, death, and resurrection of Jesus it could be comprehended by even the ignorant. Yet Christianity also developed a philosophy which commanded the respect of many of the learned. In this respect it was more successful than the mystery cults,[305] although some of the latter were fortified by elaborate intellectual systems. To the educated Christianity could offer what the rival philosophies could not. Thus Augustine said that in Neoplatonism he found philosophical concepts which he also discovered in Christianity, but that in that last great rival of the conquering faith he missed the incarnation and the humility of Christ.[306] Christianity, too, was for both sexes, whereas at least two of its main rivals were primarily for men. The Church welcomed both rich and poor. In contrast with it, the mysteries were usually for people of means: initiation into them was expensive.[307] No other cult, therefore, took in so many groups and strata of society. Here, too, the query must be raised of why this comprehensiveness came to be. It was not in Judaism. Why did it appear in Christianity?

A fifth source of strength was in the fact that Christianity was both intransigent and flexible. In its refusal to compromise with the current paganism and with many of the social customs and moral practices of the times it developed a coherence and an organization which set it over against society. The very break required to join it gave to its adherents a conviction which constituted a source of strength against persecution and of zeal in winning converts. Here it was not unlike its parent faith, Judaism. Yet Christianity proved able to adjust itself to many current intellectual beliefs and to popular practices as Judaism did not—or at least as the Rabbinic Judaism which ultimately became the dominant form of the older faith failed to do. It must also be recalled that Christianity, while adaptable, was not primarily a syncretic product. On what it deemed its essential and central doctrines the main body of the Church refused to compromise. Again one must seek to go behind the superficial reason and to ask the cause. Why this combination of intolerance and adaptability?

A sixth factor of which much is made is that Christianity supplied what the Græco-Roman world was asking of religion and philosophy, and did it better than any of its competitors. As we have seen, the ancient world, and especially those portions of it in which Hellenistic influence was strong, believed in the

---

letarian revolution. Troeltsch, *The Social Teaching of the Christian Churches*, p. 39, is quite right in declaring that Christianity was not the product of a class struggle of any kind.

[305] Nock, *Conversion*, p. 135.
[306] Augustine, *Confessions*, Book VII, **Chap. 9**.
[307] Nock, *Conversion*, pp. 56, 57.

distinction between matter and spirit. The former it regarded as evil and the latter as good. For it salvation meant the emancipation of the soul from the thraldom of matter and immortality through union with God. This was the object of the mysteries, of gnosticism, and of Neoplatonism. That salvation Christianity supplied. It had in the cross and the resurrection a dramatization of redemption which resembled the myths around which the mysteries were built. The Christians were convinced that they were heirs of a joyous immortality and in this assurance lay no small part of their appeal. Christianity had, too, the advantage of a connexion with Judaism and in the Jewish Scriptures could trace for itself what the time craved—the authority of a long tradition and the support of ancient sacred books. For the many who despaired of reason as a road to salvation it could offer a divine revelation in these Scriptures and in Jesus. For those who still wished the undergirding of reason, it provided a theology which claimed to have all that the best philosophies possessed. Some of the teachers led their pupils to Christianity by the way of philosophy. Among the apologists were those who claimed that the Greek philosophers derived many of their ideas from the Hebrew Scriptures. It will be recalled that it was in the Hellenistic world that Christianity achieved its first major successes. Again, however, it must be asked: How did it happen that Christianity could offer a way of salvation which made so powerful an appeal?

As has been suggested, its Jewish origin assisted Christianity in its growth. The Hebrew Scriptures supplied the sanctity of a long development and the authority of antiquity. Then, too, in Hellenistic Judaism Christianity found communities prepared for its message. Hellenistic Judaism, as we have seen, was an adaptation of the ancient Hebrew belief to the Greek intellectual and spiritual environment.[308] It had translated the Hebrew Scriptures into Greek. The synagogues of the Dispersion had attracted many Gentiles. Through these synagogues and their constituencies Christianity made most of its first adventures into the Gentile world. It drew to itself some of the Jewish and many of the Gentile adherents of Hellenistic Judaism. The Jews whom it did not win reacted from the direction in which Gentile Christianity was moving. Retiring within Rabbinic Judaism, they no longer reached out into the Hellenistic world. Christianity, therefore, was left the sole heir of Hellenistic Judaism. Again the question recurs, Why? What gave Christianity the qualities which enabled it to win those to whom Hellenistic Judaism had appealed?

Still another reason for the triumph of the faith was the miracles attributed to

---

[308] For an interesting description of Hellenistic Judaism, arguing an adaptation to the ideas embodied in the mystery cults, see E. R. Goodenough, *By Light, Light: The Mystic Gospel of Hellenistic Judaism*.

it. Christianity was by no means the only cult which could claim the endorsement of the miraculous, but people looked to it to do for them what they expected of other religions and were not disappointed. To the Græco-Roman world the existence of demons was almost as axiomatic as molecules, atoms, electrons, and germs have been to those reared in the science of the twentieth century. Christians claimed the power to expel evil spirits and could cite many instances of their success. The physical cures wrought by Christianity were among its claims for consideration. As we have seen, it was apparently because Constantine believed that the Christian God had aided him in achieving the mastery of the Empire and so had demonstrated his ability to do what was required by pagans of their divinities but to do it better, that he gave him his allegiance. Again the question arises as to whence came the confidence and the energy which gave rise to achievements which were regarded as manifestations of superhuman power.

In its moral qualities lay another of the reasons for Christianity's success. It was not merely that high ethical standards were held up before an age in which many were seeking moral improvement. Numbers of Christians found as well the power to forsake evil and to approximate to those standards. The experience of thoroughgoing moral and spiritual renewal was probably shared by only a minority of Christians. Enough of them had it, however, to give a tone to the Christian community. Part of the morality of Christians showed itself in the care for the unfortunate members of the community. The poor, the widows, the orphans, and the sick were the charge of the Church. As time passed thousands of underprivileged persons were supported by their fellow believers. It is important, too, to remind ourselves again that the Church did not seek retaliation against its persecutors. In the Christian writings of the period is little or nothing of bitterness or of desire for revenge against those who were hounding the faithful. In the fate of some of the persecutors Christian writers believed they saw divine retribution, but so far as we are aware no imprecatory prayers were offered against them. Once more the source of this moral and spiritual dynamic must be sought if the reason for the triumph of Christianity is to be discovered.

The more one examines into the various factors which seem to account for the extraordinary victory of Christianity the more one is driven to search for a cause which underlies them. It is clear that at the very beginning of Christianity there must have occurred a vast release of energy, unequalled in the history of the race. Without it the future course of the faith is inexplicable. That burst of energy was ascribed by the early disciples to the founder of their faith. Something happened to the men who associated with Jesus. In his contact with them, in his crucifixion and in their assurance of his resurrection and of the continued living presence with his disciples of his spirit, is to be found the major cause of the success of Christianity. That experience and that assurance were transmitted to succeeding generations. Why this occurred may lie outside the realms in which historians are supposed to move. One reason is probably to be found in the continued study of the earliest written records of Christianity and in the effort to preserve intact the belief and the experience of the circle of apostles who had been the intimates of Jesus. Whatever the cause, that the stream flowed on is clear. It is the uniqueness of Jesus which seems the one tenable explanation of the fact that Christianity is the only one of the many Jewish sects to break off from the parent stem and outstrip it in size and influence. In the impulse which came from Jesus is the primary reason for that growth and that strength which attracted Constantine, for that vitality which enabled Christianity, in the keen competition among religions, to emerge the victor, and for the vision of a fellowship of disciples which led to its organization. Here, too, is the main source of Christianity's inclusiveness. Members of both sexes and of all races, the learned and the ignorant, so Christians held, might share in the salvation made possible by Christ. This new life might express itself in many different cultural forms: hence the flexibility of Christianity. On certain matters of morals and of worship and belief, however, Christians were convinced they must not compromise: hence the intransigence of the Church. For those accustomed to the mysteries Christianity could offer in Jesus the sufferings and triumph of a Saviour-God. One appeal to those influenced by Hellenistic Judaism was the claim that the prophecies of the Jewish Scriptures pointed to Christ and had their fulfilment in him. The use of the name of Christ and faith in him were held to account for the miracles. With those touched by Christ began, too, that moral strength, that enthusiasm, and that overflowing charity which had so much to do with the success of the faith. In Jesus, therefore, and in his death and the conviction of his resurrection and of moral and spiritual rebirth and immortality through him, is to be found the chief reason for the triumph of Christianity. Without Jesus Christianity would not have sprung into existence, and from him and beliefs about him came its main dynamic.

With the question of the possible cosmic significance of Jesus we are not here concerned. Inevitably to the thoughtful mind that question obtrudes itself. It is apart from our purpose, however, to enter upon the discussion—which, it may be noted, began during his lifetime and has been in progress ever since. Simply as a plain matter of history, however, the vitality of the movement which we call Christianity, when traced back to its source, has its origin primarily in the impulse which came from Jesus.

It must be immediately added that Jesus and the beliefs about him, central though they are among the causes for the remarkable growth of Christianity in the Roman Empire, are not alone sufficient to account for it. In the course of our story we shall see the faith planted again and again by representatives as convinced and as zealous as were those who spread it in the Græco-Roman world. Yet repeatedly they have met with failure or with meagre success. Christianity has been continuously in China for a longer time than elapsed between the crucifixion and Constantine, propagated by devoted missionaries. Yet as against the probable tenth of the population of the Roman Empire who called themselves Christian at the accession of Constantine, scarcely one out of a hundred Chinese would now so denominate himself. In India, where a Christian community has been present for at least fourteen or fifteen centuries and in which missionaries from the Occident have been active for over four centuries, scarcely two out of a hundred confess to being Christian. In vast sections of Asia and Africa, Christianity, once vigorous, has died out. It requires more than the dynamic which came from Jesus, powerful though that has been, and embodied though it may be in earnest and devoted missionaries, to win and hold any large proportion of a people to Christianity. More even is demanded than the organization, the combination of compromise and unyielding adherence to principle, the active charity, and the moral and spiritual qualities which played so large a part in the triumph of the Church in the Mediterranean world. It was to the entire combination of factors which we have attempted to enumerate that the phenomenal outcome must be ascribed. We must conclude as we began by saying that the causes of the victory of Christianity were many, but that of one it can be said that without it the others would either not have existed or would have availed nothing.

May we summarize the main conclusions of this chapter? Our knowledge of the agents and the methods by which Christianity made its way in such phenomenal fashion through the Græco-Roman world is tantalizingly incomplete. Some professional missionaries there were—apostles, prophets, and teachers— but we gather that much of the work of conversion was done as an incidental part of the day's duties either by lay folk or by the clergy. Most of the converts came in one by one or in small family groups. Here and there the bulk of the population of a city, a district, or a country, following their natural leaders, moved bodily into the Church. This, however, appears to have been the exception.

The arguments used to win non-Christians were many. To the Jews and to the Gentiles on the fringes of Judaism, the chief appeal was to the fulfilment by Jesus of the expectation of the Hebrew Scriptures. To pagans the weaknesses of the current polytheism and philosophy were contrasted with the grandeur and antiquity of Christian monotheism. Here, too, emphasis was placed on the remarkable fashion in which the incarnation, death, and resurrection of Jesus were forecast in the Jewish sacred books. The ethical ideals and practices of Christians were set over against the moral frailties of current pagan society. To many the heroism of the martyrs proved impressive.

Christianity did not come to its triumph without bitter opposition. This opposition, indeed, was one of the causes of the outcome. It was severe enough to serve as at least a partial deterrent to light-hearted adoption of the faith. It gave tone to the morale of the Church and strengthened the sense of solidarity against paganism. Yet it was not severe enough seriously to threaten the existence of Christianity or even greatly to weaken the Christian community.

Opposition was chronic. Christians apparently were heartily disliked by their non-Christian neighbours. They criticized and held themselves aloof from too many current features and institutions of the life about them to avoid ill will. State officials, including some of the Emperors, took action against them, but this seems not to have been very determined until the middle of the third century, when the Church had had time to become strong enough to withstand a violent general persecution. Then, in the first half of the fourth century, the victory of Christianity was assured by the tolerance, followed by the support, of one of the most vigorous of the Emperors, Constantine.

The reasons for the remarkable outcome of the first three centuries of the spread of Christianity are many. Of these by far the most important was the original impulse which came from Jesus. It was because of what Jesus did to his intimates and because of their belief in him and in his death, resurrection, and early return that Christianity set out upon its career of conquest. It was because, for some reason, these experiences and convictions persisted in succeeding generations that the faith possessed the inner dynamic which continued to give it driving power. Here was a vast release of creative energy that revolutionized the lives which opened themselves to it. Other factors entered into the outcome, but in this was chiefly the secret of the unprecedented growth of the Christian movement.

Chapter V

THE SPREAD OF CHRISTIANITY FROM CONSTANTINE TO
A.D. 500. THE COMPLETION OF THE CONVERSION OF THE
ROMAN EMPIRE, THE BEGINNING OF THE CONVERSION OF
THE NORTHERN BARBARIANS, AND THE FURTHER EXTEN-
SION OF THE FAITH BEYOND THE ROMAN BOUNDARIES

AS WE have suggested, the reign of Constantine marked an important transition in the geographical expansion of the Christian faith. Until his time,
Christians had been only a minority of the population of the Roman Empire.
In the East, Christianity had begun to spread outside the borders of the Empire
and had made notable gains in Armenia and in the valleys of the Tigris and the
Euphrates. In numbers it was very unevenly distributed. It was strong in the
larger cities, particularly in Antioch, Alexandria, Rome, Carthage, and the ports
of Asia Minor. In Asia Minor, Christians constituted at least a large minority
and perhaps a majority. In Egypt, Christianity had begun to penetrate the non-
Greek-using older native stock. In Africa, it was firmly planted in the Latin-
speaking elements of the cities and had won some adherents among the Punic
and possibly the Berber groups. It was represented in the cities of Southern
Gaul and of South-western and Eastern Spain. It seems not to have been very
prominent in Greece itself, nor do we hear much of it in Southern Italy and
Sicily. The vast majority of the Jews had rejected it. In Syria and Palestine,
among the non-Hellenized peoples the Semitic cults remained practically un-
shaken. They were, indeed, to offer some of the most violent opposition to the
later spread of the victor. It is interesting that within the Roman Empire the
faith encountered the most determined resistance from those religions which,
like itself, sprang originally from the Semitic stock. Although Christianity
seems first to have made its way into the Gentile world through Hellenistic
Judaism, long before the time of Constantine it had reached out beyond that
environment. In Africa and to a less extent in Rome it had begun to be strong
in Latin-speaking populations. It had become the national faith of Armenia and
was widely extended among the Syriac-using peoples in the Tigris-Euphrates
Valley. It had even penetrated into Southern Arabia and perhaps to India.

Except in Armenia and parts of Asia Minor, the movement into the Church seems to have been mostly by individuals and to a less extent by families. Mass conversions appear to have been rare. The growth was made against chronic opposition which broke out from time to time into either local or general persecution.

Beginning with Constantine, the situation was greatly altered. Except for the brief reaction under Julian, Christianity was accorded the support of the government. It became a state religion and eventually the only official cult of the Roman Empire. Before many years, the Emperors were placing paganism under disabilities and after a few decades were seeking to stamp it out. Under such circumstances, conversion often ceased to be primarily from the conviction of the religious value of the faith to the individual. For many it was now a matter of policy. Others entered the Church because of official pressure or because their friends and neighbours were doing so. Christianity became identified with Græco-Roman civilization. While by the year 500 the erstwhile rivals had not been entirely eliminated, the vast majority of the population of the Empire called themselves Christian. Of the several types of Christianity, the state gave its support to one. After some vacillation, it settled down to the endorsement of that which was recognized at Nicæa as orthodox.

Even with the support of the state, the victory of Christianity was not easily achieved. The old cults were tenacious of life. In the fourth century Neoplatonism, in the form given it by Plotinus, was in the vigour of youth. Manichæism, of recent birth, was spreading rapidly and, in contrast with the faith presented by the established Church, claimed to be the true Christianity. The appeal which these systems had for many is seen in the experience of Augustine. Though reared a Christian, the future Bishop of Hippo and bulwark of the Catholic Church was in adolescence attracted to Manichæism, and then, after abandoning that system, found Neoplatonism alluring. Only in late youth did he come back, through a profound religious experience, into the Church of his mother.

In the invasions of the Empire by the northern barbarians which began on a grand scale in the latter part of the fourth century, a fresh incursion of paganism took place. To be sure, some of the Germanic peoples, notably the Goths and the Vandals, were professedly Christian before they established their control over portions of the Roman domains. However, many others of the barbarians were untouched by the faith, and their advent dealt blows to the Church. Since, however, they were generally in the minority and since Christianity was identified with the culture of the civilized majority among whom they settled, in time they usually adopted it. In some places the assimilation was delayed until after A.D. 500, but long before that date many of the earlier in-vaders had been baptized.

Christianity continued its extension beyond the borders of the Roman Empire—even outside what had been the boundaries at their widest extent. In the Persian Empire, to be sure, it now suffered under the handicap of being identified with the hereditary enemy, the Roman. In the Sassanian realms, accordingly, severe persecutions retarded its growth. In several other regions, however, it registered marked gains, notably in Ireland, in the upper part of the Nile Valley, in Arabia, and in what later became known as Abyssinia.

In spite of the disasters which in the fourth and fifth centuries overwhelmed so much of the Empire where was its chief stronghold, by the year 500 Chris-tianity was numerically many times stronger than when Constantine came to power. From being a minority cult, it had become the professed faith of the vast majority in what was still the most important civilized area of the human race, and had won minorities in some regions where other cultures were domi-nant. It is to a more detailed story of the process that we must now turn.

First of all it may be well to describe the chief actions of successive Emperors, including their legislation, which had to do with paganism and the spread of Christianity. Next we must say something of the processes by which Christianity expanded and of the arguments used to support it. Then we will cover region by region and people by people the progress of conversion, dealing first with the various sections of the Roman Empire, next with the barbarian invaders, and finally with countries outside the Empire.

The steps taken by Constantine in favour of Christianity up to 314 were only the initial ones of many. Some of these were while Licinius ruled in the East. Others were after the latter's elimination (323). In the twenty-four years which elapsed between whatever was done at Milan in 313 and his death in 337 Con-stantine adopted measure after measure increasing the privileges and prestige of that faith which in the days of his immediate predecessors had been so severely persecuted. We need not concern ourselves with the exact chronological sequence of these actions, nor ought we to undertake their exhaustive catalogue. Some of the more important, however, must be noted. Constantine exempted the Christian clergy from all contributions to the state.[1] While this was simply what was granted to priests of other recognized religions, it led to such a large influx into the ranks of the clergy that soon another edict forbade those of curial rank, on whom fell the heaviest burdens of the state, to become clergy-men, and limited ordination to those whose exemption would work little loss

---

[1] *Cod. Theod.*, xvi:2, 2 (Oct. 21, 319) ; Coleman, *Constantine the Great and Christianity*, p. 31 ; Eusebius, *Eccles. Hist.*, Book X, Chap. 7.

to the government.[2] Laws which had forbidden celibates and the childless to receive inheritances were annulled, possibly out of consideration for the clergy.[3] Wills in favour of the Church were permitted.[4] The manumission of slaves in churches in the presence of the bishop and clergy was legalized.[5] A litigant was permitted to bring suit before a bishop and the latter's decision was to be accepted by civil officials.[6] The Christian Sunday was placed in the same position as the pagan holidays by the suspension of the courts and of urban labour.[7] Constantine ordered the provincial governors to respect the days in memory of the martyrs and to honour the festivals of the churches.[8] He forbade Jews to stone such of their coreligionists as chose to become Christians.[9] He kept about him Christian ecclesiastics[10] and had his children educated in the Christian faith.[11] He erected, enlarged, and embellished churches. He encouraged the bishops to do likewise and authorized them to call on the civil officials for assistance.[12] When he moved his capital to the Bosphorus and there added to Byzantium until it became mainly a new city, he built many churches. Outwardly the New Rome must have seemed predominantly Christian.[13] Of Constantine's active attempts to promote the unity of the Church and to discourage divisions we need not speak, for that does not have much to do with our story. His efforts in this direction, however, may have strengthened the Church. Certainly they helped to determine the kind of Christianity which spread.

While Constantine thus encouraged Christianity, his restrictions on paganism were relatively few. He did not persecute the old faiths, but chiefly contented himself with giving the new every opportunity to grow peacefully. To be sure, he forbade the consultation of oracles[14] and removed from Delphi to Constantinople the famous tripod and the statue of Apollo. Even before his time, how-

---

[2] *Cod. Theod.*, xvi:2, 3 (July 18, 320); Coleman, *op. cit.*, p. 31; Huttman, *The Establishment of Christianity and the Proscription of Paganism*, pp. 59-63.

[3] *Cod. Theod.*, xi:1, 1; viii:16, 1; Coleman, *op. cit.*, p. 32; Eusebius, *Life of Constantine*, Book IV, Chap. 26.

[4] *Cod. Theod.*, xvi:2, 4; Coleman, *op. cit.*, p. 32.

[5] *Cod. Theod.*, iv:7, 1; Coleman, *op. cit.*, p. 32.

[6] *Cod. Theod.*, i:27, 1; Coleman, *op. cit.*, p. 41.

[7] Eusebius, *Life of Constantine*, Book IV, Chap. 18; *Cod. Just.*, iii:12, 2; Coleman, *op. cit.*, p. 32.

[8] Eusebius, *Life of Constantine*, Book IV, Chap. 23.

[9] *Cod. Theod.*, xvi:8, 1; Duchesne, *Early History of the Christian Church*, Vol. II, p. 52.

[10] Eusebius, *Life of Constantine*, Book I, Chap. 42; Coleman, *op. cit.*, pp. 54, 55.

[11] Eusebius, *Life of Constantine*, Book IV, Chap. 51, 52.

[12] Eusebius, *Life of Constantine*, Book I, Chap. 42; Book II, Chaps. 45, 46; Book III, Chaps. 1, 47, 50; Sozomen, *Eccles. Hist.*, Book II, Chap. 3.

[13] Eusebius, *Life of Constantine*, Book III, Chap. 48; Schultze, *Geschichte des Unterganges des griechisch-römischen Heidentums*, Vol. II, pp. 278-286; Huttman, *op. cit.*, pp. 104-118.

[14] Eusebius, *Life of Constantine*, Book IV, Chap. 25; Schultze, *op. cit.*, Vol. II, pp. 205, 206.

ever, the popularity of the oracles of Greece seems to have been declining.[15] He forbade the repair of ruined temples and the erection of new idols.[16] Here and there he ordered temples dismantled, but that usually appears not to have been so much from antipathy to the gods as from the desire to replenish the chronically overstrained imperial treasury.[17] He forbade any attempt to force Christians to take part in pagan celebrations.[18] Whether he actually prohibited sacrifice to the gods seems doubtful.[19] He showed friendship to non-Christians, especially in the West, where paganism remained stronger than in much of the East.[20] Some of his coins bore pagan symbols, as, for instance, the title of *Pontifex Maximus* and a figure representing him garbed for that office, and a cross placed beside the figures of *Sol Invictus* and *Mars Conservator*.[21] The Roman Senate, true to tradition, classed him among the gods[22] and continued the sacrifices at the altar of Victory.[23]

Little if any active resistance seems to have been offered to the pro-Christian measures of Constantine, and pagan writers appear not to have recognized that they were living in the rapidly deepening twilight of the old gods.[24] However, the Emperor himself was probably a sincere adherent of the new faith—even though he did think of it primarily as valuable for accomplishing what he expected of the old cults, only in more efficient fashion, and in many respects was far from being a model of the Christian virtues.[25] While he postponed his baptism until the latter part of his life,[26] this was probably because of the current belief that since the sacrament washed away all sins and could not be repeated, it had best be deferred as long as possible. Christians have little basis for regarding Constantine as a saint, but his measures were so wisely conceived and so skilfully executed that in his reign the outcome of the struggle of Christianity with its rivals was determined and the precedent established for accomplishing the transition with a minimum of civil disturbance.

[15] Schultze, *op. cit.*, Vol. II, pp. 205, 206.
[16] Schultze, *op. cit.*, Vol. I, pp. 51, 52.
[17] Eusebius, *Life of Constantine*, Book III, Chaps. 54-58; Schultze, *op. cit.*, Vol. I, pp. 48-50; Coleman, *op. cit.*, pp. 63, 64.
[18] *Cod. Theod.*, xvi:2, 5; Coleman, *op. cit.*, p. 37.
[19] Eusebius, *Life of Constantine*, Book IV, Chap. 25; Coleman, *op. cit.*, pp. 37-39.
[20] Eusebius, *Life of Constantine*, Book II, Chap. 22; Book IV, Chap. 55.
[21] Coleman, *op. cit.*, p. 45; Schultze, *op. cit.*, Vol. I, p. 59.
[22] Schultze, *op. cit.*, Vol. I, p. 59; Alföldi, *The Helmet of Constantine with the Christian Monogram* (*Journal of Roman Studies*, Vol. XXII, 1932, pp. 10-23). Socrates, *Ecclesiastical History*, Book I, Chap. 18, declares that Constantine had statues of himself set up in the temples.
[23] Huttman, *op. cit.*, p. 119.
[24] Coleman, *op. cit.*, p. 66.
[25] Coleman, *op. cit.*, p. 89.
[26] Eusebius, *Life of Constantine*, Book IV, Chaps. 61, 62.

Constantine was succeeded by his three sons, Constantine II, Constans, and Constantius, each of whom governed a portion of the Empire. Constantine II fell out with Constans and was eliminated in 340. Constans was assassinated in 350. This left Constantius sole ruler, especially after he had rid himself (353) of the usurper Magnentius, who had been acknowledged in Gaul and Italy. Constantius lived on until 361.

All three sons remained sufficiently true to their rearing to be supporters of Christianity, even though in personal character and public policies they were far from conforming to its ethical standards. Constans went beyond his father in his proscription of paganism and in 341, in a rescript applying to Italy, ordered that sacrifices cease.[27] Magnentius, who for about three years supplanted Constans in part of the West, had Christian symbols on his coins but proved lenient toward paganism and permitted sacrifices to be celebrated at night.[28] The pagans, still in the large majority in the West, flocked to his banners, probably out of hope of winning more concessions.[29] Constantius was more anti-pagan than Magnentius and much more so than his father. He commanded that "superstition cease and that the folly of sacrifices be abolished,"[30] a policy which led to the overturning of altars by Christians, to violent uprisings, and to much bitterness.[31] He removed from the Senate the statue of Victory which had been placed there by Augustus after the battle of Actium.[32] He ordered temples closed.[33] It must be noted, however, that of the pagan rites sacrifices were the only ones forbidden and that others, such as processions, sacred feasts, and initiations to the mysteries, including the taurobolium, were permitted and probably continued.[34]

Constantius died in 361. He was succeeded by his cousin Julian, whose brief reign of a little less than two years marked the only attempt of a Roman Emperor who controlled all the realm to reverse the policy of Constantine.

Julian is one of the most appealing figures in the long succession of Roman

---

[27] Cod. Theod., xvi:10, 1; Duchesne, Early History of the Christian Church, Vol. II, pp. 250ff.

[28] Cod. Theod., xvi:10, 5; Duchesne, op. cit., Vol. II, pp. 250ff. See also Schultze, op. cit., Vol. I, pp. 79-87. Boyd, The Ecclesiastical Edicts of the Theodosian Code, p. 22, says that the removal of the altar of Victory from the Senate was one of the causes of the revolt of Magnentius.

[29] Schultze, Geschichte des Untergangs der griechisch-römischen Heideniums, Vol. I, pp. 79-87.

[30] Cod. Theod. xvi:10, 2; Schultze, op. cit., Vol. I, pp. 75-79.

[31] Schultze, op. cit., Vol. I, pp. 75-87.

[32] Duchesne, op. cit., Vol. II, p. 501.

[33] Cod. Theod., xvi:10, 4; Duchesne, op. cit., Vol. II, pp. 250ff.

[34] Duchesne, op. cit., Vol. II, pp. 250ff.

rulers and has attracted much attention.[35] His story has often been told. After the death of Constantine and while still a child, through a series of political murders, he and his half-brother Gallus were left the sole representatives of their branch of the family. Kept under surveillance by Constantius, he was trained in the Christian faith and outwardly conformed to it. That his heart was ever committed to it seems highly improbable. As a youth he became strongly attracted to paganism as represented by Neoplatonism and yielded it enthusiastic adherence. He was initiated into the mysteries of Dionysus and of Mithra and was given to divination.

Why Julian spurned Christianity and adopted paganism is not entirely clear. It has been suggested that since Constantius favoured the Arian type of Christianity and had Julian instructed in it, the latter's acquaintance with the faith was with an intellectual, emotionally arid representation of it.[36] More probable is the conjecture that his dislike of Christianity and his espousal of paganism were due to experiences of his childhood and youth. The murder in his young boyhood of all his nearest relatives except one brother would tend to beget a hatred of Constantius and of the religion which the latter so stoutly supported. An early tutor, an ascetic eunuch, drilled him in the classics of Greek antiquity and in a simple, restrained way of life.[37] The six years of confinement, with his brother, in a lonely castle, through the jealous fear of Constantius, came in the impressionable and stormy years of adolescence. Their unhappy memory quite possibly was intertwined with recollections of the Christian books which he diligently read and of participation in Christian services. When greater liberty came and he studied in Constantinople, Nicomedia, Ephesus, and Athens, it is not surprising that Julian avidly perused non-Christian writings and sought out one of the leading pagans and gave him his allegiance.

It is clear that Julian's hearty dislike of Christianity and his zealous espousal

[35] His works are edited, with the Greek text and an English translation, in W. C. Wright, *The Works of the Emperor Julian*. Translations of excerpts from Julian are in Kidd, *Documents Illustrative of the History of the Church*, Vol. II, pp. 50-66. Some of the older accounts are in Socrates, *Eccles. Hist.*, Book III, Chap. 13; Theodoret, *Eccles. Hist.*, Book III, Chap. 15; Sozomen, *Eccles. Hist.*, Book V, Book VI, Chaps. 1, 2. The largest of the modern books on Julian is P. Allard, *Julien l'Apostat*. Other modern studies are W. D. Simpson, *Julian the Apostate*; E. J. Martin, *The Emperor Julian. An Essay on His Relations with the Christian Religion*; Alice Gardner, *Julian, Philosopher and Emperor, and the Last Struggle of Paganism against Christianity*; and J. Bidez, *La Vie de l'Empereur Julien*. A famous older account is in Gibbon, *The Decline and Fall of the Roman Empire*, Chaps. 22, 23, 24. See also Boissier, *La Fin du Paganisme*, Vol. I, pp. 85-142; Geffcken, *Der Ausgang des griechisch-römischen Heidentums*, pp. 115-141; and Labriolle, *La Réaction Païnne*, pp. 369-436. All of these have been consulted in compiling the ensuing brief summary.

[36] Allard, *Julien l'Apostat*, Vol. III, p. 314.

[37] Gardner, *Julian*, pp. 33, 34; Simpson, *Julian the Apostate*, p. 19; Bidez, *La Vie de l'Empereur Julien*, pp. 17, 18.

of paganism were more emotional than intellectual. Highly sensitive, devoted to books, religious by disposition and training, with a strong tendency to asceticism, he became an ardent adherent of Hellenism and a bitter antagonist of Christianity.

Called from his quiet by Constantius to share the rule of the Empire under the subordinate title of Cæsar, Julian was dispatched to the West to free Gaul and the Rhine country from German invaders. Here the bookish youth displayed remarkable skill as an organizer and general and performed with marked success the task to which he had been summoned. Proclaimed Augustus by his troops, the inevitable breach occurred between him and the jealous Constantius. On his march against the latter he threw off all pretense of being a Christian and openly committed himself to paganism. Constantius died before the conflict was actually joined, and Julian became the sole Emperor.

Julian now set himself to the revival of paganism and to the discrediting of Christianity. At no time did he begin any active persecution which compared at all with that of a Decius, a Valerian, or a Diocletian. He attacked Christianity by placing it under disabilities. He ordered the temples restored and commanded the stones and marble taken from them brought back.[38] He gave to pagans preference for offices[39] and deprived the Christian clergy of such privileges as free transport at the expense of the state,[40] immunity from the exacting service on the local senates,[41] and episcopal judicial jurisdiction.[42] He reserved to himself the control over professorial appointments and forbade Christians in the teaching profession to give instruction in the pagan authors.[43] This would have had the effect of turning over education to non-Christians. He showed favour to the Jews and projected the rebuilding of their temple at Jerusalem.[44] He revived pagan sacrifices.

It was not merely a restoration to which Julian set his heart and hand, but a

---

[38] Wright, *The Works of the Emperor Julian*, Vol. III, pp. xvii, 99. The latter reference is to a letter of the Emperor to his uncle. See also Sozomen, *Eccles. Hist.*, Book V Chap. 5.

[39] Letter to Atarbius in Wright, *op. cit.*, Vol. III, pp. 122, 123; Socrates, *Eccles. Hist.* Book III, Chap. 13.

[40] *Cod. Theod.*, viii:5, 12; Wright, *op. cit.*, Vol. III, p. xix. The action was taken by indirection, by more closely restricting the use of the imperial posts.

[41] *Cod. Theod.*, xii:1, 50-56; Wright, *op. cit.*, Vol. III, p. xviii; Libanius, *Oration* 18, 148, and a letter to the Byzacians given in Wright, *op. cit.*, Vol. III, pp. 124, 125 See also Martin, *The Emperor Julian*, p. 39, citing Amm. Marc., xxii, 9.

[42] Martin, *op. cit.*, p. 41, citing a letter of Julian.

[43] Wright, *op. cit.*, Vol. III, p. xix, citing a rescript which he gives in Vol. III, pp. 116-123. See also Theodoret, *Eccles. Hist.*, Book III, Chap. 8; Sozomen, *Eccles. Hist.* Book V, Chap. 18.

[44] Letter to the Jews, given in Wright, *op. cit.*, Vol. III, pp. 176-181; Sozomen, *Eccles Hist.*, Book V, Chap. 22.

eorganized paganism, purged of some of its weaknesses and strengthened by an daptation of some of its rival's methods and institutions. For instance, he established pagan almonries from state funds, sought to build a hierarchy of pagan priests somewhat resembling that of the Church, founded monasteries for retirement and meditation, introduced penance, and attempted to bring the ermon into pagan worship.[45]

Interested as he was in literature, Julian wrote against the "Galileans," as he persisted in calling the Christians, and his main treatise on the subject appeared formidable enough to draw replies from leading churchmen.[46] Among his charges were what he considered weaknesses and inconsistencies in the Pentateuch, and especially in Genesis. He declared that the Jewish law, in contrast with the mild and humane legislation of the pagans, was harsh and stern, with much of the barbarous. He declared that Jesus had been known for little more than three centuries and in his lifetime had accomplished nothing of note. He denied that some of the prophecies which the Christians regarded as pointing to Jesus could properly be so interpreted, declared that no warrant existed for the Christian appellation of Mary as "the Mother of God," and challenged the Christian neglect of the Jewish ceremonial Law and the disregard of circumcision, of the distinction between clean and unclean meats, and of sacrifices. He derided the honour which Christians paid to tombs and sepulchres and pointed out that it was contrary to the attitude of Jesus.[47]

Although Julian took pride in not resorting to the crude violence which marked the methods of his persecuting predecessors, he meted out punishments for what he believed civil offences.[48] Here and there, moreover, mobs took matters into their own hands and inflicted on Christians indignities and even death.[49] Probably in some instances this was in retaliation for the rough zeal with which Christians had, in the preceding two reigns, proceeded against paganism.[50]

In his attempt to revive and reorganize paganism Julian seems to have been actuated primarily by emotional and religious and not by political considerations. Nor does he appear to have attracted much popular endorsement. Possibly this lack of support may have been due to the fact that his efforts were centred

[45] Martin, *op. cit.,* pp. 76-78 ; Sozomen, *Eccles. Hist.,* Book V, Chap. 16.
[46] Schultze, *Geschichte des Untergangs des griechisch-römischen Heidentums,* Vol. I, pp. 310-312.
[47] The text and translation of Julian's *Against the Galileans* is in Wright, *op. cit.,* Vol. III, pp. 319-427.
[48] Sozomen, *Eccles. Hist.,* Book V, Chap. 15.
[49] Sozomen, *Eccles. Hist.,* Book V, Chaps. 9-11 ; Geffcken, *Der Ausgang des griechisch-römischen Heidentums,* pp. 124, 125.
[50] Sozomen, *Eccles. Hist.,* Book V, Chaps. 9-11.

chiefly in regions such as Asia Minor and in cities such as Antioch, where Christianity was strongest and the old faiths the most demoralized. Had he directed his attention to the West, where paganism was still fairly vigorous, he might have met with more success. As it was, the depths of religious feeling among the pagan aristocracy and proletariat were not stirred. Genuinely religious though he himself was, he could awaken little enthusiastic response. The old systems were too decrepit to be galvanized into more than a brief and deceptive revival by any such transient influence as his. Christianity had gained too much momentum to be stopped by the brief effort of a ruler. Julian came to an early death in a war with the Persians. The only permanent residuum of his dream was a tantalizing memory, execrated by the Christians and mourned by a few non-Christians. Yet for a time the succeeding Emperors, although Christian, were more moderate in their anti-pagan efforts than had been Constantius. It may be that fear of another reaction tempered their ardour.

The successor to Julian chosen by the troops was Jovian, of German descent. He is said to have declined the election on the ground that he was a Christian, but to have relented when the troops proclaimed that they too were of that persuasion.[51] In his brief reign (363-364) Jovian did not renew such energetically anti-pagan measures as Constantius had introduced. He did, however, restore to the churches, to the clergy, and to the Christian widows and virgins the privileges granted by Constantine and his sons.[52] Some of the temples were again closed and many priests discreetly retired from the public eye.[53] Jovian also called to account the officials who under Julian had destroyed churches.[54]

Valentinian I, who succeeded Jovian, was also a Christian and in the little more than a decade of his reign (364-375) favoured the Church. He is said to have been banished by Julian because of his faith[55] and naturally as Emperor would be true to it. He and his colleague, Valens (364-378), both allowed pagan priests their old rights and so preserved the Constantinian policy of toleration.[56] They also insisted on freedom for the Church and forbade officials to require Christians to guard temples.[57] Under Valens we hear of a philosopher in a high position at court who became implicated in what may have been a plot to insure to a pagan the succession to the throne and so to bring about a fresh anti-Christian reaction.[58]

[51] Sozomen, *Eccles. Hist.*, Book VI, Chap. 3.
[52] *Ibid.*
[53] Socrates, *Eccles. Hist.*, Book III, Chap. 24.
[54] Schultze, *op. cit.*, Vol. I, pp. 176-184.
[55] Sozomen, *Eccles. Hist.*, Book VI, Chap. 6.
[56] *Cod. Theod.*, xii:1, 60; Schultze, *op. cit.*, Vol. I, pp. 196, 197.
[57] *Cod. Theod.*, xvi:1, 1; Schultze, *op. cit.*, Vol. I, pp. 196, 197.
[58] Sozomen, *Eccles. Hist.*, Book VI, Chap. 35.

Gratian (367-383), a son, colleague, and successor of Valentinian I, was elevated to the purple in his teens. He was under the strong influence of the great Bishop Ambrose of Milan and supported Christianity with all the zeal of youth. He was the first to drop the title of *Pontifex Maximus* which had marked the Emperor as the head of the state paganism, and he took action against both the non-Christian cults and the non-Catholic branches of Christianity.[59] He confiscated the properties of temples and withdrew the support of the state from pagan priests and worship.[60] He restricted the privileges of paganism in the city of Rome, where the old religions were still strong, and removed once more the altar of Victory from the Senate.[61] The early death of Gratian, by assassination, brought hope to the pagan party, and in the failure of harvests in Italy, Spain, and Africa they thought they saw supernatural warning against his impiety.[62]

Theodosius I, "The Great," who reigned 379-395 but who was sole Emperor only in 394-395, had been born of Christian parents but was not baptized until he reached mature life.[63] His accession to power brought the distressed pagans to relief. He encouraged the demolition of temples, directed that entrances to temples be closed, and prohibited secret sacrifices.[64] In many places temples were destroyed by the Christians, often led by monks.[65] An imperial edict of 391 ordered the Prætorian Prefect to see that sacrifices were forbidden and that no one visit a pagan holy place. Shortly thereafter a similar edict was directed to the imperial officials in Egypt. Late in 392 Theodosius put under the ban all offerings to idols.[66] He also held that marriage between a Jew and a Christian must be legally regarded as adultery.[67] Apostates from Christianity—and presumably such must have existed or no legislation would have been thought necessary—were to be deprived of honours and hereditary rank and of the right of inheritance and of conveying by will.[68]

Late in the reign of Theodosius, a Frankish general, Arbogastes, revolted and raised to the purple Eugenius, a rhetorician. Eugenius, although nominally a

---

[59] Foakes-Jackson in *An Outline of Christianity*, Vol. I, p. 129; Schultze, *op. cit.*, Vol. I, pp. 210-216.

[60] Müller, *Kirchengeschichte*, Vol. I, pp. 190, 191.

[61] Schultze, *op. cit.*, Vol. I, pp. 218-224.

[62] Schultze, *op. cit.*, Vol. I, pp. 227-233.

[63] Sozomen, *Eccles. Hist.*, Book VII, Chap. 4.

[64] Sozomen, *Eccles. Hist.*, Book VII, Chap. 20.

[65] Sozomen, *Eccles. Hist.*, Book VII, Chap. 15; Schultze, *op. cit.*, Vol. I, pp. 270-273.

[66] *Cod. Theod.*, xvi:10, 10; xvi:10, 11; xvi:10, 12. See translations of these in Huttman, *The Establishment of Christianity and the Proscription of Paganism*, pp. 215-217. See also Schultze, *op. cit.*, Vol. I, pp. 276-279, 339.

[67] *Cod. Theod.*, xvi:8, 6; Schultze, *op. cit.*, Vol. II, p. 31.

[68] *Cod. Theod.*, xvi:7, 4; xvi:7, 5. See translation in Huttman, *op. cit.*, pp. 213-215.

Christian, was much more tender to the pagans than was Theodosius. For the brief space during which he controlled part of the West, the adherents of the old faiths breathed more easily.[69] Theodosius, however, marched against the new foe, Arbogastes and Eugenius were eliminated, and the hopes of the non Christian leaders were once more thwarted.[70]

Theodosius was followed by his two sons, Arcadius and Honorius, the former ruling in the East and the latter in the West. In the early part of the reign of Honorius, the dominant figure in the government of the West was the Vandal Stilicho, who became the Emperor's father-in-law. Honorius came to the throne in extreme youth and seems never to have displayed much energy. In his day the West was ravaged by invasions of barbarians and the Empire was shocked by the fall of Rome into the hands of Alaric and his Goths (410). In spite of this turmoil the imperial government still gave attention to religious problems. Under Stilicho its policy was one of comparative leniency to paganism, and although the statutes against the old faiths were not formally rescinded they were permitted to fall into desuetude. The ancient deities and their cult retained adherents among the aristocratic circles of Rome and the imminent danger from the barbarians appeared the confirmation of the gloomy predictions that the neglect of the gods must be followed by the ruin of the state For Africa it was ordered that festive gatherings were to be permitted and that the temples were not to be destroyed, although in both rescripts sacrifice were expressly forbidden.[71] Yet Stilicho's wife was an ardent enemy of idols and Stilicho himself gave the Sibylline books to the flames.[72]

In 409, Alaric, Christian though he professed to be, set up for a short time Attalus as a rival to Honorius and the leading members of the government were pagan.[73] However, Alaric soon withdrew the purple from his puppet With the fall of Attalus the political power of paganism in Italy disappeared.[74]

In the East commands were issued in the name of Arcadius and Honorius renewing the prohibition of including in the official holidays the special days of the ancient cults,[75] proscribing the visiting of temples and the celebration of all sacrifices,[76] withdrawing all privileges formerly enjoyed by pagans

[69] Schultze, op. cit., Vol. I, pp. 280-294; Dill, Roman Society in the Last Century of the Western Empire, pp. 28-58.
[70] Sozomen, Eccles. Hist., Book VII, Chap. 24.
[71] Cod. Theod., xvi:10, 17 and 18. Translation in Huttman, op. cit., p. 228.
[72] Schultze, op. cit., Vol. I, p. 334.
[73] Dill, op. cit., pp. 28-55.
[74] Boyd, The Ecclesiastical Edicts of the Theodosian Code, p. 31.
[75] Cod. Theod., ii:8, 22. Translation in Huttman, op. cit., p. 225.
[76] Cod. Theod., xvi:10, 13. Translation in Huttman, op. cit., pp. 225, 226.

priests,[77] and ordering the destruction of temples still standing in the rural districts.[78]

After Stilicho fell from favour and was executed, the attitude of the government in the West stiffened. The income of temples was ordered devoted to the army, the remaining images were to be destroyed, and the temples themselves were to be diverted to public purposes.[79] Pagans were to be excluded from civil offices and from the army.[80] Yet, at least in the East, those who conducted themselves peaceably and kept within the law were not to be mishandled by Christians.[81]

The old religions were slow in dying. In the fifth century the immigration of barbarians swelled the number of pagans, not only in the provinces in which imperial rule had collapsed, but in those which still remained to the Empire. Again and again in that century we find the record of governmental measures against paganism, clear evidence that former legislation had not succeeded in extirpating it. However, the power of the old religions was obviously weakening. It is clear that the imperial authorities felt much more concern over the Christian heretics and the rising religion of Manichæism than over the now obviously moribund cults of the gods. Among the orders were those which forbade bequests for the maintenance of heathen cults and prescribed the death penalty for those baptized Christians who lapsed into pagan rites.[82] Pagans were ordered to go to the churches for instruction, and exile and confiscation of property were decreed for those who declined baptism. Pagan children of tender years were to be baptized and nominal Christians who had submitted to the rite to retain military office or their property, but who had made no effort to wean from paganism their wives and children, were to suffer the loss of their goods.[83] This, it may be noted, constituted a more drastic measure than had heretofore been adopted. The state had long been content with the proscription of pagan practices and had not before commanded baptism of all its citizens.[84]

Justinian, in the first half of the sixth century, was still legislating against paganism.[85] It had ceased to be formidable, but in many places it lingered on.

[77] Cod. Theod., xvi:10, 14. Translation in Huttman, op. cit., p. 226.
[78] Cod. Theod., xvi:10, 16. Translation in Huttman, op. cit., pp. 227, 228.
[79] Cod. Theod., xvi:10, 19. Translation in Huttman, op. cit., p. 229. See also Schultze, op. cit., Vol. I, p. 334.
[80] Cod. Theod., xvi:10, 21. Translation in Huttman, op. cit., p. 235.
[81] Cod. Theod., xvi:10, 24. Translation in Huttman, op. cit., pp. 241, 242.
[82] Cod. Just., i:11, 9. Translation in Huttman, op. cit., p. 245.
[83] Cod. Just., i:11, 10. Translation in Huttman, op. cit., pp. 246-248.
[84] Schubert, Geschichte der christlichen Kirche im Frühmittelalter, pp. 100-106.
[85] Ibid.

By the time of Justinian, however, the struggle had virtually ended. The large majority of the population of the Mediterranean world professed to be Christians. Adherents of the old cults survived, but chiefly in remote regions or among the more recent barbarian invaders. Pagan beliefs and practices, thinly disguised under a Christian veneer, might persist, and the Jews still proved obdurate. Christianity, however, had become at least the nominal faith of Græco-Roman society. So far as its religious activities were concerned the state could now divert its energies into other channels.

The government was attempting to enforce religious uniformity, and sought not only to stamp out the rivals to Christianity, but to eradicate all varieties of that faith but the one which it deemed orthodox. With the autocratic trend of the imperial rule, a religious intolerance arose which was much more unyielding than had been that of the Empire at its height. This seems to have been a concomitant of political and cultural conditions. A growing, powerful state, such as was the Roman Empire in its first century and a half, could afford to be lenient. After decay set in, however, and it found itself on a waning defensive against both external and internal foes, not unnaturally it sought to repress any nonconformity. That effort was first directed against the Christians. When Christianity became the faith of the Emperors, the tables were turned. Paganism and all but one type of Christianity were discriminated against—at the outset not markedly so, but as the decades passed with increasing rigour.

Stern though the anti-pagan laws became, no such persecution was meted out to adherents of the old faiths as had been inflicted on the Christians. Here and there disorders occurred and a few fatalities are recorded. We hear, for example, of Christians slaying refractory priests of Mithra and burying them in the ruins of the Mithræa, that these sanctuaries, defiled by the presence of a dead body, might forever be unfit for the worship of that cult.[86] In the main, however, the only violence employed was against temples and idols. Often the chief exponents of the opposing positions lived in personal amity.[87] It is notable, moreover, that no serious official effort was made to stamp out Judaism. Jews were dealt with more mildly than were heretics. Attempts were made to prevent them from winning Christians to their fellowship. From the recorded legislation the chief danger of such leakage appears to have been through Christian slaves owned by Jewish masters. Except for occasional sporadic local persecutions, however, the Jews were allowed to practise their hereditary religion and to rear their children in it.[88]

---

[86] Cumont, *The Mysteries of Mithra*, p. 204.

[87] Nock, *Conversion*, p. 160; Schultze, *op. cit.*, Vol. II, p. 339.

[88] Parkes, *The Conflict of the Church and the Synagogue*, pp. 183-189.

The measures of the government were paralleled by those of the Church and of individual Christians. Indeed, the policy of the state was in part only a symptom of the movement toward Christianity. A kind of mass conversion was in progress. It was, on a huge scale, something like what occurred among various northern European peoples beginning in the fourth century and continuing for about a thousand years. It also resembled what took place in the Americas in the sixteenth and seventeenth centuries and in many tribes and social groups, such as Indian castes, in the nineteenth and twentieth centuries. In all of these instances the great influx followed the espousal of the faith by the heads of the state or of the community, leaders whom the people were accustomed to follow. In most of them some individual conversions had occurred and the Christian minority had suffered persecution before the rulers were won. In the Americas it was the new rulers, the conquering white men, who engineered the process. In the Roman Empire, before the rulers came over to the Church, a much larger body of Christians has been assembled than in almost any of these other places. Partly for this reason, while the Roman government assisted the swing toward Christianity, it was not the chief agency. It merely helped make possible the conversion of that major part of the population which at the outset of the fourth century was still pagan. Everywhere the actual work of conversion and the attendant instruction were carried on by the Church itself through many individual Christians.

Beginning with Constantine, it was much more possible than previously to pursue publicly a campaign for the spread of the faith. Especially in the fourth century do we hear of active missionaries. In an age when men of vigour and independence were rare and servility and weakness flourished, the Church could boast a number of strong leaders. Some of these must have had marked influence with pagans. More than one energetic bishop in his own diocese, or from his diocese as a centre, inspired and directed missionaries. Some bishops themselves served as missionaries. Such a one was Martin of Tours, of whom we shall hear more in a moment. Another was Ambrose of Milan. We know him to have won, by persuasion rather than by force, many pagans in Milan and to have encouraged by his letters missionaries in the Tyrol.[89] Vigilius, who directly supervised the latter mission and himself laboured and suffered in it, was the second Bishop of Trent.[90] Augustine, Bishop of Hippo, to whose remarkable conversion Ambrose contributed so notably, was earnest in winning

[89] Walter, *Die Heidenmission nach der Lehre des hl. Augustinus*, p. 1, citing A. Baunard, *Geschichte des hl. Ambrosius*, übersetz von Johann Bittl, Freiburg, 1873, pp. 379ff. Campenhausen, *Ambrosius von Mailand als Kirchenpolitiker*, pp. 186-188.
[90] Hahn, *Geschichte der katholischen Missionen*, Vol. I, p. 257.

others. In his *City of God* he gave to the world one of the most famous apologetics for Christianity. An important part of such letters of his as have reached us were to pagans, seeking to present to them his faith.[91] He and his clergy sought the conversion of non-Christians in his diocese.[92] He carefully prepared catechetical instruments for the instruction of pagans, adapting them to various grades of neophytes, such as those who entered the Church with a background of an excellent training in the traditional Greek and Roman classics, and those whose formal education had been restricted to attendance at schools of rhetoric.[93] A famous contemporary in the East, John Chrysostom, wrote an apologetic directed to Jews and pagans. As Bishop of Constantinople he sent missionaries to pagan regions and peoples, including the Goths on the borders of the Empire. While in exile in the Caucasus he employed his relative leisure to encourage missions in Cilicia and especially in Phœnicia.[94] In addition to these and the few other bishops of whose missionary efforts we know there must have been many, less prominent or less active as authors, who were zealous in seeking to propagate their faith among the pagans in their dioceses, but of whose labours no written record has reached us.

Some missionaries extended their activity very widely. For instance, a certain Philaster, dubbed a "second Paul," a man apparently of Italian origin, traversed the Empire, preaching to pagans and Jews. For a time he lived in Rome and won many by private and public disputations. After many wanderings he became the Bishop of Brixia (Brescia) and there added to his fame.[95]

An important means of attracting converts was the extensive humanitarian activity of the Church. From the beginning the Church had cared for its own poor and had enjoined hospitality to fellow Christians. Through the prosperity which followed recognition by the state it was able to do still more. It built and maintained hospitals, hospices for strangers, and houses for orphans, widows, and the indigent. When, in the fourth and fifth centuries, so much of the structure of society collapsed through internal decay and the barbarian invasions, the eleemosynary functions of the Church acquired growing importance. In many sections, notably in the West, the Church remained the one stable institution, the only protector of the weak and the sole refuge of the poor. This

[91] Walter, *op. cit.*, p. 6.

[92] Walter, *op. cit.*, p. 3.

[93] Haller, *Augustin, de catechizandis rudibus*, in *Allgemeine Missionszeitschrift* (1897), Vol. XXIV, pp. 120-129, 182-190. See also Walter, *op. cit.*, p. 7.

[94] E. Hartung, *Johannes Chrysostoms und die Heidenmission*, in *Allgemeine Missionszeitschrift* (1894), Vol. XXI, pp. 310-316.

[95] Schultze, *op. cit.*, Vol. I, pp. 313, 314. An account by his successor, Gaudentius, *Sermo XXI de vita et obita B. Philastri*, is in Migne, *Pat. Latina, Series Prima*, Vol. XX, pp. 997-1002.

must have led to numerous conversions. We know, for example, that the Church reared and instructed in the Christian faith many children of pagans who had been abandoned.[96]

Through much of the fourth and into the fifth century Christian apologetic literature continued to appear as an answer to pagan criticisms and arguments. Thus at the end of the third or the beginning of the fourth century, Arnobius, a native of North Africa who had long been a bitter opponent of the faith and did not become a Christian until late in life, wrote *Adversus Nationes*. Part of this was an arraignment of paganism such as we have seen in earlier apologists. Part of it, too, was an attempt to answer the familiar charge that the disasters from which society was suffering were the unhappy fruits of the neglect of the old gods. In reply, Arnobius declared that calamities had been known long before the advent of Christianity, and that seeming adversities must not always be regarded as pernicious.[97] He also set himself to answer such current and familiar objections to Christianity as its recent origin and the alleged vulgar authorship and crudities of its written records. He spoke of the baseness of men and the poor quality of the human soul. He declared that man can have immortality only if God cares to bestow it. He had little respect for human reason and held that because of the presence of mystery faith must be our chief dependence. In the character and miracles of Jesus he found his principal ground for belief in Christianity.[98]

Lactantius, a teacher of rhetoric and a pupil of Arnobius, who, like the latter, did not come into the Church until mature life, but who was later entrusted with the education of one of the sons of Constantine, wrote a book which he addressed to Constantine and whose title may be translated as *The Divine Institutes*.[99] He had in mind especially the educated classes and employed an excellent literary style, with frequent quotations from standard Latin authors. He appealed, too, to recognized principles of human reason.[100] He argued that the universe is governed by one God rather than many, and pilloried, as had so many others of his predecessors among the apologists, the absurdities of the prevailing polytheism and the immoralities of the gods. He dwelt on the creation of the world by God. He believed in the existence of demons, who, he maintained, were the authors of astrology, divination, oracles, and necromancy, but had no power to injure the righteous, the worshippers of

---

[96] Schultze, *op. cit.*, Vol. I, pp. 320, 321.

[97] Arnobius, *Adversus Nationes*, Book I, 1-17 (translation in *The Ante-Nicene Fathers*, Vol. VI, pp. 413-417).

[98] In addition to the text of Arnobius itself, see a discriminating summary in McGiffert, *A History of Christian Thought*, Vol. II, pp. 39-44.

[99] Translated in *The Ante-Nicene Fathers*, Vol. VII, pp. 3-223.

[100] McGiffert, *op. cit.*, Vol. II, pp. 44-53.

God. He emphasized the weaknesses of the accepted philosophies. Philosophers, he held, frequently approached the truth but erred in lacking divine authority and failed sufficiently to connect their systems with religion. True wisdom, he maintained, consists in the knowledge and worship of God, and the teachers of authentic wisdom are also the priests of God. He spoke of Christ as the *Logos*, as having been foretold by the prophets, and of his birth, passion, resurrection, and ascension. The cross, he declared, had vast power over demons. He had much to say of justice, which he said philosophers had been unable either to discover or to defend, and declared that the persecution of Christians had been against justice. The heavenly way, a compound of such virtues as justice, temperance, patience, faith, chastity, concord, truth, and wisdom, is difficult and beset by poverty, ignominy, labour, and' pain, but leads to an immortality of felicity, a reward granted by God himself. He held up an exacting standard of virtue—the abstention from evil thoughts and from even the moderate vices, the use of wealth not for the pleasure of the individual, but for the good of the many in hospitality, the ransom of captives, and the protection and defence of widows and orphans. He condemned the gladiatorial shows as homicide, saw no good in infanticide, and in the stage and the games of the circus perceived only a corrupting influence. For him, in other words, the ancient religion and philosophies and much of the ethical standards and pastimes of current society were at best imperfect and at their worst false and corrupting, drawing the soul away from its true destiny. To him Christianity was the true way, the true wisdom, the true justice, which involved a radical break with much that was usually accepted and led by a difficult path to an immortal life of bliss.[101]

Another contemporary of Constantine, Eusebius, although best known for his *Ecclesiastical History*, was also the author of two apologetic works, one of which sought to show that Christians were justified in rejecting the religion and philosophy of the Greeks and in accepting the Hebrew Scriptures, and the other upholding the general thesis that Christians were right in regarding Jesus as the Messiah and in adopting a mode of life which differed in many ways from that of the Jews.[102]

The great Augustine of Hippo was inevitably drawn into the controversy between Christians and pagans. We find in his surviving letters evidence of correspondence with cultivated non-Christians, in good temper, showing that educated men in the two camps could discuss with reciprocal respect some of the fundamental and timeless issues—the incarnation of the omnipresent Ruler

[101] A translation of *The Divine Institutes* is in *The Ante-Nicene Fathers*, Vol. VII, pp. 3-223.
[102] McGiffert in *The Nicene and Post-Nicene Fathers*, Second Series, Vol. I, p. 33.

of the universe in one human being, subject to the limitations of finite humanity, and the possibility of carrying out the Sermon on the Mount in the administration of the state.[103]

In Augustine's time came the capture and sack of Rome by Alaric and his Goths. To the pagans this appeared a spectacular confirmation of what they had long been reiterating. For generations, as we have seen, they had been declaring the neglect of the old gods brought about by the Christians was the cause of the calamities which were bringing ruin to the Empire and to civilization. Now the very centre and symbol of that Empire, the Eternal City itself, had fallen to the barbarian. Moreover, in the disaster Christians as well as non-Christians had suffered. Surely, therefore, the God of the Christians had been proved wanting in power to protect not civilization only, but his own followers as well.

Obviously such a challenge could not be allowed to pass unanswered. Orosius, a young Spanish priest, was encouraged by Augustine to prepare a refutation. As a result came a history which was to have a wide circulation in the Middle Ages and which attempted, among other things, to show that the sufferings of the present were not so severe as the many which man had experienced before the advent of Christ.[104]

Augustine himself entered the lists and gave to the world his famous *City of God*. He answered in various ways the question of why Christians suffered with pagans in the capture of Rome. He said, for instance, that while they were alike in their sufferings they differed in the manner in which they endured suffering, and that if material rewards were always meted out for goodness men would seek for these and so miss goodness. He also declared that the saints lose nothing by being deprived of their temporal goods, and that since they are sure of the resurrection it makes no difference to them if their bodies meet dishonour and remain unburied. Augustine insisted that the barbarians who sacked Rome, being Christian, showed far more mercy than had barbarians in pre-Christian times, that the churches were open sanctuaries to both pagans and Christians, and that, contrary to the former customs of war, in these even the pagans were spared for Christ's sake. He went on, as had so many of his predecessors among the apologists, to call attention to the immoralities of the gods. The gods, so he said, had whetted and abetted man's evil desires rather than thwarted them. Men did not ask to be righteous, but only that the Empire remain undefeated. As had others before him, he pointed

---

[103] Dill, *Roman Society in the Last Century of the Western Empire,* pp. 14, 15; Augustine, *Epistles* 135, 136, 233, 234, 235 (Migne, *Pat. Lat.,* Vol. XXXIII, Cols. 512-515, 1030, 1031).
[104] Dill, *op. cit.,* pp. 60-73.

out that calamities had occurred before the coming of Christianity, and that the gods had proved powerless to avert them. As to the claim that the long duration of the Empire had been due to their protection, he attempted to show that this could not be. For instance, some of the gods whom the Romans adopted had proved impotent to prevent the fall of Troy. It is God, he said, who gives earthly kingdoms to both the evil and the good. Then, in the latter half or more of the book, he contrasted the two cities, the earthly and the heavenly. He attempted to show how they both trace their course back before even the creation of man, and since then have had a continuous history. He foretold for one eternal punishment and for the other endless bliss.[105]

As with the pre-Constantinian apologies, so with these, we cannot be sure that they afford a well-rounded picture of the reasons which induced men to become Christians. We cannot prove that they led to conversions. Presumably, however, they contained the arguments which were usually put forward to the educated. Not improbably, moreover, they were also repeated orally and in more or less garbled forms were retailed by the illiterate. In them, then, we can obtain some idea of what was said to pagans. Almost certainly, however, they give us only very imperfect insight into the real motives which impelled men to seek entrance into the Church. These, presumably, were very mixed and as a rule were more emotional than intellectual. For instance, the church historian Sozomen tells us that his grandfather and all of his family were won to Christianity through knowing of a case of demon possession cured by calling on the name of Christ.[106] We hear, too, of pagans converted in one region in Gaul early in the fifth century because, when a plague attacked the herds, some of the cattle of the Christians escaped or recovered and this good fortune was attributed to the use of the sign of the cross.[107] Again and again the miraculous played a notable part in winning adherents. On the other hand, we have, also in Gaul and in the fourth century, Hilary, Bishop of Poitiers, who became the bulwark in the West of orthodox Catholicism against Arianism, who had been born of pagan parents, and who apparently came to a Christian faith by asking: What is the purpose of my life?[108]

By the middle of the fifth century the stream of apologetic literature had dwindled.[109] The old religions in the form of organized cults, espoused by

[105] Augustine, *The City of God, passim.*
[106] Sozomen, *Eccles. Hist.,* Book V, Chap. 15.
[107] Hauck, *Kirchengeschichte Deutschlands,* Vol. I, p. 36; Severus Sanctus Endelechius, *De mortibus boum,* in Lemaire, *Poet. lat. min.,* Vol. I, pp. 577ff., v. 105.
[108] Holmes, *The Origin and Development of the Christian Church in Gaul,* pp. 143-183.
[109] Schultze, *Geschichte des Untergangs des griechisch-römischen Heidentums,* Vol. I, pp. 330-333, names the end of the fourth century as the time by which the anti-pagan apologetic and polemic literature had dwindled to almost nothing, but this is a little

educated men and publicly observed, had either disappeared or had ceased to be formidable. Here and there paganism continued, in the cities perhaps among a few of the old aristocracy or of those who took pride in the ancient philosophers, occasionally in rural districts,[110] much more generally among nominal Christians as superstition or as an attitude of mind, and among some of the barbarian invaders who were not yet assimilated. Against it, however, the great leaders of the Church needed no longer to direct their literary efforts. The battle must henceforth be waged in other ways—by the continued efforts of the state, by synods, by bishops, and by missionaries.

We must now turn to the spread of Christianity by peoples and regions.

As before Constantine, so after him, the great majority of the Jews adhered to their ancestral faith. Now and then we read of conversions. Thus in the first half of the fifth century a number of Jews in Crete are said to have become Christians—in a reaction from a fanatical movement led by one of their number who claimed to be Moses and promised to bring his followers through the sea to the Promised Land.[111] A Jewish impostor, pretending to be a convert, repeatedly submitted to baptism by gullible Christians and in that manner amassed a considerable sum of money.[112] From the fourth century comes an imperial order designed to protect from their fellow Jews those in Carthage who had embraced Christianity.[113] On the other hand, from the sermons of Chrysostom "against the Jews" we infer that in Antioch in the latter part of the fourth century Christians were being attracted to the synagogue to the peril of their faith. Apparently what appealed to them was a tribunal in the synagogue which commanded their respect, the repute of the Jews in curing illness and exorcising demons, the worship of the synagogue, and the Jewish festivals.[114] Whether any Christians actually sought admission to the Jewish community there we do not know. From the imperial legislation against the circumcision of Christian slaves by Jewish masters,[115] it seems clear that some Christian servants were being absorbed into Judaism.

---

early, especially since the *City of God* did not appear until the first half of the fifth century.

[110] The word *paganus* did not mean "villager," as some have supposed who have traced its derivation to the fact that paganism often had its last strongholds in rural districts, but was used to designate a "civilian" as opposed to the *milites Christi* who had taken an oath to serve Christ.—Harnack, *Militia Christi*, pp. 68, 69; Workman, *The Evolution of the Monastic Ideal*, p. 30.

[111] Socrates, *Eccles. Hist.*, Book VII, Chap. 38.

[112] Socrates, *op. cit.*, Book VII, Chap. 17.

[113] *Cod. Theod.*, xvi, 8, 5; Leclercq, *L'Afrique Chrétienne*, Vol. II, pp. 95-97.

[114] Chrysostom, *Adversus Judæos Orationes*, in Migne, *Pat. Græc.*, Vol. XLVIII, Col. 843ff.; Kraeling, *The Jewish Community at Antioch*, p. 156.

[115] *Cod. Theod.*, xvi, 9, 1; Leclercq, *L'Afrique Chrétienne*, Vol. II, pp. 95-97.

In parts of Syria and Palestine Christianity made slow progress and then only in the face of an opposition which was often bitter. The Semitic faiths seem to have offered particularly stubborn resistance.[116] The reason would probably be significant if only it could be determined. As we have seen, Christianity succeeded in winning only a minority of the Jews. In North Africa the old Punic faith appears to have yielded slowly and with some violence.[117] In Phœnicia, the old Philistia, and sections of Syria, the disappearance of the Semitic cults was not consummated until the sixth century. Before Constantine the Christians in these regions were comparatively few. Under Julian anti-Christian riots occurred.[118] Toward the close of the fourth century we hear of a bishop storming a temple with the aid of gladiators and soldiers, but caught by the pagans and burned.[119] John Chrysostom, who was ardently missionary, dispatched zealous monks to destroy some of the temples and induced wealthy women to defray the expense. For this action he felt that he had the support of imperial decrees, and armed his messengers with them.[120] After initial successes, the monks met with a sharp reaction and a number of them were killed. The survivors were inclined to withdraw. Chrysostom, however, himself in exile, wrote them to keep up their courage and sent a messenger to hearten them.[121]

To represent Chrysostom as depending solely on force and imperial decrees to win converts would give a very distorted picture of his convictions about the Christian mission. He was persuaded that the most effective means was the example of Christian living. "There would be no more heathen if we would be true Christians," he said.[122] He urged, too, that all Christian owners of *latifundia* have chapels on their estates and work for the conversion of those who tilled the soil.[123]

In spite of the efforts of Chrysostom and other churchmen, in some places in Phœnicia and Philistia paganism was still strong at the close of the sixth century.[124] Conversion, if general, must for many have been recent or superficial

---

[116] Cumont, *The Mysteries of Mithra*, p. 62. Most of the places mentioned in Sozomen, *Eccles. Hist.*, Book VII, Chap. 15, in which pagans contended for their temples were in Semitic territories.

[117] Schultze, *op. cit.*, Vol. III, pp. 331-336.

[118] Sozomen, *Eccles. Hist.*, Book V, Chaps. 9-11.

[119] Sozomen, *op. cit.*, Book VII, Chap. 15; Schultze, *op. cit.*, Vol. I, pp. 268, 269.

[120] Theodoret, *Eccles. Hist.*, Book V, Chap. 29; Schultze, *op. cit.*, Vol. I, pp. 317, 318, 353-356.

[121] Chrysostom, *Ep.* 51, in Migne, *Pat. Græc.*, Vol. LII, Col. 636, 637; Schultze, *op. cit.*, Vol. I, pp. 317, 318.

[122] Chrysostom, I Epistle to Tim., *Homily* X, 3; Schultze, *op. cit.*, Vol. I, pp. 314-318.

[123] Chrysostom, *Homily* XVIII on Acts; Schultze, *op. cit.*, Vol. I, pp. 314-318.

[124] Schultze, *op. cit.*, Vol. II, p. 251.

when the Moslem invasion overwhelmed the land and led to defections to Islam.

Even in Antioch, probably the first large city to become predominantly Christian, in the last quarter of the sixth century paganism had a recognized head.[125] In the Lebanon, too, we hear of a monk who, entering a village first in the garb of a merchant, laboured successfully to make conversions.[126]

Moreover, in Asia Minor, where long before Constantine Christianity appears to have attracted at least the large minority of the population, we read of pagans in the second half of the fourth century, and not just as individual philosophers but as constituting a cult.[127] As late as the sixth century we learn of surviving paganism.[128]

In Greece the substitution of Christianity for the old faiths appears to have been accomplished without a very sharp struggle. Athens, to be sure, long remained a stronghold of non-Christian philosophies. Even after the time of Constantine the devout regarded it as a corrupter of the souls of those who still flocked to its teachers. Their fears seem to have been by no means baseless, for many nominally Christian youths were there led into a more or less open paganism.[129] About a decade after Julian, moreover, sacrifices at Athens were tolerated by the authorities.[130] The closing of the schools at Athens by Justinian, then, was more than a symbol of the end of an era. It had, to be sure, something of that significance. Henceforth the Greek philosophies were no longer taught at their traditional headquarters. Justinian's act, however, meant as well the elimination of a source of infection which, although no longer especially dangerous to the health of the supposedly Christian Empire, probably still affected it. Elsewhere in Greece many of the temples were transferred to Christian uses. In some places monks took possession of the shrines. It is said that in no other region do we have so much evidence of the erection of Christian churches on the sites of the holy places of the old gods.[131]

North of Greece lies territory of whose Christianization to the end of the fifth century we know all too little. It is clear that Salona, in Dalmatia, pos-

---

[125] Schultze, op. cit., Vol. II, pp. 270-272.
[126] Theodoret, Historia religiosa XVII (Migne, Pat. Græc., Vol. LXXXII, Cols. 1419-1426) ; Schultze, op. cit., Vol. I, pp. 318, 319.
[127] Basil, Ep. 258 ad Epiph., in Migne, Pat. Græc., Vol. XXXII, Cols. 951-954; Schultze, op. cit., Vol. II, pp. 313-317; Cumont, op. cit., p. 28.
[128] Holl, in Allgemeine Missionszeitschrift, 1912, p. 202, citing the Eccles. Hist. of John of Ephesus.
[129] Schultze, op. cit., Vol. II, p. 208.
[130] Zosimus, Hist., Book IV, Chap. 18. The sacrifices were to Minerva by a devotee of the old gods and are said to have saved the city and the surrounding country from the earthquakes then working destruction in Greece.
[131] Schultze, op. cit., Vol. II, pp. 212, 213.

sessed a bishop by about the middle of the third century, that in the fourth and fifth centuries the episcopal succession in that city was maintained, and that eventually large churches were constructed. From the lists of bishops and other information it is obvious that in the fourth and especially in the fifth century Christianity was growing in strength in the Danubian provinces.[132]

Egypt we know to have been one of the regions in which Christianity had made marked progress before the time of Constantine. The new faith, it will be recalled, was strongest in the Greek-speaking portions of the population and especially in Alexandria, but it had already gained some adherents among the non-Greek-using older stock.[133] In the last quarter of the fourth century an energetic Bishop of Alexandria determined to act against the remaining paganism of that city. Supported by the Emperor Theodosius, he desecrated one of the fanes and exposed to public scorn the secret and sacred symbols of the cult. This apparently led to a riot between pagans and Christians. The pagans ensconced themselves in the Serapeum, the great temple of Serapis which stood on an eminence and was the most renowned shrine of the city. Here the adherents of the old gods stood siege, but, apparently disheartened by the imperial support given the Christians, they abandoned their stronghold and their jubilant antagonists turned it into a church.[134] The destruction of other temples followed, an enterprise in which the vigorous bishop had the assistance of the civil and military authorities, and many of the images were melted down and cast into utensils for the use of the churches.[135] Yet these acts did not erase the old faiths, not even in Alexandria, and early in the next century the beautiful and learned Hypatia rose to fame as a teacher of Neoplatonism. Her brutal murder, as an incident in one of the factional disputes of the time, in Lent and in a church, by a mob said to have been led by one of the clergy, constitutes one of the darkest of the blots upon the Church of that century.[136] In the fourth century an inclusive episcopal organization arose in Upper Egypt, and by the end of the fifth century scarcely an important city in the land was without its bishop. The head of the Church in Alexandria seems usually to have been the director of the erection of this hierarchy and so helped to give system to the spread and permanence of the faith.[137] Yet paganism long

[132] Zeiller, *Les Origines Chrétiennes dans la Province Romaine de Dalmatie, passim;* Zeiller, *Les Origines Chrétiennes dans les Provinces Danubiennes de l'Empire Romain, passim.*

[133] Scott-Moncrieff, *Paganism and Christianity in Egypt,* p. 98.

[134] Sozomen, *Eccles. Hist.,* Book VII, Chap. 15; Socrates, *Eccles. Hist.,* Book V, Chap. 16. These two accounts differ in some important details.

[135] Socrates, *Eccles. Hist.,* Book V, Chap. 16.

[136] Socrates, *Eccles. Hist.,* Book VII, Chap. 15.

[137] Schultze, *Geschichte des Untergangs des griechisch-römischen Heidentums,* Vol. II, pp. 219-222.

lingered in outlying regions. Not until the sixth century was the temple of Isis on the island of Philæ transformed into a church. It was also in that century, under Justinian, that a city in the Libyan desert which still preserved its temples and its pagan cults was turned to Christianity.[138]

A vivid insight into what the transition from the old faiths to the new must have involved for many individuals of the upper classes is given in the letters of Synesius. Born in the latter half of the fourth century, in Cyrene, a scion of a wealthy and prominent family, Synesius had been educated in Alexandria and Athens and was a Neoplatonist, a warm friend of Hypatia. He also had as a protector one of the bishops of Alexandria and it is possible that it was this friendship which proved the road to his conversion. He showed initiative and ability in leading his native city in its defence against an attack of barbarians from the desert. Later the citizens of Ptolemais urged him to become their bishop. That office was not only the chief ecclesiastical but the leading political post in the province, with the direction of the army in time of war. It was probably more because of his administrative ability than the quality of his religious life that the populace desired him. At first he declined, pleading his inability to subscribe to all the doctrines of the Church. In 410 he yielded. He gave the able and courageous administration which had been expected, and assisted in the defence of the city against the raiding nomads. To the end, however, in his own life he seems to have mingled the pagan and the Christian. Certainly the imagery of his hymns is derived more from the former than the latter source—although quite possibly with no sense of inconsistency.[139]

North Africa, as we have seen, was an early stronghold of Latin Christianity and the home of the first extensive Latin Christian literature. At the accession of Constantine it was one of the regions where Christianity had been most firmly planted. In the post-Constantinian age it gave to the Church no less important a figure than Augustine. Even here, however, paganism was slow in dying. This may have been in part because of a division in the Christian forces. The Donatist movement arose in the fourth century[140] and in the fifth came the Vandals, adherents to Arianism. The Donatists seem to have joined with the Arian Vandals against their common Christian enemy, the Catholics. The Vandals expropriated some of the Catholic churches for the use of the

<hr>

[138] Schultze, *op. cit.*, Vol. II, pp. 226-229.

[139] Fitzgerald, *The Letters of Synesius of Cyrene, passim,* but especially pp. 11-69.

[140] In *c.* 330 the Donatists are said to have had in Africa 270 bishops.—Leclercq, *L'Afrique Chrétienne,* Vol. I, p. 341. It may be that the Donatist-Catholic schism represented a racial division between non-Latin peoples on the one hand and Latin-speaking elements on the other. R. P. Beaver, *The Donatist Circumcellions* in *Church History,* Vol. IV, pp. 123-133. On this see also Buonaiuti, *Il Cristianesimo nell'Africa Romana,* pp. 327, 328.

Arians. They exiled numbers of the Catholic clergy and leading laymen and sent some of the bishops to the interior at hard agricultural labour. Many Catholics were rebaptized by the Arians. The motive of this anti-Catholic policy was probably as much political as religious. In the provinces which remained under the Empire, the Catholics had the support of the state and the Arians were often persecuted. The Catholics, too, may have been drawn more from the Roman elements and the Donatists from the non-Latin speaking portions of the population. In Vandal territories, therefore, Catholic leaders were probably suspect as possible fomenters of rebellion, and pressure on Catholics in North Africa could be employed as a means of obtaining more tolerance of Arians within Roman domains. The Vandal anti-Catholic measures varied in their intensity and at times were suspended.[141] However, not until the destruction of Vandal power by Belisarius, the great general of Justinian, in 533 and 534, could the Catholics once more breathe freely. Their branch of the Church now took on new life. The tables were turned and the conquerors instituted measures against Donatists and Arians.[142]

With such prolonged and bitter divisions of the Christian forces it is not surprising that paganism in its formal dress was late in disappearing. In the time of Augustine many of social and intellectual prominence still deplored the neglect of the old cults[143]—perhaps because of that conservatism which the privileged classes nearly always show when the system under which they have flourished is threatened. Not until 391 was the famous huge Carthaginian temple of *Cælestis* (practically identical with the Phœnician Astarte) closed by imperial order. A few years later it was reopened as a Christian church. Since, however, many Christians combined in their prayers appeals to the goddess and to Christ, the shrine was destroyed.[144] Until after 398 most of the rulers were pagan.[145] In 408, so it is reported, in one city a crowd of pagans assembled and passed in procession, dancing and chanting, before a church at the hour of service. Violence followed and the next day the church was destroyed.[146] Early in the fifth century, before the Vandal occupation, paganism was still further weakened, partly by ecclesiastical action designed to carry out the imperial

[141] Leclercq, *op. cit.*, Vol. II, pp. 144-200; Duchesne, *Early History of the Christian Church*, Vol. III, pp. 433-444; Bouchier, *Life and Letters in Roman Africa*, pp. 105-108; Buonaiuti, *op. cit.*, pp. 399-414.

[142] Leclercq, *op. cit.*, Vol. II, pp. 214-273; Buonaiuti, pp. 415-423.

[143] Leclercq, *op. cit.*, Vol. II, p. 78.

[144] Leclercq, *op. cit.*, *Vol.* II, pp. 85, 86; Duchesne, *op. cit.*, Vol. II, p. 507, citing Pseudo-Prosper, *De Promissionibus*, iii, 38, Salvian, *De gubern. Dei*, Book VIII.

[145] Humphrey, *Politics and Religion in the Days of Augustine*, p. 86. On the struggle against paganism in North Africa see Humphrey, *op. cit.*, pp. 84-108, 147-169.

[146] Leclercq, *op. cit.*, Vol. II, p. 91.

anti-pagan decrees, and partly by fresh imperial orders.[147] In the year 400 Augustine could speak of temples destroyed, images broken, and sacrifices allowed to lapse.[148] Yet Augustine also tells of at least one city where the statues of the gods still graced the forum and received honour.[149] Possibly such remnants of paganism as survived until the coming of the Vandals suffered from the conquest, much as did Catholicism.[150] In the fourth and fifth centuries Christianity appears to have made progress among the indigenous Berber (or Moorish or Numidian) stock as well as among those of Latin and Phœnician descent. A number of bishops seem to have been from that element of the population.[151]

We are accustomed to think of Italy as almost uniformly Catholic and of Rome as the headquarters of the largest of the Christian Churches. Yet in many parts of Italy and the adjacent islands pagan cults were very slow to yield to the faith which later became so characteristic of the country. In the city of Rome itself many members of the aristocracy long supported the old gods. As to the intellectual validity of the pagan beliefs they may secretly have entertained a discreet scepticism. Outwardly, however, they yielded them allegiance. Their loyalty may have been in part from pride in the Roman tradition of which they considered themselves the heirs and guardians. To be sure, few if any of the aristocracy could trace their ancestry to the great families of the Republic or even of the early Empire, and the Senate had long since been shorn of most of its powers. However, membership in the Senate still meant prestige. High public offices in the city continued some of the old titles, and the glamour associated with the name and history of Rome lent them dignity. Throughout the course of the fourth and into the fifth century, therefore, a number of the leading men of Rome adhered to the traditional cults.

[147] Schultze, *Geschichte des Untergangs des griechisch-römischen Heidentums*, Vol. I, p. 374, Vol. II, pp. 162-165.
[148] Augustine, *Contra Epistolam Parmeniani*, I, 9, 15 (in Migne, *Pat. Lat.*, Vol. XLIII, Col. 44). Augustine says that this is true throughout the earth, but he must also have meant to include Africa.—Schultze, *op. cit.*, Vol. I, p. 352. Augustine seems to have looked with disfavour on this use of force and said: "Let us first extirpate the idolatry in the hearts of the heathen, and they will either themselves assist us or anticipate us in the execution of this good work."—Robinson, *The Conversion of Europe*, p. 215. Augustine was much interested in missions. He recommended that the pagan temples, statues, and groves be not destroyed, but consecrated to the service of God.—*Epist.* XLVII, 3, *ad Publicolam* (Migne, *Pat. Lat.*, Vol. XXXIII, Col. 185); Schmidlin, *Catholic Mission Theory*, p. 9. The standard work on Augustine's relation to missions is Gonsalvus Walter, *Die Heidenmission nach der Lehre des hl. Augustinus.*
[149] Schultze, *op. cit.*, Vol. II, p. 153, citing Augustine, *Epis.* 232, c. 7, Epis. 16, c. 1.
[150] Schultze, *op. cit.*, Vol. II, p. 163.
[151] Duchesne, *Les Missions Chrétiennes au Sud de l'Empire Romain*, pp. 81, 82. Yet whatever their racial origin, the great majority of the bishops had Latin names. See the lists in J. Mesnage, *L'Afrique Chrétienne. Evêchés et Ruines Antiques.*

At the close of the fourth century the majority of the Senators seem to have been pagan, although the wives and daughters of several of them had embraced Christianity.[152]

The outstanding figure of this late blooming of paganism was Quintus Aurelius Symmachus, who died in 410.[153] From a family whose members had been prominent in public affairs for a century or so, a notable orator, to him Roman dignity was inseparable from the old Roman gods. Attalus, whom Alaric and his Goths for a brief time set up as Emperor, although baptized as an Arian,[154] favoured the divination and the religious ceremonies of the old Republic.[155] Not until 416 were non-Christians formally excluded from office.[156]

However, even in the fourth century Romans of prominence were entering the Church and, apparently, some of them took the step from a genuine belief in the truth of Christianity. Thus we hear of a distinguished teacher, Victorinus, the translator into Latin of some of the writings of the Neoplatonists, and to whom had been accorded the honour of a statue in the Forum, who after careful study, much hesitation, and a growing conviction, was publicly admitted to the Church.[157] The occupation of the city by the Goths seems to have dealt the final blow to Roman paganism, perhaps because so many of the aristocratic families who were its chief support fled to Africa and Palestine.[158] The temples were closed, but at least a few were allowed to stand, and not until the sixth and seventh centuries were some of them transformed into churches. Among the last traces of the old cults were a few of the festivities. Although shorn of its too blatantly pagan features, the Lupercalia survived until almost the close of the fifth century.[159]

In parts of Italy outside of Rome, the ancient religions were even more persistent. In the fifth century the villagers of Etruria were still celebrating in the spring the rites of Osiris, and Tuscan sorcerers continued to exercise their arts.[160] In the fourth century Christianity spread rapidly in North Italy, and in 396 Ambrose hints at many churches, all but one of them supplied with

---

[152] Dill, *Roman Society in the Last Century of the Western Empire*, pp. 4, 5.

[153] Dill, *op. cit.*, pp. 16-22. The standard edition of the works of Symmachus is O. Seeck, *Q. Aurelii Summachi quae Supersunt* (Berlin, 1883), in *Monumenta Germaniae Historica*, Vol. VI.

[154] Sozomen, *Eccles. Hist.*, Book IX, Chaps. 8, 9.

[155] *Ibid.*; Dill, *op. cit.*, pp. 25, 26.

[156] Dill, *op. cit.*, pp. 25, 26.

[157] Augustine, *Confessions*, Book VIII, Chap. 2; Labriolle, *La Réaction Païenne*, pp. 360, 361.

[158] Schultze, *op. cit.*, Vol. II, pp. 169-176.

[159] Duchesne, *Early History of the Christian Church*, Vol. III, pp. 451-456; Schultze, *op. cit.*, Vol. I, p. 415; Dill, *op. cit.*, p. 74.

[160] Dill, *op. cit.*, pp. 4, 5.

clergy.[161] Yet in the middle of the fifth century the old gods were honoured in Turin by numbers of the educated, and paganism prevailed in the surrounding districts.[162] In Ravenna, in spite of the fact that there was the seat of the imperial residence, a fairly large proportion of the population seems to have remained attached to the traditional deities.[163] In 397 three of the clergy were sent to win to Christianity mountaineers in the Trentine region and were killed by those whom they wished to serve.[164] At the very end of the period which we have regarded as that of the conversion of the Roman world, Benedict of Nursia found on Monte Casino a temple to Apollo with a statue and altar at which offerings were still made.[165] Even at the close of the sixth century paganism survived in Sicily[166] and Sardinia[167] and missionary work was in progress in Corsica.[168] In the seventh century we read of missionary labours among non-Christians in the mountains between Genoa and Milan.[169]

In Spain, too, paganism died slowly. In the last decade of the fourth century the old faiths retained sufficient prestige to attract to their rites Christians who had foresworn them.[170] Near the close of the following century the acts of an ecclesiastical council at Toledo show idolatry to be deeply entrenched in Spain and Southern Gaul. While some of this may have been an importation of the Germanic invaders, part of it apparently was a survival from Roman days.[171]

However, by the time of the barbarian invasions, Christianity had been adopted by a sufficient proportion of the population to make the Church the chief refuge and bulwark of the Roman tradition. Here as elsewhere, in its learning and art it perpetuated the Roman provincial culture. Thereby it not only served civilization, but augmented its own prestige.[172]

---

[161] Ambrose, *Ep.* i, 63 (in Migne, *Pat. Lat.,* Vol. XVI, Col. 1189) ; Robinson, *The Conversion of Europe,* p. 212.

[162] Maximus Taurin, *Contra Paganos* (in Migne, *Pat. Lat.,* Vol. LVII, Col. 781).

[163] Schultze, *Geschichte des Untergangs des griechisch-römischen Heidentums,* Vol. II, p. 186.

[164] Letters of Bishop Vigilius of Trent to Simplician of Milan and John Chrysostom, in Migne, *Pat. Lat.,* Vol. XIII, Cols. 549-558; Duchesne, *op. cit.,* Vol. II, p. 511. See also Hahn, *Geschickte der katholischen Missionen,* Vol. I, p. 235.

[165] Schultze, *op. cit.,* Vol. II, p. 184.

[166] Gregory Mag., *Epist.,* Book III, 62 (in Migne, *Pat. Lat.,* Vol. LXXVII, Col. 659) ; Schultze, *op. cit.,* Vol. II, p. 167.

[167] Gregory Mag., *Epist.* IV, 24, 25, 26 (in Migne, *Pat. Lat.,* Vol. LXXVII, Cols. 693-595) ; Schultze, *op. cit.,* Vol. I, pp. 425-428.

[168] Gregory Mag., *Epist.* VIII, 1 (in Migne, *Pat. Lat.,* Vol. LXXVII, Cols. 903-905) ; Schultze, *op. cit.,* Vol. I, pp. 425-428.

[169] Robinson, *op. cit.,* pp. 221, 222.

[170] Letter of Siricius, Bishop of Rome, to Himerius of Terraco (in Migne, *Pat. Lat.,* Vol. XIII, Col. 1136) ; Schultze, *op. cit.,* Vol. II, p. 137.

[171] Schultze, *op. cit.,* Vol. II, p. 145.

[172] Schultze, *op. cit.,* Vol. II, p. 142.

As in North Africa, Italy, and a part of Gaul, so in Spain some of the invaders, while Christian, were Arian and made difficulty for the Catholic Roman provincials. The dominant invading nation, the Visigoths, were ardently Arian. They esteemed that branch of the Christian faith the national religion of the Goths and endeavoured to win to it such others of the Germanic peoples as had embraced Catholicism, notably the Suevi and the Burgundians.[173] The Suevi had invaded the Iberian Peninsula early in the fifth century and had established themselves in what is now the north and north-western part of Spain, chiefly in Galicia.[174] Before the middle of that century a number of them, including their chief ruler, had become Catholic Christians.[175] In the third quarter of the fifth century they went over to Arianism, and not until the second half of the sixth century were they brought back to the Catholic fold.[176] Eventually the Visigoths themselves were persuaded to become Catholics, but this was not until after the fifth century. By the year 500, then, Christianity was dominant in the Iberian Peninsula, but it was divided into two camps by a gulf which was at once ethnic and doctrinal. The racial and religious fusion of the erstwhile Roman provincials and their Teutonic overlords was not to be achieved for several generations.

North of the Pyrenees and the Alps, in the present France, Switzerland, Southern Germany, and Austria, Christianity, as we have seen, had obtained no very extensive acceptance before Constantine. It was found in some of the cities of Southern and Central Gaul and in a few of the cities on the Rhine.[177] Apparently, however, it had not spread into the rural districts and even in the towns Christians seem to have been small minorities. In the fourth century, as in most of the Empire, Christianity made rapid progress. In the cities it became dominant and some of the episcopal sees were occupied by scions of the Latinized Gallo-Roman aristocracy.[178] Prominent members of the lettered upper classes came over to the Church. For instance, the conversion of Paulinus, the outstanding Aquitanian noble of his time, formerly consul and governor, created a profound sensation. His adoption of Christianity was no merely nominal change, for he gave up his wealth and the literary pursuits to which

---

[173] Leclercq, L'Éspagne Chrétienne, pp. 231-234.

[174] Leclercq, op. cit., pp. 214-230.

[175] Duchesne, Early History of the Christian Church, Vol. III, p. 405. A source of information for the Suevi of which Duchesne speaks is a chronicle of Hydatius, Bishop of Aquæ Flaviæ, on the border of the present Galicia, who lived during part of the occupation of that region by the Suevi.

[176] Leclercq, op. cit., pp. 230, 246-249.

[177] Hauck, Kirchengeschichte Deutschlands, Vol. I, pp. 5-41; Harnack, The Mission and Expansion of Christianity, Vol. II, pp. 260-272.

[178] Besse, Les Moines de l'Ancienne France, p. 1.

he had been trained, and devoted himself to the preparation of his soul for the judgment.[179] Christianity also penetrated the rural districts, although there its progress was much slower than in the towns.

Here, as elsewhere, we know only a few of the more prominent of the agents of the spread of the faith and merely catch occasional glimpses of the process by which it was accomplished. Probably the most famous of those who propagated Christianity in Gaul in the fourth century was Martin of Tours. Born about 316 or 317, the son of pagan parents, as a boy Martin is said to have become a catechumen. His father was a military officer and under the rule which made that occupation hereditary, in his teens Martin entered the army. For three years before his baptism he bore arms, and it was while serving in Northern Gaul that the incident is said to have occurred, later to become famous, in which on a cold winter day he divided his cloak with a beggar, and the following night dreamed that he saw Christ clothed with the half which he had given away and saying that it was he to whom Martin had been generous. While still young, Martin resigned from the army and attached himself to Bishop Hilary of Poitiers, who won fame by championing the cause of Nicene orthodoxy against the Arians. Martin made an extended journey in an attempt to win his parents to his new faith, but succeeded only with his mother. He ardently embraced monasticism, then a comparatively new movement, and is credited with introducing it and becoming its first great exponent in Gaul. While in middle life, at the insistence of the populace, Martin became Bishop of Tours and held that post for between two and three decades, until his death, near the close of the fourth century.

As bishop Martin was an active missionary, especially in his own diocese. In this he was in accord with the imperial policy of Gratian and Theodosius and was merely paralleling, although possibly more zealously than most, what many other bishops were doing in their domains. At the time of his accession to the see, Christianity appears to have been restricted chiefly to the city of Tours, then probably a place of only a very few thousand inhabitants. The surrounding countryside seems to have been pagan. Martin led his monks in preaching, in destroying temples, and in baptizing. As a rule he built on the site of a non-Christian fane a Christian church or monastery. Possibly back of this was the belief that the gods were not imaginary, but real demonic powers which must be exorcized by the erection of the cross.[180] In the work of conversion Martin was aided by the popular belief that miracles had been wrought by him or through him. His standard biography, by Sulpicius Severus, a

[179] Dill, *Roman Society in the Last Century of the Western Empire*, p. 396.
[180] Babut, *Saint Martin de Tours*, pp. 218, 219.

younger contemporary admirer, abounds in stories of the marvellous. Martin obviously made a profound impression upon those who knew him, not by his learning, for in that his attainments were meagre, but by his energy, his courage, his unfailing poise and good cheer, a character which seemed to those of his age that of an ideal Christian,[181] and probably also by the fact that he was credited with introducing monasticism to Gaul. His reputation increased with time, and for centuries his cult was widespread. Churches and chapels bearing his name were numerous and in several lands, and the biography by Sulpicius Severus quickly achieved a wide circulation.[182]

Although the most famous, Martin of Tours, as has been suggested, was only one of a number of bishops to whom the conversion of Gaul is largely indebted. For instance, Victricius, a friend of Martin, and, like him, from the army, as Bishop of Rouen laboured to win to the faith all those of his diocese and established Christian outposts in regions not far from the present Flanders.[183] Whether by the end of the fourth century Gaul was fully divided into dioceses we do not know. If it was, presumably only part of the sees were filled and the task of many bishops must have been chiefly missionary.[184]

The extension of conversion into the rural areas was probably very fortunate for the Church. In the barbarian invasions of the fifth century the cities suffered severely, and had Christianity been confined to them, as it seems chiefly to have been earlier, it would have fared badly. As it was, this rooting in the countryside helped it to withstand the shock.[185] The Romanization of the peasant population and the adoption of Latin as the vernacular seem to have gone hand in hand with conversion to Christianity. Christianity became identified with the Romanized life of the cities and to give up the Celtic gods for the urban faith apparently meant abandoning the associated Celtic tongue and

---

[181] Sulpicius Severus said of him: "No one ever saw him angry, or annoyed, or mournful, or laughing. He was always the same and presented to every one a joy of countenance and manner which seemed to those who saw it beyond the nature of man. Nothing was in his mouth except Christ, nothing in his heart but piety, peace, and pity."—*Sulpicii Severi Vita S. Martini*, 27, 1.

[182] Among the accounts of Martin, and the sources of the above sketch, are *Sulpicii Severi Vita Sancti Martini*, in *Corpus Scriptorum Ecclesiasticorum*, Vol. I, pp. 109-141; Besse, *Les Moines de l'Ancienne France*, pp. 2ff.; Babut, *Saint Martin de Tours*; Foley, *The Greatest Saint of France*; Lecoy de la Marche, *Saint Martin*; Duchesne, *op. cit.*, Vol. II, pp. 416-418; Holmes, *The Origin and Development of the Christian Church in Gaul*, pp. 197-216. A chapter on the churches dedicated to Martin is in Lecoy de la Marche, *op. cit.*, pp. 499-594.

[183] Duchesne, *op. cit.*, Vol. III, pp. 116, 117.

[184] Holmes, *op. cit.*, p. 216.

[185] Schubert, *Geschichte der christlichen Kirche im Frühmittelalter*, p. 42.

adopting Latin, even though in vulgarized form, and so becoming Roman.[186] In the Rhineland, however, outside the cities the population seems to have been largely German and to have clung more tenaciously to its native tongue and so to its older customs and religions.[187]

Early in the fifth century came the Germanic invasions, bringing great loss of life and havoc to much of the existing civilization. In the middle of the century Attila and his Huns swept through, leaving destruction in their wake. Late in the century the Franks established a kingdom in the North. The invaders, although most of them were non-Christian, did not seek to persecute Christianity as such. The ancestral religion of the Germanic peoples had been greatly weakened or quite abandoned before they entered the Roman domains.[188] Prolonged contact with the Romans had led them to adopt many features of the civilization for which they had that mixture of admiration and contempt with which barbarians have usually regarded the cultures they have overrun. Some had been affected by the pre-Christian cults of the Empire and others had nominally accepted Christianity. They did not deliberately seek to destroy Roman culture but wished, in their rough fashion, to appropriate such of its wealth and pleasures as appealed to their untutored tastes. Yet the suffering, disorder, and exploitation of the provincial population brought by the invasions were accompanied by the weakening, and in some places the disappearance, of the Church. Toward the end of the fifth century, for instance, Roman culture, and with it Christianity, were largely erased in the region south of the Upper Danube, in what are now parts of Bavaria, Austria, and Switzerland. This was a serious loss, for the region had become predominantly Christian.[189] Through much of the territory south of the Rhine and the Upper Danube and north of the Alps and the Pyrenees, indeed, a recrudescence of paganism seems to have occurred. Part of this was of the older native cults and part that imported by the conquerors. Probably, however, the revived paganism was not highly organized, but fell within the classification of superstition and magic. The pre-Christian faiths had been too badly demoralized and the disorder of the times was too marked to allow elaborate cults to develop. The invaders made no effort to obtain homage for their hereditary gods.[190] Yet it is not surprising that, in the brigandage and anarchy of the period, many Christian altars were abandoned and church services became less frequent.[191]

[186] Hauck, *Kirchengeschichte Deutschlands,* Vol. I, pp. 5-41.
[187] *Ibid.*
[188] *Ibid.*
[189] Hauck, *Kirchengeschichte Deutschlands,* Vol. I, pp. 333-338.
[190] Duchesne, *Fastes Episcopaux de l'Ancienne Gaule,* Vol. III, p. 11.
[191] Dill, *Roman Society in the Last Century of the Western Empire,* pp. 346-382.

In the invasions themselves consecrated virgins were violated and some of the bishops fled.[192]

In most of the land, however, Christianity was not wiped out. Although some of the bishops and clergy fled, many remained by their posts. We hear of more than one bishop who was a tower of strength in protecting his flock and who won the respect of the barbarian overlords. Thus Lupus, of the educated provincial aristocracy, and who, a devout man, became Bishop of Troyes, made so profound an impression on Attila that the latter wished his assistance in his prayers.[193] Apollinaris Sidonius, well educated in the learning affected by the Gallo-Roman aristocracy and son-in-law of Avitus, who for a brief time in the fifth century was proclaimed as Emperor in the West, in 471 was made Bishop of Clermont and in that post laboured to obtain from the Goths protection for his flock.[194] When, toward the close of the fifth century, the collapse of Roman power came in what is now part of Austria, the Tyrol, and South-eastern Bavaria, a most remarkable Christian ascetic, Severinus, did much to encourage the dismayed and impoverished Christian provincials and to soften the rigours of the conquest. He seems not to have been a native of the region, but to have come, no one knew whence, in the hour of need. He heartened the Roman forces to resist the plunderers, but induced them to treat their captives with mercy. He advised in the defence of one of the towns. He had influence with some of the barbarian princes and exerted it in behalf of the Christian population. He stirred up the Christians to give for the relief of the impoverished.[195]

We learn, too, of conversions during these troubled decades. Thus we hear of a bishop in the southern part of Aquitaine who baptized many pagans and destroyed at least one temple.[196] About the middle of the fifth century a synod which met at Arles regarded it as a neglect of duty if any bishop had not stamped out the worship of idols in his territory, and decreed penalties for a landowner who permitted it on his lands. This seems to indicate that the territory covered by the synod was regarded as normally Christian and that pagans were looked upon as an anomalous minority.[197] Certainly, by the end of

---

[192] Holmes, op. cit., pp. 381-387. Holmes cites as a contemporary description a poem by Prosper of Aquitaine, given in Migne, Pat. Lat., Vol. LI, Col. 618.

[193] Vita Sancti Lupi Episcopi in Script. rer. Merov., Vol. III, p. 121, in Monumenta Germaniæ Historica; Holmes, op. cit., pp. 472-480.

[194] Dill, op. cit., pp. 346-382; Holmes, op. cit., pp. 409-442.

[195] The standard life of Severinus is by Eugippius, one of his companions. This is to be found in Migne, Pat. Lat., Vol. LXII, Cols. 1167-1200. An English translation is by G. W. Robinson. Brief summaries are in Robinson, The Conversion of Europe, pp. 286-291, and Hauck, op. cit., Vol. I, pp. 337-340.

[196] Schultze, Geschichte des Untergangs des griechisch-römischen Heidentums, Vol. II, p. 109.

[197] Hauck, op. cit., Vol. I, p. 38.

the fifth century nearly every important city in Gaul was the seat of a bishop.[198]

Monks shared in the work of conversion. Of the missionary activities of the earliest leading exponent of that movement in Gaul, Martin of Tours, we have just spoken. Others, among them some of the companions of Martin, had a part. However, in the fourth and fifth centuries monks occupied no such outstanding rôle in spreading the faith in the West as they did in the succeeding era. Monasticism was comparatively new and at the outset often met with opposition from the secular clergy.[199] Repeatedly, too, the monks were more spectators of the ruin brought by the invasions than apostles to the invaders and the victims.[200] Yet it was from some of the monasteries that new currents were to issue which did much to perpetuate Christianity through the years of turmoil. Future monastic and ecclesiastical life in Gaul and the West was deeply indebted, for instance, to communities established on islands off Cannes by monks who there sought refuge from the invasions.[201] From one of these, the monastery of Lerins, founded about 410 by Honoratus, of aristocratic lineage, came many bishops who helped to give stability to the Church in Gaul in these troubled centuries. Honoratus himself and his biographer, Hilary, became successively Bishops of Arles.[202]

The conversion of the barbarians had commenced before the invasions of the fifth century. To those beginnings we will turn a little later. As we have repeatedly noted, when they first established their rule within the Empire, many of the Goths were already Christians of the Arian type. It was, therefore, a Christian kingdom, although Arian, which the Visigoths set up in Southern Gaul in the fifth century. The Burgundians, too, became Christian, but at first were Catholics. In the first quarter of the fifth century numbers of the Burgundians moved south of the Rhine into Roman territory. The Emperor Honorius gave official recognition to what he could not remedy and permitted the invaders to remain. Here the Burgundians found a population which was already at least partly Christian and Catholic. They accepted the faith, apparently much as they took over other features of the culture of those among whom they had moved.[203] Presumably they had no desire to overthrow Roman culture, but sought to adjust themselves to it. Christianization was part of the process of voluntary assimilation. For many generations barbarians had been

---

[198] Schultze, op. cit., Vol. II, p. 113.
[199] Oulton, in Phillips, A History of the Church of Ireland, Vol. I, pp. 20-26.
[200] Besse, Les Moines de l'Ancienne France, p. 119.
[201] Oulton, in Phillips, op. cit., Vol. I, pp. 20-26.
[202] Montalembert, The Monks of the West, Vol. I, pp. 464-479.
[203] Hauck, Kirchengeschichte Deutschlands, Vol. I, pp. 90-92, citing Orosius VII, 32, 12ff., who wrote in 417-418.

enrolled in the Roman armies. In the later years of the Empire, indeed, the legions were largely recruited from these peoples. In taking service under the Roman standards, they not unnaturally willingly assumed something of the *mores* of the Empire. Now that the Empire had become officially Christian, what was more reasonable than that the barbarian settlers, whether or not formally in the army, should welcome entrance into the Church? A few years later, those Burgundians who remained on the right bank of the Rhine asked baptism of a bishop. The reputed motive was the desire for the aid of the God of the Romans against the Huns. The bishop, after giving them a brief course of instruction in some of the rudiments of Christianity, granted their request. The Burgundians are said to have defeated overwhelmingly a much larger force of the Huns and, confirmed in the faith by this proof of the superiority of their new God, to have become zealous Christians.[204] They thus were the first German Catholic tribe.[205] Later in the century the Burgundians established themselves in the Rhone Valley. There, presumably under the influence of the Visigoths, they turned Arian.[206] Still later, partly through contact with the more powerful Franks, they once more became Catholic.[207]

Because of its importance for the spread of Christianity in Western Europe, far more significant than the conversion of the Burgundians was that of the Franks. For many years some of the Franks had been in contact with the Romans. Numbers of them had seen service under the Roman state, several of them rising to high position. Often these had become Romanized and, as a corollary, had professed Christianity.[208] In the fifth century a section of the Franks mastered part of Northern Gaul and of the lower portion of the Rhine Valley. The first outstanding head of this incipient state, Childeric, although pagan, was on fairly friendly terms with such of the Roman provincials, now mostly Christian, as were his subjects. His son Clovis, who followed him in 481, was the real creator of the Frankish kingdom. Clovis inherited a small area and the overlordship of one branch of his people, the Salian Franks. By skill and energy in war, diplomacy, and administration he made himself master of much of Gaul and laid the foundations of what was to become the

---

[204] Socrates, *Ecclesiastical History*, Book VII, Chap. 30.

[205] Hauck, *op. cit.*, Vol. I, p. 94.

[206] Robinson, *The Conversion of Europe*, p. 188; Holmes, *The Origin and Development of the Christian Church in Gaul*, p. 323, citing letter of Sidonius to Bishop Patiens of Lyons, *Ep.* vi, 12.

[207] Schmidlin, *Katholische Missionsgeschichte*, p. 115; Moreau in Descamps, *Histoire Générale Comparée des Missions*, pp. 168, 169, citing an epitaph of one of the princesses who helped to prepare the Burgundian court for the change, in *Monumenta Germaniæ Historica, Auctores antiquissimi*, Vol. VI, p. 185.

[208] Hauck, *op. cit.*, Vol. I, pp. 98-102.

most important of those kingdoms which in the West succeeded the Roman Empire.

What motives led Clovis to the baptismal font we do not know. Perhaps he himself was not aware of them all. Some of the influences we can readily guess. As he extended his domains into Gaul, Clovis found himself and his warriors a small ruling minority in a region where the majority were Christians and some of the outstanding leaders Christian bishops. It was the part of prudence to keep on friendly terms with both people and clergy. Even before his conversion he was cordial to some of the bishops and showed an inclination to respect the Church. His wife was a Burgundian princess, but a Catholic, not an Arian Christian. He offered no objection to her desire for the baptism of their first-born son. The early death of the infant might have been regarded as an indication of either the futility or the unwisdom of this act, and Clovis is said to have remarked that had the child been called by the name of his gods he would have lived. Yet he permitted the baptism of the second child. The Arians sought to win him to their branch of the faith. This step might have seemed the natural one if he were to come over to Christianity at all, for the rulers of the other Teutonic states were of that persuasion. Clovis rejected it, however, perhaps because he shrewdly distrusted the breach which it might make between him and his Catholic subjects. If one reason for becoming a Christian was the desire to win the support of the Christian provincials, the profession of a type which their leaders abhorred would defeat his aim. The precise date of his baptism is somewhat uncertain, but the one most generally favoured is December 25, 496.[209] Clovis used no force to induce the Franks to conform to his example, but a large number of his warriors quickly followed him and it was almost inevitable that in time the others would do so.

Baptism seems to have wrought little if any change in the habits or character of Clovis. Probably, too, its importance can readily be exaggerated. The conquering Franks, in most regions a minority and less civilized than their subjects, would almost certainly in time have adopted the faith along with the culture of the majority. That, at least, was the fate of all other Teutonic peoples who settled within the Empire. Unlike the conquering Arabs two centuries later, they brought with them no religion which could offer effective resistance to

[209] On the conversion of Clovis and the Franks, pertinent sources are a letter of Bishop Nicetius (probably our earliest account written ante A.D. 568?), in *Monumenta Germaniæ Historica, Epistolarum,* Vol. III, p. 122, and (a little later in the sixth century) Gregory of Tours, *Historia Francorum,* Book II, Chaps. 29-31 (*Monumenta Germaniæ Historica. Scriptores Rerum Merovingicarum,* Vol. I, pp. 90-93). A good summary, with reference to and analysis of the sources, is in Hauck, *op. cit.,* Vol. I, pp. 103ff. Of the many secondary accounts the one in Holmes, *op. cit.,* pp. 327, 330-333, may be noted. On the date of the baptism of Clovis, see Hauck, *op. cit.,* Vol. I, pp. 553-557.

Christianity. If Clovis had not become a Christian, his successors would almost certainly have done so. Nor, if he had espoused Arian rather than Catholic Christianity, is it probable that the West would have abandoned its orthodoxy. Certainly elsewhere the Teutonic ruling Arian minority eventually adopted the Catholicism of their subjects. In some instances the process was hastened by the example of the Catholic Franks, but the eventual outcome seems never to have been greatly in doubt. If Clovis had become an Arian, would the Frankish state, thus ecclesiastically divided, have been as powerful as it became? We cannot know.

Whether the espousal of Nicene (Catholic) Christianity by Clovis was as important as is sometimes thought may, then, be debated. Beyond question, however, is the significance of the emergence of a powerful, Catholic Frankish monarchy. With the Frankish state, as we shall see in a later period, was to be inextricably associated the spread of Christianity through much of those portions of Northern and Central Europe to which the Roman Empire had not extended or in which Roman Christian culture had been obliterated by the invasions. The conversion of the Franks, indeed, is an important landmark in our story. More than any other event it may be used to register the close of the first main period in the expansion of Christianity and the beginning of another. It was the single most important stage in the spread of the faith among the non-Roman peoples in the north-western part of the continent of Europe.

On the island of Great Britain, whose chalk cliffs were so near the shores of Gaul, the course of Christianity seems both to have resembled that on the Continent and to have differed from it. Our knowledge of it is very imperfect. Archæological remains of pre-Anglo-Saxon Christianity in Britain are very slight[210] and literary records tantalizingly fragmentary. We know that by the fourth century much of the South and East of Britain was fairly well Romanized, and that the language of the towns was probably Latin. Contacts with the Roman world were through Gaul. The inference seems fair, therefore, that Christianity in Britain came from Gaul, centred first in the towns among the Latin-speaking part of the population, originally had few members among the wealthy, and was slightly later in coming to prominence than on the adjacent

[210] The foundations of a Christian church have been discovered at Silchester, the Roman town excavated in Hampshire.—Leclerq, *Note sur les Plus Anciens Autels Bretons* (in *Report of the Nineteenth Eucharistic Congress*, 1908, pp. 361-367). See also, for slight traces, Foord, *The Last Age of Roman Britain*, pp. 145, 146. On Christianity in Britain in the fourth and fifth centuries, see Williams, *Christianity in Early Britain*, pp. 139-331.

sections of the Continent.[211] We have the suggestion that by the close of the fourth century many of the leading families had accepted Christianity and that in some regions Christians were in the majority.[212] For this, however, the archæological proof, while real, is scanty. Probably as convincing evidence as any is the assumption by Patrick, a Briton, that Christian and Roman were identical.[213]

Shortly after the middle of the fourth century, the Church in Britain was said to be Catholic.[214] One of the most famous heretics of the West, Pelagius, is reported to have been a native of Britain.[215] While proof is lacking that his distinctive opinions originated there, the orthodox of Rome and of Gaul were alarmed at the hold which his doctrines were gaining in the island and in 429 two Gallic bishops, Germanus of Auxerre and Lupus of Troyes, were dispatched to deal with the situation.[216] Germanus is said to have preached to eager crowds in churches, at cross-roads, and in the open country. He and his colleagues also visited the forces which were attempting to hold off the invaders who, as in so much of the Empire, were then troubling civilization. Germanus, a former soldier, is reported to have been chosen commander-in-chief of the defenders and to have made it his first duty to convert and baptize thousands of the pagan soldiers thus unexpectedly placed under his influence.[217] This appears to indicate a fairly rapid spread of Christianity in the fifth century. In the latter half of the fifth century the Angles and Saxons succeeded in breaking down the resistance which had long been presented to them and began establishing themselves as permanent settlers. Themselves pagans, in the general destruction which they made of the existing order they seem to have wiped out most, if not all, of the Christianity in the eastern part of the island.[218] In the western part, to which the rule of the Teutonic invaders did not extend, the Church survived. It even grew, assisted by a fresh flow of life from its putative child, the Irish Church, of whose birth we are shortly to speak.[219] In a later chapter we shall see that when Christianity reëntered the eastern part

[211] Browne, *The Christian Church in These Islands before the Coming of Augustine*, pp. 29-35, 69; Collingwood and Myres, *Roman Britain and English Settlements*, pp. 272, 273.

[212] J. L. G. Meissner in Phillips, *A History of the Church of Ireland*, Vol. I, pp. 49-54; Collingwood and Myres, *op. cit.*, pp. 272, 273.

[213] That at least seems to be a legitimate inference from Patrick's *Letter.*

[214] Theodoret, *Eccles. Hist.*, Book IV, Chap. 3.

[215] Browne, *op. cit.*, pp. 79ff.; Foord, *op. cit.*, pp. 145, 146.

[216] Foord, *op. cit.*, p. 154. The source used is a biography of Germanus by his pupil Constantius, written about fifty years after the visit.

[217] Foord, *op. cit.*, p. 154; Gougaud, *Christianity in Celtic Lands*, p. 21.

[218] Leclercq, *Note sur les Plus Anciens Autels Bretons.*

[219] *Ibid.*; Browne, *op. cit.*, p. 137.

of the island it was not from the descendants of the Roman provincials of Britain, but from the Continent, Ireland, and the North.

This, then, completes our survey of the spread of Christianity within the Roman Empire. The story is complicated by the collapse, in the fifth century, of the structure of government in several of the provinces in Africa and the West. In many areas the inroads of pagan barbarians weakened the Church. In some regions they wiped out Roman society and with it Christianity. By the end of the fifth century, however, Christianity had become the faith of the vast majority of the population of the Empire. Even in most of those provinces which had been wrested from the imperial sway it remained strong. The Church, only two centuries before attacked as a menace to Roman culture, had in great areas now become its chief bulwark and was in turn reënforced by it. Even before the end of the fifth century the process of assimilation had commenced, and the invaders were beginning to accept the faith of their subjects. Here and there the older pagan cults survived. Usually, however, they lived on only in degenerate forms and in the rural districts. Those of the aristocracy who long proudly held to the traditional religions either died without transmitting their faith to their children, were dispossessed by the turmoil of the times, or submitted to baptism. Later we shall see how much of paganism persisted, thinly disguised by baptism and by Christian names and dress. Officially, however, it was dead. In the first two or three centuries of its spread, Christianity, as we have seen, has repeatedly been said to have been confined mainly to the lower classes in the cities and to have had its chief strength in the urban proletariat. That the Church was predominantly urban is indubitable. Whether it drew disproportionately from the humble and unlettered or contained a cross section of the city population is less clear. Before the end of the fifth century, however, it had unquestionably captured not only the cities, but the landed as well as the urban aristocracy. It was among the rural peasant stock that its victorious course was most retarded. By the end of the fifth century even here its triumph was nominally nearly complete.

It was not only within the area which the Roman Empire had once compassed that Christianity won converts. Even before the fourth century it had, as we have seen, moved outside these boundaries. In the fourth and fifth centuries it continued that spread. Upon this expansion the progressive conversion of the Empire worked important modifications.

Now began the wholesale entrance into the Church of the northern barbarians whose incursions were at once a symptom and a cause of collapse of Roman rule in so many of the provinces. Many decades before Constantine the movement of these peoples into the Empire had started. As we have suggested, among them the legions had long found their chief supplies of recruits. With the Roman livery the soldiers tended to take over the culture of the Empire. Many of the Emperors of the third and fourth centuries were from barbarian stocks. As the Empire became officially Christian, the immigrants generally adopted the faith along with the culture of which it now appeared an integral part. To be sure, before Constantine the army had been a stronghold of paganism, but when the Emperors became Christian the legions seem to have followed them into the Church. Many of the leaders of the invaders who broke the Roman rule were glad to accept titles from the regime which they were overthrowing and they and their followers took over much of the culture which their inroads weakened. Since this culture and Christianity were now wedded, in adopting the one they professed the other. Christian missionaries were apostles not only of religion, but of the Greek or Latin language. As so frequently in the spread of a religion, conversion was part of the process of acculturation.

It would not be in accord with the facts to see in the conversion of the barbarians an automatic development in which the activity of the Church and of missionaries did nothing to alter the outcome. In many instances the initiative of missionaries hastened the process. Always it modified the result.

In the conversion of the northern barbarians a movement began whose completion did not come until the fourteenth century. The fourth century saw its inception on a large scale and in it the year 500 has no significance. Even the baptism of Clovis in 496, while marking a very important stage, is, after all, only a major step in an advance which had already begun. Here, therefore, is an instance of the impossibility of making any one date serve as a division point for all the geographic and racial channels through which Christianity has spread.

The first of the northern peoples to adopt Christianity in large numbers were the Goths. These we first hear of in the earliest Christian century as dwelling in the valley of the Vistula. In the third century they laid waste Mœsia, south of the Danube, and ravaged the coasts of Asia Minor and Greece.[220] It was probably through Christian captives made in the third century that Christianity was introduced to them. These captives are said to have included some priests who won many of their masters to their faith.[221] When, in the third century, Dacia, north of the Danube, was abandoned by the Empire, the Goths moved into it (they had, indeed, already been traversing it), and were thus brought into even closer contact with Mediterranean culture. The conversion of the

[220] Hodgkin, *Italy and Her Invaders*, Vol. I, Part I, pp. 32-69.
[221] Sozomen, *Eccles. Hist.*, Book II, Chap. 6.

Goths was accomplished through contact with three types of Christianity—Catholic, Audian, and Arian. The three did not arrive in any chronological sequence, and as in so many other phases of our story most of the details of their coming are lost in the mists of time.

Catholicism seems to have been the first of the three to reach the Goths. As we have seen, there were Christians among the Goths before the Athanasian-Arian division, the converts of captives and of refugees from persecutions in the Empire.[222] A Gothic bishop appears to have attended the Council of Nicæa where that issue was fought out.[223] We are also informed that in the time of Constantine some of the Goths, defeated by the Emperor, accepted the faith by which they believed the victor had been defended[224]—a statement which, if a valid report of the motive, seems to fit in with what we know to have been an impelling reason for the adoption of a religion on many another occasion. Augustine speaks of a persecution of Gothic Catholics which probably dates from the second half of the fourth century.[225] Late in the fourth and early in the fifth century the great John Chrysostom was zealous in efforts to win converts from among the Goths. While Bishop of Constantinople he was actively interested in them,[226] and sent them a bishop.[227] Then in his exile he dreamed of raising up from the Goths missionaries and a clergy of their own.[228]

The Audians took their name from Audius, a bishop of great purity of life but accused of vagaries of doctrine, who led a movement in Syria which aroused opposition among many of his fellow bishops. Banished, at their instance, to Scythia, he was active in giving the Gospel as he understood it to non-Christians outside the Empire. He himself seems to have won many among the Goths and to have developed an ecclesiastical organization, with monasteries and bishops.[229] In the middle of the fourth century, therefore, the Audians appear to have been fairly strong among the Goths, but about A.D 370

[222] Scott, *Ulfilas, Apostle of the Goths*, pp. 21, 25.

[223] Socrates, *Eccles. Hist.*, Book II, Chap. 41. It is conjectured that this bishop was near the Black Sea and the Goths in this region are said to have remained Catholic after the majority of their people became Arians.—Zeiller, *Les Origines Chrétiennes dans les Provinces Danubiennes de l'Empire Romain*, pp. 407-417.

[224] Socrates, *Eccles. Hist.*, Book I, Chap. 18.

[225] Augustine, *City of God*, Book XVIII, Chap. 52. He says that his information came from Gothic Catholics who were boys at the time of the persecution.

[226] This at least is the inference of Scott, *op. cit.*, pp. 151, 152, from Theodoret, *Eccles. Hist.*, Book V, Chaps. 28, 30. It is not clear, however, that Scott is justified in drawing the conclusions which he reaches from the passages which he cites.

[227] Chrysostom, *Ep. ad Olympiadem*, XIV, 5 (in Migne, *Pat. Græc.*, Vol. LII, Col. 618); Scott, *op. cit.*, p. 153.

[228] Hartung, in *Allgemeine Missionszeitschrift* (1894), Vol. XXI, p. 313.

[229] Theodoret, *Eccles. Hist.*, Book IV, Chap. 9; Epiphanius, *Hæres.*, LXX, 14 (in Migne, *Pat. Græc.*, Vol. XLII, Col. 371); Duchesne, *Early History of the Christian Church*, Vol. II, p. 451.

suffered severely in a persecution by pagan Goths visited indiscriminately upon all types of Gothic Christians.[230]

The great majority of Gothic Christians were Arians. Intimately connected with the spread of that type of Christianity among them is one of the most prominent figures in the roster of Christian missionaries, Ulfilas.[231] Presumably he himself was a Goth, the report that he was descended from Christian captives from Cappadocia[232] being of dubious authenticity. The date of his birth is uncertain, but the year most generally given is 311.[233] Nor do we know how he became a Christian—whether he was reared as such or adopted the faith in his young manhood. The usual conjecture is that he came into the Church during a protracted stay in Constantinople. Probably because that was then the prevailing form of Christianity in court circles, it was a mild form of Arianism which he professed.[234] Presumably, too, it was while in the capital that he acquired his knowledge of Greek and Latin. At the age of thirty he was consecrated bishop of "the Christians in Gothia" and laboured among his people north of the Danube. After seven years, to gain for his flock surcease from persecution, he sought and obtained permission to move them into Roman territory, in Mœsia, south of the Danube. Here he spent more than thirty years. Then, summoned by the Emperor, apparently for some sort of ecclesiastical council, he died in Constantinople, probably near the end of 380

[230] Scott, op. cit., p. 76.

[231] An account, with brief biographical notes, by a contemporary and disciple, Auxentius, is in Waitz, who discovered it, Über das Leben und die Lehre des Ulfila. Other early accounts are in Philostorgius, Eccles. Hist., Book II, Chap. 5; Socrates, Eccles. Hist., Book IV, Chap. 33; Sozomen, Eccles. Hist., Book VI, Chap. 37. Comparatively recent accounts are Waitz, op. cit., Bessell, Ueber das Leben des Ulfilas und die Bekehrung der Gothen zum Christentum, and Scott, op. cit. An excellent brief summary is by C. H. Robinson in The East and the West, Vol. XIV, pp. 328-343. See also Zeiller, op. cit., pp. 440-477.

[232] So Philostorgius, Eccles. Hist., Book II, Chap. 5.

[233] Waitz, op. cit., p. 35, thinks it was 318, but Bessell, op. cit., p. 53, and Scott, op. cit., p. 48, say 311.

[234] A statement of his faith is in the life by Auxentius, given by Waitz, op. cit. Sozomen, Eccles. Hist., Book VI, Chap. 37, says that originally Ulfilas held no views at variance with those of the Nicene party and only later, to obtain imperial support, entered into communion with the Arians. Theodoret, Eccles. Hist., Book IV, Chap. 33, while not saying that Ulfilas was originally a Catholic, declares that it was he who won the Goths to Arianism, on the representation that the difference between Catholicism and Arianism was one of personal rivalry and not of doctrine. This may possibly reflect the frame of mind of Ulfilas, especially if he were a practical man of deep personal piety. Ulfilas seems to have been consecrated bishop by the Arians, which would appear to show that as early as the age of thirty he was an Arian, and that it was in this type of Christianity that he originally reared his converts.—Scott, op. cit., pp. 46, 47, 98, 99. In his mildly Arian statement of faith, moreover, Ulfilas declares that he "always so believed."—Waitz, op. cit., p. 21.

or early in 381.[235] What may have been his most noteworthy achievement was his translation of a large part of the Bible into the Gothic tongue. For this purpose he is said to have devised an alphabet.[236] If that be true, we have here what is probably the first or the second instance of what has since happened for hundreds of tongues—their reduction to writing by Christian missionaries and the translation into them by that medium of a part or all of the Scriptures.[237] Portions of what seem to be this version of Ulfilas have survived.[238] The translator appears to have been careful to give as nearly as possible a word-for-word rendering from the Greek, probably with some reference to the Latin versions. Yet he also sought to observe the Gothic idiom and, as is inevitable in translations, introduced something of his own interpretation.[239]

The connexion between the labours of Ulfilas and the conversion of the major part of the Gothic nation is by no means clear, nor is it entirely certain that it existed. Within the lifetime of Ulfilas a severe persecution harassed the Gothic Christians who were not within the Empire with Ulfilas, but north of the Danube. This may have been instituted by a native chief, Athanaric, in revenge for treatment accorded him by the Christian Romans. Opposition to Athanaric was led by one Frithigern, and it seems a fair guess that the latter posed as a friend and protector of the Christians. Frithigern obtained help from the Romans and with this aid defeated Athanaric. In association with Roman support came the adoption of Christianity, the faith of the Romans, by Frithigern and at least some of his followers. Since Arianism was then professed by the imperial court, that type of Christianity was the one accepted. A little later, pressed by the Huns, Frithigern and his followers asked imperial permission to settle in Roman territory and thus put the Danube between themselves and these terrifying enemies. Presumably the ensuing migration was accompanied by the acceptance of the faith of the Empire in its court form by many of those who may until then have remained pagan. When, therefore, dissensions broke out between the immigrants and the imperial authorities, and the settlers defeated the imperial forces at the memorable battle of Adrianople, in 378, the majority of the victors were probably Christians. It is from these Christian

[235] See the *Life* by Auxentius, in Waitz, *op. cit.,* pp. 19-21. See also Scott, *op. cit.,* p. 46.

[236] Socrates, *Eccles. Hist.,* Book IV, Chap. 33; Philostorgius, *Eccles. Hist.,* Book II, Chap. 3. The Goths possessed an alphabet before the time of Ulfilas, but he seems to have devised a new one, influenced by the Greek. See a long note in Hodgkin, *Italy and Her Invaders,* Vol. I, pp. 102-111.

[237] Robinson, *The Conversion of Europe,* p. 252.

[238] See Migne, *Patrologia Latina,* Vol. XVIII, Cols. 458-870, for a text. Scott, *Ulfilas, Apostle of the Goths,* p. 129, declares, however, that it is an unproved although generally accepted assumption that we have in the surviving texts the translation of Ulfilas.

[239] Friedrickson, *The Gothic Version of the Gospels: A Study of Its Style and Textual History,* pp. 16-22. On the translation see also Scott, *op. cit.,* pp. 124-137.

Visigoths that the Ostrogoths, Gepidæ, and Vandals seem to have received the faith. This at least appears a rational piecing together of the various fragments of evidence, some of them conflicting.[240]

It has been suggested that the Goths found Arian Christianity not unlike some phases of their ancestral religion, equating the Christian God with the All-Father, for ever removed from contact with human needs, and Christ with those subordinate deities who mediated between man and the All-Father.[241] This may, indeed, help to account for the adoption of Arian rather than Catholic Christianity.

Whatever the cause, the fact that the Goths were Arian entailed important consequences. It tended to separate them from the Romans whom they conquered, for the vast majority of the latter were Catholic, especially in the West, where the Gothic and Vandal kingdoms were established. Probably it accentuated and hastened the collapse of Roman rule in the West, for had the Gothic invaders been Catholic they might have been more quickly assimilated and the distinction between their regime and that of the imperial authorities not have been so marked.[242] It is possible, on the other hand, that had the Gothic kingdoms not been weakened by this religious cleavage, they might have achieved a greater strength and longevity.

The Arianism of the Goths could not well be permanent. The invaders were in the minority and faced a fairly strong Catholic organization which held the allegiance of the majority and represented the tradition of Roman culture. It is conceivable that the Goths might have imposed their faith on their subjects. Indeed, some of their rulers attempted to do so and have gone down into history as persecutors of the Catholics. Yet, while possible, it was scarcely probable. Not until nearly the close of the sixth century did the last of the Gothic powers, the Visigothic kingdom in Spain, go over officially to the Catholic faith.[243] The eventual outcome, however, was probably never seriously in doubt.

Not all the Goths passed through the phase of Arianism. We hear of some in the present South Russia who apparently never accepted any other than the orthodox form of Christianity and who seem to have preserved for several

[240] The various accounts are analysed in Scott, *Ulfilas, Apostle of the Goths*, pp. 79-103, and an order of events suggested which is virtually that adopted in the above paragraph. Among these accounts are Theodoret, *Eccles. Hist.*, Book IV, Chap. 33; Socrates, *Eccles. Hist.*, Book IV, Chap. 33; and Sozomen, *Eccles. Hist.*, Book VI, Chap. 37. See also Zeiller, *op. cit.*, pp. 534-542.

[241] Scott, *op. cit.*, pp. 104, 105.

[242] Some of this is suggested in Hodgkin, *op. cit.*, Vol. I, pp. 92, 93.

[243] Scott, *op. cit.*, p. 217.

centuries a partially distinct, although not fully autonomous, ecclesiastical existence.[244]

In what was probably a little less than a decade after the death of Ulfilas the island of Great Britain became the native place of another distinguished missionary, Patrick.[245] In him and his associates and contemporaries the Christianity of Roman Britain and Gaul laid important foundations for the extension of the faith beyond the Roman frontiers. Patrick lived and laboured in a time when in the West Roman political power was disintegrating. His life spanned the Gothic invasion of Italy and the capture of Rome by Alaric, the earlier Teutonic conquests in Gaul, the establishment of the Gothic power in Spain, the incursions of the Vandals and the founding of their rule in North Africa, the memorable Western raid of Attila and his Huns, and the beginnings of the Anglo-Saxon power in Britain. In his days, moreover, Christianity was making great strides in the Empire, and most notably in the West. When he was born, Martin of Tours was still alive and Christianity had only recently become the faith of the majority in Gaul. Patrick, therefore, represented the vigour of that religion, which, as the familiar world into which it had been born crumbled about its ears, was not only winning the Empire but was reaching out into regions where the Roman legions had never penetrated. Impelled by deep religious conviction, he made it the task of his life to spread the faith among a people with whom hard fate had first put him in close touch. In so doing he incidentally became the channel for some other phases of the culture of the Empire. In the succeeding period the Irish Church, with the laying of whose foundations he had so much to do, was a means of perpetuating and propagating in the West both Christianity and something of Græco-Roman culture.

It is clear that Patrick first saw the light of day in Roman Britain. From

[244] Scott, op. cit., pp. 155, 156. In 547 the Goths of the Crimea are said to have asked Justinian for a bishop.—Duchesne, Early History of the Christian Church, Vol. III, p. 450, citing Tetrarites, Bull. Goth., iv, 5. See also Zeiller, op. cit., pp. 407-417.

[245] Our most reliable sources for Patrick are his own Confession and Letter (against Coroticus), the authenticity of both of which is usually acknowledged; and three brief Dicta Patricii, the Patrician authorship of the first two of which seems fairly well assured. The "Lorica," an Irish hymn ascribed to Patrick, is more open to question, as are also the canons attributed to him. A seventh-century memoir, by Bishop Tirechan, and the earliest formal biography, by Muirchu, written in the latter part of the seventh century, are both so long after Patrick's death that error and legend seem to have crept in, mixed almost inextricably with fact. Several mediæval biographies are also extant. An excellent critical description of the sources is in Bury, The Life of St. Patrick, pp. 225-287. Another description of sources and literature is in Mrs. Concannon's Saint Patrick, pp. ix-xxxiii. A list of documents from the fifth through the fifteenth century dealing with Patrick is in Stokes, The Tripartite Life of Patrick, pp. cxxix-cxxxii. In addition to the Tripartite Life, Stokes gives, pp. 269-574, the texts of a number of other documents bearing on Patrick, including the memoir by Tirechan and the life by Muirchu.

his own words we know that his father was a decurion,[246] one of the provincial landowning class upon whom the burdens of Roman taxation fell especially heavily.[247] He was born, then, to comfortable circumstances, but probably not to great wealth. He had behind him at least two generations of Christians, for he speaks of his paternal grandfather as being a presbyter, or priest, and his father a deacon.[248] Apparently he was reared in the faith, but as a boy he seems not to have taken it seriously.[249] Probably, too, if he received any education in Latin literature and rhetoric, it was very slight, for even in his old age he was sensitive over his meagre attainments in that field.[250] What part of Britain became his childhood's home has been disputed.[251] The only safe course is tentative conjecture or a confession of ignorance. A favoured date for his birth is 389, but that also is far from certain.[252] From his own pen we learn that as a lad of fifteen Patrick was guilty of some secret fault which weighed on his conscience.[253] From the same source we know that when about sixteen years of age he was carried off from his home, with many others, to Ireland.[254] Presumably his captors were of those bands of raiders from beyond the borders of the Empire who, early in the fifth century, were harassing the provinces.

In Ireland, probably as a slave, Patrick tended flocks for at least six years.[255] To the impressionable, sensitive youth, with the soul of a mystic, suddenly torn from home and comfort, the life of lonely servitude brought religious awakening and growth. The inherited faith which at best had been nominal

[246] Patrick, *Letter* against Coroticus. The text of the letter is in Migne, *Pat. Lat.*, Vol. LIII, Cols. 814-818. English translations are to be found in the works by White mentioned in footnote 248.

[247] Bury, *Life of St. Patrick*, pp. 16-20.

[248] Patrick, *Confession*. The text of the *Confession* is in Migne, *Pat. Lat.*, Vol. LIII, Cols. 801-814. English translations are by N. J. D. White, *A Translation of the Latin Writings of St. Patrick*, pp. 5-26; N. J. D. White, *The Writings of St. Patrick*, pp. 7-27; N. J. D. White, *St. Patrick, His Writings and Life*.

[249] Patrick, *Confession*.

[250] *Ibid.*; Patrick, *Letter* against Coroticus.

[251] For a discussion see Bury, *op. cit.*, pp. x, 322-325. Bury conjectures that it was near the Severn or on the Bristol Channel. Other conjectures are Dumbarton, on the Firth of Clyde, Ireland, Armoric Britain, and Glastonbury. Todd, *St. Patrick, Apostle of Ireland*, pp. 355-362; Hitchcock, *St. Patrick and His Gallic Friends*, pp. 40, 41; White, *St. Patrick, His Writings and Life*, pp. 111, 112. Stokes, *The Tripartite Life of Patrick*, p. cxxxvii, favours Dumbarton.

[252] Bury, *op. cit.*, p. 334, places it as probably in 389. Stokes, *op. cit.*, p. cxxxvii, says it it was about 373. Another date suggested is 386.—Zimmer, *Keltische Kirche*, in Herzog-Hauck, *Realencyklopädie*, 3d ed., Vol. X, p. 218.

[253] Patrick, *Confession*.

[254] *Ibid.*

[255] *Ibid.*

now became a living reality, and he filled with prayer the solitude of his days and nights.

In the night came dreams which gave him hope of seeing his homeland and sent him forth to seek a ship. The captain at first demurred but later relented and took him. Apparently the voyage landed Patrick, not in Britain, but in Gaul, and for days he and his fellows traversed what in after years he thought of as a desert—probably a region stripped of subsistence and inhabitants by the invasions of the early decades of the fifth century.[256] It may be that not until after he reached Italy (if, indeed, he was ever there) was he able to escape from these companions.[257]

For many years after Patrick's departure from Ireland it is impossible to trace the events of his life in order or with accuracy. It may be that, after wanderings in Italy and the islands of the Tyrrhene Sea, he spent several years in that monastery at Lerins,[258] off the southern coast of Gaul, whose foundations we have noted as being laid in about 410, not far from the time when he first left Ireland.[259] Eventually Patrick made his way back to Britain and rejoined his family. He hints at the joy with which he was welcomed and at the urgent request of his kindred that he remain with them.[260]

Once more came the dreams which played so large a part in directing his life, and in them a letter called "the Voice of the Irish" and a cry, presumably also from the Irish, "We beseech thee, holy youth, to come and walk with us once more." Just when Patrick returned to Ireland we do not know, whether soon or after more years of waiting, travel, and study.[261] That sometime he

[256] *Ibid.;* Bury, *op. cit.,* pp. 34, 35. It is not certain that the land was Gaul.

[257] Patrick, *Confession,* speaks of a second captivity, probably meaning at the hands of those with whom he shipped. The first of the *Dicta Patricii,* which Bury, *op. cit.,* pp. 228-231, holds to be a genuine word of Patrick, speaks of his journeying through Gaul, Italy, and the islands in the Tyrrhene Sea, but gives no way of telling when the journey or journeys were made.

[258] Bury, *op. cit.,* pp. 37-41, thinks that he was certainly at Lerins. Montgomery, *op. cit.,* p. 115, thinks it probable. White, *St. Patrick, His Writings and Life,* p. 11, regards it as fairly certain.

[259] Bury, *The Life of St. Patrick,* p. 37, thinks it clear that Patrick was at Lerins soon after his separation from the companions with whom he left Ireland. White, *St. Patrick, His Writings and Life,* pp. 11, 12, thinks it probable that Patrick studied at Lerins. A seventh-century account, by Tirechan, gives on the authority of an older bishop the information that Patrick spent thirty years at Lerins (White, *op. cit.,* p. 249. On the date of Tirechan's memoir see Bury, *op. cit.,* p. 248).

[260] Patrick, *Confession.*

[261] Patrick's *Confession* gives no clear light on the question of just when he returned to Ireland. The earliest full life, written by Muirchu more than two centuries after Patrick's death, speaks of at least thirty or forty years' interval between these visions and the landing in Ireland (Chaps. 4-7). That, however, seems very dubious, especially in light of what is said in the *Letter* about a priest (presumably Irish) whom Patrick had trained from infancy—a longer time than would have been possible had Patrick

acquired a knowledge of the Bible which made that book an integral part of his life is obvious from the frequent Scriptural quotations in the scanty words of his which have come down to us. That he went to Ireland is certain. It is also clear that at some time in his career he was consecrated bishop, but by whom or precisely when is debatable.[262] Opposition he had to face, from his fellow clergy and from armed foes. His *Confession* seems to have been written as a defence against the one and his *Letter* against Coroticus to have been evoked by the other. He felt himself to be daily in danger of violent death, robbery, or slavery. That Patrick had marked success in his mission is seen from his writings and from the numerous traditions which found embodiment in later biographies.[263] He speaks of baptizing thousands and ordaining clergy, and of travelling through many perils to regions where none before him had ever done either. Although probably not himself a monk, under his influence sons and daughters of chieftains became monks and nuns. We see him winning his way by presents to "kings" and payments to "judges," and yet refusing the gifts of devout women lest any breath of scandal should arise.[264] Not only did he have to face perils from the Irish, but from Britain came the bands of Coroticus, a ruler who inherited the Roman name and prestige. These troops, though nominally Roman and Christian, fell on some of the Irish converts of Patrick. Almost as though it were yesterday we can picture the soldiers of Coroticus attacking the newly baptized who only the day before had been garbed in the white array of neophytes, slaughtering some and carrying off others.[265] This may, moreover, be only one of many instances of a sorrowful fate overtaking Christians in the disorders of the times. That Patrick's ministry in Ireland was of long duration seems well established. He speaks, for example, of sending to seek the release of these captives a presbyter whom he had taught from infancy.[266]

Into the details of Patrick's travels in Ireland we need not enter, and we can,

---

first returned to Ireland in late middle life. For other arguments against so long a period of preparation, see Stokes, *op. cit.*, pp. cxxxvii, cxxxviii.

[262] That Patrick was a bishop in Ireland is stated clearly in the *Letter* and is implied in the *Confession*. Muirchu's *Life* says he was consecrated, late in life, by Amathorex, presumably in Gaul. Bury, *op. cit.*, p. 347, thinks this was Amator, but that Amator ordained him as deacon, not bishop, and that the consecration came later, in 432, by other hands. Hitchcock, *St. Patrick and His Gallic Friends*, p. 45, agrees that the date was "about 432," but suggests that the consecrating bishop was Germanus of Auxerre. Meissner, in Phillips, *A History of the Church of Ireland*, Vol. I, pp. 85-103, thinks that Patrick was chosen a bishop by a British synod.

[263] See especially the *Confession* and *Letter*.

[264] Patrick, *Confession*.

[265] Patrick, *Letter* (against Coroticus). On Coroticus, see Bury, *op. cit.*, pp. 188-194.

[266] Patrick, *Letter*.

therefore, ignore the discussion as to which of the reputed ones are authentic. Probably, too, it is not important for our purpose to join the debate over the historicity of the reported visit to Rome.[267] It is clear that Patrick, through his birth, his education, his ordination, his knowledge of Latin, and his probable use of missionaries who had been at least trained if not born on the Continent, tended to keep the Christianity of Ireland in touch with that which prevailed in the Western part of the Roman world. The statement of belief which we have from his own pen, too, while not a well-rounded summary of the faith held by the Catholics of his time, is not out of accord with it and shows the influence of the dominant creed.[268] A visit to Rome, while probably strengthening this contact, presumably would not have added to it anything essentially new.

How far Patrick accommodated the message and organization of the Church to local conditions, and how far he reproduced what he had heard and seen in Britain and on the Continent, is not clear.[269] That, like so many missionaries of Christianity and other faiths before and after him, he sought at times to win the political heads of the community and through them to effect a mass conversion is probable.[270] It is obvious that if this was his method he did not always succeed, or not, at least, at the first attempt.[271] It is also certain that he sought to obtain from the chiefs official toleration.[272] Here and there we have hints of

[267] Bury, op. cit., pp. 150-154, believes it to have been made. White, St. Patrick, His Writings and Life, pp. 16-18, thinks it very doubtful. Todd, St. Patrick, Apostle to Ireland, pp. 350-364, also questions a supposed visit to Rome to receive consecration from the Pope. Mrs. Concannon, Saint Patrick, pp. 151-169, argues for the journey to Rome, as does Bury, some time after Patrick began his mission in Ireland. Anglican writers, naturally, are inclined to doubt the visit to Rome with its strengthening of the Roman connexion, and Roman Catholic authors are usually predisposed in its favour. The Confession and the Letter say nothing of a trip to Rome at any time. Patrick certainly, in these, represents his missionary call to Ireland as directly from God and says nothing of a commission of the Pope.

[268] The statement of faith is given in the early part of the Confession. It omits some of the phrases given in that of Nicæa and in the Apostles' Creed, but is not in conflict with either document.

[269] The Irish Canons ascribed to a synod held by Patrick imply a diocesan organization, each diocese headed by a bishop. See, for example, the Canon given in Stokes, The Tripartite Life of Patrick, p. 508, lines 33-39. Bury, The Life of St. Patrick, pp. 233-245, argues for the Patrician origin of these Canons, but points out that other authorities have assigned them to the eighth, ninth, or tenth century. If they are valid, they point to the introduction of a diocesan system such as existed in Gaul. Todd, op. cit., pp. 484-488, puts the Canons in the ninth or tenth century. On the organization of the episcopate under Patrick, see also Bury, op. cit., pp. 375-379.

[270] This may be implied in Muirchu's Life and the Confession. Todd, op. cit., pp. 498, 499, argues that Patrick worked through the chieftains, when possible winning them first.

[271] This is clear from the reference in the Confession to his being seized and plundered by kings.

[272] Patrick, Confession.

opposition from the leaders of the old faiths.[273] Agreement is lacking as to the date of Patrick's death, the years argued for it ranging between 460 and 493.[274]

Patrick, then, was possessed of a deep and continuous religious experience which shaped his entire life. As a part of that experience had come by inward illumination a profound conviction of his duty to be a missionary in the land of his captivity. Probably he cherished a warm admiration for what he deemed Christian Roman culture.[275] He stood in awe of the scholarship associated with that culture and was painfully conscious of his deficiencies in it. Courageous, devoted, persevering, with gifts of persuasion and leadership, he was at once the single-minded emissary of the faith which had become the controlling passion of its life and, probably only half consciously, an agent of the culture on whose fringes he had been born and which he so highly esteemed.

Patrick was probably not, however, the first Christian in Ireland, nor, even in his own lifetime, is it certain that the movement which he headed was the sole channel by which Christianity was penetrating the island. In his *Confession* are passages which may indicate that in parts of Ireland Christians had been known before him.[276] The commercial contact with Roman Britain probably brought a knowledge of the faith from a region which was rapidly accepting Christianity. Moreover, it would have been strange indeed if, in the Irish raids, Patrick was the only Christian to have been carried off or the sole one of the captives to develop a feeling of responsibility for imparting their faith to those among whom they had been involuntarily thrown.[277] A brief notice in a contemporary chronicle speaks of one Palladius being ordained by Pope Celestine "for the Scots believing in Christ" and sent "as the first bishop."[278] It is generally assumed that these Scots were in Ireland and, therefore, that Rome knew of Christians there for whom a bishop was needed.[279] The relation of the mission of Palladius to that of Patrick is one of those tantalizing questions

[273] Muirchu, *Life,* 15.

[274] Bury, *op. cit.,* pp. 382, 383, argues for 461. Stokes, *op. cit.,* p. cxliii, thinks the date was about 463. Todd, *op. cit.,* p. 497, thinks 493 is correct. The Bollandists plead for 460, and another date given is 465.—Todd, *op. cit.,* pp. 494, 495.

[275] In the *Letter* Patrick speaks with evident pride of the "fellow citizens of the holy Romans."

[276] Thus in the *Confession* Patrick speaks of journeying to regions "where never any one had come to baptize, or to ordain clergy, or to confirm the people," which may imply that in Ireland there were other regions where this had been done before him.

[277] On reasons for believing that there were Christians in Ireland before Patrick, see Bury, *op. cit.,* pp. 349-352; Gougaud, *Christianity in Celtic Lands,* pp. 27-31; Hitchcock, *St. Patrick and His Gallic Friends,* pp. 9-16; Meissner, in Phillips, *A History of the Church of Ireland,* Vol. I, pp. 47, 54.

[278] Prosper of Acquitaine, *Chronicum* (in Migne, *Pat. Lat.,* Vol. LI, Col. 695).

[279] So McNaught, *The Celtic Church and the See of Peter,* pp. 29ff.; Bury, *op. cit.,* p. 349; Todd, *op. cit.,* pp. 279ff.

to which no answer is given which satisfies all scholars, but it seems probable that Palladius died after a very brief tenure of office and that the consecration of Patrick as bishop followed.[280]

Another contemporary of Patrick was Ninian. Probably the son of a man of high rank from the north of Britain, he was taken to Rome by Theodosius as a hostage and seems to have spent a number of years there and to have received thorough instruction in the Christian faith. He appears to have been sent to his people as a missionary, about 395, and on his homeward journey to have visited Martin of Tours, then almost at the end of his long and eventful life. Martin seems greatly to have impressed the youthful missionary, and it may have been that it was both monasticism and Christianity which Ninian propagated on the northern fringe of the crumbling Roman possessions in Britain. The influence of Ninian penetrated southward to Wales, and it is not impossible that it also reached Ireland. Indeed, it has been suggested that the growth of Irish monasticism may have been due even more to the impulse given by him than to Patrick, and that this strain in time supplanted the diocesan organization introduced by Patrick from the Continent.[281] This unexpected result, however, must be largely conjecture. Here, as so often in our narrative, it is only fragments of information, frequently dimly discerned, which have reached us.

Thanks to Patrick and to his imperfectly remembered associates and contemporaries, in the declining days of the Empire in the West Christianity was securely planted in Ireland, well beyond the farthest limits reached by the legions. Here was an early example of what later was to be a commonplace. A faith whose founder had been born in the reign of the first Emperor outlived and partly perpetuated the Empire and brought into its fold those whom the Emperors, at the wildest reach of their ambition, had never dreamed of ruling. From Ireland, too, within a very few generations, Christian monks were

[290] This is the order given in Stokes, *op. cit.*, p. cxli, and in Bury, *op. cit.*, p. 59. Duchesne, *Early History of the Christian Church*, Vol. III, pp. 425-429, is less certain and gives a different conjecture as to the order. There is an interesting hypothesis, vigorously put forward by H. Zimmer in his article *Keltische Kirche* in Herzog-Hauck, *Realencyklopädie für protestantische Theologie und Kirche*, 3d ed., Vol. X, pp. 207-221, which identifies Patrick with Palladius and declares that Patrick, while labouring in Ireland, did not have the part in its conversion attributed to him by tradition. Christianity began in Ireland, so it is said, in the fourth century, as the result of commercial contact with Britain. The rapid extension of Christianity over Ireland, according to this hypothesis, was due to the great energy of the monastic movement which is associated with the name of Martin of Tours and which swept over Gaul and Britain after the middle of the fourth century and sent half-Romanized Britons in great numbers as missionaries to Ireland. This view is endorsed and argued in semi-popular form in Faulkner, *Burning Questions in Historic Christianity*, pp. 125-142. It has not found general acceptance and seems to ignore or set aside some of the evidence of the *Confession* and the *Letter*.

[281] On Ninian, see Meissner in Phillips, *op. cit.*, Vol. I, pp. 61-76.

to pour into Britain and the Continent, there to revive a faith which had decayed through the turmoil of the years and to carry it to pagan peoples.

It was not merely in the West that Christianity was overpassing the boundaries of the Roman Empire. We have already seen that long before it had won more than a minority in the West, even in the Roman provinces, it had spread eastward into Armenia, Mesopotamia, Arabia, and, possibly, even to India. Upon this eastward movement the official adoption of Christianity by the Empire had varying effects. In it, moreover, the year 500 approximates to several important transitions, but none of such consequence as occurred in the seventh century. East of the Empire the most important change in the geographic extension of Christianity after the adoption of the faith by Constantine was the emergence of Islam, which may be dated roughly from the Hegira, A.D. 622. However, the reign of Justinian I, which began in 527, saw the active initiation in the East and South of fresh missions outside the Roman boundaries. So, too, towards the close of the fifth century came the adoption of Nestorianism by most of the Church in the Persian Empire, an act which effectively separated Christianity in that area from the majority Church of the Mediterranean world. The sixth century witnessed the rapid spread of Monophysite or Jacobite Christianity in the East. While, therefore, the year 500 is for the churches in the East outside of the Roman Empire no such important dividing point as 622 and is adopted to keep our story of the non-Roman East parallel with that of events in the Roman Empire, it is not far removed from developments which were of marked significance.

Armenia, it will be recalled, had been brought into the Church *en masse* towards the close of the third century and the beginning of the fourth, under the leadership of Gregory the Illuminator and with the support of the state. So rapid and wholesale a conversion must obviously have been very superficial. For many decades outright paganism continued in the mountainous districts, and among nominal Christians customs and beliefs of pagan origin long survived.[282] The preparation of a Christian literature in the language and the education of the masses naturally required years. During the fourth century, however, progress was registered. At the end of the fourth or the beginning of the fifth century, the Bible was put into Armenian, and religious books were translated from Greek and Syriac.[283] Thus, as we have seen, a national literature was encouraged. Towards the close of the fourth century, moreover, under

---

[282] Ormanian, *The Church of Armenia*, p. 20.
[283] Duchesne, *Early History of the Christian Church*, Vol. III, p. 376; Adeney, *The Greek and Eastern Churches*, pp. 542-552; Ormanian, *op. cit.*, pp. 19, 22-25. Dowling, *The Armenian Church*, p. 105, places the adoption of the Armenian alphabet in A.D. 406 and the translation of the Scriptures in A.D. 410. The man chiefly responsible was Mesrob.

influences from Cæsarea in Cappadocia, a purification and deepening of the life of the Armenian Church was attempted, chiefly by Nerses, a descendant of Gregory the Illuminator.[284]

Armenian ecclesiastical affairs were complicated by the struggles between the Roman and Persian Empires, with the effort of each rival to control the buffer state which lay between them. In the fifth century the Persians dominated the land. For a time the new overlord contented himself with interfering in the affairs of the Church, attempting to make it subservient to him. Before long, however, official efforts were made to propagate Zoroastrianism, the faith of Persia. Perhaps Christianity, as the religion of the hereditary enemy, was regarded as a possible menace to Persian rule. Many Armenian martyrs of this period are commemorated.[285] Not until towards the end of the century, when toleration was once more attained, could the Church again breathe freely.[286]

Not far from that time the Armenian Church broke formally with the majority Church of the Empire, thus making explicit a separation which had long been in progress.[287] This breach helped to cut it off from the currents of life and thought in the rest of the Christian community and contributed to a kind of ossification. For the ensuing centuries the Church of Armenia, like the nation of which it had become an integral part, remained on the defensive, relatively static, insistently holding to its past, tenacious of life, but not reaching out into new areas of race or conduct. Threatened and at times partly overrun by powerful invaders, Armenia could do little more than preserve its own existence. In maintaining the national entity, the Church afforded marked assistance, but it could do little more.

In an earlier chapter we have noted the entrance of Christianity into Georgia, in the Caucasus north of Armenia. Georgia, like Armenia, was on the border between the Roman and the Persian Empire and was subject to influences, political and cultural, from both directions. Usually it is difficult to know to what extent, if at all, political motives complicated the religious vicissitudes. While Christianity may have arrived much earlier, our first clear glimpse of it seems to be towards the close of the third or fairly early in the fourth century. The traditional story, to which we referred in an earlier chapter, relates how Nino (or Nunia, Nina, or Nonna), a captive Christian woman, by a miracle of healing wrought in the name of Christ won a hearing and had the queen for a convert. The king, Mirian, the founder of the Georgian branch of the Sassanids, is said soon to have followed his wife into the faith, convinced by

[284] Duchesne, op. cit., Vol. III, pp. 372, 373.
[285] On the martyrs, see Dowling, op. cit., pp. 57-60.
[286] Duchesne, op. cit., Vol. III, pp. 373-378; Ormanian, op. cit., pp. 26-30.
[287] Adeney, op. cit., p. 544; Ormanian, op. cit., pp. 31-36.

his deliverance, when, hunting and lost in the darkness, he called on the name of Christ and found his way out. The populace are reported to have followed their king into the Church. It is also said that Mirian sent to Constantinople, requesting both an alliance and clergy.[288] If the story is correct, we may surmise that, as in so many other instances, a mixture of factors entered into the conversion of the land—the sincere and simple faith of a Christian captive, the widespread belief in the miraculous, the desire of the king for cultural and political contacts with the Roman Empire (perhaps because he felt that he had less to fear from that direction than from Persia), the active support by the king of the religion of the Empire, and the acquiescence of the masses. Mirian's son and successor is said to have been zealous in his support of the Church. Apparently throughout the fourth century Christianity continued to make progress, and with it the culture of the Greek East. Then followed a period of Persian invasion, with an attempt to oust Roman influence by the forcible substitution of Zoroastrianism, the official cult of the Sassanids, for Christianity. In the second half of the fifth century a king, Vakhtang I (446-499), proved strong enough to purge the land of the fire cult, built many churches, and instituted numerous bishoprics. It was probably in his reign, moreover, that the Georgian Church achieved ecclesiastical independence of Constantinople.[289]

Earlier we have suggested that the adoption of Christianity as the official religion of the Roman Empire brought misfortune to the churches in Mesopotamia. Almost inevitably the fate of Christianity was affected by the relations between that realm and its chronic enemy, Persia. While the faith was being persecuted by the Romans, the Persian state, although never friendly, was usually not especially intolerant. When, however, its rival made that religion its own and sought to obtain peace for the Christians in Persia, periodic attempts to eradicate the Church were to be expected. The amazing fact is not that Christianity remained a minority cult, but that it survived at all.

Its persistence appears to have been due to its close association with the Syriac-using portions of the population. Although Christianity won some adherents from those of Persian blood and language, its strength was chiefly among those for whom Syriac was the prevailing tongue. The emergence of Syriac as a literary language seems to have been due mainly to Christianity.[290] In Persia

---

[288] Socrates, *Eccles. Hist.*, Book II, Chap. 7. For a traditional account, with much of the miraculous, see Malan, *A Short History of the Georgian Church* (a translation of a work by the Georgian Ioselian), pp. 17-29.

[289] Tamarati, *L'Église Géorgienne*, pp. 66-70, 161-210; Schmidlin, *Katholische Missionsgeschichte*, pp. 97, 100; Adeney, *op. cit.*, pp. 344-348; Malan, *op. cit.*, pp. 35-64.

[290] Brockelmann, *Die syrische und die christlich-arabische Litteratur*, in *Geschichte der christlichen Litteraturen des Orients*, pp. 7, 22.

and Mesopotamia the two appear usually to have been closely associated. Those owning Syriac as their mother tongue as a rule were politically subject, some to the Romans, some to the Persians, and in later centuries to the Arabs. Many of them, however, living as they did on important trade routes and in commercial cities, proved enterprising merchants. As such, they accumulated wealth and, partly under the tutelage of their priests and monks, developed men of education who rose to prominence in the service of the state, especially after the Sassanids were displaced by the Abassid Caliphs. As merchants, moreover, they fared forth into distant lands and established communities in the cities of Persia and Central Asia which became fertile centres for the propagation of their faith.[291]

Never, however, did the Christianity which sprang from this source in Mesopotamia, Persia, Central Asia, and China achieve complete independence from Syrian culture. Therein lay both its strength and its weakness. In the basin of the Mediterranean Christianity became identified with the dominant Græco-Roman culture and in that association made its triumphant way among the peoples of Northern Europe who saw it as an integral part and the vehicle of the only civilization which they knew. In Mesopotamia and the East, Christianity expanded in connexion with Syriac-using peoples. Without them it might not have spread as far as it did. Without it, too, they might not have achieved such prominence and prosperity. However, politically a subject people, except in limited areas their culture was not dominant. Their faith, therefore, nearly always faced far more severe competition from other religions with their associated cultures than did Christianity in Northern Europe. While it attained to wide geographic extension, Christianity never enjoyed in the Persian domains and eastward the practical monopoly that it did in much of Europe. Eventually, in severe political vicissitudes of later centuries, it was all but stamped out.

This, however, is anticipating much of what we are to narrate more in detail in a subsequent volume. That is not entirely amiss, for in Mesopotamia and Persia, as we have suggested, the year 500 does not approximate so nearly to a logical major division in the spread of Christianity as in the Mediterranean world. At the risk of making our division a Procrustean bed, we must now return to some of the major events of the fourth and fifth centuries in the spread of Christianity in the Persian domains.

It will be recalled that the earliest strongholds of Christianity in the Tigris-Euphrates Valley were Edessa and Adiabene.[292] In the wars between the Romans and the Sassanids, in the third century and later, the Persians, when

---

[291] Budge, *The Monks of Kûblâi Khân*, p. 32.
[292] Mingana, *The Early Spread of Christianity in Central Asia and the Far East*, pp. 3-8.

successful, deported large numbers from the eastern borders of the Roman Empire into their own domains. It seems probable that among these were many Christians.[293] While the prevailing element in the Christian communities of the Sassanian domains was Syriac-using, converts were made from among the Persians, and in Middle Persian, or Pahlavi, a Christian literature arose.[294] The faith was carried still farther eastward. The majority of its adherents continued to be found in Persis, Northern and Southern Media, and Parthia, or in what are now the south-western, the north-western, and the north-eastern portions of Iran.[295] In the fifth century even such distant cities as Herat, Merv, and the present Meshed possessed bishops.[296] By the end of the fifth century some of the Hephthalite Huns and Turks were Christian.[297]

This wide extension of Christianity in the Persian domains and even east of them did not take place at once or without severe persecutions. The predominance of Syriac and Mesopotamian influence in the churches of this realm was no accident. Zoroastrianism was deeply entrenched in Persia and was closely identified with the national life. The coming to power of the Sassanids, in the first half of the third century, just when Christianity was spreading rapidly, appears to have been accompanied and assisted by a Zoroastrian revival. Both were, in a sense, parts of a national movement. In contrast with the Roman Empire, where no powerful professional priesthood of a state cult existed to offer opposition to the introduction of a rival faith, in the Sassanian realms Zoroastrianism was supported by a strong priestly body which exerted great influence among rulers and ruled.[298] In contrast, too, with the Græco-Roman world, where Christianity made its way in a time when the popularity of a wide variety of religions and systems testified at once to the active religious hunger and to the disintegration of old cultural patterns, in Persia Zoroastrianism was clearly dominant, and, in spite of what the gains of Christianity and Manichæism may have evidenced, no such widespread dissatisfaction with the old and deep yearning for something as yet unfound seems to have troubled the spirits of many. As a result, the soil was not well prepared for the entrance of a new faith. Then, too, it has been suggested that in Persia the literate, book-reading public was not so large as in the Roman Empire, and no such field existed for

[293] Labourt, Le Christianisme dans l'Empire Perse sous la Dynastie Sassanide, pp. 18-20.
[294] Mingana, op. cit., pp. 3-8.
[295] Sachau, Zur Ausbreitung des Christentums in Asien, pp. 14-17.
[296] Sachau, op. cit., pp. 14-17, 64.
[297] Mingana, op. cit., pp. 3-19.
[298] Labourt, op. cit., p. 5; Browne, The Eclipse of Christianity in Asia from the time of Muhammed till the Fourteenth Century, p. 2; Mommsen, The Provinces of the Roman Empire, Vol. II, p. 90.

written apologies as in the basin of the Mediterranean.[299] Added to all these handicaps was the espousal of Christianity by the Roman state. The recurring wars between the two empires now took on at times the aspects of a religious struggle and in the Sassanid domains Christians were suspect as protégés of the enemy and as potential and at times actual traitors. In the light of these many handicaps, it is not strange that Christianity, although often vigorous, remained a minority faith.

It is significant that severe persecution of Christians in the Sassanian territories began soon after the avowal of the faith by Constantine. Apparently Constantine believed himself the protector of his fellow believers in the Persian domains. He wrote to the Persian monarch, Sapor II, commenting on the pleasure given him by the reports that Christians were to be found in the latter's realm and commending them to his protection.[300] This must have aroused the fears of the Persian authorities, suspicions which may have been heightened when Constantine, in his preparations for the ensuing war, asked bishops to accompany him and to assist his arms with their prayers.[301] Certainly much of the long reign of Sapor II (310-379) was marked by recurring persecutions, and the number of victims is reported to have mounted to sixteen thousand. Reasons to adduce for the severity were not difficult to find. Sapor's ire is said to have been aroused by the encouragement which its bishop gave to Nisibis in its defence against his forces. Christians were accused of opposing the tenets of the state faith—of teaching men not to pay honour to the sun and fire, of defiling water with their ablutions, and of burying the bodies of men in the earth. They were also said to have refused to assist Sapor in his wars. It is not unlikely that many of them desired a Roman victory. Sapor is reported first to have ordered that Christians submit to double taxation and that the bishops collect the levies. Quickly, however, the measures passed beyond the stage of pecuniary penalties. A bishop, for instance, was martyred when he demurred at the task assigned him. While Julian was in power, persecution appears to have lagged, presumably because Christians were no longer under the ægis of Rome. When, however, Julian's successor, the Christian Jovian, bought peace by the cession of Roman territory, the Persians sought to incorporate the new regions into their realm by transporting many of the Christian inhabitants and by forcing them to renounce their faith.[302] Persecution is said not to have been general through-

[299] Browne, op. cit., p. 2.
[300] Eusebius, Life of Constantine, Book XIV, Chaps. 8-13; Theodoret, Eccles. Hist., Book I, Chap. 25.
[301] Eusebius, op. cit., Book XIV, Chap. 56.
[302] Sozomen, Eccles. Hist., Book II, Chaps. 9-15; Labourt, Le Christianisme dans l'Empire Perse sous la Dynastie Sassanide, pp. 43-93; Wigram, An Introduction to the History of

out the Sassanian domains and to have varied with the energies of the local officials. Apparently, however, it had some popular support.[303] Whether or not this was the case, it seems to have subsided towards the end of the century, when under Sapor III (383-388) and Bahram IV (388-399) peace was made with the Romans. The following monarch, Yazdegerd I (399-420) also proved tolerant.[304] His mildness towards the Church may have been due to a desire to curb the power of the great nobles and the Zoroastrian priests. It may have owed something to a bishop who was also a physician and a diplomat and who came to have influence at court.[305]

The persecutions under Sapor II seem to have been the most severe and prolonged of any under the Sassanids. They appear to have weakened the Church and to have left many bishoprics vacant.[306] With the alteration in government policy towards the end of the century, the Church once more lifted its head and entered upon a new period of prosperity. A number of prominent nobles became Christian.[307] Moreover, at a Council held in 410, a national organization was formed. At the head was placed the bishop of the capital, Seleucia-Ctesiphon, as Catholicos or Patriarch, and he was accorded state recognition. The Catholicos was made responsible for the behaviour of his people and the Christian community became a kind of state within a state, not unlike the position of the religious minorities in the Turkish Empire which persisted into the twentieth century. No state Church emerged as in the Roman Empire, Armenia, and Georgia, but the throne gave the Church recognition, assigned it certain quasi-political functions, and from time to time interfered in its affairs. Theoretically Christians were tolerated, but were supposed to make no converts from among their non-Christian neighbours.[308] This organization was not consummated without severe opposition. By giving the Church a national character, however, it probably helped to allay the suspicion which regarded Christianity as alien and pro-Roman.[309] Yet at times, when persecution was renewed, the Church obtained Roman support and so did not entirely lose its non-Persian character.[310]

The separation from the Church of the Roman Empire was emphasized by a

---

the Assyrian Church, pp. 58-76; Adeney, *op. cit.,* pp. 297-301; Burkitt, *Early Eastern Christianity,* p. 24.

[303] Wigram, *op. cit.,* pp. 58-76; Labourt, *op. cit.,* pp. 51-82.

[304] Labourt, *op. cit.,* pp. 83-93.

[305] Wigram, *op. cit.,* pp. 82-102.

[306] Sachau, *op. cit.,* p. 39.

[307] Labourt, *op. cit.,* pp. 105-118.

[308] O'Leary, *Arabia before Muhammad,* p. 130. O'Leary says the status was not unlike that already granted to the Jews in Mesopotamia.

[309] Labourt, *op. cit.,* pp. 20-28, 90-99, 326-339; Browne, *op. cit.,* pp. 4-9; Wigram, *op. cit.,* pp. 82-102.

[310] Theodoret, *Eccles. Hist.,* Book V, Chap. 39; Browne, *op. cit.,* pp. 4-9.

difference in doctrine. That did not come at once. The formation of the organization in 410 led within a few years to complete ecclesiastical independence,[311] but at first it appears not to have involved any theological breach. The Church of Mesopotamia and Persia seems not to have been particularly affected by the Arian controversy which in the West gave rise to the Nicene Creed. If we may judge from a series of homilies of the fourth century, it was more concerned with Jewish opposition, with the threat of Manichæism, native as it was to that region, and with the heretical Christian Marcionites and Valentinians.[312] However, in the fifth century it was won over to what was called Nestorianism. Into the history of Nestorius and into a description of the doctrines associated with his name we must not go. Nor need we enter upon the details of the process by which Nestorianism prevailed in the Persian Church. The main steps were the removal to Mesopotamia of some of those exiled from the Roman domains because of their Nestorian views, the winning over by some of them of the school at Nisibis, the chief educational centre of the Mesopotamian-Persian Church, and the filling of many of the leading ecclesiastical posts with those trained at Nisibis and committed to Nestorian doctrines. The new theology and the practices associated with it did not make their way easily, but eventually opposition was overcome.[313] The Sassanian monarch is said to have made Nestorian Christianity the only type entitled to official recognition and to have done this in response to the plea that Nestorians, anathematized in the Roman Empire, would be less likely to be disloyal to him than would those doctrinally in accord with the Church of his enemy.[314] To ecclesiastical independence the Church now added a theological complexion which severed it from the Christians of the Roman world but which helped to mitigate the enmity of the Persian rulers.

The acquisition of independence and individuality did not entirely remove restrictions. A number of times in the fifth century and under more than one monarch persecutions arose.[315] One of these led to a war with the Roman Empire.[316] At times, too, through the fact that the state exercised a certain amount of control over the Church, unworthy men, by political influence, obtained episcopal appointment.[317]

[311] Labourt, op. cit., pp. 326-339; Wigram, op. cit., pp. 103-125.
[312] Labourt, op. cit., pp. 28-42.
[313] Labourt, op. cit., pp. 131-152; Browne, op. cit., pp. 4-9; Wigram, op. cit., pp. 167, 176; Adeney, op. cit., pp. 477-492.
[314] O'Leary, op. cit., p. 135.
[315] Theodoret, Eccles. Hist., Book V, Chap. 39; Socrates, Eccles. Hist., Book VII, Chaps. 18-20; Labourt, op. cit., pp. 105-118, 126-130; Wigram, op. cit., pp. 103-125.
[316] Socrates, Eccles. Hist., Book VII, Chaps. 18-20.
[317] Wigram, op. cit., pp. 103-125.

In spite of persecution, dissensions, and occasional worldly bishops, Christianity continued to spread. We hear, for instance, of one Saba (died 487) who was born in Media of an aristocratic Iranian family. His father was a zealous adherent of Zoroastrianism, but his mother had him reared by a Christian nurse and he attended a Christian school. Later he distributed his property among the poor, persuaded his mother to accept baptism, and retired to a monastery. Still later he became a missionary and, with a colleague, is said to have persuaded an entire city, with its Zoroastrian priest, to become Christian. He is reported to have destroyed numbers of temples and to have built many churches and even to have braved the Kurds in their mountain fastnesses and to have won some of them to his faith.[318] Apparently it was in the fifth century that Christianity became strong enough in such Central Asian cities as Merv and Herat to establish the bishoprics there which we have noticed. It was this remarkable march eastward which carried it, in the seventh century, to China.

With all of this wide geographic extension, Christianity in the Sassanian Empire and the regions eastward remained, we must always remind ourselves, the religion of a minority. While in its westward spread, in the larger and supposedly stronger Roman Empire, it achieved dominance, on its eastward march Christianity won to itself usually only minority groups. The reasons for that difference we have seen. The fact itself had consequences of vast importance for the future of the faith. Because of it Christianity became practically identified with the culture of the Mediterranean basin and the peoples who derived their cultures from it. It became primarily the religion of the West. Except for the Church which we now usually think of by the name of Nestorian and the much smaller communities of Monophysites, when Christianity spread outside the Mediterranean basin it was practically always in connexion with the political or commercial activities of the peoples of that area and of those of Northern Europe whose cultures stemmed from it. It is one of the inviting but futile pastimes of the historian to conjecture what might have been the future had the Persian Empire, like the Roman, become Christian. Probably no great alteration would have been wrought, for presumably Persian Christianity, like Zoroastrianism, would have been all but erased by Islam.

It seems probable that by the close of the fifth century Christians were to be found in India and perhaps in Ceylon.[319] We have more than one authentic reference to Christians in what was called India, but usually uncertainty exists as to whether by that term was meant what today is denominated India, or

---

[318] Labourt, op. cit., p. 152.

[319] Macnicol, The Living Religions of the Indian People, p. 267, declares that no other immigrant faith, either Zoroastrianism or Islam, has been in India as long as has Christianity.

Southern Arabia. Probably, because of geographical propinquity and commercial contacts, much of whatever Christianity existed in India was derived from that in the Sassanian domains. At the Council of Nicæa, in 325, one of the bishops signed himself as "John the Persian of all Persia and Great India,"[320] but what was meant by India is not clear.[321] About a generation later, in the sixth decade of the fourth century, the Emperor Constantius sent "Theophilus the Indian," a native of the island of Dibous or Dibu, on a mission to Southern Arabia and the Ethiopians. Theophilus is reported to have proceeded to "other parts of India" and there to have brought into conformity to the ecclesiastical usages to which he was accustomed the practices of the Christians whom he found there.[322] Whether these "other parts of India" were in Southern Arabia or in what we now term India is debated.[323] The conjecture has also been ventured that the severe persecutions by Sapor II led some of the Christians of the Sassanian domains to seek refuge in India.[324] Cosmas Indicopleustes, writing about the middle of the sixth century, spoke, apparently from knowledge obtained on his extensive travels, of Christians on the island of Taprobana (by which is usually supposed to have been meant Ceylon),[325] in Inner India, and in Male, "where pepper grows," and said that in Kalliana was a bishop who received consecration from Persia.[326] The exact identification of these names is uncertain, but it is generally agreed that Male and Kalliana were on the west coast of India.[327] It is entirely possible that the Christian communities mentioned traced their foundations to at least as early as the fifth century. Some connexion with Persia is clear, but they may also have been indebted to Southern

[320] Germann, *Die Kirche der Thomaschristen*, p. 67, citing *Act. Synod. Nicaen* II, can. 28.

[321] It is not certain whether "Great" is here a technical term or simply a descriptive adjective. It looks like the former.

[322] The source for the account is in the epitome by Photius of Philostorgius, *Eccles. Hist.*, Book III, Chaps. 4, 5 (Migne, *Pat. Græc.*, Vol. LXV, Cols. 481-486). Secondary accounts based on the above, with discussions of the points raised, are in Germann, *op. cit.*, pp. 67-118; Rae, *The Syrian Church in India*, pp. 96-102, and Mingana, *The Early Spread of Christianity in India*, pp. 26-28.

[323] Germann, *op. cit.*, pp. 73ff., contends that he went to India. Rae, *op. cit.*, p. 97, thinks that Arabia Felix and India, as used by Philostorgius, were the same. Mingana, *op. cit.*, pp. 26-28, holds that Theophilus went to the present India. The island of Dibous has variously been suggested as located near the mouth of the Indus and as off the Arabian coast of the Red Sea near Anfuda.—Bell, *The Origin of Islam in Its Christian Environment*, pp. 34, 35. It is elsewhere declared to be the island of Socotra.—Moberg, *The Book of the Himyarites*, p. xlix.

[324] Mingana, *op. cit.*, pp. 7, 8; Germann, *op. cit.*, pp. 83ff.

[325] The evidence that Taprobana is Ceylon appears not entirely conclusive. It is called "Taprobana Island in *esotera* (perhaps "interior") India," but what is meant by *esotera* India is not certain.

[326] Cosmas Indicopleustes, *Christiana Topographia*, Book III (in Migne, *Pat. Græc.*, Vol. LXXXVIII, Cols. 169, 170).

[327] Rae, *op. cit.*, pp. 114ff., and Germann, *op. cit.*, pp. 129-139.

Arabia. Whether any of these Christians were of the older stocks of India and Ceylon, or whether they were merchants and immigrants from Arabia and the Sassanian domains, we do not know. The close commercial contacts would seem to indicate that at least some were from the latter groups.

Our information concerning Christians in Arabia, while fragmentary, is somewhat less unsatisfactory than for India. It is, to be sure, complicated by the uncertainty of what is included in the term India as we find it in the sources. Since, as we have seen, that seems often to have embraced not only the present India, but part of Southern Arabia, sometimes any satisfactory judgment as to which is meant in a given passage becomes impossible.

Geographically, by the year 500 Christianity was fairly extensively represented in Arabia. As was to be expected, its centres appear to have been mainly where contacts with the Roman Empire and Mesopotamia were the most marked. Christianity entered Arabia chiefly from these two regions, and in South-west Arabia owed much to the churches of Abyssinia. It was almost inevitable that as the Roman Empire became predominantly Christian its faith would be spread eastward and southward by merchants, official embassies, professional missionaries, and the numerous hermits who in the fourth and fifth centuries were seeking refuge in the deserts of Northern Arabia. Commercial and political contacts with the Persian Empire led to the introduction of Christianity into the eastern portions of Arabia.

It is not strange that east of the Jordan, bordering, as the region did, upon Roman territory, Christians were to be found. It is said that about the time of the reign of Valens, that is, about the second half of the fourth century, the dowager ruler of a "Saracen" people on the borders of Palestine and Arabia laid down as a condition of peace in a war in which she had defeated the Roman forces, the consecration as bishop of a monk of her choice.[328] We also read in a fifth-century historian of "Saracens" converted to the Christian faith not long before the beginning of the fifth century through priests who dwelt among them and through monks in the neighbouring desert. The erstwhile childless chief of one tribe is reported to have been baptized and to have been followed by his people when a monk promised him an heir if he would become a Christian, and when, in response to the monk's prayer, a son was born to him.[329] East of Jerusalem a sheik whose son, a paralytic, had been healed by a monk, passed over to Christianity with his entire tribe.[330] We hear, too, of a

---

[328] Rufinus, *Eccles. Hist.*, Book II, Chap. 6 (Migne, *Pat. Lat.*, Vol. XXI, Cols. 514, 515); Sozomen, *Eccles. Hist.*, Book VI, Chap. 38; Socrates, *Eccles. Hist.*, Book IV, Chap. 36.
[329] Sozomen, *Eccles. Hist.*, Book VI, Chap. 38.
[330] Duchesne, *Early History of the Christian Church*, Vol. III, pp. 395, 396, citing Cyril of Scythopolis, *Vita Euthymii*, c. 81ff.

Christian bishop on an island in the Gulf of Aqaba. In the fifth century a number of Arab tribes accepted Christianity, it is said, as they moved into Roman territory.[331] In a council which met at Antioch in the reign of Jovian (363-364) we hear of a "Bishop of the Arabs."[332]

Hira, south and west of Babylon and near the Arabian edge of Mesopotamia, became another Christian centre, having received its faith, presumably from the Tigris-Euphrates Valley, in the fourth or early in the fifth century. As early as 410 it was the seat of a bishop.[333] In the second half of the fourth century the Arab kingdom of Ghassan, on the frontier, became an ally of Rome and, not unnaturally, the faith of the Empire began making headway in it.[334] In both of these districts Christianity was to become more prominent in the sixth century.

By the year 500 Christianity was also represented along the Arabian shore of the Persian Gulf. So in the Bahrein Islands and in Oman were bishops in fellowship with those in the Persian Empire.[335] Presumably the Christians over whom they presided owed their faith to the churches in Mesopotamia. In attendance at the Council of 410 which did so much to organize the Church in the Persian Empire was a bishop of the Katars, of South-eastern Arabia.[336] The persecution in the Sassanian realm in the fourth century may have led some Christians to migrate to Arabia. To the end of the fourth century is ascribed the record of a monastery which may have been on the Arabian side of the Persian Gulf.[337]

In Southern and especially in South-western Arabia Christianity was early represented. Here various strains intermingled, for contributions probably came from the Roman Empire, the Persian domains, and the Axumite or Abyssinian kingdom. If the "India" reached by Pantænus was Southern Arabia, then towards the close of the second century Christians were to be found there who possessed "a Hebrew version of Matthew's Gospel."[338] On the other hand, if the India of Pantænus was our India, then quite possibly, in Southern Arabia, a stage on the journey, Christians were also to be found. The Theophilus sent by Constantius in the first half of the fourth century is said to have given much attention to the Himyarites, in the south-western corner of Arabia. Our record states that Theophilus was ordained bishop, and that Constantius not only gave

---

[331] Duchesne, Les Missions Chrétiennes au Sud de l'Empire Romain, pp. 112-122.

[332] Socrates, Eccles. Hist., Book III, Chap. 25.

[333] Guidi, L'Arabie Antéislamique, pp. 33-36.

[334] Guidi, op. cit., p. 19.

[335] Sachau, Die Chronik von Arbela, pp. 9-12; Mingana, The Early Spread of Christianity in India, pp. 7, 8.

[336] Mingana, op. cit., pp. 7, 8.

[337] Mingana, op. cit., pp. 18-24.

[338] Eusebius, Eccles. Hist., Book V, Chap. 10.

official sanction to the mission but equipped it munificently, provided it with gifts for the native rulers, and desired that churches be built both for the Romans engaged in commerce and for the inhabitants of the land. The story goes on to declare that Bishop Theophilus won to the faith the native ruler and that three churches were erected, one in the metropolis, another in Adan (Aden?), a city spoken of as frequented by the Romans, and the third in a famous Persian emporium at the mouth of the Persian Sea.[339] If the "other regions of India" which Theophilus is reported to have visited[340] were in Arabia, then it was there that he found those Christian communities with ecclesiastical customs differing from the ones to which he had been accustomed. In the sixth century Cosmas Indicopleustes wrote of Christians, bishops, martyrs, and monks in Arabia Felix and among the Homerites (Himyarites?).[341] One strain of Christianity represented in that region seems to have been from Persia. An eleventh-century Nestorian chronicle tells of a merchant from Najran in Yemen (in South-western Arabia) who in the early part of the fifth century became a Christian while in Hira, and, returning home, won his family and eventually many others.[342] Later we shall hear of a severe persecution which in the first quarter of the sixth century overtook the Christians of Yemen. Here it need merely be said that the records of this persecution leave no doubt that Christianity existed in the region at least as early as the fifth century, that the churches had close connexion with the Axumite state, and that they were partly under its protection.[343] These various fragments of information provide evidence of Christian communities in Southern Arabia, some of which by the year 500 may have been more than two centuries old.[344]

By the beginning of the sixth century, then, Christianity was penetrating Arabia from numerous points on its periphery. In the following hundred years its influence increased. Later we must take occasion to point out the significance of this fact for the origin and form of Islam.

[339] Philostorgius, *Eccles. Hist.*, Book III, Chap. 4 (in Migne, *Pat. Græc.*, Vol. XLV, Cols. 481-486).
[340] Philostorgius, *Eccles. Hist.*, Book III, Chap. 5 (in Migne, *Pat. Græc.*, Vol. XLV, Cols. 485, 486).
[341] Cosmas Indicopleustes, *Christiana Topographia*, Book III (in Migne, *Pat. Græc.*, Vol. LXXXVIII, Cols. 169, 170).
[342] Moberg, *The Book of the Himyarites*, p. xlix, citing the Nestorian Chronicle of Saard, Part I, pp. 218ff., edited by Addai Scher in *Patrologia Orientalis*, Vols. IV, V, VII.
[343] See a record of the persecution in Moberg, *op. cit., passim*, and in Bell, *The Origin of Islam in Its Christian Environment*, pp. 36, 37.
[344] Brief summaries of Christianity in Arabia before Mohammed are to be found by Jacquin in Descamps, *Histoire Générale Comparée des Missions*, p. 136; Schmidlin, *Katholische Missionsgeschichte*, p. 100; Smith, *Studies in Early Mysticism in the Near and Middle East*, pp. 103, 104; O'Leary, *Arabia before Mohammed*, pp. 125ff.; and a longer one in Bell, *op. cit.*

When Christianity first made its way to Abyssinia is not known. Our earliest knowledge of it there is associated with the state of Axum or Aksum and with the name of Frumentius. The territory of Axum lay along the African side of the Red Sea, in the present Eritrea and extending into what is now Abyssinia. The capital, Axum, was inland, but on the coast commercial contacts were had with the Roman world. The traditional story declares that a philosopher from Tyre, taking with him two youths, relatives, one of them Frumentius, sailed for "India." On his return voyage when the ship touched at a port, the inhabitants, who had thrown off their alliance with the Romans, attacked and massacred the ship's company, but saved the two youths. These eventually rose to high posts in the service of their captors. Frumentius set himself to the spiritual care of the Christian merchants from the Roman Empire whom he found there and built them houses of worship. Later he went to Alexandria and asked Athanasius for a bishop for the Christians in the land. Athanasius replied by appointing Frumentius to the office and the latter returned to the country of his adoption.[345] What facts lie behind the details of this story we do not know. Contemporary documents make it clear, however, that one Frumentius had been appointed Bishop of Axum by Athanasius.[346]

It seems probable that the king won to Christianity by Frumentius was 'Ezānā.[347] Archæology discloses that the earlier coins of this monarch bore pagan symbols, and the later coins a cross.[347] 'Ezānā's inscriptions also attest the change.[348] 'Ezānā seems to have been the first to have made Christianity the state religion of Axum.[349] He showed his zeal for his new faith by destroying pagan temples and killing pagan priests. He was, too, a monarch who extended his activities over a fairly wide area and even reached the Nile.[350] His motive can only be conjectured. The suggestion has been made that he was partly actuated by a desire for closer commercial relations with the Romans.[351] This, then, brings the introduction of Christianity to as early a date as the first half of the fourth century. In the second half of the fifth and in the sixth century a large number of monks made their way to Abyssinia. It was probably by them that

---

[345] Sozomen, *Eccles. Hist.*, Book II, Chap. 24.
[346] Athanasius, *Apologia ad Constantium*, c. 29, (Migne, *Pat. Græc.*, Vol. XXV, Cols. 631, 632) speaks of letters written (by the Arian Constantius) to the princes of Axum requesting that Frumentius, as a corruptor of true Christianity, be sent back to the Roman Empire. What purports to be the actual letter of Constantius is given in c. 31. This speaks of Frumentius as appointed to Axum by Athanasius.
[347] Budge, *A History of Ethiopia, Nubia, and Abyssinia*, Vol. I, pp. 147-153.
[348] Enno Littmann in *Deutsche-Aksum Expedition*, Vol. IV, pp. 32-42.
[349] Budge, *op. cit.*, Vol. I, pp. xi, xii; Enno Littmann in *Deutsche-Aksum Expedition*, Vol. I, p. 48.
[350] Enno Littmann in *Deutsche-Aksum Expedition*, Vol. I, p. 48.
[351] Budge, *op. cit.*, Vol. I, pp. 147-153.

the Bible was translated into the native tongue. Probably, too, the transition to the Monophysite type of Christianity was due to those exiled from the Roman Empire for religious reasons.[352] Certainly it appears clear that by the beginning of the sixth century the Abyssinian state was Monophysite and was exercising a kind of protectorate over the Christians in the portions of Arabia which lay opposite, across the Red Sea.[353]

In summary of this long chapter it may be said briefly that the fourth and fifth centuries witnessed the transition of Christianity from the position of a minority religion, well organized and vigorous but persecuted, to the faith of the majority of the Mediterranean basin. It thus became the professed religion of the most powerful of the civilized areas of the globe. It continued to spread beyond the confines of the Roman Empire, but chiefly in conjunction with Græco-Roman culture. Various Germanic peoples, notably the Goths, Vandals, Burgundians, and Franks became Christian, some of them within and some without the boundaries of the Empire. The faith was carried into Ireland and Georgia. In the Persian domains the Christian community grew and, after a period of persecution, partly cut itself off from that connexion with the Roman Empire which at times served as a protection and at others proved an embarrassment. While remaining a minority faith, it won state recognition and partial toleration. Christianity was carried into Central Asia and into India. It attracted followers in various places on the fringes of Arabia and became the official cult of Axum, the predecessor of Abyssinia. The two hundred years between A.D. 300 and A.D. 500, then, saw the number of professed Christians multiplied several fold and the faith officially adopted by several governments.

Why this rapid growth of Christianity? It must be attributed to a number of causes. Most of those enumerated at the close of the preceding chapter still operated. The disintegration of society, the organization of the Church, the inclusiveness, the combination of the intransigence and the flexibility of Christianity, the satisfaction afforded the religious cravings of the time, the Jewish origin, the moral qualities of the faith, and the appeal of the miraculous all contributed, as they had previously. The inner energy and conviction which characterized the first three centuries continued, due essentially to the same reasons. As earlier, zealous missionaries played an important part. We possess more nearly adequate information for more of these latter than we do for their predecessors of the preceding three hundred years. Even yet, however, our records are tantalizingly fragmentary.

To earlier factors was added the momentum of success. Having made such

[352] *Ibid;* Bell, *op. cit.,* pp. 29-32.
[353] Moberg, *op. cit.,* pp. lxii, lxxvii.

headway, the faith quite naturally continued its growth. The nominal assent without much inward conviction or comprehension of the message of Christianity which characterized a large proportion of the membership of these centuries was part of the price of popularity and tended to weaken the enthusiasm which had so much to do with the initial spread of the faith. In many even though a minority, the earlier zeal persisted. Again and again one meets it in the biographies of saints and missionaries. Given the combination of this enthusiasm and the prestige of rapid growth, continued accessions and the enlargement of the geographic boundaries of the faith were inevitable. Earlier factors, too, were now augmented by the powerful assistance of the state Toward the close of the third century the Armenian king had been the first ruler of an extensive territory to espouse the faith and to seek to induce his subjects to follow him. Soon after him Constantine took a somewhat similar step. A long succession of Roman Emperors threw their weight on the side of Christianity and against paganism. Among the Goths, the Franks, the Georgians some of the Arabs, and the Abyssinians we have seen comparable processes. Entire tribes and populations sought entrance to the Church.

As Christianity was transformed into a state religion, its fortunes became bound up with the lot of particular peoples and empires. The fact that it was Roman gave it prestige among those tribes who regarded with awe or desire the Mediterranean culture or who sought the support of the Empire. The Roman rulers sometimes exerted themselves on behalf of Christians outside their domains. Henceforward Christianity became chiefly identified with Mediterranean culture and with the peoples who derived their cultures from that source. With the emergence and spread of Islam, it was to share that distinction with its younger rival. Much more than Islam, however, Christianity caught up in itself the heritage of the Græco-Roman world, transformed by its own genius, and represented it to the rest of the human race.

This espousal by the state and the mixture of political, cultural, and religious factors in the spread of Christianity were to characterize much of the succeeding expansion of the faith and serve to make easy the transition to the next period. Before entering upon that narrative, however, we must pause to address ourselves to the questions of the effect of Christianity upon its environment in these first five centuries and of the effect of the environment on Christianity.

Chapter VI

THE EFFECT OF CHRISTIANITY UPON ITS ENVIRONMENT
TO A.D. 500

OF ALL the major questions to which we addressed ourselves at the outset of this work, none is more difficult of accurate answer than the effect of Christianity upon its environment. Some results seem fairly clear. Again and again, however, we shall be compelled to confess ourselves baffled and unable to do more than to venture suggestions which can be neither conclusively substantiated nor denied.

The reasons for our perplexity are many. Most of them are inherent in the nature of the problem. Not only do they meet us in the period before A.D. 500, but they will confront us whenever, in our pilgrimage, we have occasion to ask for the results of the faith whose spread we are recounting. Sometimes we are baffled by the paucity of the surviving evidence. Quite as frequently, especially in later centuries, we are embarrassed by its volume. Even more dismaying is the interpretation of the evidence. Not only must the historian ask, as always, whether his material is authentic, but he must seek to discover what it means. It is here that the difficulty is greatest, and for at least two reasons.

First of all is the necessity of defining the Christianity whose effects we seek to determine. Just what shall we call Christianity? Is it identical with the organized and visible Church? If we can ascertain that a particular movement or event has been due to the Church, shall we therefore assume that it must be ascribed to Christianity? The Church is itself a complex organism, displaying almost infinite variety from age to age and from region to region. It is made up partly of individual members, lay and clerical, each with his or her own characteristics, convictions, and experiences. It comprises not only members, but also sacraments, creeds, liturgies, and organizations of various kinds, and carries with it much of its past. Usually it is not united. Repeatedly in a given section two or more rival churches are found. The churches are the product not only of the original impulse out of which Christianity arose, but of many minds and experiences and of the cultures in the midst of which they have been set.

Or do we mean by Christianity the many individuals who have borne the Christian name? Obviously the original impulse given by Jesus has been only one factor, and sometimes a minor one, in determining the character and specific actions of those who have been called Christians.

Ideally, in tracing its effects, Christianity would seem best described as the continuation of the impulse given by the life, teachings, and death of Jesus, and by the convictions held by his immediate disciples concerning his resurrection. This is the definition on which we shall proceed. We will seek to discover just what results followed in the world from the presence in it of Jesus. This impulse has been seen in the churches and in individual Christians, but it has not been identical with either nor has it been confined to the churches and to those who bear the Christian name. From this standpoint, our question becomes: Just what difference has it made to the world that Jesus lived?

A second source of our difficulty is the almost inextricable fashion in which the influence of Jesus has mingled with other factors in affecting human lives and cultures. But for Jesus the Christian churches would not have come into existence. Yet many other forces have shaped them and there are those who declare that, compared with these, the influence of Jesus has been relatively minor. What is usually called Christianity is more than the impulse which came from Jesus. It is at once a growth and a series of accretions. Without Jesus it would not have been, but in it the impulse which came from Jesus is only one element and that at times a minor one. How, even in the institution which Paul declared to be the body of Christ,[1] can we determine the part played by the impulse which came from Jesus? Moreover, Christians have held that through what they have usually called the Holy Spirit a creative energy continues which owes much to Jesus, but which cannot be confined to his deeds and words in the brief years of his flesh. Into this realm the modern historian hesitates to enter, yet he must take note of the belief and of the events which gave rise to it and of those other events in succeeding centuries which have been adduced by Christians as proof of the continuing presence of the Spirit. To discover how much of what are called the works of the Spirit is due to the stream which issued from Jesus is not easy.

The individual Christian, if he is both honest and intelligent, often finds it almost impossible to judge how far even the most decisive of his actions has been due to him whom he calls Lord. If the individual is perplexed to apportion the sources of his own deeds, how much more at a loss must the historian be when he endeavours to discover the part that the influence of Jesus has played in the lives of millions of individuals and in the cultures and institutions which both mould and are moulded by these individuals.

How, too, can we possibly separate out the influence of Jesus from that of

[1] Ephesians i:23.

ose philosophies and religions older than he and quite independent of him
hich were woven into the fabric of Mediterranean life of the first five centuries
d then later into what we call Western civilization? It is often said that the
cline of slavery in the Roman Empire was due to Christianity. Yet how can
e discover to what degree this was because of the impulse which came from
sus and to what extent it is attributable to economic and political factors?

Again and again we shall be forced to say of a movement or an institution
at we cannot determine the precise potency of the influence of Jesus in bring-
g it into existence or in modifying it. Surprisingly often, however, the facts
ill permit us to say that the impulse which came from Jesus has been a major
ement. More frequently still we can be clear that this impulse has been pres-
nt, even when we find ourselves at a loss to know just how important it has
een.

Difficult though the problem is, it is fascinating. Moreover, no one who is at
ll concerned with the springs of human action and with the forces which shape
uman cultures can well ignore it. In few other phases of our story must we be
 on our guard against preconceptions and bias, both in ourselves and in the
urces and interpreters which we must use. No other question, however, is
ore important for those who wish to know why men have behaved as they
ave and what today are the moulding factors in the life of mankind.

We must also remark the close connexion between the effect of Christianity
pon its environment and the effect of the environment upon Christianity.
ecause what is usually called Christianity is at once an outgrowth from the
npulse which came from Jesus and of other, seemingly quite extraneous and
ften contradictory factors, the second question is really a subdivision of the
rst. While we are to treat the two problems separately, we must always recall
at the sharp differentiation between them is somewhat artificial. We must
ot forget, for instance, that when we are seeking to determine the extent to
hich Greek philosophy shaped the concepts of the Christian Church, we are
ealing with a problem whose obverse is the effect of the impulse derived from
sus upon the religious and philosophic concepts of the Græco-Roman world.

In attempting to ascertain the results of Christianity we do well to remember
hat the faith had greater freedom in some areas than in others. In the Persian
mpire it was never professed by the majority and was always under a govern-
ent avowedly as well as actually controlled by other presuppositions. In the
astern part of the Mediterranean basin it remained subject to the Roman state.
o be sure, in time that state came to call itself Christian and was modified by
hat fact. However, it preserved an unbroken continuity with the pre-Christian
ate and always sought to keep the Church strictly under its domination. In

the West, on the other hand, the collapse of the Roman state gave the Church a much freer hand. The Church in that region in time embodied much of the old Roman tradition and was a perpetuation of the Roman Empire in another form. However, presumably in this dominant Church of the West, tracing as it did its origin to Jesus and claiming to be his representative, the impulse which came from Jesus was less impeded than in a theoretically Christian state which had non-Christian beginnings. In the West, therefore, Christianity had larger leeway than in the East and made its influence more felt. It is in the western part of the Roman Empire, accordingly, that after about the year 500 we must look for the most distinctive fruits of Christianity. During the period with which we are dealing, that before A.D. 500, this was not the case. Throughout its course the Roman state survived in part of the West as well as in the East. Moreover, the East had ostensibly become Christian earlier than had most of the West, and by A.D. 500 the West had been more thoroughly overrun by barbarians, some of them pagan, than the East. Up to the end of the fifth century, therefore, the influence of Christianity was quite as great in the eastern part of the Roman Empire as in the western.

One other word must be added by way of general introduction. Neither here nor in later chapters will the effort be made to determine which of the results of Christianity have been good and which bad. The author, like the reader, can scarcely avoid passing judgment on the moral and social quality of the effects as they are enumerated and described. No attempt will be made, however, to place these appraisals on the written page. Every effort, rather, will be exerted to avoid doing so. Such verdicts imply standards of value and adequately to establish and test the validity of such standards would require many more pages than can properly be crowded into this book. The author must, therefore, content himself here with the rôle of the recorder who endeavours to avoid an estimate of the ethical and social worth of what he observes. That he leaves to others, perhaps to the reader or to some other pen, or postpones for possible treatment in some future work. The task of determining effects is difficult enough without complicating it with an effort to decide which were beneficent and which evil.

To come, then, to the specific period of the first five centuries of the Christian era. Here, too, before we essay a description of the concrete effects of Christianity, certain introductory generalizations must be ventured.

First of all we must recognize the fact that of late years much less attention has been paid to the influence of Christianity upon environment than of the environment upon Christianity. Possibly this is by way of a reaction from an earlier tendency to laud the transformation wrought by the faith in the Græco-

Roman world. Careful, objective studies of the effects of Christianity are much less numerous than are those which deal with the way in which what is called Christianity was shaped by the culture which it supposedly conquered.

We must next remind ourselves that Christianity was born and had its early growth in a culture already suffering from senescence. The causes of what is generally termed the fall of the Roman Empire are obscure and probably complex. Many of the symptoms are, however, obvious, and most of them were apparent long before Christians constituted more than a negligible proportion of the population. In spite of the prosperity and the apparent brilliance of those two centuries which were the initial ones both of the Roman Empire and of Christianity, the process of decay had set in before their beginning. Even as early as the second century before Christ those city states in whose halcyon days Greek culture was developed had begun to show signs of decrepitude. A revival came in the Italian cities, but in the second century after Christ that too had ceased.[2] The elimination of the small farmer and the coming of the huge landed estates, the recruiting of the legions from barbarian stock, and the disappearance of the urban middle classes were all in progress in the generations in which Christianity was beginning to make itself felt and before it had become very prominent.[3] In art and in literature the Græco-Roman spirit had ceased to say much that was new and was slavishly repeating forms created earlier. In philosophy and religion the chief product of the later Græco-Roman tradition was Neoplatonism, but that, as its very name indicates, was a conscious outgrowth of a system born in the great days of the Greek mind. If a culture can be said to die, that of the Græco-Roman world was already beginning to display the signs of a long, lingering, fatal illness when Christianity entered upon the scene.

We must go on to recognize the fact, to which we alluded in a previous chapter, that the early Christians entertained no purpose of attempting a thoroughgoing transformation of the Græco-Roman world. Whether Jesus himself did so we do not know. Certainly our brief record of his words gives us no clear evidence of such an intention.[4] Many of his followers expected the advent of an ideal society, but they believed that it would come suddenly and by an act of God and not through the deliberate effort of man. In time the majority of Christians gave over the anticipation of the early return of their Lord. However,

---

[2] Rostovtzeff, *The Social and Economic History of the Roman Empire*, pp. 478-480.
[3] *Ibid.;* Dill, *Roman Society in the Last Century of the Western Empire*, pp. 227-281; Glover, *Christ in the Ancient World*, pp. 23-33.
[4] Troeltsch, *The Social Teaching of the Christian Churches*, pp. 55-59, points out that the message of Jesus was not a programme of social reform, but a summons to prepare for the coming of the Kingdom of God.

they did not substitute for it any comprehensive plan for the remaking of the existing order.[5] The Christian apologists, indeed, took pains to rebut the charge that they were enemies of society. Some of them insisted that the Empire owed its stability and prosperity to their faith. The primary emphasis of the Church was upon the salvation of the individual for eternal life. Only as a part of its effort so to save individuals did it attack those features of society which seemed to it most to threaten the welfare of the soul. Within their own circles Christians sought to live according to what they believed to be the commands of Jesus. They constituted themselves into distinct communities in the world, but so far as might be not of the world. They passed severe strictures on many of the aspects of the life which surrounded them, but they endeavoured chiefly to prevent their own number from participating in them and, so long as they remained in the minority, did not seek to eliminate them.

When, in the two centuries after Constantine, the vast majority within the Empire came to bear the name of Christian, the official organization of the churches strove to perpetuate in the membership the same standards. If successfully carried out, this would of itself have produced a profound and sweeping transformation of the life of the realm. Even now, however, the leaders did not dream of a planned revolution which would wipe out the familiar world and substitute for it something new built on a drastic application of the words of Jesus. They endeavoured simply to eliminate a few of the features of contemporary life which the Fathers had traditionally condemned—among them the old polytheism and idolatry, the gladiatorial games, the indecencies of the theatre, infanticide, and sexual irregularities.

Even had the heads of the Church wished to bring in a fully Christian society, they would have been estopped by the alliance with the state. It was with the aid of the government that the majority of the once pagan population came into the Church. That government was conservative. Probably one of the motives of its Emperors in supporting the new faith was the hope of gaining the assistance of the Church in the preservation of the existing order against the impending disintegration.[6] Had the leaders of the Church striven for a drastic reconstruction of society, they would have forfeited the support of the state and the

[5] Troeltsch, *op. cit.*, pp. 126-128, declares that in the early Catholic Church the conception of a Christian civilization was not present and that no one dreamed that the Church might undertake social reform. See also Case, *The Social Triumph of the Ancient Church*, p. 34. It is significant that in the Christian writings of the pre-Constantinian period and in the many apologists there is nowhere any desire expressed to transform the Roman Empire as a whole.

[6] Troeltsch, *op. cit.*, pp. 126-128, declares that the temper of the times was conservative and that the many difficulties and disasters of the post-Diocletian age made it impossible for the Emperors to think of anything more than conserving what they could of civilization.

ivil authorities would quickly have replaced them with less dangerous men.
ndeed, one of the most notable results of Christianity was the preservation of
much of the vanishing culture through the agency of the Church.

The monastic movement, roughly coinciding as it did with the great influx
nto the Church, also tended to prevent the emergence of any plan for the remaking of civilization. The monastic ideal drew its devotees out of normal
ociety into communities built upon what it esteemed Christian principles.
Attracting as it did a large proportion of the most ardent Christians, it tended
o distract attention from any effort to bring all of society up to its own exacting
tandards. Indeed, it despaired of doing so and acquiesced in a division between
hose who wished to attain perfectly to the Gospel rule and those who admittedly had given over any effort to carry out more than a portion of its
precepts.

Moreover, even had Christians wished completely to reorganize the society
of the Empire, the time in which they had to work was very brief. Before Constantine they were in no position, persecuted as they often were, to effect much
change outside their own circles. Within less than a century after Constantine
hose invasions had begun which worked the final wreckage of the conven-
ional culture over a large proportion of the Mediterranean basin.[7]

Then, too, it must be noted that no ideal ever reshapes any large body of men
completely after its pattern. Always it must accommodate itself to other forces.
The result of its efforts invariably contains an element of compromise. So with
he impulse which came from Jesus. Powerful though it was, it became only
one of many factors which were working in the ancient world. It would have
been contrary to all human experience to expect it fully to remake its environment after its own likeness.

Although the vast body of Christians entertained no thought of reconstructing
society on the model of the Sermon on the Mount, the impulse emanating from
Jesus was not without profound effects upon the Mediterranean world. It is
something more than a convention which pictures human history as divided
into the two eras Before Christ and After Christ. The advent of Jesus set in
motion vast energies which placed their imprint deeply not only upon Græco-
Roman culture but also upon all the peoples and cultures which have been
touched by it and its successors. Here was a new beginning. Although modified
by them, Christianity was not the logical outcome of forces at work in Græco-
Roman culture, but a fresh departure, a new creation.[8] Deeply rooted though

[7] H. H. Scullard in Paton, Bunting, and Garvie, editors, *Christ and Civilization*, pp,
239, 240.
[8] Dawson, *Progress and Religion*, p. 157.

it was in Judaism, it was different from its parent stock and had a far wide and more transforming influence. It was born into a world, it will be recalled in which the familiar patterns of life were being broken. The years of it initial spread and earliest numerical triumphs witnessed the death throes o the culture in which it had been cradled. It had, then, an opportunity to mould what followed. Especially in the West, where the shattering of the old was mos nearly complete, it was able to exert a powerful influence on what came after. To the enumeration and brief description of these results we must now turn.

It seems almost a banality to say that one of the outstanding groups of effect of Christianity was upon the religious life of the Græco-Roman world. It was however, so important and so varied that it requires at least a brief description

Among the religious results which must be mentioned were the efforts o the rivals which Christianity eventually supplanted to copy or adapt some fea tures of their dangerous competitor. How extensive these were we do not know chiefly because the records of many of the cults have so largely disappeared. In an age characterized by syncretism, as were the early centuries of the Christia era, we would naturally expect them, and on a fairly large scale. Certainly, a we shall see in the next chapter, Christianity absorbed much from its rivals However, the surviving evidence of the influence of Christianity upon it antagonists is not very extensive. It may be that it was not so great as the reverse stream of their contributions to the victor. Yet we know or can conjecture some of the effects upon the forms of other cults.

We have already noted the attempt of Julian to incorporate into his revived paganism methods of the hated Galileans.[10] This was the most deliberate and extensive copying of Christianity of which we have record. Neoplatonism formed after Christianity had assumed portentous proportions, just possibly may also have owed something to its major competitor. Ammonius Saccas, the alleged founder of the school and a teacher of its first prominent figure Plotinus, is said to have been reared a Christian and by Christian parents,[11] but this was disputed even by his own contemporaries.[12] Porphyry, an ardent pupil of Plotinus, tended to give to Neoplatonism, it will be recalled, a strong anti

---

[9] Cadoux, *The Early Church and the World*, pp. 611-619, in summarizing the effects of Christianity on the ancient world declares that the pre-Constantinian Church was a reformative movement on a scale and with a potency unequalled elsewhere at any other time.

[10] See a summary of these measures in Martin, *The Emperor Julian*, pp. 72-78. See also Case, *op. cit.*, p. 32.

[11] Eusebius, *Eccles. Hist.*, Book VI, Chap. 19, gives Porphyry as authority for the statement that Ammonius Saccas was the son of Christian parents and had been reared a Christian.

[12] Foakes-Jackson, *Eusebius Pamphili*, p. 17.

Christian bias.[13] It is doubtful, however, whether Neoplatonism, by conscious or unconscious borrowing or by antagonism, owed many of its ideas and practices to its successful rival.[14] As to other cults, it will be remembered that Alexander Severus is said to have had in his private chapel images of Abraham, Orpheus, Apollonius, and Christ.[15] It is possible that Mithraism sought to make of the legend of the Iranian hero a parallel to the life of Jesus and was indebted to the Gospel stories for a communion meal and an ascension.[16] The Phrygian priests of the Great Mother are said to have set over against the Christian Easter their celebration of the Vernal Equinox and to have attributed to the blood shed in the taurobolium the redemptive power of the blood of Jesus.[17] It is possible that contact with Christianity spiritualized that ceremony.[18] In the reign of Septimius Severus a biography of Apollonius of Tyre was composed in which the many features similar to the life of Jesus seem to show the influence of the Gospels.[19]

The most sweeping destructive effect of Christianity upon the Græco-Roman world was the elimination of the pagan cults. If Christianity were to triumph, this was to be expected. It was against the current polytheism in all its forms that the Christian apologists directed their most trenchant attacks.[20] To be sure, not all professing Christians held themselves completely aloof from the religious practices about them,[21] and, as we are soon to note, many conceptions and customs associated with the supposedly deceased faiths persisted, though usually in more or less thinly veiled disguise. However, officially the Church was uncompromising in its purpose to eradicate all forms of the older cults, as many a writing and the actions of numerous synods show. By and large, moreover, in the Mediterranean basin the rivals of Christianity perished.

Never in human history have ancient religions so deeply entrenched in the

[13] McGiffert, in Note 1, on Book VI, Chap. 19 (pp. 264, 265) of his translation of Eusebius, *Eccles. Hist.*; Lecky, *History of European Morals*, Vol. I, p. 330.

[14] McGiffert, *loc. cit.*, declares that Neoplatonism solved in a way different from that of Christianity the problems of salvation and redemption. It is doubtful whether McGiffert is right in saying that these problems were thrown into the world of thought by Christianity. They seem, rather, to have been in the air which both Christians and Neoplatonists breathed.

[15] Healy, *The Valerian Persecution*, pp. 18, 19, citing Lampridius, *Vita Alex. Severi*, Chaps. 29, 45, 49.

[16] Clemen, *Der Einfluss des Christentums auf andere Religionen*, p. 22.

[17] Cumont, *The Oriental Religions in Roman Paganism*, p. xvii.

[18] Graillot, *Le Culte de Cybèle*, p. 543.

[19] Uhlhorn, *The Conflict of Christianity with Heathenism*, pp. 278, 279, 329-332; Labriolle, *La Réaction Païenne*, pp. 175-189.

[20] See, for instance, Tertullian, *On Idolatry*, passim, and Athenagoras, *A Plea for the Christians*, Chaps. 8, 13, 14, 17-22.

[21] As in I Cor. viii:10; x:14-21, and Tertullian, *On Idolatry*, Chap. 7. Tertullian seems to say that even some Christian clerics continued to be artificers of idols.

culture of a civilized people been eradicated so completely over so large an area. On a somewhat smaller scale we shall see the story repeated more than once in the subsequent spread of Christianity and among animistic peoples over much wider regions. The disappearance of Christianity before Islam from the seventh into the sixteenth century and under the persecuting zeal of Communism in Russia in the twentieth century might seem to equal it. In both of these instances, however, the Church has survived as the faith of a minority. Zoroastrianism, which Islam all but stamped out, has lived on, even though mostly in exile. The pre-Christian cults of the Græco-Roman world, however, all perished—with the one exception of Judaism. Since these faiths were closely entwined with economic, political, and social institutions, their disappearance inescapably worked more or less profound changes in other aspects of life. In literature their imagery has persisted to our own day. Never, however, after the fifth century was any serious attempt made to revive the ancient cults on a large scale. That they vanished so completely was partly because of the vast changes in civilization and in some areas the death of the culture with which they were associated. Christianity, however, was a major factor in the destruction.

It seems amazing that Judaism alone survived. Its persistence may shed some light upon the reasons for the fate of the others. It possessed the coherence of communities organized on the combined basis of race and religion, an asset which none of the others could show. Even more than Christianity, moreover, it was an uncompromising monotheism. It was from Judaism, indeed, that the daughter faith inherited this quality.

However, Christianity had its effect upon Judaism. Much of this must be inferred and cannot be clearly demonstrated, but the conjectures appear so in accord with the known facts as to seem at least reasonable. The main result appears to have been a reinforcement of other factors which halted Judaism in its progress toward universalization and made it turn in on itself, develop an orthodoxy which was largely an outgrowth of Phariseeism, and become a congeries of self-contained, encysted communities which exerted themselves but little to win converts and resisted efforts at assimilation to Christianity and, later, to Islam. Before the advent of Christianity, it will be recalled, many Jews were reaching out in friendly fashion to the world about them, seeking to adjust their faith to the prevailing philosophies and attracting adherents. Hellenistic Judaism had arisen, a partial accommodation to the Hellenistic world, and many synagogues of the Dispersion were being augmented by proselytes and were surrounded by a fringe of Gentiles who, while not conforming fully to the Jewish law, were adopting some features of Jewish belief, ritual, and ethics. With the coming of Christianity a sharp conflict ensued, and a separation between mother and daughter occurred with not a little rancour on both sides. The Church seems to have won most of the Gentile fringe of the synagogue.[22] Why it could do so is not entirely clear. In its fresh enthusiasm and in the type of immortality which it promised it probably seemed to offer more than could the other. It welcomed all races, whereas in formally joining with the synagogue the convert became a Jew. Still, Christians were thought of as a third race, and apparently were regarded with more popular disapproval and were subject to greater persecution than were the Jews. It seems more likely that it was the story of the life, death, and resurrection of Jesus which proved the main attraction. More nearly than anything in Judaism this was in accord with what was being sought by the more earnest spirits in that Hellenistic world in which the mystery religions flourished. Then, too, after its experience with Christian laxity toward the ceremonial law, Judaism seems to have become less tolerant of that fringe of "God-fearers" who only partly kept the Law[23] and to have become more rigid in its ritual requirements of its own constituency. It may be significant that Hellenistic Judaism itself disappeared, even within Jewish circles. The tendency represented by Pharisaism triumphed. This may have been because many of those with predilections for things Hellenistic entered the Christian movement. It may also have been because Jewish leaders, believing that Christianity showed what would come of the Hellenizing tendency, in rejecting the one reacted against the other.[24] It was probably in part because of Christianity that within Judaism a reaction set in against Messianism, and especially against its more exalted and transcendent forms.[25] Then again, in the conflict between Jews and Christians in Palestine the Jews are declared to have determined the limits of their canon by the express exclusion of the Gospels and other Christian writings.[26] It is said, moreover, that in the second and third centuries some of the rabbis attempted to make of the vicarious sacrifice of Isaac an alternative to that of Jesus.[27]

It is noteworthy that few reminiscences of the controversy with the Christians remain in the Tannaitic literature.[28] It may be that the great Jewish rebellions of the first and second centuries, with their aftermath, had more to do with

---

[22] Oesterley and Box, *The Religion and Worship of the Synagogue*, p. 8. See also Moore, *Judaism*, Vol. I, p. 92.

[23] Goodenough, *The Theology of Justin Martyr*, p. 54.

[24] The author is indebted to E. R. Goodenough for this suggestion.

[25] Montefiore, *Judaism and St. Paul*, p. 60.

[26] J. H. Ropes in *An Outline of Christianity*, Vol. I, p. 315.

[27] Parkes, *The Conflict of the Church and the Synagogue*, p. 116.

[28] Moore, *Judaism*, Vol. I, p. 92.

the disappearance of Hellenistic Judaism and the development of non-aggressive conservative orthodoxy than did the conflict with the Christians.

Whatever may have brought about the change, it did not entirely rob Judaism of its capacity to win converts. We have noted in South Arabia those who had accepted Judaism, and we shall discover them later both in Arabia and in Russia. The Church, moreover, feared the loss of Christian slaves of Jewish masters. Within the lands where Christianity had become dominant, however, Judaism probably had relatively few accessions. Its gains were from among pagans.

In general, after the sharp controversies of the first century, the relations between Jews and Christians, while seldom if ever cordial, appear not to have been bitter.[29] In the fourth century the now nominally Christian Empire meted out more severe treatment to Christian heretics than to Jews.[30] Still the Church did not give over its hope of winning the Jews. We read of at least two instances in the fourth century of Christians either destroying a synagogue or overturning a synagogue and erecting a church in its place.[31] Yet forcible conversions appear to have been much more rare than in the centuries after A.D. 500. Relatively little infiltration, either voluntary or involuntary, appears to have taken place from one community to the other.

It must be noted that the religious achievement of Christianity was not merely the negative one of the elimination of all organized rivals except Judaism. It was also the positive one of a substitution of something different. Here, indeed, was one of the major consequences of the spread of Christianity in the Græco-Roman world. Had it not been the theme of the preceding chapters, it ought logically to have been placed first, for out of it came the other results with which this present chapter deals. It was because Christianity differed from other faiths and because it supplanted them, at first among a minority and then among the majority, that the other consequences followed in institutions and in altered customs. To be sure, in many ways Christianity resembled some of its competitors. In the course of its career it was partly moulded by them, as we shall presently see. It was, however, not completely like any of them and from all of them had basic differences. Partly, as we have said, its victory is attributable to the fact that it satisfied the demands which many were making of religion, but in a more inclusive and convincing manner than other systems. It offered what some of its rivals promised, but more attractively and compellingly. Yet it also possessed qualities which the others did not have. These

[29] Parkes, op. cit., p. 305.
[30] Parkes, op. cit., pp. 183-189.
[31] Vita of Innocentius in Acta Sanc., Apr., Vol. II, p. 480; Ambrose, Ep., Book I, XL (Migne, Pat. Lat., Vol. XVI, Cols. 1103, 1109).

we have already described in our account of what the faith was at its inception and in our attempt to determine the causes of its victory. Because of these differences, the triumph of Christianity brought to the Græco-Roman world a religious life which incorporated many elements from the past, yet absorbed them all into something new. We must remind ourselves again that here was no logical evolution from the paganism of the Mediterranean world, but a fresh irruption, almost a new beginning. In its idea of God, in its concept of the nature and destiny of man, in its saviour, and in its organization, its ministry, its world view, its literature, its art, its public and private worship, and its ethics, it made original contributions. While in the complex movement which is generally called Christianity was not a little of the old and familiar, much of the essence was new and the total organism was original. Religiously Christianity gave to the waning Roman Empire a fresh complexion.

Another of the major results of Christianity which deserves our attention is the creation of the Church. Into the details of the origin and development of the Church we must not go. That is a story in itself, and a long one. The sense of the existence of a Christian community, the Christian Church, was strong at least as early as the time of Paul, and continued to be so.[32] Here was one of the major achievements of the impulse given by Jesus. The Christian Church is unique.[33] It is older than any other large organization or group of organizations now found on the planet. It has long outlasted the Roman Empire, which, as an Empire, only slightly antedated it. No other religion has created an institution quite like it. Judaism, to which it is deeply indebted, developed a community which, like the Church, has been scattered in many lands. However, the composition of Judaism is as much racial as religious. The Christian churches, in contrast, have been recruited from many races and the tie which holds them together is not one of blood. Moreover, none of the mystery religions developed so inclusive a community or so elaborate, Empire-wide an organization as did Christianity.[34] Buddhism speaks of its community, but in that has included primarily its celibates who have devoted themselves exclusively to the Buddhist law. The Buddhist laity are not nearly so closely knit

[32] For Paul, see, among other examples, I Cor. xii:1-31, Eph. iv:1-16, v:25-27. For some later examples, see The Shepherd of Hermas, Book I; The Epistle of Ignatius to the Magnesians; The Epistle of Ignatius to the Ephesians; I Clement, 44; the Epistles of Cyprian.

[33] This idea is partially developed in an editorial in The Christian Century, April 18, 1934, Vol. LI, pp. 518-520. Uhlhorn, op. cit., p. 164, declares that this congregational life of the Christians was unlike anything else in pagan antiquity. Harnack, The Mission and Expansion of Christianity, Vol. I, pp. 431-444, says that the Christian society was new and unique in Greek and Roman society.

[34] A. D. Nock in Journal of Biblical Literature, Vol. LII, p. 136.

into the community as are lay Christians into the churches. Islam has possessed a certain consciousness of solidarity, but it has never developed so elaborate an organization as are the Christian churches for the express and primary purpose of the cure of souls. It speaks volumes for the impulse which came from Jesus that in the decadent centuries of Græco-Roman culture it should have stimulated the Græco-Roman stock to the creation of this original and unique institution which has displayed such marked vitality.

The rise of the Church also sheds light on the decay of the culture by which it was enveloped. It seems to indicate that what was moribund was not the human material, for this, impelled by Christianity, produced the Church. As the Church developed and became powerful, not unnaturally it attracted to its leadership some of the ablest men of the time. It is not surprising that in the day of its triumph, in the fourth century, its outstanding figures were greater men than contemporary pagan priests, philosophers, and rhetoricians.[35] However, the Church not only drew to itself men of ability, but something in its message seems to have inspired them to utilize their powers beyond what would otherwise have been the case. This appears to have been true, for example, of an Ambrose of Milan and an Augustine of Hippo.

Closely related to the formation of the Christian Church was the emergence of the Christian ministry. Here again is a unique institution. To be sure, it has in it something of the prophetic tradition of Judaism and it shares the priestly functions not only of Judaism but of many other faiths. From the first, however, it has embraced a purpose which seems to have been derived directly from the example of Jesus himself, that of the pastor or shepherd.[36] Into the history of the development of the official leadership of the Church we must not attempt to go. It has long been a controversial subject and on it a prodigious literature exists.[37] Yet this much must be pointed out. In most of its various forms it included the pastoral function, the care of individuals, with the ideal of loving, self-forgetful effort to win them to what the Christian conceives as the highest life and to help them to grow in it.

Intimately connected, too, with the creation of the Church was the development of the Christian liturgy. Here the high-water mark was associated with the Eucharist. The details of the process by which the elaborate rituals of the

[35] Taylor, The Mediæval Mind, Vol. I, p. 50.
[36] See an article by K. S. Latourette in The International Review of Missions, Vol. XXIV (1935), pp. 113-122.
[37] Of this vast literature one of the best books is Lindsay, The Church and the Ministry in the Early Centuries. An excellent summary, but covering more than this period, is A. V. G. Allen, Christian Institutions. Well known, too, is A. Harnack, The Constitution and Law of the Church in the First Two Centuries.

later centuries grew out of the relatively simple ceremonies of the early Church lie outside the scope of this book. In another chapter we must raise the question of indebtedness to other than purely Christian sources. Here we must note that however extensive the borrowing, conscious or unconscious, from other faiths, the liturgy of the Church was essentially a Christian creation and owed its inspiration and the stories and experiences it dramatized to the example and the death of Jesus and the conviction of the disciples that he had been raised from the dead and that they continued to have contact with him as their living Lord.[38]

Upon intellectual life, literature, and language, the effect of Christianity was rather mixed. In church circles a widespread distrust of pagan philosophy and literature existed.[39] There were also neglect of and even opposition to the empirical, exact sciences—although in this Christianity was simply in accord with the spirit of declining antiquity.[40] On the other hand, many Christian teachers were ardent students of ancient philosophy and sought to present their faith in philosophical guise. Notable among these were Clement of Alexandria[41] and Origen. In post-Constantinian times, moreover, Christian teachers of the classical authors and of the traditional rhetoric were usual.[42] Yet also in the fifth century we seem to find that the conventional education was held in suspicion by some churchmen. In Phrygia we hear of a bishop who was unable to sign his name.[43]

Christianity produced a voluminous literature and in much of this were ideas quite alien to traditional Græco-Roman thought. Christian theology had an extensive inheritance from Judaism and was profoundly influenced by Greek and Hellenistic philosophy, notably Platonism and Neoplatonism. It was not, however, an eclectic medley of previous systems, but a distinctive and original contribution to human thought. As it issued from the minds and pens of the most eminent of the Christian theologians it was worthy of comparison with the non-Christian systems of philosophy. Here again the impulse which came

---

[38] Of the many books on Christian worship the following two may be mentioned as convenient brief summaries: Allen, *Christian Institutions*, pp. 399-577, by a scholarly Episcopalian, and L. Duchesne, *Christian Worship: Its Origin and Evolution. A Study of the Latin Liturgy up to the Time of Charlemagne.* See also passages in Lindsay, *op. cit.*, among them pp. 44-52.

[39] Lohmeyer, *Soziale Fragen im Urchristentum*, p. 122; Boissier, *La Fin du Paganisme*, Vol. I, pp, 200-204. Tertullian, *On Idolatry*, Chap. 10, declares that a Christian teacher could not conduct a school except by compromising with idolatry, and that a Christian could not receive such instruction without danger.

[40] Troeltsch, *The Social Teachings of the Christian Churches*, pp. 143ff.

[41] As in Clement, *Stromata*, Book I, Chaps. 2-6.

[42] Boissier, *op. cit.*, Vol. I, pp. 200-204, 215.

[43] Ramsay, *The Cities and Bishoprics of Phrygia*, Vol. II, p. 509.

from Jesus stimulated to creative activity of the highest order minds drawn from a culture from which the genius of originality seemed to have departed.

Christianity introduced, too, a philosophy of history which seems to have revolutionized the attitude of the Occident, and especially of Western Europe, towards the social process. The minds which moulded the thought of Greece did not take an optimistic view of the future of mankind. As they conceived it, human history was a succession of cycles, each terminated by progressive decline. Some of them regarded the world as created and set going by God. At its inception, as his work, it was perfect, but it carried within it the seeds of inevitable decay. At the end of the degeneration would come chaos, but God would then step in, restore conditions as at first, and the process would begin once more, to end again in complete collapse, to be followed once more by divine intervention. So, supposedly endlessly, the cycles would continue.[44] Plato seemed to endorse the view that civilizations had repeatedly arisen and, as often, had been destroyed by the gods, leaving no memory behind.[45] Aristotle held it probable that each art after being developed as far as possible, again perished.[46] In contrast with this was a conception of human history introduced by Christianity and finding what are probably its most famous expressions in *The Apocalypse* and in Augustine's *City of God*. This conception, derived from the Hebrew prophets and the Jewish apocalypses, thought of God as actively at work in human history and represented the race as moving towards a divine culmination, ushered in by God, to a society in which righteousness, peace, and happiness would prevail.[47]

How far this view of history affected Christian participation in the social process is not clear. It is not demonstrated, for instance, that because of it Christians undertook widespread reforms, hoping thereby to hasten the consummation of the age and the introduction of an ideal society. Evidence of that result appears to be lacking, probably because Christians did not contemplate such measures. Not until modern times, notably the nineteenth century, does the idea of human progress as inevitable in the nature of the universe but possible of acceleration by the effort of men seem to have become prominent. When it does emerge, sometimes it is in earnestly Christian circles and is clearly traceable to Christian roots. On other occasions a Christian origin for it cannot be

[44] Bury, *The Idea of Progress*, pp. 9, 10.
[45] Plato, *Timæus*, 21-23; *Critias*, 109 (R. G. Bury's edition of Plato, Vol. VII, pp. 30-35, 268, 269).
[46] Aristotle, *Metaphysics*, Book XI, Chap. 9.
[47] This idea is elaborated in Dawson, *Progress and Religion*, especially on pp. 137-143, 156ff. See, too, brief mentions of this Christian contribution in Goodenough, *The Church in the Roman Empire*, p. 21, and in Leclercq, *L'Espagne Chrétienne*, pp. 1, 2.

demonstrated. Of these later phases we are to speak in subsequent volumes. Here we can merely note that this Christian view of history, while giving hope for the ultimate outcome for the divine-human drama, does not before the year 500 appear to have inspired men to do much if anything to hasten it. The climax was usually believed to be in heaven, not on earth, and to be brought in, not by man, but by the act of God. Still, such works as the *City of God*, by insisting that God would not be defeated and that ultimately the ideal kingdom would come, must have heartened many who lived in the midst of a collapsing and disordered culture and who might otherwise have despaired. It may thus, indirectly, have nerved them to action. The *City of God* insisted that progress was discernible even in its day.

While out of the Christian movement came a philosophy of history, in some respects the Christian impulse seems to have vitiated feeling for the authentic in man's past. Much of the Christian so-called history and biography abounds in the miraculous. The apocryphal Gospels, which must have enjoyed wide circulation, and numerous pseudonymous works ascribed to great names of the past bear witness to a highly emotionalized atmosphere in which historical accuracy was lightly regarded.[48]

Christianity inaugurated a new literature. Almost inevitably, at the outset most of it was of a religious character or was strongly impregnated with a religious outlook. In the case of Christian literature in Latin, at its inception this was largely the work of men of action who were interested in polemics. Such popular prose literature as *The Shepherd of Hermas* also arose early.[49] As was natural, the enthusiasm generated by the new faith expressed itself partly in poetry and notably in hymns.[50] This seems to have come later in Latin, but elsewhere it began early. In the New Testament we seem to have many fragments of Christian hymns.[51] While sometimes conforming to current literary patterns, Christian literature made these ancillary to the expression of the convictions and the emotions to which the Christian dynamic had given birth. Some Christians, to be sure, among them ecclesiastics in high places who had been trained in the conventional schools of the times, in much of their

[48] Examples of this are numerous and so familiar to all who know the Christian literature of this period as not to require listing. A brief comment on this tendency is in Shotwell and Loomis, *The See of Peter*, p. xxii.
[49] Boissier, *La Fin du Paganisme*, Vol. II, pp. 2ff.
[50] Schultze, *Geschichte des Untergangs des griechisch-römischen Heidentums*, Vol. II, pp. 74-79; Glover, *Christ in the Ancient World*, p. 54.
[51] Boissier, *op. cit.*, Vol. II, pp. 2ff. Lindsay, *op. cit.*, suggests Rev. v:9-13; xi:17; xv:3, 4, as examples of these fragments of hymns. See also I Cor. xiv:26; Eph. v:19; Col. iii:16; I Tim. iii:16; II Tim. ii:11, 12. On Christian literature in Latin, see Labriolle, *Histoire de la Littérature Latine Chrétienne*, which brings the account down to the Middle Ages.

writing gave little evidence of their Christian faith, or mingled references to pagan mythology with ideas of Christian provenance. In the large proportion of the surviving Christian literature of the period, however, while the influence of literary standards inherited from non-Christian Græco-Roman culture is obvious, the dominant interest is in ideas attributable to Christian sources.

It must be noted that Christian thinkers did little or nothing to encourage the study of natural science. Augustine, in common with others of the Fathers, insisted that the Scriptures contained an authoritative account of the world and its phenomena and that further study of them was superfluous. In this indifference to independent observation of the physical universe, however, he simply reflected the temper of his time.[52]

On language Christianity made its imprint. For instance, the Greek of the New Testament, while owing much to that current at the time, the *koine*, and affected by the Aramaic-Jewish or Hellenistic-Jewish background of the authors, has its own distinctive flavour and its peculiar technical terms. Its vocabulary has been described as that of an enclosed world, living its own life, a ghetto culturally and linguistically, if not geographically.[53]

In some regions Christianity assisted the spread of Greek and in others of Latin, with the attendant destruction of the local tongues. In Asia Minor it seems to have been Christianity rather than the imperial administration which finally made Greek the universal language.[54] In North Africa Christianity appears to have been a powerful agent of the extension of Latin: at least the catechetical books which have come down to us and the inscriptions which adorned the churches were predominantly in that tongue.[55] In Gaul the Celtic idiom seems to have died out as a result of the conversion of the populace to a Christianity whose official tongue was Latin.[56]

On the other hand, in some areas Christianity provided the impulse which helped both to perpetuate local tongues and to create a literature in them. We have already noted that, in trying to familiarize the people of Armenia with Christian books, a new alphabet was formed for their language and extensive translations made through it. It was in the fifth century, under this incentive, that Armenian literature enjoyed a golden age.[57] In Georgia the chief books

[52] McGiffert, *A History of Christian Thought*, Vol. II, pp. 122, 123.

[53] A. D. Nock, *The Vocabulary of the New Testament*, in *The Journal of Biblical Literature*, Vol. LII, pp. 131-139.

[54] Ramsay, *The Church in the Roman Empire*, p. 44.

[55] Leclercq, *L'Afrique Chrétienne*, Vol. I, p. 102.

[56] Mommsen, *The Provinces of the Roman Empire*, Vol. I, p. 110.

[57] In addition to the references given, in the last chapter, see Berg, *Die katholische Heidenmission als Kulturträger*, Vol. II, p. 15; Finck, *Geschichte der armenischen Lit-*

were religious, by Christian clergy and monks. Through the same channels the language was enriched with new words, and it is to the Church that the Georgians owe two alphabets.[58]

The Syriac language was greatly indebted to Christianity. It was through that faith that Syriac literature first took on importance. The progress of Syriac as a literary language had been checked by the Hellenizing of the East and the popularity of Greek. Syriac, however, was an important vernacular, and to reach with and nourish in the faith those whose tongue it was, a Christian literature in it became necessary. A translation of the Gospels was early made. The development of Syriac literature went hand in hand with the spread of Christianity and reached its zenith at the end of the sixth century. In the seventh century the devastating wars between the Persian and Roman Empires, fought largely in the region where Syriac was spoken, followed by the Arab conquest and the coming of Arabic as the language of the rulers, dealt a blow to Syriac literature from which it never fully recovered.[59]

Christianity once more made of the native Egyptian speech a literary language. After the conquest by Alexander, the Hellenization of Egypt continued through the Ptolemaic period and was accelerated under the Romans. It was particularly marked in the urban and the upper classes. In time the hieroglyphic script fell into disuse and Greek became the polite language of the educated and the vehicle of most of the literature. The native Egyptian tongue persisted, but particularly in Upper Egypt and chiefly as the speech of the peasants and day labourers. When Christianity began to win numerous adherents among this Egyptian-using population, the need was felt for a Christian literature which could be used by them. In place of the difficult hieroglyphics a simple script was employed, based largely on the Greek letters. The Egyptian so written was called Coptic. The chief home of Coptic Christian literature was in Upper Egypt, or the Thebaïd, and the dialect which prevailed there was known as Saïdic. Translations into it were made from the Greek. That of the Bible seems to have been completed by A.D. 350. North of the Thebaïd another dialect, the Achmimian, was found, and in it some Christian literature was created. Most of this Coptic Christian literature appears to have been the work of the monks who were so prominent in Egypt. They were the educated class. From

---

teratur, in *Geschichte der christlichen Litteraturen des Orients*, pp. 77-82; Aufhauser, in *Zeitschrift für Missionswissenschaft*, Vol. VIII, pp. 83, 84.

[58] Tamarati, *L'Église Géorgienne*, p. 389, quoting in part from Josseliani, a Georgian historian.

[59] Harnack, *The Mission and Expansion of Christianity*, Vol. II, p. 145; Mommsen, *The Provinces of the Roman Empire*, Vol. II, p. 136; Brockelmann, *Die syrische und die christlich-arabische Litteratur*, in *Geschichte der christlichen Litteraturen des Orients*.

among them came not only the writers, but the best architects and physicians. The greatest author of the Saïdic literature was a monk, one Shenute, who died in 451, and by a century and a half after his death the creative period had closed.[60]

The part which the Christian missionary played in creating a Gothic literature has already been noted. Here, too, an alphabet was devised and the Scriptures translated.

It must be apparent that the linguistic influence of Christianity had effects even beyond the raising of various languages to the dignity of literary tongues and the creation of literatures in them. The spread of Greek in Asia Minor assisted in the creation of that Byzantine state and culture which in the East arose out of the Roman Empire. The extension of Latin in Gaul and in other parts of Occidental Europe was one of the causes of that sense of unity which underneath all differences and dissension characterized Western Christendom in the Middle Ages. In Armenia, Georgia, and Egypt the influence of Christianity upon language and literature augmented what would now be termed nationalism. Perhaps it helped to separate the Goths from their Roman subjects.

In art and architecture by the year 500 Christianity had begun to make pronounced and distinctive contributions. Long before the close of the fifth century, indeed, Christian art had emerged. Here again is a subject on which an appalling number of books and articles have been written and into which it is not our function to go in any detail. In Christian art many older artistic traditions and forms were utilized. As in so many other realms, however, the Christian impulse, while drawing freely on other heritages, gave rise to something distinctive in which were unmistakably the characteristic marks of its own genius. The paintings developed by it, as seen in the Roman catacombs, show indebtedness to other faiths, but usually expressed Christian sentiments. Noteworthy, for instance, is the frequency of the appearance of the figure of the Good Shepherd, and not only in Rome but in the little church of the first half of the third century at Dura-Europos, on the eastern edge of the Roman Empire, which skilful archæology has recently revealed to us.[61] If it was used prominently in two so widely separated places, probably it was a familiar figure elsewhere. The Christian cult involved congregational worship and Christian churches, when erected, were designed to house it. As the eucharist developed,

---

[60] Mommsen, *op. cit.*, Vol. II, p. 265; Leipoldt, *Geschichte der koptischen Litteratur*, pp. 133-157, in *Geschichte der christlichen Litteraturen des Orients.*

[61] On the church at Dura-Europos see C. Hopkins in Rostovtzeff (editor), *The Excavations at Dura-Europos Conducted by Yale University and the French Academy of Inscriptions and Letters. Preliminary Report of Fifth Season of Work, Oct., 1931-March, 1932*, pp. 238-253.

with its bloodless sacrifice, architectural provision became necessary for an altar in the presence of the assembled worshippers. The initiatory rite, in the early centuries largely, if not entirely, by immersion, gave rise to baptistries. Church buildings arose in many different sections, from Mesopotamia and Armenia to the western part of the Roman Empire, and incorporated several different local traditions.[62] Beginning with the recognition by Constantine and assisted by his munificent patronage, church edifices within the Empire rapidly became larger and more ornate and magnificent.[63]

Upon pagan art Christianity had a mixed effect. In general, it tended to destroy it. With the disappearance of the pagan cults, the erection of new temples and images ceased, and those already in existence were either destroyed, allowed to fall into ruin, transformed into churches, or their materials utilized for other structures. It must be recalled, however, that to some of the Popes of later centuries, notably those of the Renaissance, must be attributed the preservation of many of the surviving examples of ancient non-Christian art.

It was to be expected that Christianity would work modifications in the family and in the status of women and children. The exacting standard of sex relations set up in the Gospels,[64] even more searching than the stringent ones of Judaism, the sanctity with which the marriage tie was invested,[65] and the place accorded to women[66] and children[67] could not but have their effects. We need not accept as typical of society as a whole the laxity and the cruelty depicted in the writings of certain satirists and in pagan denunciations of the evils of the day. The fact that some non-Christians pilloried them is evidence of a body of opinion outside the Church which deplored what it deemed excesses. As we have noted, the first centuries of the Christian era witnessed, quite apart from the influence of the Church, a movement towards moral reform and humanitarianism. However, conditions existed, even if only among a minority, which Christian ethics could not condone. Moreover, some commonly accepted practices ran counter to Christian *mores*. The latter inevitably wrought changes.

[62] On the development of Christian art in Armenia and Mesopotamia, see Strzygowski, *Origin of Christian Art, passim.* Strzygowski attempts to demonstrate the influence of Armenian, Mesopotamian, and Iranian forms upon Christian art elsewhere.

[63] A very brief summary of early Christian art is in Schultze, *Geschichte des Untergangs des griechisch-römischen Heidentums,* Vol. II, pp. 53-62. See also Wulff, *Altchristliche und byzantinische Kunst;* Smith, *Early Christian Iconography and a School of Ivory Carvers in Provence;* Neuss, *Die Kunst der alten Christen;* Garrucci, *Storia della Arte Cristiana nei primi otto secoli della Chiesa.*

[64] As in Matt. v:27-30.

[65] As in Matt. v:31, 32; Mark x:2-12.

[66] Gal. iii:28.

[67] Mark x:13-16.

The Church insisted upon monogamy.[68] In at least one instance we hear of a high ecclesiastical official who allowed what legally was called concubinage between high-born women and men of lower social rank, but that was not polygamy and was tolerated because women outnumbered men among the Christians of the upper classes and a woman sacrificed her social status if she entered into formal marriage with a spouse of inferior condition.[69] The Church, moreover, attempted to bring about continence before marriage and to prevent any violation of the marriage tie.[70] Some of its strongest condemnations were for what it adjudged sexual irregularities.[71] Christianity, of course, brought to an end the prostitution carried on in temples and sacred groves under the auspices of the pagan religions.[72] While some prominent Christians assented to the customs of the times in regarding woman as "the weaker vessel,"[73] none of the Church fathers acknowledged that differences in sex affected salvation. Men and women might equally be heirs of eternal life.[74] The rise of monasticism tended to regard woman as a major temptation to the aspirant for sanctity, but long before what we think of as the beginning of the monastic movement women celibates were honoured.[75] Always, moreover, marriage was regarded as an institution deserving the Church's blessing.[76]

The Church taught that abortion was murder[77] and so protested against what seems to have been a common practice of the time.[78] Christians also condemned infanticide and the exposure of children and often sought to rescue abandoned children and to rear them in the faith—although when so reared they might be allowed to become members of the servile class.[79] The traditional

---

[68] Tertullian, *To His Wife;* Tertullian, *On Monogamy;* Troeltsch, *The Social Teaching of the Christian Churches,* pp. 129-132.

[69] Case, *The Social Triumph of the Ancient Church,* pp. 126-129.

[70] Troeltsch, *op. cit.,* pp. 129-132.

[71] Origen, *Contra Cels.,* Book III, Chap. 51; Haslehurst, *Penitential Discipline in the Farly Church,* pp. 117, 118.

[72] See instances of this temple prostitution, with references to the sources, in Uhlhorn, *The Conflict of Christianity with Heathenism,* p. 484. A popular description of the grove of Daphne with its sacred prostitutes, both men and women, is in Spencer, *Beyond Damascus,* p. 159.

[73] I Peter iii:7; Eph. v:22, 23; Chrysostom, *Hom.* 13 on Eph.; Schmidt, *The Social Results of Early Christianity,* pp. 188, 189.

[74] Gal. iii:28; Augustine, *Sermon CXC,* paragraph 2, in Migne, *Pat. Lat.,* Vol. XXXVIII, Col. 1008; Case, *The Social Origins of Christianity,* p. 145.

[75] I Cor. vii:8; Troeltsch, *op. cit.,* pp. 129-132.

[76] As in the Epistle of Ignatius to Polycarp.

[77] Athenagoras, *Apology,* Chaps. 31-36; Haslehurst, *op. cit.,* pp. 116-124, citing Basil, *Letter* 188; *The Apostolic Constitutions,* Book VII, Chap. 3.

[78] Lecky, *History of European Morals,* Vol. II, pp. 20ff.; Brace, *Gesta Christi,* p. 72.

[79] Oliver, *The Social Achievements of the Christian Church,* pp. 45ff.; Lecky, *op. cit.,* Vol. II, pp. 20ff., citing Labourt, *Recherches sur les Enfans Trouvés,* p. 25; Chastel,

authority of the father over the child, already weakening, was still further modified.[80] Christianity condemned the unnatural vices which had so large a part in the society of the time.[81] It refused to sanction suicide, an act which pagans viewed as heroic under certain circumstances.[82]

Then there was the rather superficial matter of names. Distinctively Christian names were rather slowly adopted. Not until the third and fourth centuries did they become at all common. During the first two centuries most converts retained their pagan designations, even when derived from the gods. One suggestion is that a change of name would have been tantamount to a public declaration of a change of faith and so have unnecessarily invited persecution. When distinctively Christian names were developed, they were either taken from the Bible or were ones of pagan origin which had been consecrated by early saints or martyrs.[83]

Slavery was a characteristic feature of the social and economic organization of the ancient world. Slaves cultivated the great landed estates of the Empire, provided the domestic service, and performed much of the urban labour. The supply was recruited in part as an incident of war. Often the lot of the bondman was unhappy. We hear of those who exposed or killed slaves when they could no longer serve them, and of one distinguished master who sold his old slaves at a low price or drove them away when they were no longer of use.[84] Yet manumission was frequent and the freedman constituted a prominent feature of society.[85] Various factors combined to weaken the institution and to better the lot of the slaves as the Empire progressed.[86] In general Christianity contributed to them. The Christians conducted no organized campaign against slavery. No effort was made to abolish it, even among themselves.[87] The Christian conscience of the time did not condemn the institution. Christian thinkers held it to be due to the Fall, to be a rod of discipline in the hands of God,

Etudes Historiques, p. 104; Brace, *op. cit.*, p. 72; Schmidt, *op. cit.*, p. 204; Justin Martyr, *First Apology*, Book I, Chaps. 27, 29; Lactantius, *Divine Institutes*, Book VI, Chap. 20.

[80] Oliver, *op. cit.*, pp. 45ff.

[81] Rom. i:26, 27; I Cor. vi:9, 10; Brace, *Gesta Christi*, pp. 37-40.

[82] Lecky, *History of European Morals*, Vol. I, pp. 212-224.

[83] Ramsay, *The Cities and Bishoprics of Phrygia*, Vol. II, pp. 485, 492; Schmidlin, *Katholische Missionsgeschichte*, p. 56.

[84] Suetonius, *Claudius*, c. 25; Plutarch, *Marcus Cato*, c. 4.

[85] Barrow, *Slavery in the Roman Empire*, pp. 173-207.

[86] Troeltsch, *op. cit.*, p. 41; Uhlhorn, *op. cit.*, pp. 272-278. At the close of the second century, jurists were declaring that by *jus naturale*—the law of nature—men were free and equal, and that slavery was contrary to nature and part of the *jus gentium*. Carlyle, *A History of Mediæval Political Theory in the West*, Vol. I, p. 47. See also Brace, *Gesta Christi*, pp. 50-58; Uhlhorn, *op. cit.*, pp. 133-140.

[87] Case, *The Social Triumph of the Ancient Church*, p. 118.

and one of the laws of the state appointed by God.[88] However, the Christian attitude could not but tend to rid slavery of some of its most extreme features. Paul declared that "in Christ Jesus" no distinction existed between bond and free,[89] and in a brief but famous letter charged a Christian master to receive as a brother a runaway servant of his who had become a Christian.[90] On the other hand, it is also significant that Paul did not charge the master to free the slave, but sent the latter back to his old service. He was no emancipating revolutionist.[91] Christianity helped to lighten the opprobrium from which labour suffered.[92] It emphasized the duty of work.[93] Since labour had been associated with slavery, the latter was thereby relieved from some of the obloquy which attached to it. Leading exponents of Christianity also declared that both bond and free were capable of the same moral and spiritual life.[94] Several maintained that men in their original nature were free and equal.[95] Ambrose said that the slave might be superior to his master in character and be really more free than he.[96] Augustine held that God did not create rational man to lord it over his rational fellows.[97] How far these ideas as found in the minds of these Fathers had their source in Stoicism and how far in the Gospels we do not know. It is clear, however, that they were believed to be in accord with the Christian message. Moreover, many Christians freed their slaves. Manumission was often performed in a church and on the great festival days, especially Easter, but it was looked upon not as a duty, but as an act of piety or as a means of expiating past sins.[98] Sometimes the freedom of slaves was purchased by church funds.[99] We even hear of Christians who surrendered their own freedom to ransom others.[100] Slaves were granted religious equality and were

[88] Troeltsch, op. cit., pp. 132, 133.
[89] Gal. iii:28.
[90] Philemon, 15:16.
[91] Philemon, passim. See also McGiffert, A History of Christianity in the Apostolic Age, p. 376.
[92] As illustrative of the attitude of ancient society toward labour, see Schmidt, The Social Results of Early Christianity, pp. 17, 18. Aristotle (Politics, Book III, 4) held that the good man and the statesman and the good citizen ought not to learn the crafts of inferiors except for their own occasional use.
[93] Acts xviii:1-3; Eph. iv:28; II Thes. iii:7-10; Case, The Social Triumph of the Ancient Church, pp. 58, 59; Troeltsch, The Social Teaching of the Christian Churches, p. 118; Orr, in Paton, Bunting, and Garvie, editors, Christ and Civilization, p. 231; Uhlhorn, op. cit., p. 188; Schmidt, op. cit., p. 212.
[94] Carlyle, A History of Mediæval Political Theory in the West, Vol. I, pp. 111-124.
[95] Ibid.
[96] Ambrose, De Joseph Patriarcha, Chap. 4, in Migne, Pat. Lat., Vol. XIV, Col. 649.
[97] Augustine, De Civ. Dei, Book XIX, Chap. 15.
[98] Troeltsch, op. cit., pp. 132, 133; Lecky, op. cit., Vol. II, pp. 66-70.
[99] Apostolic Constitutions, Book IV, Chap. 9.
[100] First Epistle of Clement to the Corinthians, 55.

permitted to hold office in the Church, even that of a bishop. The matrimonial ties of slaves were protected. Non-Christians were urged to liberate their slaves or to allow them to purchase their freedom, because by such servitude under non-Christians the religious welfare of the slave was supposed to be imperilled.[101] All of these actions and attitudes, while not regarded as deliberate steps toward terminating the institution of slavery, tended in that direction.

Closely allied to the deeds and beliefs which weakened slavery was the custom of the Church to seek to redeem from servitude prisoners of war. This was frequent, notably in the case of those carried off by the barbarian invasions.[102]

The Church did not conduct an egalitarian campaign to eradicate classes. Apparently its leaders entertained no thought of erasing the social distinctions which characterized the Empire, and especially the Empire in the years in which Christianity was becoming numerically dominant. Yet here, too, by proclaiming that all Christians were heirs of eternal life and that worldly position did not control eternal destiny, it released ideas which, centuries later, had marked influence in breaking down stratifications in society.

Inevitably Christians were confronted with the problem of how far they should conform to the economic standards and patterns of the world about them. It was not only in slavery that they were faced with this issue. They were compelled to consider whether, as Christians, they could hold property of any kind or in any manner. If property could be acquired, should it be held by individuals, with distinctions between rich and poor, or should it be owned in common and for the use of all—or at least of all Christians? If a Christian participated in the economic pursuits of the non-Christian world about him, should he hold aloof from some current occupations and practices?

To these questions no uniform answer was given. Well-known passages in the Gospels seemed to indicate that Jesus condemned not only wealth, but all holding of property.[103] Some of his followers, notably those who joined the monastic movement, followed these in what they regarded as their real meaning and either shunned all ownership of property or held it collectively while eschewing individual title to it. Monasticism, however, did not develop until these first five centuries were well along in their course. The early Church at Jerusalem appears to have had a community of goods,[104] but the brief surviving notice leaves the impression that this was a fleeting phenomenon and not

[101] Troeltsch, op. cit., p. 133.
[102] Troeltsch, op. cit., pp. 140-142; Lecky, op. cit., Vol. II, p. 72.
[103] Mark x:17-27; Luke vi:20, 24.
[104] Acts iv:34, 35.

regarded as obligatory.[105] The Epistle of James indicates a distrust of the rich and their riches,[106] but it does not expressly reject the rich from membership in the Christian community. The first Christians deemed riches a temptation, but the difference in form of the beatitudes in Luke[107] and Matthew,[108] the one seeming to commend poverty and to condemn the rich, and the other making poverty and wealth qualities of the spirit rather than of physical possessions, may reflect varieties of attitudes in the communities in which these records were transmitted and put into writing. Clement of Alexandria, while recognizing the spiritual peril of wealth, held that it was possible, although difficult, for a rich man to be saved and that not all those who are poor in this world's goods are blessed, but only those who are poor in spirit and who hunger and thirst after righteousness.[109] The fact that he found it necessary to discuss the issue at all, however, may indicate the presence of some in the Church who questioned his permission to hold wealth. Clement would not have the Christian conform entirely to economic customs about him, but held that, if he were a merchant, he should seek to determine what was a just price to ask for his wares and to demand no more and accept no less.[110] Some Christians held that commerce was dubious for those of their faith and rated higher agriculture and manual labour.[111] Tertullian objected to the oath-taking involved in borrowing money from pagans, but apparently this was not on the ground that borrowing was wrong, but that the oaths were a compromise with idolatry.[112] So far as our record informs us, then, the Christians of the first five centuries did not contemplate attempting any thoroughgoing economic revolution in society as a whole. Except for the monks, they engaged fairly generally in the processes by which the ancient world procured clothing and shelter. With their emphasis upon the duty of labour they even encouraged participation in it. However, some occupations were regarded as unquestionably wrong—for instance, that of the gladiator and those having to do directly with idolatry and the stage. At least one eminent churchman decried the growth of the large estates characteristic of the Empire.[113] It must be noted, moreover, that the monastic movement which, although opposed by many of

---

[105] Acts v:4.
[106] James v:1-6.
[107] Luke vi:20, 24. Ambrose of Milan denied the right to hold private property. Dudden, *The Life and Times of St. Ambrose*, Vol. II, p. 545.
[108] Matt. v:3.
[109] Clement of Alexandria, *Who is the Rich Man that Shall Be Saved?*
[110] Clement of Alexandria, *Instructor*, Book III, Chap. 11.
[111] Troeltsch, *The Social Teaching of the Christian Churches*, pp. 127, 128.
[112] Tertullian, *On Idolatry*, Chap. 23.
[113] "Epistle of Cyprian to Donatus," translated in *Ante-Nicene Fathers*, Vol. V, pp. 275-280.

the clergy, was increasingly regarded as the perfect expression of the Christian ideal, challenged the entire economic structure of existing society and the presuppositions upon which it was based. Even for Christians who remained outside of monasticism, the principles professed by their communities could not but make some difference. Riches, if not in themselves wrong, were certainly not the chief end of life and could readily be a handicap.[114]

Christians, then, were not unanimous in condemning wealth. The Christian conscience, however, seems universally to have held that property must be used freely to assist the needy, and particularly those of the "household of faith."[115] As a result came works of benevolence and charity by voluntary contributions. Here, indeed, was one of the most distinctive results of Christianity.

Many non-Christians of the Græco-Roman world had made gifts for what they conceived to be the public welfare. Such largess was very widespread. Some of it was voluntary, but public opinion and in time the state held it to be a duty of those who had means. The Emperors were lavish with their benefactions. The first of them, Augustus, set the precedent. Great numbers of public officials and private citizens were munificent. Schools and libraries were founded and endowed, temples, baths, theatres, markets, and public buildings erected, costly aqueducts constructed, roads and bridges built, and games and other public amusements provided. Especially were the first two centuries of the Empire, marked as they were by prosperity, notable for this kind of pagan public spirit. Even when, beginning with the close of the second century, the shadows of impending economic and political doom deepened and wealth diminished, the precedent was followed, though on a declining scale.[116]

In this tradition the Christian spirit partly concurred. Like it, it held that wealth entailed an obligation to the less fortunate. However, it made at least three significant changes. It increased the number of givers, modified the motive, and altered the forms of beneficence.

Whereas under the pagan society philanthropy had been the obligation primarily of the rich, Christians were taught that not only the wealthy but the poor should give, each according to his ability.[117] The collection was made a part of the ritual of public worship.[118]

[114] Among the secondary accounts of the Christian attitude toward property before A.D. 500, see Harnack, *The Mission and Expansion of Christianity*, Vol. I, pp. 147-198; Troeltsch, *op. cit.*, pp. 118, 120, 123; Cadoux, *The Early Church and the World*, especially the summary on pp. 611-619; Carlyle, *op. cit.*, Vol. I, pp. 98-101, 132-146; Case, *The Social Triumph of the Ancient Church*, pp. 55, 72, 73.

[115] Gal. vi:10.

[116] On this pagan benevolence see Dill, *Roman Society from Nero to Marcus Aurelius*, pp. 196-250; Lecky, *History of European Morals*, Vol. II, pp. 72-81; and Case, *op. cit.*, pp. 17-21, with their references to the sources.

[117] I Cor. xvi:1-3; II Cor. viii:2.

[118] Justin Martyr, *First Apology*, Chap. 67; Tertullian, *Apology*, c. 39.

The motive was modified. In the established order it seems either to have been a sense of public duty, of political expediency, or of desire for renown. As the state adopted Christianity, these motives probably were to be found among those who called themselves Christian. In primitive Christian days, however, the emphasis was laid partly on love—a love evoked by the love of God and the example and love of Jesus[119]—and partly on the hope of a future and eternal reward.[120]

The objects for which gifts were made were altered. While they were still a suspected or a persecuted minority, Christians confined their charity chiefly to their own number. They supported their unemployed (among them those thrown out of their usual occupations because of their faith), the orphans and the widows, the injured and the sick. They entertained Christian travellers. They saw that their poor were decently buried. They ransomed those of their number who were put to servile labour for their faith or who were imprisoned for debt. A church sent relief to other churches in time of famine or other calamity.[121] Christians were exhorted to fast and to give the poor what they thus saved.[122] Some of this beneficence was on a large scale. We hear of the Church in Rome supporting fifteen hundred widows and persons in distress.[123] Later, some time after Constantine, the Church in Antioch is said to have supported three thousand widows and virgins, as well as those ill in inns, prisoners, and many poor.[124] Sometimes Christians extended their care to those outside their community. Thus in time of pestilence in Alexandria and Carthage we read of them as remaining when able-bodied pagans had fled and as caring for the sick and the dying.[125] When Christians ceased to be a minority and the Church became almost co-extensive with Roman society, these forms of charity continued as predominantly those through which Christian philanthropy expressed itself.[126] Presumably through long usage under different conditions they

---

[119] II Cor. viii:9; I John iii: 16, 17.

[120] Matt. xxv:31-46.

[121] For these many types of Christian charity, see Harnack, *op. cit.*, Vol. I, pp. 147-198; Oliver, *op. cit.*, pp. 28-44; Uhlhorn, *op. cit.*, p. 202; Lohmeyer, *Soziale Fragen im Urchristentum*, pp. 100-105. Special works covering the various forms of Christian benevolence in these centuries are Chastel, *Études Historiques sur l'Influence de la Charité durant les Premiers Siècles Chrétiens;* Uhlhorn, *Die christliche Liebesthätigkeit in der alten Kirche,* of which an English translation, *Christian Charity in the Ancient Church,* appeared in 1883; Lallemand, *Histoire de la Charité,* Vols. I and II.

[122] *Apostolic Constitutions,* Book V, Chap. 20; Origen, *Hom. 10 on Levit.;* Schmidt, *The Social Results of Christianity,* p. 251.

[123] Eusebius, *Eccles. History,* Book VI, 43.

[124] Chrysostom, *Homily on Matt.,* No. 66, section 3.

[125] Pontius, *Vita Cyprian,* Chap. IX; Eusebius, *Eccles. Hist.,* Book VII, Chap. 22, Book IX, Chap. 8.

[126] James Orr, in Paton, Bunting and Garvie (editors), *Christ and Civilization,* p. 229.

had become so hallowed that they remained the conventional channels for the expenditure of the generous impulses begotten of a Christian faith. They were enlarged and at times institutionalized. We hear, for example, of a large hospital erected in 370 at Cæsarea and supported from the lands which the Emperor gave to the church there.[127] A number of hospitals were founded by rich Christians in various cities.[128] To the traditional expressions of Christian philanthropy were later added others, notably the erection and endowment of monasteries. Through the centuries, however, the early forms of benevolence, in part stereotyped when Christians were closely knit minority communities and later often extended to non-Christians as well as Christians, have persisted, with some additions, as the characteristic expressions of what has come to be known technically as Christian charity.

These differed from the expressions of pagan philanthropy. Public works, such as baths, aqueducts, and bridges, were naturally not undertaken in the early days of the Church. Such structures as theatres were regarded as evil, as were the public games involving gladiatorial combats. Indiscriminate largess, made without careful effort to determine need and worthiness, was discouraged in the primitive centuries, although, as Christians grew in numbers, probably less care was exercised to prevent pauperization.

Even the casual visitor to Rome must be impressed by the contrast between the types of public structures which survive in impressive ruins from pagan days, and those erected in the centuries since the city has been presumably modified by Christianity. Both include buildings for public worship, and more than one heathen fane survives as a Christian church. Both have structures for public games, but those of the modern city are relatively not so prominent as were the old, and no longer are buildings erected for those phases of the old Roman amusements which the Christian conscience has regarded with horror— gladiatorial contests and combats with wild animals. In both the military is prominent, in equipment and in monuments to those who have won fame on the field of battle. The forums of old are in part paralleled by the public squares of today. The ancient baths, however, are without their modern duplicate, and the huge public hospitals of the present time are confronted by no ruins of pagan predecessors. Whether for good or for ill, then, Christianity effected a change which has left its persistent impression, even on governmental charity.

In connexion with this contribution of money for charity, it must be noted that the Christian ideal held that Christians must give themselves as well as their means. Personal ministrations and not merely donations of property were

[127] Stead, *The Story of Social Christianity,* Vol. I, p. 105.
[128] Stead, *op. cit.,* Vol. I, pp. 105-108.

enjoined. Christians must visit the widows and the fatherless in their affliction.[129] With their own hands they must care for the ill and the prisoners.[130] Here was a concrete application of the law of love. This, in its emphasis, seems to have been new, not only in the Græco-Roman world, but among the rest of the human race. In these centuries it was seen in such instances as we have already noted in the pestilence in Alexandria and Carthage and in a Severinus in time of invasion. It was to come to much fuller fruition in later centuries.

While Christians were innocent of any designs for the complete and thorough-going transformation of the social and economic structure of the Mediterranean world, they dissented not only from its prevailing religions, but abstained—at least in theory—from some of the most prominent features of its secular life. For years many Christians regarded service in the army as inconsistent with their profession. Some held that for them all bloodshed, whether as soldiers or executioners, was unlawful.[131] At one stage in its history the powerful Church of Alexandria seems to have looked askance upon the reception of soldiers into its membership and to have regarded enlistment in the army as permissible only in exceptional instances.[132] Tertullian argued against Christians taking part in the army, on the ground that such service brought one under another master than Christ, that it was out of accord with the Christian obligation to the family, that it involved taking the sword, and that it made necessary inflicting punishment, when to a Christian was forbidden all revenge. Yet he declared that soldiers who were in that occupation before becoming Christians were in a different situation.[133] Presumably, then, if so strict a moralist as Tertullian took this position, even before Constantine the Church did not generally regard it as obligatory upon a soldier to renounce his profession when he entered its membership. Indeed, in its earliest days the Church seems to have regarded with complacency the baptism of soldiers and not to have required them to resign from the army.[134]

Coolness towards the enlistment of its members in the army appears to have brought no very marked embarrassment to the Church. To be sure, in 295, so we read, a boy was killed who refused to enroll as a soldier on the ground that he was a Christian.[135] To most Christians, however, at least in the first three centuries, the ethical problem involved in military service was not an issue.

[129] James i:27.
[130] Matt. xxv:31-40.
[131] Lactantius, *Divine Institutes*, Book VI, Chap. 20.
[132] *Canons of the Church of Alexandria*, translated in *Ante-Nicene Fathers*, Vol. V, p. 257.
[133] Tertullian, *De Corona*, Chaps. 1, 2. On Tertullian see Harnack, *Militia Christi*, p. 66.
[134] As in Acts x:1-48. See also Cadoux, *The Early Church and the World*, p. 121.
[135] Mason, *The Persecution of Diocletian*, p. 44.

Jews and slaves were legally disqualified from membership in the legions and, therefore, such Christians as were drawn from these groups were ineligible. The state could nearly always obtain as many soldiers as it wished through voluntary enlistment without recourse to conscription. Then, too, as time passed, the legions were filled chiefly with barbarians from the fringes of the Empire, where Christianity was late in obtaining a large following.[136] After Christianity was adopted by the state, the Church expected those of its members who served in the army to remain there. It even recognized warlike archangels and soldier saints.[137]

It was not only in looking askance at military service that Christians separated themselves from the secular life about them. Far more sweeping was their condemnation of some of the most prominent of the prevailing amusements. It is, of course, a commonplace that among the outstanding popular forms of entertainment of the pre-Christian Roman Empire were the theatre, gladiatorial combats, and contests between beasts and men. The theatre and the amphitheatre were characteristic architectural features of the typical Roman city. In Rome itself, which set the fashions for the rest of the Empire, and especially the West, some of the shows were on a prodigious scale. We hear, for instance, that after his Dacian victories Trajan sent down ten thousand gladiators into the arena.[138] So rare a spirit as Pliny approved such spectacles.[139] Even the noble-minded Marcus Aurelius, conforming with what was expected of one in his position, gave gladiatorial contests and attended them.[140] For gladiatorial combats and the theatre many of the leading Christians had nothing but condemnation. There was a time when the Church refused to receive for baptism a professional gladiator unless he promised to surrender his calling, and excluded from the communion those of its membership who attended the games.[141] Apparently the Church sometimes supported converted actors until they could find other occupations, but was inclined to forbid them to continue even to teach their former profession.[142] Tertullian explained fairly fully the reasons, as he saw them, for the prohibition to Christians of attendance at the public spectacles. He said that in origin the games were in honour of idols and that the circus was chiefly consecrated to the sun. Gladiatorial contests, he asserted, were also begun in honour of the gods. Because of their connexion with the non-Christian faiths which Christianity so vigorously fought, they

[136] Cadoux, op. cit., pp. 116-120.
[137] Harnack, Militia Christi, p. 92.
[138] Dion Cass., lxviii, c. 15.
[139] Pliny, Panegyricus Traiano Imp. Dictus, 33.
[140] Dill, Roman Society in the Last Century of the Western Empire, pp. 54-58.
[141] Lecky, History of European Morals, Vol. II, p. 37.
[142] Cyprian to Euchatius, translation in Ante-Nicene Fathers, Vol. V, p. 356.

were, therefore, improper for the faithful. Then, too, in contrast with the calm, the gentleness, and the peacefulness which are presumably the fruits of the Spirit, the shows, so Tertullian declared, stirred up rage, bitterness, and grief, and those who engaged in betting were too much agitated. He disapproved of the theatre because of its characteristic lubricity and its hypocrisy—its simulation of love, wrath, fear, and sorrow.[143] Cyprian condemned the gladiatorial contests on the ground that "man is slaughtered that man may be gratified" and "crime is not only committed, but is taught." Theatres he had no use for, saying that they portrayed the parricide and incest of the old days and that "adultery is learned while it is seen."[144] Clement of Alexandria, although much less inclined to an ascetic view of life than were some of the Fathers, denounced the theatre, the racecourse, and others of the public spectacles.[145] Tatian called the gladiatorial show "a cannibal banquet for the soul."[146] Minucius Felix denounced it as inculcating murder, objected to the theatre as picturing vice and as exciting the spectators to it, and opposed the chariot races.[147]

How far this official attitude of the Church and these strictures of leading Christians proved a factor in bringing to an end the amusements so pilloried is not clear. It is certain that many Christians abstained from attendance. Convictions strongly held by the leadership of the Church imply such a result. It is also certain that many Christians did not conform to these opinions. Tertullian deplored the attendance of some Christians.[148] Both the obscenity of the theatre and the contests in the arena continued until the Empire collapsed in the West,[149] and this long after the vast majority of the spectators must have been nominal Christians. Constantine patronized the amphitheatre for at least a decade after his toleration of the Church had begun.[150] However, he is said to have forbidden the gladiatorial combats and the punishment which condemned criminals to become gladiators.[151] It seems probable that these spectacles had little or no place in the new capital which he established on the Bosphorus.[152] We have, too, the famous story that in Rome the gladiatorial

---

[143] Tertullian, *De Spectaculis, passim;* Tertullian, *Apology,* Chap. 38.

[144] Cyprian to Donatus (See *Ante-Nicene Fathers,* Vol. V, pp. 275-280).

[145] In *The Instructor,* Book III, Chap. 11.

[146] Tatian, *Against the Greeks,* Chap. 23.

[147] Minucius Felix, Chap. 37.

[148] Tertullian, *De Spectaculis.*

[149] Dill, *Roman Society from Nero to Marcus Aurelius,* pp. 234-245; Dill, *Roman Society in the Last Century of the Western Empire,* pp. 115-142.

[150] Adeney, *The Greek and Eastern Churches,* p. 40.

[151] Eusebius, *Life of Constantine,* Book IV, Chap. 25; Socrates, *Eccles. Hist.,* Book I, Chap. 18; Cod. Theod. XV, 12, 1. It is a question whether this prohibition applied to more than the province of Phœnicia.—Lecky, *op. cit.,* Vol. II, p. 34.

[152] W. H. Hutton, in *An Outline of Christianity,* Vol. II, pp. 140ff.

shows were brought to an end when, in the reign of Honorius, the monk
Telemachus went into the arena to arrest them and was killed by an enraged
mob who objected to having their pleasures thus interrupted.[153] Probably,
however, another factor in terminating gladiatorial combats was the diminishing supply of possible victims. An impoverished society no longer able to
recruit the arena with war captives and strange beasts would probably, even
without Christianity, have been deprived of the lavish amusements of a more
prosperous age.[154]

Not only did many leading Christians labour to keep the faithful from
attending the theatre and the arena. They fought what they believed to be the
excesses of some of the spectacles which long survived the gladiatorial combats. Thus John Chrysostom, like many another bishop of the period, waged
war against the horse-races and against popular farces and pantomimes.[155] If the
Church found these too deeply entrenched to be uprooted, even from a nominally Christian society, it at least found it possible to modify and in some
instances to abolish the pagan feasts. Several long continued, such as the
Saturnalia, the Quirinalia, and the Terminalia, but without the religious features which most obviously tied them to the old cults. A list of feasts published
towards the end of the fourth century with imperial permission no longer contained the names of the gods.[156] For the celebration of the Calends of January
which marked the beginning of the civil year and which often had taken on a
lewd character, the Church endeavoured, with some success, to substitute a
time of penitence.[157] Christianity, indeed, effected marked changes in the
calendar. "The Christian year" with its festivals and holy days, while bearing
evidence of pre-Christian influence, is largely a fresh creation.

On the whole, then, while amusements and diversions were not made
entirely to conform to the Christian ethic, some eliminations and modifications
were effected.

The study of the change wrought in burial customs would prove interesting
and important. The Christian faith, and especially its conceptions of death,
inevitably brought about alterations in funerals, funerary monuments, and the
disposition of the bodies of the departed. These often came slowly. Thus in

---

[153] Theodoret, *Eccles. Hist.*, Book V, Chap. 26.

[154] Lecky, *op. cit.*, Vol. II, p. 37. Dill, *Roman Society in the Last Century of the Western
Empire*, pp. 115-142, believes that economy rather than virtue was the chief factor in the
termination of the theatre and the circus in the West.

[155] Puech, *St. John Chrysostom*, pp. 86-88; Duchesne, *Early History of the Christian
Church*, Vol. III, pp. 52-68.

[156] Schultze, *Geschichte des Untergangs des griechisch-römischen Heidentums*, Vol. II,
pp. 88-94.

[157] Leclercq, *L'Afrique Chretiénne*, Vol. I, p. 70.

Egypt the practice of mummification only gradually ceased after the land became Christian and remnants of pagan nomenclature long continued. However, Christian formularies were progressively built.[158] The catacombs and cemeteries at Rome contain numerous examples of the survival of pagan usages in Christian circles and of the innovations wrought by the new faith.

How far did Christianity affect the complexion of the state? Probably the most obvious result was one which has been repeatedly mentioned—the substitution of Christianity for the ancient cults as the official religion and the enlistment of state support in the eradication of pagan worship. This change, however, might conceivably have been made without substantially altering the moral and spiritual outlook of the government. It might simply mean that one deity and his associates had been substituted for a rival group of gods and that the new were expected to perform, only in better fashion, what the old had been regarded as doing—to ensure divine aid for the maintenance of the established order in prosperity and against internal and external foes. In that case the inward genius of Christianity might work no modifications. Only the outward form of religious observance would be altered. As a matter of fact, the official actions of the state were not made fully to conform to the moral standards of the Gospels. Moreover, in some of the changes which followed the adoption of Christianity, it is often impossible to determine how far they were due to the new faith and how far to other factors. In some areas, however, Christianity appears to have had substantial influence.

In legislation, beginning with Constantine, Christianity seems to have made itself felt. Seldom, unless they deal with ecclesiastical matters, can specific innovations be conclusively demonstrated to have sprung from the faith. Yet some of Constantine's enactments appear to be traceable to his new faith. Thus in his earlier days, in Gaul, Constantine had prisoners destroyed in gladiatorial spectacles, while in his later years he legislated against such contests.[159] He introduced milder measures for slaves and facilitated manumission,[160] issued edicts in behalf of widows, orphans, and the poor, and against immorality and immoral religious rites.[161] He made divorce more difficult and sought to strengthen the marriage tie.[162] He was the first to denounce formally

---

[158] Schmidt, *Ein altchristliches Mumienetikett nebst Bemerkungen über das Begräbniss-wesen der Kopten* in *Zeitschrift für ägyptische Sprache und Alterthumskunde*, 1894, Vol. CCCIII, pp. 52-62.

[159] Eusebius, *Life of Constantine*, Book IV, Chap. 25; Coleman, *Constantine the Great and Christianity*, pp. 42, 43.

[160] *Cod. Theod.*, ii:8, 1; iv:7, 1; iv:8, 5; iv:8, 6; ix:3, 1; ix:3, 2; xi:7, 3; Adeney, *The Greek and Eastern Churches*, p. 40.

[161] Coleman, *op. cit.*, pp. 43-45.

[162] Brace, *Gesta Christi*, pp. 26-28. See *Cod. Just.*, v:26, 1.

the ancient right of the father to kill a child, although in practice that had long since lapsed.[163] To prevent, so he said, parents from putting their offspring to death, he made provision from the treasury of the state to enable the needy to rear their children.[164] Under succeeding emperors concubinage was forbidden and adultery declared a capital crime.[165] In contrast with pagan times, when adultery was winked at for men but not for women, under Theodosius II it was made a ground on which either party to the marriage tie could claim a divorce.[166] The profession of an actress normally involved prostitution, and in the second half of the fourth century the Church scored a point in obtaining a provision that an actress who, in *articulo mortis*, asked for and received the last sacraments, was not, if she recovered, to be forced to resume her old life.[167] In general, Christian influence seems to have made for the sharpening of the punishments for the kind of sins on which the Church frowned and for the mitigation of penalties in the direction of the humanity which the faith encouraged.[168] The suggestion has also been offered that the forerunner of codes of law compiled by the state was a private collection, by a clergyman of Syria, of local customs and imperial legislation bearing chiefly on inheritance and marriage.[169] However, the measures so assembled showed little Christian influence, and it is not clear that the impulse which led to the work was from specifically Christian sources.

Christianity, by bringing the Church into existence, developed an institution which in part was a rival of the state. It created a society within the Empire which, so many believed, threatened the very existence of the latter. The conflict was very marked in the century or more before Constantine and was to be so again in Western Europe in the Middle Ages and in numerous times and places thereafter. When Constantine made his peace with the faith, however, it long looked as though the conflict had been resolved by the control of the Church by the state. Yet, even in the days of the seeming subordination of the Church to the government, ecclesiastics sought to influence the policies of the latter. At least one notable instance is on record where a bishop asserted, in spiritual matters, the authority of his office over the Emperor himself. That was the famous act of Ambrose, Bishop of Milan, in refusing to admit to his

[163] Schultze, *Geschichte des Untergangs des griechisch-römischen Heidentums*, Vol. II, pp. 34, 35.
[164] *Ibid.*
[165] Brace, *Gesta Christi*, pp. 26-28.
[166] Schultze, *op. cit.*, Vol. II, p. 39.
[167] *Cod. Theod.*, xv:7, 1.
[168] Schultze, *op. cit.*, Vol. II, pp. 23-25; Troeltsch, *The Social Teaching of the Christian Churches*, pp. 129-132.
[169] Schultze, *op. cit.*, Vol. II, p. 47.

cathedral the powerful Theodosius until the latter had made public confession and done penance for what appeared to the bishop the wanton slaughter of a number of the populace in one of the cities.[170] We have, too, Hilary of Poitiers attacking the interference of the state in matters religious.[171] Towards the end of the fifth century, moreover, Pope Gelasius I declared that the Emperor was a son of the Church, not its director.[172]

For many Christians their faith brought a diminution of the authority of the state. To be sure, more than one New Testament writer enjoined obedience to government,[173] and some of the apologists insisted that Christians were loyal subjects and offered prayers for the monarch.[174] It is noteworthy that we have no direct evidence that in the first three centuries the Christians ever withstood persecution by force.[175] However, the widespread opinion of non-Christians and the conviction of some of the pagan emperors that Christians menaced the supremacy of the state were not entirely without a basis of fact. The execution of Jesus as a threat to the established order showed real, even if crude, insight. The early disciples who insisted that they "must obey God rather than men"[176] had a numerous following. The explicit injunctions of Paul to obey the magistrate and pay taxes may imply that they were provoked by revolutionary radicalism in the Christian communities which held that Christians were bound to do neither.[177] The Basilides of Alexandria of the third century who, on his conversion, refused to take an oath on the ground that, as a Christian, it was unlawful for him to swear at all,[178] did not stand alone. The wholesale refusal of Christians to sacrifice at the command of the Emperor gave evidence that a power was at work winning thousands of citizens to an allegiance which, on at least some issues, claimed priority over that to the state. The only similar community was Judaism, and that, while here and there occasionally breaking out into desperate rebellion, was primarily

[170] Sozomen, *Eccles. Hist.*, Book VII, Chap. 25; Adeney, *op. cit.*, pp. 85, 86.

[171] Dawson, *Progress and Religion*, p. 163.

[172] McIlwain, *The Growth of Political Thought in the West from the Greeks to the End of the Middle Ages*, p. 163; Carlyle, *A History of Mediæval Politicial Theory in the West*, Vol. I, p. 187. Carlyle, as authority, gives a quotation from Gelasius I, *Ep.* x:9.

[173] Mark xii:17; Rom. xiii:1-7; I Peter ii:17.

[174] As in Tertullian, *Apology*, Chaps. 6, 30, 33, and Tertullian, *Ad Scapulam*. Christian writers tended to hold that government is a divine institution, a divine remedy for man's sin, and that the ruler is a representative of God and so must be obeyed in the name of God. Carlyle, *op. cit.*, Vol. I, pp. 147-160.

[175] Cadoux, *The Early Church and the World*, p. 101.

[176] Acts v:29.

[177] See this suggestion in Cadoux, *op. cit.*, pp. 98-100, and in McGiffert, *A History of Christianity in the Apostolic Age*, pp. 506-545.

[178] Eusebius, *Eccles. Hist.*, Book VI, Chap. 5.

racial. The Church, with its conscious striving to reach all men, was much more dangerous.

Beginning with the time of Constantine, the majority of Christians were no longer made uneasy by a feeling of conflicting loyalties. The Emperor, himself now ostensibly a Christian, would presumably not command anything contrary to the law of Christ. However, a basic change took place in the theory of the state. The Roman Emperors had been regarded as divine. That was now no longer possible. To be sure, as we have seen, the Roman Senate placed Constantine among the gods. Yet that anomaly could not persist. The Emperor might rule by the appointment of God, but he himself was no longer a god.[179] In practice, the change seems to have had few if any political consequences of immediate importance. A Constantine and even a Justinian were no less effective autocrats than a Diocletian. Not for many centuries and long after the year 500 did this alteration in political theory have widespread visible results. However, before the end of the fifth century the conception began to develop that the Church and the state equally derived their authority from God and that each was supreme in its own sphere.[180] Before then, too, the problem had begun to emerge which loomed so prominently in the Western Europe of the Middle Ages—the reconciliation of the two societies, ecclesiastical and civil.[181] The Church had grown up as a closely interrelated group of communities, largely controlling the life of its own members and acknowledging an authority ultimately superior to that of the state. Although now the state had become nominally Christian, the conflict was by no means resolved. It has been suggested that the courage of Athanasius in standing for his interpretation of the Christian faith against the entire machinery of the imperial state, bent as it was on enforcing Arianism, is an instance of the political effect of Christianity.[182] Athanasius, so it is said, advanced a theology which gave dignity to man. The claim that the Son is "of the same substance" and not of "similar substance" with the Father was to him essential. It made it possible for him to hold that the Son "was made man that we might be made God"[183] and that "the Word was made flesh that we, partaking of his Spirit, might be deified."[184] While, probably, Athanasius had no thought of repercussions upon political theory when he upheld this doctrine, a direct effect, even though he may not have been aware of it or have intended it, so it is said, was to add

---

[179] Ferrero, *Peace and War*, pp. 187-189; McIlwain, *op. cit.*, p. 144.
[180] Carlyle, *op. cit.*, Vol. II, p. 254.
[181] McIlwain, *op. cit.*, pp. 145-148.
[182] Allen, *Christian Institutions*, p. 307.
[183] Athanasius, *De Incar.*, Chap. 54; Allen, *op. cit.*, p. 307.
[184] Athanasius, *De Decretis*, Chap. 3, par. 14.

dignity to the individual and to inspire him, convinced that he was empowered by the Divine Spirit, to stand against all organized authority of man.[185] It may well be that this effect was not confined to Athanasian Christianity and that the Arian form of the faith would have been almost and perhaps quite as potent. Yet that here was one consequence of Christianity seems possible.

This, indeed, was a continuation of the tradition of the old Hebrew prophets. Many of the most impressive surviving monuments of antiquity are expressions of man's physical power and cruelty and his ability to enslave his fellows —the pyramids of Egypt, the statues and carvings of monarchs slaying their enemies, the triumphal arches of the Roman Empire, the Colosseum.[186] Here, however, in Hebrew and Christian prophets and leaders, was a different type of force, that of the individual, with no weight of arms back of him, inspired by his conviction of the mandate of God to stand against the majority and the authority which has command of overwhelming physical resources. It is a phenomenon which is not confined to Christianity, but which has probably found there its most explosive expressions.

Even in the years after the Empire had become nominally Christian, various Christian groups were impelled by their faith to ignore or defy the state. The extremists in the growing monastic movement usually endeavoured to cut themselves off from all existing society. Even the more moderate of the monks tended to remove themselves from many of the obligations currently binding on Roman citizens. In seeking to establish what they intended to be communities conforming perfectly to the Christian ideal, they sought to separate themselves from a society in which the professed Christianity was only one and sometimes a minor determining factor. In addition to the monastic movement were many of the groups regarded as heretics by the majority. Usually, in their attempt to preserve unity and so to arrest the disintegration of society, the Christian emperors sought to suppress them. However, claiming to represent true Christianity, the recalcitrants stubbornly declined to conform. By that attitude they embarrassed and weakened the state.

Moreover, the Church tended to divide regionally, and this contributed to the break-up of the Roman Empire. By creating literatures in the vernacular, as in Syriac and Coptic,[187] in several regions in the East Christianity augmented

---

[185] Allen, *op. cit.*, p. 310.

[186] Breasted, *The Dawn of Conscience*, pp. 412-420, calls attention to this, but with not all these illustrations.

[187] Cumont, *The Oriental Religions in Roman Paganism;* Mommsen, *The Provinces of the Roman Empire*, Vol. II, pp. 136, 265; Leipoldt, *Geschichte der koptischen Litteratur*, pp. 133-157, and Brockelmann, *Die syrische und die christlich-arabische Litteratur*, both in *Geschichte der christlichen Litteraturen des Orients*.

the decline of Greek as the language of polite society and so in part undid the universalizing work of Alexander and his successors.

On the other hand, in some regions this nationalizing influence of Christianity strengthened the state. In Asia Minor, as we have seen, it assisted powerfully in the spread of the Greek language.[188] It helped to give to the Greek-speaking peoples an organizational coherence such as they had not known in the palmiest days of classical Greece. The Greek nation which, with Constantinople as its centre, professed to carry on in the East the Roman tradition was in large part a Christian creation. For nearly a thousand years after the old imperial power collapsed in the West it survived the shocks not only of barbarian invasions, but also the attacks by civilized non-Christian peoples. To no small extent it was the pride, the energy, and the coherence given it by its Christian faith which enabled it to resist its foreign foes, to assimilate its barbarian invaders, and to impress its culture, if not its political authority, upon some of its neighbours.[189]

In the West, where the state did not go on without a break as in the Greek East, the Church formed the rallying-point, the bulwark, and much of the inspiration of the elements which strove to preserve the Roman tradition. It was largely through it that Roman law, the Latin language, and much of the Roman spirit and ideal persisted. The Church which bore the Roman name carried over to ensuing ages a great deal of what had traditionally been associated with the Eternal City.

Christianity, then, had profound, even if varied, political effects. However, as has been suggested, these did not all appear at once. Most of them did not attain their most striking manifestations until after the fifth century. The recognition of the Church by Constantine did not alter the form of the Roman state in many important particulars, nor did it do so until after the close of the fifth century. To be sure, the jurisdiction of ecclesiastics in some types of cases which might normally have come before the civil courts curtailed the power of the state and in later ages assumed large proportions. This was, however, merely the legalizing of a practice which Church officials had begun long before Constantine and which may have gone back to the time of Paul.[190] The tendency had been to hold that disputes between Christians should be adjusted within Church circles and without reference to the non-Christian civil courts. The imperial title of *pontifex maximus* was eventually dropped as inconsistent

[188] Ramsay, *The Church in the Roman Empire*, p. 44.

[189] Allen, *Christian Institutions*, pp. 183, 184, citing Church, *The Influence of Christianity upon National Character*, p. 31.

[190] Paul's statement is in I Cor. vi:1-7. The practice of the Church is summarized by B. S. Easton in *An Outline of Christianity*, Vol. II, pp. 66, 67.

with Christianity, but the Christian emperors, beginning with Constantine, both claimed and exercised the right of a certain amount of control over the Church, as they had over the former non-Christian official religion.[191] They encouraged the regularly constituted leaders of the Church to define orthodox doctrine, but, when it was once determined, they sought to compel conformity to it. The political theory of the accepted Fathers of the Church was that of pagan antiquity and the modifications brought by Christianity were regarded as matters of detail rather than as fundamental.[192] In some respects legislation was affected, but the general theory on which the law was based was not swept aside. In general, Christian writers held that the law of nature, of which much had been made by pagan legal thinkers, was identical with the law of God,[193] and so could be accepted by Christians. Roman law was codified under Christian emperors, but its basic concepts had largely been the work of pagan jurists.[194] The influence of the post-Constantinian Church in awakening in the Roman state and society sentiments of freedom, equality, and self-respect can probably be easily exaggerated.[195]

In the final analysis the influence of Christianity directly upon individuals is probably of more significance than is that upon general concepts, literature, art, and institutions. Changes in these latter, indeed, derive much if not most of their importance from the effect upon individual men, women, and children who are touched and more or less moulded by them. It becomes, therefore, of major interest to seek to determine how far Christianity changed individual lives. To what extent did the ethical and spiritual ideals and dynamic of Christianity transform those who professed the faith? If many individuals were profoundly altered, they would modify or even revolutionize letters, art, customs, laws, and governments, and the alterations in these would, in turn, affect other individuals. We must, then, give some time to an investigation of the evidence for the degree to which Christians conformed to the standards set up in the New Testament.

The task is not easy, nor are the results always definite enough to prove satisfying. One of the difficulties is the scantiness of the material. To be sure, a large body of the writings of Christians has come down to us. The temper of these constitutes more or less unconscious testimony to the character of the

---

[191] McIlwain, *The Growth of Political Thought in the West from the Greeks to the End of the Middle Ages*, p. 144.

[192] Carlyle, *A History of Medieval Political Theory in the West*, Vol. I, p. 195.

[193] Carlyle, *op. cit.*, Vol. I, pp. 83-85, 102-110.

[194] Lecky, *History of European Morals*, Vol. II, p. 42.

[195] Troeltsch, *The Social Teaching of the Christian Churches*, p. 145, thinks the influence very slight.

men who composed them. The bitter denunciation of heretics, for instance, is a commentary on the failure of the Christian ethic of love fully to be carried out. However, these writings are very rarely descriptions of men and women. More usually they have to do with theology or philosophy, or are homilies holding up ethical and spiritual standards. They often contain useful evidence. However, they and many other pertinent documents labour under the disadvantage on the one hand of setting forth ideals without providing exact information as to the degree to which these were incorporated in life, or, on the other hand, for homiletical reasons, of painting dark pictures of the deficiencies and vices which they denounce, when an objective survey might disclose less sombre conditions. The one is too idealized a portrayal and the other gives too sordid a report. Presumably the actual situation was a mixture of the two.

The evidence of the goals set up for Christian living is extensive and scattered through the centuries. The sayings ascribed to Jesus occupy a prominent place in the Gospels. Embodied as they were in the revered and authoritative writings of the faith which in time were made the familiar property of all Christians by regular use in the services, they must have had a marked influence upon the standards of the communities. So, too, with the Epistles of the New Testament. They also were read in Christian assemblies and were studied and preached upon. They made much of ethics and of the dynamic which the faith provided to live up to them. Paul especially spoke of a new type of life, begun through Christ and lived under the power of the Spirit, a life which men did not initiate but which depended upon their coöperation to be effective.[196] In a well-known passage he spoke of "the fruit of the Spirit" as "love, joy, peace, long-suffering, gentleness, goodness, faith, meekness, self-control," and contrasted it with the "works of the flesh"—"adultery, fornication, uncleanness, lasciviousness, idolatry, witchcraft, hatred, emulations, wrath, strife, seditions, heresies, envyings, murders, drunkenness, revellings, and such like."[197] So, also, a generation or two after the time of the Apostles, in the Epistle of Barnabas, held in high esteem by many Christians, "the way of light" was described as loving God, honouring him who had redeemed the Christian from death, obeying the commandments of Christ, simplicity of heart, hatred of hypocrisy, humility, innocence of fornication and adultery and of evil counsel against a neighbour, love for one's neighbour, peacemaking and peaceableness, lack of covetousness, consideration for servants, and generosity.[198] The Epistle to Diognetus, which professes to be for the purpose of instruction in the faith,

[196] As in Eph. ii:1-10; iv:1; v:1-5.
[197] Gal. v:19-26.
[198] *Epistle of Barnabas* (translation in *Ante-Nicene Fathers*, Vol. I, pp. 133-149).

speaks of Christians as poor, yet making many rich, as repaying insults with honour, as being imitators of God and as preservers of the world.[199] Polycarp in writing to the Philippians charged deacons not to be slanderers, double tongued, or lovers of money, but temperate, compassionate, industrious, walking according to the truth of the Lord who was the servant of all.[200] Tertullian charged women to be modest in dress and humble in deportment.[201] He described the seven deadly sins as idolatry, blasphemy, murder, adultery, fornication, false witness, and fraud.[202] Clement of Alexandria, in the *Pædagogue*, sets forth a way of life which he regards as that of the ideal Christian— not ascetic, but moderate; simple, plain food as ministering to life and not to luxury; abstention from all slavish habits and excess; decorum at meals; water as the main beverage, and only a sparing use of wine; simplicity in clothing; the avoidance of revelry, filthy speaking, excessive eating, and immoderate laughter and tears; continence; and the love which suffers long and is kind, envies not, and is not puffed up.[203] Clement, too, in his *Stromata*, emphasized love for one's enemies as necessary and Christian, and forgiveness of injuries, and declared that he who does good from neither fear of punishment or hope of reward is on his way to true knowledge.[204] Pliny, in his famous letter to Trajan, said that Christians claimed that in their services they bound themselves by a sacred formula to abstain from thefts and violence, from adultery, from the breaking of faith, and from the refusal to surrender a deposit on demand.[205] The so-called *Apostolic Constitutions*, of varying ages, denounce covetousness, recommend that Christians avoid contests, that they return blessing for cursing, that envy, jealousy, evil-speaking, and love of contention be eschewed, and command that neophytes before receiving baptism should have "left off to work sin," and be chaste, pure, holy.[206] The *Didache* began by contrasting the two ways, that of life and that of death. The former involved loving God and one's neighbour, meekness, long-suffering, returning blessing for cursing, and refraining from lying, covetousness, and fornication.[207] *The Shepherd of Hermas*, very popular reading among Christians in the second,

---

[199] *Epistle to Diognetus* (translation in *Ante-Nicene Fathers*, Vol. I, pp. 23-30).
[200] *Epistle of Polycarp to the Philippians* (translation in *Ante-Nicene Fathers*, Vol. I, pp. 31-36).
[201] Tertullian, *On the Apparel of Women* (translation in *Ante-Nicene Fathers*, Vol. IV, pp. 14-26).
[202] Tertullian, *Against Marcion*, Book IV, Chap. 9.
[203] Clement, *The Instructor* (translation in *Ante-Nicene Fathers*, Vol. II, pp. 209-298).
[204] Clement, *Stromata*, Book IV, Chaps. 14, 22; Book VII, Chap. 13.
[205] Pliny, *Epis. X* (*Epistularum ad Traianum Liber*, pp. 97, 98). A translation of the pertinent passage is in Merrill, *Essays in Early Christian History*, p. 180.
[206] *The Apostolic Constitutions*, Books I, II, III especially Book III Chap. 17.
[207] *Didache*, Chaps. 1-4.

third, and fourth centuries, commended faith, self-restraint, simplicity, guile-
lessness, chastity, cheerfulness, intelligence, and love, and abstention from
speaking evil of others and from anger and falsehood.[208] Dionysius, Bishop
of Alexandria in the middle of the third century, declared that "love is alto-
gether and for ever on the alert and casts about to do some good even to one
who is unwilling to receive it."[209] Commodianus of North Africa admonished
the faithful not to cherish hatred toward their brethren, and denounced
jealousy, greed, and envy.[210]

It is interesting to ask how far these standards were a novelty in the world
to which they were enunciated. We have one statement by an eminent scholar
that little else was required than complete conformity to the highest ethical
aspirations of the world at large and that the most distinctive elements were
love and holiness. What was peculiar to Christian ethics, so this scholar goes on
to say, was not so much the ideal as the motive behind them and, in contrast
with the aristocratic character of pagan ethics, the power with which they
appealed to the common people. This power was partly the hope of reward
and the fear of punishment, but chiefly the duty of Christians to walk worthily
of their calling as children of God.[211] On the other hand, we have the assertion
that in ascribing moral obligation in social relations to an ultimate supernatural source of command, Christianity brought into popular life something
new so far as the Roman tradition was concerned, and that it also was innovat-
ing when it taught the brotherhood of all human beings.[212] Since, moreover,
most pagan religions of the day put the chief emphasis on correct ritual and
ceremonial purity, Christianity was for many undertaking an alien and difficult
task when it strove to induce its non-Jewish adherents to conform to the
Jewish law and prophets and to the insistence of Jesus upon purity of heart
as well as of outward act.[213] So, too, we have the claim that Christianity
introduced a new ethical terminology and that the Greek words which we
translate as love, joy, peace, hope, and humility were not found in Greek
moralists before Christ.[214]

In advocating these standards, we must again remind ourselves, Christian

[208] *The Shepherd of Hermas,* Books I and II.
[209] *The Fourth Festival Epistle of Dionysius* (translation in *Ante-Nicene Fathers,* Vol.
VI, p. 110).
[210] *The Instructions of Commodianus* (translation in *Ante-Nicene Fathers,* Vol. IV,
pp. 203-218).
[211] McGiffert, *A History of Christianity in the Apostolic Age,* pp. 506-545.
[212] This was in contrast with the Stoics, who taught simply the essential equality of all
men.—Merrill, *op. cit.,* p. 34.
[213] Foakes-Jackson, *The Rise of Gentile Christianity,* pp. 99-100.
[214] Quoted from Dean Inge by Glover in *The Influence of Christ in the Ancient World,*
p. 60.

writers were not contemplating a transformation of all society. They held them up, rather, for the conduct of members of a minority group in their private lives, in their contacts with one another, and in personal relations with non-Christians. This limited application of ethical principles, so sweepingly revolutionary if applied to society as a whole, once become traditional and given sanctity by association with an idealized early Church and revered authors, tended to persist and to mould the thought of Christians in all later ages.

Many Christians, both in the first five centuries and since, have declared that these ethical standards, reinforced by the powerful dynamic which Christianity displayed, wrought marked differences in the lives of the faithful, and that, on at least the part of many, an approximation was made to the ethical requirements of the New Testament. Paul, who was keenly sensitive to the shortcomings of his converts,[215] was happy in the change which had been wrought in at least some of them.[216] Origen, in his famous reply to Celsus, declared that the name of Jesus expelled demons, took away diseases, and produced a marvellous meekness of spirit and a character marked by humanity, gentleness, and goodness.[217] He said that in the assemblies of Christians larger numbers of those were to be found who had been converted from a not very wicked way of life than of those who had committed abominable sins,[218] but he also insisted that Christians turned women away from dissolute living, from being at variance with those with whom they lived, and from a passion for the theatre and dancing, and that they trained in habits of self-restraint boys just reaching the age of puberty and feeling a desire for sexual pleasures.[219] Tertullian challenged the critics to find a Christian who had been accused of sacrilege or seduction, or who was an assassin, a cut-purse, or a stealer of bathers' clothes, and said that Christians were guiltless of lust, and that, if some are guilty, they were cut off from the Christian fellowship.[220] Justin Martyr spoke of himself and his fellow Christians as "we who formerly delighted in fornication but now embrace chastity alone; . . . we who valued above all things the acquisition of wealth and possessions [but] now bring into a common stock and communicate to every one in need; we who hated and destroyed one another and on account of their different manners would not live with men of a different tribe, [but] now since the coming of Christ

[215] As in I Cor. i:10, 11; v:1,2; vi:1-8.
[216] I Cor. i:9-11.
[217] *Origen against Celsus*, Book I, Chap. 67.
[218] *Origen against Celsus*, Book III, Chap. 65.
[219] *Origen against Celsus*, Book III, Chap. 56.
[220] Tertullian, *Apology*, Chaps. 44, 46.

live familiarly with them and pray for our enemies and endeavour to persuade those who hate us unjustly to live conformably to the good precepts of Christ, to the end that they may become partakers with us of the same joyful hope of a reward from God."[221] Athenagoras declared that among Christians were to be found uneducated persons, artisans, and old women who by their deeds showed the benefit of the teachings of their faith, who when struck did not strike again, who when robbed did not go to law, who gave to those that asked of them and loved their neighbours as themselves.[222] Tatian asserted that Christianity set men free from ten thousand tyrants, and rid them of the entire demon world, their hatred of men, and their immorality and cruelty.[223] It must be remembered, however, that all of these are *ex parte* statements by those who were seeking to defend their faith against its calumniators. Presumably they are honest but not objective appraisals.

So, too, with more recent characterizations by Christian writers. Even when made by eminent scholars, they are open to the suspicion of bias. Thus one comment on the first fourteen verses of the sixth chapter of Romans declares that Paul is keeping close to experience and to facts when he confidently assumes that his readers will know what he means when he speaks of living and moving in a new sphere of life, and that this was the experience, not of himself alone, but of Christians in general.[224] Another says that the early Christians spoke of freedom from demons, forgiveness and reconciliation with God, gladness and moral strength and peace in the Holy Spirit, and that they invariably associated them with Jesus.[225] Still another speaks of the contrast between the peace and the joy which were the fruits of Christianity and the fear of life, the cruelty, and the feeling of insecurity which lay at the heart of Hellenism.[226] We have the assertion that Christianity gave what the contemporary world lacked—peace of conscience through reconciliation with God, a new aim, and fresh moral strength—and that the Christian lived for God, for his fellows in the faith, and for humanity at large.[227] It is also said that the names adopted by Christians had significance. Many of these expressed self-depreciation, humility, resignation to insult, joy, and victory.[228] One of the greatest of modern students of Christianity in its early centuries has much to say of

---

[221] Justin Martyr, *First Apology* (translation in *Ante-Nicene Fathers*, Vol. I, pp. 150-187).
[222] Athenagoras, *A Plea for the Christians*, Chap. 11.
[223] Tatian, *Address to the Greeks*, Chaps. 7, 8, 9, 16, 17, 32, 33.
[224] Dodd, *The Epistle of Paul to the Romans*, pp. 95, 96.
[225] Glover, *op. cit.*, p. 151.
[226] Barry, *Christianity and the New World*, pp. 59-67.
[227] Dobschütz, *Christian Life in the Primitive Church*, pp. 368-370.
[228] Ramsay, *The Cities and Bishoprics of Phrygia*, Vol. II, p. 493.

the evidence that here was a faith marked by power, ethical earnestness, and holiness, and that the Spirit heightened the religious and moral attainments of the Christians.[229]

These statements by ancient and modern Christians must not be ruled out of court as hopelessly prejudiced. They afford clear evidence of the standards which were emphasized and inculcated. Clearly, moreover, these ideals became sufficiently embodied in the lives of a large number of Christians to enable the apologists to speak confidently of approximation to them as an important argument for the validity of their faith.

We are, however, given pause by evidence, also from Christians, and some-times from the very ones who paint such roseate pictures of the virtues of their fellow believers, which indicates that many adherents of the Church fell far short of the standards held up before them. Not only was this true of the third century, when the Church had begun to enroll large numbers, and of the post-Constantinian age when the majority flocked into it. Even in the first two or three generations many were found whose conduct differed markedly from that contemplated in the Gospels and the Epistles. It seems doubtful whether the Church ever had a golden age, even in the time of the Apostles, when its numbers were few and its ardour might have been supposed to be fresh with the recent memory of its Master. In the circle of intimates who surrounded Jesus, one betrayed him, another denied him, and all fled in the hour of crisis.[230] In that earliest community at Jerusalem jealousies, recriminations, race prejudice, and deliberate lying were not unknown.[231] Paul speaks of those in his churches who were guilty of sexual offences which were quite contrary to the standards he set up, hints at those who regarded the life of the spirit as freeing them from ethical requirements or as justifying laziness, and makes direct mention of quarrels, gluttony, and drunkenness on the part of those who claimed to be Christians.[232] We hear more than once of factions and divisions in the New Testament churches and even between the leaders.[233] We are told of at least one who was accused of loving power in the Christian community.[234] The last of the books of the New Testament freely accuses some Christians in the province of Asia of sexual irregularities and of compromises with idolatry.[235] *The Didache*, that picture of an early Christian com-

[229] Harnack, *The Mission and Expansion of Christianity*, Vol. I, pp. 199-218.
[230] Mark xiv:43, 44, 50, 66-72.
[231] Acts v:1-10, vi:1, 2, xi:1-3.
[232] Rom. vi:1; I Cor. v:1, 2, vi:1-6, xi:21; Phil. iii:18, 19; II Thes. iii:6-13.
[233] Acts xv:39; I Cor. i:11; James iv:1.
[234] III John, 9.
[235] Rev. ii:14, 20.

munity which in many ways seems idyllic, appears to know of those who under the guise of prophets abused the hospitality of fellow Christians.[236] From the first Christians held up love as the major ethical tenet, yet beginning even with the Gospels bitter denunciations of those who differ from them are not unknown, and often especially of those who most closely resemble them. The most virulent words of the Gospels are for the Pharisees,[237] whose ideals most nearly approached those of the Christians, and throughout the first five centuries Christians often reserved their most vitriolic attacks for those fellow Christians whom they thought of as heretics. Paul, in spite of his famous hymn of love, displayed little of the qualities he there praised when he denounced fellow disciples who wished Christians to conform in some respects to the ritual requirements of the Jewish law.[238] Tertullian, a stickler for Christian morality and who speaks of Christians as loving their enemies, declares of some with whom he disagrees "that they care for nothing so much as to obscure what they preach. The officiousness with which they guard their doctrine is an officiousness which betrays their guilt."[239] Of another opponent he says: "He is a thorough adulterer, both doctrinally and carnally."[240] Instances of this in still other Christian leaders could be multiplied. The author of *The Shepherd of Hermas* seems to have had a Christian family, yet he appears to indicate that his wife was notorious for her evil tongue and that his children had strayed into blasphemy, the denial of Christ, and various kinds of iniquities.[241] *The Apostolic Constitutions* indicate clearly that Christians, fallen into sin, had had to be disciplined and won back by the ecclesiastical authorities.[242] They also seem to indicate that some bishops were arrogant, and that some, for a money consideration, allowed sinners to remain in the Church.[243] From Cyprian we gather that on the eve of the Decian persecution covetousness, false swearing, quarrelling, and luxury had crept into the Church.[244] Tertullian tells us of those who had been excluded from membership for fornication or adultery and who had been forgiven and readmitted by those who had suffered

[236] *The Didache*, Chaps. 10-12.
[237] As in Matt. xxiii:1-33. These may not, of course, be the words of Jesus, but reflect the feelings of the first generation of Christians.
[238] As in Gal. i:9, ii:4, v:12.
[239] Tertullian, *Against the Valentinians*, Chap. 1 (translation in *Ante-Nicene Fathers*, Vol. III, p. 503ff).
[240] Tertullian, *Against Hermogenes*, Chap 1 (translation in *Ante-Nicene Fathers*, p. 477).
[241] *The Shepherd of Hermas*, Book I, Visions 1 and 2; Dobschütz, *op. cit.*, pp. 314-316.
[242] *The Apostolic Constitutions*, Book II.
[243] *The Apostolic Constitutions*, Book II, Chap. 9.
[244] Cyprian, *De Lapsis*, Chap. 6; Haslehurst, *Penitential Discipline of the Early Church*, pp. 71-80.

for the faith.[245] The canons of a Spanish synod held early in the fourth century seem to show that among the Christians were murderers, pimps, procurers, and procuresses, and that among the clergy were usurers and adulterers.[246] It was to be expected that after most of the Empire had flocked into the Church the average level of moral living of professed Christians should fall below the standards set by the New Testament. It is, therefore, not surprising to find John Chrysostom denouncing the laxity of Christians.[247] The ascetic Jerome was disposed to take a gloomy outlook of the society of his time, but after making all due allowance for his bias it seems fairly clear from his writings that many even of the monks and clergy whom he knew were far from being models of the virtues officially taught by the Church of which they were leaders.[248] We have the records of council after council which specifically denounce flagrant evils present among Christians.[249]

How shall we reconcile the idealistic statements of the New Testament, of apologists, and of modern Christians with the clear evidence of the stark failure of many Christians, some of them the most revered leaders, fully to live up to them? Did Christianity effect any change whatever in the spiritual and moral character of its adherents? Given human nature, the standards put forth in the Gospels seem impossible of full attainment. By setting a goal so different from the practice of men, was Christianity defeating its own end and producing discouragement and easy acquiescence with frailties? The answer is to be found partly in the discipline evolved by the Church to enforce its standards and partly in what we are able to ascertain of a few of the lives of the Christians of these centuries.

From what we know of the disciplinary measures of the Church it is obvious not only that many Christians were deemed to have fallen short of their calling but also that a conscience was at work which sturdily and persistently sought to mould the human stuff that made up the membership. The details of the ecclesiastical machinery which endeavoured to inculcate and enforce Christian ideals we must not take the space to describe. These can be found elsewhere.[250]

[245] Tertullian, *On Modesty*, Chap. 22.

[246] Harnack, *op. cit.*, Vol. II, pp. 297-306.

[247] As in Chrysostom, *Hom. VII on Matt.*, Chap. 7; *Hom. XLIX on Matt.*, Chap. 5; Puech, *St. John Chrysostom*, p. 53.

[248] Jerome, *Epis. XXII ad Eustochium*, Chap. 13; *Epis. LII ad Nepotean; Epis. CXXV ad Rusticum*, Chap. 10; Dill, *Roman Society in the Last Century of the Western Empire*, pp. 115-142; Lea, *History of Sacerdotal Celibacy*, Vol. I, pp. 81-84.

[249] We have the record of some of these in Spain and Gaul.—Lea, *op. cit.*, Vol. I, pp. 81-84; Schultze, *Geschichte des Untergangs des griechisch-römischen Heidentums*, Vol. II, p. 134; Dale, *The Synod of Elvira and Christian Life in the Fourth Century*, *passim*.

[250] Among the books on the subject see Lea, *A History of Auricular Confession and*

It seems certain that from the very beginning the Christian communities disciplined their members for moral lapses and usually sought to do so in such fashion that penitence would be evoked and restoration be possible.[251] *The Didache* tells of a confession of sins in the Church and of a segregation from their fellows of those who sinned after baptism.[252] In the second century Justin Martyr seems to hint that means were found of keeping from the Eucharist those who had lapsed.[253] In the third century, in a frequently quoted passage Origen declares that Christians counted as dead those of their number who had succumbed to licentiousness or to any other sin, but that if they displayed real repentance as evidenced by a change in conduct, they were readmitted—although only after a longer probation than for baptism and never to any office in the Church.[254] Elsewhere Origen seems to say that for lighter sins repentance was possible with penance, but that for graver sins after baptism penance was granted but once.[255] In still another passage he appears to indicate that forgiveness of sins was granted at baptism, but that afterward no pity was shown for sin nor was any forgiveness granted.[256] Clement of Alexandria seemed to allow a second repentance to those Christians who fell into sin, but regarded frequent repentance as counterfeit and not genuine.[257] Tertullian told of the severe discipline through which the lapsed were required to go to give evidence of the sincerity of their repentance.[258] In the third century the bishop and his presbyters adjusted or, failing adjustment, adjudicated controversies between Christians and encouraged reconciliation.[259] Beginning with the fourth century our knowledge of disciplinary measures becomes much fuller,[260] and it is clear that the Church was making valiant if at times futile efforts to bring about among the multitudes who thronged into it conformity to its traditional ethical requirements. Then and earlier many believed the majority to be overlax, and in protest arose such movements as Montan-

---

Indulgences in the Latin Church; Haslehurst, *The Penitential Discipline of the Early Church,* and Watkins, *A History of Penance.*

[251] See, for instance, I Cor. v:1-5; II Cor. ii:5-8, vii:8-12; Gal. vi:1.

[252] *The Didache,* iv:14, xiv:1, and Chap. xx. See also Lea, *op. cit.,* Vol. I, pp. 9-13, and Haslehurst, *op. cit.,* p. 44.

[253] Justin Martyr, *First Apology,* Chap. 66; Haslehurst, *op. cit.,* p. 47.

[254] *Origen against Celsus,* Book III, Chap. 51.

[255] Origen, *Hom. in Lev.* xv:2 (*Lev.* xxv), translated in Haslehurst, *op. cit.,* p. 65; Watkins, *op. cit.,* Vol. I, pp. 133-135.

[256] Origen, commentary on Leviticus ii, translated in Haslehurst, *op. cit.,* p. 69.

[257] Clement, *Strom.,* Book II, Chap. 13.

[258] Tertullian, *De Poenit,* Chap. 11. See also Lea, *op. cit.,* Vol. I, pp. 22, 23.

[259] B. S. Easton in *An Outline of Christianity,* Vol. II, pp. 66, 67.

[260] Haslehurst, *op. cit.,* pp. 86-91. See an account in Watkins, *op. cit.,* Vol. I, pp. 260-465.

ism, Novatianism, and monasticism which in one way and another strove to realize in practice what they believed to be Christian moral and spiritual ideals.

It seems clear that in Christianity was a force which on an increasingly large scale was working to effect a change in the conduct of men and women. The earnestness and the persistence of the effort appear to indicate both partial failure and partial success.

When we come to an examination of the lives of particular individuals, the mixture of failure and success becomes even more obvious. The best-known Christian of the first century is Paul. His surviving letters are more numerous than are those of any of his Christian contemporaries and are so spontaneously self-revealing that it is fairly clear what manner of man he was. Obviously he was convinced that his new faith had wrought a revolutionary change. To him, "if any man is in Christ he is a new creature. Old things are passed away; behold, all things are become new."[261] Clearly he believed this to have been his own experience and upon it he kept ringing the changes. Joy, peace, love, and hope, and the other qualities which he regarded as characteristic of the new life he thought of as present in himself. However, he recognized his own failure fully to reach the goal and hopefully pressed on towards it.[262] Growth was to him part of the essence of the new life.[263] He did not expect perfection of his converts and spoke of them, with himself, as those who were in process of being saved.[264]

Cyprian, Bishop of Carthage in the middle of the third century, had reached maturity when he became a Christian. His new faith led him to devote to charity a large part of his inherited fortune, to turn aside from a successful career as a teacher of rhetoric, and to be strictly continent.[265] He believed that following his conversion had come a fresh moral power. To him the birth into a new spiritual and moral life was a reality.[266]

To take a few of the Christian rulers. It is difficult to know just what, if any, change was made in the character of Constantine. It seems probable that he thought of Christianity as a cult which brought the help of the supreme heavenly power in military conflicts and political crises and whose rites insured eternal happiness.[267] Constantius, his son, reared a Christian, was implacable when once his easy suspicions were aroused, but amid the enervating influences

[261] II Cor. v:17.
[262] Phil. iii:12-14.
[263] Eph. iv:7-16.
[264] I Cor. i:18.
[265] McGiffert, *A History of Christian Thought*, Vol. II, pp. 24-38.
[266] Cyprian to Donatus (translation in *Ante-Nicene Fathers*, Vol. V, pp. 275-280).
[267] Coleman, *Constantine the Great and Christianity*, pp. 82, 88-94.

of an Oriental court he seems to have preserved a reputation for chastity and temperance and to have been in part guided by conscience in civil, military, and ecclesiastical affairs.[268] Theodosius the Great is said to have been chaste and temperate, but to have been at times a victim of a quick temper and to have varied long periods of indolence with spurts of energy.[269] Ambrose had sufficient influence with him to induce him to do penance for one of his volcanic outbursts of violence. Theodosius the Younger is reported to have been learned in the Scriptures and very devout and to have sought to establish a school at Constantinople which would aid in reviving Roman culture and, by a thoroughly Christian atmosphere, counteract the pagan influence of the schools at Athens.[270] In the case of all these nominally Christian emperors it is clear that their faith, although producing some changes of attitude, did not work a thoroughgoing revolution.

Synesius of Cyrene, in his later years bishop, we have noted in the preceding chapter. Whether his acceptance of Christianity, in mature life, was followed by any pronounced alteration in his character is very doubtful. A high-minded, public-spirited Neoplatonist, his new faith probably seemed to him but little different from his older philosophy and such modifications as it wrought in him came slowly, if at all.[271]

For an Augustine of Hippo, however, reared as a nominal Christian, and passing, in mature life, through Manichæism and Neoplatonism into a vivid Christian experience, his childhood's faith, now become a sudden and powerful reality, worked fundamental moral and spiritual change. An increased sensitivity of conscience and an accession of vigour to follow what he believed right, with a sense of peace and of fellowship with God, though not complete, were very marked.[272] The wide popularity of his writings in the West served to reproduce his experience and his standards among later generations of Christians.

Among the members of the Gallic aristocracy of the fifth century the adoption of Christianity appears, as elsewhere, to have been varied in its effects. On the whole, the nominal Christians of this group seem not to have been given to gross vice, but, wealthy and cultivated in the conventional manner of the Empire, to have shown much class pride and at times an absence of public spirit. Here and there one of its number became a bishop, and at least

---

[268] Gardner, *Julian*, p. 74.
[269] Gibbon (Bury's edition), *Decline and Fall of the Roman Empire*, Vol. III, pp. 160-169.
[270] Boyd, *The Ecclesiastical Edicts of the Theodosian Code*, p. 11.
[271] FitzGerald, *The Letters of Synesius of Cyrene, passim*, especially pp. 11-69.
[272] The classic, although not the only, record of Augustine's experience is, of course, his *Confessions*.

one of these churchmen, Apollinaris Sidonius, in his pre-episcopal days almost pagan in his letters,[273] as bishop gave devotedly of himself and his wealth to his flock and proved a tower of strength and stability in the disorder and suffering of the barbarian invasions. To him, and presumably to some others, an active acceptance of his professed faith meant an accession of unselfishness. One of his friends, of high rank and large fortune, a devout Christian who spent much of his time reading the Scriptures and chanting the Psalms, regarded his position and wealth as a trust, was considerate to his subordinates, and was honoured by them.[274] Apparently in him Christianity was bearing some of its expected fruits. We hear, too, of members of that same aristocracy who joined the monastic movement and so, by their faith, were led to adopt a way of life very different from that in which they had been reared.[275]

From these few examples, drawn from the governing or educated classes, it seems clear that Christianity worked alterations in the lives of many individuals. They are not a cross section of the Christian communities. Our object is not to determine with exactitude the extent of the change in the moral practices and spiritual outlook of the Christians of the first five centuries. That would be an impossible task. Our point is that modifications were made, even though we cannot accurately measure them. In some individuals very slight, in others they were extensive. Christianity was releasing a force which, through various channels and by various agencies, was shaping the practices of men. Few, if any, conformed completely to the ideals set forth in the New Testament. In many, perhaps in the majority of, Christians these were much less prominent than their opposites. They were, however, at work, and among many were having marked results. We must remind ourselves again that we are here not attempting to determine whether these results were good or bad. That would take us too far afield into the establishment of criteria for value judgments. High-minded men and women had existed in paganism as they existed in Christian circles. We are, however, trying to say that in many Christianity wrought modifications and in some brought revolution in moral character.

In appraising the effect of Christianity upon the individual, we have deliberately passed over what seemed to Christians of primary importance—the attainment of immortality. An eternal life of joy in fellowship with other Christians, with Christ, and with God, in likeness to Christ, begun here and now and continued in the heavenly city, was what the believer held to be the

---

[273] Hauck, *Kirchengeschichte Deutschlands*, Vol. I, pp. 18-23.
[274] Dill, *Roman Society in the Last Century of the Western Empire*, pp. 187-223.
[275] Dill, *op. cit.*, pp. 142-166.

goal of his striving and the supreme gift of God.[276] Into this realm the historian cannot go. The evidence is not of the sort with which he is accustomed to deal. He must, however, note that here was the hope of the Christian and that such ethical and cultural results as came out of Christianity cannot be understood apart from it. It was that hope and that faith which inspired the Church, moulded liturgy, affected literature and art, and contributed to changes in customs, institutions, and ethical practices.

The effects of Christianity, both on group behaviour and on individuals, were seen more clearly in minorities than in the great body of the Church. It was difficult and perhaps impossible to conduct oneself conformably to the ethics of the Gospels in the midst of a culture which in so many of its features, both superficial and fundamental, was in contrast with them. In such a situation, a Christian might adopt one of four courses. He might seek to transform the society in which he lived, striving to make it fully conform to what he conceived of as Christian ideals. That few, if any, sought to do in this age. He might, in the second place, give over any thought of remaking completely the world about him, but endeavour to mend or to eliminate some of its features which were in most flagrant contradiction with his ideals and strive to live as nearly in conformity to the New Testament as existence in the current society would permit. This was the course adopted by some thoughtful Christians after Constantine. It meant abstention from pagan religious rites, from most of the contemporary amusements, and from some prevalent practices in sex and possibly in business. A third procedure, and the one probably followed by most nominal Christians after Constantine and by some before his time, was to refrain from most pagan religious rites, but in other ways to conform as closely to current customs as the Church would allow. Or, as a fourth procedure, the Christian might seek to establish a society as nearly as possible divorced from the life about him and which would embody what he believed to be Christian standards. In a moderate form this was the effort of the official organization of the Church before Constantine. In a somewhat more drastic manner it was pursued by such minorities as the Montanists and Novatians, of whom we are to say more in the next chapter. Its most extreme manifestations were in monasticism. Of these, too, we are to speak later. Again and again we shall see the experiment recurring. Every age has had Christians who, regarding the society about them as evil, have set themselves to form, as distinct from it as possible, communities in which they could realize their ideals and build a

[276] As in John xvii:2; Rom. viii:12-17; Eph. ii:19-22, iv:1-32; Phil. iii:8-14; I Thes. iv:13-18.

culture on the New Testament model. Such was many a monastic community and such were numerous Protestant groups, especially in North America.

All four courses, it must be noted, involved greater or less tension. None could be followed, not even the most easygoing, without conflicting with the pre-Christian life of the Empire. For the minorities, the conflict was often very severe. It brought on the persecutions of pre-Constantinian times. It led the monks to withdraw more or less completely from society to communities or to solitary existence in the deserts or other relatively inaccessible places. All four entailed changes in the established order. Of the four, the last two prob ably had the least effect upon society as a whole. The relatively tolerant attitude which, so far as possible, conformed to prevailing customs, naturally wrought few alterations. The method of drastic divorce from the world despaired of the existing structure as hopelessly evil and tended to abandon it to its fate. Obviously its influence would be chiefly that of lives who by word or example rebuked their fellow Christians for their laxity. Beginning as early as the fifth century, however, monks became active as missionaries and in alleviating the woes of those upon whom society pressed heavily. We have already seen the precursors of these on the Arabian frontier, here and there in Persia, in Martin of Tours, and in Severinus. In succeeding centuries and down into the present day monks were to have a major part in the propagation of Christianity and in works of mercy. Never, however, did they seek to bring all mankind fully to their ideals. They were content to rebuke some of what they regarded as the vices of their fellow Christians, to eradicate pagan religious practices, and to relieve the ill and underprivileged. Wherever they had charge of a community or were influential in it, they sought to inculcate such of the Christian virtues as they thought those who were not monks should follow. In some instances, as in the famous Jesuit missions in Paraguay, they strove to build a Christian society in which the majority, although not monks, were under their tutelage. All this, however, was after the year 500. Before then, only here and there were monks beginning to have much effect upon the *mores* outside their circles.

Inevitably the question arises as to how far Christianity was responsible for the decay of Græco-Roman society—for what is often termed the "fall of Rome." The query is an old one. Indeed, often it has not been a query but an accusation. As we have seen, one of the earliest charges of non-Christians was that Christians were turning the world upside down.[277] Repeatedly the apologists were forced to address themselves to the indictment that Christians were responsible for the misfortunes which were overtaking the Empire. Of

[277] Acts xvii :6.

ate years we have heard the same assertion, although in different terms.[278]

On the face of it, some of the evidence seems on the side of the prosecution. t is true that Christianity, before Constantine, discouraged its adherents from aking office or serving in the army.[279] Later, when such occupations were not leemed inconsistent with the profession of an ordinary Christian, the monastic movement led many of the middle and upper classes to shun the burdens of iublic office and, by devoting their goods to the poor or the Church, to deprive he ever-needy public treasury of some of what might have come to it. It is ust possible that Christian asceticism, by its scorn for this-worldly wealth nd culture, contributed to the decay of industry and wealth and to the decline f letters and art.[280] We have noted that Christians attacked outstanding fea-ures of ancient society. They denounced its religion and condemned many f its amusements. Many of them looked askance at its literature and dominant ihilosophies. Much of its art, too, they could not tolerate, for its association vith polytheism and for what they deemed its obscenity.

It is clear that at least some of the diseases which sapped the strength of the ncient world had set in before Christianity had assumed sufficient proportions greatly to affect the Empire.[281] Because the growth of Christianity coincided vith the development of these maladies to acute stages it must not be assumed hat the one was responsible for the other. May it not be, however, that Christianity, even if not the main or even a major factor, aggravated the ill-lesses of society, and to such an extent as to render recovery impossible? One Christian scholar has said that if the faith had no share in bringing about the lownfall of the Empire, at least it did nothing to arrest it.[282]

It must be said in reply that experts are still debating the causes of the tagnation and decline of the Græco-Roman world.[283] Amid such disagreement t would be rash dogmatically to assert that Christianity was a determining actor. Perhaps, however, it would be equally premature to pronounce its

[278] Troeltsch, *The Social Teaching of the Christian Churches*, p. 87, declares that Chris-ianity broke to pieces the ancient world, not only in its spirit, but also in its outward form. errero, *The Ruin of Ancient Civilization and the Triumph of Christianity*, pp. 74-76, ays that Christianity was destroying the Empire by abstention.

[279] Glover, *Christ in the Ancient World*, p. 35.

[280] Dill, *Roman Society in the Last Century of the Western Empire*, p. 11, summarizes ome of these views.

[281] Rostovtzeff, *The Social and Economic History of the Roman Empire*, pp. 478-480, ays that what from the intellectual and spiritual point of view was the main phenomenon f the decline of ancient culture, the decay of the city civilization of the Græco-Roman vorld, had begun in the second century B.C., followed by a revival in the cities of Italy vhich stopped almost completely in the second century after Christ.

[282] Duchesne, *Early History of the Christian Church*, Vol. III, p. 3.

[283] See a summary of the usual reasons assigned and a discussion of them in Rostovtzeff, p. cit., pp. 480-487. For some features of the decay see Dill, op. cit., pp. 227-281.

innocence. Still, the trend of opinion seems to be that whatever the infections which brought about the decay of the ancient world, Christianity was at least not an important one.[284] Politically Christianity seems not to have hampered the efforts of the Emperors of the third and fourth centuries to reorganize the realm. It appears not to have had any perceptible effect on the army, largely because, as we have said, very few of any religion of the areas from which the Church was chiefly drawn in the days of the Christian disapproval of military service were enrolling in the legions. It is improbable that Christianity hastened the "fall" of the Empire.

Moreover, it must also be said that in some areas Christianity seems to have retarded the decay, that in others it prevented the collapse from being as great as would have been the case without it, that it contributed to salvaging much from the ruins, and that it hastened the appearance and largely determined the form of the new culture which emerged out of the wreckage of the old.

We have already noticed that Christianity helped to weld together the Greek elements and to give unification in language and sentiment to Asia Minor, Greece, and the Ægean. It was, too, a powerful agency in aiding the assimilation of the barbarian peoples who moved into these areas. It had, therefore, an important share in the continuation of the tradition of civilization in the East and in the transition from the Roman Empire to that Byzantine state that did so much to perpetuate civilization in an age when Western Europe was near to chaos.

In the West, where the collapse was most marked, the Church was the chief conservator of Roman traditions. It was the one great institution which passed over from the old era to the new, and it carried with it, although in forms altered by its own genius, much of the old tradition. More than once a bishop led the citizenry in resistance to invasion and served as a stabilizing centre in times of despair.[285]

Moreover, long before the disappearance of Roman power in the West Christianity was giving rise to new institutions and ideas which were to have a large part in shaping the cultures that followed. In a culture which was largely clinging to old forms and repeating and reworking accepted ideas, Christianity was producing the Church and its own theology and literature. In it was an energy which galvanized the Græco-Roman world to its last notable creative efforts. That energy was to pass on to the next age, transmitting much, but placing its own peculiar stamp upon the new cultures. Here it was to have a much freer hand than it could while the old survived.

The preservation of the past and yet the putting on it of a new and distinctive mark is seen in many ways. There is the perpetuation of the Latin language as a vehicle for living thought and action and yet largely for ecclesiastical and theological purposes. There is canon law, carrying over so much of the Roman tradition, yet informed by the Christian impulse. There are the painting and sculpture of the Middle Ages and the Renaissance, with much of the classical and yet often used for ecclesiastical subjects. There is the use of ancient architectural forms, and yet their modification and their devotion to the erection of churches. It is thought-provoking to contrast that most prominent surviving building of pre-Christian Rome, the Colosseum, with its memories of gladiatorial combats "to make a Roman holiday," and the outstanding physical creation of Christian Rome, St. Peter's, with its bloodless sacrifice of the mass offered for the present and eternal welfare of man. There is, too, the preservation of Trajan's Column, but its use as a pedestal for a statue of the Galilean fisherman, and, of much more recent erection, but after the model of the columns of imperial Rome, the monument to the Immaculate Conception. The Roman Catholic Church itself, in its name, temper, and organization, has transmitted much of the spirit and form of imperial Rome. Yet it is more than "the ghost of the Roman Empire." Both subtly and openly it has perpetuated much of the old, yet it is a fresh creation, containing motives and ideals quite alien to the Rome of the Emperors and arising from clearly Christian sources. It is primarily a product of the Christian spirit. It has, moreover, shown much more vitality than the Roman Empire. It has gathered into its fold more peoples than ever owned the sway of the Cæsars and has extended its message and its organization over territories many times broader than those which heard the tramp of the Roman legions. It has, moreover, displayed an ability to survive, to adapt itself to various cultures, and to influence those cultures far greater than ever did imperial Rome.

Whether the new is more or less admirable than the old is, of course, important. For our present purposes, however, it is sufficient to point out that Christianity was the agency for preserving much of the Roman world and at the same time using it to express its own peculiar ideas. It helped create new cultures to which it brought over much of the past and yet upon which it placed its own distinctive impress in a way it was never free to do under the ancient regime. It was both conservative and revolutionary. It has shown, too, a vigour and a power to survive and to propagate itself far greater than that of the political structure which it outlived and even than the ideas and the concepts of the Greek and Roman sages and artists. Time after time it has, indeed, as we shall see, provided the vehicle by which these have spread. Into the Græco-Roman world there was born, in Christianity, a force which, while not destroying it, outlived it, and by its own exuberant vitality carried much of it, often made over in a new fashion, to future ages and alien peoples.

In conclusion and summary we may say that the effects of Christianity upon its environment were not the result of a deliberately planned effort of Christians at a wholesale reconstruction of society. That was quite foreign to their purpose. Few, if any, dreamed of reshaping all, even of the Mediterranean world, into conformity with the ideals of the New Testament. Many Christians, indeed, vehemently repudiated the charge that their movement was a menace to the established order. With some features of it they felt they could not conscientiously have anything to do. However, with most of the main outline of the political, intellectual, economic, and social structure of Græco-Roman civilization the majority of Christians were not consciously out of accord. To be sure, in the New Testament and notably in the sayings of Jesus were to be found ideals which, if fully carried out by all men, would entirely change society. In its earlier stages, too, the Christian communities tended to hold themselves apart from the currents about them and to have their own distinctive life moulded on their own principles. Always, after the Church swept into its fold the vast majority of the population of the Empire, minority movements sought to emphasize the antinomy of what they thought of as true Christianity to the manner of life of the general run of mankind. The pre-Constantinian Church, however, and the intransigent minorities cherished no purpose of remaking the world. They were content to allow it to go its own way, hitting out against a few of its salient features and keeping more or less aloof from it, but planning neither to destroy it nor to reconstruct it. Some features of Græco-Roman culture Christians did attack—especially its religion, some of its sex *mores*, and its amusements. They sought to relieve on a large scale the distresses of their own number and, to a more limited extent, of those outside their fold. For themselves they inculcated ethical standards which, while partially in accord with some of the non-Christian philosophies and religions, yet in practice differed widely from those of the majority. The Christian movement displayed, too, an inner power which even apart from the formal discipline of the Church seemed to inspire many to an approximation to these standards. One of its characteristic features was its ability to transform individuals. All this, however, was not meant to destroy society.

Christianity had its growth in the midst of a crumbling world. Probably it did not contribute in any decisive fashion to that disintegration. While the decay was in progress it was changing the religious complexion of the Empire, it was creating a new organization, the Church, a fresh philosophy, its theology, and was bringing into existence its own peculiar forms of worship, literature, art, and architecture. In a few regions it stimulated what today would be called nationalism. In some areas it aided resistance against disintegration. In many it was a major factor in transmitting contributions from the disappearing culture to those which succeeded it, and had an important rôle in inspiring and shaping the new age. In the midst of a culture whose springs of originality and creativity seemed to have dried up, Christianity was introducing a fresh dynamic which, in the face of the general senescence, was producing young and vigorous institutions and which was to have a major part in making the subsequent period something new.

Chapter VII

THE EFFECT OF THE ENVIRONMENT UPON CHRISTIANITY TO A.D. 500

TO THE effect of the environment upon Christianity in the first five centuries more attention has been paid of late years than to the effect of Christianity upon the environment. A large literature has arisen. Some writers are inclined to magnify the contributions from other sources and to ascribe little significance to the impulse which came from Jesus. To them Christianity is primarily a syncretistic religion, owing its strength chiefly to its success in adapting itself to the atmosphere of the times and to absorbing attractive features from its rivals. Others have arisen to minimize the foreign content and to deny that Christianity is merely a variant of Judaism or just the survivor of a number of mystery religions.

It need not surprise us that Christianity absorbed extensively from the many faiths and cultural streams with which it came in contact, and especially during these formative centuries. Jesus, as will quickly be recalled, took few, if any, of the precautions which prudence might have suggested to preserve his message uncontaminated. So far as our surviving records show, he did not commit it to writing nor encourage his disciples to do so. He framed no creed nor easily remembered short formula to summarize his teaching. If he contemplated a permanent organization of his followers, our documents do not indicate that he elaborated even its main outlines. Certainly it does not seem to have made a very profound impression upon the intimate circle which was most in his confidence. A short prayer which he taught was cherished and transmitted, as was what came to be known as the eucharist. In general, however, he inculcated no ritual of worship. Without the protection of the devices which other founders of the most widespread religions have adopted, it is not surprising that the impulse given by his life and teachings and by the story of his death and the belief in the resurrection clothed itself in many widely diverse ways as it moved out into different cultural circles and as it was felt by individuals with variant backgrounds.

The early belief in the Spirit accentuated the diversity, for it implied continued messages from an invisible and risen Lord which might be independent of what had been told his followers in the days of his flesh.[1]

The process of borrowing and assimilation seems to have been augmented by the habit of many Christians of regarding their faith as the legitimate heir of all the goodness which had existed before Jesus. The Old Testament was thought of as fulfilled in Jesus. Some of the Christian apologists were inclined to claim a Jewish and so a divine origin for what they regarded as acceptable in pagan philosophies. Many Christian thinkers held non-Christian Greek philosophy in high esteem. Augustine said that "the very thing which is now called the Christian religion existed among the ancients nor was it absent even at the beginning of the human race. Yet not until Christ himself came in the flesh did the true religion which already existed begin to be called Christian."[2] Very much earlier it had been said of the Logos that "that was the true light which lighteth every man as he comes into the world."[3] Under such circumstances it is not remarkable that Christians appropriated freely from other systems or that pagans charged Christians with plagiarism and declared that all the essentials of Christianity were to be found elsewhere.[4]

Long before the year 500 what we call Christianity had taken on fairly well stereotyped forms in organization, creed, sacred books, and ritual. The most prominent of these have persisted to our times and the major part of what we denominate Christianity still largely conforms to them. In the formative generations, however, the flexibility must have been great and the effect of environment very marked.

We must, indeed, ask ourselves again and again to what extent the original impulse survived, and how far, if at all, it dominated what claimed to perpetuate it. We must also inquire as to how it happened that so much of it persisted. To anticipate briefly what will be later elaborated, it may be said that the very dangers of losing contact with the original impulse and the many movements claiming to derive from it but which seemed to be distorting or diluting it proved an incentive to safeguard it. What developed into the main streams of Christianity became such largely because they were believed to have been effective in transmitting the primitive historical content of the faith. Repeatedly through the centuries Christians have harked back, as to an authoritative standard, to what appear to be the most authentic reports of what

[1] II Cor. v:16.

[2] Augustine, *Retract.* Book I, Chap. 13, paragraph 3 (Migne, *Pat. Lat.,* Vol. XXXII, col. 603. Compare Augustine, *Confessions,* Book VII, Chap. 9, paragraph 13).

[3] John i:9.

[4] Case, *The Evolution of Early Christianity,* pp. 178-194, presents an interesting summary and contains a useful bibliography.

Jesus said and did and of what his immediate disciples experienced in his death and resurrection and in the coming of the Spirit.

It is important to trace, even if only in brief summary, the course of the development of Christianity and of its reaction to its environment in these centuries, partly because then were evolved those forms of the faith which propagated themselves in the succeeding thousand years, and, with some additions and modifications, down into our own day. If we are to know what it was which spread between the years 500 and 1500 and even between the years 1500 and the present time, we must see something of the varied garb which Christianity took by the close of its fifth century. It is to this story that most Church histories devote the major portion of their space. We need not, therefore, recount it in any detail. We can content ourselves by outlining the salient features, and especially those most germane to our purpose.

Before embarking upon an account of the effect of the environment, however, we must inquire into what is meant by that term. In its broadest sense it is very inclusive. In it is comprehended the various cultures and races into which Christianity moved. It embraces, too, the religions with which Christianity came in contact, the philosophies with which it dealt, and the artistic and literary traditions which touched it. In it must be counted the political structures with which Christianity had to do, and geographic and climatic conditions. In it ought ideally to be considered the many millions of individuals who professed the faith. Each Christian has had his peculiar background and temperament and it is probable that to no two has the faith seemed exactly the same. The Christianity of each individual who has claimed that religion as his own differs, even if only slightly, from that of every other.

In this inclusive sense of the term, it would be quite impossible to trace exhaustively the effect of environment. All we can hope to do is to consider some of the impress made by the most outstanding features of the milieu of the first centuries. We will cover the manner in which Christianity was moulded by the cultures, the religions, and the philosophies which affected it most profoundly, and say something of traditions which modified its art, its literature, its customs, and its festivals. We will speak of the manner in which the organization of the Church reproduced the political and geographic setting. We will describe briefly the ways in which the main types of the Christianity of these centuries reflected the racial, geographic, and cultural divisions of the world of the time, and how far they arose out of the experiences and convictions of outstanding Christians. We shall be especially interested in those branches of Christianity which spread most widely, particularly in the succeeding centuries.

In its earliest days the chief cultural and religious influences with which the infant Christianity was in contact were Judaism, Hellenistic culture, and the belief of attainment to immortality through the processes of cults which centred about saviour-gods. These three currents had different sources. Often they did not operate together. Yet at times they intermingled. Thus we have strains which we are at a loss to know whether to term Judaistic Hellenisticism or Hellenistic Judaism.[5] Then, too, the spirit of the Hellenistic world and probably of Hellenistic Judaism was profoundly modified by the mystery cults.

The nascent religion was in danger of absorption by one or all of these powerful forces. For a brief time it seemed merely another sect of Judaism, one of the many begotten by that virile faith. One of the earliest struggles which convulsed the Christian communities was over the question of whether they should remain within Judaism. Very soon, too, apparently through the channels of Hellenistic Judaism, Christianity began to move out into the Hellenistic world of the Orient with its attitudes of mind and spirit derived from Greek philosophy and the mystery religions. Here it faced the peril of losing itself and of becoming just another philosophy or merely one more of the many mystery cults. What eventually proved numerically and in their ability to survive and propagate themselves the main forms of Christianity displayed sufficient strength to overcome these dangers. However, other types of the Christian movement so far conformed that they sacrificed most of whatever distinctiveness came from the impulse given by Jesus. Moreover, even the predominant schools passed on to the present time evidences of having been in intimate touch with these three powerful currents. Sometimes, indeed, it is asserted that Christianity became simply a blend of certain strains from Judaism with Hellenistic doctrines of redemption by the incarnation of a divine saviour.[6]

First of all, of course, Christianity carried over much from Judaism.[7] From that faith it inherited a belief in God—God a personal being, the creator and sovereign of the universe, the judge of all men, whose will is the law of men's lives, is righteous, and must in the end prevail.[8] In this conception of God Christians had to find room for what they believed they had learned through Jesus and through that continuing experience which they ascribed to the Spirit.

[5] Goodenough, *The Theology of Justin Martyr*, p. vii.
[6] Bacon, *Studies in Matthew*, p. xi, contains a succinct statement of that position.
[7] For one summary analysis of Christianity's debt to Judaism, see Levison, *The Jewish Background of Christianity*, pp. 188-195.
[8] A study of both Old and New Testaments must make this apparent. See comments on it in McGiffert, *A History of Christian Thought*, Vol. I, pp. 30-36; Scott, *The Kingdom of God in the New Testament*, p. 15; McGiffert, *The God of the Early Christians*, p. 179; Scott, *The Gospel and Its Tributaries*, pp. 23-46.

Around this attempted adjustment, complicated by relations with Greek philosophy, some of the most acute controversies of the Church centred. Some who called themselves Christians, notably the Marcionites, entirely rejected the God of the Jews. Some tended to make Jesus their God.[9] Indeed, the echoes of the controversy have not yet subsided. For the majority of Christians the result was what they believed to be an enlarged conception of God, one in which that inherited from the Hebrews was still present, but profoundly modified, and, they held, enriched by what they had derived from Jesus and the Spirit.[10]

From Judaism, too, came the strong ethical note of Christianity. Although most Christians broke with those ritual requirements of the Jewish Law which would have assimilated them to the parent faith, and although some appear to have claimed release from all its other Commandments,[11] the great majority regarded as binding at least the non-ritualistic portions of the Law, and even held to some of the ritual. To this they added what they believed to be the precepts and the interpretations of Jesus. The Ten Commandments and the Sermon on the Mount both had a place in Christian teaching.

From Judaism Christianity inherited its intransigence and the closely associated martyr complex. The Pharisaic type of Judaism with which Christianity, at its inception, was so closely allied, was particularly uncompromising and held in honour those who had perished for the faith. On many points, too, the major strains of Christianity, while in some respects showing an extraordinary capacity of absorption, were adamant. Christians both expected persecution and gloried in it.

Christianity shared in the Jewish dream of universalism but carried it much farther. Many of the Jews had long claimed universality for their faith and had foretold a time when all men would benefit from it.[12] Few if any, however, had been able to divorce themselves from their racial exclusiveness. The main currents of Christianity broke the bounds set by this restrictive racialism. Here lay much of the secret of their power.

While Christianity went farther toward inclusiveness than did Judaism, it inherited something of the latter's pride. Christians thought of themselves as the true Israel, the people whom God had chosen from among the nations

---

[9] This tendency to make Jesus the God of the Christians is stressed—probably over-stressed—in McGiffert, *The God of the Early Christians.*

[10] The Spirit is, of course, to be found in the Old Testament, but the doctrine concerning it developed further among the Christians. See a brief mention of this in Gavin, *The Jewish Antecedents of the Christian Sacraments,* p. 99.

[11] Rom. vi:1; I Cor. v:1.

[12] As in the book of Jonah and as in Isaiah ii:1-4.

after the majority of the Jews, by their refusal to accept his Messiah, had been cast off.[13] Salvation, so they held, was only through Christ. Hospitable though they often were to practices and intellectual conceptions from other faiths and systems, toward the systems themselves they continued intolerant and often scornful.[14] Seers and philosophers outside the Jewish-Christian tradition might have some angles of the truth, but the full truth was in the Christian revelation.

This belief in its own universal validity, with a concomitant desire to have all men share its blessings, and this sense of exclusive possession of the full truth of God through his election, while possibly involving a paradox and presenting presuppositions difficult of reconciliation, have characterized most of Christianity through the centuries and have been among the sources of its persistence and its missionary zeal.

From Judaism, moreover, Christianity took over what it came to call the Old Testament.[15] Some there were among the Christians who rejected the Jewish Scriptures. To the majority, however, these latter were divinely inspired. Yet they must, so Christians held, be interpreted in light of the further revelation in Jesus. So interpreted, the Scriptures, Christians declared, pointed toward Jesus, contained many explicit prophecies of him, and were fulfilled by him. Read in this fashion, therefore, the Scriptures became quite a different collection than when taught by an orthodox Jew. This acceptance of the Old Testament, it may be noted, was an important factor in preventing Christianity from becoming identical with the pagan cults which it supplanted, monotheistic and sacramental though some of them tended to be.[16]

Christians were influenced by the extra-canonical literature of the Jews. Especially did they reflect some of the views of the apocalypses. As we have noted, First Enoch particularly appealed to Christian writers.[17] From the apocalypses and the general spirit of much of Judaism and of its literature came that philosophy of history which we have already noted.

In some writings the Jewish and Christian strains are so intermingled that experts are divided as to whether they are Jewish documents with Christian interpolations or whether they are of purely Christian authorship. This is the case with *The Odes and Psalms of Solomon*[18] and *The Testaments of the*

[13] As in Rom. ix:1—xi:32; Gal. iv:28-31; I Peter ii:7-10.

[14] This is seen again and again in the Apologists.

[15] On this see a useful summary in Harnack, *The Mission and Expansion of Christianity*, Vol. I, pp. 279-289.

[16] Burkitt, *Church and Gnosis*, p. 138.

[17] Moore, *Judaism*, Vol. I, pp. 127, 128; Charles, *The Book of Enoch*, pp. xcv-ciii.

[18] Harris and Mingana, *The Odes and Psalms of Solomon*, *passim*, especially pp. 61, 8, 187, 197, in which various views of the composition of the collection are given.

Twelve Patriarchs.[19] In either event they evidence strong Jewish influence on Christians. So, too, part of the Christian *Didache* is believed to be of Jewish origin.[20]

Naturally, Jewish influence is strong in much of the style and form of early Christian literature. It is suggested that we owe the collections of the sayings of Jesus which are incorporated in the Synoptic Gospels to a contemporary Jewish practice of preserving so far as possible the exact words of their more prominent rabbis.[21] Paul's method of argument is sometimes rabbinic.[22] The allegorical treatment of the Old Testament made famous by Philo, that outstanding figure in Hellenistic Judaism, was used by Paul,[23] Justin Martyr,[24] and other Christian writers.[25] The designation of Jesus as Lord, which many have thought an importation from the mysteries, may also have Hebrew roots and have been derived from the Aramaic with little or no connexion with Hellenistic-Oriental cults.[26]

The oldest of the Christian sacraments appear to owe much to Judaism. Baptism seems clearly not to have been a Christian innovation. It had been used as a Jewish initiatory rite for proselytes.[27] The Christian practice may well have been derived from that of John.[28] It is possible, too, that the Christian use of oil in connexion with baptism and, later, in association with confirmation, came from Jewish sources.[29]

Whatever its affiliations, the Christians gave to baptism distinctive meanings. As a symbol of the believer's beginning a new life and of his sharing the death and resurrection of his Lord it had similarities to the mysteries, but it possessed a peculiar flavour which it owed to Jesus and to the Christian experience of moral and spiritual transformation.[30]

So with the eucharist. One of the earliest Christian beliefs was that the

---

[19] Moore, *Judaism,* Vol. I, pp. 190-192.

[20] Moore, *Judaism,* Vol. I, pp. 187, 188.

[21] Streeter, *The Four Gospels,* p. 369.

[22] As in Gal. iii:16.

[23] Gal. vi:21-31. See also Dodd, *The Epistle of Paul to the Romans,* p. 105.

[24] Goodenough, *The Theology of Justin Martyr,* pp. 113-116.

[25] Paul Heinisch, *Der Einfluss Philos auf die älteste christliche Exegese,* pp. 1-41.

[26] Dodd, *op. cit.,* pp. 167, 168, citing some of the special literature on the subject; Rawlinson, *The New Testament Doctrine of the Christ,* pp. 37, 76-79, 231-237; Burkitt, *Christian Beginnings,* pp. 44-52. This, of course, is different from the well-known thesis of Bousset *Kyrios Christos,* which derives the title "The Lord" from contemporary popular Gentile religion and regards it as a development of the Hellenistic Church.

[27] Gavin, *The Jewish Antecedents of the Christian Sacraments,* pp. 30-40, 55-58.

[28] Clemen, *Primitive Christianity and Its Non-Jewish Sources,* pp. 212-237; Bacon, *The Gospel of the Hellenists,* pp. 66-69, 70, 99.

[29] Gavin, *op. cit.,* p. 112.

[30] Foakes-Jackson, *The Rise of Gentile Christianity,* p. 34. However, on the new birth in Philo see Reitzenstein, *Die Vorgeschichte der christlichen Taufe,* pp. 103 ff.

acrament was instituted by Jesus himself.[31] Some, while not denying this, ee in it an outgrowth from Jewish precedents. The question is debated as to vhether it was originally the Passover meal or in accord with a Jewish custom •y which a group of friends met together periodically for a common repast and eligious fellowship.[32] It is held that Jewish influence is evident in early ucharistic liturgies.[33]

As with baptism, so with the eucharist, it must be said that while some of the lements and background were Jewish, a thoroughly distinctive Christian :haracter was given to the sacrament.[34]

It ought also to be added that if something akin to sacramentalism may have •een found in Judaism (and this is by no means proved), in Christianity it ecame much more fully and explicitly developed.[35]

Christianity's debt to Judaism in special days for religious observances was very marked. So Easter seems to have arisen out of the Jewish paschal feast and originally not to have been celebrated primarily to commemorate the esurrection. Only gradually was it Christianized.[36] Pentecost was continued, or obvious reasons.[37] The early Jewish Christian community seems to have ollowed the Jewish custom of fasting twice a week.[38] Up to the middle of the ifth century Christians were still observing the Jewish Sabbath, although even n the second century this was not universal or generally binding.[39] The Jewish veek, with its naming of the days by numbers and not by planets, and the Jewish divisions of the day were also taken over.[40]

Yet here again, Christians made characteristic additions and modifications. They kept the first day of the week—possibly although not certainly (and perhaps even improbably) in memory of the resurrection of Jesus.[41] Paul :ended to think of the observance of "days and seasons" as a matter of personal preference and of little consequence, and to teach his churches to do likewise.[42] Some Jewish feasts, such as the Day of Atonement and the Day of Taber-

---

[31] I Cor. xi:23-26. In this early Christian document Paul speaks of having received the story from others, still earlier than this letter.

[32] Gavin, *op. cit.*, pp. 64-67, 81; Oesterley, *The Jewish Background of the Christian Liturgy*, pp. 157-179.

[33] Gavin, *op. cit.*, p. 86; Oesterley, *op. cit.*, pp. 205-230.

[34] Gavin, *op. cit.*, p. 96.

[35] Gavin, *op. cit.*, pp. 3-25.

[36] Loeschke, *Jüdisches und heidnisches im christlichen Kult*, pp. 9-11.

[37] Acts ii:1-41.

[38] Lietzmann, *Geschichte der alten Kirche*, Vol. I, pp. 55-57.

[39] Loeschke, *op. cit.*, pp. 5-8.

[40] Loeschke, *op. cit.*, pp. 1-3.

[41] Acts xx:7; I Cor. xvi:2; Rev. i:10; Lietzmann, *op. cit.*, Vol. I, pp. 60-62; Duchesne, *Christian Worship*, p. 228.

[42] Rom. xiv:5; Col. ii:16.

nacles, were disregarded.[43] For fasting, Christians set aside two days of the week different from those used by the Jews.[44] The new wine was doing something to the old wineskins.

In liturgy the Christian debt to Judaism was very great.[45] Early Christians had been accustomed to the worship of the synagogue and naturally carried over into their own conventicles some of its customs and forms, hallowed as these were to them by long association. Not until the fourth century do we have more than partial glimpses of the Christian liturgy. It seems, however, fairly clear that from the synagogue came the practice of the public reading of the Scriptures, the responsive "Amen," and the chanting of the Psalms. The Christian forms and customs of prayer appear to display some evidence of Jewish heritage. Obviously, Christians did not slavishly follow Jewish models, but out of their own peculiar beliefs and experiences were fashioning something new. They were adding, too, their own types of services.[46]

In giving to charity, Paul inculcated a practice which seems to have been akin to Jewish custom.[47]

The organization of the Christian Church bore, and continues to bear, marks of the Jewish heritage. The idea of a distinct religious community may be derived from Judaism. Certainly when Christians came to form their own groups, the synagogue, with which a large proportion of them had been familiar, provided useful and familiar precedents.[48] The title and function of elder may have been borrowed from that institution, although it may have been taken over from Greek associations for worship,[49] or from municipal constitutions, or even have arisen spontaneously.[50]

It is often impossible to determine whether an ecclesiastical form or office is derived from a Jewish or a Gentile precursor, or whether it is entirely original.[51]

In general, however, Christians appear to have developed their own types of organizations with surprisingly little transfer from the somewhat similar religious associations about them.[52] The Christian Church was and is distinctly a Christian creation. Even the separation of the clergy and laity, with the similarity of the former to the Jewish priesthood, seems to have come about

---

[43] Duchesne, op. cit., p. 235.

[44] Duchesne, op. cit., p. 228; Loeschke, op. cit., pp. 1-3.

[45] On the influence of Jewish on Christian liturgy, see Oesterley, op. cit., passim, and Loeschke, op. cit., pp. 11-15.

[46] As in Acts i:12-14, ii:42, xx:7, 11; I Cor. x:16, xi:20-34; Oesterley, op. cit., pp. 91-97.

[47] Spencer, Beyond Damascus, p. 98.

[48] Harnack, The Constitution and Law of the Church in the First Two Centuries, p. 45.

[49] Clemen, Primitive Christianity and Its Non-Jewish Sources, p. 209.

[50] Harnack, op. cit., p. 58.

[51] Harnack, op. cit., pp. 43, 44.

[52] Lindsay, The Church and the Ministry in the Early Centuries, pp. 131, 132.

by a spontaneous development from within and not from imitation of anything in the world without.[53]

Cardinal concepts of Christianity which owed much to Judaism were those of faith, righteousness, and justification. The Christian belief in the Spirit had a Jewish ancestry. From Judaism, too, came much of the Christian conviction of the supremacy of the religious obligation, the prior claim of God's will upon the allegiance of men.

Some popular beliefs appear to have entered Christianity from Judaism, notably that in angels. This angelology was probably a purely Jewish development which passed over into its daughter faith,[54] there to have a further evolution. From Judaism came in part the belief in demons and the practice of exorcism. From entirely outside Judaism were derived conceptions of various discarnate intelligences. They had standing in both Stoic and Platonic circles and were easily correlated with the idea of angels.[55] We find that in Antioch the Church honoured the seven Jewish brethren put to death there by Epiphanes. In Antioch, too, many Christian converts, especially women, visited synagogues on the Sabbath and festival days and observed Jewish rites.[56] Some Christians, moreover, long continued to observe Easter according to the dating of the Jewish Passover.

Very early, perhaps within a very short time after the crucifixion, Christianity began to move into the Hellenistic world. Its first steps in that direction were by way of Hellenistic Judaism. In the primitive Christian community at Jerusalem were Hellenistic Jews, among them that Stephen whose radical views led to his untimely death. It was, indeed, largely by the avenue of Hellenistic Judaism that the new faith escaped the bonds of the parent faith and started on its course as a new and universal religion. It was mostly in Greek-speaking communities, as we have seen, that Christianity first gained its extension throughout the Roman Empire. Inevitably, therefore, the faith was influenced by that environment.

Contributions from the Hellenistic world seem to have come in, at least at first, not primarily by conscious copying and adaptation, or by way of those who were expert in the philosophies or the mystery cults, but from the general atmosphere and attitude of mind and spirit which had been bred by these systems. They entered with the very language.[57] Phrases current on everyone's

---

[53] Allen, *Christian Institutions,* p. 128.
[54] Clemen, *op. cit.,* pp. 83-96.
[55] Dodd, *The Epistle of Paul to the Romans,* p. 185.
[56] Bouchier, *A Short History of Antioch,* pp. 130-132; Kraeling, *The Jewish Community at Antioch,* p. 154.
[57] Adeney, *The Greek and Eastern Churches,* p. 7.

tongue brought with them, even if only vaguely understood, philosophic and religious concepts. Of this Paul seems to have been an example. Proud of his Jewish lineage and orthodoxy, and probably without much technical training in either Greek rhetoric or philosophy, in his letters are echoes of Greek thought[58] and notions which appear associated with the mystery cults.

It is not easy to trace accurately the effect of this Hellenistic atmosphere on Christianity. It is a fascinating field for speculation, but it is difficult, particularly for the early centuries, to arrive at dependable results. It is clear that here was an environment which favoured compromise and syncretism.[59] To it, moreover, contributed Greek philosophy and those mystery cults which, although largely if not entirely non-Greek in origin, played so large a part in the Hellenistic world. Through this world ran a contrast between spirit and matter, the one good and immortal, the other evil and perishable. Men, compounded of the two, were struggling to free themselves from the corruption of fleshly matter and to attain the immortal life of the spirit. For many, salvation was by union with the divine and thousands sought this by way of the mystery cults. Then, too, the Hellenistic mind emphasized reason. It felt that the salvation which it sought was to be largely by the way of knowledge.[60] The philosophical habit was strong upon it. As Paul so clearly saw and so succinctly stated, "The Greeks seek after wisdom."[61]

Christians who had been reared in this atmosphere, who came into the Church from it, and who, in their contacts outside the Church, continued to be in touch with it, inescapably had their attitudes in part moulded by it. Their Christianity, therefore, developed certain trends. It was inclined to be interested in an intellectual interpretation of the faith which would be defendable against the systems round them. It was concerned about theology,[62] about definitions and speculation.[63] In some of its more extreme forms it became almost, if not quite, as much a philosophy as a religion.[64] In time it sought to formulate creeds, concrete verbal statements which could be made a test of orthodoxy and a basis of union, and the acceptance of which was regarded as evidence of faith.[65] Creeds, however, were a relatively late development. The Christianity of Hellenistic converts became interested in the problem of how God, who was transcendent and pure spirit, could pass into the sphere of the

[58] McGiffert, A History of Christianity in the Apostolic Age, pp. 114, 115.
[59] Scott, The Gospel and Its Tributaries, pp. 100ff.
[60] Bertrand, L'Evangile de la Grâce, pp. 176-182.
[61] I Cor. i:22.
[62] B. S. Easton in An Outline of Christianity, Vol. I, pp. 297, 298.
[63] Hatch, The Influence of Greek Ideas and Usages upon the Christian Church, pp. 134ff.
[64] Hatch, op. cit., pp. 123-126.
[65] Hatch, op. cit., pp. 310, 334.

phenomenal and come in touch with matter.[66] For it the question of the incarnation and of the relation of Jesus to God became important. It was greatly concerned about immortality. The apocalyptic Kingdom of God tended to fade into the background and to find meaning only as it was associated with immortality.[67] Asceticism naturally developed—the attempt here and now to be freed from the trammels of the body and this present evil world.[68]

With different currents in the Hellenistic world Christianity came in contact in varying degrees. The Epicureans had small effect and were usually dismissed by Christians as unworthy of the name of philosophers.[69] Aristotle and his followers, the Peripatetics, had little prominence in the world of the early Christian centuries. They had a part in shaping the thought of Christians of the first five hundred years.[70] Aristotle did not, however, come to his position of large influence in Christian theology until the Western Europe of the Middle Ages. Yet in the eighth century John of Damascus, the last of the great theologians of the Eastern Church, in some phases of his thinking followed him closely.[71] The Cynics, who in popular harangues proclaimed their views to the multitudes, probably had some effect upon the form and perhaps the content of Christian ethics and upon the Christian book and sermon.[72] The Pythagoreans made themselves felt, as in the world at large at that time, chiefly through Neoplatonism and Stoicism. The philosophic systems which most affected the Christianity of the first five centuries were Stoicism and Platonism, with that development from the latter, Neoplatonism. This was natural. These were the schools most in vogue among the educated of the time and were, therefore, the most prominent of the philosophies which were forming the intellectual, moral, and religious views of the age.

Stoicism affected Christianity through a number of channels. Its ideas were common property, even though often in garbled and attenuated forms. Some modern scholars ascribe to it a substantial part in shaping Christianity,[73] but to

[66] Hatch, *op. cit.*, pp. 134ff., 194-200, 239-282.
[67] Case, *Experience with the Supernatural in Early Christian Times*, pp. 264-299.
[68] B. S. Easton in *An Outline of Christianity*, Vol. I, pp. 297, 298.
[69] Goodenough, *The Theology of Justin Martyr*, pp. 19, 20.
[70] Justin Martyr may have derived some ideas from him.—Goodenough, *op. cit.*, p. 67. The suggestion is made that Arianism had something of Aristoteleanism in it.—Adeney, *op. cit.*, p. 43.
[71] McGiffert, *A History of Christian Thought*, Vol. I, pp. 316, 317.
[72] Troeltsch, *The Social Teaching of the Christian Churches*, p. 110; Stelzenberger, *Die Beziehungen der Frühchristlichen Sittenlehre zur Ethik Stoa*, pp. 466ff.
[73] Case, *The Evolution of Early Christianity*, pp. 278, 279, citing a fairly extensive bibliography; Clemen, *Primitive Christianity and Its Non-Jewish Sources*, pp. 41-77; Steck, *Der Galaterbrief*, pp. 249-265, discussing the possible interdependence of Paul and Seneca; Bultmann, *Der Stil der paulinischen Predigt und die kynisch-stoische Diatribe*, arguing the influence, although not an overwhelming one, of the Cynic-Stoic diatribe upon

venture upon an exact appraisal of its influence is to touch upon debatable ground.[74] How far the idea of the Logos, so prominent in John's Gospel and in the first chapter of Hebrews, was derived ultimately from Stoicism must still largely be conjectural.[75] Some Stoic ideas and even Stoic phraseology have been found in Paul,[76] but it is not at all certain that they came from the famous school of Tarsus with its distinguished Stoic head.[77] More probably Paul obtained them, as he probably did some of the literary forms which he used, from listening in the market-places to popularizing preachers of Stoicism.[78] It has been suggested, indeed, that the paucity of Stoic terms in the New Testament is evidence of a deliberate avoidance by the authors of all words having objectionable associations.[79] It may have been that the Church, with its universal inclusiveness, was aided by the Stoic ideal of the unity of mankind.[80] The Stoic insistence on duty, Providence, moral freedom, the equality of women, children, and slaves, and upon independence of externals is akin to much in Christianity.[81] Some students of Stoic ethics may have believed that in Christianity was the philosophical religion which they sought and among the Christians were those who thought that they found in Stoicism ideas borrowed from the Scriptures.[82] On several prominent Christians the influence of Stoicism is obvious. Thus Clement of Alexandria founded much of his ethics on the Stoic Musonius[83] and in other ways seemed to show the effect of that philosophy.[84] As the head of the important Christian school in that great intellectual centre, he was both familiar with Hellenistic thought and in a position to affect the attitude of the Church. Lactantius was much influenced by the Stoicism of Cicero and Seneca and took over from the Stoic Chrysippus an interpretation of virtue as the successful struggle with evil and therefore as

---

Paul's literary style, and consequently some transfer of thought; Stelzenberger, *Die Beziehungen der frühchristlichen Sittenlehre zur Ethik der Stoa.*

[74] Arnold, *Roman Stoicism*, p. 409.

[75] Clemen, *op. cit.*, pp. 73, 74.

[76] As in I Cor. viii:6. See Porter, *The Mind of Christ in Paul*, pp. 172-176, citing Norden in *Agnostos Theos.* See also Clemen, *op. cit.*, p. 63; Stelzenberger, *op. cit.*, pp. 112-114, 192.

[77] Spencer, *Beyond Damascus*, pp. 10, 11.

[78] Dodd, *The Epistle of Paul to the Romans*, pp. 30, 36. In Romans ii:1-16, Dodd says, Paul followed a literary form used by Stoic preachers. In Romans ii:15, Dodd suggests, Paul speaks like a Stoic.

[79] Nock in *Journal of Biblical Literature*, Vol. LII, pp. 131-139.

[80] D. C. Munro in *An Outline of Christianity*, Vol. II, p. 2.

[81] Angus, *The Religious Quests of the Græco-Roman World*, p. 67; Troeltsch, *op. cit.*, pp. 64-68.

[82] Troeltsch, *op. cit.*, pp. 64-68.

[83] Geffcken, *Der Ausgang des griechisch-römischen Heidentums*, p. 232.

[84] McGiffert, *A History of Christian Thought*, Vol. I, pp. 177-207; Moody, *The Mind of the Early Converts*, p. 256; Stelzenberger, *op. cit.*, pp. 118-121, 226, 283, 323, 419.

dependent upon evil for its existence.[85] Tertullian assumed the Stoic position that the soul is corporeal.[86] Ambrose of Milan, in a book which had much to do with the development of the moral philosophy of Mediæval Europe, boldly endeavoured to combine much of Stoicism with Christianity.[87] Epictetus, re-edited in a Christian form, was widely popular in church circles.[88] Christian monasticism was sometimes presented as the attainment of the Stoic ideal of perfect dominion over the inclinations of nature.[89] It seems to have been from Stoicism that the conception of natural law passed into its prominence in Christian thought.[90]

Yet between Christianity and Stoicism fundamental differences existed. The underlying pantheism which would deny the opposition of God to the world and sin, the looking to the past for a golden age and not to the future for the coming Kingdom of God, and the faith in the upper classes were all in contrast with Christianity.[91] Christians seem to have taken from Stoicism only what they believed to be in accord with the genius of their faith and to have rejected what appeared to them in contradiction with it.

Platonism and Neoplatonism made a particularly marked impression on Christianity. Hellenistic Judaism, and notably Philo, owed much to Plato and the ideas associated with his name—although Philo may have been more Pythagorean than Platonic. While, in accordance with the prevailing syncretism of the times, Platonism was not followed meticulously and contributions from other sources were welcomed and may even have predominated, much of that school had passed into the warp and woof of the Judaism of the Dispersion. Since early Christianity drew so extensively from the constituency of Hellenistic Judaism, something from the Platonic attitude must early have made itself felt. It is often asserted, but is by no means conclusively proved and is vigorously questioned, that the "Logos doctrine" of John's Gospel was descended ultimately from Plato.[92] Philo seems to have been largely used by some of the Christian Fathers, and through him whatever of Plato had shaped his thought tended to pass on into Christianity.[93] Justin Martyr, who apparently had made a fairly extensive philosophic pilgrimage before finding satisfaction

[85] McGiffert, op. cit., Vol. II, p. 49; Stelzenberger, op. cit., pp. 125-128.
[86] McGiffert, op. cit., Vol. II, pp. 8-10.
[87] Hatch, The Influence of Greek Ideas and Usages upon the Christian Church, p. 168; Stelzenberger, op. cit., p. 129; Dudden, The Life and Times of St. Ambrose, Vol. II. pp. 502ff.
[88] Matheson's edition of Epictetus, Discourses and Manual, Vol. I, p. 16.
[89] Workman, The Evolution of the Monastic Ideal, p. 37.
[90] Troeltsch, The Social Teaching of the Christian Churches, p. 144.
[91] Troeltsch, op. cit., pp. 64-68.
[92] Burkitt, Church and Gnosis, p. 93.
[93] Kennedy, Philo's Contribution to Religion, pp. 1-3.

in Christianity, wove into his theology much from Platonic sources—although also drawing some from Aristoteleanism.[94] The Alexandrian school which, led by Clement and Origen, did so much to acclimatize Hellenistic philosophy in Christian circles, brought in Platonic as well as other contributions from the syncretistic atmosphere of its native city.[95] Augustine passed from Neoplatonism into his vivid Christian conversion. He continued to feel sympathy with many of the teachings of that school and held that it was nearer to Christianity than were any of the other philosophies.[96] The Neoplatonic elements in the Bishop of Hippo can easily be exaggerated, for it was not they but his experience in his final faith which brought him into prominence,[97] but he could not, even if he had so desired, quite have erased the impression made on him by his former associations. His developed theology was largely a combination of Neoplatonism with traditional Christian views.[98]

Platonism has continued in Christian thought. Through Augustine something of it must have entered the minds of those who held his writings in reverence. It has, although probably with some exaggeration, been called the intellectual side of Christianity.[99] From time to time Platonism has had revivals in Christian mysticism and theology—as in Eckhart and other German mystics of the late middle ages, in the Cambridge Platonists of the second half of the seventeenth century,[100] and in the nineteenth and twentieth centuries in Inge. It has, indeed, been dubbed the father of European mysticism.[101]

Yet again, Christianity has not become just a continuation of Platonism and Neoplatonism. Its own peculiar genius welded their contributions, along with others, into a new and living whole, in which the story of Jesus and the type of experiences which arose from contact with him were the unifying elements. Platonism, with other philosophies, was made ancillary.

For a time in the second century some observers might have thought that the Christian movement was in danger of being dissolved into schools led by teachers, in the guise and according to the organization of the philosophies of the time. Occasionally at least, popular Christianity was deliberately given the

[94] Goodenough, The Theology of Justin Martyr, p. 67.

[95] See, as a summary of the large literature on Clement and Origen, McGiffert, op. cit., Vol. I, pp. 177-231. See also Moore, Ancient Beliefs in the Immortality of the Soul, pp. 83-92.

[96] Augustine, Confessions, Book VIII, Chap. 2; Augustine, De Civ. Dei, Book VIII, Chap. 5.

[97] Geffcken, op. cit., p. 232.

[98] McGiffert, op. cit., Vol. II, pp. 83, 84.

[99] Muirhead, The Platonic Tradition in Anglo-Saxon Philosophy, p. 26.

[100] Muirhead, op. cit., pp. 27-71; Inge, Christian Mysticism, p. 78; Inge, The Platonic Tradition in English Religious Thought.

[101] Inge, Christian Mysticism, p. 78.

form of a philosophic school, probably to protect it from a suspicious state and to commend it to a hostile community. We hear of a number of local schools led by prominent Christians who, presumably, there taught their faith as a kind of philosophy. By the beginning of the third century, however, the peculiar organization which the Church developed around the episcopate had largely obviated that danger. When not divided theologically, the Christians in any given city constituted a single community headed by a bishop.[102] In organization, as in life and thought, Christianity was more than a philosophy.

The part which the mystery cults had in shaping Christianity, like the effect of so many other phases of the environment upon Christianity, has been warmly debated.[103] It is clear that the mystery religions, although a number of them were not of Greek origin and entered the Hellenistic world late, were prominent in the culture which was being moulded by a popularized Greek thought. They fitted in with that climate of opinion which looked upon matter as evil and spirit as good, for they professed to provide a way by which initiates, by union with a saviour-god who had suffered but had later attained victory, could escape the blight of the flesh and achieve immortality.

Superficially, the story of the death and resurrection of Jesus bears striking similarities to the myths round which the mysteries centred. Accommodation to that type of religion, therefore, would presumably be easy, especially since the latter was strong in those very circles from which Christianity won so large a proportion of its adherents and since the syncretistic temper of the age would make the process easy and natural.

The accommodation might come about by deliberate copying. Of that little or no clear evidence exists. Such information as we possess seems against the theory. The Christian apologists, as we have suggested, do not have as much to say of the mystery religions as of the state cult and the traditional deities of the Greek and Roman pantheons. If anything, they held them in contempt. Probably little or no conscious borrowing took place from cults looked upon by Christians in this fashion. The repugnance to competing paganism was probably too strong to permit of that.[104]

[102] Harnack, *The Constitution and Law of the Church in the First Two Centuries,* pp. 106-109.

[103] In addition to the references given below, the literature includes Gustav Anrich, *Das antike Mysterienwesen in seinem Einfluss auf das Christentum;* Reitzenstein, *Die hellenistischen Mysterienreligionen;* A. Jacoby, *Die antiken Mysterienreligionen und das Christentum;* Bousset, *Kyrios Christos;* Clemen, *Der Einfluss der Mysterienreligionen auf das älteste Christentum,* arguing that the mystery religions had little effect on early Christianity, first had a deep influence on Christianity in its Gnostic forms, and left some marks on Catholic Christianity; A. Loisy, *Les Mystères Païens et le Mystère Chrétien;* Grill, *Untersuchungen über die Entstehung des vierten Evangeliums,* Part II.

[104] Allen, *Christian Institutions,* pp. 441, 442.

More likely is the possibility of the unconscious reshaping of Christianity in partial likeness to the mysteries. Phrases and ideas derived from the mystery cults were, presumably, a constituent part of the language and thought of the world into which Christianity moved and might well influence that faith, especially since the latter contained features which, at least superficially, appeared akin to them. This process might readily be accentuated by the presence in the Christian communities of converts who had been initiated into the mysteries. Half-consciously they would interpret their new faith in terms of the old and tend to adjust its ceremonies and teachings to accord with what they had known before their Christian days.

Statements that this influence was present, and in powerful form, are numerous. Thus it is said that the Gentile convert saw in Jesus a Lord like the lords of the cults, and in baptism and the eucharist, with liturgies depicting a drama, perceived "mysteries" offering a new birth and eternal life to those who partook of them.[105] It is suggested that Jesus, dead and risen, must have reminded the Gentiles who came into the Church of divine lords whom they had known—Attis, Adonis, Serapis, and the like—and that many Gentile Christians tended to make Christ their god and were only slowly educated up to monotheism.[106] Christians to whom the identification of Jesus with the Messiah corresponded to nothing in their background would equate him, so it is suggested, with the dying and risen saviours whom they knew.[107] It is hinted that the antinomian movement in the churches which tended to take the Pauline doctrine of freedom as an excuse for license came from the mysteries with their amoral characteristics.[108] The hypothesis is also ventured that the practice of baptism for the dead which was found at Corinth[109] strayed in from the mysteries and that at Colossæ[110] were ascetic practices associated with mystery terminology.[111] We have the quite natural, even if debatable assumption that the eucharist was much influenced by the mysteries.[112] It is also suggested that, since mystery fraternities were scattered over the Græco-Roman world, they very probably furnished, along with the synagogue, models for the organization of early Christian communities, especially of the house-churches.[113] The theory

[105] Lake, *The Earlier Epistles of St. Paul*, pp. 44-46; Holl, *Urchristentum und Religions-geschichte*, pp. 7-10.
[106] McGiffert, *The God of the Early Christians*, pp. 41, 42.
[107] McGiffert, *A History of Christian Thought*, Vol. I, pp. 18, 19.
[108] Lake, *op. cit.*, pp. 44-46.
[109] B. S. Easton in *An Outline of Christianity*, Vol. I, p. 220.
[110] Col. ii:18-23.
[111] B. S. Easton in *op. cit.*, Vol. I, p. 220.
[112] Goodenough, *The Church in the Roman Empire*, pp. 95-99.
[113] Angus, *The Religious Quests of the Græco-Roman World*, p. 80.

is advanced that the influence of the mysteries made Christian associations more secret and modified baptism.[114] The imprint of the mysteries is said to have been stronger on Gnostic than on Catholic Christianity. However, Catholicism is declared to owe to the mystery cults its ideas of secrecy, symbolism, mystical brotherhood, sacramental grace, and the three stages of the spiritual life.[115] A notable opponent of Christianity seemed to class it with "other mysteries" and Origen, in replying, did not deny that his faith was of that type of religion, but spoke of "initiation into the mysteries of Jesus."[116] The conversion of Constantine is said to have aided the transition of Christianity into a mystery equipped with the requisite sacramental apparatus.[117]

Some hold that Paul aided the transformation of Christianity into a mystery cult.[118] It is suggested that the vision of Jesus to which Paul owed his conversion was of a divine being who had come down from heaven and assumed human flesh and then laid it by again that men, identifying themselves with him in his death and resurrection, might die to the flesh and live a new life in the spirit. This interpretation, so it is said, was original with Paul.[119] It is also said that Paul frequently employed terms which had received a more or less technical meaning in connexion with the mysteries.[120]

The hypothesis is put forward that the basic purpose of the famous miracle at Cana in which water was turned into wine was Dionysiac, derived from the popularity of the cult of Dionysus in Syria.[121] The statement "except ye eat the flesh of the Son of Man and drink his blood ye have no life in you"[122] is thought possibly to indicate Mazdean and Mandæan influence.[123] The coincidence of the Christian Sunday with the resurrection day of ancient Oriental belief is regarded as so striking as to indicate some borrowing.[124] The ideas of hell and the devil are conjectured to have a Persian source and to have entered Christianity partly through pre-Christian Mazdean influence on Judaism and partly through Mithraism.[125] Mithraism is reported to have helped to give precise form to Christian ideas concerning the powers of hell

---

[114] Hatch, *The Influence of Greek Ideas and Usages upon the Christian Church*, pp. 294-307.

[115] Inge, *Christian Mysticism*, p. 354.

[116] *Origen against Celsus*, Book III, Chaps. 59, 60.

[117] Angus, *op. cit.*, p. 152.

[118] Kennedy, *St. Paul and the Mystery Religions*, p. 2.

[119] McGiffert, *A History of Christian Thought*, Vol. I, pp. 20-28.

[120] Kennedy, *op. cit.*, p. 117.

[121] Bacon, *The Gospel of the Hellenists*, pp. 162, 163.

[122] John vi:53.

[123] Clemen, *Primitive Christianity and Its Non-Jewish Sources*, pp. 262-266.

[124] Clemen, *op. cit.*, p. 189.

[125] Cumont, *Oriental Religions in Roman Paganism*, p. 154.

and the end of the world.[126] From the doctrines and the ritual of that same faith are said to have come contributions to the teaching and language of some of the early Christian apologists.[127] The idea that the body is a prison in which we are pent is declared to be derived from the Orphic cults,[128] and in the realm of eschatology Christian writers are reported to offer ideas which may have had their origin in the Orphic books.[129] The Christian emphasis upon the Virgin Mary as the "Mother of God" is alleged to owe much to the *Magna Mater* so familiar in some of the mysteries.[130] The Madonna of Southern Italy, so it is asserted, is probably Isis renamed,[131] and some have seen an identity between the cult of Isis and Horus and the honour paid to the Virgin and Child.[132]

The most convinced and enthusiastic adherents of this power of the mysteries hold that Christianity was transformed into a mystery cult, carrying over, no doubt, distinctive elements from its Jewish past and with some features peculiar to itself, but in its emphasis and in many of its symbols and ceremonies conformed to the popular cults which thus constituted the major factor in shaping its growth.[133]

Against this extreme view a number of considerations have been urged. Paul, it is said, did indeed compare the Christian God and the Christian Lord with rival claimants for the allegiance of men, but as totally different, and presented Christian worship as the uniquely valid and wholly other way of serving God.[134] The assertion is made that the mysteries belong to an atmosphere entirely alien to that in which Paul moved, that nothing in them corresponded to Paul's concept of the cross of Christ, and that in contrast with the mysteries the essential feature of Paul's religious attitude was his detachment from ceremonial.[135] As to the derivation from the mysteries of the title Lord as applied to Jesus, it is suggested that the expression *Marana tha*, "Our Lord, come!"[136] was probably from the ritual of the primitive Aramaic-speaking Christian communities, that it had a Semitic origin, and that to Paul with

---

[126] Cumont, *The Mysteries of Mithra*, p. vi.

[127] Geden, *Select Passages Illustrating Mithraism*, p. 4.

[128] Baillie, *And the Life Everlasting*, p. 21.

[129] Guthrie, *Orpheus and Greek Religion*, pp. 266-271.

[130] Farnell, *Cults of the Greek States*, Vol. III, p. 304; Angus, *The Religious Quests of the Græco-Roman World*, p. 86.

[131] Glover, *Conflict of Religions in the Early Roman Empire*, p. 23.

[132] Budge, *Legends of Our Lady Mary the Perpetual Virgin and Her Mother Hannâ*, p. lix. Budge believes great differences to exist, however, between the two cults.

[133] See a summary in McGiffert, *A History of Christian Thought*, Vol. I, pp. 328-330.

[134] Nock, *The Vocabulary of the New Testament*, in *Journal of Biblical Literature*, Vol. LII, pp. 131-139.

[135] Kennedy, *St. Paul and the Mystery Religions*, pp. 280-299.

[136] I Cor. xvi:22.

Hebrew usage in view it meant that God had conferred on Jesus his own name as the covenant God of Israel.[137] The conception in the mysteries of a new birth, it is said, differs markedly from Paul's teaching of a new creation.[138] Paul, too, while bringing into relation with his mysticism the sacraments which he found in the early Christian community, took a very different attitude toward them than did the mysteries, so it is pointed out.[139] Paul never mentions his own baptism, and while he speaks of the Lord's Supper he never calls it "eating the flesh and drinking the blood" of Christ as does John's Gospel.[140] It must be noted, moreover, that Paul's conception of the characteristic Christian experience as a moral empowerment, with ethical fruits in character,[141] seems in contrast with those of the mysteries who had little to say of morals. Moreover, the mysteries do not seem to have pointed beyond their saviours to God[142]—not, at least, quite as did Christianity. Then, too, Christians thought of the crucifixion of Jesus as a voluntary self-sacrifice, not like the deaths of the saviour-gods of the mysteries, and the Christian drama of salvation from the sin of Adam differed markedly from that of the mysteries.[143] Nor does any parallel seem to exist in Hellenistic non-Christian theology to belief in a divine being who for the love of men took on him the form of a servant and submitted to the humiliation of the cross.[144] Baptism, too, was probably of Jewish origin, and the eucharist showed Jewish roots and is traced back to its institution by the words and example of Jesus himself.[145] The early Christian designation of "the breaking of bread" has been said to have no exact counterpart in the mysteries.[146] It is only fair to add that this statement has been challenged. However, when in the fourth century the eucharist acquired added dignity of ceremonial, no deliberate copying from the mystery dramas has been proved.[147] Moreover, it has been pointed out that in such Christian writings of the close of the first and of the second century as the

[137] Dodd, *The Epistle of Paul to the Romans*, pp. 167, 168. Burkitt, *Christian Beginnings*, pp. 49-52, thinks, too, that the application of the title Lord to Jesus by the first disciples had no connexion with the mystery cults. See also Case, *The Evolution of Early Christianity*, pp. 107-122.

[138] Reitzenstein, *Die hellenistischen Mysterienreligionen*, p. 423, declares that Paul's religion was new and his own. See also Burkitt, *op. cit.*, p. 108.

[139] Schweitzer, *The Mysticism of Paul the Apostle*, p. 20.

[140] Glover, *Paul of Tarsus*, pp. 162, 163.

[141] Kennedy, *St. Paul and the Mystery Religions*, p. 199. Among pertinent Pauline passages are Rom. vii:7-25; Gal. v:22-24; Eph. ii:1-10, iv:1-3, v:1-5; Col. iii:1-15.

[142] As in Eph. ii:10, 16, iii:14-19; Col. i:10, 11.

[143] Guthrie, *Orpheus and Greek Religion*, pp. 266-271.

[144] Edwyn Bevan, *Hellenism and Christianity*, p. 108; Halliday, *The Pagan Background of Christianity*, p. 135.

[145] Raven, *Jesus and the Gospel of Love*, pp. 259, 262.

[146] Holl, *Urchristentum und Religionsgeschichte*, p. 12.

[147] Nock, *Conversion*, p. 204.

epistles of Clement, the *Shepherd of Hermas*, the *Didache* and the Epistle of Barnabas, the picture obtained of the faith is not of a mystery religion, but of a moral system based on divine sanctions, a divine law from obedience to which comes eternal life and from disobedience eternal torment.[148] Through the centuries Christian teachers insisted that he who had entered the new life had become a new man morally and that union with God meant oneness with his moral nature. They also assumed that the new life included a communion of believers with one another. Both of these ideas appear to have been alien to the mysteries. For most of the latter salvation was non-moral and purely individualistic.[149] Except possibly Mithraism and a few others, they seem not to have been so highly ethical as Christianity and none developed so closely knit and widely spread a community.

The conclusion of the matter must be that our information is insufficient to afford conclusive proof or disproof either of conscious or of unconscious specific borrowing from the mystery religions. It is possible that Christianity, especially in some of its branches, was affected by the atmosphere generated by these cults. Basically, however, it seems clear that the main stream of Christianity retained features quite unlike anything in these particular rivals. In their Jewish heritage, in the teachings and character of Jesus, in certain outstanding features of the beliefs concerning the death and resurrection of Jesus and of the Christian experience, and in the origin of the two chief sacraments, those churches in which the majority of Christians were comprised differed profoundly from the mysteries with which the ancient world was familiar. Faith and love, as seen in the words and deeds of Jesus, making for moral and spiritual renewal, and as echoed in other writings in the New Testament, including those of Paul, and, following in their train, in later Christian authors, created an atmosphere of another colour than anything of which we have evidence in the mysteries.

The religious and thought world into which Christianity of the first five centuries was forced to make its way contained not only Judaism, Greek philosophy, and the mysteries, but views of the universe, many a cult, and still more numerous gods, beliefs, and practices not embraced in these three. They also are said to have made contributions to the varied movements embraced in Christianity. Here, too, we have many conjectures drawn from suggestive but usually tantalizingly inadequate evidence. Only a few fairly typical ones can here be selected and put down in somewhat random fashion.

[148] McGiffert, *A History of Christian Thought*, Vol. I, pp. 67-98.
[149] Scott, *The Kingdom of God in the New Testament*, pp. 158-167.

We have the quite understandable theory that the orientation of church buildings toward the rising sun stems from a pagan root.[150] *The Apocalypse of Peter,* of which fragments are preserved in a papyrus, is said to show the influence of the Egyptian *Book of the Dead.*[151] The account of the descent of Jesus into Hades, mentioned briefly in the New Testament[152] and developed much more fully in later centuries, has aroused the curiosity of scholars. Its origin is debated. The victorious descent of the saviour-god into the underworld appeared both in Babylonian and in Egyptian religion, and Greek heroes were pictured as having visited Hades in their lifetimes. A Babylonian background influenced by Iran is a favoured source. However, it has been pointed out that in its inception the story might have been purely Christian, an understandable attempt to provide the deceased ancestors of Christians with an opportunity to hear the Gospel. Yet later accretions from foreign myths and folklore are held possible.[153] It is suggested that the seven archangels, the twenty-four elders, the four living creatures, and the horsemen of the Apocalypse were ultimately derived from Babylonia.[154] Both Babylonian and Persian contributions may have come into Christianity through Judaism. From Persia through this channel may have been derived the belief in the devil and some eschatological ideas.[155] We also have the thesis learnedly argued that the Christian belief in the Antichrist came ultimately from the ancient dragon myth, although by way of Judaism.[156] The use of holy water, it is hinted, may have been transferred, the abbreviated and symbolic substitute for the purificatory bath found in pagan temples.[157] The Christian priesthood, while admittedly a development within the Church from indigenous beginnings, was, in some of its features, so it is held, the result of both heathen and Jewish precedent.[158]

The pagan custom of raising men to the rank of gods or demigods against which Christian apologists so vigorously protested crept into the Church in the honours paid to the apostles, martyrs, and angels.[159] The Christian Theodoret openly rejoiced that the martyrs had been substituted for the pagan gods and

---

[150] Loeschke, *Jüdisches und heidnisches im christlichen Kult,* pp. 16-18.

[151] Boulanger, *Orphée,* pp. 127-134.

[152] I Peter iii:18-20.

[153] See a review by C. H. Kraeling of J. Kroll, *Gott und Hölle* in *Journal of the American Oriental Society* (Sept., 1933), Vol. LIII, pp. 290-292. See also Clemen, *Primitive Christianity and Its Non-Jewish Sources,* pp. 198-200.

[154] Clemen, *op. cit.,* pp. 366-373.

[155] Clemen, *op. cit.,* pp. 23-39, 117-167, 372.

[156] This thesis is presented in Bousset, *The Antichrist Legend,* especially p. 144.

[157] Goodenough, *The Church in the Roman Empire,* pp. 95-99.

[158] Harnack, *The Constitution and Law of the Church in the First Two Centuries,* p. 118.

[159] Harnack, *The Mission and Expansion of Christianity,* Vol. I, pp. 297-299; Loeschke, *op. cit.,* p. 28; McGiffert, *A History of Christian Thought,* Vol. II, p. 62.

given their glory.[160] Sometimes, as did Gregory Thaumaturgos, officials of the Church encouraged the practice.[161] Often pagan divinities and heroes, more or less thinly transformed or disguised, persisted under Christian names or were displaced by Christian substitutes. When, as often happened, a pagan site or temple was appropriated for Christian purposes, something of its previous associations might remain. Thus in Cappadocia in a community of horse-raisers a cult of the Greek *Dioscuri*, said probably to have been associated with an old god of the place, became a triad of Christian saints.[162] We have evidence which is declared to point to other instances of the continuation of the divine twins in Christian guise.[163] The cult of the Virgin Diana may have contributed to the worship of the Virgin Mary and more than a coincidence may possibly be seen in the facts that one of the earliest churches in honour of Mary rose at Ephesus on the site of the famous temple of Diana, and that in the same city in 431 a synod was held which first officially designated Mary the Mother of God.[164] In some places in Italy the ancient Lares are said to have been replaced by the Virgin, or the saints, or figures of the child Jesus.[165] Presumably under such circumstances something of the functions assigned to the old were transferred to their successors. In Sicily the Virgin is said to have taken possession of all the sanctuaries of Ceres and Venus, and the pagan rites associated with them are reported to have been perpetuated in part in honour of the Mother of Christ.[166] At Naples lamps burning before the image of the Virgin are said to have replaced those before the family gods.[167] At Naples, too, the popular cult of the Madonna is conjectured to have proceeded from that of Vesta and Ceres.[168] In Asia Minor sites held sacred long before the advent of Christianity continued to be regarded as such when the population became Christian, and then, centuries later, when the region became Moslem, still preserved their aura of sanctity. Once associated with a pagan god and then with a Christian saint, they were eventually held dedicated to Moslem or Turkish personages. Some pre-Christian practices are also held to have come down through Christian into

[160] Theodoret, *Græc. Affectionum Curatio*, Sermo viii, 923, in Migne, *Pat. Gr.*, Vol. LXXXIII, Col. 1033.

[161] Harnack, *op. cit.*, Vol. II, pp. 203-210.

[162] Harnack, *op. cit.*, Vol. II, p. 195, citing H. Gregoire, *Saints Jumeaux et Dieux Cavaliers* (Paris, 1905).

[163] J. R. Harris, *The Dioscuri in the Christian Legends;* Geffcken, *Der Ausgang des griechisch-römischen Heidentums*, p. 235.

[164] Laing, *Survivals of Roman Religion*, pp. 92-96.

[165] Laing, *op. cit.*, pp. 19-24. For what seems to have been the substitution of martyrs labelled saints and victors for pagan cults of victor gods see Rütten, *Die Victorverehrung im christlichen Altertum*, pp. 50-87.

[166] Maury, *La Magie*, p. 153.

[167] Maury, *op. cit.*, p. 152.

[168] Maury, *op. cit.*, p. 151.

Moslem times.[169] It may be significant that in Phrygia in many cases a Christian bishopric succeeded to the priesthood of an old *hieron*.[170] In Asia Minor, too, the ancient sacrificial meal is said to have lived on in honour of the martyrs.[171] At Siena the Temple of Quirinus became the Church of St. Quirino and thus a pagan god was given Christian canonization.[172] The transfer of Aphrodite Pelagia into St. Pelagia seems to be proved.[173] It is natural to assume an historic connexion between pagan ceremonies on the one hand and on the other the offering of lamps and flowers to the saints, the placing of food before the dead, the feasts in memory of the martyrs, and visits paid to them deep in the night.[174] In pagan times popular belief spoke of the protection of an individual by a *genius*. In Christian times this function was readily transferred to saints and angels.[175] How far the pagan use of relics passed over into the well-known Christian custom is not clear. Marked differences separated the two. The pagan relics, for instance, were not divided as were the Christian, and no spiritual power was supposed to go out from them.[176] Nor is it at all certain that the Christian pilgrimages to the shrines of martyrs and as a means of penance sprang directly from pagan precedents. Apparently some connexion existed between the pagan division of dæmons into good and bad and the distinction drawn by Christians between the host of Christ and of his angels on the one hand and the hosts of evil on the other. Christians easily identified the old gods with evil spirits.[177] A direct transfer from the pagan use of idols to the Christian utilization of images is very doubtful, but it is impossible not to view the latter as arising in part from the same sense of need which presumably was one of the sources of strength of the former. Certainly much the same arguments to defend the custom seem to have been employed by the Christians as were advanced by the pagans.[178]

It would be difficult to demonstrate an indubitable connexion between the emphasis by Christians upon prophecy as a proof of the validity of their faith and the strong desire of the day for oracles, secret passwords, and inspired

[169] Ramsay, *The Cities and Bishoprics of Phrygia*, Vol. I, p. 29.

[170] Ramsay, *op. cit.*, Vol. I, p. 29.

[171] Schultze, *Geschichte des Untergangs des griechisch-römischen Heidentums*, Vol. II, p. 317.

[172] Robinson, *The Conversion of Europe*, p. 216.

[173] Geffcken, *op. cit.*, p. 235, citing Usener, *Legenden der Pelagia* in *Festschrift für die XXXIV Versammlung deutscher Philologen und Schulmänner zu Trier, 1879.*

[174] Geffcken, *op. cit.*, p. 234.

[175] Schultze, *op. cit.*, Vol. II, pp. 364-366.

[176] Geffcken, *op. cit.*, p. 235.

[177] Tatian, *Ad. Gr.*, Chap. 8; Clement of Alexandria, *Ad. Gent.*, Chap. 3; Minucius Felix, Chap. 27.

[178] Angus, *Religious Quests of the Græco-Roman World*, p. 345.

books. That more than a similarity exists seems, however, probable.[179] It is interesting, too, to find a Christian substitution for the oracle in the incident in which the Emperor Theodosius, before his campaign against Arbogastes and Eugenius, sent to Egypt to ask the Christian hermit John of Lycopolis the outcome of the expedition and was reassured by a prediction of victory.[180]

It was almost to be expected that processes utilized by pagans for obtaining divine aid in the treatment of disease should be duplicated by Christians.[181] The presence of miracles in the accounts of the life of Jesus seemed to give such efforts sound standing. So Origen declared that the repetition of the name of Jesus, especially if done in faith, would drive out demons, and gave instances in which the use of the name even by evil men had been followed by that desirable result.[182] He also declared that Christians expelled evil spirits and performed many cures according to the will of the Logos.[183] The church historian Sozomen relates that Aquiline, an advocate, a convert from paganism, had told him of his recovery from a disease which had baffled the physicians. Aquiline ordered his servant to carry him to a house of prayer, and while lying there at night a divine direction came to him to adopt a therapy which went contrary to the rules of the physicians. He obeyed and was cured.[184] It is not difficult to see a transfer here from the pagan custom of incubation in shrines for the sake of healing. It was probably to prevent this practice, regarded as superstitious, that the Canons of Hippolytus, perhaps dating from the end of the second or the beginning of the third century, forbade the sick to sleep in the churches or even to remain there beyond the hours of prayer.[185]

What probably must be regarded as magic, or at least as closely akin to it, could be seen in Christian circles. The attitudes which created it presumably had persisted from pre-Christian times. Thus the worship paid the Labarum by the soldiery of Constantine[186] was in all likelihood a continuation of that accorded the pagan standards. The use of Christian names came late, and was not general until sometime in the fourth century. It has been suggested that, arriving as it did in the age when multitudes were flooding into the Church and bringing superstitions with them, the growth of the custom was due, not to the end of the fear that the adoption of Christian names would

---

[179] Case, *Experience with the Supernatural in Early Christian Times*, pp. 68-105; Goodenough, *The Theology of Justin Martyr*, p. 73.

[180] Sozomen, *Eccles. Hist.*, Book VII, Chap. 22.

[181] On the miraculous in the early centuries of Christianity, see Th. Trede, *Wunderglaube im Heidentum und in der alten Kirche*.

[182] Origen, *Contra Cels.*, Book I, Chap. 6. On the use of the name of Jesus to work cures, see Conybeare, *Myth, Magic, and Morals*, pp. 239-244.

[183] Origen, *Contra Cels.*, Book I, Chap. 46.

[184] Sozomen, *Eccles. Hist.*, Book II, Chap. 3.

[185] Lindsay, *The Church and the Ministry in the Early Centuries*, p. 258.

[186] Sozomen, *Eccles. Hist.*, Book I, Chap. 4.

draw unnecessary attention to one's faith, as has been conjectured, but to a belief that by taking the name of a saint the miraculous power which dwelt in the very word itself would serve as a protection against danger. That seems to have been a reason back of the pagan custom of naming children Dionysius or Serapion, and it may be that the same intention carried over.[187] So, too, the pagan employment of amulets was replaced by the Christian use of relics,[188] of portions of the Gospels, crosses, medals, and the like.[189] Chrysostom preached against the inroads of such practices in Christian circles, including the hanging of Gospels round the necks of children.[190] In Egypt, in which sacred charms had long been popular, the use of spells carried over into Christian times.[191] Charms under a Christian blessing were employed in the treatment of disease and over a magic drink the name of the Trinity was invoked.[192] A papyrus of the eighth century, presumably by Christians, dealing with matters of magic, has in it a piece of ancient Egyptian mythology.[193] Long after the nominal conversion of the land, what seems to have been a succinct recension of the essential elements of the ancient *Book of the Dead* was attributed to Christ and the Virgin Mary and employed by Abyssinian Christians to render men holy on earth, to preserve their bodies after death, and to ensure their souls life beyond the grave and entrance into heaven.[194] We have already noticed that in Gaul Christians employed the sign of the cross to protect their cattle against a plague—with what were reported to be excellent results.[195] In another region racehorses were sprinkled with water from the horn of St. Hilarion.[196]

Belief in miracles was a normal and persistent feature of Christianity. How far, if at all, this was due to pagan example, how much it must be attributed to the atmosphere of the times, and to what extent it was a purely spontaneous development from the original Christian tradition must be a matter of con-

---

[187] Harnack, *The Mission and Expansion of Christianity*, Vol. I, pp. 422-430.

[188] Lea, *A History of Auricular Confession and Indulgences in the Latin Church*, Vol. II, p. 126.

[189] Schultze, *Geschichte des Untergangs des griechisch-römischen Heidentums*, Vol. I, p. 309.

[190] Hartung in *Allgemeine Missionszeitschrift*, Vol. XXI, p. 323, giving pertinent passages from Chrysostom's sermons.

[191] Harnack, *op. cit.*, Vol. II, pp. 176, 177.

[192] Erman, *Ein koptischer Zauberer*, in *Zeitschrift für ägyptische Sprache und Alterthumskunde*, Vol. XXXIII, pp. 43-46.

[193] Erman, *op. cit.*, pp. 47-51.

[194] Review by H. S. Gehman of Budge, *The Bandlet of Righteousness—an Ethiopian Book of the Dead* (London, 1929) in *Journal of the American Oriental Society*, Vol. LIII, pp. 293-295.

[195] Severus Sanctus Endelechius, *De Mortibus Boum*, in Lemaire, *Poet. Lat. Minor.*, Vol. I, pp. 577ff.

[196] Loeschke, *Jüdisches und heidnisches im Christlichen Kult*, pp. 28-30, citing Hieron, *Vita Hil.*, 20.

jecture. Probably the latter two factors were the most important. Certainly lives of the saints abound in stories of the miraculous. This is true not only of those composed in later centuries, when time had given opportunity for accretion, but in those written by contemporaries and intimate friends. This brief paragraph is by no means proportionate to the place which the miraculous came to occupy in the life of the Church and in the belief of Christians. A fairly wide reading of the surviving documents of the Christianity of the first five hundred years leaves the impression that in the fourth and fifth centuries the emphasis on miracles increased. This may be an erroneous conclusion. If correct, it may indicate that the flooding of the Church with many poorly prepared in its traditions and in whom pre-Christian attitudes persisted had something to do with the change. It may also possibly be traced to an alteration in the general intellectual climate with a decline in the critical spirit and a growing willingness to give credence to the marvellous. The examples are so numerous as to make selection of any kind run the risk of not giving a balanced picture. However, two instances among many may be chosen at random. Of a bishop in Cyprus of the fourth century, a man of peasant stock, it is said that robbers who came to steal his sheep were miraculously held by invisible bonds until the good man, arriving in the morning, reproved them, gave them a ram, and released them. Of the same bishop it is told that by calling on the spirit of a dead person who had concealed it, he learned the location of a hidden treasure and returned the lost property to the owner.[197] The ethics here seem to be of Christian provenance, but the type of miracle is by no means characteristic of the New Testament and is akin to what one finds in other traditions. It may indicate alien influence.

In the art developed by Christians for religious purposes, many previous traditions were made to yield tribute. Thus the phœnix, whose story had been told by Herodotus and Pliny, was employed as a symbol of the resurrection.[198] The familiar figure of Orpheus was utilized to portray the Good Shepherd.[199] Only gradually, possibly from the desire of Christian leaders to be rid of such suggestive traces of paganism, were the elements of Orpheus eliminated from the representation of Christ.[200] The figure of Jesus, too, is said to have been modelled on that of Apollo,[201] and less certainly on that of Aesculapius.[202]

[197] Sozomen, *Eccles. Hist.*, Book I, Chap. 11.
[198] As in I Clement, 25.
[199] Guthrie, *Orpheus and Greek Religion*, p. 264.
[200] Boulanger, *Orphée*, pp. 149-163.
[201] Adeney, *The Greek and Eastern Churches*, p. 185.
[202] Harnack, *The Mission and Expansion of Christianity*, Vol. I, pp. 101-124, deals with the problem of the influence of the cult of Aesculapius upon the Christian Church.

Mithraic sculptures are asserted to have provided Christian marble-cutters with models which they adopted or adapted.[203] The suggestion is also offered that the Christian picture of a mounted saint fighting evil had a Mazdean origin.[204] The cherubs and other winged figures seen in the paintings discovered at Pompeii and Herculaneum suggest a non-Christian source of figures well known in Christian portrayals. The existence of a connexion between pagan and Christian iconography in Egypt has been held unproved,[205] but the earliest Christians in Egypt seem freely to have employed pagan designs and to have made sparing use of Christian symbolism.[206] The conjecture is offered that figures of Isis and Horus suggested the form for pictures of the Virgin.[207] The hypothesis is developed that in the second half of the fifth century Egyptian Christians, in a reaction against the Byzantine type of the faith, turned to symbols used by their pagan forefathers and so gave to their art a new bent, but this has been questioned.[208] In building their churches, moreover, it is said that the Egyptian Christians showed no interest in imitating the temples of their pagan antiquity, but made a clean break.[209]

The influence of the non-Christian basilica upon the construction of churches is well known. One theory, however, declares that the Christian basilica stems not from the Roman house or the temples of Greece and Rome, but from the sanctuaries of Oriental cults.[210] It is also suggested that Christian basilicas followed the models of Jewish synagogues—perhaps even in an orientation towards Jerusalem. Probably at the outset Christian architecture took many forms and in part adopted the tradition of the various lands in which it developed. Perhaps, too, these local types were transmitted to other areas and tended to coalesce.[211] Thus the hypothesis has been advanced that in Armenia in the fourth century was first introduced for ecclesiastical purposes the square building with a single dome and axial and diagonal niche-buttresses,[212] that the barrel vault came from Mesopotamia,[213] that the Church in the Sassanian

---

[203] Cumont, *The Mysteries of Mithra*, pp. 195, 196.
[204] Strzygowski, *Origin of Church Art*, pp. 174, 175.
[205] Scott-Moncrieff, *Paganism and Christianity in Egypt*, pp. 133-147.
[206] Scott-Moncrieff, *op. cit.*, pp. 101-132.
[207] Budge, *Legends of Our Lady Mary*, p. xli.
[208] Carl Schmidt, *Über eine angebliche altkoptische Madonna-Darstellung*, in *Zeitschrift für ägyptische Sprache und Alterthumskunde* (1895), Vol. XXXIII, pp. 58-62, citing, in disagreement, Gayet in *Les Monuments Coptes du Musée de Boulaq* (*Mém. de la Mission arch. française au Caire*, III, 3) and *La Sculpture Copte* in *Gazette des Beaux Arts*, May, July, August, 1892.
[209] Clarke, *Christian Antiquities in the Nile Valley*, p. 18.
[210] Laing, *Survivals of Roman Religion*, p. 189.
[211] Strzygowski, *op. cit.*, pp. 1-10.
[212] Strzygowski, *op. cit.*, pp. 36, 58-62.
[213] Strzygowski, *op. cit.*, pp. 67-70.

Empire employed decorated walls and both domed and barrel vaulting,[214] and that the famous St. Sophia at Constantinople was built in a form which originated in Armenia.[215]

As to the distinctive dress and robes of the clergy, it is said that in the early centuries ecclesiastical vestments were unknown[216] and that garb for the clergy different from that of the laity was frowned upon.[217] Some of the special vestments of the clergy in the West are declared to be conventionalized and modified derivatives from civilian dress and particularly that of the Roman magistracy.[218]

Christians seem sometimes to have carried over pre-Christian rites for such occasions as marriage and burial. Thus down to the end of the fifth century in the West marriages were still celebrated in Christian families with some of the forms customary in pagan times[219] and the nuptial rite prescribed by Pope Nicholas I in the ninth century was that in use in imperial Rome with the substitution of the mass for the pagan sacrifice.[220] In Egypt the mummification of the bodies of the dead continued, although with diminishing frequency, into Christian times, with, presumably, some of the old customs of pagan origin.[221] Probably, however, in most if not all instances the more obviously pagan portions of the ceremonies were eliminated or replaced by features of distinctly Christian parentage and the original significance of such pagan forms as persisted was sooner or later forgotten.

Several festivals celebrated as Christian were of pagan birth, baptized and purged of some of the features which were too obviously from the older religions. Thus in the town of Gubbio a fiesta called the Elevation of the *Ceri*, patronized by the bishop and celebrated by processions in which are figures of the saints, may go back to pre-Christian times.[222] The Christmas festival on December 25th seems to have developed in Rome and not until the second half of the fourth century. The day had been observed as the birthday of the Sun. Since this was associated with Mithraism, it is possible that it was appropriated by Christians to compete with that faith.[223] Probably it was not intended to

[214] Strzygowski, *op. cit.,* pp. 21, 22.

[215] Strzygowski, *op. cit.,* p. 46.

[216] Lindsay, *The Church and the Ministry in the Early Centuries,* p. 353.

[217] Duchesne, *Christian Worship,* pp. 379-385.

[218] Lindsay, *op. cit.,* p. 353; Duchesne, *op. cit.,* pp. 379-385.

[219] Dill, *Roman Society in the Last Century of the Western Empire,* p. 446.

[220] Duchesne, *op. cit.,* pp. 433, 434.

[221] Scott-Moncrieff, *Paganism and Christianity in Egypt,* pp. 101-132; Schmidt, *Ein altchristliche Mumienetikett nebst Bemerkungen über das Begräbnisswesen der Kopten* in *Zeitschrift für ägyptische Sprache und Alterthumskunde* (1894), Vol. XXXII, pp. 52-62.

[222] Conway, *Ancient Italy and Modern Religion,* pp. 7-11.

[223] Cumont, *Oriental Religions in Roman Paganism,* p. xvii; Allen, *Christian Institutions,* p. 473; Loeschke, *Jüdisches und heidnisches im christlichen Kult,* pp. 19-22.

replace the Saturnalia,[224] although some connexion may have existed.[225] More than once the deliberate effort seems to have been made to place a Christian sacred day upon the date of a pagan feast, supposedly to displace pagan customs which enjoyed popularity by others which could be given a clearly Christian significance. The *Litania Major* was put on the date of the old *robigalia* and the Christian procession on that day followed in large part the route traversed by its pagan predecessor.[226] In Gaul and Spain a fast was set for the calends of January to detach the faithful from the pagan customs which had marked that occasion.[227] The feast of the Epiphany on January 6th seems originally to have been designed to erase the pagan celebrations of that day.[228] In the rites of All Saints' Day may be survivals of the Parentalia.[229] How far pagan ideas were carried over in these festivals is debatable. Certainly under Christian auspices features were developed which were quite alien to what had gone before, and which, therefore, brought in something new, of Christian rearing.

Inevitably Christian writers adopted literary models which they found ready to hand and with which they were familiar. Paul's Letter to the Romans follows, with modifications, the form usually employed in Greek letters of the period.[230] We have noted, too, that Paul resorted on occasion to the technique of the *diatribe* evolved by the Cynics and Stoics.[231] Luke's Gospel conforms in its methods to the biographies composed by such famous contemporaries as Plutarch and Tacitus.[232] The literary custom of Greek and Hellenistic authors was not to attempt to reproduce verbatim the words of those whose speeches they were recording, but to catch the spirit of the speaker and to put in his mouth what he might be supposed to have said under given circumstances. This, it has been opined, was the device followed in John's Gospel,[233] the most Hellenistic of the New Testament accounts of Jesus. On the other hand, as we have noted, to the Jewish practice of preserving exactly the words of revered teachers we seem to owe the collections of the sayings of Jesus which are so prominent in Matthew's and Luke's Gospels.[234] The literature which grew up around pagan philosophers, particularly Pythagoras, is said to have

[224] Duchesne, *op. cit.,* pp. 258-261.
[225] Farnell, *Outline History of Greek Religion,* pp. 122-137.
[226] Loeschke, *op. cit.,* p. 23.
[227] Duchesne, *op. cit.,* p. 286.
[228] Geffcken, *Der Ausgang des griechisch-römischen Heidentums,* p. 233.
[229] Laing, *Survivals of Roman Religion,* p. 84.
[230] Dodd, *The Epistle of Paul to the Romans,* pp. 3, 6.
[231] Dodd, *op. cit.,* p. 148; Weiss, *Urchristentum,* pp. 303-320.
[232] Streeter, *The Four Gospels,* p. 365.
[233] Streeter, *op. cit.,* pp. 370-372.
[234] Streeter in *An Outline of Christianity,* Vol. I, pp. 349, 350.

had marked influence on the early Christian legends of the saints.[235] The allegorical method of interpreting the Scriptures, so widely employed by Christians of the early centuries, was in accord with a practice which had enjoyed a marked development in Hellenistic Judaism.[236] For a time, many Christians entertained a prejudice against Greek and Roman literature, with its imagery taken from the hated polytheism. Gradually, however, this largely disappeared.[237] Men like Jerome and Augustine, trained in the accepted forms of the day and of high repute in the Church, probably helped to give the current style respectable standing in ecclesiastical circles.[238] Rhetorical traditions of pre-Christian origin were followed in the Christian sermon.[239] In the fourth and fifth centuries eloquent preaching which conformed to these models won loud acclaim from huge audiences.[240]

Again the question arises as to how far the original content of Christianity was distorted or lost by the process of seeking to transmit and interpret it through these media of non-Christian development. Many writers and speakers would no doubt have hotly and quite sincerely repudiated the suggestion that they were thus distorting or clouding the purity of the truth which they championed. Inevitably, however, something of a mixture took place. The old wineskins proved sufficiently flexible to hold the new vintage, but the latter took on something of the taste of the containers.

We must decline, as we have said, to attempt to go into the organization of the Church in any detailed fashion. We must, however, note certain reflections of the political and social structure in which it developed. The Church, we have noted, was one of the most remarkable fruits of the Christian movement. It was, too, a real creation, the result of the impulse and ideals which came from Jesus, of much experience, and of large numbers of men working over the course of centuries. No one or two men of outstanding genius built it. Nor was it constructed on the model of any previous institution. Yet while it was an original outgrowth of Christianity, existing organizations—religious, social, and political—had more or less marked effect upon it. Almost inevitably, moreover, partial conformity was seen to current political divisions and to the geographic and racial environment. In this, indeed, the creators and administra-

[235] Nock, *Conversion*, p. 176.

[236] McGiffert's translation of Eusebius, *Eccles. Hist.*, in *Nicene and Post-Nicene Fathers*, Vol. I, p. 266, Note 13 on Book VI, Chap. 19; Hatch, *The Influence of Greek Ideas and Usages upon the Christian Church*, pp. 50-59, 69.

[237] Case, *The Social Triumph of the Ancient Church*, p. 140; Dill, *Roman Society in the Last Century of the Western Empire*, p. 385.

[238] Dill, *op. cit.*, pp. 386, 387.

[239] Hatch, *op. cit.*, pp. 107-113.

[240] Foakes-Jackson in *An Outline of Christianity*, Vol. II, p. 131.

tors of the Church displayed the wisdom which helped to make that institution so powerful and unique. It would have been the height of folly not to have learned from other types of organizations or to refuse to take into account the political and geographic setting in which the Church must, perforce, carry on its work. Converts often unconsciously brought to the Church the habits and methods to which they had previously been accustomed, and the manner in which society was carried on outside almost automatically carried over into the Christian organization. External influences, therefore, which had a share in giving form to the Church were probably very numerous. A few of them seem apparent. Others we can only conjecture. Of still others we must remain unaware.

Those outside factors of which we know or from which it seems reasonable to suppose that some influence entered into the shaping of the Church were Judaism, including the synagogue, pagan religious and social societies, guilds and clubs, the family, the official religion of the Empire, the imperial, provincial, and municipal political organization, and the schools of philosophy.[241] Of the part played by the synagogue and the schools of philosophy we have already spoken. Of the others we must make only brief mention. It has been suggested that when, as seems fairly early to have been the case, Christianity made its way into the noble families of Rome, the latter probably opened their houses to their fellow Christians, allowed their basilicas to be used for worship, and became "patrons" of their poorer brethren.[242] Under this guise, so nearly in accord with established custom as to tend to quiet suspicion, some of the early communities took shape. In the days in which Christianity was spreading, the Roman Empire teemed with voluntary associations, *collegia,* many of them for the proletariat. Some provided their members with proper burial, others were for athletics, many were akin to trade and craft guilds. All had religious rites attached to them, and usually they adopted a patron deity and had their meeting-place in a temple. Often they had the custom of a common meal.[243] Some were recognized by the government, *collegia licita.* Some, *collegia illicita,* were not so licensed, and, while often tolerated, were subject to repression on suspicion of endangering the public weal. Before their conversion, many Christians had probably held membership in these associations. Naturally they brought over with them into the Church some of the

[241] Harnack, *The Constitution and Law of the Church in the First Two Centuries,* pp. 41, 167; Raven, *Jesus and the Gospel of Love,* p. 233.

[242] Lindsay, *The Church and the Ministry in the Early Centuries,* p. 124.

[243] Dill, *Roman Society from Nero to Marcus Aurelius,* pp. 250-286; Case, *The Social Triumph of the Ancient Church,* pp. 22-27, in which a selected bibliography is given; Lindsay, *op. cit.,* pp. 125-136.

organizational habits of mind to which the *collegia* had accustomed them. It has been suggested that conscious adaptation took place, and especially to the burial clubs, in an attempt to escape persecution. This, however, has been debated and is not generally accepted as proved.[244]

It has also been surmised that the structure of the state cult was in part reproduced by the Church. The hierarchical organization of the Church, with its distinction between metropolitans and other bishops, and its multiplication of the lower orders of the clergy with gradations among them, is said to reflect the form of the state religion.[245] It is held to have been shown that in Gaul the pagan organization was the forerunner of the Christian and that every city in which a *flamen* was in charge of the worship of Augustus became the seat of a Christian bishop.[246] How far this was borrowing and how far both arose in response to the same set of conditions must be conjectural. It seems clear, however, that the Church differed from what is held to be its prototype in that, unlike the latter, it did not reserve its higher positions for members of the upper classes, but kept open the way for advance from the very lowest to the most exalted ranks.[247] Some connexion seems also to have been shown between the two cults in the fact that in the Province of Asia the councils of the Church were established in the cities where assemblies had met under the presidency of the provincial priests of the imperial cult and that the Christian bodies often had the same number of members as had the pagan.[248]

The political structure of the Empire was partly reflected in the Church. The conjecture has been offered that the transition from the Kingdom of God of the Gospels to the City of God of Augustine and even to "the holy city, the New Jerusalem" of the Apocalypse, betrays the influence of a society in which the city was prominent.[249] The growing autocracy in the Empire in the third and fourth centuries is said to have been paralleled in the Church.[250] The doctrine of Apostolic Succession, of which so much was made in the Church, so the theory is, arose naturally in an age which sought authority for existing teachings or institutions in continuous contact through the past to an original precedent or founder. This is said to be seen in the Roman law and

---

[244] Lindsay, *op. cit.*, pp. 125, 129; Uhlhorn, *The Conflict of Christianity with Heathenism*, p. 487; Duchesne, *Early History of the Christian Church*, Vol. I, p. 37.

[245] Lindsay, *op. cit.*, pp. 350, 354.

[246] Desjardins, *Géographie Historique et Administrative de la Gaule Romaine*, Vol. III, p. 524.

[247] Lindsay, *op. cit.*, p. 354.

[248] Lindsay, *op. cit.*, pp. 351-353, citing Paul Monceaux, *De Communi Asiae Provinciae*, pp. 117ff.

[249] Glover, *Christ in the Ancient World*, p. 36.

[250] Lindsay, *op. cit.*, p. 357.

constitution, in the philosophical schools, and in Judaism.[251] Paul, in his missionary work, thought in terms of the political provinces. He grouped together Corinth and Achaia and wrote to the Christians in Galatia. John addressed the churches of Asia. As the episcopate developed, provincial capitals became the centres of the main ecclesiastical divisions. The bishop of the church in a provincial city naturally enjoyed a certain preëminence over the other churches of the civil province.[252] In Aquitaine the Church reproduced the divisions of Roman administration.[253] In his reorganization of the Empire, Diocletian increased the number of provinces and created dioceses, each of which included several provinces. In the East, in the fourth century the groupings of the bishops corresponded almost everywhere to the new political divisions. The bishop in the metropolis, the city in which the governor resided, became the head of the episcopacy of the region. The system spread later to the greater part of the West.[254]

It must be noted, however, that the Church did not necessarily copy the political structure. Both, rather, largely conformed to geographic realities.[255] All inclusive organizations, civil or religious, covering the Mediterranean world would, if astutely planned, correspond to much the same geographic pattern. It was natural that the bishops in the main cities—Antioch, Alexandria, Carthage, Rome, and, later, Constantinople—should be the outstanding figures in the Church. Nor was it due merely to the vigour of an Ambrose that when Milan was an imperial residence its bishop became a person of importance.[256] Moreover, it was almost an inevitable even though regrettable outgrowth of human nature that each of these chief sees should be jealous of its own prerogatives.

In its palmy days the Empire was a political unity. Never, however, was it racially or culturally fully one. Particularly in the Orient the regions which composed it had their own antecedent histories and cultures which preserved something of local consciousness. In some instances these reasserted themselves as the power of the central authority declined and made their impression on the Church. The dream of a Christian body which should embrace all believers everywhere was never lost. In practice, however, the organization which most nearly embodied it was almost coextensive with the boundaries of the Empire

[251] Harnack, *op. cit.*, p. 123.
[252] Harnack, *op. cit.*, pp. 158-160; B. S. Easton in *An Outline of Christianity*, Vol. II, pp. 67, 68; D. C. Munro in *An Outline of Christianity*, Vol. II, p. 3.
[253] Duchesne, *Fastes Episcopaux de l'Ancienne Gaule*, Vol. II, p. 17.
[254] Duchesne, *Early History of the Christian Church*, Vol. II, p. 5; Duchesne, *Christian Worship*, p. 24.
[255] Duchesne, *Christian Worship*, pp. 17-23.
[256] Duchesne, *Christian Worship*, pp. 32-36.

and, with some exceptions, was limited by them. As the Empire weakened, the Church tended to divide along racial, national, and cultural lines.[257] These non-ecclesiastical sources of division coincided with differences in doctrine and ritual. Every local area tended to develop its own liturgy, or, rather, to accept that of the church in the leading city of the district. Thus in the sixth century those regions dependent on Antioch and Alexandria each had a distinctive liturgy, dignified by apostolic names.[258] So, too, the Nestorian theology came to be identified with the Church of the Persian Empire, one form of Monophysitism with that in Syria, and the Coptic Church became Monophysite. To these national, racial, and cultural schisms we must return a little later and slightly more in detail. Here we must simply notice the factors which brought them into existence.

We must also remind ourselves that, although these extra-ecclesiastical factors made for division, and often successfully, the Church remained more nearly united than did the political realm. In many instances the dream of the union of all Christians, the conviction of the urgency of conforming to a body which was believed to transmit the true faith and to be backed by the authority of Christ, overrode entirely or in part racial, cultural, and geographic barriers and maintained in visible form and in the consciousness of believers the fellowship of the Christian community.

We have already suggested that the changing political environment had its effect on the Church. The adoption of Christianity by the Roman government worked alterations. The Church now was largely controlled by the state. It became necessary, for example, for the Church to reverse its attitude towards military service and office-holding and to permit what it had once frowned upon.[259] Matters of church doctrine now became the concern of the state, which was interested, for its own sake, in preserving unity.[260] As the Roman Empire collapsed in the West, the Church preserved some of its ideals and took over some of its functions and was thereby modified. The various barbarian kingdoms also made changes.

It must be noted again, however, that much as the organization of the Church reflected its environment and tended to assimilate suggestions from preëxistent or contemporary institutions, practices, modes of thought, and

[257] Schubert, *Geschichte der christlichen Kirche im Frühmittelalter*, p. 146.
[258] Streeter, *The Four Gospels*, p. 43. See also the introductory note on liturgies in *Ante-Nicene Fathers*, Vol. VII, pp. 533, 534.
[259] So at the synod of Arles, in A.D. 316, the first held after Constantine's change of front, the deeply rooted conviction against military service was censured and difficulties removed which had long stood in the way of Christians accepting high official posts.— Hauck, *Kirchengeschichte Deutschlands*, Vol. I, p. 37.
[260] Goodenough, *The Church in the Roman Empire*, p. 43.

regional distinctions, it was, in the main, an original creation. In the conception of the place and functions of the Church and of the clergy, in the sacraments, in theology, in ritual, in the main features of the episcopate, and in the means of legislation and of discipline, the Christian impulse displayed unique fruitage, a fruitage which indeed was affected by the soil in which it was rooted, the air by which it was surrounded, and the weather to which it was subject, but which owed, in the main, its distinctive features to the life germ out of which it sprang.

We must turn, now, for most of the remainder of this chapter, to note some of the main types of Christianity which arose in response to the various forms of the environment. We ought not to devote space to the thrice-told story of the growth and characteristics of the various branches of the faith and of the novel movements on the periphery. Our particular interest must be in the manner in which these well known developments were a reflection of their setting. It must be recalled, too, that the milieu included outstanding leaders, with their particular convictions, characteristics, and experiences, as well as institutions, philosophies, religions, races, and geography.

The varying responses to environment became apparent in the first two generations of Christians. Left as it was by its founder without elaborate organization or carefully formulated creed or ritual, but with the powerful impulse of a transforming experience and a gripping enthusiasm, it is not remarkable that, thrown into the Mediterranean world, Christianity should early develop many forms.

The evidence for the existence of these primitive differentiations is written into the very texture of the New Testament. Paul's letters, among them the earliest Christian documents to reach us in approximately their original form, bear testimony to Paul's own revolutionary experience and to the guise which that gave to his thinking about the new faith. In them, too, are glimpses of the struggle between those, on the one hand, who wished to have Christians conform fairly closely to Judaism, and those, on the other, who believed it to be the genius of Christianity, if it were true to the revelation made through Jesus, to break with many of the ritual requirements of the parent faith and to become a distinct religion, while holding to what in the old was in accord with the message, life, death, and resurrection of the Master. In the Gospels which introduce the New Testament are vivid contrasts—between the interest in the deeds and the career of Jesus represented by the Gospel of Mark, and in his words, represented in the collections of sayings incorporated in Matthew and Luke; between the interpretation of Matthew, with its kinship for much of Judaism, its Davidic descent of Jesus, and its apocalypticism, and that of

John, with its virtual substitution of the coming and work of the Paraclete for the visible return of the Lord and with its identification of Jesus with the Logos. If, as is often held, each of the four Gospels originated in a particular locality[261] and both reflected and moulded the views of the Christians of that vicinity, they were at once products and nourishers of various early strains of the faith. The chief contrast is between John and the Synoptists. It is not so clear that the differences between the latter are expressive of local points of view. The antinomy between Paul's letters and the Epistle of James[262] may possibly indicate different types of constituencies. Whether the Apocalypse was the product of a trend represented by special communities, or, more likely, embodied views held, along with others, in several localities, may be open to question.

It is clear that the books which found their way into the New Testament incorporated views which, in the main, were near enough together not to make it seem inconsistent to bring them all into one Christian canon. In the New Testament, however, are hints of variants so far removed from what became the convictions of the majority as to be regarded with abhorrence by the latter. The Epistle of Jude, for example, denounces some who appear to be akin to the Gnostics, of whom more in a moment.[263] The Johannine Epistles show intense disapproval of what also may have been the same tendency.[264] The Apocalypse condemns views represented in the churches in the Province

[261] This takes us at once into a vast literature marked by much difference of opinion and heated debate. More scholars would agree to the theory that the Gospels (at least Matthew and John) were revered in particular localities, each being the Gospel of that region, than would coincide in their judgment as to the locality in which each originated. Mark seems to have had a more general circulation, for it was known to the authors of Matthew and Luke and possibly of John. Streeter (*The Four Gospels*, pp. 1, 16) presents in summary one view of the localities in which each circulated—Mark in Rome, John in Ephesus, and Matthew in Antioch. Streeter (*op. cit.*, pp. 397-421) thinks that the author of John knew Mark. Luke, Streeter suggests (*op. cit.*, pp. 230, 233) may have used traditions of Jesus collected at Cæsarea. Bacon (*Studies in Matthew*, pp. 20, 21, 498) puts forward the thesis that Matthew originated in Syria in some place where the Jewish tradition lingered, that it was not composed in Antioch, but was later backed by the church there. He thinks that Edessa may have exerted some influence. Bacon (*The Gospel of the Hellenists*, pp. 10-14) would agree that John's Gospel arose from a type of teaching known in Asia Minor, but to Asia Minor he would also add Northern Syria. Bacon (*The Gospel of the Hellenists*, pp. 116, 117) holds that the author of the Fourth Gospel wrote late enough to know the Synoptics, but was not overawed by their prestige. We must not, of course, enter upon the literature in this moot field, nor into the interesting claim of Torrey (*The Four Gospels: A New Translation*) that all four Gospels are Greek translations of Aramaic originals, nor into "Formgeschichte."

[262] Weiss, *Urchristentum*, pp. 578-584, thinks that the Epistle of James dealt with a locally circumscribed circle with definite social and religious conditions.

[263] McGiffert, *A History of Christianity in the Apostolic Age*, pp. 584-588.

[264] I John iv:1-3, II John, 7.

of Asia,[265] but of which we know almost nothing more than the brief references there given us. It may be that the Fourth Gospel was written to refute Gnostic Hellenizers.[266] It seems also possible that Simon Magus founded a school or a religious cult akin to Christianity which gained numerous adherents in Samaria and even won converts in Rome.[267] The "false Christs" against whom the New Testament contains warnings may have been actual persons who preached a faith so like that of the main bodies of Christians as to attract followers from their ranks.[268]

Early, perhaps from the very beginning, as we have suggested, the professed followers of Jesus displayed not only a markedly fissiparous tendency, but also the conviction that in some manner unity should be preserved. That dream of one Church, the body of Christ, was strong in Paul. It is found elsewhere as well—in John's Gospel[269] and in Acts,[270] for instance. The efforts to make it a reality began early, and as Christianity spread it gave rise to a group of communities, the majority of them in fellowship with one another, with the episcopate regarded as deriving its authority and its teachings in direct succession from the inner circle about Jesus, with creeds, and with a collection of writings looked upon as the valid record of what Jesus and the first missionaries had taught and done. In a certain sense the creation of the Catholic Church was an attempt of the descendants of the converts to perpetuate inviolate the message of the first missionaries. It was to have interesting parallels in later centuries.

With this Catholic Church the majority of those who called themselves Christian were eventually in communion. However, either apart from it or from within it arose from time to time movements whose adherents, while thought of by the majority as heretics, esteemed themselves more worthy of the name Christian than the others.[271]

Of these minority groups, the earliest were those which preserved closer kinship to Judaism than did the majority. Of the original Christian community at Jerusalem a large proportion remained so far as possible on friendly terms

[265] Rev. ii:2, 6, 15, 20.
[266] Bacon, *The Gospel of the Hellenists*, p. 89.
[267] Bacon, *op. cit.*, p. 82; B. S. Easton, in *An Outline of Christianity*, Vol. I, p. 121.
[268] As in Mark xiii:6, 21, 22.
[269] John xv:12, xvii:11.
[270] Acts xv:1-33.
[271] An interesting thesis is developed in Bauer, *Rechtgläubigkeit und Ketzerei im ältesten Christentum*. Bauer emphasizes the great variety in early Christianity. What became orthodoxy, he holds, was not necessarily at the outset the faith of the majority of Christians. Its stronghold, he maintains, was in Rome, with some centres in Asia Minor. It owed its victory in part, he holds, to the failure of the "heresies" to present a united front.

with Judaism. They continued to frequent the Temple[272] and to observe the usual ritual and moral requirements of their ancestral religion.[273] What distinguished them from their fellow Jews was their belief that Jesus was the Messiah and their expectation of his early return to inaugurate a new age.[274] The Judaism of the time contained many schools and parties, and to these they seemed simply to have added another. Such intolerance as they experienced from their fellow Jews appears to have been chiefly because of their attempt to win others to this belief, and their accusation that the leaders of the nation had been responsible for the execution of the Messiah.[275]

Earnest efforts were made to hold in one fellowship the Christians who attempted to remain within Judaism and that more rapidly growing number of believers, both Jews and Gentiles, who regarded the ritual requirements of Judaism as having for them no validity and even as being an obstacle to entrance into the life opened by Jesus.[276] Of these attempts only the most fragmentary records have reached us.[277] Temporarily at least they seem to have met with some success.[278] In the second century, and even later, indeed, some leaders in the main stream of Catholic Christianity looked upon the Jewish Christians with friendly or at least tolerant eye.[279] Other Gentile Christians, however, regarded them as heretics.[280] They even forgot the origin of the name, Ebionite, by which they knew them. They thought that it came from an early leader, whereas it was almost certainly derived from a word meaning "poor"—perhaps harking back to the "poor" of the Sermon on the Mount.[281]

Only now and again do we catch glimpses of the Jewish Christians. Presumably they were to be found not only in Jerusalem, but in other places, chiefly in Palestine.[282] Before the final investment of Jerusalem by the Roman armies in A.D. 70 those who remained in the city, in response to what they

[272] Acts ii:46, iii:1, xxi:23-26.
[273] Acts xxi:20.
[274] Acts ii:14-38, iii:13-26.
[275] Acts iv:18, v:17, 18, 27-34.
[276] As in Gal. v:2.
[277] Acts xv:1-33; Gal. ii:1-10. To these efforts must also be joined the collection which Paul gathered among his churches for the Christians in Judea.—Acts xxiv:17, I Cor. xvi:1-3. See on the relations between the Jewish and Gentile churches Lake, Landmarks in the History of Early Christianity, pp. 57-97.
[278] Acts xv:30-33, xviii:21, 22, xxi:17. However, Acts may present the harmony thus attained in too roseate hues.—Weiss, Urchristentum, pp. 3-7.
[279] Justin, Dialogue with Trypho, Chap. 47; Moore, Judaism, Vol. I, p. 186; Duchesne, Early History of the Christian Church, Vol. I, pp. 89-93.
[280] Irenæus, Adv. Hær, Book I, Chap. 26, Book III, Chap. 21, Book IV, Chap. 33, Book V, Chap. 1.
[281] Duchesne, Early History of the Christian Church, Vol. I, pp. 89-93; McGiffert, Eusebius, Ecclesiastical History, pp. 158-160; Weiss, Urchristentum, p. 569.
[282] Duchesne, op. cit., Vol. I, pp. 89-93.

regarded as a divine command, fled to Pella, twenty miles south of the Sea of Galilee.[283] It has been surmised that the fall of the city seemed to them a punishment for the rejection of the Messiah and that with this as their argument they engaged, with some success, in missionary work among their fellow Jews. If they did so, this would provide an explanation for the action of the rabbis in introducing into the daily prayers a modification which made it impossible for any Christian to lead the service in the synagogue or to join in it. Whether this drove the Christians from the synagogue is not known.[284] In the first half of the second century came another rebellion of the Jews, led by Bar Cochba, who professed to be the Messiah. Since the Jewish Christians, in loyalty to Jesus, would not recognize this claim, they were persecuted by him and his followers.[285] The Romans, in their turn, would not allow any Jews, not even Christians, to return to the site of the demolished Jerusalem, and the episcopate there, when reëstablished, became Gentile.[286] Yet some of the "Ebionites" lived on and we hear of them in both the first and the second half of the fourth century.[287]

Apparently these Jewish Christians were not all of one type. It may have been, for instance, that from one group came the Odes of Solomon.[288] Some, we hear, did not hold to the virgin birth of Jesus, while others found no difficulty with the virgin birth but refused to believe in the preëxistence of Jesus.[289] Some gladly recognized Paul.[290] We read of others, represented both in Syria and in Rome, who rejected Paul's letters and showed other peculiarities.[291] Some were much affected by Gnosticism.[292]

How widely spread these Jewish Christians were we do not know. From what we have just said they seem to have been represented in Rome. Those whom Pantænus found in "India" (probably South Arabia) using "a Hebrew version of Matthew's Gospel"[293] may possibly also be classified among them. It need scarcely be added that eventually they died out.

The main bodies of both Jews and Christians repudiated those who wished to hold to the one while having affinities with the other. Orthodox Jews

[283] Eusebius, Eccles. Hist., Book III, Chap. 5.
[284] Moore, Judaism, Vol. I, pp. 90-92; Parkes, The Conflict of the Church and the Synagogue, pp. 77, 78.
[285] Justin Martyr, First Apology, Chap. 31; Moore, Judaism, Vol. I, pp. 90-92.
[286] Moore, Judaism, Vol. I, pp. 90-92.
[287] Eusebius, Eccles. Hist., Book III, Chap. 27; Moore, Judaism, Vol. I, p. 186.
[288] Kraeling, The Jewish Community at Antioch, p. 154.
[289] Eusebius, Eccles. Hist., Book III, Chap. 27.
[290] Moore, Judaism, Vol. I, p. 186.
[291] Duchesne, Early History of the Christian Church, Vol. I, pp. 94-96.
[292] Epiphanius, Panarion hær., XIX, XXX.
[293] Eusebius, Eccles. Hist., Book V, Chap. 10.

refused to consider Jesus as Messiah and the vast majority of Christians were Gentiles who, while thinking of themselves as the true Israel, had no intention of continuing within the fold of historic Judaism. The effort to remain within the Jewish faith and to win all of the seed of Abraham to acknowledge the Nazarene Messiah had failed. It was as a universal religion unhampered by an inherited racialism that Christianity went on its way.

Yet the result was a compromise. The majority of Christians did not break entirely with Judaism. They claimed its Scriptures as their own, held its ethical precepts authentic commands of God, and in other ways which we have noted carried on many of the traditions of the parent religion. It was the fuller conformity practised by the Jewish Christians which they rejected.

A movement of an opposite nature was Gnosticism. The Ebionites represented those who would have Christianity remain within Judaism. The Gnostics, on the other hand, wished a more nearly complete divorce from Judaism than the masses of Christians would assent to, and sought fully to incorporate the new faith into some ranges of the world of thought and religion of the time. The Gnostics were not one school, but many, and displayed a very wide variety. However, they had much in common. Far more than those who came to be the majority of Christians they responded to the syncretizing tendencies of the age.[294] They attempted to make a place for Jesus and the impulse given by him in widely prevalent currents of thought and mysticism. These currents antedated Christianity.[295] They were strong in the Hellenistic world, but, like the mystery cults with which they had kinship, are probably not to be identified completely with it and had in them much of Oriental provenance.[296] In general, they endeavoured to take Jesus and Christianity out of their Jewish dress and to garb them in a manner less objectionable to non-Jews. They wished to set forth the living essence of the new faith uncontaminated by the Jewish envelope in which it had reached them[297] and to explain it in terms of the thought and philosophy with which they were familiar.[298]

The general trend of the teaching is quickly stated. Gnostics believed in the distinction between spirit and matter, the one good, the other evil. They were dualists, although some would reconcile dualism with a primitive monism. To all of them, God, pure spirit and supreme good, could have no direct

---

[294] Müller, Kirchengeschichte, Vol. I, pp. 69-72.

[295] For instance, W. Anz, Zur Frage nach dem Ursprung des Gnostizismus, argues a Babylonian origin for Gnosticism. Faye, Gnostiques et Gnosticisme, pp. 470, 471, does not believe it is possible to discover any one primitive type of Gnosticism.

[296] Angus, Religious Quests of the Græco-Roman World, pp. 377-413. Leisegang, Die Gnosis, pp. 5-8.

[297] Burkitt, Church and Gnosis, pp. 27, 28.

[298] Burkitt, op. cit., pp. 3, 87, 88.

contact with matter and the creation of this present evil world. They provided, therefore, for a succession of emanations from him. It was through the demiurge or creator, one of the more remote of these emanations, or æons, that the world came into existence by a bridging of the gap between spirit and matter. Into this world were introduced by a higher æon sparks of divinity which found lodgment in human beings. The problem for men equipped with this spark was to be freed from contamination with matter and to be restored to the realm of pure spirit. Not all men had the spark of divinity, but even though they possessed it they could not save themselves. That must be done by God. This saving work of God had been performed by Christ, whom the Gnostics identified with one of the æons. He, of course, could not have become man, for that would have involved too close a touch with evil matter. Some held that the divine Christ had descended on the man Jesus at baptism and left him before the crucifixion. Others maintained that Jesus possessed a heavenly, not an earthly, body. Still others taught that the human Jesus was a mere phantom and that from birth to death he seemed to men real but was not actually such.[299]

The variations in Gnosticism were multitudinous. Many teachers existed, some for at least a time within the Christian fellowship and some on its fringes. Some accepted parts of the Old Testament. Others rejected it entirely.[300] Many took extremely ascetic attitudes, particularly towards marriage.[301] Others were accused of license and antinomianism.[302] Some are reported to have shared in the repasts associated with non-Christian worship, to have sacrificed to idols, taken part in heathen festivals, and attended gladiatorial spectacles.[303] Some,

[299] There are many accounts of Gnosticism. Useful brief summaries are in Angus, *Religious Quests of the Græco-Roman World*, pp. 377-413, McGiffert, *A History of Christian Thought*, Vol. I, pp. 45-58, and in Bousset, *Hauptprobleme der Gnosis*, pp. 320-331, to which the last few lines are much indebted. A fuller, but still a brief treatment, is in Leisegang, *Die Gnosis*. Some of the ancient summaries, much fuller, by Christian opponents of Gnosticism are in Irenæus, *Against Heresies* (translation in *Ante-Nicene Fathers*, Vol. I, pp. 309-567); Tertullian, *Against All Heresies* (translation in *Ante-Nicene Fathers*, Vol. III, pp. 649-654); Tertullian, *Against Hermogenes* (translation in *Ante-Nicene Fathers*, Vol. III, pp. 477-502); and Hippolytus, *The Refutation of All Heresies* (translation in *Ante-Nicene Fathers*, Vol. V, pp. 9-162). These have the disadvantages of being written by bitter critics. A Gnostic document is given in Mead, *Pistis Sophia*. Others are mentioned in Duchesne, *Early History of the Christian Church*, Vol. I, pp. 139, 140. A selected bibliography is in Case, *Evolution of Early Christianity*, pp. 326, 327. A list of the early "heresies," including Gnosticism, is in Hilgenfeld, *Die Ketzergeschichte des Urchristenthums, passim*.

[300] Irenæus, *Against Heresies*, Book I, Chap. 18; McGiffert, *A History of Christian Thought*, Vol. I, pp. 45-58.

[301] Irenæus, *Against Heresies*, Book I, Chaps. 6-28.

[302] Irenæus, *Against Heresies*, Book I, Chaps, 25, 28.

[303] Irenæus, *Against Heresies*, Book I, Chap. 6.

too, are said to have used images, and to have associated that of Jesus with those of non-Christian worthies and divinities.[304] In cosmologies and cosmogonies the Gnostics did not agree.[305] Among the Gnostics, too, were those who taught transmigration of souls.[306] Several were friendly to the mystery cults, or at least were said to attend regularly the ceremonies in honour of *Magna Mater*.[307] Suggestions, indeed, leave us wondering whether we do not here have one or more Christian mystery cults.[308] Some Gnostics were accused of dealing in magic and love philtres, and of making much of dreams.[309]

By no means all the Gnostics rejected the Catholic Christians as unsaved. For these, they held, the morality inculcated by the Church was a way to salvation. It might be, indeed, for some, a necessary road. They regarded it, however, as an inferior path from which those who, like themselves, were purely spiritual by nature and had true knowledge were fortunately exempt.[310]

Apparently Gnosticism had in it ample room for individualism and contradictory views. Indeed, if a divorce were effected, as it seems to have been by the Gnostics, between historic fact and religious speculation, speculation, freed from the annoying restrictions of observed and recorded data, could become exuberant and need conform to no existing patterns. To be sure, the Gnostics did not completely disown history. All made room for the Jesus of the Gospels. Some professed, however, to supplement that figure and the teachings transmitted to ordinary Christians with esoteric instructions of Jesus handed down through other lines of tradition.[311] Jesus the man, moreover, they fitted into their systems by means of their interpretation of the records.

With all their diversity, the Gnostics, as we have suggested, had much in common in their sharp distinction between spirit and matter, in their belief in a supreme, unknown God, in their views as to the nature of salvation, and

[304] Irenæus, *Against Heresies*, Book I, Chap. 25.
[305] Irenæus, *Against Heresies*, Book I; Hippolytus, *The Refutation of All Heresies, passim*.
[306] Irenæus, *Against Heresies*, Book I, Chap. 25.
[307] Hippolytus, *The Refutation of All Heresies*, Book V, Chaps. 1-6.
[308] Tertullian, *Against the Valentinians*, Chap. 1, says that the Valentinians had devised Eleusinian dissipations of their own. Sulpicius Severus, *Sacred Hist.*, Chap. 46, says that in his day Gnosticism in Spain concealed itself under mystic secret rites. Guthrie, *Orpheus and the Greek Religion*, p. 265, speaks of a seal or amulet of the third or fourth century which by some is supposed to have originated with a Gnostic sect which combined Orphic and Christian ideals. He questions this. See also Hippolytus, *The Refutation of All Heresies*, Book I, Chap. 5.
[309] Irenæus, *Against Heresies*, Book I, Chaps. 13, 25.
[310] Tertullian, *Against the Valentinians*, Chap. 1; Irenæus, *Against Heresies*, Book I, Chap. 6.
[311] So *Pistis Sophia* (see Mead, *Pistis Sophia, passim*) represents Jesus, after rising from the dead, as spending eleven years with his disciples, revealing to them mysteries. See also Irenæus, *Against Heresies*, Book I, Chap. 3.

in their explanation of how the world came to be and how salvation was to be attained.[312]

Gnosticism had a long course. Traces of it, or of the views which led to it, were probably present as early as the time of Paul.[313] What seems at least related to it appears to have aroused the apprehension of the authors of the Johannine epistles.[314] The movement reached its height towards the end of the second century and then began to wane.[315] Echoes of it, however, were heard much later. Manichæism had much in common with it. The ascetic tendencies represented in some strains of it found permanent expression in monasticism.[316]

Gnosticism was not without effect upon what became the main stream of Christianity. The majority of Christians rejected it and teachers of Gnosticism were denounced as heretics. Yet the very vigour of the repudiation and the lengthy treatises evoked are evidence that many Christians were attracted by Gnosticism, and that some may even have feared that a large minority, and perhaps even a majority, might be diverted to it. The leaders of what came to be thought of as Catholic Christianity, therefore, were forced to define and defend their position. They were constrained to clarify and to develop their own views, and in doing so helped to shape the doctrine and practice of that type of Christianity which won and held the allegiance of the majority of the faithful.

The precise forms and limits of that unintended debt to Gnosticism are not ascertainable. Just how far, if at all, the doctrine of apostolic succession, what is usually called the Apostles' Creed, and the fixing of the canon of what we term the New Testament, arose out of the desire to define and defend the main stream of Christianity against the Gnostic efforts to divert it into other channels is not clear. How far, too, the struggles with the Gnostics helped to develop the consciousness of a Catholic Church and to give it organization, is

[312] Bousset, *Hauptprobleme der Gnosis*, pp. 320-331.

[313] As in Col. ii:18. Burkitt, *The Church and Gnosis*, pp. 9, 10, questions the usual theory which makes Gnosticism older than Christianity and holds that it was dominantly a Christian creation. Clemen, *Der Einfluss des Christentums auf andere Religonen*, pp. 20, 21, holds that Gnosticism antedated Christianity. He believes it is seen, too, in Hermetic literature. Scott, *The Gospel and Its Tributaries*, pp. 188-220, holds that Gnosticism, at the beginning, was purely pagan but became mainly associated with Christianity and is evidence of the wide influence and deep impression made by that faith.

[314] I John iv:3; II John 7. B. W. Bacon, in *An Outline of Christianity*, Vol. I, pp. 329-339, believes that we have evidence of the Gnostic controversy in First and Second Timothy, Titus, Hebrews, James, First and Second Peter, Jude, and the Epistles and Gospel of John. Bacon believes that Paul's principles of liberty and spirituality lent themselves to the growth of Gnosticism.

[315] McGiffert, *A History of Christian Thought*, Vol. I, pp. 45-58.

[316] Workman, *The Evolution of the Monastic Ideal*, pp. 38-66.

not certain.[317] The answer depends in part upon what should be included in Gnosticism—whether, for example, the Marcionites, as some of their opponents claimed, belonged to it. That the struggle left its imprint, and a fairly permanent one, upon the main bodies of Christians is, however, fairly evident.

Inevitably the question emerges, Why did not Gnosticism win? Why did it not capture the majority of Christians? At first sight the advantages would have seemed to lie with it. By adjusting Christianity, as they did, to much of the thought and the religious sentiment of the contemporary Hellenistic and Oriental world, by acclimatizing it to its cultural surroundings, the Gnostics seemed to have much more likelihood of gaining converts from among non-Christians and of avoiding the sharp dislike which Christianity chronically evoked as alien, destructive, and intransigent. Why, then, was it not Gnosticism rather than what was eventually called Catholic Christianity which became orthodox, the faith of the majority of the believers?

Probably no answer can be infallibly authenticated. We must be here in the realm of speculation. It may be that the wide variations among the Gnostics kept them from presenting a united front. Giving, as they did, a minimum place to objective history, they had little basis of agreement. What became orthodox Christianity, on the other hand, insisted upon holding to history, to the Jewish Scriptures, to what the first missionaries had taught or had received from those who had been intimates of Jesus, and to those earliest written records of the faith which were being collected and sifted to form the New Testament. In this objective history which would, at least in a rough fashion, be authenticated and subscribed to by all, there was a common basis which made for agreement. This unity proved an element of great strength. Then, too, the very refusal of Catholic Christianity to compromise with non-Christian faiths probably was an asset of no mean value. As we have pointed out in an earlier chapter, this intransigence gave solidarity to the Christian community and encouraged tenacity of purpose. What became orthodox Christianity was profoundly influenced, as we have seen, by its environment. It displayed remarkable capacity for adaptation and assimilation. Always, however, it insisted upon making primary what it believed to be the original revelation in Jesus as that had been transmitted by the companions of the Lord. Everything else it sought, perhaps not always successfully, to subordinate. With the non-Christian

[317] Harnack, *The Mission and Expansion of Christianity*, Vol. I, pp. 483, 484, believes that the Catholic confederation, embracing the majority of the churches East and West and with its headquarters at Rome, came into existence in the Gnostic controversies and assumed relatively final shape under the Montanist controversy. He holds that the feeling of unity and fellowship begotten by the Catholic confederation helped greatly in the spread of Christianity.

faiths it would have no fellowship, even when refusal meant bitter persecution. These two reasons seem fairly clear. It may be, too, although here we are on less secure ground, that in thus holding to history those whom we now regard as orthodox better perpetuated the original Christian impulse and experience and the gripping, compelling, and contagious enthusiasm which so characterized them.

A kindred question must be: What would have been the fate of Christianity had Gnosticism won? If the great majority of Christians had been swept into the Gnostic camp, would Christianity have become the dominant religion of the Roman Empire? If it had done so, would it have succeeded in perpetuating itself after the fall of that Empire and in winning the place which Christianity has since achieved?[318] Here we are on the edge of the realms of the might-have-beens, regions which the historian, if he be wise, resolutely avoids, or, if he ventures upon at all, treads warily and declines to enter far. Yet they are very alluring. This much can be said without departing from observed fact. Gnosticism disappeared, and that not primarily because of persecution by the orthodox. Long before Catholic Christianity had become the religion of the state or could invoke the aid of the civil arm against heretics, Gnosticism had begun to wane. So far as being able to coerce each other out of existence was concerned, the two streams of Christianity had about an equal chance. Gnosticism, because of the willingness of many of its exponents to make Christianity comfortably at home in the contemporary world of thought and religion, seemingly had the advantage. Yet Gnosticism died out or passed on into other forms whose debt to it is difficult to prove.[319] It is a fair guess that this would have been the fate of Christianity had it been fully captured by the Gnostics.[320] The suggestion may possibly also be ventured that Gnosticism, by so belittling the objective historic roots of Christianity—the Old Testament, and the story of Jesus—and by so interpreting the life of Jesus and the original Christian experience as to make them fit into current intellectual and religious conceptions, would have fatally identified Christianity with a particular climate of opinion. When men had moved out of that climate into another, Christianity, in this Gnostic form, would presumably also have been abandoned. Chris-

[318] On these questions see Foakes-Jackson in *An Outline of Christianity*, Vol. II, pp. 26-28.
[319] In Spain the Church was successfully struggling against Gnosticism in the fourth and fifth centuries.—Bouchier, *Spain under the Roman Empire*, pp. 176-179. Burkitt, *Church and Gnosis*, pp. 100-120, holds that the Mandæans, in Lower Babylonia, are Gnostics and the only ones to survive. Workman, *The Evolution of the Monastic Ideal*, pp. 38-66, feels that Gnosticism persisted in monasticism.
[320] Uhlhorn, *The Conflict of Christianity with Heathenism*, p. 347, believes that if Gnosticism had won, Christianity would have split into a hundred sects and the line between it and heathenism would have been erased.

tianity has had no small part of its strength in its capacity for outliving the cultures with which it has been associated and in its ability to win a commanding place for itself among different races and ages. Part of the secret of this timelessness is very probably in the adherence of the major existing forms of Christianity to the historic events and experiences out of which the faith arose. Those types of Christianity which have attempted to keep these in the forefront and to make them standard seem to have been the ones which usually have survived. To this generalization exceptions can readily be pointed out. It appears to be, however, a sufficient approximation to the facts, even though only a rough one, to be worthy of attention. If the generalization has any validity whatever, then a Gnostic Christianity would probably have disappeared with the decay of the strains of thought and faith with which it had too intimately identified itself.

The struggles between variant forms of Christianity that we have so far recounted affected the future of the entire Christian movement. The choice between remaining a Jewish sect and going out frankly into the Gentile world was of primary importance. Its outcome determined that Christianity was to be a distinct religion seeking to appeal to non-Jews for the major proportion of its adherents. The decision, on the one hand, between holding to the Jewish roots, to the historic facts of the beginnings and the verifiable teachings of the founder as the norm, and, on the other hand, seeking to integrate and, if necessary, subordinate this history to a prevailing style in religion and thought, was equally important. It determined the character of the forms of Christianity which have since predominated and possibly insured for Christianity ultimate triumph in the Roman world and persistence after that world had collapsed.

Of the contests between the many other types of Christianity which appeared in the first five centuries none was so vital for the future of the faith as were these two. Most, though not all, of the others were localized and did not involve so markedly the whole future of the Christian movement. Yet several of them had great significance and helped to determine the kinds of Christianity which were to spread in later centuries.

Resembling the Gnostics were the Marcionites. Some classify the two together, making the latter a subdivision of the former. Similarities between the two give ground for this association, but its correctness is not incontestable.[321] If we think of the Marcionites as the result of environment we must make the latter include not only much in the atmosphere of the time, but the individuality of a powerful teacher. Marcion, the founder of the sect, was

[321] McGiffert, *A History of Christian Thought*, Vol. I, pp. 58-66.

probably a native of Sinope, then the most important Greek commercial centre
on the south coast of the Black Sea, and is reported to have been a son of a
bishop of that city.[322] Coming to Rome about the year 140, he affiliated himself
with the church there. His beliefs, however, led to a separation from that
body, and his followers formed distinct communities. He held that the great
run of contemporary Christianity was too much encumbered with Judaism and
so was an incompatible mixture of the essence of the faith with elements which
were a negation of it. Unadulterated Christianity he professed to find in Paul
and as an authoritative literary source for it he constructed a canon composed
of the Gospel of Luke and ten letters ascribed to Paul, so emended as to purge
them of Jewish corruptions. He denounced the Old Testament and the God
whom it portrayed. That Old Testament Jewish deity, he held, was the author
of wickedness and of this evil world, delighted in war, and was infirm of
purpose. It was this deity who spoke through the Jewish Law and prophets.
However, Jesus, derived from the true God, the Father who is above the god
of the Old Testament, abolished the Law and the prophets and all the works
of the god who had inspired them. For proof of the authenticity of Jesus,
Marcion maintained, we must look not to the Old Testament prophecies, as
Christians usually had done, but to the miracles. To be consistent, Marcion had
to deny that Jesus had been born of woman, for birth through a human womb
would have contaminated the Christ with the evil world created by the god
of the Old Testament. The communities which Marcion inspired preserved an
austere morality. Complete abstinence from sexual intercourse was enjoined,
for procreation was sharing in the work of the evil god who had made the
world. Vegetarianism was the rule, with an exception in favour of fish. The
Marcionites were, therefore, marked by great moral earnestness, but apparently
were free from those ebullitions of the spirit which have characterized some
other ascetic movements.[323]

A sect which made such severe demands on its adherents and which could
not perpetuate itself through physical heredity might have been expected to be
foreordained to a limited spread and a brief existence. Yet, even if it did not
enjoy the broad diffusion or the longevity of monasticism, it was widely
extended and persisted for centuries. It was strong in Rome and was to be

[322] Tertullian, *A Prescription Against Heretics*, Chap. 30.
[323] On Marcionism, see early accounts in Tertullian, *Against Marcion*; Tertullian,
A Prescription Against Heretics; Tertullian, *On the Flesh of Christ*; Irenæus, *Against
Heresies*, Book I, Chap. 26. More recent secondary accounts are in Harnack, *Marcion*;
Wilson, *Marcion*; and Hastings, *Encyclopædia of Religion and Ethics*, Vol. VIII, pp.
407-409.

found as far east as Mesopotamia.[324] Eventually the Marcionites passed out of existence, but they had profound effects upon other movements. It may be that Manichæism was in their debt.[325] Moreover, the conjecture has been offered that it was in opposition to them that the so-called Apostles' Creed and the New Testament canon of the majority wing of the Christian movement were developed[326]—or, at least, their formation hastened. It is also suggested that Marcion was an organizing genius and that some of the features of the structure of his sect influenced the Catholic Church.[327] If these hypotheses are true, then the Marcionites left on Christianity permanent traces of their existence.

Roughly contemporary with the Marcionites in origin, and also inspired by a native of Asia Minor, was Montanism. It need not surprise us that both such prominent movements should spring from scions of that region, for here, as we have seen, Christianity had its most extensive following in the first three centuries. More than the Marcionites, the Montanists seem to have reflected the characteristics of Asia Minor. In them were found the ecstatic features of some of the mystery cults which appear to have been indigenous there. They gave a prominent place to women, which also may have been in accord with the long-established tradition of the country.[328]

The founder, Montanus, before his conversion had been a priest of Cybele, and apparently was a man of enthusiastic and neurotic temperament, tendencies presumably accentuated by his experiences in the priesthood. His was the cult of a convert of the first generation, a reaction of one who had been reared in another faith. As a Christian he believed that he had direct messages from the Spirit, that the age of the Spirit foretold in the Gospel of John had returned, and that the second coming of Christ was at hand. In him and his followers the early Christians with their emphasis on continuing revelation through prophecy seemed to have returned. The Montanists, too, protested against what they deemed the growing laxity of the majority of Christians. They declined to readmit to fellowship those who had been guilty of grievous sin after baptism. While not forbidding matrimony, they prized celibacy and

[324] Burkitt, *Church and Gnosis*, p. 112; Burkitt, in Mitchell, *S. Ephraim's Prose Refutations of Mani, Marcion, and Bardaisan*, Vol. II, pp. cxvii-cxx.

[325] Burkitt, *Church and Gnosis*, p. 112.

[326] McGiffert, *A History of Christian Thought*, Vol. I, pp. 149-165; Bacon, *Studies in Matthew*, p. 452; Foakes-Jackson in *An Outline of Christianity*, Vol. II, p. 35; A. S. Peake in *An Outline of Christianity*, Vol. I, p. 371; McGiffert, *The Apostles' Creed, passim*. Yet, Lietzmann, *Geschichte der alten Kirche*, Vol. II, pp. 100-119, in reviewing the origin of the creeds, gives to the Marcionites little or no place in the history.

[327] Wilson, *Marcion*, p. 122.

[328] Ramsay, *The Church in the Roman Empire*, p. 67.

frowned on second marriages. They inculcated respect for their prophets rather than for the regularly established clergy. They gave a higher place to women than did the rest of the Church, and counted in their number prophetesses and possibly women bishops. They spread widely and were found in Rome, in North Africa, and elsewhere in the East and West. In North Africa the famous Tertullian became an ardent adherent, and in so doing lost caste with the orthodox. After more or less hesitation the majority branded the Montanists as heretics, but, in spite of persecution by fellow Christians and zealously correct Christian Emperors, the sect persisted in Asia Minor down at least into the eighth century. Montanism, too, left its impress upon the majority and, by way of reaction, the main stream of Christianity hastened the development of certain features and accentuated the emphasis upon them. Among these were the conviction that the age of prophecy had closed with that of the Apostles, a distrust of teachers who claimed direct inspiration but were not sanctioned by the bishops, an addition to the authority of the episcopate as against prophets, more emphasis upon the writings collected in the New Testament as apostolic and so authoritative as against the fresh utterances of the prophets, and a coldness towards any proclamation of the near approach of the Second Advent.[329]

The Marcionites and the Montanists were not the only groups who sought to observe a stricter standard of living than did the majority of Christians. As the number of converts multiplied, a natural and widespread tendency arose to relax rules which could be maintained when Christians constituted only small minorities. This trend was probably accentuated by the increasing proportion of those who had inherited the faith through one or more generations, took it as a matter of course and did not have the zeal of the convert to an unpopular cause. Against this leniency protests were almost inevitable. These became especially vigorous when, after the persecutions of the third and the early part of the fourth century, the Church seemed to some remiss in readmitting those who, under pressure, had denied the faith. It is probably more than a coincidence that the two more prominent of these protests, Novatianism and Donatism, arose, respectively, after the first severe general persecution, that of Decius, and after the last and the most devastating of the general persecutions, that which bears the name of Diocletian. Novatian, who claimed

[329] On Montanism, see Labriolle, *La Crise Montaniste;* Labriolle, *Les Sources de l'Histoire du Montanisme;* Ramsay, *The Cities and Bishoprics of Phrygia,* Vol. I, p. 118, Vol. II, pp. 574-576; Haslehurst, *Some Account of the Penitential Discipline of the Early Church,* p. 52; note in McGiffert, *Eusebius' Ecclesiastical History,* p. 229; McGiffert, *A History of Christian Thought,* Vol. I, pp. 166-174; Duchesne, *Early History of the Christian Church,* Vol. I, pp. 196-206.

to be the legal bishop of Rome, had the support of members of the strict party. The sect spread widely in both the East and the West and continued at least into the sixth century. It attracted some of the Montanists.[330] The Donatists were predominant in North Africa, where they persisted through the Vandal occupancy and probably to the Moslem-Arab conquest. They seem to have been strongest among the indigenous, non-Latin population. With them the Catholics, who prevailed among the Roman elements of the region, argued the question of the validity of clerical functions performed by unworthy priests. The Donatists held that the character of the officiating clergyman determined the efficacy of the sacramental act, while the Catholics maintained that the sacraments were effective no matter what the personal misdeeds of the administrant.[331]

Into the long and complicated struggle between Arianism and the views which were eventually established as orthodox we must not take the time to go. After the conflicts over Gnosticism it proved the most severe of the many schisms which troubled the Church in the first five centuries. In its essence it appeared primarily theological and concerned with the difficult but, to Christians, important question of the relation of Jesus to God. Was Christ created by God, and subordinate to him, perhaps of similar but certainly not of "the same substance"? Or was Christ from all eternity an integral part of the Godhead, and of "the same substance" with the Father? This was, of course, modified by the influence of Greek philosophy and by conceptions inherited from Judaism. It was affected, too, by the religious convictions and experiences of the great majority of Christians, for probably to them Jesus had the value of God. Many, indeed, tended to make him their only God and to think of God the Father and Creator either as vague and unreal or to have, for them, practically no existence. Here some would see the influence of the atmosphere generated by the mystery cults. For Athanasius, the leading protagonist of the view which prevailed, if man were to attain divinity God must become man. To him God became man that man might become God.

The outcome could never seriously have been long in doubt. For the majority of Christians the Lord whom they met in Gospel story was more vivid,

[330] Eusebius, *Eccles. Hist.*, Book VI, p. 43; note by McGiffert on p. 286 of his edition of *Eusebius*; Harnack, *The Mission and Expansion of Christianity*, Vol. II, pp. 308-311. See Migne, *Pat. Lat.*, Vol. III, Cols. 861-970, which includes writings of Novatian; Hastings, *Encyclopædia of Religion and Ethics*, Vol. IX, pp. 398-401.

[331] Duchesne, *op. cit.*, Vol. II, pp. 72-97, Vol. III, pp. 76-103; McGiffert, *A History of Christian Thought*, Vol. II, pp. 107, 108. For Augustine's writings against the Donatists, see Migne, *Pat. Lat.*, Vol. XLIII; Hastings, *Encyclopædia of Religion and Ethics*, Vol. IV, pp. 844, 845. R. P. Beaver, *The Donatist Circumcellions*, in *Church History*, Vol. IV, pp. 123-133.

concrete, and near than what must have seemed the rather vague and abstract Being of the philosophers and theologians, or even the God of the Old Testament and the God and Father of whom Jesus and the Apostles spoke. They would not, therefore, consent to any formula about the Christ which would give him a subordinate, even though an exalted place.

While in its simplest forms the issue was approximately what the last two paragraphs have attempted to set forth, in its history it was complicated by many factors. Into the struggle entered the personalities of the leaders of the two groups and of the subdivisions of these groups. Each prominent figure coloured the controversy with his own characteristics. Into it, too, came political considerations, notably the desire of the Emperors for unity. Regional and racial interests were present. Eventually, as we have seen, by steps which we are not able to trace but whose sequel is clear, Arianism became almost exclusively identified with the Goths and Vandals and some of the other Germanic peoples in contact with them. As the Goths, and these others, nearly always in former Roman territory a conquering minority, were assimilated to the subject majority, they took on the faith of the latter. In some places the outcome was long delayed. Everywhere it was all but inevitable.[332]

The number of distinct currents within the Christian stream sooner or later branded as heresies by the majority must have been legion. Of the Nestorian and Monophysite movements we will speak in a moment. Of the others we must take time for only a few, and some of them not the most prominent.

There were those who, in accord with much of the religious temper of the day, were more interested in personal salvation to an immortal life of joy than in problems of the creation of the world. They were inclined to make Christ their God. This tendency, indeed, has been repeatedly seen in human history. Some theologians attempted to put this conception into ordered philosophical form. As one result came Modalism, to which Sabellius gave its most elaborate dress and which insisted that God is one person and one substance. Some said that it was the Father who had been born of a virgin and died on the cross. They were, therefore, dubbed Patripassians.[333]

Some thought of Jesus as a mere man who at his baptism was adopted by

[332] McGiffert, A History of Christian Thought, Vol. I, pp. 246-257, contains a brief summary of the Arian controversy. A much longer study, very good in quality, is H. M. Gwatkin, Studies in Arianism, Chiefly Referring to the Character and Chronology of the Reaction which Followed the Council of Nicæa. Of value is C. E. Raven, Appollinarianism. P. E. More, Christ the Word, pp. 114-183, contains a brief, semi-popular summary.

[333] McGiffert, A History of Christian Thought, Vol. I, pp. 232-245; Harnack, History of Dogma, Vol. III, pp. 51-98.

God as his Son. This "adoptionism" had vogue in both East and West and was given the powerful support of Paul of Samosata, Bishop of Antioch.[334]

From Pelagius, a British monk who had long lived in Rome, comes the name of another school of thought which had a wide following and from which Augustine vigorously dissented. A man of sterling character who wished to improve the morals of the masses of the membership of the Church, Pelagius seems to have believed that the doctrine of original sin gave men an excuse for delinquency. To this he opposed a view which, while leaving room for the grace of God, accorded larger place than did Augustine to freedom of the will and to the native ability of man to live a life of righteousness. Presumably the conflicting views were in part the fruit of varying experiences. Augustine had in his own past what seemed to him a confirmation of his convictions. We know less of Pelagius, but he may well have been one to whom had never come any abrupt conversion with its striking transition from moral impotence to moral victory explained as an act of God. For a time Pelagianism attracted something of a following, particularly in Gaul and Britain, but eventually the views of Augustine won out, although in a modified form.[335]

A movement on the fringes of Christianity was Manichæism.[336] It was profoundly influenced by the older faith, especially in regions where the latter was strong. At times its adherents claimed that it was the only true Christianity. It spread from Europe and North Africa to China and persisted for over a thousand years. Whether it should be classified under Christianity or whether, like Islam, it should be called a separate religion may be debatable. Probably

[334] McGiffert, op. cit., Vol. I, pp. 232-245; Harnack, op. cit., Vol. III, pp. 14-50.

[335] McGiffert, op. cit., Vol. II, pp. 125-145; Migne, Pat. Lat., Vols. XLIV-XLV, for Augustine's writings against Pelagianism; the translation of Augustine's anti-Pelagian writings in Nicene and Post-Nicene Fathers, Vol. V; A. Souter, Pelagius's Expositions of Thirteen Epistles of St. Paul; E. Jauncey, The Doctrine of Grace up to the End of the Pelagian Controversy, pp. 173-285; Bede, Eccles. Hist., Book I, Chap. 17.

[336] Of the extensive literature on Manichæism, the following have been employed in preparation of this sketch: Burkitt, The Religion of the Manichees; Schmidt and Polotsky, Ein Mani-Fund in Ägypten; Jackson, Researches in Manichæism; Mitchell, S. Ephraim's Prose Refutations of Mani, Marcion, and Bardaisan; DeStoop, Essai sur la Diffusion du Manichéisme dans l'Empire Romain; Clemen, Der Einfluss des Christentums auf andere Religionen, p. 21; Holl, Urchristentum und Religionsgeschichte, p. 11; Jackson in An Outline of Christianity, Vol. II, pp. 271-282; Ante-Nicene Fathers, Vol. VI, pp. 179-235, 241-253; Waldschmidt and Lentz, Die Stellung Jesu im Manichäismus. Among the references to Manichæism by early Christian writers are Eusebius, Eccles. Hist., Book VII, Chap. 31, and Socrates, Eccles. Hist., Book I, Chap. 22. These are of dubious value. See treatises by Augustine dealing with Manichæism, in Migne, Pat. Lat., Vol. XXXIV, Cols. 172-246, Vol. XLII, Cols. 93-602. See also Epiphanius, Panarion haer., LXVI, 1-87, Kata Manixaion. Much more authoritative for an objective study are the Manichæan documents discovered within the past few decades in Turfan and Egypt. See a bibliography in Burkitt, op. cit., pp. 12-16, 48.

the determining factor should be the reply to another question: was the primary impulse back of Manichæism from Christian sources? Here no one answer is generally accepted. Several notable scholars in the field hold Manichæism to have been an offshoot of Zoroastrianism, or at least Iranian in its foundation. Another scholar esteems it primarily an outgrowth from Christianity. Another finds in it late Judaism, another bases it upon the Mandæans, and still another maintains that the prevailing element is Buddhist.

The founder, Mani, was born early in the third century, of Persian stock, with some of the blood of the Parthian Arsacids in his veins. He spent much of his youth and early manhood in Seleucia-Ctesiphon, then the chief city of Babylonia, a mart where East and West met. In this cosmopolitan centre he could imbibe ideas of many origins. Presumably he was profoundly and sincerely religious, a man of intense emotions, marked imagination, and unusual poetic gifts. In A.D. 242, at about the age of twenty-six, inspired by what he declared to be a divine revelation, he came forward as a prophet. At first he met with some success, but eventually aroused the antagonism of the dominant and jealous Zoroastrian hierarchy, and was driven out of the Persian Empire. For years he wandered abroad and is said to have preached widely in Central Asia and North India. Then he returned to his native land and for a brief time won royal favour. However, under the next monarch he was martyred (perhaps in 273 or 274) and his followers, persecuted, probably scattered both eastward and westward, carrying their faith with them.

Mani preached a syncretic religion. The sources of all his concepts are not yet agreed upon by those who have made him a special study. He believed in divinely inspired predecessors, among them Zoroaster and Jesus. Into his system entered ideas of Zoroastrian, old Babylonian, Jewish, and Christian provenance. In his journeys eastward he may have been receptive to suggestions from Buddhism. Certainly his followers in Central and Eastern Asia tended to emphasize elements from the faiths of these regions. He wrote extensively, both in Syriac and in Persian, but mostly in Syriac, and that language seems to have been the one in which he felt most at home. He was familiar with at least parts of the Old and New Testaments. His contact with Christianity appears to have been chiefly through the Gnostics, the Marcionites, and Bardaisan, a prominent writer of Syriac Christianity whose original views won him eventual classification with the heretics. Jesus, Mani held, was the undying light of the Father who brought the knowledge of the truth from heaven to earth. In agreement with some of the Gnostics, he thought of him as a divine being who appeared among men but was never born of woman. The sharp distinction which he drew between spirit and matter would naturally have made offensive a human birth for Jesus. Nor did he think Jesus was really crucified. Whether this cleavage between good and evil, the realms of light and of darkness came from Persian, Babylonian, or Christian sources is undetermined. Mani is reported, however, to have begun all his letters with "Mani, Apostle of Jesus Christ."[337] Certainly he declared either that the Paraclete promised by Jesus spoke through him or that he was the Paraclete. We seem here to have one, receptive to ideas from many sources, who regarded himself as in the Christian succession, but with a later revelation than that possessed by the Catholic Christians of his day. His followers he divided into two groups, the elect or perfect who led celibate and austerely ascetic lives, and the auditors who might marry, engage in business, and support the elect.

In the Roman Empire Manichæism achieved a wide vogue. It seems to have appeared in Syria, in Asia Minor, in Judea, in Constantinople, and in Rome itself. In Egypt it greatly troubled the Church and in North Africa the young Augustine for a time had fellowship with it. It appears to have left a permanent impression upon him—for instance, in his distinction between the *Civitas Dei* and the *Civitas Mundi*. Many others reared as Catholic Christians must, like himself, have been attracted to it. It had a strong appeal to those inclined to the mystery faiths, including Mithraism, and to some of the Gnostic sects. It may, indeed, in part have become the heir of these systems.[338] Better than Mithraism, it offered a via media between Christianity and Zoroastrianism. Mithraism prepared the way for it. It professed to give an explanation of the universe more in accord with the learning of the time than could Christianity. Then, too, and perhaps more important still, it accorded with the syncretizing temper of the times by making room for the Old Testament antediluvians, the Buddha, Zarathustra, Jesus, and Mani, and placing them all in one religious system.

It was not only in the Roman Empire that Manichæism attracted followers. In Persia and Central Asia it gained adherents and in China it persisted down into the seventeenth century. That the Cathari of the European Middle Ages and the Bogomils of the Balkans were its lineal descendants is sometimes asserted but by others of the expert is declared unproved.

Why, with all these advantages and these many footholds, did Manichæism die out and find a lasting place only in the museum of bygone faiths? Obvious

[337] Augustine, *Contra Faustum Manichæum,* Book XIII, Chap. 4 (Migne, *Pat. Lat.,* Vol. XLII, Col. 283).

[338] Harnack, *Mission and Expansion of Christianity,* Vol. II, pp. 308-311, holds that Manichæism absorbed some of the Gnostics and of the Marcionites. Cumont, *The Mysteries of Mithra,* pp. v, 207, says that Mithraism prepared the way for Manichæism. See also Nock, *Conversion,* p. 252.

answers can readily be suggested. When it appeared in the Roman Empire, orthodox Christianity, with a much better organization, was already powerful and soon had back of it the support of the state. The sharp distinction between the perfect and the auditors must have been chilling to the majority, who found much more assurance of salvation in the Catholic Church. In Persia Manichæism faced the unrelenting enmity of the state-reinforced Zoroastrian hierarchy and then, after the Sassanids had been displaced by the caliphs, the hostility of the ruling Moslems. In Central Asia it won a considerable section of the Uighurs. However, never did it succeed in making itself the dominant faith of any major culture or of any people of outstanding political power. For this failure other more subtle and perhaps more weighty factors may be accountable. Whatever the reasons, this once powerful religion into which the impulse which came from Jesus entered so prominently, completely disappeared. The final, devastating blows were dealt it by the later Mongols and Tamerlane.

A movement characteristic of most of the main branches of Christianity was monasticism. It became an outstanding feature of all those divisions of the Church which persisted through the thousand years between A.D. 500 and A.D. 1500, the next period of our story. In that millennium, moreover, the vast majority of Christian missionaries were from its ranks. From the fifteenth century to the present time the majority of Roman Catholic missionaries have been from the regulars—those who have perpetuated the monastic tradition. Of the remainder of the Roman Catholic clergy, the seculars, one of the three outstanding features of monasticism, celibacy, has been required. Monasticism, then, has had a large part in the expansion of Christianity and has had marked influence in shaping the concepts of converts as to what constitutes an ideal Christian. Except for Protestantism, the Christianity which has spread has consciously or unconsciously exalted the monastic life.

In its origin and early development monasticism must be attributed to a number of factors, some of them inherent in Christianity from its first century, some arising out of the history of the Christian movement in its first five centuries, and some finding entrance from the world outside the Church. Jesus himself was a celibate, and a saying attributed to him has been repeatedly quoted as giving sanctity to that state.[339] Moreover, although he was not an ascetic, he pointed out the dangers of the ownership of property and seemed to exalt voluntary poverty.[340] Paul was unable to discover any word of Jesus

[339] Matt. xix:12.
[340] Mark x:21, 23, 24; Luke xi:33, 34.

which enjoined celibacy,[341] but believed that state preferable to matrimony and was of the somewhat hesitant opinion that in this he had the confirmation of the Spirit.[342] In the second century many Gnostics and the Marcionites and Montanists, as we have seen, advocated ascetic practices. It has been claimed, indeed, that monasticism is the legacy of Gnosticism to its opponents.[343] Then, too, from the very start Christians, instead of attempting to transform all society in accordance with the standards of the Gospels, formed themselves into groups more or less distinct from the world about them in which these standards could be observed. As larger numbers came into the Church and the descendants of converts remained in it, Christians tended to conform more and more to the social order in which they were set. Against this, as we have said, came protests in the form of efforts to organize communities which would live according to the precepts of Jesus and the Apostles. Of these the monastic movement was the most widespread and the most persistent. The factors arising out of the nature of Christianity and the inescapable tension between its ethical standards and those of non-Christian society might have been sufficient to give birth to movements resembling monasticism. Certainly Protestantism, which reacted vigorously against Roman Catholic monasticism, often assumed forms akin to it. Almost none of these latter, however, enjoined celibacy or forbade private ownership of property. What seems to have given monasticism some of its main characteristics were elements in the religious atmosphere and practice of the surrounding non-Christian society. The Cynics, who long antedated Christianity, resembled the early monks, and facile passage from one group to the other was not unknown.[344] The widespread belief in the antinomy between flesh and spirit and the conception of salvation as escape from the trammels of the one into the realms of the other engendered rigid asceticism both within and outside the Christian movement. It was within Christianity, however, that in the Græco-Roman world asceticism enjoyed its most extensive development. To account for monasticism, both the Christian impulse and the non-Christian environment seem necessary.

On the familiar story of the birth and growth of monasticism we need not linger.[345] The movement began to assume shape toward the close of the third century and had its earliest prominent centre in Egypt. Anthony, the most famous example of Egyptian monasticism and who lived in the latter half of

---

[341] I Cor. vii:25.

[342] I Cor. vii:25-40.

[343] Workman, *The Evolution of the Monastic Ideal*, pp. 38-66.

[344] Dill, *Roman Society from Nero to Marcus Aurelius*, pp. 353, 361. Dill mentions an Egyptian Cynic of the fourth century who wore the distinctive marks of his philosophic brotherhood until he was installed Bishop of Constantinople, and tells of a man who joined a Christian brotherhood in Palestine, left it, and assumed the dress of a Cynic.

[345] Workman, *op. cit.*, gives an excellent brief account.

the third and the first half of the fourth century, as a young Copt of inherited wealth, struck by hearing the passage in the Gospel in which Jesus commanded the rich ruler to sell all that he had and give to the poor, took the word as applying to himself. After fulfilling it he retired to the desert. In the West the best-known early exponents were Jerome, a man of education, and Martin of Tours, the ex-soldier. The immense circulation of the biographies of Anthony and Martin attests the quick popularity of the movement. Monasteries achieved prominence in both East and West and in the churches of Armenia, Syria, and Persia.[346] The monks lived either as hermits or in communities. The model for the communities of the West was established by Benedict of Nursia. So important in the conversion of Western Europe were those living according to the Benedictine rule or modifications of it that we have suggested, as will be recalled, the setting up of Benedict's community as one reason for beginning a new stage of our story with about the year 500.

At its inception, monasticism was not at all welcome to the large proportion of the hierarchy of the Church.[347] Particularly at its outset and in its eremetical forms, it was individualistic[348] and restive under constituted authority.[349] However, it proved too popular to be frowned down. The clamour of the masses brought some monks into episcopal position. Yet even a Martin of Tours, when reluctantly forced into the episcopate, was not welcomed by the clergy of his diocese and had little to do with his fellow bishops.[350]

With the growth of the ascetic ideal, although by no means always as a result of monasticism, went the increase, especially in the West, of the celibacy of all the clergy. A Roman synod of 384 insisted upon the celibacy of the higher ranks[351] and Ambrose of Milan indicates that in his time that state was generally recognized as necessary for all the clergy, although the practice was neglected in some of the remoter districts.[352]

Long before the end of the second century, as we have seen, the ideal of the unity of all Christians in one visible community had brought into being what has sometimes been called a federation of Christian groups. This tended to uniformity of creed, of a canon of Scriptures, and of organization, and professed to preserve the teachings of the original disciples of Jesus. The struggle

[346] See a short account of one of these monks who was Bishop of Edessa from 411 to 435 in Burkitt, *Early Eastern Christianity*, pp. 49-61.
[347] Workman, *op. cit.*, pp. 15-24.
[348] Allen, *Christian Institutions*, p. 156.
[349] Monks tended to be insubordinate to bishops. Duchesne, *Early History of the Christian Church*, Vol. III, pp. 22-25.
[350] Hauck, *Kirchengeschichte Deutschlands*, Vol. I, pp. 50-60.
[351] Lea, *History of Sacerdotal Celibacy*, Vol. I, p. 62.
[352] Lea, *op. cit.*, Vol. I, p. 66.

against movements which threatened to disrupt it had helped to give it form. In practice this Catholic Church was about coextensive with the Roman Empire. Theoretically it knew no racial, cultural, or geographic divisions. Actually, however, it was inclined to take on the colour of the various regions and peoples among whom it was found and to divide in accordance with them. No organization or appeal to loyalty to an ideal, a person, or a doctrine proved strong enough entirely to thwart the drift and often outright schism followed.

The main territorial divisions which appeared before the close of the fifth century we have already mentioned. It remains to add a further word about them, partly because it was through these regional and national churches that the spread of Christianity in the succeeding period was chiefly accomplished.

Of the Armenian Church no more need be said. Its separation from the other churches was primarily for reasons of nationality. While in the main conforming to the type of its sister churches of the East it developed institutional peculiarities. It was a major factor in giving cohesion to the Armenian nation, but it did not reach outside its own borders in missionary effort. In the future expansion of Christianity it had no active part.

Christians in the Syriac-speaking regions long lived their lives somewhat apart from the currents which disturbed the Græco-Latin sections of the Church. Although Gnosticism vexed them, in general on most of the disputed issues they remained in doctrinal accord with the majority of Christians until about the close of the fifth century. In the sacraments, too, they differed little in essentials from Greek and Roman Catholics. Yet the Arian controversy which brought such upheaval among their brethren of Greek and Latin speech seems not to have loomed large on their horizon. In the fourth century their Christianity had changed less from that of the second than had that of the Greek world.[353] They developed, too, a Christian literature in their own tongue.[354]

Politically they were divided. A large proportion were in the Tigris-Euphrates Valley, a region mainly incorporated in the Persian Empire. The western and north-western borders of that empire fluctuated in the shifting fortunes of the centuries-long struggle with Rome, but the rich lower part of the valley was consistently within the Persian boundaries. In the Persian Empire the Church, as we have suggested, reflected its surroundings. Some Persian-speaking converts were added to its fold. Eventually it devised a national organization which may have resembled the hierarchy of the established

[353] Burkitt, Early Christianity Outside the Roman Empire, pp. 8-12, 17, 54.
[354] Burkitt, op. cit., pp. 17-26.

Zoroastrianism[355]—although this latter seems unproved. In adopting Nestorianism, moreover, a process which was not completed until after the fifth century, this Persian Church took on theological aspects which deepened the rift between itself and the churches of the Roman Empire and heightened its national character.

The Syriac-using Christians who remained within the Roman Empire were thus cut off from their brethren in the East. Most of them, in turn, as we shall see in a later chapter, adopted Monophysite doctrines. These eventually separated them from Greek and Roman Christians and, while zealously propagated in the Persian domains, never won there the majority of Christians.

In Egypt before the end of the fourth century the Church had begun to be identified with local nationalism—if the use of this nineteenth-century term for features of that period be not an anachronism. The tradition of absolutism represented by the Pharaohs and the Ptolemies and carried into the Roman regime may have accentuated the authority of the Bishop of Alexandria over the Church in Egypt.[356] As Christianity spread to the masses it became predominantly Coptic in language. We have already seen that some old Egyptian customs were perpetuated in Christian burial rites. In the long and bitter Arian controversy, native Egyptian opinion seems to have been increasingly on the side of the repeatedly exiled and as often restored Bishop of Alexandria, Athanasius.[357] Arianism, at the times when it enjoyed imperial support, retained in Egypt a precarious foothold only in the Greek-speaking population and with the aid of imperial troops. It is not surprising that later, when Monophysite views made headway, they should be adopted and vehemently held against the views declared orthodox by the alien Greek rulers.

So, too, the Church in the Greek-speaking portions of the Mediterranean world took on features which in part reflected its background. It became the church of those who were loyal to Greek rule as represented by the Emperors in Constantinople. In contrast with the West, where the collapse of the imperial power left the Bishop of Rome the chief representative of cultural unity and the Roman tradition and where the Church tended to be independent of the civil power, in the Greek world the authority of the Emperors continued without a break and controlled the Church. In practice, too, the Greek Church, perhaps because of the interest in salvation as the achievement of immortality inherited from the Hellenistic world, emphasized Easter and the resurrection. The Latin world, on the other hand, possibly by reason of its legal background,

[355] Duchesne, *Early History of the Christian Church*, Vol. III, p. 381.
[356] Duchesne, *op. cit.*, Vol. III, p. 56.
[357] Duchesne, *op. cit.*, Vol. II, pp. 209-215.

stressed the cross and the atonement. In the Greek Church, moreover, mysticism seems earlier to have been more at home than in the West, perhaps because of the influence of Neoplatonism. The treatises purporting to be by Dionysius the Areopagite which had much to do with fostering this spirit bear markedly the impress of Neoplatonism.[358] The Greek Church, possibly through the intellectual heritage from Hellenism, stressed creed as the basis of unity. The Western Church, while holding to uniformity of creed, placed emphasis upon the recognition of the authority of the Bishop of Rome as the test of fellowship, here showing itself the heir of the organizing genius of the Roman Empire. With such distinct characteristics it is not strange that in reality, although for centuries not in theory, a broadening gulf existed between the church whose Patriarch resided at Constantinople and the Pope whose headquarters were in Rome.

This geographic and cultural differentiation was also seen in that branch of the Church which became the largest and most extensive of all, the one bearing the name of Rome. It was natural that the Church of Rome should enjoy a certain pre-eminence in the Empire. Was it not in the capital of the Græco-Roman world, and did not the very name of Rome inspire awe? Rome was more than a city and the headquarters of empire. It was the symbol of law and order, of a unity which had bound together under one sway more of mankind than had ever before acknowledged any one political allegiance. In the West especially the name of Rome carried prestige. Here were no competing indigenous cultures of greater antiquity, and no other cities, except perhaps the conquered rival, Carthage, which might lift their heads against it. Moreover, in the West Rome had the one church which could boast early associations with the Apostles, while in the East were many such.[359]

It was natural that the Roman tradition should place its peculiar stamp upon the portions of the Church which most looked to Rome for leadership. Rome's was the spirit of world-wide empire made tangible in a visible organization bound together by allegiance to a single ruling authority centralized in one man. Rome, too, meant law. It symbolized the dominance of the practical, the utilitarian, the ethical. It was conservative. It visualized success in terms of an orderly, civilized society. All of these characteristics were reflected in the Roman Catholic Church. Within the city itself was need, as nowhere else, to form a united church out of heterogeneous elements, for here, to the cosmopolitan capital of the Empire, came, as to no other place, representatives

[358] McGiffert, *A History of Christian Thought*, Vol. I, pp. 292-307.

[359] For a summary of the steps by which the Bishop of Rome rose to hegemony in the Church, see Shotwell and Loomis, *The See of Peter*, pp. 213-227.

of the various racial and doctrinal strains of Christianity.[360] Then, too, as the seat of political authority was moved elsewhere, the Bishops of Rome were increasingly left without rivals and became the perpetuators of the Roman ideals. This was especially true after the Empire collapsed in the West. Here centred, then, a church which dreamed in terms of universal empire represented by a highly articulated organization, with Latin as its language, with its laws, and in the hands of a skilful and forceful administrator an instrument for immense influence. More than any other of its sister churches, it dreamed of transforming and ordering human society. Theology it had and mysticism it was to know, but its genius was that of the practical, organizing, administrating, civilizing empire. Under it Christianity took on distinctive forms. The very use of the Latin language gave to some of its ideas connotations which dated back to pre-Christian days.[361] Into the Roman Catholic Church and its hierarchy has come, too, something of the pride of empire, the scorn of all outside the fold, which were so familiar in the old Rome.

Yet the Roman Catholic Church is far more than the continuation of the Roman Empire. In the inherited Roman tradition the Christian impulse wrought many modifications and to it brought many additions. If the Roman Catholic Church is the joint product of the ancient Roman imperial spirit and of what came from Judea and Greece, the Judean element is by no means the least influential. By the Roman Catholic Church the scope of empire has been vastly broadened. It has been made to include not only the Mediterranean world, but all the earth. It not only claims sway over the faithful in this life but professes divine authority to extend its power in certain broad realms beyond the grave. The ideal, too, which the Church holds before men is chiefly non-Roman. Those whom it canonizes as worthy of the emulation of all Christian people are seldom its mightiest rulers, for some of the most justly famous of these have never been accorded that honour, but more often are the humble who have given their lives in radiant self-devotion to the underprivileged and to God. Its favourite emblem is a cross, to the Romans a gibbet. While it wishes to transform society, it esteems its chief function as constituting a channel for divine powers which transform the inward spirit as well as the outward conduct of man, and which insure for the regenerated soul an eternal life in company with the redeemed of all ages and climes and in the beatific vision of God. Whether this conception of its mission be true or false, the Roman Catholic Church is much more than Roman. The Roman tradition

[360] La Piana, *The Roman Church at the End of the Second Century*, p. 210.
[361] Fowler, *The Religious Experience of the Roman People*, pp. 459-465, calls attention to the pre-Christian connotation carried over into Christian usage in such words as *religio, pius, sanctus, sacer,* and *sacramentum.*

has entered into both its spirit and its form, but is only one and often not the most powerful ingredient.

It was through these five regional types of Christianity, Syrian-Persian-Nestorian, Syrian-Monophysite, Egyptian-Monophysite, Greek Orthodox, and Roman Catholic, that the faith was to spread in the thousand years between the close of the fifth and the close of the fifteenth century. All bore striking likenesses to one another, growing out of their common Catholic heritage. As we have seen, all acknowledged as canonical Scriptures made up of the Old and New Testaments. All had an episcopal organization, all had at least some of the sacraments. In all, monasteries had a part. Of the five, the first three were in regions which in the seventh century fell under Moslem Arab sway and so were compelled to live and work under the dominance of a victorious and aggressive Islam. The first two, moreover, had direct access only to peoples most of whom already professed advanced types of religion. The third touched more nearly primitive peoples up the narrow Nile corridor to the South, but from the animistic Negro folk of Africa was shut off by the Sahara. The fourth was always under the control of the state and in addition for centuries confronted Islam and finally became subject to Moslem rulers. On its northern frontiers, however, it faced folk of primitive cultures and religious beliefs and here it had opportunity to widen its boundaries. Of the five, the Roman Catholic form of Christianity enjoyed the fullest opportunity for expansion. It, too, had Islam on its southern border but never more than a minority of its adherents were subject to Moslem rulers, and alone of the five it permanently regained ground temporarily lost to the followers of the Prophet. Usually freer from state control than was the Greek Orthodox Church, it enjoyed more liberty to express its own genius. On the north, moreover, it had access to vigorous, semi-barbarous peoples who stood in awe of the culture with which Christianity was associated and who desired to assume it while they plundered the folk who possessed it.

In our hurried pilgrimage through the first five centuries of the spread of Christianity we have watched that faith moulded by element after element of its environment. Left to begin its career with a minimum of organization, without a literature, and with no formulæ with which to define and defend its content, and thrust into a world in which syncretism was the fashion, Christianity might well have seemed foredoomed to absorption and to lose whatever distinctiveness it may have inherited from the teaching and the story of the life, death, and resurrection of its founder. The primitive belief in the continued guidance of the Spirit seemed to lead in the same direction, for would not every convert interpret its supposed inward promptings in accordance with his past beliefs and experiences?

That Christianity was modified by many elements of its environment we have seen. The faith out of which it sprang, Judaism; the philosophic and religious atmosphere in which it long made its largest numerical gains, Hellenistic culture and the mystery cults; the other religions which it displaced; the popular festivals; the political structure of the Empire; the artistic and literary traditions of the various peoples from which converts came; the geographic and racial setting; the many individual leaders—all left their marks.

In response to these influences, now one and now another, or to varying combinations of these factors, Christianity took on many different forms. Among those which claimed to be heirs of the Christian tradition were groups who preserved more of the Jewish heritage than did the majority. Most of the many types of Gnosticism, on the other hand, made less of the Jewish background and fitted in more extensively with much of the current religious and intellectual atmosphere than did those who are usually thought of as Catholic Christians. The Marcionites denounced Judaism and all its works. The Montanists attempted to perpetuate and accentuate the prophetic and ecstatic features of early Christianity. Donatists and Novatians strove for more rigid adherence to standards of ethics nominally accepted by most Christians than the majority thought best. A religion, Manichæism, which was widely diffused both East and West, arose on the fringes of the Christian movement.

Early the majority of Christians were included in an Empire-wide fellowship which, while adopting a kind of via media between all the conflicting forces, sought to hold to the original message of Jesus and his Apostles and believed that it had done so. Even within this large body, however, external factors combined with internal ones to bring variations and divisions. Monasticism came into being and, while remaining within the Church, divided it into two main groups of Christians—those who thought of themselves as seeking to conform perfectly to the commands of Jesus and those whom they regarded as having in part compromised with the world. Division amounting eventually to actual schism took place for reasons which combined geography, race, and culture, with, usually, the added bitterness of differing theological views. So in Armenia, Persia, Syria, and Egypt national churches arose. Most of the Goths and Vandals and some affiliated German peoples adhered to Arianism. Between the Greek East and the Latin West fellowship, long precariously maintained, eventually came to an end.

Yet these many exterior forces and all the varying experiences and convictions of strong leaders did not succeed in erasing the effect of the impulse which had originally given rise to Christianity. None of the numerous forms of the faith was simply a combination of extraneous or later elements. On all the original impulse made a profound impression. In most it was the one factor in which the others found their unity and by which they were combined into an entirely fresh synthesis. Different though they were, the many movements which sprang out of the impulse given by Jesus had a striking family likeness which can be explained only on the basis of their common origin. We need not, and, indeed, must not, enter upon a discussion of which of the groups most nearly represented him. That would mean entanglement in ancient and highly controversial issues. It must be noted, however, that all the forms, except Manichæism, which propagated themselves in the next period, were offshoots of that Catholic Church which had professed to preserve, undiluted, and to put foremost the message of Jesus and of the original Apostles. It must also be remembered that the most authoritative records of the life and teachings of Jesus together with some of the writings of the leaders of the early Church had been collected and accorded canonical standing. As such they served as a norm, even if not the only one, by which doctrines and practices were supposedly judged. With whatever conscious or unconscious distortions or developments, the message and mission of Jesus were ostensibly kept central.

However, we must not attempt to disguise the plain fact: in the year 500 Christianity was not the same as at its inception. Thrust, still plastic, into the Mediterranean world, it had been largely shaped by its environment. Some of the features then acquired persisted into succeeding ages and were accorded sanctity and regarded as norms. Indeed, the vast majority of Christians in the centuries since A.D. 500 have been in churches whose creeds, ritual, and organization are lineal descendants of the Christianity which took form in the period which we have been describing. Would Christianity have been different had the original impulse appeared in some other cultural area—in India or China? Undoubtedly. How different we cannot know. In future generations, as its cultural environment changes or as it is introduced to non-Occidental peoples may it not acquire still other forms? Very probably. Some of the actual alterations we are to record in later volumes. Through all our story, however, we shall discover that the cultural environment of these initial centuries has left an indelible impress, sometimes weak but more frequently strong upon all that is later called Christianity. For better or for worse the Christianity of subsequent ages has borne the marks of the world and the cultures in which it was cradled.

Chapter VIII

TO A.D. 500. IN SUMMARY AND ANTICIPATION

AT THE outset of this work, it will be recalled, seven major questions were propounded: What was the Christianity which spread? Why did it spread? Why at times did it suffer reverses and on occasion meet only partial success? By what processes did it spread? What effect did it have upon its environment? What effect did the environment have upon Christianity? What bearing did the processes by which Christianity spread have upon the effect of Christianity upon its environment and of the environment upon Christianity?

As we reach the end of the first major period of the expansion of Christianity, we may do well to pause for a moment to see in retrospect the distance we have traversed, to note in summary fashion the answers which have been given to the first six questions, and to say a word concerning the seventh, for to that only scattered and incidental references have thus far been made. We should also remind ourselves of the factors which brought this period to an end and which ushered in the succeeding one and gave it distinctiveness.

The Christianity which spread, as we have seen, began as an offshoot of Judaism, the only one which ever succeeded in disengaging itself from the parent stock and pursuing a robust independent existence. To Judaism Christianity owed not only its monotheism, much of its ethics, and, if measured by bulk, the major portion of its Scriptures, but the many other characteristics which we have noted and contributions from the numerous religions and cultures which had touched and influenced Judaism. Through Judaism Christianity was an heir of the cultures and religions of Persia, Mesopotamia, and of the Mediterranean basin east of Italy. Yet Christianity, as its very name implies, owed its inception and its impelling and integrating impulses to Jesus and to the beliefs held about him. Among these were his teachings, his life and death, and the experiences of his early followers which led them to regard him as still living and with enhanced power and as touching believers through the Spirit and at least one of the sacraments. It was a faith of great enthusiasms and which gloried in the moral and spiritual transformation of individuals. It appealed to both sexes and to members of all classes and of many races.

From the outset it possessed a strong sense of the essential unity of all believers and a desire to give that unity tangible expression in a body bound together by a common faith and by love. Yet it also carried within itself the seeds of multitudinous variations and divisions. As the decades and centuries passed it gave birth to new forms, so that what was spreading in the year 100 was not the same as what was spreading in the year 50. So, too, by A.D. 500 still other changes and schisms had occurred.

For the expansion of Christianity a number of factors were accountable. Christianity had the good fortune to be born into the largest cultural centre of mankind, the Mediterranean world. By becoming the faith of the vast majority in that world it achieved a position of advantage for expansion into other areas of the globe. It came into that world at a period extraordinarily propitious for the spread of a new religion. Never before in the history of the race had conditions been so favourable for the acceptance of any one faith by so large a proportion of mankind. The formation of the Roman Empire had brought political unity to a larger number of civilized human beings than had ever over a long period acknowledged any one allegiance. The *pax Romana*, maintained so admirably during most of the first two centuries of the life of Christianity, the extensive commerce, the Roman roads, the freeing of the seas of pirates, the wide use of the two tongues, Greek and Latin, all furthered the dissemination of ideas through the Mediterranean basin. The very unity and the resulting interchange of cultures accelerated a loss of belief in many of the existing religious systems. Outwardly these were still imposing and were deemed essential to social coherence and political well-being. They had, however, failed to satisfy the inward needs of thousands of individuals. The conflicting philosophies brought scepticism and a desire for certainty through an intellectually acceptable divine revelation. A rising hunger for some faith which would insure a blissful immortality for the individual and, in some quarters, a movement for moral improvement prepared the way for a religion which would give assurance of a divine revelation, of immortality in fellowship with God, and of moral renewal and strength.

To meet this need many systems competed. Out of them all Christianity won partly because of its organization, with the fellowship and protection which the deracinated individuals of the Græco-Roman world craved, partly because of its inclusiveness, partly because of its happy combination of adaptability and intransigence, partly because it supplied better than any other what the ancient world was asking of religion and philosophy, partly because of its Jewish heritage, its moral earnestness and power, and its miracles, but chiefly because of the quality of the life and the death of Jesus and the experiences which followed among his disciples. In the last analysis it was from Jesus that those qualities stemmed which gave to Christianity its victory over its rivals.

During these five centuries Christianity suffered no major reverses comparable to those in later periods. To be sure, it encountered recurring persecutions, but in the Roman Empire none of these was severe enough or sufficiently prolonged to bring any great loss of territory. In one direction, eastward of the Roman Empire, in the Persian realm, Christianity met only limited success. Here a well-entrenched state religion offered effective resistance and, beginning with the fourth century, the fear that the now Christian Roman Empire would use the faith as a cloak for aggression strengthened official opposition.

Of the processes by which Christianity spread in these five centuries, and especially in the first three, we have all too little information. Missionaries who, like Paul, made the propagation of the faith their main passion undoubtedly had a large part. Prophets and professional teachers also had a share. Probably individual lay folk did something incidental to their everyday tasks. An extensive apologetic literature may have reached some, either directly or indirectly, by providing arguments which could be employed orally. The public address and attendance on services were of assistance. Catechetical instruction and careful testing of applicants helped to insure intelligent comprehension, sincerity, and approximation to the ethical standards of the Christian community. During the first three centuries, conversion seems to have been chiefly by individuals and families. Always it was primarily individual change rather than the complete transformation of society which Christians envisaged—except as that latter was expected to come in cataclysmic fashion by the sudden act of God. Yet mass movements there were. Towards the close of the third century they came in Armenia and in parts of Asia Minor. Then, in the fourth century, the Roman state took an increasingly friendly attitude and eventually commanded compulsion in the destruction of the pagan religions. This brought millions into the Church, and often from very superficial motives and without much knowledge of any but a few outward formalities of the Christian cult, some of the ethical requirements, and a hope of an immortal life of happiness.

Upon its environment Christianity had varying results. As we have more than once suggested, no thoroughgoing reconstruction of society by human effort was planned. Yet some effects were profound. The old cults, except Judaism, were swept away. The Graeco-Roman world, so stereotyped and decadent, was stimulated into the creation of the Christian Church and Christian theology. The Christian ministry, in many ways a new creation, came into existence. A Christian philosophy of history was developed. A new literary tradition was created. Some languages were given written form and others were stimulated to the production of the first voluminous literature which they had known. In several regions what would now be called nationalism was furthered, and in some assimilation to a dominant tongue and culture was hastened. Christians objected vigorously to certain features of the life about them, especially to most of the prominent amusements. In the abolishment of a number of these, notably the exhibitions of the amphitheatre, Christianity had a part, even though not always the most important one. Although it did not directly attack slavery, Christianity joined with other forces which were ameliorating the lot of slaves. It altered family customs and sought, not always successfully, to revolutionize sex *mores*. Probably it affected warfare but little, in either its extent or its nature. Christianity fostered physical care for the poor, the ill, the orphans, the widows, and others who were underprivileged and had suffered from the existing social order. This philanthropy was conducted on a huge scale by the gifts of the many in a fashion never before equalled. Among individuals Christianity sought thoroughgoing moral transformation. The standards it enjoined were in sharp contrast with the practice of the majority in the Mediterranean world, as they were, for that matter, with that of the rest of humankind. These standards the Christian community sought valiantly to enforce. Even in the most exemplary, however, a frank failure fully to attain the ideals was sometimes acknowledged, and for the masses of Christians the disparity between profession and practice was even more marked. This lack of accord between goal and attainment was, however, due in part to the vast difference between the objectives and the prevailing customs. Nor does it argue an entire lack of effect. Changes in habits were wrought in thousands of instances. In altering the ethical tenor of men's lives Christianity proved one of the most powerful agencies which the race had thus far known.

Christianity was modified by its environment. Cast, without literature or formal creeds and almost without organization, into a world where reciprocal borrowing was a highly respected religious custom, this new faith took on colour from the religions and philosophies with which it was thrown in intimate contact. It was also affected by the political structures, races, and geographic features of its surroundings. In some of its forms it seemed to minimize its own historic past. In those in which it prevailed, however, while showing markedly the effects of its environment and displaying much development, it clung tenaciously to the traditions in which it had been cradled and took as standard what it believed had been handed down from Jesus and the circles of his intimate friends.

Of the seven major questions which we have propounded, the last is probably the most difficult to answer. Partly for that reason it must be dismissed with a few brief comments. First of all, as to the effect upon environment of the methods of spread, we need to note that at the outset Christianity was propagated by private individuals, at first a small minority, who were seeking to reach other individuals and to build them up into a community in the world yet not of the world. It was hoped within that community to attain Christian ideals. In the sharp antithesis between the Church and the world, the latter was often thought of as foredoomed to complete destruction by God, to be replaced, also through divine fiat, by a perfect world order. Consequently, as we have suggested, no campaign was carried on for the eradication of customs and institutions contrary to the Christian ethic. Some institutions and practices were forcefully denounced, notably polytheism and many traditions which the Christian deemed immoral. In so far as converts were withdrawn from society into the Christian community, the existing order was weakened. Until the time of Constantine, however, Christians were so much in the minority that probably their actions had done little to modify the structure of society in which the vast majority, non-Christians, passed their lives. Non-Christians denounced and persecuted Christians as a threat to the existing order. Their charge seems never to have been, however, that Christians were deliberately planning to upset the Empire or the economic or social fabric. They contended, rather, that by being "atheists," completely denying the accepted gods and cults, Christians were threatening the continuation of that divine favour with which the Empire had been built and without which it could not hope to go on. Christians disavowed any attempt to overthrow the Empire, but insisted that to their prayers and the presence of their faith was due the prosperity of the first two centuries of the Christian era. Later, when decay became obvious, the Christian apologists held that the faith they professed was conserving society.

Still later, when Christianity was adopted by the state, and the government furthered its spread, obviously the official Church continued its earlier policy of not contemplating revolution. With the aid of the state it rooted out all opposing faiths except Judaism and it sought to reform morals, but this latter was not beyond what most high-minded pagans had advocated. The Church, indeed, became a conservative force in an age of disintegration. In the West especially, such of the old as survived did so largely under its ægis. Monks and some of the more ascetic Christian sects demanded of themselves and those who would join them a more or less complete renunciation of the world, but never did they seek to reorganize it. They abandoned it as hopelessly evil.

The methods by which Christianity spread, then, often worked a revolution in the lives of individuals and gave rise to communities which sought, in greater or less separation from society, to practice ideals which differed from those of the world. However, such general social results as followed were not planned, but were incidental to changes in individuals.

What we know of the results of the methods of spread upon Christianity itself and upon the effect of the environment on Christianity can also quickly be stated. Before Constantine Christianity remained a group of communities seeking to draw individuals to their fellowship, but leading, so far as possible, self-contained lives and with the minimum of intercourse with the surrounding world. On the part of some groups claiming a Christian origin, among them a few of the Gnostic schools, this was not the case. These favoured accommodation to the world. Of the majority, however, the opposite was true. This attempt to win individuals out of the world into a community with distinct standards helped to give strength and solidarity to the Church. It helped to make the Church much less responsive to outside influences than it might otherwise have been.

When, beginning with Constantine, the state reversed its policy and came to the support of the Church and assisted it in eliminating its religious rivals, the effect of the altered method of spread was fairly obvious and has again and again been noted. The multitudes who flocked into the Church brought with them from their pre-Christian environment customs and beliefs against which the official Church might struggle, but which it was powerless to eliminate. At times ecclesiastical leaders seem deliberately to have given the blessing of the Church to customs of pagan origin freed from some of the features too obviously in contradiction of Christianity. The Church, in alliance with a state of pre-Christian origin and flooded by those who had come over light-heartedly from paganism, was found acquiescing to much in its membership and in the society which it now embraced within its fold which was quite antagonistic to its professed principles. Before Constantine, the Church had striven, by and large, to keep itself aloof from the world and so had left the latter undisturbed. Beginning with Constantine, except for the more palpably antagonistic religious cults, it still allowed the world mostly to go its own course, but it had now taken into its membership those who made up this world. As a result of this wholesale conversion with its tolerances came reaction. Protesting groups arose, before Constantine usually in the guise of such sects as the Donatists and Novatians, and after Constantine chiefly in the monastic movement. Indeed, in one sense, although this is by no means the complete explanation, monasticism was the product, by the process of reaction, of some of the missionary methods of the Catholic Church of the third, fourth, and fifth centuries.

At the close of its fifth century of expansion Christianity was in a very different position than at its outset. From being one of the smallest of Jewish sects, it had become the religion professed by the majority in the most populous of the cultural areas of mankind. Never in the history of the race had so complete a religious revolution been wrought in so short a time among so large a proportion of civilized man. Christianity was almost entirely confined to this Mediterranean world, but in Ireland, the Persian Empire, Arabia, Armenia, the Caucasus, the west coast of the Red Sea, and possibly in India it had begun to move outside these borders. It was principally represented by off-shoots of an earlier Catholic Church—in Armenia, in the Persian Empire, in Syria, in Egypt, in the Greek East, and in the Latin West. It was through all but the first of these branches that it was chiefly to expand in the next thousand years. In whatever form Christianity spread, however, the active missionaries were usually to be monks. It was a religion seen through the eyes of monasticism which was propagated.

By the year 500 the world in which Christianity had achieved these triumphs was disappearing. Internal weaknesses and pressure from without were disrupting the Roman Empire and bringing to an end the Græco-Roman culture in which Christianity had been born and where it had lived its lusty youth. A new age was dawning. In the western portions of the Mediterranean basin barbarians from the North were destroying much of the old regime and were setting up new states. From the South-east another irruption was soon to come, overwhelming Arabia, Persia, Syria, Palestine, Egypt, North Africa, and most of the Iberian peninsula and bringing with it a faith, itself bearing traces of Christian influence, which, though often scornfully tolerant, was the most obdurate and dangerous foe which Christianity had so far encountered. Given this new and strange world, could Christianity continue to expand? Could it even continue to exist? If it persisted and spread into new areas, could it mould the new age and its peoples, or would it be itself made over into new forms which, while perpetuating the name, would have little real kinship with the past? To these issues we must address ourselves in the next volume.

BIBLIOGRAPHIES

A S WILL quickly be seen, the following bibliographies are arranged by chapters. Under each chapter a bibliography is given of the works cited in that chapter. Titles are listed in the order in which they are first mentioned in the footnotes. Within the bibliography of a given chapter each title referred to in the footnotes of that chapter is cited once but only once. In the case of some of the well-known sources no bibliographical notation has been deemed necessary. For most of these the texts can be found in J. P. Migne, *Patrologiæ . . . Latinæ* (Paris, 221 vols., 1844-1864) and J. P. Migne, *Patrologiæ . . . Græcæ* (Paris, 161 vols., 1857-1866). For a large proportion of the early Christian documents cited translations are in *The Ante-Nicene Fathers*, edited by A. Roberts and James Donaldson (the American reprint and revision of the Edinburgh edition, by A. C. Coxe; Buffalo, The Christian Literature Publishing Co., 10 vols., 1885-1887), and in *A Select Library of Nicene and Post-Nicene Fathers of the Christian Church*, New York (The Christian Literature Co., first series, 14 vols., 1886-1890, second series, 14 vols., 1890-1900). In many instances the English translation of the title rather than the original title is used.

CHAPTER I

The pre-Christian development of religion. Arthur Keith, *The Antiquity of Man* (London, Williams and Norgate, 2 vols., 1925); a standard work. George Grant MacCurdy, *The Coming of Man. Pre-Man and Pre-Historic Man* (New York, The University Society, 1932, pp. 156); by a well known specialist in the field. George Grant MacCurdy, *Human Origins. A Manual of Pre-History* (New York, D. Appleton and Co., 2 vols., 1924). Arthur Keith, *New Discoveries Relating to the Antiquity of Man* (London, Williams and Norgate, 1931, pp. 512); also by an outstanding expert. V. Gordon Childe, *New Light on the Most Ancient East. The Oriental Prelude to European Prehistory* (New York, D. Appleton and Co., 1934, pp. xviii, 327); by a professor of prehistoric archæology in Edinburgh University. James Henry Breasted, *The Dawn of Conscience* (New York, Charles Scribner's Sons, 1933, pp. xxv, 431); semi-popular, by an eminent Egyptologist. K. S. Latourette, *The Chinese, Their History and Culture* (New York, The Macmillan Company, 2 vols., 1934); a general survey.

The Græco-Roman world into which Christianity was born: general. M. Rostovtzeff, *A History of the Ancient World,* translated from the Russian by J. D. Duff (Oxford, The Clarendon Press, 2 vols., 1930); by an eminent authority. M. Rostovtzeff, *The Social and Economic History of the Roman Empire* (Oxford, The Clarendon Press, 1926, pp. xxv, 695); a standard work. Arthur Cushman McGiffert, *A History of Christianity in the Apostolic Age* (New York, Charles Scribner's Sons, 1897, pp. xii, 681); long standard, but in need of revision to take account of recent scholarship. Ludwig Friedländer, *Roman Life and Manners under the Early Empire,* translated by L. A. Magnus from the seventh edition (London, George Routledge and Sons, 3 vols., no date). Adolf Harnack, *The Mission and Expansion of Christianity in the First Three Centuries,* translated and edited by James Moffatt (New York, G. P. Putnam's Sons, 2d ed., 2 vols., 1908); authoritative. Baron Descamps, editor, *Histoire Générale Comparée des Missions* (Paris, Librairie Plon, 1932, pp. viii, 760); a useful handbook by a number of Roman Catholic scholars. Samuel Dill, *Roman Society from Nero to Marcus Aurelius* (London, Macmillan and Co., 1904, pp. xxii, 639); standard.

The Græco-Roman world into which Christianity was born: morals, philosophies, and religions. S. Angus, *The Mystery Religions and Christianity* (New York, Charles Scribner's Sons, 1925, pp. xvi, 357); scholarly, with a pro-Christian bias. Shirley Jackson Case, *The Social Origins of Christianity* (The University of Chicago Press, 1923, pp. vii, 263); by a well-known specialist of markedly liberal tendencies. Harold R. Willoughby, *Pagan Regeneration. A Study of Mystery Initiations in the Græco-Roman World* (The University of Chicago Press, 1929, pp. ix, 307); a semi-popular, useful summary of existing authorities. Gilbert Murray, *Five Stages of Greek Religion* (New York, The Columbia University Press, 1925, pp. 276); by an eminent classicist; a revised edition of his *Four Stages of Greek Religion.* James Henry Breasted, *Ancient Times* (Boston, Ginn and Co., 1916, pp. xx, 742); an elementary textbook by a distinguished specialist. E. G. Hardy, *Christianity and the Roman Government. A Study in Imperial Administration* (London, George Allen and Unwin, 1925—reprint of the 1894 edition—pp. xiii, 161); carefully done, with no extreme views. Elmer Truesdell Merrill, *Essays in Early Christian History* (London, Macmillan and Co., 1924, pp. viii, 337); by a professor of Latin in the University of Chicago. *Epictetus, The Discourses and Manual, together with Fragments of His Writings,* translated with introduction and notes by P. E. Matheson (Oxford, The Clarendon Press, 2 vols., 1916). A. D. Nock, *Conversion. The Old and the New in Religion from Alexander the Great to Augustine of Hippo* (Oxford University Press, 1933, pp. xii, 309); competent, with some fresh points of view. Lewis Richard Farnell, *Outline-History of Greek Religion* (London, Duckworth and Co., 1921, pp. 160); a short manual by an eminent authority. T. R. Glover, *The Conflict of Religions in the Early Roman Empire* (London, Methuen and Co., 1909, pp. vii, 359); charmingly written, pro-Christian, based upon wide reading. *Plutarch's Morals. Ethical Essays,* translated by Arthur Richard Shilleto (London, George Bell and Sons, 1898, pp. ix, 408). *Plutarch's Morals. Theosophical Essays,* translated by C. W. King (London, George Bell and Sons, 1898, pp. xii, 287). George La Piana, *Foreign Groups in Rome during the First Three Centuries of the Empire* (Harvard University Press, 1927; from *Harvard Theological Review,* Oct., 1927, vol. xx, pp. 183-403); thorough and careful. W. Warde Fowler, *The Religious*

Experience of the Roman People from the Earliest Times to the Age of Augustus (London, Macmillan and Co., 1911, pp. xviii, 534); the Gifford Lectures for 1909-1910. Lily Ross Taylor, *The Divinity of the Roman Emperor* (Middletown, Conn., American Philological Association, 1931, pp. xv, 296); well done. Kenneth Scott, *The Identification of Augustus with Romulus-Quirinus* in *Transactions and Proceedings of the American Philological Association,* vol. xlvi, pp. 82-105. Shirley Jackson Case, *The Evolution of Early Christianity. A Genetic Story of First Century Christianity in Relation to Its Religious Environment* (The University of Chicago Press, 1914, pp. ix, 385); especially useful for its bibliographies. H. Leclercq, *L'Afrique Chrétienne* (Paris, Librairie Victor Lecoffre, 2 vols., 1904); based on extensive research. Gerhard Uhlhorn, *The Conflict of Christianity with Heathenism,* edited and translated by E. C. Smyth and C. J. H. Ropes (New York, Charles Scribner's Sons, 1879, pp. 508); from a strongly Christian point of view. Erwin R. Goodenough, *The Theology of Justin Martyr* (Jena, Frommannsche Buchhandlung, 1923, pp. viii, 320); by a competent specialist. W. R. Halliday, *The Pagan Background of Early Christianity* (The University Press of Liverpool, 1925, pp. xvi, 334); careful, semi-popular lectures. E. Zeller, *The Stoics, Epicureans and Sceptics,* translated by O. J. Reichel (London, Longmans, Green and Co., 1870, pp. xix, 548); based upon extensive reading in the sources. Thomas Whittaker, *The Neo-Platonists. A Study in the History of Hellenism* (Cambridge University Press, 2d ed., 1918, pp. xv, 318); one of the best accounts of its subject. E. Vernon Arnold, *Roman Stoicism* (Cambridge University Press, 1911, pp. ix, 468); a handbook with extensive references to the sources. *The Thoughts of Marcus Aurelius,* translated by John Jackson (Oxford University Press, 1928, pp. xx, 135). Leonard Alston, *Stoic and Christian in the Second Century* (London, Longmans, Green and Co., 1906, pp. lx, 147). Edwin Hatch, *The Influence of Greek Ideas and Usages upon the Christian Church* (London, Williams and Norgate, 1890, pp. xxiii, 359). Williams Ralph Inge, *The Philosophy of Plotinus* (New York, Longmans, Green and Co., 2 vols., 1923). Shirley Jackson Case, *Experience with the Supernatural in Early Christian Times* (New York, The Century Co., 1929, pp. vii, 341). Franz Cumont, *Astrology and Religion among the Greeks and Romans* (New York, G. P. Putnam's Sons, 1912, pp. xxvii, 208); by a distinguished specialist. Franz Cumont, *The Oriental Religions in Roman Paganism,* translated from the second French edition (Chicago, The Open Court Publishing Co., 1911, pp. xxiv, 298).

The Mystery Cults. H. A. A. Kennedy, *St. Paul and the Mystery-Religions* (London, Hodder and Stoughton, 1913, pp. xvii, 311); scholarly, inclined to discount the alleged influence of the mystery religions upon Paul. S. Angus, *The Religious Quests of the Græco-Roman World* (New York, Charles Scribner's Sons, 1929, pp. xx, 444); carefully done, with a pro-Christian bias. John Baillie, *And the Life Everlasting* (New York, Charles Scribner's Sons, 1933, pp. xvi, 350); a Christian view of immortality. R. Reitzenstein, *Die hellenistischen Mysterienreligionen nach ihren Grundgedanken und Wirkungen* (Leipzig, B. G. Teubner, 3d ed., 1927, pp. viii, 438). Erwin Rohde, *Psyche. The Cult of Souls and Belief in Immortality among the Greeks,* translated from the eighth edition by W. B. Hillis (New York, Harcourt, Brace and Co., 1925, pp. xvi, 626); a standard work. Lewis Richard Farnell, *The Cults of the Greek States* (Oxford, The Clarendon Press, 5 vols., 1896-

1909); a standard work. F. A. Spencer, *Beyond Damascus. A Biography of Paul the Tarsian* (New York, Harper & Brothers, 1934, pp. xiii, 466); in a popular style, based upon extensive reading. Jane Ellen Harrison, *Prolegomena to the Study of Greek Religion* (Cambridge University Press, 1903, pp. xxii, 680); scholarly, illustrated. W. K. C. Guthrie, *Orpheus and Greek Religion. A Study of the Orphic Movement* (London, Methuen and Co., 1935, pp. xix, 287); excellent. W. M. Ramsay, *The Cities and Bishoprics of Phrygia, being an Essay on the Local History of Phrygia from the Earliest Times to the Turkish Conquest* (Oxford, The Clarendon Press, 2 vols., 1895, 1897); based upon prolonged archæological investigation. J. G. Frazer, *Adonis Attis Osiris* (Part IV of *The Golden Bough,* London, Macmillan and Co., 1907, pp. xix, 452). Franz Cumont, *The Mysteries of Mithra,* translated from the second revised French edition by T. J. McCormack (Chicago, The Open Court Publishing Co., 1903); semi-popular lectures by an outstanding authority based upon his large work, *Textes et Monuments Figurés aux Mystères de Mithra.* A. S. Geden, *Select Passages Illustrating Mithraism* (London, Society for Promoting Christian Knowledge, 1925, pp. vi, 87); drawn largely from Cumont. Kirsopp Lake, *Landmarks in the History of Early Christianity* (London, Macmillan and Co., 1920, pp. x, 147); semi-popular lectures. T. R. Glover, *The Influence of Christ in the Ancient World* (Yale University Press, 1929, pp. 122).

Hermeticism. C. H. Dodd, *The Bible and the Greeks* (London, Hodder and Stoughton, 1935, pp. xv, 264); excellent. Walter Scott, *Hermetica. The Greek and Latin Writings which Contain Religious or Philosophic Teachings Ascribed to Hermes Trismegistus, edited with English translations and notes* (Oxford, The Clarendon Press, 4 vols., 1924-1936); the third and fourth volumes posthumous; the standard English work. Jos. Kroll, *Die Lehren des Hermes Trismegistos* (in *Beiträge zur Geschichte der Philosophie des Mittelalters,* edited by Clemens Baeumker, vol. xii, Münster i.W., Aschendorffsche Verlagsbuchhandlung, 1914, pp. xii, 441); excellent.

Judaism. George Adams Smith, *Atlas of the Historical Geography of the Holy Land* (London, Hodder and Stoughton, 1915, pp. xxxvi, 54); a standard work. W. O. E. Oesterley and Theodore H. Robinson, *A History of Israel* (Oxford, The Clarendon Press, 2 vols., 1932); excellent. Charles Foster Kent, *A History of the Hebrew People* (New York, Charles Scribner's Sons, 2d ed., 2 vols., 1898); a popular account. Henry Preserved Smith, *The Religion of Israel. An Historical Study* (New York, Charles Scribner's Sons, 1914, pp. x, 369). Christopher Dawson, *Progress and Religion. An Historical Enquiry* (New York, Longmans, Green and Co., 1929, pp. xvii, 254); by a Roman Catholic, very suggestive. George Foot Moore, *Judaism in the First Centuries of the Christian Era. The Age of the Tannaim* (Harvard University Press, 2 vols., 1927); a standard work by a distinguished scholar. W. O. E. Oesterley and G. H. Box, *The Religion and Worship of the Synagogue* (London, Sir Isaac Pitman and Sons, 1907, pp. xv, 443); scholarly, for non-Jewish readers. Hans Lietzmann, *Geschichte der alten Kirche. 1. Die Anfänge* (Berlin, Walter de Gruyter und Co., 1932, pp. vii, 323); semi-popular. R. H. Charles, *Religious Development between the Old and the New Testaments* (New York, Henry Holt and Co., pp. 256); one of the Home University Library series. R. H. Charles, *A Critical History of the Doctrine of the Future Life in Israel, in*

Judaism, and in Christianity (London, Adam and Charles Black, 1899, pp. x, 428); the Jowett Lectures for 1898-1899; the result of more than a decade of study of the sources. Emil Schürer, *Geschichte des jüdischen Volkes im Zeitalter Jesu Christi* (Leipzig, J. C. Hinrichs'sche Buchhandlung, 3d and 4th ed., 3 vols., 1898-1901); a standard. Burnett Hillman Streeter, *The Four Gospels. A Study of Origins Treating of the Manuscript Traditions, Sources, Authorship, and Dates* (New York, The Macmillan Co., 1925, pp. xiv, 622); by a distinguished specialist. W. O. E. Oesterley, *The Jewish Background of the Christian Liturgy* (Oxford, The Clarendon Press, 1925, pp. 243); scholarly, arguing for an extensive influence of Jewish upon Christian liturgy. R. H. Charles, *The Testaments of the Twelve Patriarchs*, translated and edited (London, Adam and Charles Black, 1908, pp. xciv, 247). Ernest F. Scott, *The Kingdom of God in the New Testament* (New York, The Macmillan Co., 1931, pp. 197); by a highly esteemed New Testament scholar. N. Levison, *The Jewish Background of Christianity. A Manual of the Political, Religious, Social and Literary Life of the Jews from 586 B.C. to A.D. 1* (Edinburgh, T. and T. Clark, 1932, pp. xvi, 205); by a Christian, a converted Jew, favourable to Judaism. R. H. Charles, *The Book of Enoch or I Enoch*, translated (Oxford, The Clarendon Press, revised ed., 1912, pp. cx, 331); a standard edition. Shailer Mathews, *The Messianic Hope in the New Testament* (The University of Chicago Press, 1905, pp. xx, 338); a semi-popular summary from a liberal, historical standpoint. Albert Schweitzer, *The Quest of the Historical Jesus. A Critical Study of its Progress from Reimarus to Wrede*, translated by W. Montgomery with a preface by F. C. Burkitt (London, Adam and Charles Black, 1910, pp. x, 410); a famous work emphasizing the apocalyptic side of Jesus' teaching. *Josephus, with an English Translation*, by H. St. J. Thackeray (London, William Heineman, 5 vols., 1926-1934, to be 8 vols. in all); the fifth volume by Ralph Marcus; Greek text, English translation, and notes. *The Works of Flavius Josephus*, Whiston's translation revised by A. R. Shilleto (London, George Bell and Sons, 5 vols., 1889-1890); without the Greek text. Benjamin W. Bacon, *The Gospel of the Hellenists*, edited by Carl H. Kraeling (New York, Henry Holt and Company, 1933, pp. xiii, 432); a posthumous work of a distinguished New Testament scholar. Carl H. Kraeling, *The Jewish Community at Antioch* (New Haven, Antioch Index Publications, No. I, 1932, pp. 31). H. A. A. Kennedy, *Philo's Contribution to Religion* (London, Hodder and Stoughton, 1919, pp. xi, 245); scholarly, with a pro-Christian bias. Arthur Cushman McGiffert, *A History of Christian Thought* (New York, Charles Scribner's Sons, 2 vols., 1932, 1933); by a liberal Protestant scholar. Kirsopp Lake, *The Earlier Epistles of St. Paul. Their Motive and Origin* (London, Rivingtons, 1911, pp. xi, 466); by an eminent New Testament scholar, an advanced radical in some of his views. Erwin R. Goodenough, *By Light, Light. The Mystic Gospel of Hellenistic Judaism* (Yale University Press, 1935, pp. xv, 436); by a competent scholar setting forth hypotheses which have not yet won general acceptance.

CHAPTER II

Jesus. Albert Schweitzer, *The Quest of the Historical Jesus. A Critical Study of its Progress from Reimarus to Wrede*, translated by W. Montgomery, with a preface by F. C. Burkitt (London, Adam and Charles Black, 1910, pp. x, 410); a famous work whose appearance caused a stir in the circles of New Testament scholarship. Shirley Jackson Case, *The Historicity of Jesus* (The University of Chicago Press, 1912, pp. vii, 352); by a liberal scholar. Benjamin W. Bacon, *The Story of Jesus and the Beginnings of the Church. A Valuation of the Synoptic Record for History and for Religion* (New York, The Century Co., 1927, pp. viii, 326); by a distinguished New Testament scholar with radical views. Shirley Jackson Case, *Jesus: a New Biography* (The University of Chicago Press, 1927, pp. ix, 453); containing some radical positions. Charles Cutler Torrey, *The Four Gospels. A New Translation* (New York, Harper & Brothers, 1933, pp. xii, 331); by a thorough and competent scholar and based on the conviction that the accepted texts of all four Gospels are Greek translations of Aramaic originals. Frank Chamberlain Porter, *The Mind of Christ in Paul* (New York, Charles Scribner's Sons, 1930, pp. xiii, 323); a work of ripe scholarship and deep religious insight. T. R. Glover, *The Jesus of History* (New York, Association Press, 1917, pp. xiv, 225); a sympathetic, brilliantly written interpretation. George Foot Moore, *Judaism in the First Centuries of the Christian Era. The Age of the Tannaim* (Harvard University Press, 2 vols., 1927); the major work of a great scholar. Hans Lietzmann, *Geschichte der Alten Kirche. I. Die Anfänge* (Berlin, Walter de Gruyter und Co., 1932, pp. vii, 323); a semi-popular summary. F. C. Burkitt, *Christian Beginnings* (University of London Press, 1924, pp. 152); three semi-popular lectures by a distinguished New Testament scholar. Karl Kundsin, *Topologische Überlieferungsstoffe im Johannes-Evangelium* (Göttingen, Vanderhoeck und Ruprecht, 1925, pp. 80). Benjamin Wisner Bacon, *Studies in Matthew* (New York, Henry Holt and Company, 1930, pp. xxvi, 533); by an eminent authority. Ernest F. Scott, *The Kingdom of God in the New Testament* (New York, The Macmillan Company, 1931, pp. 197); by a competent scholar. Arthur Cushman McGiffert, *A History of Christianity in the Apostolic Age* (New York, Charles Scribner's Sons, 1897, pp. xii, 681); long a standard, but now in need of revision to take account of recent scholarship. Shailer Mathews, *The Messianic Hope in the New Testament* (The University of Chicago Press, 1905, pp. xx, 338); from a liberal, Protestant, historical standpoint. R. H. Charles, *Religious Development between the Old and the New Testaments* (New York, Henry Holt and Company, pp. 256); in the Home University Library series. Vladimir G. Simkhovitch, *Toward an Understanding of Jesus and Other Historical Studies* (New York, The Macmillan Co., 1921, pp. vii, 165); an interesting interpretation based upon Jewish nationalism in the time of Jesus. Lionel Curtis, *Civitas Dei* (London, Macmillan and Co., 1934, pp. xxiii, 297); by a brilliant non-expert. Gerald Friedländer, *The Jewish Sources of the Sermon on the Mount* (London, George Routledge and Sons, 1911, pp. xxix, 301); from an orthodox Jewish standpoint, critical of Jesus and of Christianity. C. G. Montefiore, *Rabbinic Literature and Gospel Teachings* (London, Macmillan and Co., 1930, pp. xxii, 442); by a liberal, distinguished Jewish scholar. Ernest F. Scott, *The Gospel and Its Tributaries* (New York, Charles Scribner's Sons, 1930, pp. 295); competent, semi-popular. Johannes Weiss, *Das Urchristentum* (Göttingen, Vanderhoeck und Ruprecht, 1914, 1917, pp. iv, ix, 681); a standard work.

The earliest Christianity. Thomas M. Lindsay, *The Church and the Ministry in the Early Centuries* (London, Hodder and Stoughton, 4th ed., 1910, pp. xxii, 398);

the author believes in a visible Catholic Church and a valid ministry. T. R. Glover, *The Conflict of Religions in the Early Roman Empire* (London, Methuen and Co., 1909, pp. vii, 359); charmingly written; based upon wide reading. James Hardy Ropes, *The Apostolic Age in the Light of Modern Criticism* (New York, Charles Scribner's Sons, 1906, pp. viii, 327); by an excellent scholar. Charles Cutler Torrey, *The Composition and Date of Acts* (Harvard University Press, 1916, pp. 72); contending for an Aramaic original for the first fifteen chapters of Acts. Arthur Cushman McGiffert, *The God of the Early Christians* (New York, Charles Scribner's Sons, 1924, pp. 200); by a distinguished specialist. Shirley Jackson Case, *The Evolution of Early Christianity. A Genetic Study of First-Century Christianity in Relation to Its Religious Environment* (The University of Chicago Press, 1914, pp. ix, 385). Benjamin Wisner Bacon, *Stephen's Speech. Its Argument and Doctrinal Relationship,* in *Biblical and Semitic Studies* (Yale Bicentennial Publication, 1901), pp. 213-276. Benjamin Wisner Bacon, *The Founding of the Church* (Boston, The Pilgrim Press, 1909, pp. 89). R. Reitzenstein, *Die Vorgeschichte der christlichen Taufe* (Leipzig, B. G. Teubner, 1929, pp. vii, 399).

CHAPTER III

For the period covered by the entire chapter the standard work is Adolf Harnack, *Die Mission und Ausbreitung des Christentums in den ersten drei Jahrhunderten* (Leipzig, J. C. Hinrichs'sche Buchhandlung, 1902, pp. xii, 561). Citations are from the English edition, *The Mission and Expansion of Christianity in the First Three Centuries,* translated and edited by James Moffatt (New York, G. P. Putnam's Sons, 2d ed., 2 vols., 1908).

The Apostolic Age. An Outline of Christianity. The Story of Our Civilization (New York, Bethlehem Publishers, 5 vols., 1926); semi-popular, by various authors, most of them well-known specialists in their respective fields. Johannes Weiss, *Das Urchristentum* (Göttingen, Vanderhoeck und Ruprecht, 1914, 1917, pp. iv, ix, 681); a standard work. F. C. Burkitt, *Christian Beginnings* (University of London Press, 1924, pp. 152); three semi-popular lectures by a distinguished expert. Burnett Hillman Streeter, *The Four Gospels. A Study of Origins, Treating of the Manuscript Traditions, Sources, Authorship, and Dates* (New York, The Macmillan Company, 1925, pp. xiv, 622); by a well-known scholar. C. H. Dodd, *The Epistle of Paul to the Romans* (New York, Ray Long and Richard R. Smith, 1932, pp. xxxv, 246); competent. Arthur Cushman McGiffert, *A History of Christianity in the Apostolic Age* (New York, Charles Scribner's Sons, 1897, pp. xii, 681); standard, but in need of revision to take account of later scholarship. A. D. Nock, *Conversion. The Old and the New in Religion from Alexander the Great to Augustine of Hippo* (Oxford University Press, 1933, pp. xii, 309); competent, with some fresh points of view. E. S. Bouchier, *A Short History of Antioch 300 B.C.-A.D. 1268* (Oxford, Basil Blackwell, 1921, pp. xii, 324); based in part on the sources. C. R. Haines, *Heathen Contact with Christianity during Its First Century and a Half, being All References to Christianity Recorded in Pagan Writings during that Period* (Cambridge,

Deighton, Bell and Co., 1923, pp. 124); convenient. Adolf Deissmann, *Paul. A Study in Social and Religious History,* translated by William E. Wilson (London, Hodder and Stoughton, 2d ed., 1926, pp. xv, 323); a standard work by an expert. T. R. Glover, *Paul of Tarsus* (New York, George H. Doran Co., 1925, pp. 256); popularly written by a competent scholar. F. J. Foakes-Jackson, *The Rise of Gentile Christianity* (New York, George H. Doran Co., 1927, pp. xiii, 231); semi-popular, by a well-known scholar. C. G. Montefiore, *Judaism and St. Paul. Two Essays* (London, Max Goschen, 1914, pp. 240); by a distinguished liberal Jewish scholar. Charles E. Raven, *Jesus and the Gospel of Love* (New York, Henry Holt and Company, 1931, pp. 452); by a scholar-preacher. Albert Schweitzer, *The Mysticism of Paul the Apostle,* translated by William Montgomery, with a prefatory note by F. C. Burkitt (London, A. and C. Black, 1931, pp. xv, 411); arguing for the dominance in Paul of the eschatological outlook. F. A. Spencer, *Beyond Damascus. A Biography of Paul the Tarsian* (New York, Harper & Brothers, 1934, pp. xiii, 466); written in a popular style; based upon extensive reading. Hans Lietzmann, *Geschichte der alten Kirche. I. Die Anfänge* (Berlin, Walter de Gruyter und Co., 1932, pp. vii, 323); a standard, semi-popular summary. Benjamin Wisner Bacon, *The Story of St. Paul. A Comparison of the Acts and Epistles* (Boston, Houghton Mifflin and Co., 1904, pp. x, 392); by a distinguished New Testament scholar. James Hardy Ropes, *The Apostolic Age in the Light of Modern Criticism* (New York, Charles Scribner's Sons, 1906, pp. viii, 327); by a competent scholar. Frank Chamberlain Porter, *The Mind of Christ in Paul* (New York, Charles Scribner's Sons, 1930, pp. xiii, 323); a work of ripe scholarship and deep religious insight. *The Ante-Nicene Fathers. Translations of the Fathers down to A.D. 325,* edited by Alexander Roberts and James Donaldson. American reprint of the Edinburgh edition, revised and rearranged, with brief prefaces and occasional notes by A. Cleveland Coxe (Buffalo, The Christian Literature Publishing Co., 10 vols., 1885-1887); standard English translations. Hans Lietzmann, *Petrus und Paulus in Rom* (Berlin, Walter de Gruyter und Co., 2d ed., 1927, pp. viii, 315); critical, careful, thorough. W. M. Ramsay, *The Church in the Roman Empire before A.D. 170* (New York, G. P. Putnam's Sons, 1893, pp. xv, 494). Kirsopp Lake, *The Earlier Epistles of St. Paul, Their Motive and Origin* (London, Rivingtons, 1911, pp. xi, 466); by an eminent New Testament scholar with advanced radical views. Shirley Jackson Case, *The Evolution of Early Christianity. A Genetic Study of First-Century Christianity in Relation to Its Religious Environment* (The University of Chicago Press, 1914, pp. ix, 385); especially useful for its summaries and bibliographies. *The Church History of Eusebius,* translated . . . by A. C. McGiffert, in *A Select Library of Nicene and Post-Nicene Fathers,* vol. i (New York, The Christian Literature Society, 1890, pp. x, 403); a standard translation of this most famous of early Church histories, a work especially valuable for its incorporation and use of earlier sources. Benjamin Wisner Bacon, *The Gospel of the Hellenists,* edited by Carl H. Kraeling (New York, Henry Holt and Company, 1933, pp. xii, 432); a posthumous work of a distinguished New Testament scholar. J. Schmidlin, *Katholische Missionsgeschichte* (Steyl, Missionsdruckerei, 1924, pp. xi, 598); by an outstanding Roman Catholic authority on missions. Karl Müller, *Kirchengeschichte* (Freiburg i.B., J. C. B. Mohr, 2 vols., 1892, 1919); a standard handbook. George Foot Moore,

Judaism in the First Centuries of the Christian Era. The Age of the Tannaim (Harvard University Press, 2 vols., 1927); the major work of a distinguished scholar. Shirley Jackson Case, *The Social Origins of Christianity* (The University of Chicago Press, 1923, pp. vii, 263).

From the Apostolic Age to Constantine: General. M. Rostovtzeff, *A History of the Ancient World,* translated from the Russian by J. D. Duff (Oxford, The Clarendon Press, 2d ed., 2 vols., 1930); by an outstanding specialist. Guglielmo Ferrero, *The Ruin of Ancient Civilization and the Triumph of Christianity with Some Considerations of Conditions in the Europe of Today,* translated by the Hon. Lady Whitehead (New York, G. P. Putnam's Sons, 1921, pp. vii, 210); stimulating, but to be used with care. Patrick J. Healy, *The Valerian Persecution. A Study of the Relations between Church and State in the Third Century A.D.* (London, Archibald Constable and Co., 1905, pp. xv, 285); by a Roman Catholic, diligent, but not always critical.

From the Apostolic Age to Constantine: Asia Minor. Theodor Mommsen, *The Provinces of the Roman Empire from Caesar to Diocletian,* translated by W. P. Dickson (New York, Charles Scribner's Sons, 2 vols., 1906); a standard work. W. M. Ramsay, *The Cities and Bishoprics of Phrygia, being an Essay on the Local History of Phrygia from the Earliest Times to the Turkish Conquest* (Oxford, The Clarendon Press, 2 vols., 1895, 1897); based on prolonged archæological research. *C. Plinii Cæcilii Secundi Epistolæ,* edited by Moritz Döring (Freyberg, J. G. Engelhardt, 2 vols., 1843). Joseph Cullen Ayer, *A Source Book for Ancient Church History from the Apostolic Age to the Close of the Conciliar Period* (New York, Charles Scribner's Sons, 1913, pp. xxi, 707); translations with comments. *Luciani Samosatensis Opera Græce et Latine,* edited by J. T. Lehmann (Leipzig, Libraria Weidmannia G. Reimer, 9 vols., 1822-1831). James Orr, *Neglected Factors in the Study of the Early Progress of Christianity* (New York, A. C. Armstrong and Son, 1899, pp. 235); argues against some of the accepted views. J. P. Migne, *Patrologiæ Cursus Completus . . . Patrologiæ Græcæ* (Paris, 161 vols., 1857-1866); standard, with Greek texts and Latin translations. Louis Duchesne, *Early History of the Christian Church from Its Foundations to the End of the Third Century,* translated from the fourth edition (New York, Longmans, Green and Co., 3 vols., 1909-1924); a standard work by an eminent Roman Catholic scholar.

Greece, The Balkan Peninsula, the Danube. Jacques Zeiller, *Les Origines Chrétiennes dans les Provinces Danubiennes* (Paris, E. de Boccard, 1918, pp. iv, 667); carefully done, well documented. Jacques Zeiller, *Les Origines Chrétiennes dans la Province Romaine de Dalmatie* (Paris, Librairie Honoré Champion, 1906, pp. xviii, 188); well documented.

Egypt. Frederic G. Kenyon, *Recent Developments in the Textual Criticism of the Greek Bible* (London, published for the British Academy by Oxford University Press, 1933, pp. 119). *New Sayings of Jesus and Fragment of a Lost Gospel from Oxyrhynchus,* edited by B. P. Grenfell, Lucy Wharton Drexel, and A. S. Hunt (Oxford University Press, 1904, pp. 46). Hugh G. Evelyn White, *The Sayings of Jesus from Oxyrhynchus* (Cambridge University Press, 1920, pp. lxxvi, 48); contains an excellent bibliography.

North Africa West of Egypt. H. Leclercq, *L'Afrique Chrétienne* (Paris, Librairie

Victor Lecoffre, 2 vols., 1904); based upon extensive research. M. Rostovtzeff, *The Social and Economic History of the Roman Empire* (Oxford, The Clarendon Press, 1926, pp. xxv, 695); authoritative. Stuart A. Donaldson, *Church Life and Thought in North Africa, A.D. 200* (Cambridge University Press, 1909, pp. xii, 200); a careful, objective account. J. Mesnage, *Le Christianisme en Afrique* (Algiers, Adolphe Jourdan, 3 vols., 1914, 1915); carefully done by one of the White Fathers. J. Mesnage, *Évangélisation de l'Afrique, Part que Certaines Familles Romano-Africaines y ont Prise* (Algiers, Adolphe Jourdan, 1914, pp. 98); excellent. Ernesto Buonaiuti, *Il Cristianesimo nell' Africa Romana* (Bari, Gius. Laterza e Figli, 1928, pp. xxiv, 454); a history from the beginning through the Moslem conquest.

Italy, including Rome. George La Piana, *Foreign Groups in Rome during the First Centuries of the Empire* (Harvard University Press, 1927. From *Harvard Theological Review,* Oct., 1927, vol. xx, pp. 183-403); thorough and careful. *C. Suetonii Tranquilli Vita Divi Claudii,* edited by H. Smilda (Groningen, J. B. Wolfers, 1896, pp. 192); text and full notes; a doctoral dissertation. James T. Shotwell and Louise Ropes Loomis, *The See of Peter* (New York, Columbia University Press, 1927, pp. xxvi, 737); in large part a collection of the pertinent texts translated and commented upon. Edward Gibbon, *The History of the Decline and Fall of the Roman Empire,* edited by J. B. Bury (London, Methuen and Co., 4th ed., 7 vols., 1908).

Spain. E. S. Bouchier, *Spain under the Roman Empire* (Oxford, B. H. Blackwell, 1914, pp. 200); based upon the sources. H. Leclercq, *L'Espagne Chrétienne* (Paris, Librairie Victor Lecoffre, 1906, pp. xxxv, 396); by a Roman Catholic; based upon careful research. Alfred Winter Winterslow Dale, *The Synod of Elvira and Christian Life in the Fourth Century* (London, Macmillan and Co., 1882, pp. xxviii, 354). Charles Joseph Hefele, *A History of the Christian Councils from the Original Documents,* translated from the German and edited by W. R. Clark and H. N. Oxenham (Edinburgh, T. and T. Clark, 5 vols., 1871-1896. Vols. ii-v bear the title, *A History of the Councils of the Church*); a standard work, carrying the story to A.D. 787.

Gaul and Germany. L. Duchesne, *Fastes Episcopaux de l'Ancienne Gaule* (Paris, Albert Fontemoing, 3 vols., 1900-1915); excellent. Albert Hauck, *Kirchengeschichte Deutschlands* (Leipzig, J. C. Hinrichs'sche Buchhandlung, 5 vols., 1922-1929); standard, by a Protestant. Walter Alison Phillips, editor, *A History of the Church of Ireland from the Earliest Times to the Present Day* (Oxford University Press, 3 vols., 1933, 1934); by several members of the clergy.

Britain. Hugh Williams, *Christianity in Early Britain* (Oxford, The Clarendon Press, 1912, pp. vii, 484); carefully done. Henry Gee and William John Hardy, *Documents Illustrative of English Church History* (London, Macmillan and Co., 1896, pp. xii, 670).

Outside the Roman Empire. M. P. Charlesworth, *Trade-Routes and Commerce of the Roman Empire* (Cambridge University Press, 2d ed., 1926, pp. xxiii, 296); a semi-popular, competent account. G. F. Hudson, *Europe and China. A Survey of their Relations from the Earliest Times to 1800* (London, Edward Arnold and Co., 1931, pp. 336); readable and scholarly. F. Crawford Burkitt, *Early Eastern Christianity. St. Margaret's Lectures 1904 on the Syriac-Speaking Church.* (New York, E. P. Dutton and Co., 1904, pp. viii, 228); in a popular style by an expert.

F. Crawford Burkitt, *Early Christianity outside the Roman Empire* (Cambridge University Press, 1899, pp. 89). F. C. Burkitt, *Euphemia and the Goth with the Acts of Martyrdom of the Confessors of Edessa,* edited and examined (London, Williams and Norgate, 1913, pp. xii, 187); text, translation, and extensive notes and comments. Victor Schultze, *Geschichte des Untergangs des griechisch-römischen Heidentums* (Jena, Hermann Costenoble, 2 vols., 1887, 1892); based largely on the sources. J. Labourt, *Le Christianisme dans l'Empire Perse sous la Dynastie Sassanide (224-632)* (Paris, Librairie Victor Lecoffre, 1904, pp. xix, 372); a standard work. Eduard Sachau, *Die Chronik von Arbela. Ein Beitrag zur Kenntnis des ältesten Christentums im Orient* (Berlin, Königl. Ak. der Wissenschaften, 1915, pp. 94); important. W. A. Wigram, *An Introduction to the History of the Assyrian Church or the Church of the Sassanid Empire 100-640 A.D.* (London, Society for Promoting Christian Knowledge, 1910, pp. 318); by an English missionary to the Assyrians. Alphonse Mingana, *The Early Spread of Christianity in Central Asia and the Far East. A New Document* (Manchester, The University Press, 1925, pp. 80); by a well-known expert. M. I. Rostovtzeff, editor, *The Excavations at Dura-Europos Conducted by Yale University and the French Academy of Inscriptions and Letters. Preliminary Report of Fifth Season of Work, October, 1931-March, 1932* (Yale University Press, 1934, pp. xviii, 322). Fred C. Conybeare, *The Key of Truth. A Manual of the Paulician Church of Armenia. The Armenian Text Edited and Translated with Illustrative Documents and Introduction* (Oxford, The Clarendon Press, 1898, pp. cxcvi, 201). Victor Langlois, *Collection des Historiens Anciens et Modernes de l'Armenie* (Paris, Librairie de Firmin Didot Frères, Fils et Cie, vol. i, 1867, pp. xxxi, 421). Michel Tamarati, *L'Église Géorgienne des Origines jusqu'a nos Jours* (Rome, Imprimerie de la Société Typographico—Editrice Romaine, 1910, pp. xv, 710); based upon extensive research. Walter F. Adeney, *The Greek and Eastern Churches* (New York, Charles Scribner's Sons, 1928, pp. xiv, 634); scholarly. Ladislas-Michel Zaleski, *The Saints of India* (Mangalore, The Codialbail Press, 1915, pp. 424); by a Roman Catholic Delegate Apostolic of the East Indies. Joseph Dahlmann, *Die Thomas-Legende und die ältesten historischen Beziehungen des Christentums zum fernen Osten im Lichte der indischen Altertumskunde* (Frieburg i.B., Herder, 1912, pp. 174); by a Jesuit who argues for the authenticity of the mission of the Apostle Thomas to India. F. A. D'Cruz, *St. Thomas, the Apostle, in India* (Madras, 2d ed., 1929, pp. xix, 182); by a Roman Catholic, contending that Thomas was in India. J. N. Farquhar, *The Apostle Thomas in North India* (Manchester, The University Press, 1926, pp. 34); thinks it quite probable that Thomas was in North-west India. J. N. Farquhar, *The Apostle Thomas in South India* (Manchester, The University Press, 1927, pp. 33); holds the story as probably true. A. E. Medlycott, *India and the Apostle Thomas* (London, David Nutt, 1905, pp. xviii, 303); displays much erudition in support of the traditional thesis. George Milne Rae, *The Syrian Church in India* (Edinburgh, William Blackwood and Sons, 1892, pp. xii, 388); semi-popular, anti-Roman Catholic.

Size and composition of the Christian Community at the end of the third century. Shirley Jackson Case, *The Social Triumph of the Ancient Church* (New York, Harper & Brothers, 1933, pp. vii, 250); by a well-known expert. Gerhard Uhlhorn,

The Conflict of Christianity with Heathenism, edited and translated from the third German edition by E. C. Smyth and C. J. H. Ropes (New York, Charles Scribner's Sons, 1879, pp. 508); from a strongly Protestant and Christian standpoint. C. J. Cadoux, *The Early Christian Attitude to War. A Contribution to the History of Christian Ethics* (London, Headley Brothers, 1919, pp. xxxii, 272); from a pacifist standpoint; well documented. Ed. Freiherr von der Goltz, *Der Dienst der Frau in der christlichen Kirche* (Potsdam, Stiftungsverlag, 1914, pp. 257, 202); a scholarly but brief survey covering the entire course of Christian history. Lydia Stöcker, *Die Frau in der alten Kirche* (Tübingen, J. C. B. Mohr, 1907, pp. 31). Elfriede Gottlieb, *Die Frau im frühen Christentum* (Leipzig, U. Klein, 1928, pp. 47); a semi-popular summary.

CHAPTER IV

Agents. Benjamin Wisner Bacon, *The Gospel of the Hellenists,* edited by Carl H. Kraeling (New York, Henry Holt and Company, 1933, pp. xii, 432); a posthumous work of a distinguished New Testament scholar. Adolf Harnack, *The Mission and Expansion of Christianity in the First Three Centuries,* translated and edited by James Moffatt (New York, G. P. Putnam's Sons, 2d ed., 2 vols., 1908); the standard work. Thomas M. Lindsay, *The Church and the Ministry in the Early Centuries* (London, Hodder and Stoughton, 4th ed., 1910, pp. xxii, 398); the author believes in a visible Church and a valid ministry. Eusebius, *Ecclesiastical History,* translated by A. C. McGiffert in *Nicene and Post-Nicene Fathers,* second series, Vol. I (New York, The Christian Literature Society, 1890, pp. x, 403); the best of the early Church histories, incorporating many older sources. Baron Descamps, *Histoire Générale Comparée des Missions* (Paris, Librairie Plon, 1932, pp. viii, 760); a Roman Catholic work, by a number of authors; excellent.

Methods. Gerhard Uhlhorn, *The Conflict of Christianity with Heathenism,* edited and translated by E. C. Smyth and C. J. H. Ropes (New York, Charles Scribner's Sons, 1879, pp. 508); strongly Protestant and Christian in its bias. *An Outline of Christianity. The Story of Our Cvilization* (New York, Bethlehem Publishers, 5 vols., 1926); popular, by a number of experts. Henry Charles Lea, *A History of Auricular Confession and Indulgences in the Latin Church* (Philadelphia, Lea Brothers and Co., 3 vols., 1896); based upon the sources.

Processes and motives of conversion: the arguments of the apologists. C. H. Dodd, *The Epistle of Paul to the Romans* (New York, Ray Long and Richard R. Smith, 1932, pp. xxxv, 246); by a recognized specialist. M. I. Rostovtzeff, editor, *The Excavations at Dura-Europos Conducted by Yale University and the French Academy of Inscriptions and Letters. Preliminary Report of the Fifth Season of Work, October, 1931-March, 1932* (Yale University Press, 1934, pp. xviii, 322). A. D. Nock, *Conversion. The Old and the New in Religion from Alexander the Great to Augustine of Hippo* (Oxford University Press, 1933, pp. xii, 309); competent, with some fresh points of view. Erwin R. Goodenough, *The Theology of Justin Martyr* (Jena, Verlag Frommannsche Buchhandlung, 1923, pp. viii, 320); by a competent specialist. Dora Askowith, *The Toleration and Persecution of the Jews in the Roman Empire. Part I. The Toleration of the Jews under Julius Cæsar and Augustus* (New York, 1915, pp. xiii, 234); a doctoral dissertation at Columbia University. Jean Juster, *Les Juifs dans l'Empire Romain. Leur Condition Juridique, Économique et Sociale* (Paris, Paul Geuthner, 2 vols., 1914); extensively documented. Aimé Puech, *Les Apologistes Grecs du IIe Siècle de Notre Ère* (Paris, Librairie Hachette et Cie, 1912, pp. vii; 344). James Parkes, *The Conflict of the Church and the Synagogue. A Study in the Origins of Anti-semitism* (London, The Socino Press, 1934, pp. xxvi, 430); well documented, assigning anti-semitism to the Church rather than to popular prejudice. F. A. Wright, *Fathers of the Church. Tertullian: Cyprian: Arnobius: Lactantius: Ambrose: Jerome: Augustine. A Selection from the Writings of the Latin Fathers, Translated with an Introduction and Biographical Notes* (New York, E. P. Dutton and Co., 1929, pp. vii, 351). Arthur Cushman McGiffert, *A History of Christian Thought* (New York, Charles Scribner's Sons, 2 vols., 1932, 1933); a standard work by a distinguished Protestant scholar.

Reasons for the Opposition to Christianity. Herbert B. Workman, *Persecution in the Early Church. A Chapter in the History of Renunciation* (Cincinnati, Jennings and Graham, 2d ed., preface 1906, pp. xx, 382); an excellent survey. Elmer Truesdell Merrill, *Essays in Early Christian History* (London, Macmillan and Co., 1924, pp. viii, 337); by a professor of Latin in the University of Chicago. E. G. Hardy, *Christianity and the Roman Government. A Study in Imperial Administration* (London, George Allen and Unwin, 1925, reprint of the 1894 edition, pp. xiii, 161); carefully done, with no extreme views. C. R. Haines, *Heathen Contact with Christianity during the First Century and a Half, being all References to Christianity Recorded in Pagan Writings during that Period* (Cambridge, Deighton, Bell and Co., 1923, pp. 124). Otto Glöckner, *Celsi αληθής λόγος excusit et restituer conatus est* (Bonn, A. Marcus and E. Webers Verlag, 1924, pp. xiv, 72). Pierre de Labriolle, *La Reaction Païenne. Étude sur la Polémique Antichrétienne du Ier au VIe Siècle* (Paris, L'Artisan du Livre, 1934, pp. 519). F. J. Foakes-Jackson, *Eusebii Pamphili, Bishop of Cæsarea in Palestine and First Christian Historian. A Study of the Man and His Writings* (Cambridge, W. Heffer and Sons, 1933, pp. ix, 153); semi-popular essays. Amos Berry Hulen, *Porphyry's Work Against the Christians, an Interpretation* (Scottdale, Pa., 1933, pp. 56, *Yale Studies in Religion*, Vol. I); a doctoral dissertation. *A Select Library of Nicene and Post-Nicene Fathers of the Christian Church* (New York, The Christian Literature Co., First series, 14 vols., 1886-1890, second series, 14 vols., 1890-1900). Paul Allard, *Histoire des Persécutions pendant les Deux Premiers Siècles* (Paris, J. Gabalda et Cie, 4th ed., 1911, pp. xl, 499); favourable to the Christians, by a Roman Catholic.

Persecutions. Erwin R. Goodenough, *The Church in the Roman Empire* (New York, Henry Holt and Company, 1931, pp. xii, 132); a brief handbook by an able scholar, viewing Christianity as a mystery religion. Arthur Cushman McGiffert, *A History of Christianity in the Apostolic Age* (New York, Charles Scribner's Sons, 1897, pp. xii, 681); standard, but in need of revision to take account of more recent scholarship. F. J. Foakes-Jackson, *The Rise of Gentile Christianity* (New York, George H. Doran Co., 1927, pp. xiii, 231); semi-popular. C. H. Dodd, *The Epistle of Paul to the Romans* (New York, Ray Long and Richard R. Smith, 1932, pp. xxxv, 246); by a recognized scholar. Leon Hardy Canfield, *The Early Persecutions of the Christians* (New York, Columbia University Press, 1913, pp. 215); an excellent critical summary. James T. Shotwell and Louise Ropes Loomis, *The See of Peter* (New York, Columbia University Press, 1927, pp. xxvi, 737); in large part a collection of the pertinent texts, with translations and comments. Hans Lietzmann, *Petrus und Paulus in Rom* (Berlin, Walter de Gruyter und Co., 2d ed., 1927, pp. viii, 315); critical, thorough. Benjamin W. Bacon, *Studies in Matthew* (New York, Henry Holt and Company, 1930, pp. xxvi, 533); by an eminent authority with radical views. A. Linsenmayer, *Die Bekämpfung des Christentums durch den römischen Staat bis zum Tode des Kaisers Julian (363)* (Munich, J. J. Lentner'schen Hofbuchhandlung, 1905, pp. 301); scholarly. Shirley Jackson Case, *The Social Triumph of the Ancient Church* (New York, Harper & Brothers, 1933, pp. vii, 250); by a well-known expert. Louis Duchesne, *Early History of the Christian Church from Its Foundations to the End of the Third Century,* translated from the fourth edition (New York, Longmans, Green and Co., 3 vols., 1909-1924); by an eminent Roman Catholic authority. W. M. Ramsay, *The Church in the Roman Empire before A.D. 170* (New York, G. P. Putnam's Sons, 1893, pp. xv, 494); by a distinguished scholar. Patrick J. Healy, *The Valerian Persecution. A Study of the Relations between Church and State in the Third Century A.D.* (London, Archibald Constable and Co., 1905, pp. xv, 285); by a Roman Catholic, diligent but not always critical. *Eusebii Pamphili Chronici Canones* . . . edited by J. K. Fotheringham (London, Humphrey Milford, 1923, pp. 352). *Sulpicii Severi Libri qui supersunt* . . . edited by C. Halm in *Corpus Scriptorum Ecclesiasticorum* (Vinobonæ apud C. Geroldi Filium Bibliopolam Academiæ, 1866, pp. xiv, 278). E. G. Hardy, *C. Plinii Cæcilii Secundi Epistolæ ad Traianum Imperatorem cum eiusdem Responsis* (London, Macmillan and Co., 1889, pp. x, 251). E. C. E. Owen, *Some Authentic Acts of the Early Martyrs, translated with notes and introduction* (Oxford, the Clarendon Press, 1927, pp. 183). M. Rostovtzeff, *A History of the Ancient World,* translated from the Russian by J. D. Duff (Oxford, the Clarendon Press, 2d ed., 2 vols., 1930); by a well-known authority. Karl Johannes Neumann, *Die römische Staat und die allgemeine Kirche bis auf Diocletian* (Leipzig, Veit und Co., 2 vols., 1890); based upon the sources. Paul Allard, *Histoire des Persécutions pendant la Première Moitié du Troisième Siècle* (Paris, Librairie Victor Lecoffre, 1886, pp. xv, 524); a standard work by a Roman Catholic scholar. Karl Bihlmeyer, *Die "syrischen" Kaiser zu Rom (211-35) und das Christentum* (Rottenburg, Wilhelm Bader, 1916, pp. vii, 166); carefully done, with extensive references to the sources. John A. F. Gregg, *The Decian Persecution* (Edinburgh, William Blackwood and Sons, 1897, pp. xiv, 304); the Hulsean Prize Essay for 1896; Shirley Jackson Case, *The Social Origins of Christianity* (The University of Chicago Press, 1923, pp. vii, 263); by a Church historian of markedly liberal tendencies. E. A. Wallis Budge, *George of Lydda, the Patron Saint of England. A Study of the Cultus of St. George in Ethiopia* (London, Luzac and Co., 1930, pp. xviii, 210); by a distinguished orientalist. Paul Allard, *Les Dernières Persécutions du Troisième Siècle (Gallus, Valérien, Aurélien) d'après les Documents Archéologiques* (Paris, Librairie Victor Lecoffre, 1887, pp. xvii, 411). Edward

Gibbon, *The History of the Decline and Fall of the Roman Empire,* edited by J. B. Bury (London, Methuen and Co., 4th ed., 7 vols., 1908). Arthur James Mason, *The Historic Martyrs of the Primitive Church* (London, Longmans, Green and Co., 1905, pp. xi, 423); popularly written by an able scholar. H. Leclercq, *L'Afrique Chrétienne* (Paris, Librairie Victor Lecoffre, 2 vols., 1904); based upon extensive research. H. Leclercq, *L'Espagne Chrétienne* (Paris, Librairie Victor Lecoffre, 1906, pp. xxxv, 396); by a Roman Catholic expert. W. M. Ramsay, *The Cities and Bishoprics of Phrygia, being an Essay on the Local History of Phrygia from the Earliest Times to the Turkish Conquest* (Oxford, The Clarendon Press, 2 vols., 1895, 1897); based upon prolonged archæological investigation. T. Scott Holmes, *The Origin and Development of the Christian Church in Gaul during the First Six Centuries of the Christian Era* (London, Macmillan and Co., 1911, pp. xiv, 584); carefully done. Paul Allard, *La Persécution de Dioclétien et le Triomphe de l'Église* (Paris, Librairie Victor Lecoffre, 2 vols., 1890). Arthur James Mason, *The Persecution of Diocletian* (Cambridge, Deighton Bell and Co., 1876, pp. ix, 379); long a standard work. *Corpus Scriptorum Ecclesiasticorum Latinorum, editum Consilio et Impensis Academiae Litterarum Cæsareæ* (Vindobonensis, 66 vols., 1866-1932). *Bede's Ecclesiastical History,* translation . . . by A. M. Sellar (London, George Bell and Sons, 1907, pp. xliv, 439); a revision of the translation by Giles based upon the Latin text of Plummer. Herbert B. Workman, *The Martyrs of the Early Church* (London, Charles H. Kelly, no date, pp. 152); for a popular constituency. Henri Grégoire, *La "Conversion" de Constantin,* in *Revue de l'Université de Bruxelles,* Vol. XXXVI, 1930-1931, pp. 231-272. Walter F. Adeney, *The Greek and Eastern Churches* (New York, Charles Scribner's Sons, 1928, preface 1908, pp. xiv, 634); scholarly.

The Conversion of Constantine. Norman H. Baynes, *Constantine the Great and the Christian Church* (London, Humphrey Milford, 1930, pp. 107); from the *Proceedings of the British Academy,* Vol. XV. Christopher Bush Coleman, *Constantine the Great and Christianity, Three Phases, the Historical, the Legendary, and the Spurious* (New York, The Columbia University Press, 1914, pp. 258); based upon extensive use of the sources. J. Schmidlin, *Katholische Missionsgeschichte* (Steyl, Missionsdruckerei, 1924, pp. xi, 598); especially useful for its footnotes and bibliographies. Andreas Alföldi, *The Helmet of Constantine with the Christian Monogram (The Journal of Roman Studies,* Vol. XXII, 1932, pp. 10-23).

Reasons for the Victory of Christianity. Donald W. Riddle, *The Martyrs. A Study in Social Control* (University of Chicago Press, 1931, pp. ix, 231); from the standpoint of the control of the Church over its members. W. E. H. Lecky, *History of European Morals from Augustus to Charlemagne* (New York, D. Appleton and Co., 3d ed., 2 vols., 1854). Arnold J. Toynbee, *A Study of History* (Oxford University Press, vols. 1-3, 1934); stimulating. George La Piana, *Foreign Groups in Rome during the First Centuries of the Empire* (Harvard University Press, 1927, from *Harvard Theological Review,* Vol. XX, pp. 183-403); thorough and careful. S. Angus, *The Mystery Religions and Christianity* (New York, Charles Scribner's Sons, 1925, pp. xvi, 357); scholarly, pro-Christian. Karl Holl, *Urchristentum und Religionsgeschichte* (Gütersloh, C. Bertelsmann, 1925, pp. 48). Ernest Troeltsch, *The Social Teaching of the Christian Churches,* translated by Olive Wyon (New York, The

Macmillan Company, 1931, pp. 1019). Erwin R. Goodenough, *By Light, Light. The Mystic Gospel of Hellenistic Judaism* (Yale University Press, 1935, pp. xv, 436); a suggestive and original study based largely upon a careful examination of Philo.

CHAPTER V

Attitudes and actions of the Emperors. (Codex Theodosianus) Theodosiani Libri XVI cum Constitutionibus Sirmondianis edidit adsumpto apparatu P. Kruegeri Th. Mommsen (Berlin, Weidmann, 1905, pp. ccclxxx, 931, cix, 219). Christopher Bush Coleman, *Constantine the Great and Christianity. Three Phases: the Historical, the Legendary, and the Spurious* (New York, The Columbia University Press, 1914, pp. 258); based upon extensive use of the sources, *The Church History of Eusebius,* translated . . . by A. C. McGiffert, in *A Select Library of Nicene and Post-Nicene Fathers of the Christian Church, Second Series,* Vol. I (New York, The Christian Literature Society, 1890, pp. x, 403). Maude Aline Huttman, *The Establishment of Christianity and the Proscription of Paganism* (New York, Columbia University, 1914, pp. 257); a doctoral dissertation. *The Life of Constantine by Eusebius . . . a* revised translation . . . by Ernest Cushing Richardson, in *Nicene and Post-Nicene Fathers of the Christian Church, Second Series,* Vol. I (New York, The Christian Literature Society, 1890). *Codex Justinianus recognovit et retractavit Paulus Krueger in Corpus Juris Civilis* (Berlin, Weidmann, 1925). Victor Schultze, *Geschichte des Untergangs des griechisch-römischen Heidentums* (Jena, Hermann Costenable, 2 vols., 1887, 1892); based largely upon the original sources. Louis Duchesne, *Early History of the Christian Church from Its Foundations to the End of the Third Century,* translated from the fourth edition (New York, Longmans, Green and Co., 3 vols., 1909-1924); by an eminent Roman Catholic specialist. Socrates, *Ecclesiastical History . . . from the accession of Constantine to the 36th year of Theodosius, Jun. A.D. 445,* translated from the Greek (London, Samuel Bagster and Sons, 1844, pp. xxiv, 556); by a native and resident of Constantinople who drew his history partly from public records, episcopal letters, acts of synods, and works of other ecclesiastical writers. William K. Boyd, *The Ecclesiastical Edicts of the Theodosian Code* (New York, Columbia University Press, 1905, pp. 122). Wilmer Cave Wright, *The Works of the Emperor Julian with an English translation* (London, William Heinemann, 3 vols., 1913-1923); Greek texts and English translations. B. J. Kidd, *Documents Illustrative of the History of the Church* (London, Society for Promoting Christian Knowledge, 2 vols., 1920, 1923). Sozomen, *Ecclesiastical History . . . from A.D. 324 to A.D. 440,* translated (London, Samuel Bagster and Sons, 1846, pp. xvi, 448); Sozomen claims that his sources are largely laws, proceedings of synods, and letters of kings and priests. Paul Allard, *Julien l'Apostat* (Paris, Librairie Victor Lecoffre, 3 vols., 1900-1903); pro-Roman Catholic. W. Douglas Simpson, *Julian the Apostate* (Aberdeen, Milne and Hutchison, 1930, pp. xi, 127); a pleasantly written essay. Edward J. Martin, *The Emperor Julian. An Essay on His Relations with the Christian Religion* (London, Society for Promoting Christian Knowledge, 1919, pp. 126);

objective, judicious. Alice Gardner, *Julian Philosopher and Emperor and the Last Struggle of Paganism against Christianity* (New York, G. P. Putnam's Sons, 1906, pp. xx, 364); semi-popular in style. J. Bidez, *La Vie de l'Empereur Julien* (Paris, Société d'Édition "Les Belles Lettres," 1930, pp. x, 408); semi-popular, appreciative of Julian. Edward Gibbon, *The History of the Decline and Fall of the Roman Empire,* edited by J. B. Bury (London, Methuen and Co., 4th ed., 7 vols., 1908). Gaston Boissier, *La Fin du Paganisme. Étude sur les Dernières Luttes Religieuses en Occident au Quatrième Siècle* (Paris, Librairie Hachette et Cie, 2d ed., 2 vols., 1894); gives major attention to the manner in which Christianity and paganism mixed. Johannes Geffcken, *Der Ausgang des griechisch-römischen Heidentums* (Heidelberg, Carl Winters Universitätbuchhandlung, 1920, pp. 365); extensive references to sources and secondary literature. Pierre de Labriolle, *La Réaction Païnne. Étude sur la Polémique Antichrétienne du Ier au VIe Siècle* (Paris, L'Artisan du Livre, 1934, pp. 519). Theodoret, *Ecclesiastical History . . . from A.D. 322 to the Death of Theodore of Mopsuestia A.D. 427, translated* (London, Samuel Bagster and Sons, 1843, pp. xxiv, 360). *An Outline of Christianity. The Story of Our Civilization* (New York, The Bethlehem Publishers, 5 vols., 1926); semi-popular, by various experts. Karl Müller, *Kirchengeschichte* (Freiburg i.B., J. C. B. Mohr, 2 vols., 1892, 1919); a standard handbook. Samuel Dill, *Roman Society in the Last Century of the Western Empire* (London, Macmillan and Co., 2d ed., 1906, pp. xxviii, 459); readable, scholarly. Hans von Schubert, *Geschichte der christlichen Kirche im Frühmittelalter, ein Handbuch* (Tübingen, J. C. B. Mohr, 1921, pp. xxiv, 808); excellent. Franz Cumont, *The Mysteries of Mithra,* translated from the second revised French edition by T. J. McCormack (Chicago, The Open Court Publishing Co., 1903, pp. xiv, 239); a semi-popular account by an expert. A. D. Nock, *Conversion. The Old and the New in Religion from Alexander the Great to Augustine of Hippo* (Oxford University Press, 1933, pp. xii, 309); competent, with some fresh points of view. James Parkes, *The Conflict of the Church and the Synagogue. A Study in the Origins of Antisemitism* (London, The Soncino Press, 1934, pp. xxvi, 430); well documented.

Efforts of the Church and of individual Christians to effect conversions. Gonsalvus Walter, *Die Heidenmission nach der Lehre des hl.Augustinus* (Münster i.W., Aschendorff, 1921, pp. viii, 216); based upon the sources; by a Capuchin. Heinrich Hahn, *Geschichte der katholischen Missionen seit Jesus Christ bis auf neuste Zeit* (Cologne, Commissions-Verlag der M. Du Mont-Schauberg'schen Buchhandlung, 5 vols., 1857-1863); almost entirely lacking in footnote references to the sources. Hans Freiherrn v. Campenhausen, *Ambrosius von Mailand als Kirchenpolitiker* (Berlin, Walter de Gruyter und Co., pp. xv, 290); well documented. *The Ante-Nicene Fathers. Translations of the Fathers down to A.D. 325* (Buffalo, The Christian Literature Publishing Co., 10 vols., 1885-1887). Arthur Cushman McGiffert, *A History of Christian Thought* (New York, Charles Scribner's Sons, 2 vols., 1932, 1933); by a distinguished liberal Protestant scholar. *A Select Library of the Nicene and Post-Nicene Fathers of the Christian Church,* translated (New York, The Christian Literature Company, First series, 14 vols., 1886-1890; Second series, 14 vols., 1890-1900). J. P. Migne, *Patrologiæ Cursus Completus . . . in qua Prodeunt Patres*

Doctores Scriptoresque Ecclesiæ Latinæ . . . (Paris, 221 vols., 1844-1864); a standard collection of sources. Augustine, *The City of God* (a translation is to be found in Vols. 1 and 2 of *The Works of Aurelius Augustine, Bishop of Hippo. A New Translation*, edited by Marcus Dods. Edinburgh, T. and T. Clark, 1888). Albert Hauck, *Kirchengeschichte Deutschlands* (Leipzig, J. C. Hinrichs'sche Buchhandlung, 5 vols., 1922-1929; first edition, 1887 ff.); a standard work, by a Protestant. Adolf Harnack, *Militia Christi. Die christliche Religion und der Soldatenstand in den ersten drei Jahrhunderten* (Tübingen, J. C. B. Mohr, 1905, pp. vii, 129). Herbert B. Workman, *The Evolution of the Monastic Ideal from the Earliest Times down to the Coming of the Friars* (London, The Epworth Press, 2d ed., 1927, pp. xxi, 368); excellent, semi-popular, sympathetic with monasticism.

The Jews. H. Leclercq, *L'Afrique Chrétienne* (Paris, Librairie Victor Lecoffre, 2 vols., 1904); based upon extensive research. J. P. Migne, *Patrologiæ Cursus Completus . . . Patrologiæ Graecæ* (Paris, 161 vols., 1857-1866); with Greek texts and Latin translations. Carl H. Kraeling, *The Jewish Community at Antioch* (New Haven, Antioch Index Publications, No. I, 1932, pp. 31); competent.

Greece. Zosimi Historiæ Græce et Latine, edited by J. F. Reitemeier (Leipzig, Weidmann; Heredes et Reichium, 1784).

Dalmatia and the Danubian Provinces. Jacques Zeiller, *Les Origines Chrétiennes dans la Province Romaine de Dalmatie* (Paris, Librairie Honoré Champion, 1906, pp. xviii, 188); carefully documented. Jacques Zeiller, *Les Origines Chrétiennes dans les Provinces Danubiennes de l'Empire Romain* (Paris, E. de Boccard, 1918, pp. iv, 667); based upon extensive research.

Egypt. Philip David Scott-Moncrieff, *Paganism and Christianity in Egypt* (Cambridge University Press, 1913, pp. viii, 225). Augustine Fitzgerald, *The Letters of Synesius of Cyrene, translated . . . with introduction and notes* (Oxford University Press, 1926, pp. 272); carefully done.

North Africa. E. S. Bouchier, *Life and Letters in Roman Africa* (Oxford, B. H. Blackwell, 1913, pp. 128); based upon the sources. Edward Frank Humphrey, *Politics and Religion in the Days of Augustine* (New York, privately printed, 1912, pp. 220); carefully done. Charles Henry Robinson, *The Conversion of Europe* (London, Longmans, Green and Co., 1917, pp. xxiii, 64); good, but in need of revision to take account of more recent scholarship. Joseph Schmidlin, *Catholic Mission Theory*, translated from the German (Techny, Ill., Mission Press, 1931, pp. xii, 544); by an expert, a careful scholar. J. Mesnage, *L'Afrique Chrétienne. Evêchés et Ruines Antiques* (Paris, Ernest Leroux, 1912, pp. xii, 592); erudite, primarily for reference purposes. Ernesto Buonaiuti, *Il Cristianesimo nell'Africa Romana* (Bari, Gius. Laterza e Figli, 1928, pp. xxiv, 454).

Spain. H. Leclercq, *L'Espagne Chrétienne* (Paris, Librairie Victor Lecoffre, 1906, pp. xxxv, 396); based upon careful research, by a Roman Catholic.

Gaul and regions to the North and East. J.-M.Besse, *Les Moines de l'Ancienne France (Période Gallo-Romaine et Mérovingienne)* (Paris, Librairie Veue C. Poussielgue, 1906, pp. xii, 571); based upon the sources. E.-Ch. Babut, *Saint Martin de Tours* (Paris, Librairie Ancienne H. Champion, no date, pp. viii, 320); objective, carefully done. Louis Foley, *The Greatest Saint of France* (Milwaukee, Morehouse

Publishing Co., 1931, pp. xi, 321); popularly written, based upon careful research, containing critical notes. A. Lecoy de la Marche, *Saint Martin* (Tours, Alfred Mame et Fils, 1881, pp. xv, 735); a standard work. T. Scott Holmes, *The Origin and Development of the Christian Church in Gaul during the First Six Centuries of the Christian Era* (London, Macmillan and Co., 1911, pp. xiv, 584); carefully done. L. Duchesne, *Fastes Episcopaux de l'Ancienne Gaule* (Paris, Albert Fontemoing, 3 vols., 1900-1915); a standard work. George W. Robinson, *The Life of Saint Severinus by Eugippius* (Harvard University Press, 1914, pp. 141). Walter Alison Phillips (editor), *A History of the Church of Ireland from the Earliest Times to the Present Day* (Oxford University Press, 3 vols., 1933-1934); by several members of the clergy. The Count de Montalembert, *The Monks of the West from St. Benedict to St. Bernard,* authorized translation (Edinburgh, William Blackwood and Sons, 7 vols., 1861-1876); based upon extensive research; ardently sympathetic with the monks and with Christianity. J. Schmidlin, *Katholische Missionsgeschichte* (Steyl, Missionsdruckerei, 1924, pp. xi, 598); especially useful for its footnotes and bibliographies. Baron Descamps, *Histoire Générale Comparée des Missions* (Paris, Librairie Plon, 1932, pp. viii, 760); by several Roman Catholic scholars.

Great Britain. Edward Foord, *The Last Age of Roman Britain* (London, George G. Harrup and Co., 1925, pp. 294); based upon careful and extensive research. Hugh Williams, *Christianity in Early Britain* (Oxford, The Clarendon Press, 1912, pp. vii, 484); carefully done. R. G. Collingwood and J. N. L. Myres, *Roman Britain and the English Settlements* (Oxford, The Clarendon Press, 1936, pp. xxv, 515); especially useful for its summary of recent archæology. G. F. Browne, *The Christian Church in These Islands before the Coming of Augustine* (London, Society for Promoting Christian Knowledge, 1895, pp. 156); popular lectures by an expert. Louis Gougaud, *Christianity in Celtic Lands* (London, Sheed and Ward, 1932, pp. lxii, 458); by an expert, a Benedictine. H. Leclercq, *Note sur les Plus Anciens Autels Bretons* (Reprinted from *The Nineteenth Eucharistic Congress Report*, 1908, pp. 361-367).

The Goths. Thomas Hodgkin, *Italy and Her Invaders* (Oxford, The Clarendon Press, 2d ed., 8 vols., 1892-1899); a standard work. Charles A. Anderson Scott, *Ulfilas, Apostle of the Goths, together with an Account of the Gothic Churches and their Decline* (Cambridge, Macmillan and Bowers, 1885, pp. xiv, 239); excellent. Georg Waitz, *Über das Leben und die Lehre des Ulfila* (Hanover, Verlag des Hahn'schen Hofbuchhandlung, 1840, pp. 62); dealing especially with a hitherto unpublished life of Ulfilas. W. Bessell, *Ueber das Leben des Ulfilas und die Bekehrung der Gothen zum Christentum* (Göttingen, Vanderhoeck und Ruprecht's Verlag, 1860, pp. 119). G. W. S. Friedrichsen, *The Gothic Version of the Gospels. A Study of Its Style and Textual History* (Oxford University Press, 1926, pp. 263).

Patrick and the Irish. J. B. Bury, *The Life of St. Patrick and His Place in History* (London, Macmillan and Co., 1905, pp. xv, 404); the standard critical biography. Mrs. Thomas Concannon, *Saint Patrick, His Life and Mission* (Dublin, The Talbot Press, 1931, pp. xxxiv, 260); a popular life by a Roman Catholic; contains a valuable critical bibliography. Whitley Stokes, *The Tripartite Life of Patrick and Other Documents Relating to that Saint,* edited with translations and indices (London,

Her Majesty's Stationery Office, 2 vols., 1887). Newport J. D. White, *The Writings of St. Patrick* (London, Society for Promoting Christian Knowledge, 1932, pp. 41). Newport J. D. White, *St. Patrick. His Writings and Life* (London, Society for Promoting Christian Knowledge, 1920, pp. 142); a translation, with notes and introduction, of Patrick's *Confession, Letter, Lorica, Sayings,* and of Muirchu's *Life of St. Patrick.* Newport J. D. White, *A Translation of the Latin Writings of St. Patrick* (London, Society for Promoting Christian Knowledge, 1918, pp. 32). James Henthorn Todd, *St. Patrick, Apostle of Ireland. A Memoir of His Life and Mission* (Dublin, Hodges, Smith and Co., 1864, pp. xii, 538); based upon the sources. F. R. Montgomery Hitchcock, *St. Patrick and His Gallic Friends* (London, Society for Promoting Christian Knowledge, 1916, pp. 164); by an Anglican clergyman, with an anti-Roman Catholic bias, but based upon extensive critical study of the sources. John Campbell, *The Celtic Church and the See of Peter* (Oxford, Basil Blackwell, 1932, pp. xv, 118); contends that the Celtic Church was in communion with the Bishop of Rome and acknowledged him as the visible head of the Church. John Alfred Faulkner, *Burning Questions in Historic Christianity* (Cincinnati, The Abingdon Press, 1930, pp. 235); by a Methodist scholar.

Armenia. Malachia Ormanian, *The Church of Armenia, her History, Doctrine, Rule, Discipline, Liturgy, Literature, and Existing Condition,* translated from the French by G. M. Gregory (London, A. R. Mowbray and Co., 1912, pp. xxx, 27); often uncritical, but containing important information. Walter F. Adeney, *The Greek and Eastern Churches* (New York, Charles Scribner's Sons, 1928, preface, 1908, pp. xiv, 634); scholarly. Archdeacon Dowling, *The Armenian Church* (London, Society for Promoting Christian Knowledge, 1910, pp. 160); given chiefly to recent and contemporary history and organization.

Georgia. S. C. Malan, *A Short History of the Georgian Church, translated from the Russian of P. Ioselian and edited with additional notes* (London, Saunders, Otley and Co., 1866, pp. ix, 208). Michel Tamarati, *L'Église Géorgienne des Origines jusqu'a Nos Jours* (Rome, Imprimerie de la Société Typographico-Editrice Romaine, 1910, pp. xv, 710); based upon extensive research.

The Persian Empire, including Mesopotamia. C. Brockelmann and others, *Geschichte der christlichen Litteraturen des Orients* (Leipzig, C. F. Amelangs Verlag, 1907, pp. viii, 281). E. A. Wallis Budge, *The Monks of Kûblâi Khân . . . or the History of the Life and Travels of Rabban Sâwmâ . . . and Markôs. . . . Mar Yahbhallâhâ III . . .* translated from the Syriac (London, The Religious Tract Society, 1928, pp. xvi, 335). Alphonse Mingana, *The Early Spread of Christianity in Central Asia and the Far East: A New Document* (Manchester, The University Press, 1925, pp. 80); by a specialist. J. Labourt, *Le Christianisme dans l'Empire Perse sous la Dynastie Sassanide (224-632)* (Paris, Librairie Victor Lecoffre, 1904, pp. xix, 372); the best work on its subject. Eduard Sachau, *Zur Ausbreitung des Christentums in Asien (Abhandlungen der preus. Ak. der Wis. 1919, phil. hist. Klasse,* pp. 1-80); a scholarly summary. Laurence E. Browne, *The Eclipse of Christianity in Asia from the Time of Mohammed till the Fourteenth Century* (Cambridge University Press, 1933, pp. 198); an excellent survey. Theodor Mommsen, *The Provinces of the Roman Empire from Cæsar to Diocletian,* translated by W. P. Dickson (New

York, Charles Scribner's Sons, 2 vols., 1906). W. A. Wigram, *An Introduction to the History of the Assyrian Church, or the Church of the Sassanid Persian Empire 100-640 A.D.* (London, Society for Promoting Christian Knowledge, 1910, pp. 318); by an English missionary to the Assyrians. F. C. Burkitt, *Early Eastern Christianity* (New York, E. P. Dutton and Co., 1904, pp. viii, 228); popular lectures by an expert. DeLacy O'Leary, *Arabia before Muhammad* (London, Kegan Paul, Trench, Trübner and Co., 1927, pp. ix, 234); based upon source material, but does not give the authority for many statements.

India. Nicol Macnicol, *The Living Religions of the Indian People* (London, Student Christian Movement Press, 1934, pp. 324); by a Protestant expert. W. Germann, *Die Kirche der Thomaschristen* (Gütersloh, C. Bertelsmann, 1877, pp. x, 792); scholarly, fairly critical. George Milne Rae, *The Syrian Church in India* (Edinburgh, William Blackwood and Sons, 1892, pp. xii, 388); semi-popular, anti-Roman Catholic. Richard Bell, *The Origin of Islam in Its Christian Environment* (London, Macmillan and Co., 1926, pp. vii, 224); semi-popular, by an expert. Axel Moberg, *The Book of the Himyarites. Fragments of a hitherto unknown Syriac Work* (Lund, C. W. K. Gleerup, 1924, pp. clxxii, 61); introduction, translation, and text.

Arabia. L. Duchesne, *Les Missions Chrétiennes au Sud de l'Empire Romain* (Rome, Spithöver, 1896, pp. 79-122 in *École Française de Rome Mélanges d'Archeologie et d'Histoire*). Ign. Guidi, *L'Arabie Antéislamique* (Paris, Paul Geuthner, 1921, pp. 88); by an eminent scholar. Eduard Sachau, *Die Chronik von Arbela* (Berlin, Königl. Ak. der Wis., 1915, pp. 94); important. A. Mingana, *The Early Spread of Christianity in India* (Manchester, The University Press, 1926, pp. 82). Margaret Smith, *Studies in Early Mysticism in the Near and Middle East* (London, The Sheldon Press, 1931, pp. x, 276); carefully done.

Abyssinia. E. A. Wallis Budge, *A History of Ethiopia, Nubia, and Abyssinia* (London, Methuen and Co., 2 vols., 1928); by a specialist. *Deutsche Aksum Expedition, herausgegeben von der Generalverwaltung der königlichen Museen zu Berlin* (Berlin, Georg Reimer, 4 vols., 1913).

CHAPTER VI

Introductory generalizations. M. Rostovtzeff, *The Social and Economic History of the Roman Empire* (Oxford, The Clarendon Press, 1926, pp. xxv, 695); by an eminent authority. Samuel Dill, *Roman Society in the Last Century of the Western Empire* (London, Macmillan and Co., 2d ed., 1906, pp. xxviii, 459); readable, scholarly. T. R. Glover, *The Influence of Christ in the Ancient World* (Yale University Press, 1929, pp. 122); pro-Christian, by a specialist. Ernst Troeltsch, *The Social Teaching of the Christian Churches,* translated by Olive Wyon (New York, The Macmillan Company, 1931, pp. 1019); a standard work. Shirley Jackson Case, *The Social Triumph of the Ancient Church* (New York, Harper & Brothers, 1933, pp. vii, 250); a series of lectures by a well-known expert. John Brown Paton, Percy William Bunting, and Alfred Ernest Garvie, editors, *Christ and Civilization. A*

Survey of the Influence of the Christian Religion upon the Course of Civilization (London, National Council of Evangelical Free Churches, 1910, pp. xi, 546); semi-popular, warmly appreciative of Christianity. Christopher Dawson, *Progress and Religion. An Historical Inquiry* (New York, Longmans, Green and Co., 1929, pp. xvii, 254); stimulating, by a Roman Catholic layman. John Cecil Cadoux, *The Early Church and the World. A History of the Christian Attitude to Pagan Society and the State down to the Time of Constantinus* (Edinburgh, T. and T. Clark, 1925, pp. li, 675); thoroughly documented.

The Effect of Christianity upon Religion. Edward J. Martin, *The Emperor Julian. An Essay on His Relations with the Christian Religion* (London, Society for Promoting Christian Knowledge, 1919, pp. 128); objective, judicious. *The Church History of Eusebius,* translated . . . by Arthur Cushman McGiffert in *A Select Library of Nicene and Post-Nicene Fathers of the Christian Church,* Second series, vol. i (New York, The Christian Literature Company, 1890, pp. x, 403). F. J. Foakes-Jackson, *Eusebius Pamphili. . . . A Study of the Man and His Writings* (Cambridge, W. Heffer and Sons, 1933, pp. ix, 153); semi-popular essays. William Edward Hartpole Lecky, *History of European Morals from Augustus to Charlemagne* (New York, D. Appleton and Co., 3d ed., 2 vols., 1854); supporting the intuitive theory of ethics against the utilitarian theory. Patrick J. Healy, *The Valerian Persecution. A Study of the Relations between Church and State in the Third Century A.D.* (London, Arnold Constable and Co., 1905, pp. xv, 285); by a Roman Catholic, diligent, but not always critical. Carl Clemen, *Der Einfluss des Christentums auf andere Religionen* (Leipzig, A. Deichertsche Verlangsbuchhandlung D. Werner Schall, 1933, pp. 122); well documented. Franz Cumont, *The Oriental Religions in Roman Paganism,* a translation (Chicago, The Open Court Publishing Co., 1911, pp. xxiv, 298); by a distinguished expert. Henri Graillot, *Le Culte de Cybèle Mère des Dieux à Rome et dans l'Empire Romain* (Paris, Fontemoing et Cie, 1912, pp. 599); a doctoral dissertation presented at the University of Paris. Gerhard Uhlhorn, *The Conflict of Christianity with Heathenism,* translated from the third German edition (New York, Charles Scribner's Sons, 1879, pp. 508); strongly pro-Christian and Protestant. Pierre de Labriolle, *La Réaction Païenne. Étude sur la Polémique antichrétienne du Ier au VIe Siècle* (Paris, L'Artisan du Livre, 1934, pp. 519). W. O. E. Oesterley and G. H. Box, *The Religion and Worship of the Synagogue* (London, Sir Isaac Pitman and Sons, 1907, pp. xv, 443); scholarly, written for non-Jewish readers. George Foot Moore, *Judaism in the First Centuries of the Christian Era. The Age of the Tannaim* (Harvard University Press, 2 vols., 1927); the major work of a distinguished scholar. Erwin R. Goodenough, *The Theology of Justin Martyr* (Jena, Verlag Frommannsche Buchhandlung, 1923, pp. viii, 320); by a competent specialist. C. G. Montefiore, *Judaism and St. Paul* (London, Max Goschen, 1914, pp. 240); by a distinguished liberal Jewish scholar. *An Outline of Christianity. The Story of Our Civilization* (New York, Bethlehem Publishers, 5 vols., 1926); semi-popular, by various experts. James Parkes, *The Conflict of the Church and the Synagogue* (London, The Soncino Press, 1934, pp. xxvi, 430); well documented.

The creation of the Church. Adolf Harnack, *The Mission and Expansion of*

Christianity in the First Three Centuries, translated and edited by James Moffatt (New York, G. P. Putnam's Sons, 2d ed., 2 vols., 1908); the standard work in its field. *Journal of Biblical Literature* (1881 *et seq.*). Henry Osborn Taylor, *The Mediæval Mind. A History of the Development of Thought and Emotion in the Middle Ages* (London, Macmillan and Co., 2 vols., 1911); a standard work. *International Review of Missions* (London, 1912 *et seq.*); the most scholarly of the Protestant journals on missions. Thomas M. Lindsay, *The Church and the Ministry in the Early Centuries* (London, Hodder and Stoughton, 4th ed., 1910, pp. xxii, 398); believing in a visible Catholic Church. Alexander V. G. Allen, *Christian Institutions* (New York, Charles Scribner's Sons, 1897, pp. xxi, 577); a scholarly history. Adolf Harnack, *The Constitution and Law of the Church in the First Two Centuries,* translated by F. L. Pogson, edited by H. A. J. Major (London, Williams and Norgate, 1910, pp. xiv, 349). L. Duchesne, *Christian Worship. Its Origin and Evolution. A Study of the Latin Liturgy up to the Time of Charlemagne,* translated by M. L. McClure (London, Society for Promoting Christian Knowledge, 5th ed., 1931, pp. xx, 593); by a distinguished Roman Catholic scholar.

The effect upon intellectual life, language, and literature. Ernest Lohmeyer, *Soziale Fragen im Urchristentum* (Leipzig, Quelle und Meyer, 1921, pp. 136); one of a series of short handbooks; by an expert. Gaston Boissier, *La Fin du Paganisme. Étude sur les Dernières Luttes Religieuses en Occident au Quartième Siècle* (Paris, Librairie Hachette et Cie, 2d ed., 2 vols., 1894); gives major attention to the manner in which Christianity and paganism mixed. W. M. Ramsay, *The Cities and Bishoprics of Phrygia, being an Essay on the Local History of Phrygia from the Earliest Times to the Turkish Conquest* (Oxford, The Clarendon Press, 2 vols., 1895, 1897); the fruit of extensive archæological research. J. B. Bury, *The Idea of Progress. An Inquiry into Its Origin and Growth* (London, Macmillan and Co., 1920, pp. xv, 377). Erwin R. Goodenough, *The Church in the Roman Empire* (New York, Henry Holt and Company, 1931, pp. xii, 132); by an expert with some radical views. H. Leclercq, *L'Espagne Chrétienne* (Paris, Librairie Victor Lecoffre, 1906, pp. xxxv, 396); by a Roman Catholic scholar. James Shotwell and Louise Ropes Loomis, *The See of Peter* (New York, Columbia University Press, 1927, pp. xxvi, 737); in large part a collection of pertinent texts, translated and annotated. Victor Schultze, *Geschichte des Untergangs des griechisch-römischen Heidentums* (Jena, Hermann Costenable, 2 vols., 1887, 1892); with extensive references to the sources. Pierre de Labriolle, *Histoire de la Littérature Latine Chrétienne* (Paris, Société d'Édition "Les Belles Lettres," 1920, pp. viii, 741); well documented, bringing the story down to the Middle Ages. Arthur Cushman McGiffert, *A History of Christian Thought* (New York, Charles Scribner's Sons, 2 vols., 1932, 1933); by a distinguished liberal Protestant scholar. W. M. Ramsay, *The Church in the Roman Empire before A.D. 170* (New York, G. P. Putnam's Sons, 1893, pp. xv, 494); excellent. H. Leclercq, *L'Afrique Chrétienne* (Paris, Librairie Victor Lecoffre, 2 vols., 1904); based upon extensive research. Theodor Mommsen, *The Provinces of the Roman Empire from Cæsar to Diocletian,* translated . . . by W. P. Dickson (New York, Charles Scribner's Sons, 2 vols., 1906). Ludwig Berg, *Die katholischen Heidenmission als Kulturträger* (Aachen, Aachener Missionsdruckerei, 3 vols., 1927); warmly pro-Roman Catholic, well documented. C. Brockelmann and others, *Geschichte der christlichen Litteraturen des Orients* (Leipzig, C. F. Amelangs Verlag, 1907, pp. viii, 281). *Zeitschrift für Missionswissenschaft* (Münster i.W., 1911 *et seq.*); the best of the Roman Catholic scholarly journals on missions. Michel Tamarati, *L'Église Géorgienne des Origines jusqu'a Nos Jours* (Rome, Imprimerie de la Société Typographico-Editrice Romaine, 1910, pp. xv, 710); based upon extensive research.

The effect upon art and architecture. M. I. Rostovtzeff, *The Excavations at Dura-Europos Conducted by Yale University and the French Academy of Inscriptions and Letters. Preliminary Report of Fifth Season of Work, October, 1931-March, 1932* (Yale University Press, 1934, pp. xviii, 322). Josef Strzygowski, *Origin of Christian Art. New Facts and Principles of Research,* translated from the German by O. M. Dalton and H. J. Braunholtz (Oxford, The Clarendon Press, 1923, pp. xvii, 267); emphasizing the part of the Semites, Iranians, and Armenians in the development of Christian art. Oskar Wulff, *Altchristliche und byzantinische Kunst* (Berlin-Neubabelsberg, Akademische Verlagsgesellschaft Athenaion M. B. H., 2 vols., 1914). E. Baldwin Smith, *Early Christian Iconography and a School of Ivory Carvers in Provence* (Princeton University Press, 1918, pp. xv, 276); based upon extensive rsearch. Wilhelm Neuss, *Die Kunst der alten Christen* (Augsburg, Benno Filser, 1926, pp. 152, 92); profusely illustrated. Raffaele Garrucci, *Storia della Arte Cristiana nei primi otto secoli della Chiesa* (Prato, G. Gvasti, 6 vols., 1872-1881); profusely illustrated.

The effect upon the family and upon the status of women and children. R. S. T. Haslehurst, *Some Account of the Penitential Discipline of the Early Church* (London, Society for Promoting Christian Knowledge, 1921, pp. vii, 162); quoting extensively from the sources. F. A. Spencer, *Beyond Damascus. A Biography of Paul the Tarsian* (New York, Harper & Brothers, 1934, pp. xiii, 466); based upon wide reading; written in a popular style. C. Schmidt, *The Social Results of Early Christianity,* translated by Mrs. Thorpe, with a preliminary essay by R. W. Dale (London, William Isbister, 1889, pp. xxxii, 480); appeared first in French about 1853; thoroughly documented; an apology for Christianity. Shirley Jackson Case, *The Social Origins of Christianity* (The University of Chicago Press, 1923, pp. vii, 263); by an expert, a Protestant with markedly liberal tendencies. Edmund H. Oliver, *The Social Achievements of the Christian Church* (Toronto, Board of Evangelism and Social Service of the United Church of Canada, 1930, pp. 192); meant for class use, decidedly pro-Christian; containing excellent selected bibliographies. C. Loring Brace, *Gesta Christi or A History of Human Progress under Christianity* (London, Hodder and Stoughton, 1889, pp. xxiii, 520); frankly pro-Christian; widely read in its day. J. Schmidlin, *Katholische Missionsgeschichte* (Steyl, Missionsdruckerei, 1924, pp. xi, 598); especially valuable for its footnotes and bibliographies.

The effect upon slavery. R. H. Barrow, *Slavery in the Roman Empire* (London, Methuen and Co., 1928, pp. xvi, 259); carefully done; well documented. R. W. and A. J. Carlyle, *A History of Mediæval Political Theory in the West* (Edinburgh, William Blackwood and Sons, 5 vols., 1928-1932); based upon the sources. Arthur Cushman McGiffert, *A History of Christianity in the Apostolic Age* (New York,

Charles Scribner's Sons, 1897, pp. xii, 681); excellent, but in need of revision to take account of later scholarship.

Economic issues. Samuel Dill, *Roman Society from Nero to Marcus Aurelius* (London, Macmillan and Co., 1904, pp. xxii, 639); well written, authoritative. F. Homes Dudden, *The Life and Times of St. Ambrose* (Oxford, The Clarendon Press, 2 vols., 1935).

Charity. Ernst Lohmeyer, *Soziale Fragen im Urchristentum* (Leipzig, Quelle und Meyer, 1921, pp. 136); a handbook by an expert. Etienne Chastel, *Etudes Historiques sur l'Influence de la Charité durant les Premiers Siècles Chrétiens, et Considerations sur son Rôle dans les Sociétés Modernes* (Paris, Capelle, 1853, pp. xv, 419); valuable for its references and for its quotations from the sources. G. Uhlhorn, *Die christliche Liebesthätigkeit* (Stuttgart, D. Gundert, 3 vols., 1882-1890. An English translation of the first volume, by Sophia Taylor, was published in Edinburgh, by T. and T. Clark, in 1883). Francis Herbert Stead, *The Story of Social Christianity* (London, James Clarke and Co., no date, 2 vols.); laudatory of the changes wrought by Christianity.

Military Service. Adolf Harnack, *Militia Christi. Die christliche Religion und der Soldatenstand in den ersten drei Jahrhunderten* (Tübingen, J. C. B. Mohr, 1905, pp. vii, 129). Arthur James Mason, *The Persecution of Diocletian. An Historical Essay* (Cambridge, Deighton Bell and Co., 1876, pp. ix, 379); a standard work.

Amusements. Samuel Dill, *Roman Society from Nero to Marcus Aurelius* (London, Macmillan and Co., 1904, pp. xxii, 639); well written, carefully done. Walter F. Adeney, *The Greek and Eastern Churches* (New York, Charles Scribner's Sons, 1928, pp. xiv, 634); an excellent survey. *An Outline of Christianity. The Story of Our Civilization* (New York, Bethlehem Publishers, 5 vols., 1926); semi-popular, by a number of experts. Aimé Puech, *Saint John Chrysostom (344-407),* translated by Mildred Partridge (London, R. and T. Washbourne, 2d ed., 1917, pp. ix, 192); popularly written; by a Roman Catholic; based upon the sources. Louis Duchesne, *Early History of the Christian Church from Its Foundation to the End of the Third Century,* translated from the fourth edition (New York, Longmans, Green and Co., 3 vols., 1909-1924); by an eminent Roman Catholic scholar.

Burial customs. Zeitschrift für ägyptische Sprache und Alterthumskunde (Leipzig, 1863 et seq.).

Effect upon the state. Christopher Bush Coleman, *Constantine the Great and Christianity: Three Phases, the Historical, the Legendary, and the Spurious* (New York, The Columbia University Press, 1914, pp. 258); based upon extensive use of the sources. Charles Howard McIlwain, *The Growth of Political Thought in the West from the Greeks to the End of the Middle Ages* (New York, The Macmillan Co., 1932, pp. vii, 417); excellent. Guglielmo Ferrero, *Peace and War* (London, Macmillan and Co., 1933, pp. vii, 244). James Henry Breasted, *The Dawn of Conscience* (New York, Charles Scribner's Sons, 1933, pp. xxvi, 431); by an eminent Egyptologist.

Influence upon individuals. The Ante-Nicene Fathers. Translations of the Fathers down to A.D. 325 (Buffalo, The Christian Literature Publishing Co., 10 vols., 1885-1887). Elmer Truesdell Merrill, *Essays in Early Christian History* (London, Macmillan and Co., 1924, pp. vii, 337); by a professor of Latin in the University of Chicago. *C. Plini Cæcili Secundi Epistularum Libri Novem. Epistularum ad Traianum Liber*, by Henry Keil and Theodor Mommsen (Leipzig, Teubner, 1870, pp. xlvii, 432). F. J. Foakes-Jackson, *The Rise of Gentile Christianity* (New York, George H. Doran Co., 1927, pp. xiii, 231); semi-popular, by a well-known scholar. T. R. Glover, *The Conflict of Religions in the Early Roman Empire* (London, Methuen and Co., 1909, pp. vii, 359); charmingly written, pro-Christian, based upon wide reading in the sources. C. H. Dodd, *The Epistle of Paul to the Romans* (New York, Ray Long and Richard R. Smith, 1932, pp. xxxv, 246); by a competent scholar. F. R. Barry, *Christianity and the New World* (New York, Harper & Brothers, introduction 1931, pp. xvi, 317); by an Anglican clergyman. Ernst von Dobschütz, *Christian Life in the Primitive Church*, translated by George Brenner and edited by W. D. Morrison (London, Williams and Norgate, 1904, pp. xxxix, 438); pro-Christian, based upon the sources. Henry Charles Lea, *History of Sacerdotal Celibacy in the Christian Church* (New York, The Macmillan Co., 3d ed., 2 vols., 1907); carefully done, but with an anti-Roman Catholic bias. Alfred William Winterslow Dale, *The Synod of Elvira and Christian Life in the Fourth Century* (London, Macmillan and Co., 1882, pp. xxviii, 354). Henry Charles Lea, *A History of Auricular Confession and Indulgences in the Latin Church* (Philadelphia, Lea Brothers and Co., 3 vols., 1896). Oscar D. Watkins, *A History of Penance* (Longmans, Green and Co., 2 vols., 1920); the first volume is to A.D. 450, the second to A.D. 1215; carefully done, with extensive excerpts from the sources. Alice Gardner, *Julian Philosopher and Emperor and the Last Struggle of Paganism against Christianity* (New York, G. P. Putnam's Sons, 1906, pp. xx, 364); semi-popular. Edward Gibbon, *The History of the Decline and Fall of the Roman Empire*, edited by J. B. Bury (London, Methuen and Co., 4th ed., 7 vols., 1908). William K. Boyd, *The Ecclesiastical Edicts of the Theodosian Code* (New York, The Columbia University Press, 1905, pp. 122). Augustine FitzGerald, *The Letters of Synesius of Cyrene*, translated into English, with introduction and notes (Oxford University Press, 1926, pp. 272); carefully done. Albert Hauck, *Kirchengeschichte Deutschlands* (Leipzig, J. C. Hinrichs'sche Buchhandlung, 5 vols., 1922-1929); standard, by a Protestant scholar.

Christianity and the "fall of Rome." Guglielmo Ferrero, *The Ruin of Ancient Civilization and the Triumph of Christianity with Some Considerations of Conditions in the Europe of Today*, translated by the Hon. Lady Whitehead (New York, G. P. Putnam's Sons, 1921, pp. vii, 210); stimulating but not always convincing.

CHAPTER VII

The Influence of Judaism. Shirley Jackson Case, *The Evolution of Early Christianity. A Genetic Study of First-century Christianity in Relation to Its Religious Environment* (The University of Chicago Press, 1914, pp. ix, 385); especially useful for its summaries and bibliographies. Erwin R. Goodenough, *The Theology of Justin Martyr* (Jena, Verlag Frommannsche Buchhandlung, 1923, pp. viii, 320); by a competent specialist. Benjamin Wisner Bacon, *Studies in Matthew* (New York, Henry Holt and Company, 1930, pp. xxvi, 533); by an eminent authority. N. Levison, *The Jewish Background of Christianity. A Manual of the Political, Religious, Social, and Literary Life of the Jews from 586 B.C. to A.D. 1* (Edinburgh, T. and T. Clark, 1932, pp. xvi, 205); by a Christian Jew, favourable to Judaism. Arthur Cushman McGiffert, *A History of Christian Thought* (New York, Charles Scribner's Sons, 2 vols., 1932, 1933); a standard work. Arthur Cushman McGiffert, *The God of the Early Christians* (New York, Charles Scribner's Sons, 1924, pp. 200). Ernest F. Scott, *The Kingdom of God in the New Testament* (New York, The Macmillan Company, 1931, pp. 197); by a competent New Testament scholar. Ernest F. Scott, *The Gospel and Its Tributaries* (New York, Charles Scribner's Sons, 1930, pp. 295). F. Gavin, *The Jewish Antecedents of the Christian Sacraments* (London, Society for Promoting Christian Knowledge, 1928, pp. viii, 120). Adolf Harnack, *The Mission and Expansion of Christianity in the First Three Centuries,* translated and edited by James Moffatt (New York, G. P. Putnam's Sons, 2d ed., 2 vols., 1908); the standard work in its field. F. C. Burkitt, *Church and Gnosis. A Study of Christian Thought and Speculation in the Second Century* (Cambridge University Press, 1932, pp. ix, 154); semi-popular lectures by a distinguished authority. George Foot Moore, *Judaism in the First Centuries of the Christian Era. The Age of the Tannaim* (Harvard University Press, 2 vols., 1927); the major work of a great scholar. R. H. Charles, *The Book of Enoch or I Enoch,* translated and edited (Oxford, The Clarendon Press, new edition, 1912, pp. cx, 331). Rendel Harris and Alphonse Mingana, *The Odes and Psalms of Solomon, reëdited* (Manchester, at the University Press, 2 vols., 1916, 1920); text and translation. Burnett Hillman Streeter, *The Four Gospels. A Study of Origins, Treating of the Manuscript Traditions, Sources, Authorship, and Dates* (New York, The Macmillan Company, 1925, pp. xiv, 622); important. C. H. Dodd, *The Epistle of Paul to the Romans* (New York, Ray Long and Richard R. Smith, 1932, pp. xxxv, 246); competent. Paul Heinisch, *Der Einfluss Philos auf die älteste christliche Exegese* (*Barnabas, Justin und Clemens von Alexandria*) (Münster, Verlag der Aschendorffschen Buchhandlung, 1908, pp. viii, 296). A. E. J. Rawlinson, *The New Testament Doctrine of the Christ* (London, Longmans, Green and Co., 1926, pp. xv, 288); the Bampton Lectures for 1926. F. C. Burkitt, *Christian Beginnings* (University of London Press, 1924, pp. 152); semi-popular lectures by an expert. Wilhelm Bousset, *Kyrios Christos. Geschichte des Christusglaubens von den Anfängen des Christentums bis Irenæus* (Göttingen, Vanderhoeck und Ruprecht, 1913, pp. xxiv, 474); famous for its thesis of the influence of the mysteries and of other non-Jewish cults upon Christianity. Carl Clemen, *Primitive Christianity and Its Non-Jewish Sources,* translated by R. G. Nisbet (Edinburgh, T. and T. Clark, 1912, pp. xiii, 403); careful, conservative in its judgments, employing the sources. Benjamin W. Bacon, *The Gospel of the Hellenists,* edited by C. H. Kraeling (New York, Henry Holt and Company, 1933, pp. xii, 432); a posthumous work of a distinguished New Testament scholar. F. J. Foakes-Jackson, *The Rise of Gentile Christianity* (New York, George H. Doran Co., 1927, pp. xiii, 231); semi-popular, by a well-known scholar. R. Reitzenstein, *Die Vorgeschichte der christlichen Taufe* (Leipzig, B. G. Teubner, 1929, pp. vii, 399). W. O. E. Oesterley, *The Jewish Background of the Christian Liturgy* (Oxford,

The Clarendon Press, 1925, pp. 243); attempting to prove that Jewish liturgy left many marks upon Christian liturgy. Gerhard Loeschke, *Jüdisches und heidnisches im christlichen Kult* (Bonn, A. Marcus und E. Weber's Verlag, 1910, pp. 36). Hans Lietzmann, *Geschichte der alten Kirche* (Berlin, Walter de Gruyter und Co., vol. i, 1932, pp. vii, 323); a semi-popular summary. L. Duchesne, *Christian Worship. Its Origin and Evolution. A Study of the Latin Liturgy up to the Time of Charlemagne,* translated by M. L. McClure (London, Society for Promoting Christian Knowledge, 5th ed., 1931, pp. xx, 593); by a Roman Catholic. F. A. Spencer, *Beyond Damascus. A Biography of Paul the Tarsian* (New York, Harper & Brothers, 1934, pp. xiii, 466); based upon extensive reading; written in a popular style. Adolf Harnack, *The Constitution and Law of the Church in the First Two Centuries,* translated by F. L. Pogson, edited by H. D. A. Major (London, Williams and Norgate, 1910, pp. xiv, 349). Thomas M. Lindsay, *The Church and the Ministry in the Early Centuries* (London, Hodder and Stoughton, 4th ed., 1910, pp. xxii, 398); by one who believes in a visible Catholic Church. Alexander V. G. Allen, *Christian Institutions* (New York, Charles Scribner's Sons, 1897, pp. xxi, 577); scholarly. E. S. Bouchier, *A Short History of Antioch 300 B.C.-A.D. 1268* (Oxford, Basil Blackwell, 1921, pp. xii, 324); based in part upon the sources. Carl H. Kraeling, *The Jewish Community at Antioch* (New Haven, Antioch Index Publications, No. I, 1932, pp. 31); competent.

Contributions from the Hellenistic World. Walter F. Adeney, *The Greek and Eastern Churches* (New York, Charles Scribner's Sons, 1928, preface 1908, pp. xiv, 634); an excellent survey. Arthur Cushman McGiffert, *A History of Christianity in the Apostolic Age* (New York, Charles Scribner's Sons, 1897, pp. xii, 681); excellent, but in need of revision in the light of more recent scholarship. A. N. Bertrand, *L'Évangile de la Grace* (Paris, Editions "Je Sers," 1934, pp. 241); thoughtful, popular. *An Outline of Christianity. The Story of Our Civilization* (New York, The Bethlehem Publishers, 5 vols., 1926); semi-popular, by a number of experts. Edwin Hatch, *The Influence of Greek Ideas and Usages upon the Christian Church,* edited by A. M. Fairbairn (London, Williams and Norgate, 1890, pp. xxiii, 359); the Hibbert Lectures for 1888. Shirley Jackson Case, *Experience with the Supernatural in Early Christian Times* (New York, The Century Co., 1929, pp. vii, 341). Ernst Troeltsch, *The Social Teaching of the Christian Churches,* translated by Olive Lyon (New York, The Macmillan Company, 1931, pp. 1019). Rudolf Steck, *Der Galaterbrief nach seiner Echtheit untersucht* (Berlin, Georg Reimer, 1888, pp. xiv, 386). Rud Bultmann, *Der Stil der paulinischen Predigt und die kynisch-stoische Diatribe* (Göttingen, Vanderhoeck und Ruprecht, 1910, pp. 109). Johannes Selzenberger, *Die Bezeihungen der frühchristlichen Sittenlehre zur Ethik der Stoa* (Munich, Max Hueber, 1933, pp. xx, 525). E. Vernon Arnold, *Roman Stoicism* (Cambridge University Press, 1911, pp. ix, 468); a handbook with extensive references to the sources. Frank Chamberlain Porter, *The Mind of Christ in Paul* (New York, Charles Scribner's Sons, 1930, pp. xiii, 323); a work of ripe scholarship and deep religious insight. S. Angus, *The Religious Quests of the Græco-Roman World* (New York, Charles Scribner's Sons, 1929, pp. xx, 444); carefully done, with a pro-Christian bias. Johannes Geffcken, *Der Ausgang des griechisch-römischen Heidentums* (Heidelberg, Carl Winters Universitätbuchhandlung, 1920, pp. 365);

extensive references to sources and to other pertinent literature. Arthur Cushman McGiffert, *A History of Christian Thought* (New York, Charles Scribner's Sons, 2 vols., 1932, 1933); a standard survey. Campbell N. Moody, *The Mind of the Early Converts* (London, Hodder and Stoughton, 1920, pp. xii, 310); a stimulating comparison between the Early Church and what the author has known among the converts in Formosa. F. Homes Dudden, *The Life and Times of St. Ambrose* (Oxford, The Clarendon Press, 2 vols., 1935). *Epictetus, The Discourses and Manual together with Fragments of His Writings,* translated with introduction and notes by P. E. Matheson (Oxford, The Clarendon Press, 2 vols., 1916). Herbert B. Workman, *The Evolution of the Monastic Ideal from the Earliest Times down to the Coming of the Friars* (London, The Epworth Press, 2d ed., 1927, pp. xxi, 368); competent, semi-popular, sympathetic with monasticism. H. A. A. Kennedy, *Philo's Contribution to Religion* (London, Hodder and Stoughton, 1919, pp. xi, 245); scholarly, with a pro-Christian bias. Clifford Herschel Moore, *Ancient Beliefs in the Immortality of the Soul, with Some Account of Their Influence on Later Views* (New York, Longmans, Green and Co., 1931, pp. xi, 188). John H. Muirhead, *The Platonic Tradition in Anglo-Saxon Philosophy. Studies in the History of Idealism in England and America* (London, George Allen and Unwin, 1931, pp. 446); carefully done. William Ralph Inge, *Christian Mysticism* (London, Methuen and Co., 6th ed., 1925, pp. xv, 379); the Bampton Lectures for 1899. William Ralph Inge, *The Platonic Tradition in English Religious Thought* (New York, Longmans, Green and Co., 1926, pp. vii, 117); the Hulsean Lectures, 1925, 1926. Gustav Anrich, *Das antike Mysterienwesen in seinem Einfluss auf das Christentum* (Göttingen, Vanderhoeck und Ruprecht, 1894, pp. viii, 237); argues for the influence of the mysteries upon Christianity. R. Reitzenstein, *Die hellenistischen Mysterienreligionen nach ihren Grundgedanken und Wirkungen* (Leipzig, B. G. Teubner, 3d ed., 1927, pp. viii, 438). Adolf Jacoby, *Die antiken Mysterienreligionen und das Christentum* (Tübingen, J. C. B. Mohr—Paul Siebeck—1910, pp. 44). Carl Clemen, *Der Einfluss der Mysterienreligionen auf das älteste Christentum* (Giessen, Alfred Töpelmann, vormals J. Ricker, 1913, pp. 88); scholarly. Alfred Loisy, *Les Mystères Païens et le Mystère Chrétien* (Paris, Émile Nourry, 1919, pp. 368); holds that Christianity is a mystery, but nevertheless unique. Julius Grill, *Untersuchungen über die Entstehung des vierten Evangeliums* (Tübingen, J. C. B. Mohr—Paul Siebeck—two parts, 1902, 1923); the second part deals with the mystery religions and their relation to Christianity. Kirsopp Lake, *The Earlier Epistles of St. Paul, their Motive and Origin* (London, Rivingtons, 1911, pp. xi, 466); holding some advanced views. Erwin R. Goodenough, *The Church in the Roman Empire* (New York, Henry Holt and Company, 1931, pp. xii, 132); a brief textbook by an expert, stressing Christianity as a mystery religion. H. A. A. Kennedy, *St. Paul and the Mystery Religions* (London, Hodder and Stoughton, 1913, pp. xvii, 311); scholarly; inclined to discount the influence of the mystery religions upon Paul. Franz Cumont, *Oriental Religions in Roman Paganism,* a translation of the second French edition (Chicago, The Open Court Publishing Co., 1911, pp. xxiv, 298); by a distinguished specialist. Franz Cumont, *The Mysteries of Mithra,* translated from the second French edition (Chicago, The Open Court Publishing Co., 1903, pp. xiv, 239); semi-popular account based upon a larger and authoritative work. A. S. Geden,

Select Passages Illustrating Mithraism (London, Society for Promoting Christian Knowledge, 1925, pp. vi, 87); drawn largely from Cumont. John Baillie, *And the Life Everlasting* (New York, Charles Scribner's Sons, 1933, pp. xvi, 350); a Christian view of immortality. W. K. C. Guthrie, *Orpheus and the Greek Religion. A Study of the Orphic Movement* (London, Methuen and Co., 1935, pp. xix, 287); semi-popular, scholarly, cautious on moot questions. Lewis Richard Farnell, *The Cults of the Greek States* (Oxford, The Clarendon Press, 5 vols., 1896-1909); based upon extensive research. S. Angus, *The Religious Quests of the Græco-Roman World* (New York, Charles Scribner's Sons, 1929, pp. xx, 444); carefully done, pro-Christian. T. R. Glover, *The Conflict of Religions in the Early Roman Empire* (London, Methuen and Co., 1909, pp. vii, 359); charmingly written, based upon wide reading; pro-Christian. E. A. W. Budge, *Legends of Our Lady Mary the Perpetual Virgin and Her Mother Hannâ translated from the Ethiopic.* . . . (London, The Medici Society, 1932, pp. lxxv, 317). Shirley Jackson Case, *The Evolution of Early Christianity. A Genetic Study of First-century Christianity in Relation to Its Religious Environment* (The University of Chicago Press, 1914, pp. ix, 385); especially useful for its summaries and bibliographies. Albert Schweitzer, *The Mysticism of Paul the Apostle,* translated by William Montgomery, with a prefatory note by F. C. Burkitt (London, A. and C. Black, 1931, pp. xv, 411); emphasizing the eschatological outlook of Paul. T. R. Glover, *Paul of Tarsus* (New York, George H. Doran Co., 1925, pp. 256); popularly written by a competent scholar. Edwyn Bevan, *Hellenism and Christianity* (London, George Allen and Unwin, 1921, pp. 275). W. R. Halliday, *The Pagan Background of Early Christianity* (The University of Liverpool Press, 1925, pp. xvi, 234). Charles E. Raven, *Jesus and the Gospel of Love* (New York, Henry Holt and Company, 1931, pp. 452); by a preacher-scholar. Karl Holl, *Urchristentum und Religionsgeschichte* (Gütersloh, C. Bertelsmann, 1925, pp. 48). A. D. Nock, *Conversion. The Old and the New in Religion from Alexander the Great to Augustine of Hippo* (Oxford University Press, 1933, pp. xii, 309); excellent.

Contributions from paganism aside from those from philosophy and the mystery religions. André Boulanger, *Orphée. Rapports de l'Orphisme et du Christianisme* (Paris, F. Rieder et Cie, 1925, pp. 171); scholarly, with conservative conclusions. W. Bousset, *The Antichrist Legend,* translated from the German with a prologue on the Babylonian dragon myth by A. H. Keane (London, Hutchison and Co., 1896, pp. xxxi, 307). J. Rendel Harris, *The Dioscuri in the Christian Legend* (London, C. J. Clay and Sons, 1903, pp. 64). Gordon S. Laing, *Survivals of Roman Religion* (New York, Longmans, Green and Co., 1931, pp. xiii, 257); scholarly, with excellent footnotes. Felix Rütten, *Die Victorverehrung im christlichen Altertum. Eine Kulturgeschichte und hagiographische Studie* (Paderborn, Ferdinand Schöningh, 1936, pp. 182); well done. Alfred Maury, *La Magie et l'Astrologie dans l'Antiquité et au Moyen Age* (Paris, Didier et Cie, 3d ed., 1864, pp. 481). W. M. Ramsay, *The Cities and Bishoprics of Phrygia. Being an Essay on the Local History of Phrygia from the Earliest Times to the Turkish Conquest* (Oxford, The Clarendon Press, 2 vols., 1895, 1897); arising from extensive archæological research. Victor Schultze, *Geschichte des Untergangs des griechisch-römischen Heidentums* (Jena, Hermann Costenable, 2 vols., 1887, 1892); a standard work. Charles Henry Robinson, *The Conversion of Europe* (London, Longmans, Green and Co., 1917, pp. xxiii, 640); fairly good. Shirley Jackson Case, *Experience with the Supernatural in Early Christian Times* (New York, The Century Co., 1929, pp. vii, 341). Th. Trede, *Wunderglaube im Heidentum und in der alten Kirche* (Gotha, Friedrich Andreas Perthes, 1901, pp. 273). Frederick Cornwallis Conybeare, *Myth, Magic, and Morals. A Study of Christian Origins* (London, Wattband Co., 1910, pp. xxviii, 382). Henry Charles Lea, *A History of Auricular Confession and Indulgences in the Latin Church* (Philadelphia, Lea Brothers and Co., 3 vols., 1896); a standard work. *Allgemeine Missionszeitschrift* (Berlin, 1874-1923); a standard Protestant periodical on missions. *Zeitschrift für ägyptische Sprache und Alterthumskunde* (Leipzig, 1863 *et seq.*). *Journal of the American Oriental Society* (1881 *et seq.*). N. E. Lemaire, *Poetæ Latini Minores* (Paris, N. E. Lemaire, 7 vols., 1824-1826).

Art, architecture, and dress. Josef Strzygowski, *Origin of Church Art. New Facts and Principles of Research,* translated from the German by O. M. Dalton and H. J. Braunholtz (Oxford, The Clarendon Press, 1923, pp. xvii, 267); maintaining that Semitic, Iranian, and Armenian influences were important in the development of Christian art. Philip David Scott-Moncrieff, *Paganism and Christianity in Egypt* (Cambridge University Press, 1913, pp. viii, 225). Somers Clarke, *Christian Antiquities in the Nile Valley. A Contribution towards the Study of Ancient Churches* (Oxford, The Clarendon Press, 1912, pp. 234).

Rites and festivals. Samuel Dill, *Roman Society in the Last Century of the Western Empire* (London, Macmillan and Co., 2d ed., 1906, pp. xxviii, 459); readable, scholarly. Robert Seymour Conway, *Ancient Italy and Modern Religion* (New York, The Macmillan Company, 1933, pp. 150); the Hibbert Lectures for 1932. Lewis Richard Farnell, *Outline History of Greek Religion* (London, Duckworth and Co., 1921, pp. 160); a handbook by an eminent authority.

The Church. Samuel Dill, *Roman Society from Nero to Marcus Aurelius* (London, Macmillan and Co., 1904, pp. xxii, 639); readable, carefully done. Shirley Jackson Case, *The Social Triumph of the Ancient Church* (New York, Harper & Brothers, 1933, pp. vii, 250); by a well-known expert. Gerhard Uhlhorn, *The Conflict of Christianity with Heathenism,* translated from the German (New York, Charles Scribner's Sons, 1879, pp. 508); from a strongly Christian and Protestant point of view. Ernest Desjardins, *Géographie Historique et Administrative de la Gaule Romaine* (Paris, Librairie Hachette et Cie, 4 vols., 1876-1893). L. Duchesne, *Fastes Episcopaux de l'Ancienne Gaule* (Paris, Albert Fontemoing, 3 vols., 1900-1915); a standard work. Louis Duchesne, *A History of the Christian Church from Its Foundations to the End of the Third Century,* translated from the fourth edition (New York, Longmans, Green and Co., 3 vols., 1909-1924); by a distinguished Roman Catholic scholar. Hans vons Schubert, *Geschichte der christlichen Kirche im Frühmittelalter* (Tübingen, J. C. B. Mohr, 1921, pp. xxiv, 808); a handbook by an eminent authority. Albert Hauck, *Kirchengeschichte Deutschlands* (Leipzig, J. C. Hinrichs'sche Buchhandlung, 5 vols., 1922-1929); standard, by a Protestant scholar.

Variations in Christianity in the Apostolic age. Charles Cutler Torrey, *The Four Gospels, a New Translation* (New York, Harper & Brothers, 1933, pp. xii, 331); maintaining the thesis that all four Gospels were first written in Aramaic. Johannes Weiss, *Das Urchristentum* (Göttingen, Vanderhoeck and Ruprecht, 1914, 1917, pp. iv, ix, 681); in part posthumous. Walter Bauer, *Rechtgläubigkeit und Ketzerei im ältesten Christentum* (Tübingen, J. C. B. Mohr, 1934, pp. vii, 247); contends that originally the "orthodox" were not clearly in the majority.

Jewish Christianity. James Parkes, *The Conflict of the Church and the Synagogue. A Study in the Origins of Antisemitism* (London, The Soncino Press, 1934, pp. xxvi, 430); well documented. Kirsopp Lake, *Landmarks in the History of Early Christianity* (London, Macmillan and Co., 1920, pp. x, 147); semi-popular lectures, with some radical views. Epiphanius, *Panarion hær.* (edited by Karl Holl in *Die griechischen Schriftsteller der ersten drei Jahrhunderte.* Leipzig, J. C. Hinrichs'sche Buchhandlung, 1915, 1922, 1933).

Gnosticism. Karl Müller, *Kirchengeschichte* (Freiburg i.B., J. C. B. Mohr, 2 vols., 1892, 1919); a handbook. Wilhelm Anz, *Zur Frage nach dem Ursprung des Gnostizismus* (Leipzig, J. C. Hinrichs'sche Buchhandlung, 1897, pp. 112). Eugene de Faye, *Gnostiques et Gnosticisme. Étude Critique des Documents du Gnosticisme Chrétien aux IIe et IIIe Siècles* (Paris, Paul Geuthner, 2d ed., 1925, pp. 546). F. C. Burkitt, *Church and Gnosis. A Study of Christian Thought and Speculation in the Second Century* (Cambridge University Press, 1932, pp. ix, 154); semi-popular lectures by a distinguished expert. Wilhelm Bousset, *Hauptprobleme der Gnosis* (Göttingen, Vanderhoeck und Ruprecht, 1907, pp. vi, 398). Hans Leisegang, *Die Gnosis* (Leipzig, Alfred Kröner, 1934, pp. vii, 404). G. R. S. Mead, *Pistis Sophia. A Gnostic Gospel* (London, The Theosophical Publishing Society, 1896, pp. xliv, 394). Adolf Hilgenfeld, *Die Ketzergeschichte des Urchristenthums* (Leipzig, Fuess Verlag—R. Reisland—1884, pp. x, 642); based upon a painstaking examination of the sources. Gilbert Murray, *Five Stages of Greek Religion* (New York, The Columbia University Press, 1925, pp. 276); by an expert. Carl Clemen, *Der Einfluss des Christentums auf andere Religionen* (Leipzig, A. Deichertsche Verlagsbuchhandlung D. Werner Schall, 1933, pp. 122); carefully done. E. S. Bouchier, *Spain under the Roman Empire* (Oxford, B. H. Blackwell, 1914, pp. 200); based upon the sources.

Marcion and his followers. Adolph von Harnack, *Marcion. Das Evangelium vom Fremden Gott* (Leipzig, J. C. Hinrichs'sche Buchhandlung, 2d ed., 1924, pp. xv, 235, 455); a standard work. Robert Smith Wilson, *Marcion. A Study of a Second-century Heretic* (London, James Clarke and Co., 1933, pp. 190); based partly upon Harnack, but also upon the sources; carefully done. C. W. Mitchell, *S. Ephraim's Prose Refutations of Mani, Marcion, and Bardaisan, of which the Greater Part has been transcribed from the Palimpsest B.M. Add. 14623 and is now first Published* (London, for the Text and Translation Society by Williams and Norgate, 2 vols., 1912, 1921); the second volume compiled by A. A. Bevan and F. C. Burkitt. Hans Lietzmann, *Geschichte der alten Kirche, Vol. 2, Ecclesia Catholica* (Berlin, Walter de Gruyter und Co., 1936, pp. viii, 339).

Montanism. W. M. Ramsay, *The Church in the Roman Empire before A.D. 170* (New York, G. P. Putnam's Sons, 1893, pp. xv, 494); by a distinguished scholar. Pierre de Labriolle, *Les Sources de l'Histoire du Montanisme. Textes Grecs, Latin, Syriaques, publiés avec une introduction critique, une traduction française . . .* (Paris, Ernest Leroux, 1913, pp. cxxxviii, 282). Pierre de Labriolle, *La Crise Montaniste* (Paris, Ernest Leroux, 1913, pp. xx, 607); carefully done.

Arianism. Henry Melvill Gwatkin, *Studies in Arianism, Chiefly Referring to the Character and Chronology of the Reaction which Followed the Council of Nicaea* (Cambridge, Deighton, Bell and Co., 1882, pp. xxvi, 303). Charles E. Raven, *Apollinarianism. An Essay on the Christology of the Early Church* (Cambridge University Press, 1923, pp. viii, 312). Paul Elmer More, *Christ the Word* (Princeton University Press, 1927, pp. vi, 343); a semi-popular summary of early heresies. Adolph Harnack, *History of Dogma,* translated from the third German edition by Neil Buchanan (London, Williams and Norgate, 7 vols., 1894-1899).

Pelagius. Alexander Souter, *Pelagius's Expositions of Thirteen Epistles of St. Paul* (Cambridge University Press, 3 vols., 1922-1931). Ernest Jauncey, *The Doctrine of Grace up to the End of the Pelagian Controversy* (London, Society for Promoting Christian Knowledge, 1925, pp. vii, 299).

Manichæism. F. C. Burkitt, *The Religion of the Manichees* (Cambridge University Press, 1925, pp. viii, 130); a popular series of lectures on Manichæan literature, by an expert. Carl Schmidt and H. J. Polotsky, *Ein Mani-Fund in Ägypten. Originalschriften des Mani und seiner Schüler* (Berlin, Akademie der Wissenschaften, 1933, pp. 89). A. V. Williams Jackson, *Researches in Manichaeism with Special Reference to the Turfan Fragments* (New York, Columbia University Press, 1932, pp. xxxviii, 393); by an outstanding expert. Ém. De Stoop, *Essai sur la Diffusion du Manichéisme dans l'Empire Romain* (Gand, Librairie Scientifique E. Van Goethem, 1909, pp. viii, 151); well documented. E. Waldschmidt and W. Lentz, *Die Stellung Jesu im Manichäismus* in *Abhandlungen der preussischen Akademie der Wissenschaften, Phil. hist. Klasse,* 1926, pp. 131).

Monasticism. F. C. Burkitt, *Early Eastern Christianity* (New York, E. P. Dutton and Co., 1904, pp. viii, 228); semi-popular lectures by an expert. Henry Charles Lea, *History of Sacerdotal Celibacy in the Christian Church* (New York, The Macmillan Company, 3d ed., 2 vols., 1907); carefully done, with a bias against celibacy and the Roman Catholic Church.

Regional Churches. F. C. Burkitt, *Early Christianity outside the Roman Empire* (Cambridge University Press, 1899, pp. 89). George La Piana, *The Roman Church at the End of the Second Century* (*Harvard Theological Review,* Vol. XVIII, pp. 201-277). W. W. Fowler, *The Religious Experience of the Roman People from the Earliest Times to the Age of Augustus* (London, Macmillan and Co., 1911, pp. xviii, 534); the Gifford Lectures for 1909-1910.

INDEX

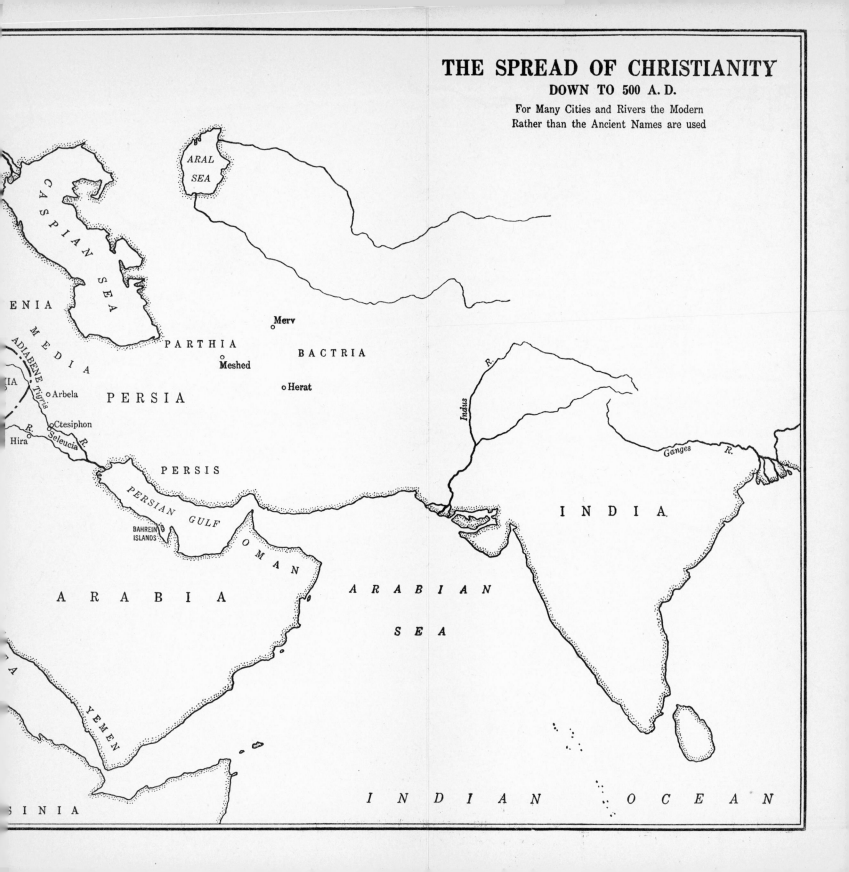

THE SPREAD OF CHRISTIANITY
DOWN TO 500 A. D.
For Many Cities and Rivers the Modern
Rather than the Ancient Names are used

ARAL
SEA

CASPIAN SEA

ENIA

MEDIA

ADIABENE

IA

Tigris

Arbela

Ctesiphon

R.

Hira

Seleucia

R.

PARTHIA

Meshed

Herat

Merv

BACTRIA

Indus R.

PERSIA

PERSIS

PERSIAN GULF

BAHREIN
ISLANDS

OMAN

Ganges R.

INDIA

ARABIA

ARABIAN

SEA

YEMEN

INDIAN OCEAN

SINIA